PROFESSIONAL
SEWING TECHNIQUES
FOR DESIGNERS

Director of Sales and Acquisitions: Dana Meltzer-Berkowitz

Executive Editor: Olga T. Kontzias

Acquisitions Editor: Olga T. Kontzias

Assistant Acquisitions Editor: Jaclyn Bergeron

Senior Development Editor: Jennifer Crane

Development Editor: Michelle Levy

Production Director: Ginger Hillman

Assistant Editor: Blake Royer

Cover Art: Julie Johnson and Ron Carboni

Copy Editor: Donna Frassetto

Technical Illustrations: Ron Carboni

Fashion Illustrations: Julie Johnson

Text Design: Renato Stanisic Design

Page Composition: SR Desktop Services, Ridge, NY, and Renato Stanisic Design

Library of Congress Catalog Card Number: 2006939040

ISBN-13: 978-1-56367-516-4

GST R 133004424

Printed in the United States of America

TP08

PROFESSIONAL
SEWING TECHNIQUES
FOR DESIGNERS

PROFESSIONAL SEWING TECHNIQUES FOR DESIGNERS

JULIE COLE   SHARON CZACHOR

Fairchild Books, Inc.
New York

Director of Sales and Acquisitions: Dana Meltzer-Berkowitz

Executive Editor: Olga T. Kontzias

Acquisitions Editor: Olga T. Kontzias

Assistant Acquisitions Editor: Jaclyn Bergeron

Senior Development Editor: Jennifer Crane

Development Editor: Michelle Levy

Production Director: Ginger Hillman

Assistant Editor: Blake Royer

Cover Art: Julie Johnson and Ron Carboni

Copy Editor: Donna Frassetto

Technical Illustrations: Ron Carboni

Fashion Illustrations: Julie Johnson

Text Design: Renato Stanisic Design

Page Composition: SR Desktop Services, Ridge, NY, and Renato Stanisic Design

Library of Congress Catalog Card Number: 2006939040

ISBN-13: 978-1-56367-516-4

GST R 133004424

Printed in the United States of America

TP08

To Jules' dear Mum, Megan Clark, and Sharon's dear mother, Marie Rose Novotny, who encouraged us in our love of fashion and pursuit of design excellence.

CONTENTS

EXTENDED CONTENTS

PREFACE

Jules:

As a new immigrant to America from Australia, I thought my career would continue just as it had in Sydney and Melbourne and I would carry on designing collections as I had done for the past 30 years. Little did I know that the course of my life was about to change. Instead the opportunity came to teach fashion design at Harper College and the International Academy of Design and Technology, both in Illinois. Over the past 6 years it has been my privilege to impart my fashion design knowledge and skills to students in their pursuit of a career in fashion.

Sharon:

Design and bringing the design to completion through excellent construction have been the focus of my 14 years of teaching. Although I have been an owner of a sewing business, an award-winning designer, and now an instructor at Harper College, the opportunity to share the knowledge I have gained through these experiences with students in the fashion design program continues to excite and challenge me.

Our passion for design and construction has always been a part of our lives. The methods detailed in this book are a result of many long hours of designing, patternmaking, sample making, and refinement of techniques developed over years of designing collections, teaching, and sewing. Our mutual passion for fashion design and dedication to excellent sewing skills are evidenced in this book.

It is impossible to have good designs without having accurate patternmaking and quality construction. This book presents a source of continuing education in the pursuit of excellent construction skills for the designer, from the beginning stages as a student through the development of the working designer.

The book is organized to reflect the stitching order of any garment and offers many insights into techniques appropriate to varying levels of proficiency. Each chapter is enriched with detailed sketches to provide visual support to the text. We hope it will increase your sewing skills, inspire your confidence, and stimulate your further creative experimentation. Sewing skills are a continuing process, the basis from which design is supported, interpreted, and reinforced through effort and informed instruction.

This book is a resource to be returned to, over and over, throughout your design/sewing career. As you develop the accompanying workbook, a visual reminder of the techniques in each chapter will be compiled for future reference.

ACKNOWLEDGMENTS

Jules:

I would like to thank Cheryl Turnauer (Harper College) and Kathy Embry (International Academy of Design and Technology Chicago) for giving me the opportunity to teach in the fashion design programs and for their encouragement and support while writing this textbook. I also want to express my gratitude to my husband, Graham, who has loved, encouraged, and supported me and shown patience when I had such tight work schedules. My family and friends, who have also walked this journey with me, I would also like to thank them for their faithful support. I also thank my colleagues who kindly allowed me to ask questions and run ideas by them. Lastly I need to thank the students at both Harper College and the International Academy of Design and Technology, who have allowed me to test my work in a classroom setting.

Sharon:

I'd like to thank Cheryl Turnauer for providing me with the opportunity to develop and teach a class that introduces industrial sewing methods to fashion design students; also thank you to Neal Tufano, who supports this class with his tireless devotion to teaching students how to use industrial equipment; and to the students who have passed through my classes, who have been a source of continuing inspiration and challenge. Never having written a book (only thousands of handouts), I had no idea how much I would come to rely on my family and friends during this process. And so, I must express my deep appreciation for all the help I received from my husband, Ken, and my children, Lauren and Christopher, who never showed any irritation over my repeated requests for computer advice. To my many dear friends (and you know who you are) who have held my hand, listened to my ideas, and kept me going, thank you.

This book was made possible as a result of a very fortunate meeting between Dana Meltzer-Berkowitz, Director of Sales and Acquisitions at Fairchild Books, and the authors at a book fair. Both Dana and Olga Kontzias, Executive Editor, have our deepest appreciation for the opportunity to publish the results of our combined teaching methods and sewing and design experience.

And, many thanks to Michelle Levy, our Development Editor, and Jessica Rozler, Associate Production Editor, who put our massive amounts of material in order and kept us on schedule; and to the art department at Fairchild, who have worked so hard to organize our sketches to coordinate with our text.

INTRODUCTION

This book is written for the student designer. Patternmaking tips are suggested throughout the textbook, as correct pattern and correct stitching are closely linked and depend on each other. The professional sewer who desires to increase sewing proficiency, knowledge of professional techniques, and expand creativity supported by excellent construction methods will also find this textbook helpful.

The order of the book follows the stitching order of a garment. Each chapter builds on the previous one and offers simple to advanced instruction. References to the detailed sketches move the student along from step to step.

Chapter 1: The Design Process

In this chapter, the designer is on view. Each part of the design process is highlighted. The chapter focuses on why construction should matter to the fashion design student.

Chapter 2: Getting Prepared

The necessary sewing tools, their uses and functions, a detailed explanation of fabric (the designer's medium), grainlines, fabric layout—everything needed to begin the actual construction is discussed.

Chapter 3: Introduction to Stabilizers

Choosing the best stabilizer for the style can make or break the design; stabilizers are a crucial part of the success of a design. A thorough explanation and examination of stabilizers is provided.

Chapter 4: Darts

Shaping and contouring the garment with darts is the focus of this chapter; various styles of darts, and how to sew and press, complete this chapter.

Chapter 5: Pockets

Correct stitches, suitable stabilizers and linings, matching the appropriate pocket to the garment, and functional and decorative pockets are covered in this chapter. Facings, trims, braids, piping, and other decorative elements are discussed.

Chapter 6: Seams

Sample, sample, sample! This chapter emphasizes that choosing the appropriate seam and seam finish for the fabric of the garment is critical to the success of the garment, and learning to analyze the best seam and seam finish is accomplished through sampling.

Chapter 7: Tucks and Pleats

This chapter details the techniques used to create tucks and pleats that are both functional and decorative.

Chapter 8: Zippers

This chapter discusses and illustrates the many applications of zippers, their styles, the appropriate zipper for the design, and how to match the zipper type to the fabric.

Chapter 9: Waistbands

Specifying the construction and proper stabilizing of both functional and decorative waistbands, this chapter provides the details for a professional finish.

Chapter 10: Ruffles and Flounces

This chapter explains and illustrates the sewing techniques involved in the fabrication of soft, delicate texture imparted to a garment through ruffles and flounces.

Chapter 11: Collars

An important area for creativity that must be properly supported through the correct stabilizers, collars in all their variety are presented in this chapter, which details the construction of a range of collar styles.

Chapter 12: Facings

This chapter on facings examines professional techniques that are used to finish raw edges on garments. Facings, bias bindings, and decorative facings are covered in detail.

Chapter 13: Cuffs and Other Wrist Finishes

As the completion of a sleeve, the cuff must be in harmony with the details of the garment. Cuffs can be both functional and decorative, and this chapter explains and illustrates sewing techniques to enhance the finished look of the garment.

Chapter 14: Sleeves

Sleeves alter the silhouette of the garment and are an important aspect of the design. This chapter explains, illustrates, and instructs the student how to sew sleeves in many variations.

Chapter 15: Hems

Various hem techniques using different methods that are suitable for the fabric and different garment hem shapes are explained and illustrated in this chapter.

Chapter 16: Linings

Linings make the garment beautiful on the inside as well as functionally covering the interior of the garment, adding warmth and comfort. This chapter explains and illustrates various lining treatments and the techniques used to apply the linings.

Chapter 17: Closures

This chapter details the opening and closing of garments, the functional and decorative applications that are suitable to the design, and the techniques used to stitch closures.

Chapter 18: Finishing Touches

The final phase of the garment is at hand—what needs to be done to finish the garment? Working through the stitching order in the checklist, this chapter ensures that every step has been carefully, thoughtfully, and beautifully completed.

Each chapter in the book includes the following helpful features:

Style I.D.—a visual example of what the chapter is all about, highlighted through detailed sketches of garments and garment sections.

Key Terms—appearing in bold type in each chapter and defined in the Glossary in the back of the book

Gather Your Tools—a list of necessary equipment and supplies to complete the sewing steps in that chapter

Now Let's Get Started—detailed information and step-by-step sewing instructions specific to the subject of each chapter

Stitching Tricky Fabrics—detailed information on how to execute the subject of the chapter in difficult-to-work-with fabrics

Transfer Your Knowledge—where you are encouraged to take what you know and transfer it to what you don't know

Stretch Your Creativity—providing suggestions for furthering the techniques of each chapter

Self-Critique—a useful tool to develop the designer's eye for recognizing what is good construction and what is not

Review Checklist—a summary feature, enabling the student/designer/professional to identify and explore techniques that need further development and practice

All the skills covered in this book, and more, are necessary for a career in fashion design. Tune in just once to *Project Runway* and listen to what the judges have to say about any poorly sewn garment; those contestants just don't make it. Think of how your work is a reflection of who you are as a designer, and what your work ethic is, and remember, there is no good design without good construction!

STYLE KEY

Listed below are colored swatches indicating the various materials used in this textbook. Each swatch is uniquely colored to show the correct and wrong sides of the fabric, interfacing, underlining and lining. As you use this book refer to the style key for any clarification needed.

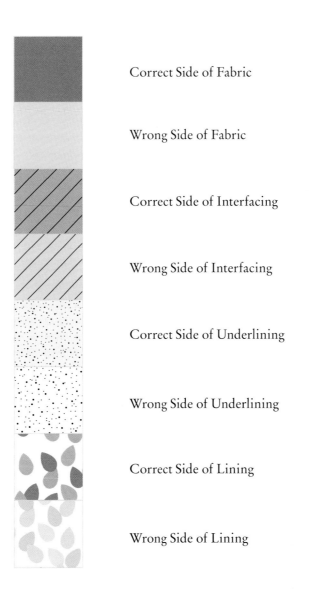

Correct Side of Fabric

Wrong Side of Fabric

Correct Side of Interfacing

Wrong Side of Interfacing

Correct Side of Underlining

Wrong Side of Underlining

Correct Side of Lining

Wrong Side of Lining

The Design Process: Why Construction Should Matter to the Fashion Designer

Vivienne Westwood said fashion is "life-enriching and, like everything that gives pleasure, it is worth doing well."[1] Even though this textbook is primarily about how to construct garments, this chapter focuses on why excellent construction skills should matter to the fashion designer. By focusing on the design process, from researching trends to the production of the collection, this chapter emphasizes why one needs to have a working knowledge of all these

areas to be a well-rounded designer. Combined with researching trends, fabric is both the entry point of this process and the designer's artistic medium. Knowing how to stitch fabric into clothes empowers the designer with more knowledge of design possibilities.

Patternmaking is also part of the design process: if the patterns are not made correctly, the seams cannot be stitched correctly. The type of seam stitched is determined by the fabric type, which in turn determines the amount of seam and hem allowances added to the pattern. This is why stitching knowledge is essential for making patterns.

Knowing how to stitch garments is a skill on which the fashion designer will rely during his or her entire career. For this reason, fashion students need to know how to sew.

STYLE I.D.

Here is the designer at work with the basic essential equipment at her (or his) fingertips. A tape measure is swinging around her neck. Fabric, the designer's medium, the dress form, scissors, and pins, all essential equipment to the designer, are used for shaping and manipulating fabric to fit a woman's body.

KEY TERMS

Collection
Cutting
Designing
Draping
Dress Form
Fabric
Fashion Designer
Grading
Manufacturing
Notions/Trims
Patternmaking
Production
Quality Control
Research Trends
Sample
Sample Hand
Sewing/Construction
Sketching

FIGURE 1.1 THE DESIGNER

Style I.D.

DRESS
FORM

GATHER YOUR TOOLS

The designer's tools are **fabric**, a **dress form**, pins, scissors, and a tape measure. As a new design student, you will soon be using these essential tools along with other tools outlined in Chapter 2. These are the first few key tools needed to begin working as a fashion designer. Figure 1.1 shows the designer at work with these essential tools.

NOW LET'S GET STARTED

Fashion designers have a "passion for fashion" and love working in the rush and bustle of its seasonal calendar. It is easy to get caught up in the creativity and vibrancy of the fashion industry. The rewards are great—they may not be ones of fame and fortune, but other rewards such as working in a fun and creative environment are enticing.

THE FASHION DESIGNER

The fashion designer is an artist. Many students want to become fashion designers because they think it will be a glamorous job, and to some degree it is. Students are also attracted to the

NOTE

A dress form is a replica of a woman's body shape. In this book, we use two forms: one form without limbs sits on a stand and the other form has legs and hangs free from the stand. Dress forms are available in various sizes and shapes, padded and covered in linen or jersey. They are pinnable and adjustable in height.

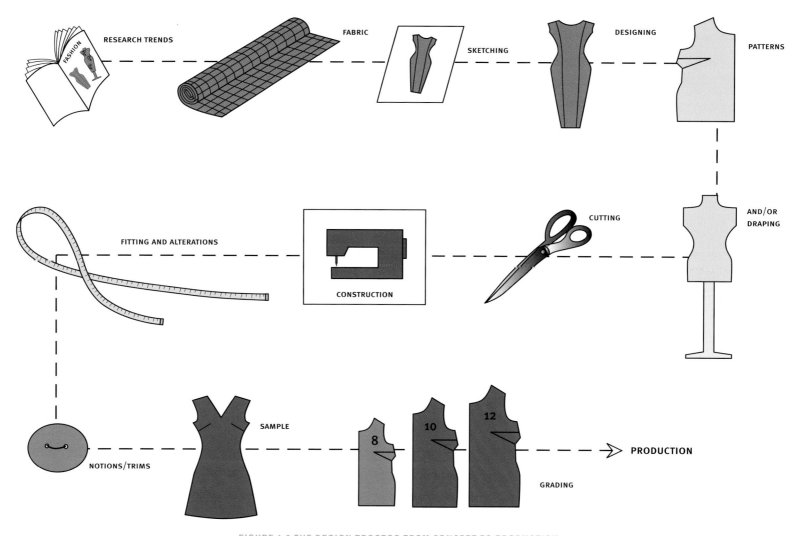

FIGURE 1.2 THE DESIGN PROCESS FROM CONCEPT TO PRODUCTION—
A FASHION DESIGNER NEEDS TO HAVE A WORKING KNOWLEDGE OF ALL THESE AREAS.

artistic component of the job. Students can imagine themselves working in a charming design studio **sketching** marvelous **collections** for the rich and famous, and playing with amazing fabrics. And of course in between **designing** collections, trips to Paris, Milan, New York, and London would be a necessity.

Yes, this can be part of what a fashion de-

signer does but it is not the whole story. Some fashion designers work in this type of environment, but only a few make it to the very top. Depending on the size of the company, the designer may be involved with the whole design process or be part of a design team and occasionally do humdrum work.

The designer is the fashion library of the fac-

tory. The designer is often called on to resolve **manufacturing** or **quality control** problems. These problems could be assessing poor-quality fabric, badly made patterns, wrong color fabric, poor stitching, or a fitting problem. Having knowledge of all aspects of the design process will prepare the design student for what is ahead. Figure 1.2 sets out all the steps involved in the design process from the conceptualization of ideas to the production.

Fashion design programs teach a vast number of design subjects, including sketching, **patternmaking**, **draping**, designing, textiles, clothing construction, and **grading,** along with important computer subjects in the course curriculum. This comprehensive education prepares design students so they *do* have a *working knowledge* of the skills needed to work in the fashion industry. Notice it says a *working knowledge*; this doesn't mean you have to know about everything! However, the more you know, the better you will be as a designer.

When creating a collection, a designer may produce as few as 10 or as many as 60 or more coordinating garments. As the designer develops the collection, all the components—the fabric, patternmaking, construction, and trims—should be in his or her mind as each aspect connects together (Figure 1.3).

Sometimes students struggle with learning how to sew, especially when they have had no stitching background. This process can be hard—however, stitching is an essential part of the design process, which will become clear as this book unfolds. So don't give up if you find stitching tough—it takes time and patience to learn!

THE IMPORTANCE OF HAVING CONSTRUCTION KNOWLEDGE

Clothing **construction** refers to the stitching of garments and all the **sewing** techniques involved in this process. Construction tech-

niques involve stitching darts, pockets, seams, tucks and pleats, zippers, waistbands, ruffles and flounces, collars, facings, cuffs, sleeves, hems, linings, and closures, all of which are covered in this book. Clothing construction also involves understanding fabric, the sewing machine, and the equipment needed to accomplish this task.

A student once commented, "Skip the stitching and let's just design!" This comment shocked us! A fashion design student needs to see the relevance in learning how to sew garments and realize how connected it is to the design process. Obviously this person hopes to be the designer described at the beginning of this chapter, who

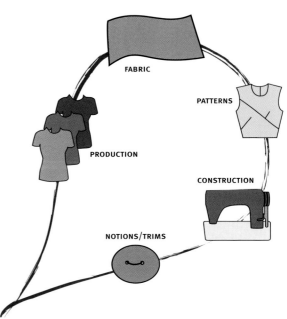

FIGURE 1.3 AS THE DESIGNER SKETCHES, ALL THESE ASPECTS OF THE DESIGN PROCESS NEED TO CONNECT IN HER MIND.

sits in a design studio sketching and playing with fabrics and is uninvolved with the whole **production** of the collection. Two questions we would ask the student are, "How can you design if you can't sew?" and, "How can you design if you don't know patternmaking?" These two aspects are closely linked.

Having these skills equips a designer to oversee manufacturing or the production of a collection. Very often the designer instructs the **sample hand** (the person who stitches the first prototype, or "proto," sample) how to stitch the garments in the collection. Without these skills, the designer is limited in her or his ability to oversee the quality of garments. Zac Posen, a very successful designer, has arranged his studio in the style of a European atelier so he can be involved in the production of his collections. He notes, "Nearly all of the studio is given over to actually making up clothes, with all the sewers and patternmakers, so that we can oversee the quality construction."[2]

The most exciting thing about teaching in a fashion design program is seeing how each element of the design process, from research to the final garment, interconnects. Figure 1.2 illustrates how the design process connects from concept to production; each aspect of the design process needs the others.

The first step in the design process is to **research trends** for inspiration. A designer's inspiration can come from anywhere—architecture, cars, landscapes, color, different cultures, or movies, just to mention a few. The design process progresses to fabric, sketching, designing,

patternmaking, draping, **cutting**, stitching, fitting, **notions,** and **trims,** which all contribute to making the first "proto" **sample** garment. The design process is repeated over and over as the collection is built. From there the final sample goes into production, where the patterns are graded in preparation for **manufacturing** the garment.

THE DESIGN PROCESS

The sections of the design process outlined in Figure 1.2 are explained here to emphasize how each connects together, and the importance of having this knowledge.

The Importance of Fabric to the Designer

The designer is a fabric sculptor. Design students need to become experts in fabric. Choosing a suitable fabric for the design is one of the most important aspects of the design process. Fabric selection and style development act in tandem. If an unsuitable fabric is chosen for a style, then the design won't work.

Start by understanding the variety and qualities of each fabric before they are applied to a design. This involves learning the differences between natural and synthetic fibers, fabric weaves (plain, twill, satin), and woven and knitted fabrics. These fabric details are important, as each type of fabric can influence the design. Each fabric has a different structure, and understanding each will help the designer design to the fabric. For example, knit and woven fabrics need very different designs, because knit fabric stretches and woven fabrics don't. For this reason, it is advisable to use fewer design

IMPORTANT

To know fabric—
Use fabric.
Look at fabric.
Touch and *feel* fabric.
Cut fabric.
Stitch fabric.
Design to the fabric.

The only way to learn about fabric is by actually working with different ones. Then, eventually, like the experienced designer, the design student will be able to look at a fabric and envision the designs into which it can be made. In Chapter 2, "Know Your Fabric" will explain more about the qualities of each fabric type.

lines in a knit garment than in one of woven fabric. Becoming knowledgeable about fabric also involves observing different fabric surface patterns and textures, and this is discussed more fully in Chapter 2. We suggest you take a peek at Figure 2.15, as it illustrates this point. Notice the interesting one-way fabric print and the simplicity of the design. The designer in this case has observed the fabric surface pattern and lets the fabric speak for itself. The design is uncomplicated, with no design lines to speak of, except for the side seams; too many design lines would spoil this bold fabric pattern.

To get acquainted with fabric, the designer also plays and drapes with fabric on the form to determine how it performs when pleated, folded, tucked, gathered, or scrunched. By draping two very different fabric weights, such as silk taffeta and silk georgette, it will become obvious how different each looks on the form. Taffeta is crisp to the hand and when gathered or tucked it holds its shape. On the other hand, silk georgette is soft to the hand, sheer, and delicate, and it drapes softly to skim the body when cut to its best advantage. Refer to Chapter 2, "Know Your Fabric."

Why the Designer Needs to Know How to Sketch

Sketching is the first part of the design process. It is the fundamental tool used to communicate a seam, a dart, a pocket, a zipper, topstitching, or buttons, so it is not only an artistic pleasure but also a phase during which functional and structural design need to be taken into consideration.

Why the Designer Needs to Know How to Draft Patterns

Learning how to construct patterns mathematically and knowing where to place each line for darts, seams, pockets, ruffles, and other design details empowers the designer in knowing how line in design can be used to enhance a woman's body. Structuring patterns is like architecture—we use line and shape to build form. Making patterns is all about using line, proportion, balance, and shape as each pattern is drafted. Each seam is placed to fit the curves of a woman's body—placement is not arbitrary. Many students find line placement difficult because they have not thought this through at the sketching stage.

Why the Designer Needs to Know How to Drape Fabric

Some designers like to draft flat patterns mathematically using specs and measurements, while others like to drape the fabric on the form, then take the draped fabric pieces and make the pattern from them. Draping fabric helps the design student understand the shape of the form and how fabric can be molded to enhance a woman's body. This in turn empowers the designer with more design possibilities for placing line in the design.

Why the Designer Needs to Know How to Cut Fabric

Knowing how to cut fabric following the grainlines is essential, as they must be correctly placed parallel to the selvage. Refer to Chapter 2, "Placing the Patterns 'On Grain.'" Placing the grainlines in certain directions can also change the look of the fabric surface. The fabric surface can have a texture, a bold large print, stripe, check, one-way pattern, or have a furry pile. The designer needs cutting knowledge so that when the darts, seams, gathering, and tucks are stitched, the fabric surface looks its best. This is explored in Chapter 2, "Laying Out and Cutting Fabric."

Why the Designer Needs to Know How to Sew Garments

The designer needs to learn how to sew darts, pockets, seams, zippers, ruffles, tucks, pleats, waistbands, collars, facings, cuffs, sleeves, hems, and linings, and how to embellish fabrics and stitch closures. *All empower the designer* by imparting an overall knowledge of design. Not every fabric is stitched in exactly the same way; seams and hems are not stitched in a uniform way on every garment. The construction method needs to match the type and weight of fabric, as we shall see in Chapter 2.

Why the Designer Needs to Know about Notions and Trims

Notions and trims are all the supplies needed for constructing garments other than the fabric. Notions can be buttons, snaps, zippers, thread, tape, elastic, ribbon, piping, interfacing, or a lace trim. The designer needs to be involved in choosing these details and therefore needs an artistic eye to harmonize them with the fabric and design. A designer can learn what notions and trims are available by researching the Internet for the latest items. The designer also directs the choice of what basic items to use, such as the type, weight, and length of a zipper; the type, size, and design of a button; and the color of the topstitching.

The notions and trims that are used matter, as you will learn by using this textbook. For example, the weight of the zipper needs to suit the fabric weight, and the zipper needs to be long enough so the garment will open comfortably, allowing the customer to get in and out easily. The type of button (glass, metal, wood, or leather) needs to be compatible with the fabric type and suitable for laundering. The interfacing also needs to suit the fabric weight and the part of the garment in which it is being used. All these aspects of the construction process will be discussed as you read further in the textbook, in Chapters 3 and 7.

Why the Designer Needs to Know about Production

Being involved in production is an aspect of the design process that fashion designers often find difficult and irksome, as they just want to get on with designing clothes and back to the design studio! How involved the designer is with production depends on the size of the company. In a large company the designer's role in production may be minimal, but students who plan to have their own design business in the future will need to be totally involved. Designers need to keep their eyes open and look at the quality of garments being produced, and at the top of the list is *quality stitching*.

As the collection develops, the designer may be involved with ordering fabrics and trims, an important part of the design process. In some companies, designers may also be involved with grading patterns into larger and smaller sizes that are ready for production. When the garments are completed, quality control personnel may also call on designers for their expertise when a stitching or fabric problem occurs.

The production of a collection keeps to a strict schedule, and completing your assignments by their due dates is a great way to learn how to organize your schedule. This is excellent practice for your future responsibilities as a designer!

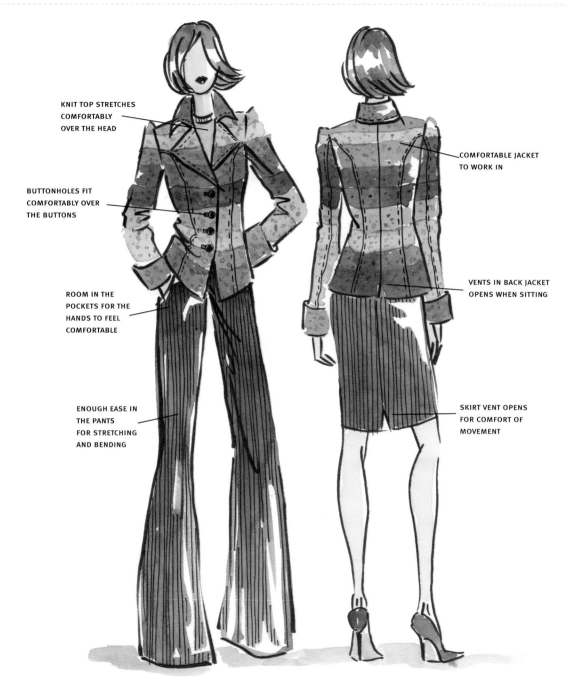

KNIT TOP STRETCHES COMFORTABLY OVER THE HEAD

COMFORTABLE JACKET TO WORK IN

BUTTONHOLES FIT COMFORTABLY OVER THE BUTTONS

VENTS IN BACK JACKET OPENS WHEN SITTING

ROOM IN THE POCKETS FOR THE HANDS TO FEEL COMFORTABLE

ENOUGH EASE IN THE PANTS FOR STRETCHING AND BENDING

SKIRT VENT OPENS FOR COMFORT OF MOVEMENT

FIGURE 1.4 FUNCTIONAL DESIGN: JACKET, SKIRT, AND PANTS

THE COLLAR IS HIGH
ENOUGH TO PROVIDE
WARMTH

THE FABRIC IS
WATERPROOF AND
THE COAT LARGE
ENOUGH TO WEAR
OVER OTHER
GARMENTS

SEAMS, TOPSTITCHING,
HEMSTITCHING, BUTTONHOLES,
BUTTON STITCHING – NEED TO
BE GOOD QUALITY
CONSTRUCTION AND HOLD
THE GARMENT TOGETHER

THE COAT IS LONG ENOUGH
FOR PROTECTION FROM THE
ELEMENTS

Why the Designer Needs to Know about Functional, Structural, and Decorative Design

A designer needs to address these three aspects—functional, structural, and decorative design—when designing garments. Each of these aspects has equal value. If these areas of design are ignored, it can ultimately affect the sale of the collection. And without sales, the designer does not have a job!

It is the designer's responsibility to create clothes that function, feel comfortable, and are user-friendly in the way they work. Garments that represent interesting designs made in quality fabrics that are comfortable to move in, and stitched with quality stitches, are what women want! This is what makes one design and designer stand out from the rest. Coco Chanel, one of the most famous designers in fashion history, knew how important this was. Chanel said, "I make fashion women can live in, breathe in, feel comfortable in, and look younger in."[3] Her revolutionary designs changed the way women dressed, from being confined to feeling comfortable. As design students, let's continue Chanel's tradition!

Each of the garments in Figure 1.4, Figure 1.5, and Figure 1.6 demonstrates each area of design: functional, structural, and decorative.

Functional Design

Functional design refers to how the garment works physically on the body. This is an important aspect on which the designer needs to focus. Garments need to work physically for the purpose they are made for (police or firefighter's uniform, ball gown, swimwear, and more).

- Garments need to feel comfortable on the body and be made from pleasant-feeling fabric.
- Garments need to provide adequate room for movement yet hold their shape to the form.
- Garments need to be made in a suitable fabric type and weight to suit the style and provide protection, warmth, or coolness.

HOW THE GARMENT WORKS PHYSICALLY

This aspect of designing is the designer's responsibility. A customer trying on a garment does not want to struggle getting in and out of the garment. If the garment is complicated to put on, or uncomfortable in some way, or too tight to walk in, the customer will leave the fitting room and look for another brand. Busy people don't want to be bothered with complicated openings and uncomfortable clothing.

Here are a few practical tips pertaining to some areas of functional design that the designer needs to attend to when designing clothes:

- The *closure* of a garment *must* work simply and efficiently. Buttonholes need to fit comfortably over the button and not feel too tight or too loose. Snap closures need to hold the garment securely closed. Dysfunctional closures that easily "pop" open are not going to sell. All of the garments in Figures 1.4, 1.5, and 1.6 have closures—do take a look at them.
- A *pocket* needs to be positioned so the hand enters at a comfortable level. The size of the pocket needs to be generous enough for the hand to rest in it, and maybe hold keys and some cash. Notice that the pants in Figure 1.4 and the raincoat in Figure 1.5 show comfortable, adequately sized pockets. In Chapter 5, "Pocket Styles" will explain more about the placement and size of pockets.
- A *skirt vent* must be long enough to allow a person to walk easily. Similarly, a jacket vent allows room for the jacket to spread when a person is sitting. Figure 1.4 illustrates how important a vent is for functional design in a jacket and skirt. Refer to Chapter 15, "Vent."
- A *strapless bodice* must be structured with underlining and boning so it won't slip down when the wearer is on the dance floor—a customer does not want to keep tugging at the garment to keep it up all evening—this would be dysfunctional design. The zipper also needs to open from the top edge of the garment to 7 inches below the waistline so the customer can comfortably get in and out of the garment (see Figure 1.6). Refer to Chapter 3, "Underlining," and Chapter 6, "Boning."
- *Neck openings* must be large enough in a knit or woven fabric to slip comfortably over the head without feeling too tight—women do not want to spoil their hair! Men also do not want to feel choked or suffocated. Many students forget about this aspect of functional design—a garment is utterly dysfunctional when it can't slip over the head. In Figure 1.4 a knit top has been slipped comfortably over the head and paired with the jacket.

COMFORT

Comfort is all about how the garment feels when it is worn. Customers should not feel restricted when sitting in the office, walking the dog, jumping for joy, running to catch the train, crouching to pick up the baby, or reaching for that hidden candy on the top kitchen shelf. To enable comfort and movement in a garment, "ease" is incorporated into the garment at the patternmaking stage. Ease is the excess fabric that can be pinched from both sides of your garment. Different amounts of ease will be added depending on the style, silhouette, and fabric type—some fabrics have more "give" than others—and the age group of the target customer also defines the amount of ease used. For example, the strapless dress in Figure 1.6 would not have any ease in the bodice, as it must fit tightly to the body. In comparison, the raincoat in Figure 1.5 needs excess fabric ("ease"), as it is worn over other clothing.

FABRIC SELECTION NEEDS TO SUIT THE FUNCTION OF THE GARMENT

The function of the garment influences the fabric selection. This aspect of functional design is the designer's responsibility. Some examples to consider:

- A raincoat is designed to keep out rain; therefore, the fabric needs to be weatherproof or waterproof (or both). The cut of the coat *must* be large enough and long enough to wear over other clothes with the neck high enough to help keep the rain out—this is an example of functional design (Figure 1.5).

- Winter coats need to be made from fabrics that keep wearers warm and insulate the body from the cold; fabrics such as wool, cashmere, fur, or leather are ideal choices. A coat underlined and lined will also have added warmth. Refer to Chapter 3, "Underlining."

- A summer jacket needs to be made from breathable fabrics that keep the wearer cool. Natural fibers such as cotton, linen, or silk are ideal choices.

- When a business wear collection is designed, the fabric choice becomes very important, especially when traveling is part of the job. Fabrics with synthetic fibers prevent crushing—this is how fashion meets function (Figure 1.4).

- Fabric needs to be taken into consideration when designing for sportswear; the fabric *must* stretch in the width and length so it can move with the body when a person swims, runs, or jumps. For functional sportswear, the following attributes in the fabric are advantageous: lightweight, heat and moisture regulated, stable when wet, good air and water vapor permeability, low water absorption, absence of dampness, quick to dry (to prevent feeling cold), durable, easy to care for, and soft and pleasing to touch. However, it is not possible to achieve all these properties in one simple structure of fabric using one fiber.[4] So a fabric with moisture-wicking properties is needed to regulate the body temperature, improve performance, and delay exhaustion.

STRUCTURAL DESIGN: THE BODICE IS STRUCTURED WITH UNDERLINING AND BONING AND STITCHED WITH QUALITY CONSTRUCTION

FUNCTIONAL DESIGN: THE ZIPPER IS LONG ENOUGH TO COMFORTABLY GET IN AND OUT OF THE DRESS

THE BEADS AND BOW ARE PART OF THE DECORATIVE DESIGN

FIGURE 1.6 FUNCTIONAL, STRUCTURAL, AND DECORATIVE DESIGN: STRAPLESS PARTY DRESS

This is achieved by placing the right type of fiber in the right place. Blending the fibers will not achieve this; however, fibers in a multilayer structure will. The layer closest to the skin absorbs, evaporates, and pulls moisture away from the skin.

Figure 1.7 illustrates a swimsuit. The customer wants it to be functional, so part of the designer's responsibility is to choose synthetic high-spandex knit, elastic in both vertical and cross-wise directions. Spandex is an elastic fiber that is often mixed with other yarns to produce combinations such as nylon/spandex, cotton/spandex, and polyester/cotton/spandex. Spandex gives a fabric excellent stretch and recovery so the garment retains its shape and doesn't sag. Swimwear is commonly made from nylon/spandex to enable it to be figure-hugging, fast-drying, flexible enough for movement, and shape-retaining.[5] Garments made in fabrics that have spandex don't need zippers; however, they do need to be stitched with stretch seams. (Refer to Chapter 6, "Stretch Seams.")

Even though swimwear and active wear are made from fabrics with spandex, elastic also needs be applied to the garment edges to help it stay put and cling to the body.[6] To see where swimwear elastic (which is especially treated to stand up to chlorine) has been applied, refer to Figure 1.7. Also refer to Chapter 6, "Stretch Seams."

Spandex is not just limited to use in knit fabrics; it can also be added to woven fabrics. For example, the jacket, pants, and skirt in Figure 1.4 could be made in wool/spandex. The amount

STRUCTURAL DESIGN: SWIMWEAR ELASTIC IS APPLIED TO ALL THE EDGES TO HELP THE SWIMSUIT CLING TO THE BODY

THE FABRIC PATTERN DECORATIVE DESIGN

PART OF THE FUNCTIONAL DESIGN IS TO CHOOSE THE CORRECT FABRIC TYPE TO SUIT THE FUNCTION AND PURPOSE OF THE GARMENT

FIGURE 1.7 FUNCTIONAL, STRUCTURAL, AND DECORATIVE DESIGN: SWIMWEAR

of spandex is not added in the same percentage as swimwear but a minimal amount would offer extra comfort when wearing these garments. Refer to Chapter 2, "Some Differences between Knit and Woven Fabrics."

Structural Design

The second aspect the designer needs to attend to is the *structural design*. Structural design refers to all the seamlines that are stitched to hold the garment together. It also refers to the thread used for stitching. When choosing the stitches and seam finishes, the wear and tear of the garment must be considered.

The first and most important area of structural design, which is necessary to pass quality control, is to have quality permanent seam stitching. A certain number of stitches per inch securely hold the seams together. Too few stitches will not hold the seam adequately; too many stitches may pucker the fabric. Refer to Chapter 2, "Stitch Lengths." Garments made from stretch fabrics need to be stitched with stitches that stretch so the seams can stretch during wear. If stretch stitches are not used, the stitches will "pop" open and eventually the garment will split apart and be returned to the manufacturer. Refer to "Knits" in the section "Stitching Seams in Tricky Fabrics" in Chapter 6.

Buttons are another example; they need to be stitched for closures using quality thread with enough stitches to hold the buttons permanently to the garment so they don't fall off. Refer to Chapter 17, "Stitching Buttons."

Decorative Design

Decorative design refers to the decorative additions to the fabric surface. Decorative design is an important aspect of design because ultimately it may be what attracts a customer to purchase the garment—the special detail that distinguishes one garment from another.

Embroidery, lace, ribbon, bows, buckles, and buttons are just a few of the many items that can be used for decorative design. Choosing just the right decorative item requires time and patience. Decorative design can also encompass the vibrant fabric color or fabric texture, print, or pattern. This is the case in Figure 1.4. Observe the vibrant variegated color in the fabric, which is quite eye-catching.

In Figure 1.5 the decorative design details are the buttons and topstitching used to define the seamlines. In Figure 1.6 the beaded lace and the bow represent the decorative design. The swimsuit in Figure 1.7 also attracts the eye by using an all-over, energetic fabric pattern.

When you hear the following statement about the garment you have designed and manufactured, then you have combined functional, structural, and decorative design together as one: "This garment is so comfortable (functional design) and beautifully stitched together (structural design), and wow . . . this beaded lace adds just the touch that makes the garment stand out from the rest (decorative design)." All three aspects are working together to create one fabulous garment!

REVIEW CHECKLIST

- Do I understand that learning how to sew is a necessary part of designing clothes?
- Do I understand that knowing how to make patterns and stitch garments empowers my knowledge as a design student?
- Do I understand that a designer needs to be connected with every aspect of the design process in order to have a good general knowledge of producing fashion?
- Do I see the importance of functional, structural, and decorative design and how they combine fashion and function?
- Do I see that great designs that function well, have quality stitching, and are made in fabrics that are "just the right weight" are all key to achieving excellent sales?
- Do I understand that designers need to keep their eyes on the entire design process when overseeing the birth and production of a collection?

Getting Prepared: Avoiding Snags

We cannot stress enough the importance of the preparation needed in any sewing project before you begin. Many design students don't prepare and end up in a tangle and discouraged in their sewing ability. This chapter outlines the importance of preparation and shows you how to do it. Every fabric—from silk georgette to a knit jersey—behaves differently. Silk georgette is a soft, drapable, lightweight, sheer fabric, whereas wool jersey is a medium-weight knit fabric that stretches. Understanding the fabric you are working with is vital to successful stitching. Since fabric is the designer's medium, the choices for notions and trims are fabric driven. It can't be assumed that the same notions, such as the thread type, needle type, and interfacing, can be used on all fabric. These aspects need to be individualized for each fabric type and weight.

In this chapter, we explain the importance of taking the time before beginning to stitch any garment to find the right notions to suit each fabric. Sampling first gives a clear direction for the project, and an idea of the notions needed to get started. Ultimately it will prevent mistakes. If one needle or thread type doesn't work, try another size or type until you come up with "just the right one" to suit your fabric.

We still practice this sewing preparation after years of experience and we would never think of skipping this valuable process. Take our advice and get prepared to avoid snags!

STYLE I.D.

The tools needed in your sewing kit are pictured in Figure 2.1.

KEY TERMS

Bulk
Embroidery Scissors
Grainlines
Ironing Board
Matchpoints
Needle Board
Notches
Pressing Cloth
Rotary Cutter/Mats
Scissors
Seam Allowance
Seam Roll
Sleeve Board
Steam Iron
Tailor's Ham
Thread Clippers
Velvaboard

FIGURE 2.1:
STYLE I.D.: TOOLS

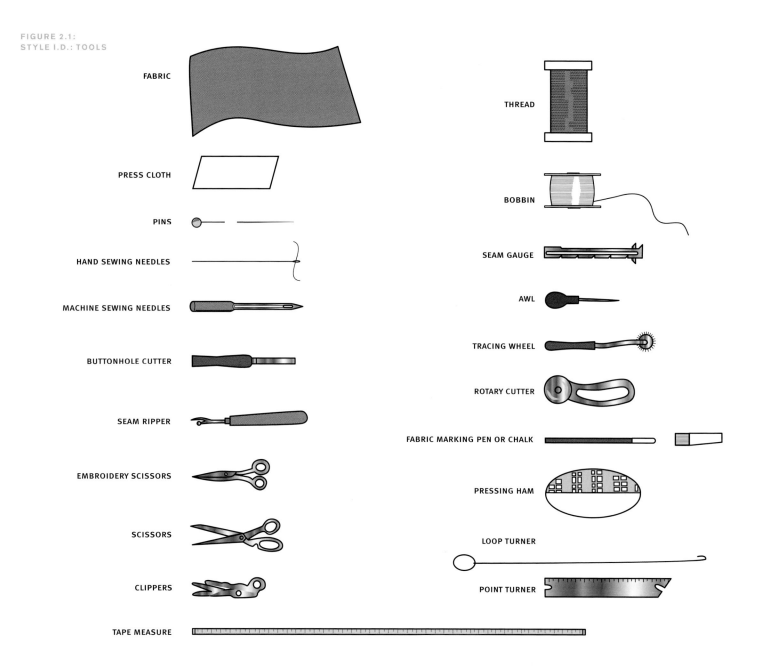

FABRIC

PRESS CLOTH

PINS

HAND SEWING NEEDLES

MACHINE SEWING NEEDLES

BUTTONHOLE CUTTER

SEAM RIPPER

EMBROIDERY SCISSORS

SCISSORS

CLIPPERS

TAPE MEASURE

THREAD

BOBBIN

SEAM GAUGE

AWL

TRACING WHEEL

ROTARY CUTTER

FABRIC MARKING PEN OR CHALK

PRESSING HAM

LOOP TURNER

POINT TURNER

GATHER YOUR TOOLS

These are the essential tools used for stitching garments:

Fabric—the designer's medium.

Scissors—to cut fabric.

Tape measure—to measure patterns and fabric.

Thread—to stitch fabric.

Pins—to pin patterns to fabric, and pin seams together in preparation for stitching.

Seam ripper—to remove unwanted stitching.

Thread clippers—to snip threads after stitching.

Point turner—to get perfect angled corners on collars and cuffs.

Buttonhole cutter—to cut open machine-stitched buttonholes.

Embroidery scissors—for precise cutting into a point.

Machine sewing needles—for stitching seams with the sewing machine.

Hand sewing needles—for stitching seams and hems by hand.

Fabric marking pen or chalk—for marking seams, darts points, and matchpoints.

Loop turner—for turning bias loops.

Pressing ham—a pressing aid.

Pressing cloth—to protect the fabric surface from the iron.

Iron—for pressing garments.

Bobbin—for stitching seams; both top thread and bobbin threads are needed to stitch seams.

Seam gauge—for measuring the seam allowance.

Awl—for marking dart points and matchpoints on the pattern and fabric.

Tracing wheel—for tracing the pattern line in patternmaking and seamlines for stitching; can be either plain edge or serrated.

NOW LET'S GET STARTED

Before cutting and stitching fabric, a design student needs to understand what fibers the fabric is made from, as this influences how the fabric behaves, how to stitch it, and what notions to use.

KNOW YOUR FABRIC

The design process begins with fabric. Fabric is the designer's artistic medium. Choosing a suitable fabric for a style is one of the most important aspects of the design process. Fabric selection and style development *must* work in tandem. If an unsuitable fabric is chosen for a style, then the design won't work.

The designer must understand different varieties and qualities of fabric before attempting a design. Silk georgette won't make a tailored jacket. Designers need to be experts in fabric selection to understand which fabric suits which style. The experienced designer is a fabric sculptor who can look at a fabric, feel it, and envision a design that will suit the fabric. The designer develops this ability through continuous experimentation with fabric. Some designers work directly with the fabric while others sketch designs first and then search for a suitable fabric for the design. **To know fabric, *use it!***

In each chapter, detailed information on handling specialty fabrics will be discussed in the section "Stitching Tricky Fabrics."

Table 2.1 lists some of the categories of fabrics, along with their general uses and care.

The following fabrics are a joy to work with and have become our favorites over the many years of our sewing. This list can be added to as you work with fabric and find your own favorites.

- *Wool crepe:* Easy to sew, it doesn't wrinkle in higher qualities, has a pebbly surface, is stable, and drapes well. It's great for suits, tailored pants, bias-cut garments, and dresses.
- *Wool flannel/worsted:* Easy to sew, wool has a soft, spongier surface, and worsted has a harder, stronger, flatter surface. The weight of the wool determines its use—heavier wools and double-faced wool make great coats and outer jackets, while lighter-weight wools can be used for tailored jackets, pants, skirts, and dresses, all of which should be lined to avoid bagging out.
- *Silk dupioni:* Easy to sew, stable, and crisp, it has a nubby textured surface and is available in a range of colors. It works well for tops, dresses, skirts, jackets and pants, and evening wear.
- *Jersey knit:* Once you learn the correct way to pattern, cut, and stitch knits, they will soon transform from being a tricky fabric to a favorite fabric to work with. Rayon or silk jersey drapes beautifully; it is light to medium weight; and, combined with silk,

TABLE 2.1   CATEGORIES OF FABRIC: THEIR GENERAL USES AND CARE

Type of Fiber: Natural Fibers	Characteristics	Uses	Care
Cotton	Strong, absorbent, versatile, takes dye well, comes in many weights, textures, and weaves. No static cling, tends to wrinkle, and shrink. Works well blended with other fibers.	Lightweight to heavyweight garments, bed linens, upholstery and other home furnishing items, quilting	Wash, hot water, hand or machine, bleach whites, use fabric softener to reduce wrinkling, tumble dry; press while damp or use steam iron.
Wool	Warm, absorbent, resists wrinkling, weakens and stretches when wet, comes in many weights, colors, weaves, and textures; shrinks, tends to "pill," is flame resistant and water repellent. Can be damaged by incorrect pressing.	Coats, suits, pants, skirts, especially tailored styles	Dry clean; some wools are washable by hand in mild soap and cool water. Careful steam pressing is most effective, allow garment to cool before moving
Linen	Absorbent, comfortable, comes in many weights, strong, slightly stiff hand, wears at edges, shrinks, and wrinkles; often mixed with cotton to reduce wrinkling	Warm-weather garments, dresses, blouses, pants, suits	Dry clean, or launder if preshrunk
Silk	Absorbent, strong, deep luster, takes dye well, may bleed, comes in many weights and weaves; medium and heavier weights resist wrinkles; prone to static cling; often woven with linen.	Dresses, suits, blouses, linings, lingerie, evening, and bridal wear	Dry clean; may be hand washable; test a sample for bleeding
Synthetic/ Man-made Fibers:			
Rayon	Weaker than natural fibers, somewhat absorbent, dries fast; tends to wrinkle, is prone to static cling, resists stretching and shrinking.	Is used to make luxurious, silky fabrics such as brocade, crepe, faille, satin, jersey, tricot, and lace, for lingerie, blouses, dresses, and linings	Dry clean; test for hand washing. Avoid high iron temperatures, which melt rayon acetate or viscose
Acrylic	Soft, warm, lightweight, wrinkle resistant; slightly absorbent, dries quickly, may "pill."	Often blended with other fibers to make sheer fabrics, knits, and pile fabrics that are used for dresses, sweaters, sport, and work clothes.	Can be dry cleaned but usually laundered, warm, tumble dry. Press with low setting on wrong side of fabric.
Nylon	Strong, low absorbency, smooth, elastic, resists wrinkles and shrinkage	Often blended with other fibers for wide variety of textures and weights for use in blouses, dresses, linings, and swimwear	Hand or machine wash, rinse thoroughly; drip dry or tumble dry at low setting. Warm iron only if needed.
Polyester	Strong, low absorbency, quick drying, resists wrinkles, stretching, and abrasion; can pill, and have static cling.	Often combined with other fibers to form many weights and textures; used for garments for all types of clothing.	Machine wash depending on the other fiber if blended. Warm iron. Fabric softener reduces static cling
Microfiber	Durable, densely woven, fine fibers, can be water repellent	Usually polyester; used for all types of clothing	Machine wash low temperature; tumble dry low; low temperature iron if needed.

it is luxurious and feels wonderful in tops, tanks, turtlenecks, dresses, pants, cardigans, hoodies, scarves, and lingerie.

- *Wool double knit:* Easy to sew, medium weight, and stable, wool double knit can be a combination of several fibers, including rayon, cotton, and synthetics. It looks great as a cardigan, tank, T-shirt, skirt, unstructured pants, and jackets.
- *Felted wool:* This type of wool is produced by washing wool or wool double knit in hot water and drying it in a hot dryer. The agitation causes the wool fibers to mesh together, creating a dense fabric that needs no finishing.
- *Brocade:* Easy to sew (surprise!) but beautiful, it lends itself to dramatic designs in many weights. It looks great stitched as formal wear and casual wear, too, such as tops, coats, vests, and bags.
- *Upholstery fabric:* Many fabrics found in the home-decorating section are suitable for structured garments. After prewashing, to soften and remove sizing or other fabric treatments, fabulous jackets, coats, and bags can be sewn.
- *Cotton:* A natural fiber, it comes in many weights and textures. Over time, cotton becomes softer and softer. It blends well with other fibers, combining its best qualities of softness and durability. The muslin used in the classroom by design students is 100% cotton.
- *Denim:* Denim has a twill weave, which makes it super durable, and now comes in many weights and can be blended with other

fibers such as Lycra to give it some stretch. Denim ravels and is prone to shrinking, so it needs to be pretreated in the way the garment will be cared for before stitching. This fabric can be stitched into anything.

Table 2.2 categorizes the weights of fabric, types of fabric, thread, and machine needles to use when stitching, as well as recommended stitch lengths. Although the table doesn't include all fabrics, it can be used as a reference point when sampling.

Tricky Fabrics—What They Are and How to Prepare to Use Them

Tricky fabrics require more time and effort to become successfully stitched garments. They have special requirements that must be thought of before cutting into the fabric. Often they require special interfacing or stabilizing, a particular needle for the best-quality stitch, or a notion that is not readily available at the local chain fabric store. Additional yardage may be required for the garment. After sampling the fabric, the design student may find his or her stitching skills are not up to the challenge of the fabric or that this particular fabric is not suitable for the garment after all.

Matching Stripes, Plaids, Patterns, and Repeat Patterns

Extra yardage is required to accommodate fabrics that must be matched up to create a continuous pattern around the body. Add approximately ¼ yard for small plaids, ½ yard

for medium plaids, and 1 yard for large plaids. Crosswise and lengthwise stripes require about the same extra yardage as plaids. When working with a repeat, it is essential to measure the distance between the beginning of one motif and the beginning of the next motif. Placement of the pattern pieces on these motifs, especially if they are spaced far apart, will require additional yardage and this should be measured at the fabric store before purchasing the fabric. If the fabric is being ordered via the Internet and it is not possible to physically measure it, ask for help. Otherwise, order at least one garment length of extra yardage. These are suggested amounts, and the designer may wish to add even more yardage as a safeguard. These fabrics require careful, thoughtful layout of the pattern onto the fabric and accurate transfer of markings. At all costs, avoid placing the center of a flower or a geometric shape directly over the bust area! Extra time may be needed to handbaste seams, or darts to prevent slippage of the seam when stitching.

Sheer Fabrics

Many sheer fabrics are slippery (for example, chiffon, organza, and tulle), and special attention must be paid when cutting them. Additional pattern pieces may need to be drawn and cut for each side of the garment when cutting in a single layer. Use tissue paper or pattern paper under the fabric in a single layer, and pin through the fabric, pattern, and tissue to prevent the fabric from slipping while cutting or sewing. When cutting, use fabric weights to avoid marking the fabric with holes from the pins.

TABLE 2.2 THREAD, NEEDLE, AND STITCH RECOMMENDATIONS FOR SELECTED FABRICS

Fabric Weight	Fabric Type	Thread	Machine Needles	Stitch Length (mm)
Sheer	Batiste, chiffon, nylon tricot, fine lace, organza, net	All-purpose polyester; heirloom sewing thread; silk thread or fine machine embroidery thread 60/2	Universal or Microtex/ MSharp 60/8 65/9	2.0
	Handkerchief linen, lawn, sheer crepe, voile	Mercerized cotton 50/3; silk thread	Universal 70/10 or 80/12	2.5
Light	Crepe de chine, cotton, gauze, georgette, gingham	All-purpose polyester	Universal 60/8 or 65/9	2.0
	Knits, double knits, velour	For knits woolly nylon in bobbin or for serger loopers	Stretch 75/11	Zigzag 0.5/2.5
	Satin	Fine cotton or silk	Microtex 70/10	2.0
	Taffeta, silk	All-purpose polyester or fine cotton	Universal 70/10	2.5
	Wool challis	All-purpose polyester or fine cotton, silk	Universal 80/12	2.5
	Microfiber	Fine machine embroidery	Microtex 60/8	1.5
Medium	Brocade	All-purpose polyester; Mercerized cotton 50/3	Universal 70/10	2.5
	Corduroy, linen, muslin, pique, poplin, wool, wool crepe, tweed	Same as above	80/12	2.5
	Shantung	Same as above	70/10	2.5
	Sweatshirt	All-purpose polyester	Stretch 75/11	Zigzag 0.5/3.0
	Swimwear	All-purpose polyester	Stretch 75/11	0.75/2.5
	Synthetic suede	All-purpose polyester	Jeans/Denim 75/11	2.5
	Terry cloth, velveteen	All-purpose polyester or cotton	Universal 80/12	2.5 or 3.0
Medium–heavy	Coat-weight wool	All-purpose polyester	Universal 90/14	3.0–3.5
	Faux fur	All-purpose polyester or cotton	80/12 or 90/14	Hinged seam
	Felt, fleece, gabardine	All-purpose polyester	80/12	3.0
	Leather, lightweight, heavier weight		Jeans/Denim 70/10 Leather 90/14	3.0
	Faux leather, suede	All-purpose polyester	Stretch 75/11	2.5
	Quilted fabric	All-purpose polyester or cotton	Quilting 75/11 or 90/14	3.0
	Sweater knits	All-purpose polyester	Stretch 75/11	Zigzag 0.75/2.5
	Upholstery fabric	All-purpose polyester or cotton	Jeans/Denim 90/14	3.0

(TABLE CONTINUED ON NEXT PAGE)

Fabric Weight	Fabric Type	Thread	Machine Needles	Stitch Length (mm)
Very heavy	Upholstery, heavy denim	All-purpose polyester; upholstery	Jeans/Denim 100/16	3.0
	Double-faced coating	All-purpose polyester; silk	Universal 90/14	3.0–3.5
	Canvas	All-purpose polyester; upholstery	Jeans/Denim 100/16 or 110/18	3.5

Lace

This beautiful fabric is available in different weights and can be sheer and fine or heavily embellished. When working with lace, keep in mind that there is definitely a pattern, or repeat, to work with. Additional pattern pieces may need to be cut when cutting out the lace in a single layer. Stitching the garment with tissue paper will protect the lace from snagging on the feed dogs, as explained in Chapter 6. Choose tissue paper in a color that blends with the lace, in case little bits of paper remain after stitching. Often, lace is expensive; however, a small amount used in a section of a garment can be effective. Careful measuring and layout of the pattern piece on the lace ensures efficient use of the lace—again, avoid placing a prominent motif in the bust area.

Satin

In any blend, in any weight, satin needs the most delicate handling. The designer *must* sample everything before stitching this fabric. Marking pen could bleed through the fabric, and removing the markings with water will spot the satin; the wrong-sized pins could mar the surface of the fabric with pulled threads; the slightest nick or rough surface could snag the threads that float on the surface of the satin. Be careful to cover the cutting surface with paper or tissue paper. All pattern pieces should be cut and laid out in one direction to ensure that no shading occurs. The wrong needle or thread weight will cause pulled threads, or holes in the fabric that cannot be removed. Plus, overpressing can cause the satin to look limp and worn out. Satin is a difficult fabric to work with and requires patience and a clear understanding of how to handle the fabric.

Beaded Fabrics

Often beading is done by hand or machine on silk chiffon as a base, so working with beaded fabrics requires knowledge of several things: the beading is usually a pattern or a repeat; the threads that hold the beading to the cloth must be reinforced before cutting; the beads must be removed from the seam allowances before stitching; and the correct needle and thread must be chosen for the weight of the base fabric. Pressing can damage the beads, so steam and finger-press from the wrong side of the garment. Place tissue paper or pattern paper beneath the fabric when cutting and stitching to prevent snagging and to help feed the fabric along the feed dogs.

Knits

The very thing that makes knits wonderful is also what makes them tricky—stretch. Too much stretch and the garment fit could be a disaster; not enough stretch and it could be a disaster! The amount of stretch in a knit replaces many fitting details such as darts, so it is important to have the right amount of stretch in the fabric. Some knits stretch only in the width and/or the length. The huge variety of weights, blends, and textures of knits requires careful consideration of the use of the knit for the style of the garment. If the knit is tubular, avoid using the creased fold unless the permanent crease is desired for the design. When laying out knits for cutting, it is especially important that the entire piece of fabric be supported, and not hanging off the edge of the cutting surface. This would cause distortion of the pieces being cut. Nap or surface finish on knits can cause shading on the fabric. Check to see if the knit can be cut "top and tail" (with one piece facing up and one piece facing down) or whether it must be cut with all pattern pieces lying in the same direction to ensure that no shading occurs. Sharp pins and sharp cutting tools are critical for smooth, accurate cutting, as often ¼-inch seam allowances are used when working with knits. Knits can be stitched on either sergers or sewing machines. Proper stabilizing of the shoulder, neckline, and armhole areas prevents the seams from stretching while stitching. Use stretch needles for knits to avoid skipped stitches. Pressing the seams can leave impressions on the garment; use strips of paper underneath to prevent this, and set the temperature of the iron to match the fibers of the knit. *Never* apply the iron directly on the surface of a knit; it will scorch the fibers, create a shine that can't be removed, and flatten the fibers. Keep pressing to a minimum.

Denim

Although denim is considered the "workhorse" of cottons, it comes in many weights, blends, and surface treatments. Pretreat denim to shrink the yardage and remove excess dye, which could bleed onto other garments. Press the denim while still slightly damp to prevent permanent creases. When cutting denim, it is critical to be on the straight-of-grain, otherwise problems such as twisting occur. When seams intersect, or when hemming, pound the seams with a mallet to flatten, making them easier to stitch through. A strong, sturdy denim/jeans needle should be used to avoid skipped stitches and accommodate the heavier thread available for topstitching the seams and hems.

Velvet

Velvet is a short pile fabric that is made by weaving extra loops on the surface of the fabric, and then cutting to produce the pile. The direction

in which this pile lies is called the *nap*. When you run your hand against the nap, the fabric feels rough and shows the deepest, richest color. When you run your hand in the other direction, with the nap, the fabric is smooth and appears lighter. The designer decides in which direction to place the nap, but this should be consistent when laying out the pattern pieces on the fabric. Because the beauty of velvet is the nap, avoiding crushing the nap is a consideration at every step of construction when using this fabric. Marking must be visible, but must not mar the surface of the velvet. Velvet slips when cutting and stitching, so use tissue paper or pattern paper beneath the fabric to prevent this problem. Handbasting the seams and using silk thread helps to eliminate slippage; using silk thread leaves no visible marks or holes on velvet. Pins can leave unattractive dents if left in the fabric too long, or if accidentally left in the fabric while steaming a seam. Velvet ravels and is messy to work with, as the short fibers of the pile are released from the surface after cutting. Velvet garments are almost always lined, and the seams are covered by the lining. Placing an iron on velvet crushes the nap and creates shine, which cannot be removed. Use a **Velvaboard** or **needle board** to support the velvet while steaming above the seam from the wrong side of the fabric. After the steam has penetrated the fabric, finger-press the seam open, patting along the seam as it cools. Allow each section to cool before moving the fabric. For synthetic velvets, use the lowest iron temperature that will produce steam, but be very careful to prevent water from spitting

onto the fabric at low temperatures. Velvet can be steamed while on the dress form, but this must be done very carefully to avoid crushing the pile—once the pile has been crushed, it can't be revived. The quality of velvet varies—always use the best quality that is cost effective for the garment being stitched.

Leather

Leather is sold by the individual skin or hide, in many weights (the number of ounces per square foot), colors, and textures. Many skins have imperfections, which affect the way the pattern pieces can be placed. It is essential to have full pattern pieces for each section of the garment. All leather should be cut in a single layer. Leather does not actually have a grain, but it is easy to distinguish the length versus width of the skin. The pattern pieces should be placed on the skin lengthwise as much as possible, since the width has more give. Use weights to hold pattern pieces in place, and mark with chalk or dressmaker carbon, using a smooth-edged tracing wheel. Binder clips or glue sticks can be used in place of traditional basting. A Glover needle is used for any hand stitches, and waxed thread is used to sew on buttons. A leather machine needle in the appropriate size for the weight of the leather is necessary to prevent skipped stitches. *Never* backstitch—it cuts the leather. After stitching the seams, tie off the threads, topstitch, or use leather cement, and pound with a rubber mallet to flatten and hold seams in place. To press leather, use a warm iron with no steam, covering the leather with brown paper.

Faux Fur

Faux fur is a pile synthetic fabric with either a knitted or a woven backing of cotton or synthetic fiber. It is available in an amazing assortment of plush textures that mimic real furs. Additional yardage of approximately ½ to ¾ yard is required for these fabrics, which should be cut out with the nap (pile feeling smooth, going down) in a single layer. A razor blade can be used to cut the backing to avoid cutting the fur that gives a blunt look to the cut edges. Remove the fur from the seam allowances before stitching the seams, and handbaste to prevent the fur from creeping or puckering when machine stitching. Stitch directionally, with the nap. Reinforce stress areas with tape and slightly clip curved edges. Seams cannot be pressed in the traditional manner due to the pile; either steam and then finger-press, or use a Velvaboard and press lightly with the tip of the iron over a press cloth. The temperature of the iron should be as low as possible to avoid melting the backing if it is synthetic. The choice of a specific faux fur should be based on its use in the garment, and whether it is washable or must be dry cleaned. Using contrasting fabric such as satin or taffeta or the lined-to-the-edge method reduces the bulk of traditional facings.

Heavyweight Fabrics

These fabrics require special treatment simply because of their bulk. Heavyweight fabrics are often stiff; match the style of the garment being designed to the weight of the fabric. Notched collars can be difficult to sew because of the bulk

and the difficulty of pressing the seams flat. Full pattern pieces are necessary for laying out the garment on a single layer of fabric. Trying to cut out a double layer of heavyweight fabric results in the fabric shifting. Some pieces end up being too big and some too small. Pattern weights are needed to hold the pattern pieces in place while cutting, as pins often get lost in the depth of the fabric. Snip (⅛" into the fabric) to mark notches in the seam allowances; thread tracing, chalk, or temporary marking pens also work—sample to see what shows up best on the fabric. Directionally sew the seams with the nap, lengthen the stitch length, and adjust the pressure on the presser foot (Figure 2.23) if possible. A presser foot holds the fabric against the feed dogs, moving the fabric along as stitches are formed. Instead of using self-fabric for facings or the under collars, use a contrasting, lighter-weight fabric or line the garment, edge-to-edge. Pressing heavyweight fabrics involves lots of steam, muscle, a wooden clapper to flatten the seams, and avoiding visible impressions from the seams on the front of the garment.

This is by no means a complete list of what might be considered tricky or difficult-to-work-with fabrics but rather represents the fabrics most often encountered by design students in class projects.

As you approach each chapter, the section on tricky fabrics will guide you through the dos and don'ts at each construction step. For example, if you are unsure whether a collar can be made of a particular tricky fabric, consult Chapter 11 for details.

IT ALL BEGINS WITH THE PATTERN

Correct stitching begins with correct pattern-making; correct pattern marking communicates how the fabric is to be cut. If the patterns are not made and marked correctly, then the fabric cannot be cut correctly and the garment cannot be stitched correctly! In our classes, we often notice students who are confused and unsure of how to stitch the garment, and why is this? No pattern markings! The students then scramble in their bags or lockers trying to locate the patterns while valuable class time is lost. When they finally locate the pattern, they realize they never marked the patterns, and this explains why they couldn't stitch the garment together. Let's look at each pattern marking in more depth.

Grainlines

Grainlines are one of the most important pattern markings, as they affect the way the garment hangs and retains its shape. The grainline communicates the direction in which each pattern is to be placed on the fabric and cut. As the pattern is plotted, the grainline is one of the first pattern markings to be drawn on the pattern. (Refer to Table 2.3 later in this chapter for more information.) Without marked grainlines, a pattern might be cut in any direction you chose; this could result in a peculiar, twisted-looking garment that would be difficult to stitch together, and would drape and fit poorly.

Lengthwise Grain

• This grainline is drawn parallel to the center front/center back of the pattern (Figure 2.2).

- Make sure the pattern has two arrows drawn at both ends of the grainline to indicate that the pattern can be placed on the fabric in either direction (Figure 2.2).
- Draw a T-bar at one end and an arrow at the other end of the grainline if the fabric needs to be cut directionally. The T indicates the *top* of the pattern and the arrow indicates the direction for the pattern to be placed on the fabric. Some fabrics have a one-way fabric design or the fabric has a pile. Garments cut in these fabrics need every pattern piece cut in one direction so the fabric falls in one direction when the garment is worn. For more information on directional cutting, refer to Figure 2.15. Observe how the grainline shown there indicates the direction for cutting the fabric.

Crosswise Grain

- This grainline is drawn at a 90-degree angle to the center front/center back (see Figure 2.2).

Bias Grain

- This grainline is drawn at a 45-degree angle to the center front/center back (Figure 2.2).

Notches

Notches are marked on the pattern when the pattern is being drafted. A notch is marked with a 1/8-inch pencil mark drawn at a 90-degree angle to the seamline. Notches can indicate the width of a dart, which fabric pieces are to be placed together, and the amount of seam and hem allowance to be stitched.

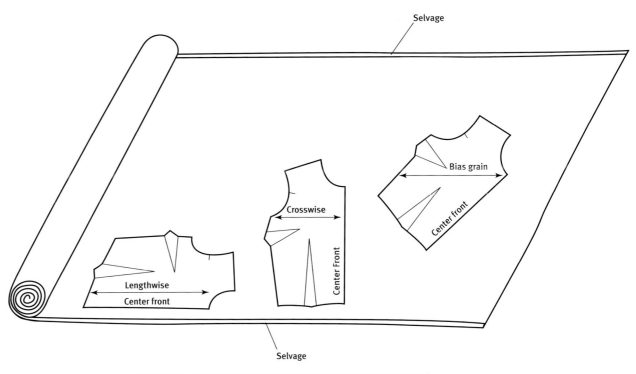

FIGURE 2.2 LENGTHWISE, CROSSWISE, AND BIAS GRAINLINES

To indicate the front of the garment, one notch is placed on the seamlines (Figure 2.3a). To indicate the back of the garment, two notches are placed on the seamlines (Figure 2.3a). Very long seams may need more than one set of notches. Notches are also placed in different positions along the seamline (Figure 2.3b). Make sure that if the pattern was flipped in the opposite direction, the notches could not be matched to any other seam.

When two fabric pieces are stitched to form a seam, each end of the seam is pinned together. After this, the notches are pinned together and then the seam is pinned in between these points.

You can see how important notches are and how they make a huge difference in the stitching process—this is why correct pattern marking results in correct stitching. When the notches have been marked on the pattern, snipped in the fabric, and matched together in the stitching process, the garment will sit perfectly and drape beautifully on the body.

Matchpoints and Dart Points

Matchpoints indicate precisely the points that must come together when stitching a seam or applying a pocket, pocket tab, or ruffle to the surface of the garment.[1] Both matchpoints are marked with a small pencil dot on the pattern. Correct marking sets the sewer up for success! In Figure 2.4, the matchpoints are indicated on the pattern to mark the pocket placement on the *right side of the garment only.*

Pattern Labeling

Labeling of each pattern piece is important to communicate the part of the garment the pattern is meant for, the size of the pattern, and how many fabric pieces need to be cut.

Figure 2.3a shows the pattern marking and labeling that *must* be communicated on the patterns for designs that are symmetrical. Notice the bodice in this figure is the same on both sides—this is what makes the bodice symmetrical—both sides are equal and mirror images of each other.

In Figure 2.3b the bodice is asymmetrical; this means that both sides of the garment *are not equal or the same.* Notice that every pattern piece is a different shape, and each piece says "Cut 1." The pattern is also labeled "R.S.U."— this stands for "Right Side Up." When the pattern is placed on the fabric, it must be facing *up* on the correct side of the fabric; this ensures the garment can be stitched correctly if it is cut correctly. If the patterns were to be turned over to the other side and cut, it would be impossible to stitch the garment! Refer to Figure 2.3b.

Patterns for asymmetrical designs can also be labeled "W.S.U." (Wrong Side Up), which indicates the pattern is placed on the wrong side of the fabric. How the pattern is laid on the fabric is guided by the fabric surface.

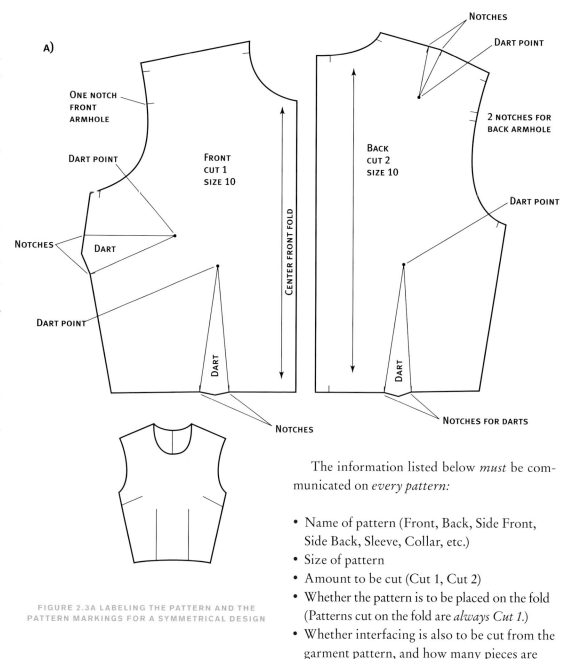

A)

NOTCHES

DART POINT

ONE NOTCH FRONT ARMHOLE

2 NOTCHES FOR BACK ARMHOLE

DART POINT

FRONT CUT 1 SIZE 10

BACK CUT 2 SIZE 10

DART POINT

NOTCHES

DART

CENTER FRONT FOLD

DART POINT

DART POINT

DART

DART

NOTCHES

NOTCHES FOR DARTS

FIGURE 2.3A LABELING THE PATTERN AND THE PATTERN MARKINGS FOR A SYMMETRICAL DESIGN

The information listed below *must* be communicated on *every pattern:*

- Name of pattern (Front, Back, Side Front, Side Back, Sleeve, Collar, etc.)
- Size of pattern
- Amount to be cut (Cut 1, Cut 2)
- Whether the pattern is to be placed on the fold (Patterns cut on the fold are *always Cut 1.*)
- Whether interfacing is also to be cut from the garment pattern, and how many pieces are

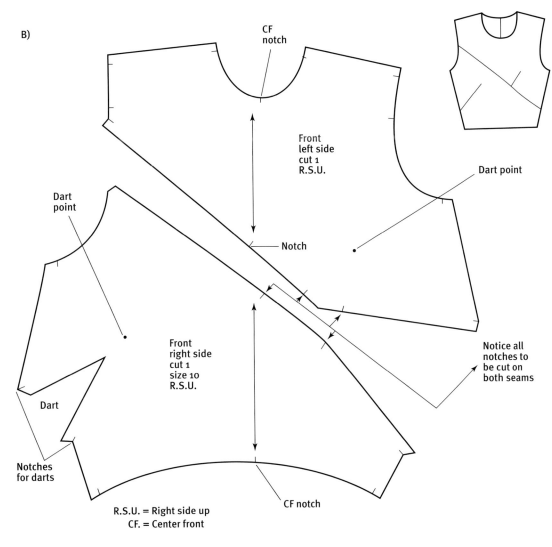

B)

CF
notch

Front
left side
cut 1
R.S.U.

Dart point

Dart
point

Notch

Dart
point

Front
right side
cut 1
size 10
R.S.U.

Notice all
notches to
be cut on
both seams

Dart

Notches
for darts

CF notch

R.S.U. = Right side up
CF. = Center front

FIGURE 2.3B LABELING THE PATTERN AND THE PATTERN
MARKINGS FOR AN ASYMMETRICAL DESIGN

to be cut (Label to communicate this—Cut 1 or Cut 2 from self fabric, Cut 1 or Cut 2 interfacing, as shown in Figure 2.5a and b.)

Interfacing for some garments is not cut from the garment pattern. In these cases, a separate interfacing pattern is needed. This is illustrated in Figure 2.6, which shows pocket interfacing that will be applied to pants. Separate interfacing patterns *must* be included in the overall patterns and labeled as "Interfacing Only."

Math for Fashion Designers

Many students struggle to use a ruler or tape measure and find it hard to measure precisely. This can slow them down in their patternmaking and stitching skills. These difficulties cannot be ignored, as knowledge of measurements is crucial for accurate patternmaking and stitching. For example, designers often measure

PATTERN TIP

If the pattern markings and notches are not plotted on the pattern and then snipped and marked in the fabric, when the machinist stitches the garments together, he or she will *not* know which seams go together or how much seam allowance to use. If notches are not snipped, garment pieces can be turned upside down or stretched to fit another garment piece. This can swing the garment "off grain," making it look twisted and badly stitched. In the classroom, this would affect one garment, but in production it could affect thousands.

a dress form before patternmaking takes place. The important measurements for making women's patterns are illustrated on the model shown in Figure 2.7b. Guessing about measurements is never going to be good enough, and the designer who guesses will soon be out of a job!

You'll need to be familiar with the various measurements illustrated in Table 2.3. Make sure you understand these measurements before beginning to make patterns. Study this table, and get help from your instructor if necessary.

Seam allowance must be added onto all patterns before the fabric can be cut. The amount of seam and hem allowance that is added determines whether the garment can be stitched correctly, and how it looks once stitched. If the seam or hem allowances are too small, it will be nearly impossible to stitch the seams. If the seam or hem allowances are too wide, then bulk will be added, and bulk always spoils the look of any garment when it is worn.

SEAM ALLOWANCE

The **seam allowance** is the space between the seamline and the edge of the pattern or the seamline and the cut fabric edge. After the seams are stitched, the seam allowance is hidden unless the garment has exposed seams, which will then show on the correct side of the garment—this is referred to as a deconstructed look (refer to Figure 6.2). The seam allowance protects the stitches from fraying. The seam allowance allows the garment to be fitted; the seam allowance can be stitched wider if the garment is too big, or let out if too tight. Seam allowance

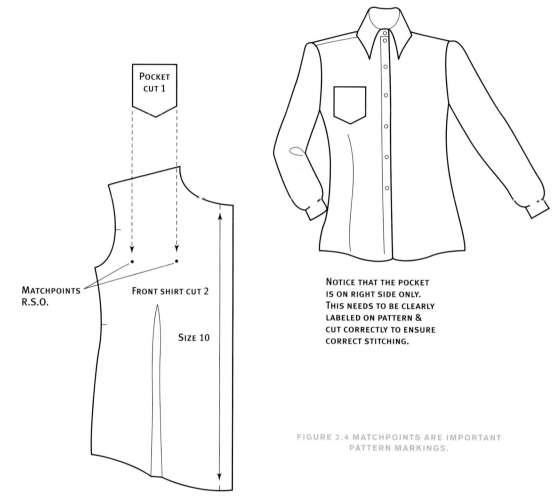

FIGURE 2.4 MATCHPOINTS ARE IMPORTANT PATTERN MARKINGS.

can be added in inches (imperial measurements) or in centimeters (metric measurements).

If you have your own design business, you'll need to set a standard seam allowance for everyone to use. When seam allowances keep changing, it confuses the machinists. Whatever seam allowance you decide to use, for your company or in school, the important thing is to keep it consistent.

Adding Seam Allowance to the Pattern

Figure 2.8a illustrates the four seam allowances that are generally used when stitching garments. Figure 2.8a and b illustrate the seam allowances used when stitching woven fabric. Hem allowances are driven more by the garment silhouette and the fabric weight (Figure 2.9).

When seams are enclosed or shaped, as for a curved neckline or collar seam, allow ¼-inch

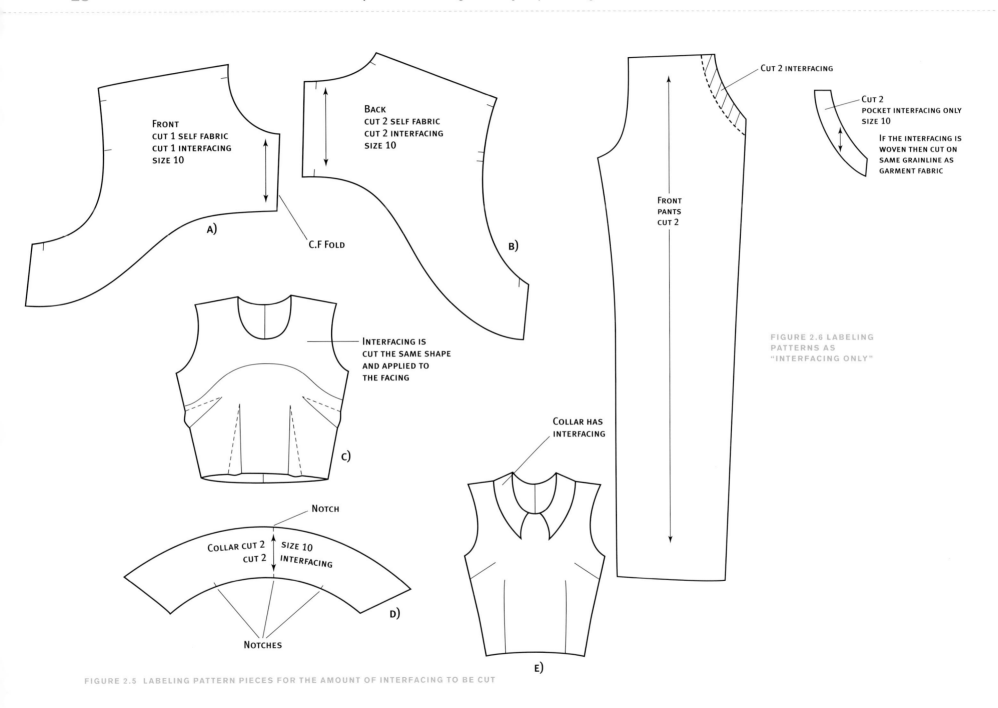

FRONT
CUT 1 SELF FABRIC
CUT 1 INTERFACING
SIZE 10

A)

C.F FOLD

BACK
CUT 2 SELF FABRIC
CUT 2 INTERFACING
SIZE 10

B)

CUT 2 INTERFACING

CUT 2
POCKET INTERFACING ONLY
SIZE 10

IF THE INTERFACING IS
WOVEN THEN CUT ON
SAME GRAINLINE AS
GARMENT FABRIC

INTERFACING IS
CUT THE SAME SHAPE
AND APPLIED TO
THE FACING

C)

FRONT
PANTS
CUT 2

FIGURE 2.6 LABELING
PATTERNS AS
"INTERFACING ONLY"

NOTCH

COLLAR CUT 2   SIZE 10
CUT 2   INTERFACING

D)

NOTCHES

COLLAR HAS
INTERFACING

E)

FIGURE 2.5 LABELING PATTERN PIECES FOR THE AMOUNT OF INTERFACING TO BE CUT

IMPORTANT MEASUREMENTS

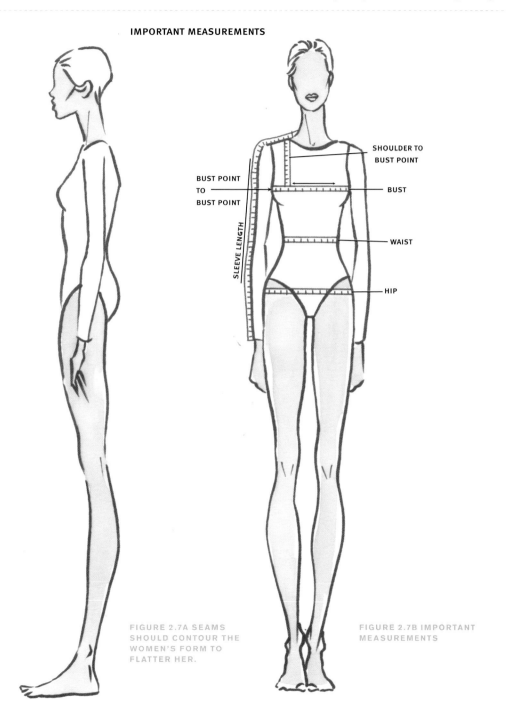

SHOULDER TO
BUST POINT

BUST POINT
TO
BUST POINT

BUST

WAIST

SLEEVE LENGTH

HIP

FIGURE 2.7B IMPORTANT
MEASUREMENTS

seam allowances (see Figure 2.8a and b). It is far easier to stitch narrower seam allowances around curved seams. If a ½-inch seam allowance were to be used for an armhole or neck opening, it would need to be trimmed back to ¼ inch to reduce bulk, and this is a waste of time. The seam can still be carefully clipped, graded (depending on the thickness), and understitched before turning. (Refer to Chapter 11 for collar seam allowance and to Chapter 6 for further information about seams.)

- Add ½ inch for all seams: side, shoulder, armhole, waist, princess seams, yokes, and any other seams not mentioned (see Figure 2.8a and b).
- Add ¾-inch seam allowance at center back and for any other seams where a zipper will be stitched (see Figure 2.8b). If the garment has a side seam zipper (a side seam normally has a ½-inch seam allowance), then make *a step* in the seam allowance to allow ¾ inch for the zipper to be stitched as well as the ½-inch side seam. The fabric layout for a one-way fabric design illustrates how the step looks on the side seam (see Figure 2.15).
- For fitting purposes, add wider seam allowances.
- Stretch knit garments only need ¼-inch seam allowances, as knits do not fray. Most knit garments are stitched with a serger, and ¼ inch is the perfect width. For firm knits such as wool double knit, use ½-inch seam allowances for woven fabric widths.

TABLE 2.3 MATH FOR FASHION DESIGNERS

FRACTIONS—MEASUREMENTS USED IN PATTERNMAKING

³/₄"   ¹/₂"   ³/₈"   ¹/₈"   ¹/₁₆"

SEAM ALLOWANCES

¼" ⎯⎯ Enclosed seams: facings, collars, and knit seams
½" ⎯⎯ Side seam, shoulder seam, princess seams, and other seams
¾" ⎯⎯ Center-back seam
1" ⎯⎯ Seams for fittings

HEM ALLOWANCES

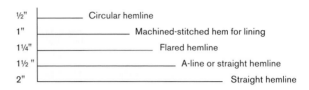

½" ⎯⎯ Circular hemline
1" ⎯⎯ Machined-stitched hem for lining
1¼" ⎯⎯ Flared hemline
1½" ⎯⎯ A-line or straight hemline
2" ⎯⎯ Straight hemline

GEOMETRY—GRAINLINES

Lengthwise grainline is a line drawn parallel to the center front.

Crosswise grainline is a horizontal line drawn at right angles to the center front. It is also referred to as *90-degree right angle.*

Bias grainline is a diagonal line drawn at a *45-degree angle* to the center front.

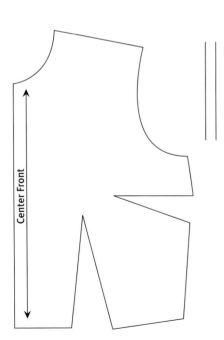

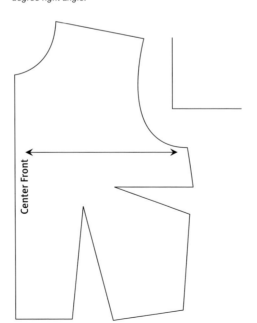

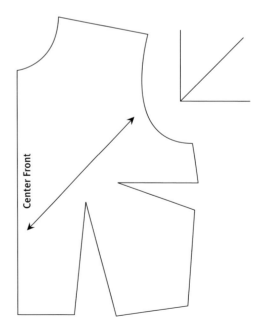

FIGURE 2.8A SEAM ALLOWANCES FOR THE FRONT GARMENT

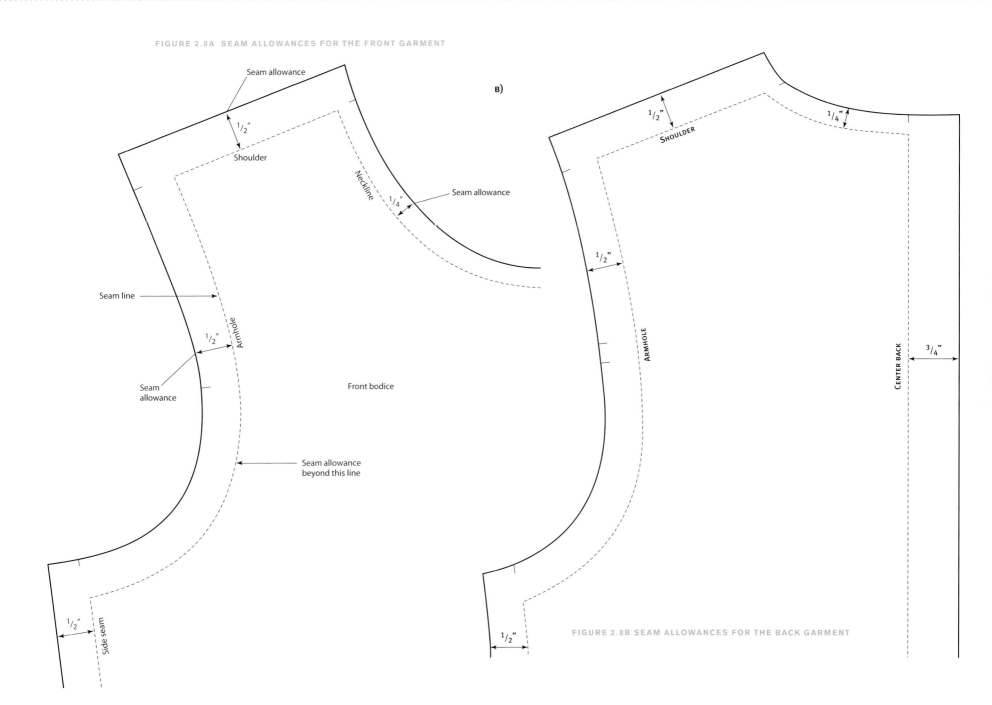

B)

FIGURE 2.8B SEAM ALLOWANCES FOR THE BACK GARMENT

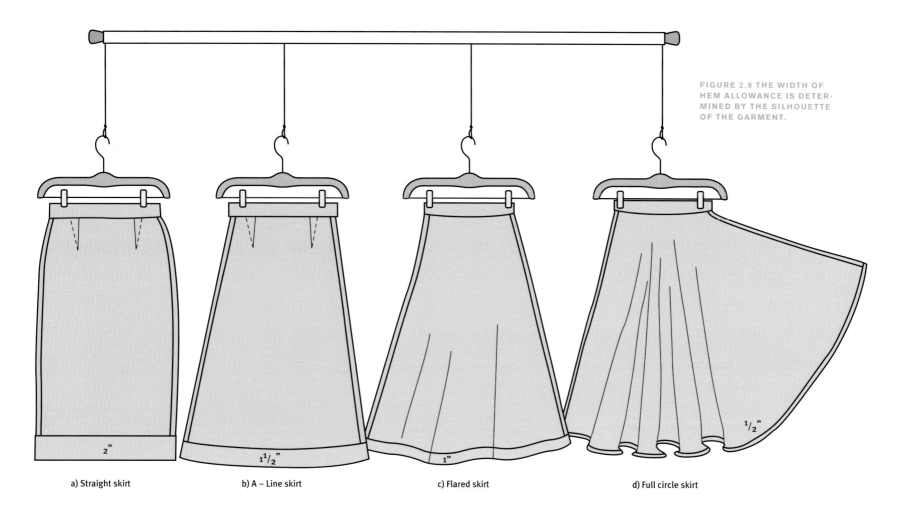

FIGURE 2.9 THE WIDTH OF HEM ALLOWANCE IS DETERMINED BY THE SILHOUETTE OF THE GARMENT.

a) Straight skirt   b) A – Line skirt   c) Flared skirt   d) Full circle skirt

Hem Allowances

The hem allowance is the width between the hemline and the hem edge. The hem allowance is folded back under the garment to the wrong side of the fabric; the clean finished edge is the finished hemline. There are times that the designer leaves a raw deconstructed hem edge as a design detail. When stitching hems, the fabric and garment silhouette determine the width of the hem

allowance. Wide, bulky hems look thick and ugly and show a ridge from the correct side of the garment; this does not give a quality finish to the garment. In general, the wider and fuller the skirt, the narrower the hem width needs to be. This is how bulk is reduced. The following tips will help define the hem allowance used for different garment silhouettes. Also refer to Chapter 15 for more information about hems.

- Straight skirts made in a medium to heavyweight fabric can have 1½-inch to 2-inch hem allowances (Figure 2.9a).
- A-line skirts have a wider silhouette, so reduce the hem allowance to 1½ inches to reduce bulk (Figure 2.9b).
- A flared skirt is wider again, so reduce the hem allowance to 1 inch (Figure 2.9c).
- A full-circle skirt is full and flouncy: reduce

the hem width to ½ inch so bulk will not be a concern. In sheer fabrics a narrow hem will not shadow and will look inconspicuous from the correct side of the fabric (Figure 2.9d).

- Hem allowances in knits are reduced to ½ to 1 inch regardless of the style. Refer to Chapter 15 for information about stitching hems in knits.

Table 2.4 shows the seam allowances used for imperial and metric measurements. The amount of seam allowance added is important to achieving quality stitching; incorrect seam allowance will result in badly stitched seams.

Table 2.4 shows fabric width in both metric measurements and imperial measurements. This chapter has explained about fabric in some depth and now it is time to cut the fabric, so let's begin.

LAYING OUT AND CUTTING FABRIC

Before the fabric can be cut, it must be prepared. Fabric preparation ensures excellent cutting; excellent cutting ensures excellent stitching; excellent stitching ensures a beautiful garment on the body! Fabric preparation is an essential step.

Know Your Fabric

First, know what fabric you are working with. It is amazing how many students *don't know* what fibers make up the fabric they are working with. If you were a visual artist, you would definitely know what type of paint you were working with, as it would influence how you paint. It is no different when using fabric! Look at the

TABLE 2.4 SEAM ALLOWANCES

	Enclosed Seams	All Seams	Center Back Seam with Zipper	Extra Width for Fitting Purposes
Woven Fabrics and Firm Knits				
Imperial (inches)	¼"	½"	¾"	1" or more
Metric	1 cm	1½ cm	2 cm	½"–1"
Knit Fabrics				
Imperial (inches)	¼"	¼"	Stretchy knits don't need zippers	¾"
Metric	1 cm	1 cm		2 cm

end of the roll of fabric and jot down the fabric content. If it is not documented, ask the salesperson, who may know, or ask your instructor.

Even before the design is sketched, know the fabric structure as well as the impact it will have on the design, patterns, cutting the fabric, stitching the seams, thread and needles used, and how the fabric is pressed. Understanding and knowing fabric begins by understanding the fabric structure. Fabric structure falls into two categories: knitted and woven.

Knitted fabric is created by forming a row of loops, and then drawing another row of loops through that row, again and again, just as you would do when knitting a sweater with knitting needles.

Woven fabric has warp and weft yarns that interlace at right angles to each other. Refer to Table 2.3 to see an example of a right angle. Along both edges of the warp fabric direction is the selvage, which finishes the fabric edges and is more tightly woven. The warp yarns

run along the length of the fabric, which is the lengthwise grain; the weft yarns run across the fabric, which is the crosswise grain. Take a look at Figure 2.10 and notice how the crosswise and lengthwise yarns intersect at a 45-degree angle; this is called the bias grain.

Some Differences between Knit and Woven Fabrics

- *Knit* and *woven* fabrics can have spandex, a manufactured synthetic fiber, added to them. The most widely used spandex today is Du Pont's Lycra. When Lycra is added to a woven fabric, it adds stretch capacity, but not enough to do away with darts and fitting lines. When spandex is added to a knit fabric, it's like adding an elastic band into the fabric. Knit fabric that contains spandex has more stretch capacity, allowing it to be fitted more tightly. Spandex also helps a garment retain its shape, and prevents woven or knit fabrics from wrinkling.

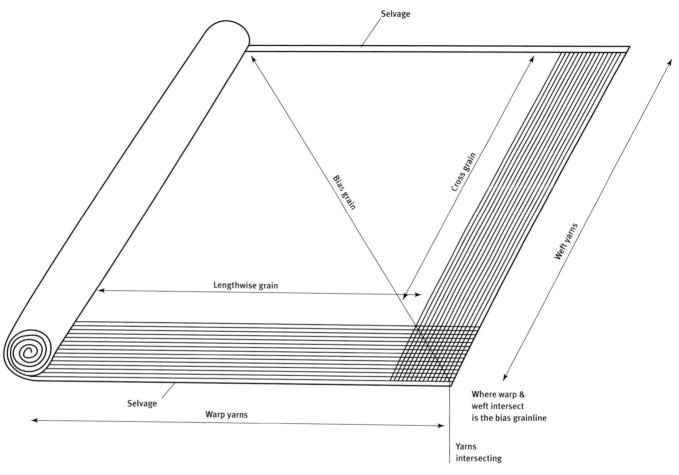

Selvage

Bias grain

Cross grain

Weft yarns

Lengthwise grain

Selvage

Where warp &
weft intersect
is the bias grainline

Warp yarns

Yarns
intersecting

FIGURE 2.10 FABRIC GRAINLINES: LENGTHWISE, CROSSWISE, AND BIAS GRAINS

- Woven fabrics don't stretch like knits. Although the fabric width does have a little give, this is not to be confused with a stretch fabric.
- Both woven and knit fabrics stretch across the *bias grain* and stretch at any angle between lengthwise and crosswise grains.
- The difference between a knit and a woven fabric influences how the pattern is made, and how the garment fits on the body. Gen-

erally, patterns for knit fabrics don't need ease, darts, or fitting lines other than those required for fitting the side seams. The stretch element replaces the need for ease. However, this aspect is individualized depending on the amount of stretch in each knit fabric. Knits can be stable, moderately stretchy, or stretchy. Ease *must* be incorporated into the patterns for woven fabrics if the garment is to fit the body.

- Whether you are working with a knit or woven fabric will influence the stitches and hem finishes used on the garment. When the seams are stitched in woven fabrics, the edges need to be finished because woven fabric frays easily; on the other hand, knit fabrics need to be stitched with a stretch stitch and do not fray. However, the edges are frequently serged to add a quality finish to the garment.

- Whether a knit or woven fabric is being stitched also influences the choice of notions used, as thread and needle types differ for each fabric type and weight (Table 2.5).

Know Your Grainlines

The decision about which grainline to use in cutting a garment is fabric and design driven. The grainline on which the garment is cut makes a difference in how the garment drapes on the body. It also makes a difference when stitching the garment.

Woven Fabric

Lengthwise Grain

The lengthwise grain is the most frequently used grainline for cutting woven fabric. One reason for this is that it has very little give; in other words, it doesn't stretch. Consequently, when vertical seams such as side seams or princess seams are stitched, the lengthwise grain helps to control the stitching and prevents seams from stretching in the stitching process. Another reason is very practical: the fabric layout is more economical. (Refer to Figure 2.18.)

Crossgrain

The crossgrain has more give and causes garments to fall differently. A gathered skirt that is cut on the crossgrain will have a fuller look and the fabric will not drape in the same way as it would if the fabric were cut on the lengthwise grain. Take a piece of fabric and observe this for yourself. Cutting garments on the crossgrain produces more "give" across the fabric, and this *may*

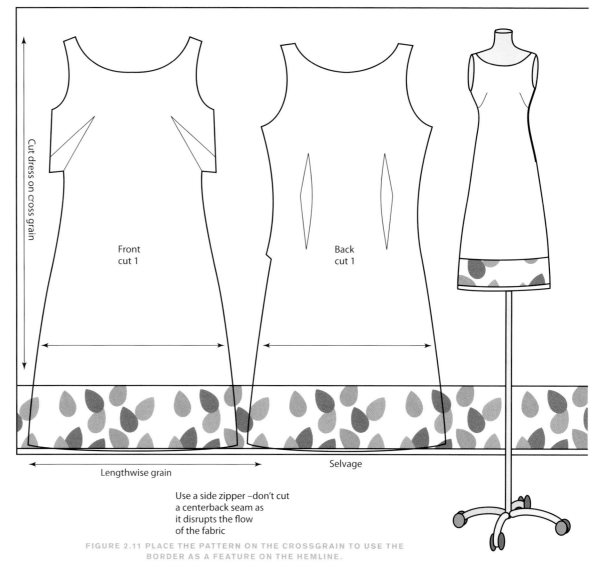

Use a side zipper –don't cut a centerback seam as it disrupts the flow of the fabric

FIGURE 2.11 PLACE THE PATTERN ON THE CROSSGRAIN TO USE THE BORDER AS A FEATURE ON THE HEMLINE.

have an impact on the fit of the garment. When a decision is made to cut a garment on the crossgrain, it is usually fabric driven, as is the case in Figure 2.11. Notice that the fabric border adds a bold accent on the hemline when cut on the crossgrain. Also notice that the garment has no centerback seam so it does not interrupt the flow of the border design; a left side seam zipper is used and the neckline is large enough to slip over the head. This is how fashion meets function.

Bias Grain

Bias grain stretches the most and is therefore more difficult to cut and stitch, but it is well worth the effort! A bias-cut garment drapes beautifully, especially in lightweight, sheer fabric. Cutting a striped fabric on the bias grain influences how the stripe looks in the final design (Figure 2.12).

Knit Fabric

Knit fabric also has a grainline, but different terminology is used to describe it. The lengthwise grain is comprised of loops called *wales*. The number of wales across the fabric depends on the count (size or thickness) of the yarn used. The crosswise grain on knit fabrics is formed by loops called *courses*. Examine the vertical ribs on knit fabric before cutting; to find the lengthwise grain, follow the direction of the wales, as knits generally don't have a selvage. The courses need to be at right angles to the wales for the fabric to be "on grain."

Fabric Layout Preparation

Preshrinking the Fabric

If you were to take the fabric and immediately cut it without doing the necessary preparation first, it could have disastrous effects on the final garment. Many fabrics shrink when they are laundered or dry cleaned. The most common of these are 100 percent cotton, wool, linen, rayon, and knit fabrics. Many fabrics need to be preshrunk so the fit of the garment is not affected after laundering.

- To preshrink machine-washable fabrics,

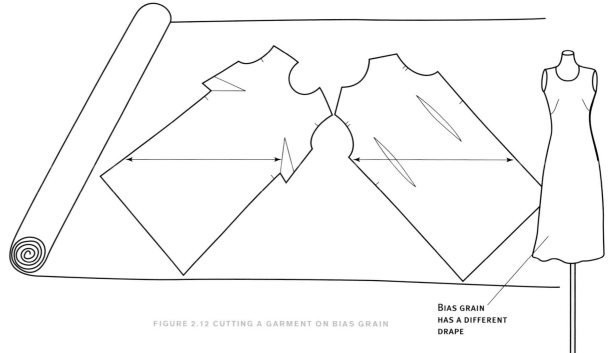

FIGURE 2.12 CUTTING A GARMENT ON BIAS GRAIN

BIAS GRAIN HAS A DIFFERENT DRAPE

place them in the washing machine on the rinse cycle using the minimum amount of water. Then place the fabric in the dryer; the heat will shrink the fabric.
- To preshrink fabrics that must be hand washed, prewash them by hand in cold water.
- To preshrink wool, first lay the fabric on a flat surface that fully supports the entire piece; next, place an iron directly above the fabric and continuously release steam into the fabric. Allow the fabric to dry completely before moving it. Or, finish the cut ends of the yardage with serging or a zigzag stitch and take it to the dry cleaners for shrinking.
- All knit fabrics shrink to some degree, so it is best to prewash washable knit fabrics; wool

knits benefit from the same process described earlier regarding wool.
- Do not prewash fabric that requires dry cleaning.
- Many fabrics do not need to be prewashed. Fabrics such as silk, rayon, polyester, and other synthetic fabrics do not need to be preshrunk; however, if you intend to hand wash a garment made in silk, then do prewash it first.

Fabric Alignment

Before the patterns are laid on the fabric, the fabric needs to be aligned so the lengthwise and crosswise grains are positioned exactly at right angles to each other. To begin, align the fabric on the crossgrain, from selvage to selvage, so it is straight and "on grain." This is *not* done by ruling a line across the fabric and cutting along the line. To align the crossgrain, use one of the following three methods:

- *Method 1:* Tear the fabric firmly across the crossgrain. This method of aligning the fabric graininess is the most accurate. However, many fabrics cannot be torn because the action of tearing the fibers would be too harsh. Synthetic fibers, some cottons, and silk fabrics can be torn successfully, but fabrics with a coarse or loose weave cannot. Some delicate fabrics may be affected by the action of tearing, which can cause little pulls to appear in the lengthwise grain. Knits will not tear; only woven fabric can tear on the crossgrain. Always sample first to see if the crossgrain of the fabric can be torn. To tear the fabric, snip the selvage with scissors and tear the fabric; snip the other selvage with scissors. The selvage can easily rip up the lengthwise grain if you don't cut with scissors.

- *Method 2:* If the fabric is coarsely woven, get close up to the fabric and, using good eye judgment, carefully cut across the weft crossgrain. Checks and stripes can also be cut "on grain" this way.

- *Method 3:* The third method is to pull a weft thread across the fabric. This is quite easily done in coarsely woven fabrics. To do this, snip into the selvage; pull out a weft fiber with a pin and gently pull the fiber that shows the weft grain on the fabric; cut along the pulled thread.

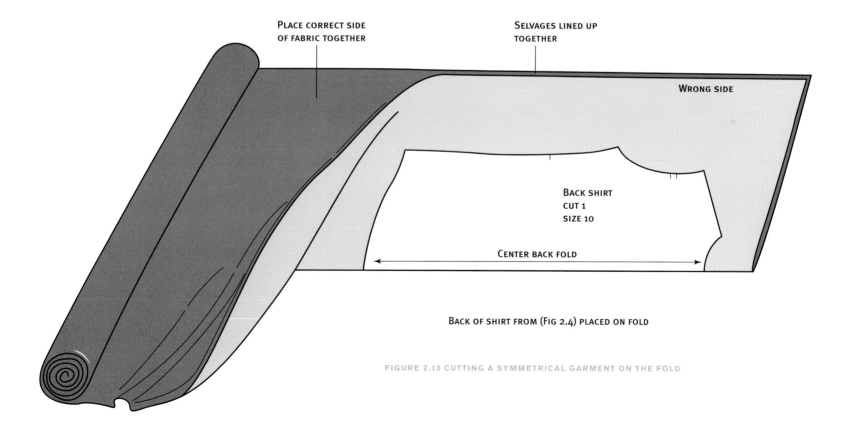

PLACE CORRECT SIDE OF FABRIC TOGETHER

SELVAGES LINED UP TOGETHER

WRONG SIDE

BACK SHIRT
CUT 1
SIZE 10

CENTER BACK FOLD

BACK OF SHIRT FROM (FIG 2.4) PLACED ON FOLD

FIGURE 2.13 CUTTING A SYMMETRICAL GARMENT ON THE FOLD

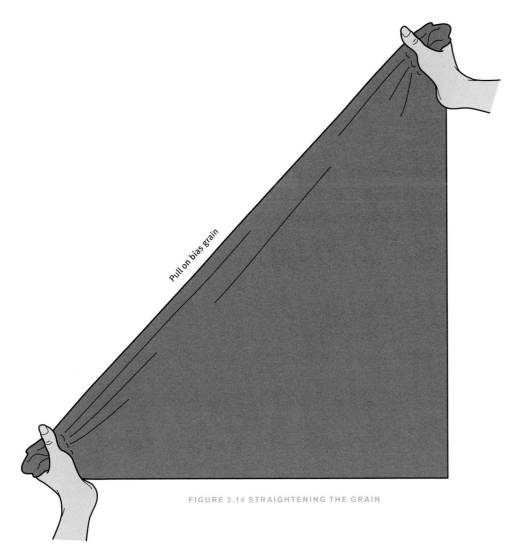

Pull on bias grain

FIGURE 2.14 STRAIGHTENING THE GRAIN

Observing the Fabric Surface and Design

After the fabric is aligned, it is important to observe the fabric surface, as some fabrics need special attention when laying the patterns on the fabric. One-way surface designs, stripes, and checks take more time to plan and cut. Some fabric designs are printed or embroidered in all directions and do not need the same attention when laying out the patterns on the fabric.

One-Way Design

The garment in Figure 2.15 has been cut from a one-way fabric design. Notice how the fabric surface design in the layout all point in one direction; this is what classifies the fabric as a one-way design. The fabric design also has a repeat pattern, which must be matched across the fabric at the side seams so when stitched, the fabric design will continue around the garment. The front and back pattern pieces have also been *centered* on the fabric design. Fabrics with one-way designs need this special attention in the cutting for the garment to look spectacular. Keep the garment design simple in these types of fabric and let the fabric be the focus of the design.

Napped Fabric

A one-way fabric layout is also needed when cutting a pile weave or a napped fabric. When a fabric is napped, the short fiber ends of spun yarns are raised with a soft fabric, surface and the fibers lie smoothly in one direction. Because of this, *all* napped fabric *must* be cut in one direction. When you touch napped fabric you will notice that one direction ("with the nap")

After the crossgrain is perfectly cut "on grain," fold the two selvages together as illustrated in Figure 2.13. Observe how the fabric lays; if it is perfectly flat, then the fabric is in alignment. If it does not lay flat and looks distorted or twisted, then the fabric is out of alignment. To pull the

fabric back into alignment, fold the fabric on the bias grain, hold at both ends, and gently pull the fabric, stretching the bias grain (Figure 2.14). Then refold the fabric with the selvages together to see if the fabric is in alignment. If the fabric still doesn't lie flat, repeat the process until it does.

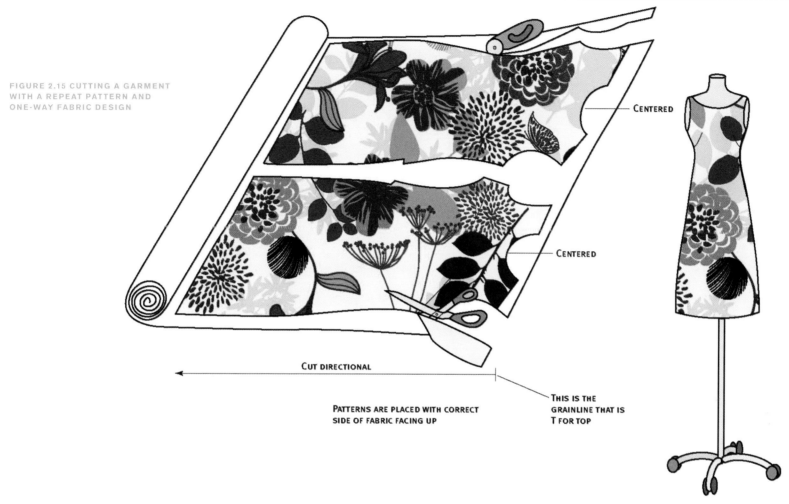

FIGURE 2.15 CUTTING A GARMENT WITH A REPEAT PATTERN AND ONE-WAY FABRIC DESIGN

CENTERED

CENTERED

CUT DIRECTIONAL

PATTERNS ARE PLACED WITH CORRECT SIDE OF FABRIC FACING UP

THIS IS THE GRAINLINE THAT IS T FOR TOP

feels smooth while the other direction ("without nap") feels rough. As the light catches the fabric surface, the color will look different from different directions. Hold the fabric against your body and look downward along the fabric. Fabric "without nap" has a rich depth of color. When holding the fabric "with nap," it looks lighter and more delicate in color. The fabric can be cut in either direction; however, the darker option is often preferred because of its richness.

Although the fabric can be cut in either direction, cutting *must* be directional; that is, all patterns *must* be placed on the fabric one way. Some pile weave fabrics are velvet, terry cloth, corduroy, and suede-cloth.

Repeat Pattern

The fabric in Figure 2.15 is not only a one-way fabric design but it also has a repeat pattern. Fabrics that have a repeat fabric need *extra-*

special care when laying out the pattern and cutting the fabric so the fabric pattern matches together on all seamlines. Fabrics with repeat patterns require extra yardage, so make sure you purchase enough fabric initially.

Large Prints

Plan carefully; don't place large flowers or circles on the bust and backside. Place the patterns on the print so any motifs are centered on the garment, as this is aesthetically pleasing to the eye. Be careful how the seams are planned on large prints, as cutting too many design lines could take away from the beauty of the large fabric print—let the fabric be the focus of the design. Figure 2.15 has a large print, one-way fabric, and repeat pattern; notice how the large print is centered on the garment.

Checks

Plaids and checks need to be cut carefully so that when the garment is stitched together the checks match horizontally and vertically on the garment (at the shoulder seams and other horizontal seams). Again, time and careful preparation are required when laying patterns on checked or plaid fabric. Garments with bold checks that do not match draw attention to a badly designed and constructed garment. Checks can be even or uneven; uneven checks cannot be matched in both directions. The fabric in Figure 2.16 is a one-way check fabric. Can you see this? If the garment patterns were turned upside down, the color blocking would be in a different order. So, this fabric has to be cut directionally, and the grainline indicates this clearly. The pattern also needs to be centered.

When placing the patterns on the fabric, make sure the notches and pattern markings match in the same check. Place the underarm seams of the sleeve and body on the same check.

FIGURE 2.16 CUTTING A GARMENT IN CHECK FABRIC

You will notice that the *front* underarm seam does not match the back underarm seam on the same check. It is impossible to match the underarms for the entire seam length when there is a dart in the side seam. So match the checks from the hem up to the first dart leg.

Stripes

Stripes can be lots of fun to work with. They offer the designer broad scope to be creative in how the fabric is cut. Striped fabric can be cut on the lengthwise, crosswise, or bias grain. The cutting of a wide stripe takes more time and thought to plan than a tiny, narrow stripe, which does not need matching. Stripes cut across the fabric *must* match on the side seams. If the stripes are cut to match, then they will be stitched to match. Figure 2.17 illustrates how a striped fabric can be cut on all three grainlines.

Fabric Border

Fabrics with borders have a decorative design running down the length of the fabric. Garments are usually cut on the crossgrain to take advantage of the border design. Very often the border is scalloped, or it may be a fabric print, as in Figure 2.11. Bordered fabrics are often embroidered, with eyelet designs or scalloped lace. Let the border be used to the design's advantage.

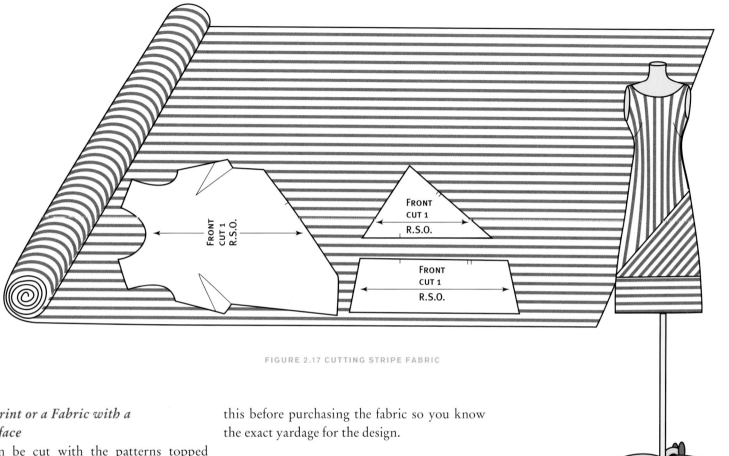

FIGURE 2.17 CUTTING STRIPE FABRIC

Allover Print or a Fabric with a Plain Surface

Fabric can be cut with the patterns topped and tailed. This means that the patterns can be turned in either lengthwise direction, as illustrated in Figure 2.18. The print in this figure has an allover fabric print and does not have a predominant design to be matched or centered on the fabric. Many fabrics can be cut this way.

Fabric Layout

Before cutting the fabric, do a practice layout to plan how the pattern pieces will be placed on the fabric. This ensures you will have adequate yardage before you begin. It is a good idea to do

this before purchasing the fabric so you know the exact yardage for the design.

- When laying out the fabric, it can be folded in half down the length by bringing the selvage edges together. Place the correct sides of the fabric together and pin the selvage edges together every 4 to 5 inches. This is an ideal method for cutting designs that are symmetrical (Figure 2.13).
- If the design is asymmetrical, then the patterns must be placed on a single layer of fabric. Be sure to place the patterns correctly following the pattern directions (R.S.U. or W.S.U.) so they will be cut correctly (Figure

2.3b). Clean the cutting surface first. Lay a piece of pattern paper on the table when cutting delicate fabric so it does not snag. Place the correct side of the fabric facing down on the table. Figures 2.18 and 2.19 both illustrate fabric cut in a single layer.

- Delicate fabrics such as chiffon, georgette, and silk charmeuse can be slippery to cut. When the fabric is delicate and slippery, draw

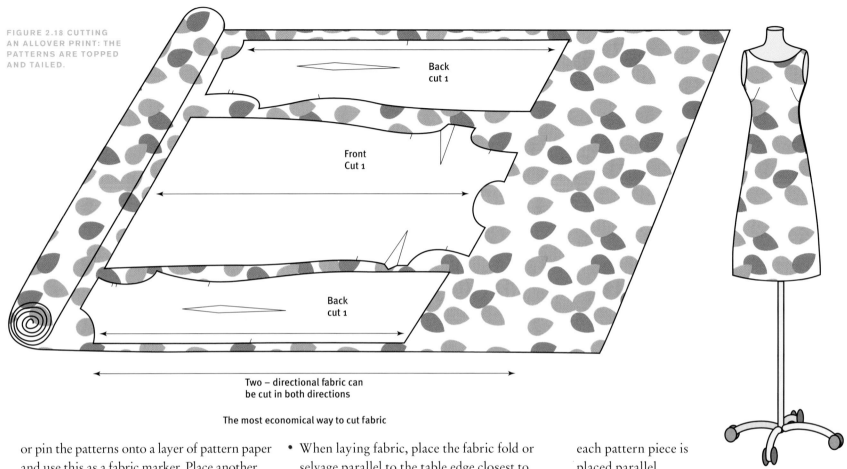

FIGURE 2.18 CUTTING
AN ALLOVER PRINT: THE
PATTERNS ARE TOPPED
AND TAILED.

Back
cut 1

Front
Cut 1

Back
cut 1

Two – directional fabric can
be cut in both directions

The most economical way to cut fabric

or pin the patterns onto a layer of pattern paper
and use this as a fabric marker. Place another
piece of pattern paper on the cutting table with
one end cut at a right angle. Lay the fabric directly on top of the paper; then lay the pattern
marker on top of the fabric, and cut (Figure
2.19). The fabric is now sandwiched between
two layers of paper that will hold it stable when
cutting. Pin the layers together or place weights
on the fabric layout to stabilize it when cutting.
The best way to cut slippery fabric is with a
very sharp rotary cutter; don't use blunt scissors to cut these fabrics!

- When laying fabric, place the fabric fold or
selvage parallel to the table edge closest to
you and about 2 inches away (Figure 2.13).
After laying the fabric on the table so it is at
right angles, place weights on the fabric to
keep it stable.

Placing the Patterns "On Grain"

- Place the patterns on the fabric *on grain. All
pattern grainlines are placed parallel to the
selvage of the fabric, regardless of whether
the grainline is lengthwise, horizontal, or
bias grain. Figures 2.2 and 2.20 show how

each pattern piece is
placed parallel
 to the selvage. If the fabric
is folded, then place the patterns
parallel to the foldline (Figure 2.13). Use
your tape measure and measure from the
selvage to the pattern grainline and place
each pattern piece on the fabric "on grain."
When all grainlines are placed parallel to the
selvage, the finished garment will fall beautifully and "on grain."

- The patterns are pinned to the fabric by
placing the pins in the seamlines. Place the

pins on the corner of each pattern section and place some pins in between (Figure 2.20). Don't overpin, as this takes too much time and is not necessary; just use a sufficient number of pins to hold the patterns to the fabric. Place weights on the fabric to stabilize it before you begin cutting.

Cutting Equipment

Figure 2.1 shows the hand cutting equipment needed to cut fabric, interfacing, underlining, lining, and threads.

Scissors

Purchase a quality pair of **scissors** for cutting fabric and *never* use them for cutting paper. Bent-handled scissors are shaped for comfort; the handles accommodate more fingers so you have better control when cutting fabric. A good, average pair of scissors to use in design school would be 7 to 8 inches long. In manufacturing settings, larger scissors are used, at least 10 to 12 inches long. Right- or left-handed scissors are available. Have your scissors sharpened if they are not cutting fabric accurately.

Rotary Cutter/Mats

Some students like to use a **rotary cutter,** as they find them quick and efficient for cutting. They also come in a variety of shapes and sizes. Make sure a **mat** is placed underneath the fabric when using the rotary cutter. Otherwise, the cuts will indent the table, and later, if delicate fabrics are placed on the table, they could snag.

Embroidery Scissors

Embroidery scissors are approximately 4 to 6 inches long; they are small and used for detailed cutting such as cutting into a point or cutting the end of each buttonhole. It is better to use embroidery scissors when cutting into these areas, as small scissors are easier to control than large scissors.

Thread Clippers

Thread clippers should sit right by your side as you stitch. The *SEW, CLIP, PRESS* method of stitching is what you use to clip the threads when stitching. Sit the thread clippers by the machine so they can be easily picked up to snip threads. Using thread clippers is faster and more efficient than scissors—time efficiency is important in manufacturing, so try to be conscious of this while in design school. When threads are snipped with larger scissors, you run the risk of cutting the fabric by mistake. Using thread clippers gives you more control over what you are doing. Oh yes—thread clippers are *not* for cutting fabric!

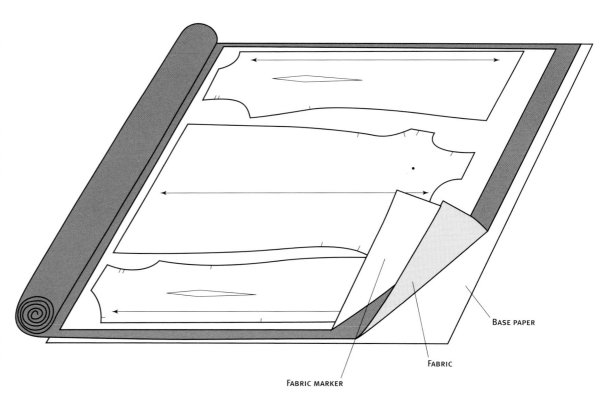

BASE PAPER

FABRIC

FABRIC MARKER

FIGURE 2.19 CUTTING DELICATE FABRIC

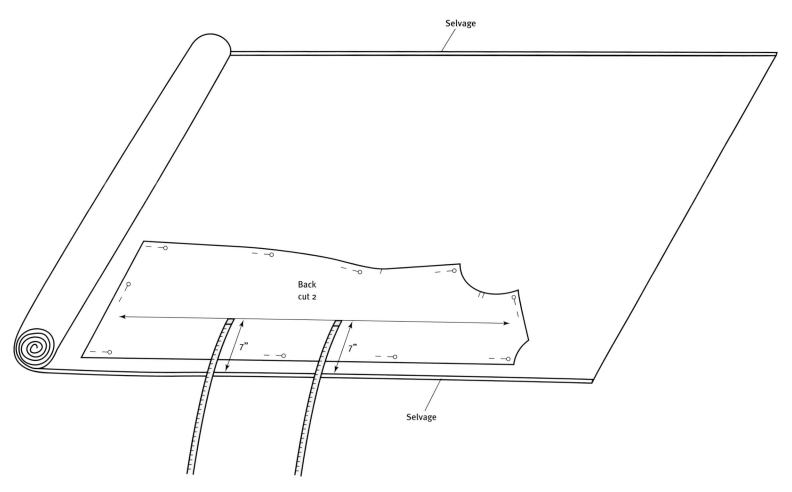

Selvage

Back
cut 2

7"   7"

Selvage

FIGURE 2.20 PATTERNS PLACED ON THE FABRIC "ON GRAIN"

Cutting the Fabric

Once the fabric is laid on the table and cutting begins, the fabric *must not* be moved; once each piece is cut, then it can be moved. Many students sit and cut and then twist the fabric this way and that to cut armholes and necklines and other difficult angles. *No*—this is not the way to cut! Stand up and be in control of your work.

If you have a difficult angle to cut, then *move your body* so you can cut at any angle rather than moving the fabric. Fabric that is moved can easily slip out of alignment and move off grain.

When cutting fabric, use sharp scissors or shears. Cut outside the edge of the pattern; don't cut off any of the pattern. And don't add any extra fabric when cutting around each pat-

tern piece, as this will misshape your garment and change the fit. Smooth, accurate cutting is essential.

After the fabric is cut, the pattern markings are transferred to the fabric to give the direction for how to stitch the garment together. We cannot stress enough how important it is to transfer all the pattern markings to the wrong side of the fabric before you begin to stitch—ultimately it is going to save time!

Snipping Notches

Notches snipped in the fabric should be no longer than ¹/8 inch in length. It is important that notches not be cut longer than this length. Many students cut *very long notches* and cut into the seamline, which makes it impossible to stitch the most basic seam.

Marking Dart Points and Matchpoints

Dart points, along with notches, indicate the position where the dart is to be stitched. Matchpoints indicate where a seam is to be stitched to or joined to another piece of fabric. They are an alterative to using notches to match seams together. Matchpoints also indicate where to place pockets or other garment parts on the surface of the fabric (Figure 2.4). When the pattern is made, indicate the dart and matchpoints by placing an awl through the pattern. Place the awl mark ½ inch back from the bust point and ¹/8 inch in and down from the pocket placement position. Patterns markings that are transferred to the fabric in this way will not be visible on the fabric sur-

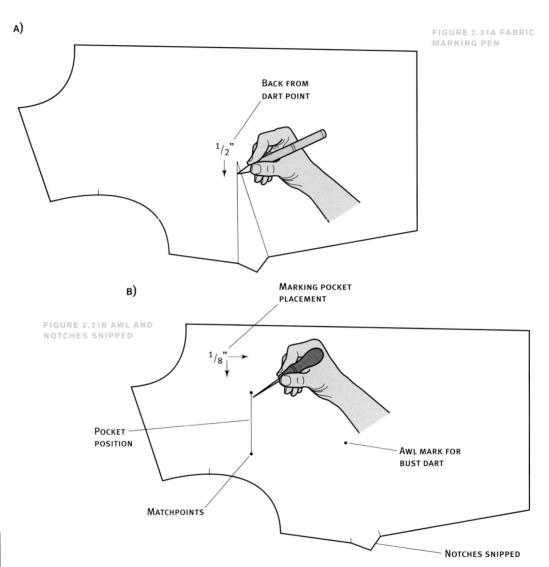

FIGURE 2.21A FABRIC MARKING PEN

A)

BACK FROM DART POINT

¹/2"

B)

MARKING POCKET PLACEMENT

FIGURE 2.21B AWL AND NOTCHES SNIPPED

¹/8"

POCKET POSITION

AWL MARK FOR BUST DART

MATCHPOINTS

NOTCHES SNIPPED

IMPORTANT

Always sample the tracing paper on your fabric, checking to see if it can be easily removed from the fabric with a damp cloth, brush, or fabric eraser. Applying heat to the traced markings will set the markings into the fabric.

face when stitched. An awl can also be used to mark these positions on fabric, as indicated in Figure 2.21b. Push the awl gently through the fabric and don't make the hole too big.

Dart and matchpoints can also be marked with a fabric marking pen, such as Mark-B-Gone, or chalk (a Chaco-liner dispenses the chalk in a fine line), on the wrong side of the fabric (Figure 2.21a). To mark, place a pin through both layers of fabric (if cut on the fold)

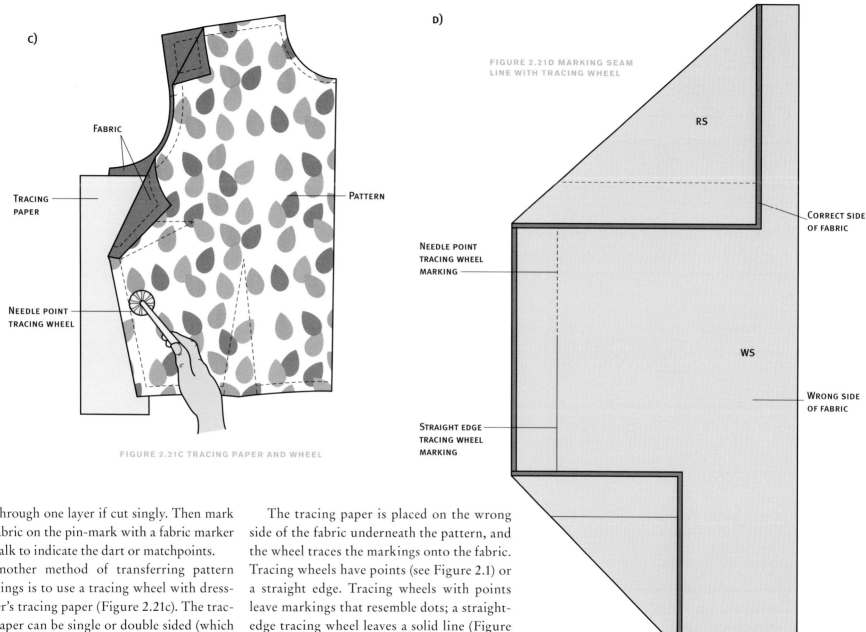

c)

FABRIC

TRACING PAPER

PATTERN

NEEDLE POINT TRACING WHEEL

FIGURE 2.21C TRACING PAPER AND WHEEL

D)

FIGURE 2.21D MARKING SEAM LINE WITH TRACING WHEEL

RS

CORRECT SIDE OF FABRIC

NEEDLE POINT TRACING WHEEL MARKING

WS

WRONG SIDE OF FABRIC

STRAIGHT EDGE TRACING WHEEL MARKING

and through one layer if cut singly. Then mark the fabric on the pin-mark with a fabric marker or chalk to indicate the dart or matchpoints.

Another method of transferring pattern markings is to use a tracing wheel with dressmaker's tracing paper (Figure 2.21c). The tracing paper can be single or double sided (which allows tracing of two layers at one time), and have chalk or a wax-based carbon coating.

The tracing paper is placed on the wrong side of the fabric underneath the pattern, and the wheel traces the markings onto the fabric. Tracing wheels have points (see Figure 2.1) or a straight edge. Tracing wheels with points leave markings that resemble dots; a straight-edge tracing wheel leaves a solid line (Figure 2.21d).

THREAD TYPES

The goal when stitching your project is to find the combination of fabric, needles, and threads that gives the best results. That is why sampling is so important. Poor-quality thread can affect the tension of the stitches by feeding through the tension discs unevenly, resulting in unbalanced stitches. This creates weak seams, which results in precious time spent ripping out and redoing stitches. The wrong-sized needle can ruin the fabric by pulling threads in the fabric, causing runs; or leave holes in seam allowances that have to be ripped out; or worse, break in the middle of a seam, causing a rip or tear in the fabric. Most often, the thread used in the needle of the sewing machine is also used in the bobbin. Keep in mind the following:

- Create a sample using the fabric, the needle, and the thread that will be used for the final garment. Make a note of the information on the sample worksheet; keep this handy for reference when stitching the same fabric again.
- Industrial sewing machines have the timing set to stitch a balanced stitch with thread on cones of several thousand yards, usually supplied in black and white—check with your instructor to see if other types of thread such as Gutterman or Mettler will work in the machines, or *sample!*
- When stitching will be visible on the surface of the garment, color match the thread or use a contrasting color; if a matching color is not available, choose a slightly darker shade to blend into the background—dark colors

> **NOTE**
>
> Several liquid sewing aids, such as Sewer's Aid, have been developed to help the thread pass through the tension discs for smoother stitching. If you find that the thread is not passing smoothly along the threading path, add a drop of the Sewer's Aid, very sparingly, to the spool and the bobbin thread. This is especially helpful when using decorative threads.

recede. To highlight stitching on the surface, use a contrasting color.

How Do I Choose the Appropriate Thread for My Fabric?

Choosing the correct thread for the fabric being used is critical to good stitching. Without well-formed stitches, the seams won't hold, and without good seams, you won't have a quality garment! Threads should be selected for their color, weight, and the type of stitching being done. The thread must be compatible in weight with the fabric being stitched—you wouldn't use jeans thread on silk charmeuse. Different threads can be used for different purposes, and more than one thread can be used in a project.

NEEDLES

Sewing machine needles are small but hugely important—needles can make or break your stitch. The type should be selected according to the construction of the fabric, and the size should be selected according to the weight of the fabric. It's always a good idea to have on hand a supply of general-purpose needles and a few specialty needles, in all sizes. This may seem like a lot of needles, but remember that needles break frequently, particularly when students are rushing to meet deadlines. The parts of the needle are shown in Figure. 2.22a. The different components of the needle are:

- The *shank*—the top section of the needle that fits into the sewing machine
- The *shaft*—the long body of the needle
- The *groove*—found on the front of the shaft in home sewing needles and on the back of

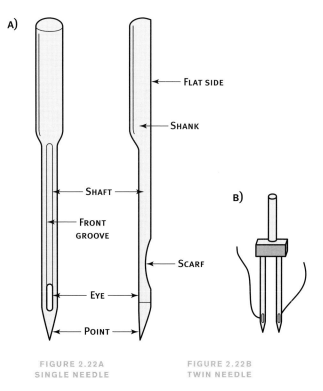

A)

FLAT SIDE

SHANK

SHAFT

FRONT GROOVE

SCARF

EYE

POINT

B)

FIGURE 2.22A
SINGLE NEEDLE

FIGURE 2.22B
TWIN NEEDLE

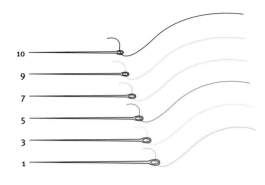

FIGURE 2.22C HAND SEWING NEEDLES

industrial needles (It becomes larger as the needle size increases.)

- The *eye*—the opening in the needle into which the thread is inserted (It varies according to the needle type.)
- The *tip*—the point of the needle (It varies in roundness.)
- The *scarf*—the indentation on the back of the eye of the needle. Different types and sizes of needles have different shapes and sizes of scarves, which eliminate skipped stitches when correctly matched to the fabric weight.

When threading the sewing machine needle, cut the thread at a slight angle. This makes the end of the thread narrower and helps it to pass through the eye without catching and untwisting. If it is still difficult to thread the needle, use a needle threader (the type with the long wire works best). The threader usually comes with an assortment of hand sewing needles but can

also be purchased separately. It's very handy to have! To use the needle threader:

- Insert the wire through the eye of the needle.
- Place the thread at the end of the wire, looping it around the wire.
- Gently pull the wire through the eye of the needle; the thread will follow.

Needle Sizing

Industrial sewing machines use a variety of needle sizing systems, and each system works only with particular machines. The sizes range from 1 up to 400! The needles are not interchangeable between industrial sewing machines and home sewing machines. When purchasing needles for a home sewing machine, consult the manual for information on what system the machine uses. Almost all home sewing machines use a 130/705H needle system, which is indicated on the needle case. The needle name and size are also indicated as two numbers that appear on the packaging; these numbers refer to the American and European sizes. European needles range in size from 60 to 120; the number refers to the diameter taken on the shaft right above the eye. American needles are sized from 8 to 19 and are paired with corresponding European sizes, for example, 60/8 or 70/10; the larger the number, the larger the needle will be.

Determine the appropriate needle size based on the fabric weight. After choosing the needle size, match the needle point to the fabric. The needle type and name is usually determined by

the characteristics of the needle's point. Fabric, thread, and needle must all work together toward the same goal: a well-stitched garment.

- Industrial sewing machines used in classrooms require specific needles designed for the particular machine—home sewing machine needles are not long enough to fit into industrial sewing machines and will not produce properly formed stitches.
- When beginning a project, start with a new needle. This may be difficult in a classroom situation, as many classes of students rotate through the sewing labs, but ask your instructor if you may purchase a sewing machine needle that can be kept in your supply kit and placed in the machine when you are sewing your project. Remember, it is your responsibility to keep track of this needle!
- Poor stitch quality or a clicking noise as the needle enters the fabric indicates a dull needle; ask for a new or different-sized needle to sample before stitching on your garment.
- Finer fabrics require smaller needles, and heavier fabrics require larger needles.
- Needles can be damaged by running the machine too fast, creating "burrs" (distortions of the needle point). Burrs are a common problem for students new to industrial equipment and can also occur from pushing the fabric too hard or hitting the needle on a pin that has been stitched over—*always* remove pins before stitching over them.
- Pulling on the fabric while stitching can also bend the needle, causing it to weaken and break.

Sewing Machine Needle Types

The type of needle required depends on the weight of your fabric, and the needle size is an essential contributor to the way the needle works. The needle should be small enough to pierce the fabric without leaving a hole; if the needle is too large, it can leave holes in the fabric or cause the thread to shred. The thread must lie along the groove of the needle to form good stitches. If the thread is too thick, it will move out of the groove, causing the thread to break or skip stitches. If the thread is too fine, the stitches might be loose on top of the fabric.

Just as there are good-quality threads, so are there good-quality needles. A cheaper needle might seem like a bargain, but it will wear out faster, cause damage to your fabric, and possibly damage the sewing machine. Sewing machine needles cannot be sharpened; replace the sewing machine needle after each project or approximately every four to eight hours of sewing time. Synthetic fabrics, fleece, and heavy upholstery fabric dull needles faster. Embroidery designs with thousands of stitches require fresh needles frequently.

The needle types and sizes recommended for particular fabrics are listed in Table 2.2 and described below.

IMPORTANT
Always sample the thread, needle, and fabric before beginning the garment.

- *Universal:* The universal needle has a modified ballpoint tip and works well on both woven and knit fabrics. Because of its shape, it also helps to prevent skipped stitches. It is available in sizes 8 to 19.
- *Ballpoint:* The ballpoint needle is specifically designed for knit and elastic fabrics and has a rounded point rather than a sharp point. The needle pushes between the yarns rather than piercing them. This needle is available in sizes 9 to 16; the larger the needle size, the more rounded is the needle point.
- *Leather:* This needle has a special wedge-shaped cutting tip that allows it to pierce heavy leathers. Do not use this needle on imitation leathers, suede, vinyl, or woven fabrics—it will cut the fabric rather than pierce it. This needle is available in sizes 10 to 19.
- *Microtex/Sharp:* This needle has a very sharp point for sewing microfibers, silk, synthetic leather, or suede and can also be used for heirloom stitching. It is available in sizes 8 to 16.
- *Jeans/Denim:* This needle has a strong, slender shaft and sharp tip to pierce heavy, tightly woven fabrics such as denim, canvas, upholstery fabric, artificial leather, and canvas. It has a longer eye, which makes it suitable for topstitching as well. This needle is available in sizes 10 to 18.
- *Topstitching:* This extra-sharp needle is not as rounded as the universal. It has a longer eye and deeper groove to accommodate heavier topstitching and decorative threads. This type of needle is available in sizes 10 to 16.

NOTE
Twin needles are used only in front-to-back threading machines with zigzag features. The needles must be able to fit into the width of the throat plate of the machine.

- *Metallic needle:* Metafil and Metallica needles are used for sewing with decorative metallic threads. These needles have a large elongated eye and groove that allows fragile metallic and synthetic threads to flow through the eye smoothly. They are available in sizes 11 and 14.
- *Embroidery needle:* This needle is designed to stitch with the fine threads used in machine embroidery. Because it is a very stable needle, it can withstand the high stitching speeds of machine-embroidered designs. Available in sizes 11 and 14, this needle is suitable for woven fabric or knits.
- *Twin needles:* This needle is actually two needles on a single shaft that produces two rows of straight stitching on the surface with a zigzag stitch underneath (Figure 2.22b). Suitable for both woven and knit fabrics, these needles come with two sets of numbering. The first number indicates the needle size. For instance, 4.0/80 indicates there are two size 80 (12) needles set 4.0 mm apart. Twin needles are available in universal, ballpoint, jeans, and stretch variations, with needle widths set 1.6 to 8.0 mm apart and needle sizes of 70 to 100.
- *Other specialty needles:* Many needles on the

TABLE 2.5 NEEDLES AND THREADS TO USE WHEN STITCHING TRICKY FABRICS

Fabric Type	Needle and Size	Thread Type
Sheer Fabrics	Universal 60/8 or 60/9	All–purpose polyester Fine heirloom Silk Fine machine embroidery 60/2
Lace	Stretch 75/11	All-purpose polyester Fine heirloom
Satin	Universal 60/8–80/12, depending on weight of satin	All-purpose polyester Mercerized cotton Silk for hand sewing
Beaded Fabrics	Universal 60/8–90/14, depending on weight of fabric	All-purpose polyester
Knits	Sewing Machine Needles Ballpoint 130/705 H SUK (have a slightly rounded tip); purchase assorted sizes Stretch 130/705 H-S (sizes 60/8–90/14) Stretch twin (for stitching necklines and hems); purchase two sizes: 2.5/75 and 4.0/75	Long-staple polyester (Guterman brand adds elasticity to seams) Woolly nylon in loopers of serger
Denim	Jeans/Denim 90/14, lightweight Jeans/Denim 100/16, heavyweight	Machine stitching All-purpose polyester Jeans thread-cotton wrapped polyester
Velvet **Stretch Velvet**	Universal 60/8–80/12, depending on weight of velvet Stretch needle 75/11	All-purpose polyester Silk for hand sewing
Leather	Machine Needles Leather needle and universal needle in sizes to suit leather weight Hand Sewing Needles Glovers needle–a triangular-tipped hand sewing needle for sewing buttons	Machine Stitching Polyester thread–do not use 100% cotton Topstitching thread Hand Sewing Heavy waxed thread–for sewing on buttons Upholstery thread
Faux Fur	Universal 80/12–short pile fur Universal 90/14–thicker, stiffer fur	All-purpose polyester Heavy-duty or topstitching
Heavyweight Fabrics	Universal 90/14	All-purpose polyester Silk

market address other stitching techniques, such as triple, hemstitch, spring, quilting, self-threading, and titanium-coated needles. It is up to the student designer to research which needle will produce the best result in tandem with the thread and fabric being used.

Needles and Threads to Use When Stitching Tricky Fabrics

Table 2.5 lists needle and thread information for use in stitching the tricky fabrics that are covered in every chapter.

How Do I Choose the Appropriate Machine Needle for My Project?

- Determine the needle size by the fabric weight.
- After choosing the needle size, match the needle point to the fabric.
- The needle type and name are usually determined by the characteristics of the point.
- The style of seam being constructed often requires a specialty needle, such as for topstitching, in addition to the needle being used for general garment construction. Refer to Chapter 6 for detailed information.

Hand Sewing Needles

Even though the design student uses the sewing machine to do the majority of stitching on a garment, there are some steps that require hand sewing. Many of the same principles that apply to machine needles also apply to hand sewing needles. Hand sewing needles are shown in Figure 2.22c and discussed in detail in Chapter 15.

Threading the Sewing Machine

Although the method of threading each industrial sewing machine is similar, it will differ slightly for each brand of machine. Refer to Figure 2.23 to see the threading path and identify the various parts of the machine.

Bobbins

A bobbin is a small spool that holds approximately 50 or more yards of thread, placed into a bobbin case, which is inserted into the sewing machine (Figure 2.1). All sewing machines require a specific type of bobbin in order to be

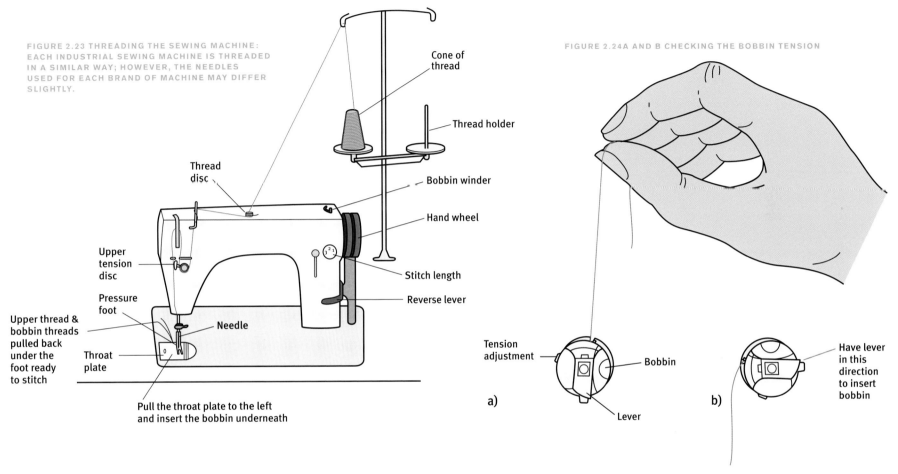

Cone of thread

Thread holder

Thread disc

Bobbin winder

Hand wheel

Upper tension disc

Stitch length

Pressure foot

Reverse lever

Upper thread & bobbin threads pulled back under the foot ready to stitch

Needle

Throat plate

Pull the throat plate to the left and insert the bobbin underneath

FIGURE 2.24A AND B CHECKING THE BOBBIN TENSION

Tension adjustment

Bobbin

a)

Lever

Have lever in this direction to insert bobbin

b)

able to form stitches with the upper thread of the sewing machine. If the bobbin is wound too fast, it will be uneven and lumpy, resulting in poor stitch quality.

Winding the Bobbin

On industrial sewing machines, the bobbin winder is located on the outside of the machine. A spindle holds the bobbin (only) in place after a small lever is pushed forward to lock it in place. The thread is threaded through a spool holder and a separate tension disc that winds the thread smoothly onto the bobbin. If the spool holder is not threaded properly, the thread will wind onto the bobbin in a mess—and it will not feed properly through the bobbin case to form good stitches. When student designers are becoming familiar with industrial sewing machines, problems with the stitch qual-

ity usually stem from improperly wound bobbins. The only answer is to remove the bobbin and the thread, and start over, *slowly* winding the thread onto the bobbin.

Tension

Check the bobbin tension. To do this, thread the bobbin and hold the thread in one hand with the bobbin hanging below (Figure 2.24a). Shake the thread; the bobbin should bounce down with the thread still holding the bobbin in place. If the bobbin does not move, then the tension is too tight. If the thread lets the bobbin run away, then tension is too loose.

Inserting the Bobbin into the Machine

The bobbin is placed inside the bobbin case, with the thread placed through the tension slot. A small, hinged lever is opened to slide the bobbin/bobbin case onto the spindle located under the throat plate of the machine (Figure 2.24b). The lever must close with a click, indicating that the bobbin/bobbin case is indeed locked into position. If it is not clearly locked into place, the needle thread will not meet the bobbin thread to form a stitch, and the needle will break, causing possible damage to the

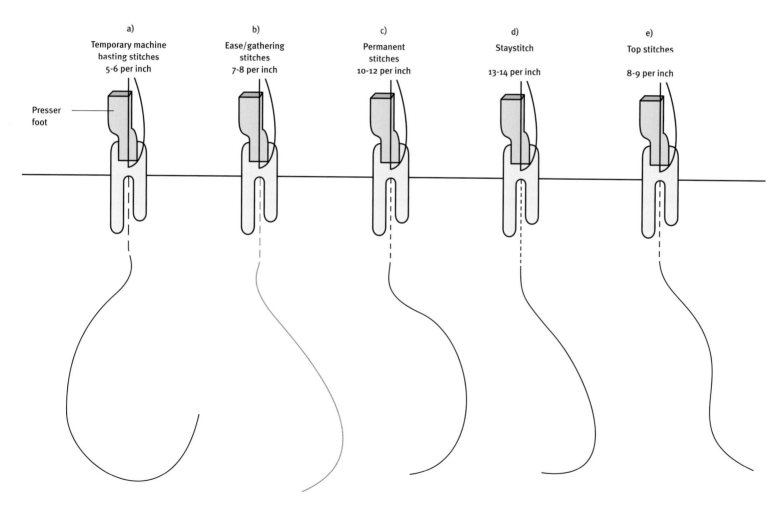

a) Temporary machine basting stitches 5-6 per inch

b) Ease/gathering stitches 7-8 per inch

c) Permanent stitches 10-12 per inch

d) Staystitch 13-14 per inch

e) Top stitches 8-9 per inch

Presser foot

FIGURE 2.25A, B, C, D, E STITCH LENGTHS FOR MUSLIN

bobbin case and to the timing of the machine. As every industrial sewing machine is different, and each bobbin/bobbin case is individualized to the sewing machine for which it is manufactured, it is impossible for the bobbins/bobbin cases to be interchanged. Turn the hand wheel one full turn to bring the bobbin thread to the needle plate opening. This forms a loop with the upper thread and is pulled up and under the presser foot, ready to begin stitching.

STITCHES
Stitch Lengths
Not all seams will be stitched using the same stitch lengths. The number of stitches stitched per inch needs to be adequate to hold the garment securely together. The stitch length determines the stitch durability. Longer stitches are temporary, and shorter stitches are stronger. The stitch length is also determined by the purpose of the stitching. Figure 2.25 sets out the length of stitches used when stitching muslin, the fabric that is most often used to teach sewing at school:

- Machine basting stitches (Figure 2.25a)
- Ease/Gathering stitches (Figure 2.25b)
- Permanent stitches (Figure 2.25c)
- Staystitch (Figure 2.25d)
- Topstitching (Figure 2.25e)

Stitches are scrutinized in production in quality control. Garments with too few stitches will not hold together and will be sent back to the manufacturer, and this will incur a huge cost for the manufacturer.

The stitch length is most important, as the stitches need to hold the garment together.

LET'S STITCH!
There is rhythm to sewing and it goes like this: *SEW, CLIP, PRESS*. This stitching rhythm should be used from the start when you begin your first row of stitching. This method of stitching needs to be firmly planted in the sewer's mind from the beginning; with experience, it will become second nature to you. Be assured it will ultimately be quicker as you methodically sew, clip, and press.

- S stands for *SEW*—Sew the seam.
- C stands for *CLIP*—Clip the threads as you sew.
- P stands for *PRESS*—Press the seams as you sew.

Following the *SEW, CLIP, PRESS* method of stitching will help to produce a professional-quality garment. There's a lot of competition out there, so while at school learn to sew at the highest standard possible.

Why Is This Method of Stitching Important?
- The garment will always be clean with no threads to get tangled up; this helps to keep your work manageable.
- Pressing as you sew ensures that after every seam is stitched, it lays flat, ready to stitch the next seam to this section. Little pleats or puckers can be stitched into unpressed seams very easily. Pressing each seam flat, direc-

tionally as it was sewn, is called melding the stitches. This simply means that the stitches are being set into the fabric by pressing in the direction in which they were sewn. So the wise person presses as he/she sews!

- At the end of your project the garment should only need a light press. Students always feel rushed to meet deadlines (we see this constantly) and if you follow this process of *SEW, CLIP, PRESS*, the finishing touches to the garment will be minimal. Getting to the deadline will not be as stressful. Refer to Chapter 18 for details on finishing the garment.

Stitching Seams
- Insert the correct needle size to suit the fabric type and weight.
- Use muslin fabric to practice stitching, as muslin is a good, medium-weight fabric on which to practice.
- When sampling, place *two layers* of fabric together with the correct sides together. As you stitch, check to make sure the needle is not making little pulls in the fabric. If it is, stop stitching and use a different needle size to avoid damaging your fabric. Table 2.2 lists the needle sizes that best suit each fabric weight.

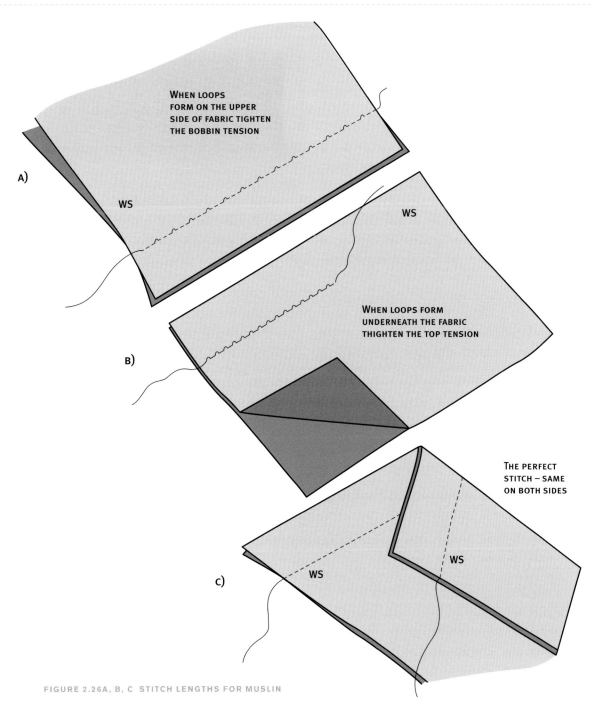

WHEN LOOPS
FORM ON THE UPPER
SIDE OF FABRIC TIGHTEN
THE BOBBIN TENSION

A)

WS

WS

WHEN LOOPS FORM
UNDERNEATH THE FABRIC
THIGHTEN THE TOP TENSION

B)

THE PERFECT
STITCH – SAME
ON BOTH SIDES

WS

WS

c)

- Practice the different stitch lengths as shown in Figure 2.25a–e.
- Make sure the machine and bobbin tensions are adjusted correctly. Loops forming on the top side of the seam indicate that the bobbin tension needs tightening (see Figure 2.26a). When loops form on the underside of the seam, the top tension needs to be tightened (see Figure 2.26b). A perfectly balanced stitch looks flat and smooth on both the top and bottom of the stitched seam (see Figure 2.26c).
- Adjust the bobbin tension (see Figure 2.24a) *only* after checking that the sewing machine is properly threaded, the needle is inserted correctly, and the correct thread weight is being used for the fabric.
- Practice sample stitching.
- Experiment with seam finishes that you think may suit the fabric and the design. Seam finishes and fabric are also a tandem pair—they must work together. If one seam finish doesn't work, then try another until you come up with just the right one for your fabric and design.

Reducing Bulk

Bulk occurs when several layers of fabric are stitched together and refers to the thickness of the seams. Thick seams can produce an ugly ridge on the correct side of the fabric if the bulk is not reduced. It is most important to attend to reducing bulk as seams are stitched, rather than thinking you can get back to it later. It's not always possible to get back inside a garment section after it's been stitched.

Fabric weights are not all uniform; they divide into heavyweight, medium weight, and lightweight fabrics. Depending on the fabric weight and the type of seam stitched, bulk is more prevalent in some seams than others. Bulk needs to be reduced from collar corners, overlapping pleats, intersecting seams, seam insertions (when a trim or binding is added into a seam), and any other thick seams. The following references from other chapters will help you to understand bulk.

- Figure 6.29a shows how *bulk* is cut away from an intersecting seam to reduce the thickness.
- Figure 6.34b shows how *excess fabric* is cut away from a flat-felled seam to reduce bulk.
- Figure 6.18d shows a seam with piping; this type of seam becomes very thick with four layers of fabric and *bulk needs to be reduced* so the seam does not show a ridge from the correct side of the fabric.
- Figure 15.27 shows how to *reduce bulk* from a scallop seam allowance.
- *Bulk* is also reduced in hems to prevent ugly ridges from showing on the correct side of the fabric. Look at Figure 15.7 to see how to reduce bulk on hems.

How to Use a Seam Ripper to Remove Unwanted Stitches

No matter how carefully we stitch, occasionally the stitches are off, the stitch quality is not good, the stitching is not the correct length—in short, the stitches need to be removed. In order to remove the stitches without damaging the fabric, they must be taken out with consideration of the fabric and the thread using a seam ripper (Figure 2.27).

A very handy tool, the seam ripper is available in many configurations, but the best seam ripper is one that feels comfortable in the hand and is large enough to grip without the fingers going numb. The point of the seam ripper should be very sharp, and the small, curved section (which is actually the cutting blade) should be sharp as well, to easily slice through any thread.

When faced with removing a long section of stitches, carefully place the point of the seam ripper under a stitch, lifting it slightly away from the fabric and cutting through it with the curved area of the ripper. Continue this process every inch or so. Once you remove the bobbin thread from the other side of the seamline, the short, cut threads will pull out easily. *Do not* attempt to pull the entire length of stitches out by yanking on the thread—the threads will tighten up and be even more difficult to remove while possibly ripping the fabric. *Never* attempt to remove stitches by pulling the fabric apart.

PROJECT PREPARATION

It is really important to begin any new project with preparation. Students who start stitching the garment without first planning it can get into a muddle. We advise you think through every garment project first before beginning to stitch.

Filling in a design worksheet (Figure 2.28) will help you to define the fabric type, weight, and fibers, along with the seam and hem stitches

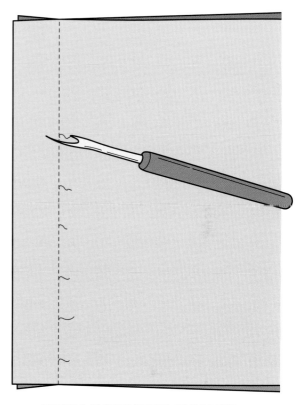

FIGURE 2.27 SEAM RIPPER: HOW TO USE

you plan to use, interfacing choice, and the supplies needed. It also gives a clear direction for the stitching order (Figure 2.29) you will use to stitch the garment together. Even though there is a general stitching order (and this book is written in this order), that order may change for each style. For example, a pocket may be stitched to the fabric surface as the first step in the stitching order, or it could be stitched last in the stitching order. So individualize your own stitching order for each garment.

Stitch seam and hem samples after cut-

IMPORTANT

Order now all the sewing supplies needed!

ting the fabric. All this information is then documented and the sample is mounted on the worksheet and used as a guide as you stitch your garment (Figure 2.30). This preparation will help you avoid mistakes such as using a zipper that is too short, interfacing that is too stiff, or forgetting to order the buttons you need. Sampling and preparation will ultimately save time.

Here is the list of sampling that will help to direct the stitching of your garment:

- Interfacing (Attach to the fabric following the directions for sampling, and assess whether the fabric and interfacing weights are compatible; see also Chapter 3, "Interfacing.")
- Seam finishes, seam stitching, and pressing
- Hem finish and pressing
- Embellishments

FITTING THE GARMENT

When a student writes an essay, several drafts may be written before the final essay is completed. For the designer creating fashion, it is no different. The designer makes muslins as the draft design. One, two, or three muslins may be made to fit the dress form, and in that time seams may change position, the length may be short-

Design Worksheet

Description of Garment _____

_____

_____

_____

_____

Fabric Type ____ Woven ____ Knit ____ Other ____

Garment Fabric Content _____

Garment Care _____

Garment Fabric:

Lightweight ____ Medium ____ Heavyweight ____

Stabilizer—Fusible ____ Sew-in ____ Fusible/Knit ____

Location _____

Lining Type _____ Woven ____ Knit ____

Lining Fiber Content _____

Seam Type _____ Location _____

Seam Type _____ Location _____

Seam Type _____ Location _____

Hem Stitching Technique _____

Type of Closure _____ Location _____

List Notions _____

_____

Trim/Embellishment _____

_____

Sketch of Design

Front   Back

Fabric Swatches
Outer Fabric/Lining/Interfacing

FIGURE 2.28 DESIGN WORKSHEET

Stitching Order

Before beginning your garment, think through the stitching order. Write down the constructional order of how the garment will be stitched together.

1. _____
2. _____
3. _____
4. _____
5. _____
6. _____
7. _____
8. _____
9. _____
10. _____
11. _____
12. _____
13. _____
14. _____
15. _____

Sample Worksheet

Before beginning any garment stitch some samples to decide on the best stitching techniques to suit your fabric and design. Several samples need to be stitched before deciding on the best one for the project. This preparation is well worth the time involved as it may save making stitching mistakes on the actual garment. Also sample some stabilizers to find the one to suit your fabric.

Cut 4" x 4" fabric swatch and apply 2" x 2" Interfacing	Hem Stitching
Seam Stitching	Other—Embellishment or Topstitching

FIGURE 2.29 STITCHING ORDER   FIGURE 2.30 SAMPLE WORKSHEET

ened, the sleeve cut shorter, and so on, until the designer is satisfied with the new proportions and fit of the garment. Muslin is the fabric (100 percent cotton) most often used to fit garments, and the term *making muslin* refers to this activity. Once the muslin version is satisfactory, the garment is cut in the final fabric. However, the fitting does not stop there. In fact, the garment is in development until the last stitch!

It is always best to make all muslins using a weight that is similar to the fabric that will be used in your final garment. At school, stitching and patternmaking fittings are made using muslin fabric, and this is an excellent choice for practicing. However, it is very difficult to get an accurate first fit in muslin when the final garment you are making will be constructed of a heavier-weight fabric, for example, a coat of heavy wool tweed. It is impossible to get an accurate fit and drape when your final garment will be made of a fabric that is lighter in weight than the muslin, for example, if 100 percent cotton muslin is used to make a draft garment that will be manufactured as a final garment from lightweight, sheer silk georgette.

When making a muslin for leather, use felt; this an ideal substitute fabric. For coats and jackets made in wool or cashmere, use upholstery fabric as the muslin.

PRESSING EQUIPMENT

Having the correct pressing tools helps to achieve quality workmanship. Pressing is important, as you are about to find out. It may take time to acquire your own equipment, but you will soon find you are unable to live without these tools, as they really do give great support when pressing beautiful fabric.

Ironing Board

An **ironing board** is used for ironing clothes and linen (Figure 2.31a). Ironing boards can be free-standing, built in, pullout, or fold away. Whichever style of ironing board is used, the padded work surface should be heat resistant. An ironing board has a cotton ironing board cover that should be replaced when damaged or worn.

Steam Iron

A **steam iron** is used for pressing seams, hems, and the final garment (Figure 2.31b). The iron has a metal plate that smoothly glides over the fabric. An iron has a temperature dial to control the heat. On domestic irons the dial is marked with fabric types such as "linen/cotton," "wool/silk," and "synthetic." At school it's not that simple, as the dial is numbered 1, 2, 3, 4, 5. The numbers on the dial indicate the following settings: number 1 is the lowest setting and corresponds to fabrics that require low temperatures, such as synthetics, rayons, and so forth; number 2 corresponds to silk without steam; number 3 corresponds to wool and is the beginning of adding steam; number 4 corresponds to linen; and number 5 is the highest setting, with the most amount of heat, which in the case of the gravity-feed irons is really hot! Change the heat temperature to match the fabric type when pressing. It is advisable to press a fabric sample first before pressing the garment.

Pressing Cloth

A **pressing cloth** is a square of open-weave cotton or muslin fabric about the size of a men's handkerchief (Figure 2.31c). Actually, a white men's handkerchief is the perfect pressing cloth! The pressing cloth is placed over the fabric surface for protection and to prevent the iron from leaving shine marks. The cloth can be dampened to provide extra steam when pressing. A natural-colored piece of silk organza also makes an excellent pressing cloth; since it is sheer you can see what you are doing when pressing.

Wool/mohair can be used as a press cloth for tweeds and knits; it works like a needle board, preventing the nap from being flattened when pressed. A rectangle of wool/mohair can be stitched to have a single layer of cotton such as muslin on one side and be finished on all sides with a serger.

Seam Roll

A **seam roll** is a firm cylinder-like cushion covered with cotton on one side and wool on the other (Figure 2.31d). A seam roll is used to press long, narrow seams such as the inseam or outseam of a pant leg or underarm seams. Use the cotton side for pressing most fabrics; the wool side can be used for pressing woolen fabrics. Using a seam roll helps to avoid seam impressions that might otherwise show to the correct side of the garment after pressing.

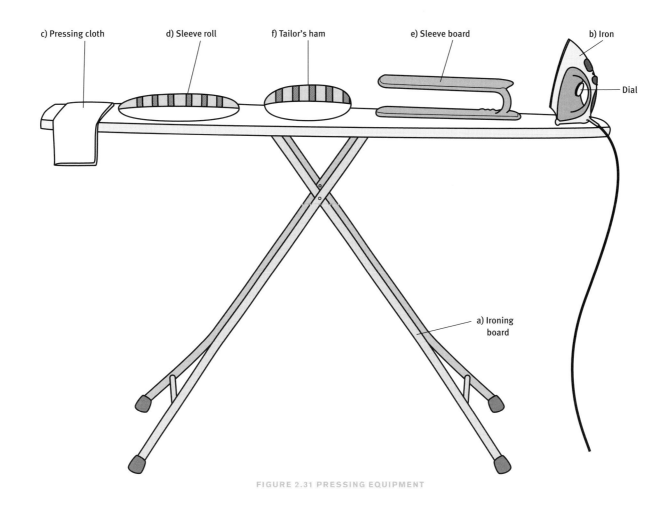

c) Pressing cloth   d) Sleeve roll   f) Tailor's ham   e) Sleeve board   b) Iron

Dial

a) Ironing board

FIGURE 2.31 PRESSING EQUIPMENT

Sleeve Board

A **sleeve board** is a small-scale wooden ironing board with rounded, padded ends (Figure 2.31e). It is a wonderful pressing tool. It is used for pressing sleeves, short seams, and hard-to-get-at areas that do not fit over a regular-sized ironing board; it can also be used on the rounded ends to steam out ease at the cap of sleeves. If you make half-size muslins at school, the sleeve board is excellent for pressing a smaller size.

Tailor's Ham

A **tailor's ham** is a firm, rounded, or oval cushion that provides a pressing surface to shape darts, sleeve head, lapels, collars, and curved areas of a garment (Figure 2.30f). The covering is usually of wool and cotton.

HOW TO PRESS A GARMENT

Construction pressing has a basic aim: to press a specific detail without pressing the entire area.

The garment has to be positioned correctly and the proper equipment must be used to press a detail. Always press on the grain in the same direction the stitching was done. Don't skip steps, because pressing makes the next construction step easier. Keep all pressed garment sections as flat as possible rather than rolled up in a ball, or thrown in a bag (and thus needing to be pressed *again* before you are able to continue sewing). Overpressing can ruin fabric! Take pride in the work accomplished from the very beginning of each garment.

Remove pins and basting before pressing—pins can mar the fabric as well as the iron. Use silk thread to baste to avoid leaving impressions in the fabric when pressing.

Always press the seams as they are stitched, pressing the seams flat as they are sewn, and then open to either side. Then place the seams on a seam roll, a tailor's ham, or on the edge of the sleeve board. Smooth the fabric crosswise and open the seam. Press the point of the iron in the direction of the grain. Finally, press the seam on the outside of the garment, using a press cloth.

Areas that are to be shaped are placed over a section of the tailor's ham or a seam roll that properly fits the area to be pressed. Garment areas that must be shaped in this way are:

- Curved seams such as a yoke or bodice seam.
- Bust and waistline curves on a fitted seam.
- Waistline seams—press toward the bodice.
- Darts and tucks—place a strip of paper under the fold of the dart to avoid leaving an impression on the front of the garment.
- Bust darts—press down.
- Waistline and shoulder darts—press toward center front or center back of the garment.
- Double-pointed darts or contour darts— clip at the widest point to lie flat and press toward the center front or center back of the garment.
- Darts in heavyweight fabric—slash to within ½ inch of the dart point, place over the tailor's ham, and press open with the point of the iron. Then press again along each side of the stitching line.
- Elbow darts—press before the sleeve is constructed. Then press the seam open on a sleeve board.
- Sleeve cap easing—steam press easing to shape.
- Shoulder seams—press crosswise, the way the shoulder curves away from the seamline, and press the seam open on the underside from the neckline to the armhole. Then, from the correct side of the fabric, shape and press the back shoulder line on the lengthwise grain around the edge of the curved seam roll or tailor's ham.
- Armhole seam—lay the top sleeve seam (between the notches) with edges together, over the edge of the sleeve board with the sleeve side up. Use the point of the iron to press the seam allowances only. (The underarm section of the seam should not be pressed open; it's trimmed.)
- Understitched facings—are pressed and turned to the inside of the garment shape with the fingers to perfect the line of the faced edges.
- Hems—press with the wrong side of the garment facing out, using a lifting rather than a gliding motion. Always press the hem along the fabric grain from hemline to hem edge.
- Gathers and shirring—press by working the point of the iron into the gathers and pressing toward the stitching line. Avoid creases by lifting the folds away from the iron as pressed.
- Pleats—these are basted before pressing on the wrong side of the fabric along the foldline to set the crease. From the correct side of the garment, remove the basting; press, using a strip of paper under each pleat to prevent leaving an impression.

Final pressing can be kept to a minimum touch-up here and there if each step of construction pressing has been done with care. Hang the garment properly to maintain its shape—choose a strong, contoured hanger. Fasten buttons or closures and zippers to retain the garment shape. Refer to Chapter 18 for more information on final pressing.

TRANSFER YOUR KNOWLEDGE

Once you get into the rhythm of sampling a project, transfer this system of stitching to all other stitching. Just don't sample muslin fabric; transfer your knowledge and sample every fabric before beginning a new garment.

STRETCH YOUR CREATIVITY

Stretch your creativity by practicing how to sew. Use different stitches with different-colored thread stitched at various angles, in various decorative stitches on different weights of fabric.

Stretch your creativity by sketching some designs, and find some fabric swatches to suit the styles. Look at your design and fill in the design worksheet as a practice step; this will help you to think about the functional, structural, and decorative design aspect of the garment.

STOP! WHAT DO I DO IF . . .

. . . I don't know what I'm doing? I feel overwhelmed when I sit at the machine. Is it best to just give up?

Relax—get help—go to the learning center in your school for extra help. Ask your teacher for help. Ask questions. Read the section again, over and over if you need to, until you have more understanding—and practice, practice, practice stitching and threading the machine. There are no quick fixes other than to stitch!

. . . I can't be bothered to use the *SEW, CLIP, PRESS* method of stitching, as it takes far too long; is that OK?

Using the *SEW, CLIP, PRESS* method ensures that your final garment will reflect quality workmanship.

. . . my stitches are skipping?

Change the needle, as it could be blunt, or try a different needle size. Rethread the machine; the machine won't stitch if it is threaded incorrectly. Check to be sure the thread has been pulled up around and into the tension disc; if it is not pulled up well in the tension disc, the machine won't stitch.

SELF-CRITIQUE

- Do I see the importance of using the stitching method of *SEW, CLIP, PRESS*?
- Do I understand how to press my seams, darts, and other garments parts?
- Do I understand the necessity of pressing as I sew?

REVIEW CHECKLIST

- Do I have all the supplies and equipment needed to begin to sew a garment?
- Do I know how to thread the sewing machine and insert the bobbin?

Having prepared for your project by gathering all your equipment, did you see a difference in the way the garment came together? We're sure it will continue to make a difference if you stick with it! It takes practice and time to plan each garment by way of sampling; however, this preparation is an integral part of the design development of any garment. The samples made and stitched in this way will become a wonderful resource for future reference for the design student or designer. So keep sampling, and don't give up on this process! Start a folder, and keep adding your samples to it.

Introduction to Stabilizers: Fabricating a Stable Foundation

This chapter discusses the importance of using stabilizers to add structure, shape, and reinforcement to garments. Our first impression of a garment is the silhouette, which is the outside shape of the garment. Whether the garment silhouette has volume or is close fitting, attention needs to be given to the foundation of the garment and how it is going to be built or structured. Sometimes when a garment is on the runway in a student fashion show, the struc-

ture is not supported and the garment silhouette looks limp. To prevent this from happening, a designer needs to know how to structure and support garments from the foundation up. The foundation of a garment can be built by using a variety of stabilizers, such as underlining, interfacing, stabilizing tape, boning, or by simply staystitching.

The structural foundation of the garment needs to be considered before stitching any darts or seams. It is important to choose the correct type, weight, color, and texture of stabilizers. Adding a stabilizer to a garment will add

to the cost of the garment, but it will also add to the quality of the garment and extend its life. Using an inappropriate stabilizer for the fabric, or leaving it out completely when needed, will affect how the final garment looks.

STYLE I.D.

The garments in the Style I.D. have all been stabilized to varying degrees, and in different ways, to help hold the structure and shape of the garment (Figure 3.1). Some fabrics need to be entirely stabilized to help hold the garment shape. Other styles need only partial stabiliz-

Style I.D.

POCKET FLAPS
INTERFACED

INTERFACING

CANVAS

INTERFACING
IN COLLAR

INTERFACING
IN CUFF

UNDERLINING

STABILIZING BIAS
WITH TAPE

FULLY
UNDERLINED

INTERFACING
IN FRONT
FACING

TWEED WOOL COAT
A

INSIDE VIEW OF COAT
B

PLAID WOOL DRESS
C

INSIDE VIEW OF DRESS
D

"LITTLE BLACK DRESS"
E

INSIDE VIEW OF "LBD"
F

FIGURE 3.1: INTERFACING AND STABILIZERS

ing, such as at the collar and cuffs. Still other garments only need their edges stabilized with tape for reinforcement and to prevent the fabric from stretching in the construction process. The tweed wool coat, plaid wool dress, and the popular "little black dress" (LBD) in Figure 3.1 have all been stabilized to different degrees. Inside views show how each garment has been structured with a stabilizer (see Figure 3.1b, d, and f). Each style in the Style I.D. will be referred to throughout this chapter.

GATHER YOUR TOOLS

Think ahead and purchase a variety of fusible and nonfusible stabilizers, a few yards of interfacing in different weights and colors, and stabilizing tapes (bias and straight grain tapes). Don't depend on your local fabric store to have these items in stock. It is recommended that you look online for these products and *order now!* It is important to use *good-quality* products, as the final garment will reflect the quality of its components. Refer to the "Where to Buy" section in this text for ordering supplies.

NOW LET'S GET STARTED

The underlying structure of a garment is the first and most important part of clothing construction. Remember, the stabilizer is the foundation on which the garment is built.

WHAT ARE STABILIZERS?

The architecture of clothing is everything. When a building is erected, it needs a foundation to support its structure. The same concept applies to clothing. The foundation in clothing is the stabilizer; it is an additional layer that offers light-, medium-, or heavyweight support to a fabric before or during the construction process to hold the garment shape. Some fabrics don't have the crispness and body needed to hold the shape of the garment. For example, a skirt made in medium-weight taffeta, gathered at the waistline, will hold a crisp structured shape, while a floaty silk georgette fabric won't hold the shape in the same way—it drapes quite differently. Stabilizers can be added in many different ways to give support and structure to the garment when needed.

A stabilizer can add structure to the entire garment, as illustrated by the coat in Figure 3.1b, or to individual parts, such as the collar, cuffs, and midriff section of the plaid wool dress in Figure 3.1d. A stabilizing tape can also add lightweight support to garment edges, as in the armhole and neckline illustrated in Figure 3.1f. To view other important key application points for stabilizing other garments, refer to Figure 3.2.

WHY USE A STABILIZER?

Using a stabilizer *correctly* can transform your garment from one that is quite ordinary-looking to one that is quite extraordinary.

A stabilizer:

- Helps hold the shape of the garment.
- Helps the appearance and performance of the garment by adding support, strength, stability, and reinforcement.

- Adds quality and extends the life of the garment.
- Can add softness; stabilizers don't necessarily make the garment feel stiff.
- Prevents the garment from wrinkling.
- Can improve the fit of the garment.
- Prevents the garment from sagging or stretching out of shape.
- Prevents seams from stretching or puckering in the stitching process; seams lay flatter with a stabilizer.
- Reinforces loosely woven fabric.
- Prevents seam slippage.
- Provides crisp edges so they don't cave in.
- Give support to areas that are clipped.

Learning how to judge when a stabilizer is needed is an important aspect of studying fashion design, because a stabilizer helps to hold the **silhouette** or shape of the garment.

HOW TO JUDGE IF THE GARMENT NEEDS A STABILIZER

Following are three steps to help the student designer ascertain if a stabilizer is needed in a garment.

FIGURE 3.2 KEY APPLICATION POINTS FOR STABILIZERS

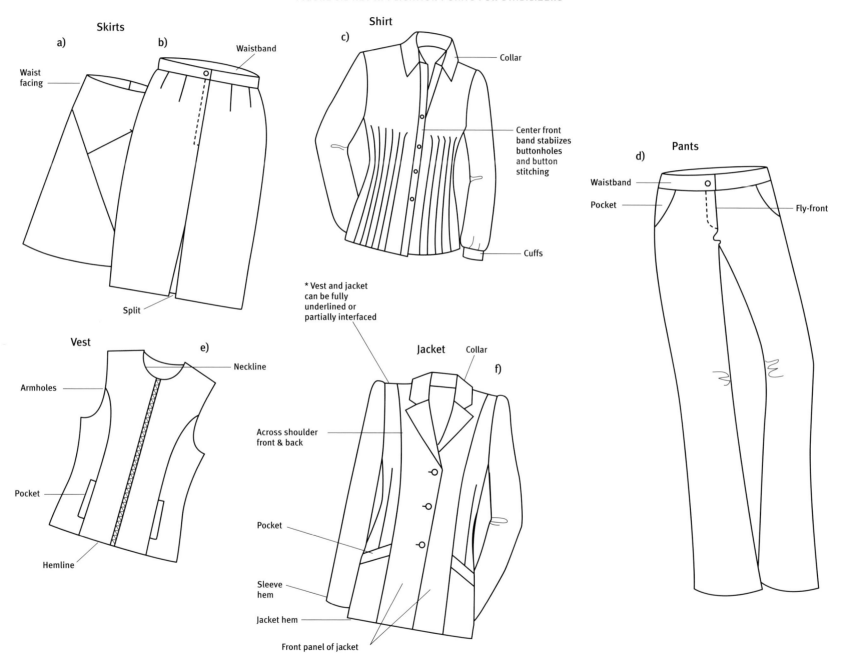

Skirts

a)

Waist facing

b)

Waistband

Split

Shirt

c)

Collar

Center front band stabiizes buttonholes and button stitching

Cuffs

Pants

d)

Waistband

Pocket

Fly-front

Vest

e)

Neckline

Armholes

Pocket

Hemline

* Vest and jacket can be fully underlined or partially interfaced

Jacket

Collar

f)

Across shoulder front & back

Pocket

Sleeve hem

Jacket hem

Front panel of jacket

TWILL TAPE

BONING

FORM

UNDERLINING

PADDING

LINING

NETTING
LAYER 1

NETTING
LAYER 2

NETTING
LAYER 3

PADDING AND NETTING
ADDED TO HOLD THE
STRUCTURE OF THE DRESS

- - - - - = SKIRT SILHOUETTE

SILK STRAPLESS COCKTAIL DRESS
A

INSIDE OF DRESS WITH
DRESS FORM VISIBLE
B

STRUCTURING THE SILK
STRAPLESS COCKTAIL DRESS
C

FIGURE 3.3 A SILK STRAPLESS COCKTAIL DRESS

Analyze the Design

The first step is to analyze the sketch of the design and have a clear picture in your mind of the overall garment shape or silhouette you want to create. When the garment is worn, the human body gives the garment form. How-ever, the body cannot always fully support the entire shape of the garment.

The garment parts that stand away from the human form are the ones in which stabilizing needs to be considered. Figure 3.3a is a sketch of a strapless cocktail dress with a gathered skirt that stands away from the human form. Figure 3.3b is a transparent view of the dress, showing the space between the form and the silhouette of the garment. The designer's responsibility is to think through how the strapless bodice would be stabilized to fit to the form and how

the skirt would be stabilized and structured to hold this shape.

First, notice in Figure 3.3b that the entire garment has been is underlined. Then the bodice seams are boned and a stabilizing tape applied to the top edge of the strapless bodice to add structure and reinforcement. Second, notice in Figure 3.3c that further structure has been added by padding the strapless bodice and adding three layers of netting, which are stitched to the lining to hold the structure of the skirt silhouette. For instruction on how these stabilizers are stitched, refer to Chapter 6, "Boning," and Chapter 15, "Hem Stabilizers."

Analyze the Fabric

The designer's artistic medium is fabric. Careful study of the fabric is therefore the second step.

The designer relies on the fabric to take on many different shapes. The type, weight, and drape of the fabric either give shape and form or allow the fabric to softly drape.

Take the fabric in your hands; feel it, fold it, and scrunch it to assess whether the weight of the fabric suits the design. Drape the fabric on the form; observe whether the fabric is crisp and firm enough to hold the shape required for the design. If it's not, then consider using a stabilizer to support the fabric. Figure 3.4 shows the designer with a length of floral fabric, determining how the fabric drapes.

When fullness and volume are added by gathering, tucking, scrunching, pleating, and draping the fabric, this extra fullness may hold the garment shape—but sometimes it won't be sufficient. In Figure 3.5 the skirt has been stitched in a crisp, medium-weight cotton. Lots of triangular-shaped pieces of fabric, called godets, have been inserted into the hem of the skirt to add volume. In this case the volume, combined with the type and weight of fabric, holds the shape of the skirt and a stabilizer is not necessary. Also notice in this design how the flowers on the jacket hold their shape and stand away from the fabric surface; the fabric has the stiffness combined with the fullness to also structure the flowers. Refer to Chapter 6, "Godets," for stitching instructions.

It is not only garments that stand away from the human form that need structure. Some form-fitting garments also need stabilizing because the fabric does not have the required body, and for the reasons set out in the previous section, "Why Use a Stabilizer?"

The original "little back dress" designed by Hubert de Givenchy, was worn by Audrey Hepburn in the movie *Breakfast at Tiffany's.* This legendary dress has inspired many designers to create their own versions, and the elegant, form-fitting LBD in Figure 3.1e is one version.[1]

We have already touched on the fact that this dress could be structured with a lightweight seam stabilizer. However, let's discuss the LBD further. There are no rules as to how this dress *should* be structured; there are many options, but there is no one *right* way. Figure 3.7a also shows the option of fully underlining the dress. Figure 3.7b illustrates how the dress could be stabilized with an interfacing applied to the facing as an alternative method. The decision about whether to fully or partially stabilize a formfitting dress is fabric driven, as you have learned in this section.

Analyze the Garment Edges

Now, for the third step, take a look at Figure 3.7 and observe the shape of the garment edges. In particular, look at the armholes and neckline. Notice in this illustration how these sections are partially cut on the bias grain. Any part of the garment cut on bias grain is stretchy, as you learned in Chapter 2. These three garment pieces—one front piece and two back pieces—when stitched together form the LBD in Figure 3.1e.

Any garment edges that are fully or partially cut on the bias, such as neckline and armholes, have the potential to stretch in the construction process. To prevent this from happening, they need to be stabilized. The designer needs to consider how to do this. There are three options: underlining, interfacing, or using stabilizing tape.

WHO CHOOSES THE STABILIZER FOR THE GARMENT?

In garment manufacturing, someone needs to be responsible for deciding whether or not to use a stabilizer in the garment, and where to place it if used. This chapter is so important because it is the *designer's responsibility* to make this decision.

When designers create collections, they begin by sketching their ideas. To do this, they define the outside edges of the garment (that is, the silhouette) by defining the neckline, shoulder line, armhole, sleeve, side seams, and hemline. The designer then uses line to create shapes within the silhouette. This is done by arranging and rearranging the design elements of line, shape, color, and texture. It is then the designer's responsibility to transform each design into a real garment. This is only made possible by understanding the medium, which is *fabric.*

If the fabric needs a stabilizer, then the designer chooses the type of stabilizer and its placement. It is important for the manufacturing of the garment that the designer understand stabilizers and what they can do for a garment. Stabilizers may be a new concept for the student designer. Now is the time to begin learning their importance, and the key application points where they need to be placed. Refer back to Figure 3.2 if you need to refresh your memory about these points.

Stabilizers are a crucial part of any successful garment. There is no checklist that says, "You need a stabilizer in this fabric!" If only designers did have this formula their jobs would be so much easier. Yet part of the creativity and excitement of creating clothes is the discovery of what works and what doesn't work.

Deciding whether a stabilizer is needed in the garment is the first important decision,

GODETS

FIGURE 3.5 VOLUME AND FULLNESS HOLD THE STRUCTURE OF THE SKIRT AND FLOWERS WITHOUT NEEDING A STABILIZER.

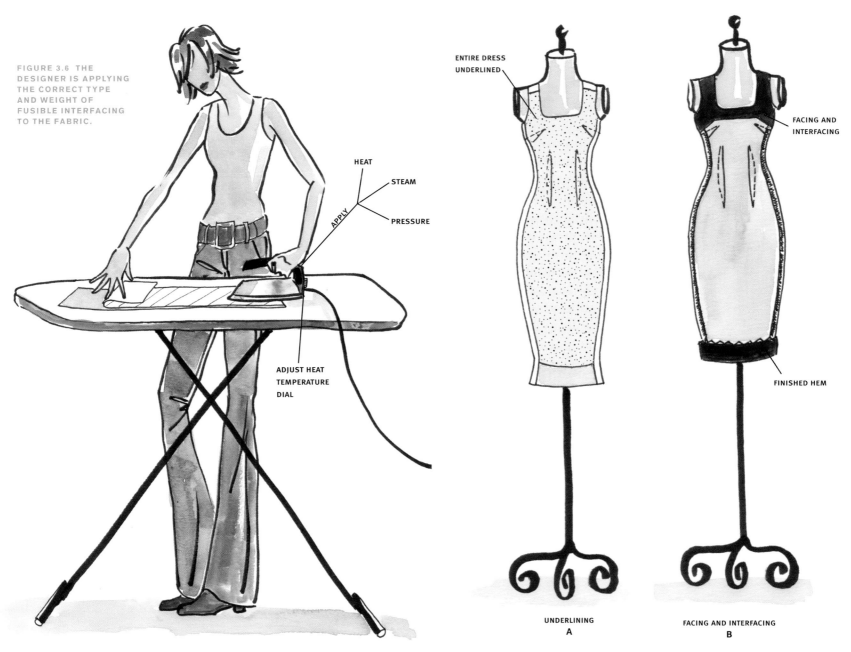

FIGURE 3.6 THE DESIGNER IS APPLYING THE CORRECT TYPE AND WEIGHT OF FUSIBLE INTERFACING TO THE FABRIC.

HEAT

STEAM

APPLY

PRESSURE

ADJUST HEAT TEMPERATURE DIAL

ENTIRE DRESS UNDERLINED

FACING AND INTERFACING

FINISHED HEM

UNDERLINING
A

FACING AND INTERFACING
B

FIGURE 3.7 STRUCTURING THE "LITTLE BLACK DRESS" UNDERLINING

which will influence the stitching order of the garment. Next, how each stabilizer will be applied must be decided, step by step.

TYPES OF STABILIZERS

The term **stabilizer** refers broadly to anything that can be used to help structure the fabric. This encompasses interfacing, fabric, boning, wire, fishing line, netting, tulle, and mesh stretch knit. For the purposes of this chapter, we will concentrate on all-fabric stabilizers.

The three stabilizing categories discussed in this chapter are stabilizing tape, interfacing, and underlining. Other types of stabilizers are discussed in later chapters: boning, in Chapter 6; fishing line, netting, and tulle, in Chapter 15. It is impossible to outline every stabilizer available. If you need to know more about other stabilizers, ask your instructor for more information.

Many stabilizers are interchangeable; an interfacing can be used as an underlining, an interfacing, or a stabilizing tape. This chapter explains each of these uses, and describes how to apply them in garment construction.

Interfacing

Interfacings are the most common stabilizers used in garments today. Interfacings are manufactured in three different structures: woven, nonwoven, and knit. Within each type, different weights, widths, hand, color, and weaves are available. They are produced in popular colors such as black, white, natural, red, and dark and light charcoal. Check the width of each inter-

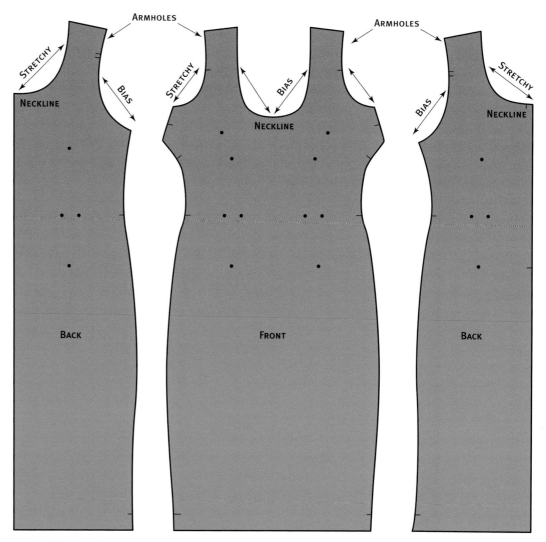

FIGURE 3.8 SHAPED GARMENT EDGES OF "LITTLE BLACK DRESS" IN FIG. 3.1E NEED STABILIZING

facing before purchasing; some interfacings are 60 inches wide, others, 30 inches wide, and yet others somewhere between these two widths. It is also important to take notice of the manufacturer's instructions describing how each one is to be applied.

Woven Interfacing

Woven interfacings are no different from fabric in the way they are formed. Warp and weft threads are woven vertically and horizontally and intersect with each other. Just as fabrics come in a variety of fibers, so do inter-

FIGURE 3.9 CUTTING WOVEN INTERFACING

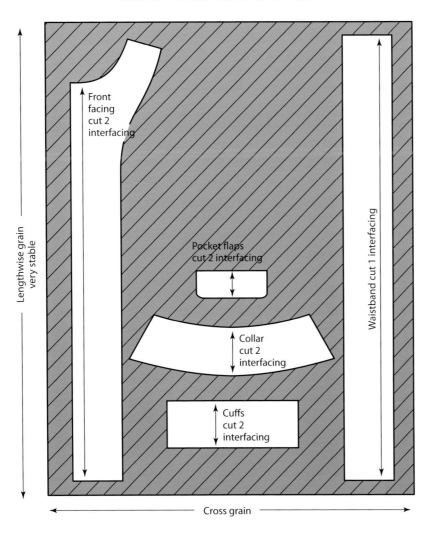

Nonwoven Interfacing

Nonwoven interfacings are considered bonded fabrics. A nonwoven interfacing is created with synthetic fibers that have been chemically or thermally compressed together with the use of heat. Nonwoven interfacings don't fray and are usually reasonably priced. They don't have an actual grainline; however, it is advisable to cut garment parts that need the most stability, such as collars, waistband, or cuff, in the lengthwise direction, as it ensures the most stability (Figure 3.10).

Knit Interfacing

Knit interfacings are made with interlooping yarns that give them a stretch capacity. They are mostly made from synthetic fibers and are mostly fusible. Knit interfacings provide a softer hand than woven interfacings. Not all knit interfacings have the same stretch capacity; some have little stretch while others have greater stretch. It is important to sample first to check that the stretch capacity of the interfacing matches that of the fabric. The stretch is usually in the width, with firmness in the length. For garment parts (such as collar, cuffs, or waistband) that need firmness, position the pattern in the direction that gives stability rather than using the stretch capacity.

Take a few minutes to look at Figure 3.11. Notice that the same front-facing pattern used in Figures 3.9 and 3.10 has been redirected. This is done so the interfacing gives stability when the buttonholes are stitched, ensuring that they will not stretch in the stitching or wearing process. If the interfacing stretches in both directions, use

facings; they can be made from natural, synthetic, or a blend of both fibers. Woven interfacings are very stable and don't stretch in the length or the width. It is important, then, that they be cut following the pattern grainlines. Because woven in-

terfacing is stable in both directions, patterns can be placed on the lengthwise or crosswise grain, as illustrated in Figure 3.9. Woven interfacings include cotton batiste, organza, broadcloth, and canvas, to name just a few.

an alternative nonstretch interfacing for garment parts that need stability. For interfacing garment parts that need to retain the stretch capacity, place the pattern on the interfacing in the direction that stretches.

Knit interfacings are not restricted to use in stretch fabrics only; they are also an *ideal* option for underlining or interfacing of woven fabrics. (When used in woven fabrics, the stretch of the knit interfacing is eliminated.) When a soft hand and light- to medium-weight hold are required, a knit interfacing can be just the one to use! Among the knit interfacings on the market are Tricot (crosswise stretch only), Fusi-Knit (or French Fuse, crosswise stretch only), and SofKnit (all-bias, which stretches in all directions).

If the stabilizer is nonfusible, it is classified as sew-in. Fusible and sew-in interfacings can be applied to the entire fabric as an underlining, applied to smaller portions as an interfacing, or used as stabilizing tapes; both types are discussed in more detail below.

Fusible Interfacing

Fusible interfacings can be woven, nonwoven, or knit. What makes interfacing fusible is the shiny resin, like tiny dots on one side. When heat is applied, the resin bonds to the fabric. The size of the adhesive dots determines how the interfacing clings to the fabric. In general, interfacings with smaller dots work well on lightweight fabrics and those with larger dots combine well with heavyweight and textured fabrics.

Fusibles are quick and easy to use; however, they may not be compatible with the fabric that

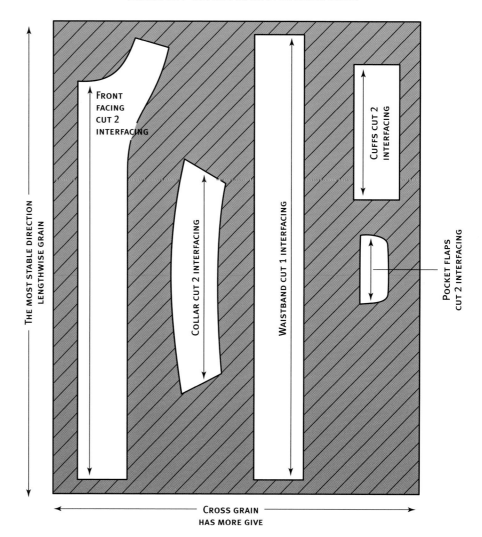

FIGURE 3.10 CUTTING NONWOVEN INTERFACING

will be used in a garment. Some fabrics do not react well to heat and moisture, which may damage their surfaces. If after sampling this is the case, try another type of interfacing, or change to a nonwoven stabilizer.

Sew-in Interfacing

A **nonfusible** stabilizer is referred to as a **sew-in interfacing** because it does not have a resin on the back, which glues to the fabric. A sew-in stabilizer needs to be hand or machine stitched to individual cut fabric pieces. Proceed with caution when machine stitching a sew-in interfacing as it can easily be pulled out of alignment in the stitching process.

Some fabrics *must* have sew-in stabilizers. These fabrics are velvet, faux fur, synthetic leather, lace, some brocades, some sheers, some silks, sequined and beaded fabrics, open-weave fabrics, metallics, vinyls, and water-repellent fabrics. Refer to "Interfacing Tricky Fabrics" later in this chapter for more detail. If a fusible stabilizer were to be used on these fabrics, the fabric surfaces would be damaged because they do not react well to heat.

Following are some sew-in stabilizers commonly used to stabilize garments:

- Organza is a lightweight, sheer fabric that adds a lightweight support; it adds stiffness without adding weight. One hundred percent sheer silk is much easier to use than polyester organza.
- Hair canvas is another sew-in available in light, medium, and heavy weights. It adds exceptional body to tailored garments. Canvas can be made from a mixture of fibers. One combination of fibers is 41 percent acrylic, 19 percent hair, 15 percent polyester, 15 percent viscose, and 10 percent cotton; this fiber mix means it must be dry cleaned. (Fusible canvas is also available.) Cotton batiste also gives a lightweight support. (Fusible batiste is also available.)
- Netting used as a stabilizer also helps to hold the shape of the garment silhouette. Skirts

and sleeves can be supported by netting. Refer back to Figure 3.3c to view how netting structures the skirt in the silk strapless cocktail dress in Figure 3.3a. Notice the netting has been stitched to a lining, as it can be very scratchy on the skin.

- Textured weft is a woven/fusible interfacing and blends superbly with textured fabrics such as tweed, silk dupioni, and boucle. The texture and weave of the interfacing blends and does not change the fabric surface. Our all-time favorite weft interfacing is Superior Soft Superior. It gives exceptional structure when used as an underlining for jackets and coats. It adds body without feeling stiff.
- Muslin is used not only for garment-fitting purposes (toile) but also as a sew-in underlining. Drapery fabrics, used for curtains, also make an excellent sew-in underlining.

HOW TO CHOOSE THE BEST STABILIZER FOR YOUR PROJECT

Here are some tips to help you when choosing which stabilizer to use. Let the *fabric* be your guide when choosing the stabilizer. The color, weight, and type of stabilizer—whether woven, knit, or fusible or nonfusible—must suit the fabric.

Type

Like fabric, interfacing is characterized by fiber content, weight, finish, and texture. The stabilizer used should never change the appearance of the fabric surface. The stabilizer needs to be compatible with the weight, hand, or stretch of the garment fabric. For example, if the fabric

you are using has a stretch capacity, then choose a stabilizer that stretches—in other words, combine like with like. To understand why matching the type of interfacing to the specific needs of the fabric is so important, let's consider velvet. Velvet is a short-pile fabric with a nap. Fabrics such as these cannot have an iron placed directly onto the fabric, as it will damage the surface. (Refer to Chapter 2, "Tricky Fabrics.") In this case, don't use a fusible stabilizer; instead, use a sew-in stabilizer.

Weight

The fabric and stabilizer weights need to be compatible and equal to each other; this is a good general rule. The final weight of the fabric and stabilizer together should not drastically change the weight or appearance of the fabric. When choosing a stabilizer, always keep in mind the integrity of the fabric—the sheerness or heaviness. For example, if a heavy interfacing were to be used to stabilize a lightweight sheer fabric, the two would work against each other and not be compatible. Don't choose a stabilizer that is heavier than the fabric you are stabilizing; rather, choose like with like. There are no "rules" to say which weight of interfacing goes with each fabric weight—it is always best to sample.

Color

The color of the stabilizer is important. If the wrong color is chosen, it could change the color of the garment fabric. The color of the stabilizer needs to blend with the overall background color of the fabric. If the overall fabric is dark, then choose a dark-colored stabilizer; if the overall fabric color is light, then choose a white or a beige-colored stabilizer. A natural color stabilizer neutralizes white fabric; a white stabilizer placed under white fabric makes it look even whiter!

Care

Always choose a stabilizer that needs the same care as the garment fabric. If the fabric is washable, then choose a washable underlining or interfacing. Some fabrics and stabilizers are preshrunk before they are combined together. If the fabric must be dry cleaned, then the stabilizer and fabric do not need preshrinking.

Purpose and Function—Combining Different Types of Interfacing in One Garment

The choice of stabilizer is also dependent on the garment's purpose and function and the final desired look. When it comes to using stabilizers, a mixture of different weights and types can be applied to the one garment. For example, let's go back and study the coat in Figure 3.1a of the Style I.D. In this coat, four different stabilizers have been used for different purposes and functions. It is important to note that both fusible and nonfusible stabilizers have been used in this coat.

Now let's take a look inside the coat.

- The body section of the coat (front and back) has been underlined with a fusible *medium-weight interfacing* to add structure to the coat.
- The sleeves have been underlined with a *lightweight interfacing* to give a softer structure; this ensures that the sleeves will not feel bulky

and uncomfortable when the arm is bent. If a fusible interfacing is appropriate, SofKnit is ideal as it gives a light structure. Note that applying a stretch knit interfacing to a woven fabric will eliminate the stretch element.

- The front facing and pocket flaps have been interfaced with the same lightweight interfacing as the sleeves. A lighter weight of interfacing is used at the front facing of the coat so it will not be too heavy and bulky to stitch buttonholes. However, it will still give a firm base on which the buttonholes and buttons can be stitched. Care needs to be taken when two layers of interfacing are used so the combination is not too heavy and bulky.
- The top shoulder/chest of the front and back coat has been stabilized with woven medium-weight hair canvas to add extra support and ensure a smooth fit over the shoulders.
- There are several possible choices for the collar. A fusible SofKnit interfacing could be applied to one side of the collar, and canvas to the other side. Or, the designer may decide to apply SofKnit to both sides of the collar and apply a canvas interfacing to one side of the collar, giving three layers of interfacing and more structure. In some collars (but not the one shown in Figure 3.1b) interfacing may be applied to the top collar only. Refer to Chapter 11 for more detail.

By mixing and matching stabilizers, individual attention is given to the purpose and function of each part of the garment. Although this com-

ponent may seem tedious, it must not be viewed this way. Function and purpose are both important aspects to consider when designing clothes. Coats and jackets have an amazing fit when they are structured using a variety of interfacings. The important thing is to choose interfacing of a suitable type and weight to compliment the fabric.

It is worth noting that the Italian couturier Giorgio Armani, an expert in tailoring jackets, incorporates several different stabilizers in each of his jackets. He uses mostly fusible interfacings, cotton twill tape, bias and straight grain strips of rayon lining, and cotton broadcloth when tailoring jackets.[2]

Sampling

Deciding which stabilizer to use can pose a dilemma. We cannot emphasize strongly enough the importance of sampling—even experienced designers still make decisions by trial and error. To avoid disaster, it is vital to sample first before making any final decisions regarding the stabilizer. Many students add fusible interfacing to the garment fabric without sampling first; only when the garment is finished do they realize interfacing of the wrong type and weight has been used. Disappointment follows, because now it's permanently adhered to the fabric and cannot be removed.

HOW TO APPLY STABILIZERS

Whether a stabilizer is added before or during the construction process or whether the fabric is underlined, interfaced, or a stabilizing tape is applied, there are two basic methods of application.

- *Fusible method:* a fusible stabilizer is pressed to the wrong side of the fabric.
- *Sew-in method:* a nonfusible stabilizer is handbasted to the wrong side of the fabric.

The directions that follow explain how to sample fusible and sew-in stabilizers. To begin sampling, cut a 4-inch-square piece of fabric. Then cut half this width for the stabilizer (Figure 3.12).

Fusible Stabilizer

How to Fuse

- Set the iron to the "wool" setting.
- Place the resin side of the interfacing to the wrong side of the fabric; take time to place and smooth out the interfacing onto the fabric. (Figure 3.12a).
- It is advisable to use a pressing cloth to prevent the interfacing from adhering to the bottom of the iron. At school, with everyone using the iron, it can overheat and easily scorch or melt the interfacing.
- Press the interfacing to the fabric by using heat, steam, and pressure. This is not to be confused with ironing; ironing consists of gliding the iron back and forth over the fabric surface. To fuse, start on one edge, place the iron straight down, lean in, and add pressure

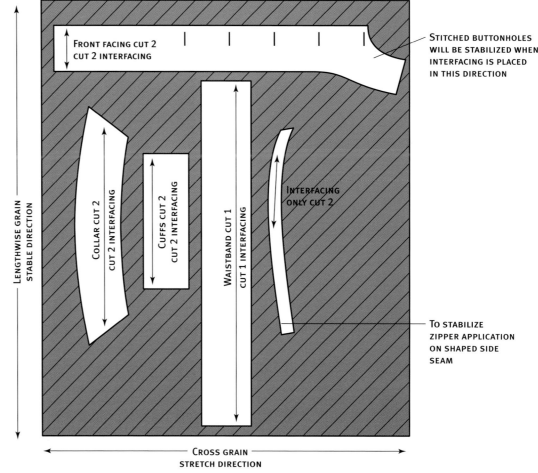

FIGURE 3.11 CUTTING KNIT INTERFACING

for 20 seconds; lift the iron and place the iron down again on the unfused area.

- When all of the interfacing has been fused, give the fabric a quick press from the correct side. Cover the fabric with a pressing cloth if the fabric surface is delicate (organza is an ideal pressing cloth, as you can see through it).

- Check the bonding by trying to peel the interfacing away from one corner of the fabric. The fusing should be secure. If it isn't, take more time to press using heat, steam, and pressure.
- Using a damp cloth can help to create more steam, which can make it easier to fuse interfacing to the fabric.

- The fabric surface should not have changed; if bubbles appear from the fusible interfacing, then choose another type and sample again.
- It is tempting to whip the fused fabric from the ironing board to begin stitching; however, don't do this. Let the fused fabric cool down first.
- After fusing, the interfacing and fabric will be stitched as *one piece* of fabric.

Sew-in Stabilizer

A sew-in interfacing is handbasted to the fabric swatch as shown in Figure 3.12b. **Handbasting** is a technique in which temporary stitches are used to lend support in the construction of a garment; these stitches are later removed. When handbasting, always work on a flat surface, and use a thread color that matches your garment. Stitch long stitches. They can be even or uneven—the style of handbasting is not important. The stitch length of handbasting will vary according to the fabric type. Use a shorter stitch length for lightweight fabric and a longer stitch for heavier-weight fabric. In Chapter 6, you will see how handbasting stitches also hold seams in place before machine stitching.

Testing the Stabilizer

- Fold the fabric in half and "hand feel" (the stabilizer will be sandwiched between both layers of fabric) to see if the two weights are compatible together. The fabric weight should not have changed all that much. If it feels too limp, consider a crisper, heavier stabilizer or add a second layer. If it feels too heavy, choose an alternative stabilizer of lighter weight.
- *Roll* the sample and observe whether it forms a smooth roll without creasing. This is important, especially for stabilizing collars.
- *Observe* the fabric *face* to see if it has changed.
- *Experiment* with as many samples as you need to find the "correct" one.
- *Keep* any correct samples, label each, and put them on a ring or in a notebook. Refer to the samples for reference as a resource for the future.

FABRIC STABILIZERS

The next sections of this chapter describe three types of fabric stabilizers: stabilizing tapes, underlining, and interfacing. An underlining covers the entire fabric piece, while an interfacing is applied to the facings and individual garment pieces, such as collars, cuffs, pockets, and waistbands, so they hold their shape. A stabilizing tape gives lightweight support because it is applied to the garment seamlines only.

To view how each stabilizer looks from the inside of a garment, turn to Figures 3.1f and 3.7a. Each figure provides an inside view of the LBD dress in Figure 3.1c of the Style I. D. Once the area has been stabilized with a stabilizing tape, underlining, or interfacing, it will feel slightly heavier and crisper, but to different degrees depending on the type and weight of stabilizer used.

You may be asking, How do I choose the best fabric stabilizer for my garment? The way forward is for the designer to feel the fabric weight, drape the fabric, and then sample so that he or she can make an informed decision about the appropriate stabilizer. Some garments may need both an underlining and an interfacing; there are no rules. It has been said before—the decision is fabric and design driven!

STABILIZING TAPES

Stabilizing tapes are narrow tapes approximately ¼ inch to ½ inch wide. They are applied to the seamline to prevent the seams from stretching in the stitching process. A variety of different tapes can be used to stabilize seams (Table 3.1). Stabilizing tapes can be purchased on the roll or cut on straight or bias grains from fusible or nonfusible interfacing yardage. This last option is discussed later in the chapter.

Fusible tapes are pressed to the seamline, and sew-in tapes handbasted to the seamline. Match the type and weight of stabilizer tape to the fabric, and color-match the tape as closely as possible to the fabric background color. Stabilizing tapes can be used in place of an underlining or interfacing and are successfully used on lightweight fabrics, as they reduce bulk.

Let's turn back to the LBD in Figure 3.1e and 3.1f to see where the stabilizing tape has been positioned in a *single layer* around the neckline and armholes of the garment. The tape stabilizes the garment edges so they will not stretch in the construction process. The dress would be lined edge-to-edge, that is, both fabric and lining go all the way to the edges. The inside construction would then be covered with the lining. Refer to Chapter 16, "Open Edge-to-Edge Lining."

TABLE 3.1 **STABILIZING TAPE CHART**

Type of Stabilizer	Fabric Suitability	Support
Sew-in Tape		
Twill tape **Straight grain tape**	Medium- to heavyweight woven fabrics that need to fit firmly to the body	Firm support to waistlines and top edge of strapless bodice and other garment edges
Selvage cut ¼-inch wide **Straight grain tape**	Sheer woven fabrics	Firm support to waistlines and top edge of strapless bodice and other garment edges
Tricot Seams Great **Straight grain tape**	Sheer woven fabrics	Lightweight support; stitch to straight and slightly curved seams; also use for seam slippage
Bias-cut tape	Sheer woven fabrics and knits	Lightweight support; stitch to knits, shaped woven fabric seams, and for stabilizing bias-cut zipper seams
Fusible Tape		
Straight grain tape	Light-, medium-, and heavyweight fabrics	Straight, slightly curved seams only; use for seam slippage
Bias-cut **Shaped tape**	As above	Round shaped seamlines such as the neckline and armholes; ideal for use on edge-to-edge lined garments instead of using an interfacing; use for seam slippage

Seam slippage is another reason why a stabilizing tape may be applied to the seams. **Seam slippage** happens when the yarns separate, pulling away from the seams. This usually only affects seams under stress and not seam edges, such as necklines and armholes—it may affect sleeves, as they have stress on them. Seam slippage is more likely to occur in smooth-yarn fabrics such as microfibers and polyesters, and in loosely woven fabrics. If you think this may be a problem, then test the fabric first. To do this, cut two 4-by-6-inch swatches, stitch a ½-inch seam, and press open; hold the swatches in both hands with the seam running vertically,

and pull out simultaneously with both hands. This would equal the stress the garment would be subject to. If seam slippage occurs, you *must* reinforce *every* seam (this means both sides of the fabric are taped) under pressure or choose an alternative fabric for the garment (Figure 3.13).

Types of Stabilizing Tapes
Fusible Tape
Fusible lightweight straight or bias grain tape is available on the roll in 100 percent cotton and comes in black and white. If you cannot purchase one to match your fabric, you can cut your

own tape. Refer to "Cutting Stabilizing Tapes" further on in this chapter for cutting directions.

Sew-in Tape
Twill tape is a narrow, sturdy, woven, straight grain tape that is purchased by the yard. It is available in black and white only, and comes in a variety of widths. You will find the ¼-inch tape an ideal width for stabilizing seams; a wider tape will add too much bulk. Polyester twill tape is less bulky than 100 percent cotton tape. Figure 3.14 shows how twill tape looks when applied to a seam. How it is stitched will be explained under "Stitching Order" later.

Since twill tape is firm, it is an excellent stabilizer for woven fabrics that need to fit firmly to the body. Seams that have been stabilized with twill tape will never stretch when worn or during washing.

Don't try to stitch twill tape around shaped seams, such as necklines and armholes, as it isn't flexible enough for use there. It can, however, be stitched to contoured, curved seamlines.

Fabric selvage makes an excellent sew-in stabilizing tape for sheer fabrics. It is the perfect substitute for twill tape when a firm hold is needed on a lightweight sheer fabric. The beauty of using the selvage is that it will perfectly match your fabric in color and weight and will never add bulk. Carefully cut off the firm ¼-inch narrow woven finished edges on either side of the woven fabric.

Tricot is a lightweight stabilizing tape made from 100 percent nylon. It is available in black, white, and ivory. One brand on the market, which is ideal for stabilizing lightweight fabrics

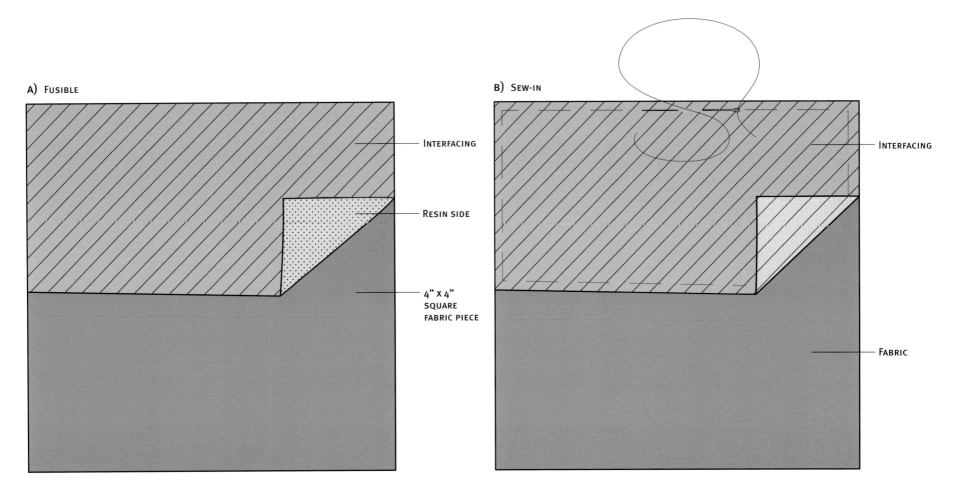

A) FUSIBLE

INTERFACING

RESIN SIDE

4" X 4"
SQUARE
FABRIC PIECE

B) SEW-IN

INTERFACING

FABRIC

FIGURE 3.12 SAMPLING INTERFACING FUSIBLE

and knit fabrics, is Seams Great. Its beauty is the sheerness and lightweight touch, which doesn't add any bulk or shadow from the correct side of the fabric. It is available cut on the bias or straight grain. If Seams Great is not available in the store nearest you, then cut to your own specifications from tricot interfacing.

Seams Great *will not* give the firmness required to hold the waistline or the top edge of a strapless bodice firmly to the body. We advise not to use it for these purposes—it is a *lightweight stabilizer*. Remember, the stabilizer, fabric, and end use must fit together—use twill tape or the selvage instead.

Cutting Stabilizing Tapes

Stabilizing tape can be cut on straight or bias grain ⅜-inch wide, or cut to follow the shape of the seam. The criteria for choosing the grain along which to cut the tape is directed by the shape or angle of the seam it is being applied to.

Straight grain tape is excellent for stabilizing

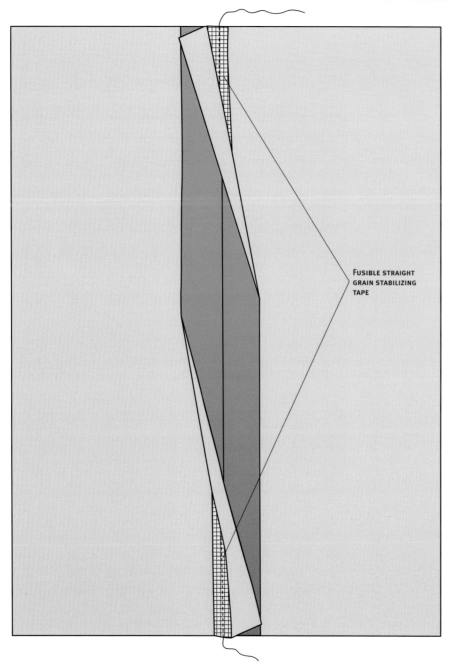

FUSIBLE STRAIGHT
GRAIN STABILIZING
TAPE

FIGURE 3.13 STABILIZING TAPE HAS BEEN APPLIED TO BOTH SIDES
OF THE FABRIC TO PREVENT SEAM SLIPPAGE.

straight seams or slightly curved or contoured seams. It can be cut from nonwoven or woven interfacing and will give a stable hold to a seam. Let's refer back to the "Key Application Points for Stabilizers" and review the pants in Figure 3.2d. The pant has an angled pocket opening, which is cut on the bias grain. A straight grain tape can be applied to a straight or slightly curved seam to prevent the seam from stretching in the stitching process. The tape also prevents the pocket from stretching in response to constant use. Figure 3.14 shows twill tape being applied to the curved pocket of these pants. A straight grain tape will also stabilize a curved waistline seam in place. Refer to Chapter 9 for more information.

Bias-cut tape has the flexibility to be shaped and can be used to stabilize curved, round, or other shaped seams. The stabilizing tape for the LBD in Figure 3.1f would be bias cut, because the seams it is applied to are shaped. For a closer view of how the neckline and armhole seams are shaped for the LBD, refer to Figure 3.7. Figure 3.15 illustrates bias grain (fusible and sew-in) tapes applied to the neckline and armhole.

Shaped tape is cut *exactly* as a mirror image of the seamline shape that needs to be stabilized. Use the pattern to cut the shape to be stabilized. Place the pattern on the interfacing along the same pattern grainline (if woven interfacing is being used). Draw around the outer edge, then cut the tape approximately ⅜ inch wide, parallel to the outer edge. When the tape is positioned on the seamline, the seam allowance will have been eliminated, which reduces bulk (Figure 3.16).

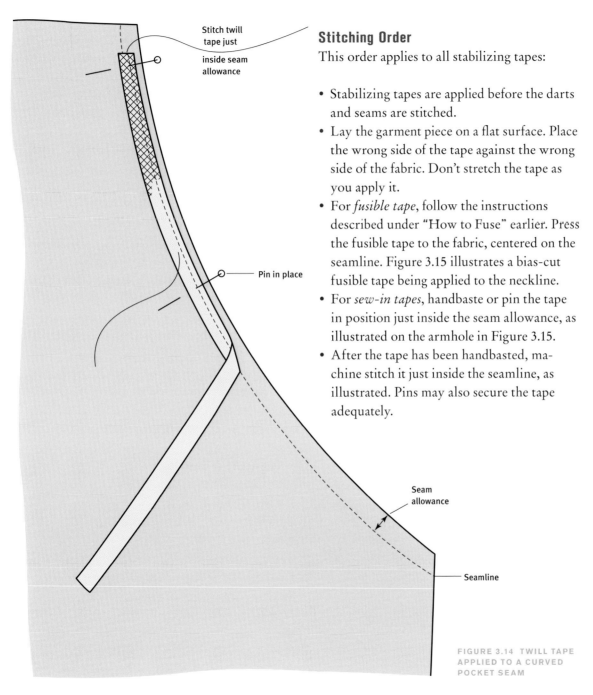

Stitch twill
tape just

inside seam
allowance

Pin in place

Seam
allowance

Seamline

FIGURE 3.14 TWILL TAPE
APPLIED TO A CURVED
POCKET SEAM

Stitching Order

This order applies to all stabilizing tapes:

- Stabilizing tapes are applied before the darts and seams are stitched.
- Lay the garment piece on a flat surface. Place the wrong side of the tape against the wrong side of the fabric. Don't stretch the tape as you apply it.
- For *fusible tape*, follow the instructions described under "How to Fuse" earlier. Press the fusible tape to the fabric, centered on the seamline. Figure 3.15 illustrates a bias-cut fusible tape being applied to the neckline.
- For *sew-in tapes*, handbaste or pin the tape in position just inside the seam allowance, as illustrated on the armhole in Figure 3.15.
- After the tape has been handbasted, machine stitch it just inside the seamline, as illustrated. Pins may also secure the tape adequately.

> **IMPORTANT**
> Keep a store of tapes, fusible and nonfusible, cut on the bias and straight grains, in both black and white.

- Figure 3.15 also illustrates a straight grain tape stitched to the shoulder seam of a knit garment to prevent the seam from stretching when the garment is worn.
- Stitch the seam as you normally would, using the allotted seam allowance. The stitching is centered on the tape.
- Seams with any tape, even twill tape, can still be clipped, understitched, and pressed open.

UNDERLINING—FULLY COVERING THE FABRIC

An **underlining** is another layer of fabric or interfacing applied to the entire garment fabric or parts of the garment fabric to stabilize and to add structure or even warmth without adding bulk. An underlining can also be referred to as a *backing*.

Here are some good reasons to underline a garment:

- It helps the appearance and performance; it adds support, strength, stability, and body to the fabric and overall garment. Underlining is what makes a jacket look well-tailored.
- It acts as a base for the hem stitching, and ensures the stitches will never show on the correct side of the fabric.

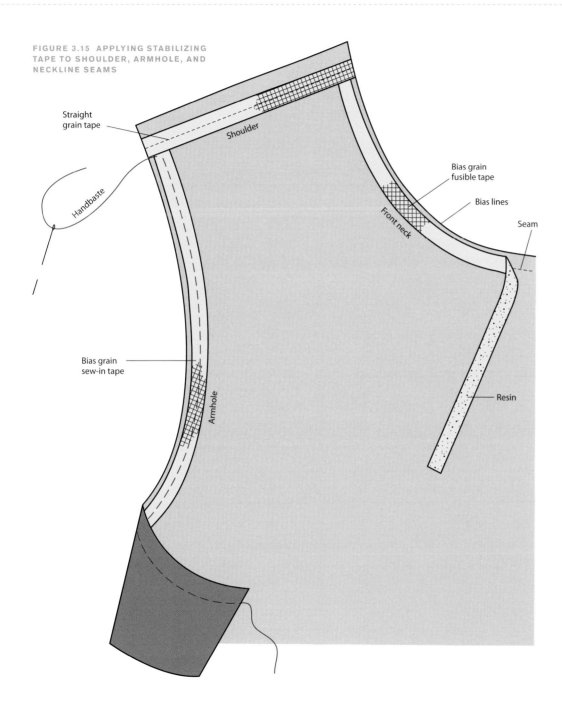

FIGURE 3.15 APPLYING STABILIZING TAPE TO SHOULDER, ARMHOLE, AND NECKLINE SEAMS

Straight grain tape

Handbaste

Shoulder

Bias grain fusible tape

Bias lines

Front neck

Seam

Bias grain sew-in tape

Armhole

Resin

- It adds a base to an open-weave or eyelet fabric.
- It can purposely change the color of sheer transparent outer garment fabric and shadow through to influence the color. A patterned underlining, such as checked, floral, or striped, can create an interesting look.

Suggested Underlining Options

Here is a selection of underlining options that can be used: interfacing, fusible and nonfusible, silk organza, cotton batiste and other light-to-medium-weight cottons, china silk, canvas, satin, muslin, wigan, curtain linings, flannel, batting, broadcloth, wool flannel, cotton flannelette, buckram, netting, or two layers of the garment fabric. Thinsulate is another underlining that adds warmth without adding bulk. Try it in winter jackets or coats. When it comes to choosing an underlining, use what works—there are no rules as to which is the "correct" stabilizer to use, except that it must suit the fabric!

How to Apply a Sew-in Underlining (or Interfacing)

Stitching Order

- Unless it is dry cleanable, the fabric may need to be preshrunk.
- Lay each garment fabric piece on a flat surface with the wrong side facing up.
- Place the wrong side of the underlining or interfacing against the wrong side of the fabric; smooth it over the fabric so it lies flat; don't worry if it goes over the fabric edges, as that can be trimmed off later (Figure 3.17).

- Handbaste the two pieces of fabric together $1/16$ inch inside the seam allowance. For directions, refer to the explanation of handbasting under "Sew-in Stabilizer" earlier. After the two fabrics have been stitched together, treat them as one fabric in the construction process.
- After the two pieces are basted together, place the pattern back on top of the fabric pieces. Snip the notches and apply the pattern markings to the underlining. When underlining a garment, don't add the pattern markings until after the underlining has been applied.
- Handbaste the center of all darts to stabilize the two fabrics together before they are stitched so they don't shift in the stitching process (Figure 3.17).
- Stitch open seams when the fabric has a sew-in stabilizer; stitching closed seams will add too much bulk. Refer to Chapter 6, "Open or Closed Seams."
- If the seams and darts feel bulky (too thick) after they are stitched, cut away the underlining, leaving $1/16$ inch of fabric intact (Figure 3.18). Darts can also be cut and pressed open after they are stitched, to reduce bulk. Refer to Chapter 4, "What Is a Dart?"

Fusible Underlining

Fusible interfacing can be applied as an underlining in one of two ways: as individual pieces fused to the fabric, garment pieces, or as block fusing. Both methods are outlined here. When underlining the entire garment or parts of the garment, use the same pattern pieces you would use to cut the outer garment fabric.

Individual pieces fused to the garment fabric are cut separately first before they are fused together. The wrong side of the interfacing is then placed to the wrong side of each garment piece, and the two pieces are fused together. This is the same method that is used to fuse an interfacing to a facing. Refer to "How to Fuse" earlier in this chapter for more detailed instructions.

In manufacturing, a steam iron with a flat bed presser[3] would be used to fuse large sections at a time; this is extremely efficient. It is worth inquiring whether your dry cleaner can fuse a large amount of fabric on a clamshell press.

Block fusing involves cutting lengths of garment fabric to fit the size of the pattern pieces. The same length of *fusible* interfacing is cut and *block fused* to the fabric. After fusing the pieces together, each pattern piece is placed on the fused fabric following the grainlines and cut. Notches are snipped and pattern markings applied. This method is recommended when the garment fabric is fine and slippery. Figure 3.19 illustrates how the fabric is blocked, fused, and cut before constructing the tweed wool coat in Figure 3.1a of the Style I.D.

If you attempt to do this at school, you will need help; it is hard to manage on your own, as the interfacing must be perfectly aligned to the fabric and then pressed. The interfacing *must* be perfectly smooth without any wrinkles after it is completed. This method *cannot* be done as a "rush job"—it takes time and patience.

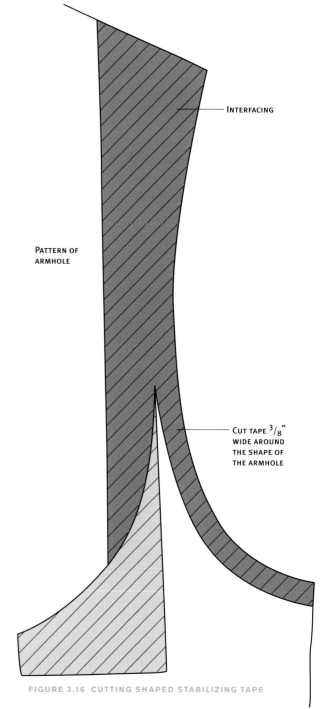

INTERFACING

PATTERN OF ARMHOLE

CUT TAPE $3/8$" WIDE AROUND THE SHAPE OF THE ARMHOLE

FIGURE 3.16 CUTTING SHAPED STABILIZING TAPE

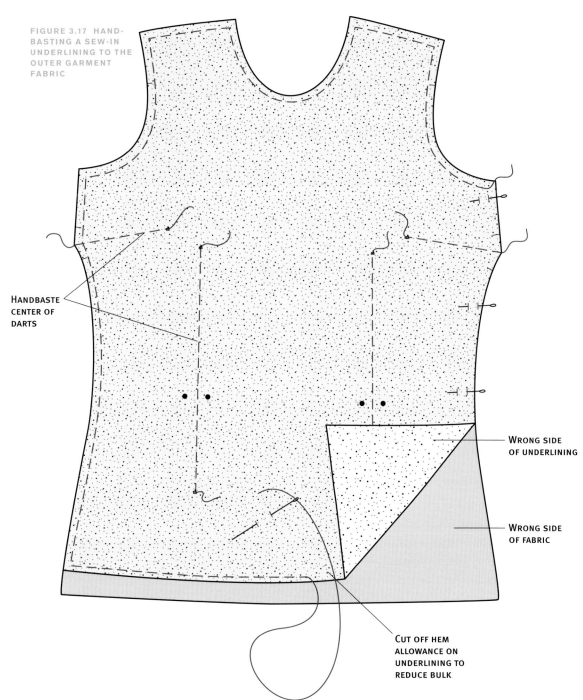

FIGURE 3.17 HAND-
BASTING A SEW-IN
UNDERLINING TO THE
OUTER GARMENT
FABRIC

HANDBASTE
CENTER OF
DARTS

WRONG SIDE
OF UNDERLINING

WRONG SIDE
OF FABRIC

CUT OFF HEM
ALLOWANCE ON
UNDERLINING TO
REDUCE BULK

INTERFACING GARMENT PARTS

The appropriate weight of interfacing depends on the amount of structure needed and the fabric used. Interfacing garment parts such as collars, cuffs, waistbands, and openings helps to maintain shape, reinforces and prevents seams from stretching in the stitching process, and also gives firmness. Refer back to Figure 3.2 and the "Key Application Points" that were highlighted earlier in the chapter.

Let's now look at each garment in more detail.

- Collars and cuffs are key application points for interfacing to help hold the structure (Figure 3.2c).
- Any area of the garment where *buttons* and *buttonholes* are applied needs to be stabilized; buttonholes can easily stretch if the fabric has not been stabilized. The following figures show buttonhole placements: Figure 3.2b, back waistband; Figure 3.2c, front shirt band; Figure 3.2d, waistband; and Figure 3.2f, front jacket.
- Skirt and pant waistbands and waist facings need firmness and stability around the waistline so they fit firmly to the body (Figure 3.2a, b, and d).
- Hems of jackets are often stabilized if not underlined (Figure 3.2f). The hem of the vest is stabilized in Figure 3.2e; the skirt split is also stabilized in Figure 3.2b.
- Neckline and armhole facings need interfacing or stabilizing tape applied to prevent

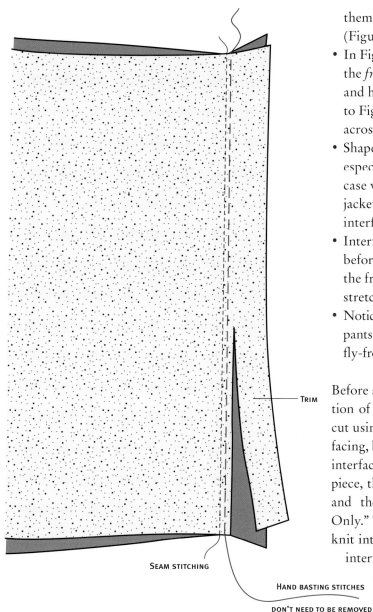

TRIM

SEAM STITCHING

HAND BASTING STITCHES
DON'T NEED TO BE REMOVED
AS THEY WILL NOT BE VISIBLE
AFTER SEAMS ARE STITCHED

FIGURE 3.18 TRIM UNDER-
LINING FROM THE SEAM AL-
LOWANCE TO REDUCE BULK.

them from stretching in the stitching process (Figure 3.2e).

- In Figure 3.2f, canvas has been applied across the *front and back* shoulders to stabilize and help hold the shape of the jacket. (Refer to Figure 3.1b to see the canvas placement across the shoulders.)
- Shaped pocket openings need stabilizing, especially if cut on the bias grain as is the case with the pant design in Figure 3.2d. The jacket pocket band is also stabilized with interfacing in Figure 3.2f.
- Interfacing is applied down the front vest before the zipper is applied; this stabilizes the front section and prevents the fabric from stretching. (Refer to Figure 3.2e.)
- Notice in Figure 3.2d that the fly-front of the pants is also stabilized; whether to stabilize the fly-front or not depends on the fabric weight.

Before stitching a garment, determine the position of the interfacing. Interfacing is generally cut using the same pattern piece as the garment facing, but there can be exceptions to this. If the interfacing differs in shape from the garment piece, then a separate pattern *must* be provided and the pattern clearly labeled "Interfacing Only." Turn back to Figure 3.11 and look at the knit interfacing layout. Notice that the narrow interfacing strip for the zipper is labeled to be cut in interfacing only. This communicates that this pattern piece is *not* to be cut in fashion fabric. Whatever interfacing is used, the pattern must

be labeled accordingly: "Cut 1 Interfacing" or "Cut 2 Interfacing." Figures 3.9, 3.10, and 3.11 point this out clearly.

For direction on how to apply fusible and sew-in interfacing to facings, refer to the earlier sections on "How to Fuse" and "How to Apply a Sew-In Underlining (or Interfacing)." Figure 3.20a and b illustrate fusible and sew-in interfacing being applied to the facings.

INTERFACING TRICKY FABRICS
Sheer Fabrics

Do use *woven stabilizers* such as organza or cotton batiste.

Do check that the color of the stabilizer blends well with the overall color of the fabric; neutral colors blend beautifully with most fabrics, as they appear like skin color.

Do sample first to make sure the resin won't seep through to the correct side of the fabric if a fusible interfacing is used.

Do use the selvage of the fabric as a seam stabilizer in sheer fabrics.

Don't use a heavy stabilizer on sheer lightweight fabric.

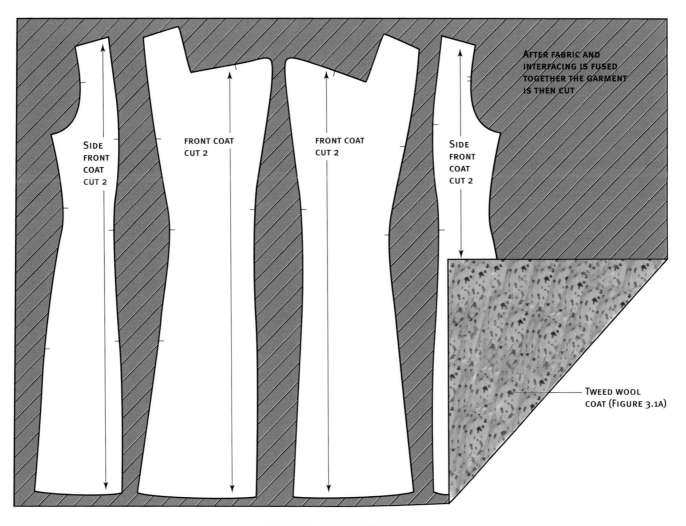

SIDE
FRONT
COAT
CUT 2

FRONT COAT
CUT 2

FRONT COAT
CUT 2

SIDE
FRONT
COAT
CUT 2

AFTER FABRIC AND
INTERFACING IS FUSED
TOGETHER THE GARMENT
IS THEN CUT

TWEED WOOL
COAT (FIGURE 3.1A)

FIGURE 3.19 BLOCK FUSING

Lace

Do always use sew-in stabilizers on lace fabric.
Do use 100 percent silk organza as a stabilizer for lace fabric—then the lace will retain its openness.

Do consider using netting as a stabilizer for lace fabric.
Do match the weight of interfacing to the weight of the lace; remember, when using stabilizers, match like with like.
Do take care in color-matching the stabilizer to the lace, as it will be visible.
Do use the selvage of the silk organza color-matched to the lace fabric as a seam stabilizer.
Don't use a fusible interfacing on lace, as the resin will seep through to the correct side of the fabric, which will look ugly.

Satin

Do consider using a sew-in stabilizer on satin; if a fusible stabilizer is chosen, the fabric surface may bubble and change.

Do test different weights of stabilizers on satin fabric to determine the required hold and stiffness.

Do mix and match different weights of stabilizers on different parts of satin garments.

Do consider underlining satin garments, especially evening gowns.

Beaded Fabric

Do use 100 percent silk sew-in organza as a stabilizer on beaded fabric.

Do always use sew-in stabilizer on beaded fabric.

Do always use a sheer stabilizer in sheer beaded fabric; always match the weight of the stabilizer to the weight of the fabric.

Don't use a fusible interfacing on beaded fabrics; it will be impossible to fuse together.

Knits

Don't assume that stabilizers are unnecessary in knit fabrics; there are times when interfacing is needed to stabilize parts of garments and prevent certain areas from stretching, such as collars, cuffs, buttonholes, and zipper seams (Figure 3.11).

Do match the color, weight, and stretch capacity of stabilizer to each knit fabric.

Do stabilize seams in knit fabrics when a zipper is being inserted so the seam does not bulge or ripple after stitching. To do this:

• Cut two strips of interfacing 1 inch wide and the length of the zipper opening, contouring the shape of the seam. Cut the interfacing with no stretch in the lengthwise grain (see Figure 3.11).

• Fuse each piece of interfacing to the wrong side of the knit.

• Stitch the invisible zipper into the seam using the same stitching process that you would for a woven fabric. Do not stretch the seam while stitching. Refer to Chapter 8 for more information.

Don't use woven stabilizers on knit fabric in areas that need to stretch.

Don't stabilize loose knits with fusible interfacing, because the resin will seep through open-weave knits. In loose-weave knits, design garments that don't need stabilizing; use a knit lining instead.

Don't use fusible interfacing on ribbed knit, as it does not fuse well to this surface.

Denim

Do test whether a stabilizer is needed on denim fabric; some denim fabric may be too heavy for a stabilizer.

Do sample interfacing first if it's used to find the correct weight for the denim.

Don't waste time using a sew-in stabilizer on denim. Fusible interfacing works perfectly on all denim; however, if a stretch element has been added into the denim, then a stretch interfacing may be needed, depending on where it is placed. For example, a skirt or pant waistband in stretch denim needs a stable interfacing, without stretch, to stabilize the waistband.

Velvet

Do be careful when choosing a stabilizer to use on velvet fabric, as it is very delicate and needs to be treated with care.

Do always use a sew-in stabilizer.

Do match the weight of stabilizer to the weight of the velvet.

Don't use fusible stabilizers on velvet, as the iron will flatten the pile and leave shiny marks on the surface.

Leather

Do use fusible stabilizers on leather. (Is this a surprise?)

Do only use *low-temperature* fusible stabilizers on leather, such as SofKnit and Touch-o-Gold[6].

Do protect the leather from the heat of the iron by placing a brown paper over the surface when applying interfacing.

Do use a sew-in stabilizer in leather.

Don't handbaste. Instead, machine baste.

Don't use steam to fuse stabilizers to leather.

Faux Fur

Do use only sew-in stabilizers for faux fur.

Do use different weights of stabilizers to hold different parts of the garment.

Do test the weight of the stabilizer with the fur; a heavyweight stabilizer may make the garment too heavy to wear and add too much bulk.

Don't use a fusible stabilizer on the back of faux fur, as it will not fuse well on the knitted backing and would flatten the fur.

Heavyweight Fabric

Do use a stabilizer that matches the weight of the fabric and holds the structure of the garment without adding bulk.

Don't use a stabilizer that's too heavy, which would make the garment feel stiff and weighty.

As students complete each semester, they learn and grow in their clothing construction knowledge. We encourage you to apply what you have learned by transferring your knowledge to other areas of clothing construction—and one area in which to do this is when using stabilizers.

TRANSFER YOUR KNOWLEDGE

To transfer your knowledge, think about what you already know about stabilizers and apply this to stabilizing fabrics and garment parts with which you have not yet had experience. Knowing what to use by way of stabilizers begins with sampling different types and weights of stabilizers on the fabric you are using.

Here are some ways of transferring your knowledge:

- Netting can used to pad a bustle. To do so, scrunch up the netting and fill the area, making sure it is held in place with a few invisible hand stitches that don't show on the correct side of the fabric. Because netting is

lightweight, it won't make the garment feel heavy and bulky when worn.

- Try using batting as a stabilizer; it works beautifully to fill in areas where women are hollow. Place it across the shoulders and down the front (above the bust) of jackets and coats. Batting also works well to pad and hold the shape of raglan sleeves in coats and jackets. Wherever the batting is placed, slipstitch to secure it in place to the seams only. Batting can also be used to stabilize and pad the collar and cuffs. If the collar and cuffs are topstitched (one or several rows of stitching), the stitching will sink into the fabric.

As a design student, you have a wonderful opportunity to stretch your creativity as much as possible and try new ideas.

STRETCH YOUR CREATIVITY

Here is an opportunity to stretch your creativity when using stabilizers. This list of ideas is not exhaustive but should whet your appetite for investigating stabilizers further.

- We encourage you to keep a box of different stabilizers on hand in different types, fusible and nonfusible, woven and knits, in a variety of colors and weights. If you have these available at all times, then you can easily stretch your creativity by trying a variety of stabilizers in one garment. If you don't have them on hand, then you won't have the opportunity to think creatively.

NOTE

As this technique was sampled, we found that silk dupioni worked wonderfully well to create this texture, as it did not create too much bulk. The outcome was the perfect structured fabric. Other fabrics will also give excellent results, but do sample first to make sure the glue doesn't show through to the correct side of the fabric.

- For an interesting look, try using a differently patterned fabric as underlining for a sheer fabric.
- A fun fabric texture can be created by fusing scrunched fabric to an interfacing. To do this, lay a large piece of paper on a flat table to protect the surface. Place the fabric on top of the interfacing, arranging the placement by scrunching the fabric until it looks aesthetically pleasing. To hold the fabric, place weights on each corner and in any other position to hold the interfacing taut as you fuse. Take the iron and fuse the fabric to the interfacing (Figure 3.21); follow the instructions outlined earlier in "How to Fuse." Begin fusing from one corner and work your way across the fabric. The fabric can be rearranged and adjusted as you fuse. Lift the weights off as each section is fused and then replace them to help hold the fabric taut. When the fusing is completed, the fabric is ready to cut. Some machine or hand stitching may also be needed to hold the fabric in place.

- Figure 3.22a illustrates a padded band around the neckline and hemline of an evening jacket. Refer to Chapter 15.
- To go against the tide of what is deemed "correct," designers like to stretch the limits. So why not try underlining a sheer organza with wool. This is certainly thinking outside the box!
- In Figure 3.22b, a cute lace cocktail dress is shown. Netting has been scrunched and inserted (and secured by hand stitching) between the outer fabric and lining to structure the silhouette of the skirt.
- Why not stitch some quality stabilizers to the outside of the garment instead of the inside—aren't designers supposed to stretch the design limits? Figure 3.22c will give you the idea.

No matter what stage you have reached, whether you are at the beginning or well along the path of your fashion course, there will still be construction problems that arise and need resolving. Even the most experienced sewer will encounter challenging stabilizing problems.

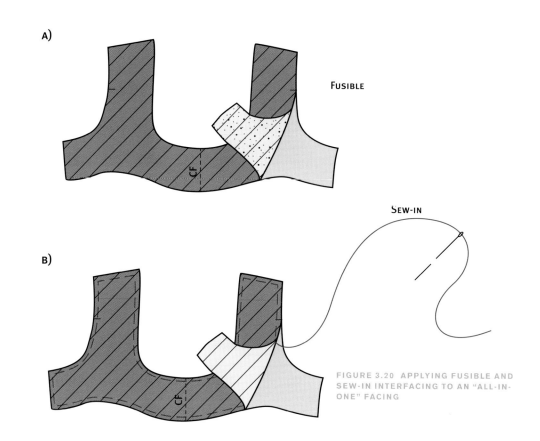

A)

FUSIBLE

CF

SEW-IN

B)

CF

FIGURE 3.20 APPLYING FUSIBLE AND SEW-IN INTERFACING TO AN "ALL-IN-ONE" FACING

STOP! WHAT DO I DO IF . . .
. . . the interfacing won't adhere properly?

Check that the iron temperature is correct; repeat fusing a new test sample and make sure that heat, pressure, and steam are applied. If it still doesn't work, sample another type of stabilizer. Also, if the fabric hasn't been preshrunk, the sizing may interfere with adherence of the resin to the fabric surface. Steaming or sponging the fabric and allowing it to dry may help remove some of the sizing, allowing the resin to adhere.

. . . I have run out of an interfacing and I can't purchase the same one to finish my project?

It doesn't matter how many different types of stabilizers are used on the one garment. The customer will never know! What is important is that the fabric and stabilizer type and weight are compatible. If the stabilizer you ran out of was fusible, then find another fusible stabilizer to take its place in a similar weight; if it was sew-in, then choose another sew-in stabilizer.

. . . I've fused my interfacing onto the fabric and the area doesn't hold the shape?

If the stabilizer is too light, then add another layer on top of the first layer (making two layers in total). If the garment is already stitched, it will be too hard to fuse another layer of interfacing, as it needs to be lying flat to be fused correctly. You could try adding a sew-in stabilizer on top of the fusible. To do so, cut off the seam allowance and another $1/16$ inch, carefully position the interfacing, and hand stitch to the seamline.

FIGURE 3.21 STRETCH YOUR CREATIVITY: SCRUNCHED FABRIC APPLIED TO AN INTERFACING

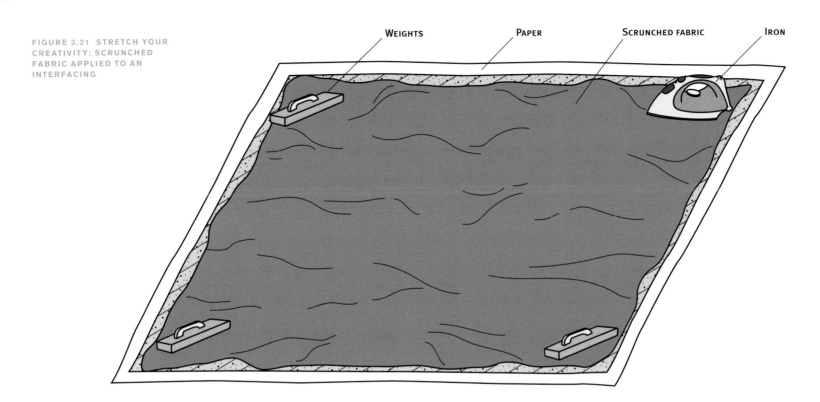

FIGURE 3.21 STRETCH YOUR CREATIVITY: SCRUNCHED FABRIC APPLIED TO AN INTERFACING

WEIGHTS PAPER SCRUNCHED FABRIC IRON

. . . the interfacing has bubbled?

We hope this has only happened at the sampling stage. Here are a few reasons why this might have happened: First, the sizing might have prevented the interfacing from adhering. Second, the iron temperature could have been too hot. Third, the interfacing might have been pulled when fusing. Reheat the fusible interfacing with steam. To do this, hold the iron just above the fused fabric and *carefully peel off* the fusible interfacing after steam has been applied. Then try another interfacing—sampling first, of course!

. . . there is a dramatic change to the garment fabric after I have fused the interfacing?

Don't use this interfacing! You need to sample another type of stabilizer that better suits the fabric. There are many types and weights of stabilizers available, so keep sampling until you find the "perfect match."

. . . the stabilizer is too heavy for my garment and it looks too stiff?

If the stabilizer is fusible and has been correctly adhered, it should be permanent and will not pull off. For this reason it is crucial that the fabric and stabilizer be compatible before you go ahead to stabilize the fabric—let this be a learning experience for the future. You may need to begin all over again—if more of the same fabric is still available. Do a sample first!

. . . the fusible interfacing melts when I put the iron to it?

Lower the iron temperature and fuse again; if this doesn't work, try another type of interfacing or change to a sew-in. Also, use a pressing cloth.

Stretch Your Creativity

FIGURE 3.22 STRETCH
YOUR CREATIVITY

CANVAS

LACE BODICE

STABILIZING TAPE

SKIRT IS STIFFENED
WITH NETTING TO
CREATE THIS SHAPE

STRETCH THE DESIGN
LIMITS BY PLACING
THE STABILIZER ON THE
OUTSIDE OF THE GARMENT

LACE APPLIQUED
TO THE NETTING

PALAZZO
EVENING
PANTS

NETTING

WOVEN BIAS
STABILIZING
TAPE

CANVAS

EVENING JACKET
A

LACE COCKTAIL DRESS
B

C

. . . the fabric and fusible interfacing shrink by different amounts when I apply heat, steam, and pressure, leaving a bubbly-looking surface? Should I keep using this interfacing?

Yes, sample again, this time without steam. Also, lower the heat temperature and lessen the fusing time. What is happening is that the fabric and stabilizer are reacting differently to heat and moisture. If it still doesn't work, try a different fusible stabilizer.

. . . I didn't add a stabilizer to my collar, and it looks limp?

Carefully detach the collar from the garment, using a seam ripper—there is no need to seam rip around the collar edge. Then cut one layer of a sew-in stabilizer to suit the fabric weight. Don't use a fusible stabilizer. It would be impossible to press into the collar. Cut the stabilizer without seam allowance, and another $1/16$ to $1/8$ inch smaller again. Slip the stabilizer in between the two collar pieces, placing the stabilizer on top of the seam allowance of the upper collar. Smooth the interfacing so it lies flat; if it doesn't lie flat, trim more interfacing away until it does. Lightly hand catchstitch the interfacing in a couple of places to the seam allowance. Pin the collar to the neckline. Then place the garment on the form to make sure the collar is sitting correctly and the interfacing is laying flat. Complete stitching the collar to the neckline.

To help you assess areas where you may need to continue improving your understanding of stabilizers, use the self-critique questions listed below. Follow up on areas you did not understand. Perhaps ask an instructor for further information about particular aspects of stabilizers if you don't understand their importance or use.

SELF-CRITIQUE

To critique the garment in terms of the stabilizer, in particular, first place the garment on a dress form or ask a fellow student to wear the garment. Do not lay it flat on the table. Now observe the structure of the garment and ask yourself the question, "Would I proudly wear this garment or purchase it from the store, or would I feel that it looks too limp and unstructured?" If the answer is "No, I wouldn't wear this garment," ask yourself why not.

Then ask yourself the following questions to continue critiquing your work:

- Is the garment structured to present the look you want?
- Did you sample enough types and weights of stabilizers to make an informed decision regarding the best stabilizers to use for the fabric?
- If you used a stabilizing tape, did you choose one that was appropriate for the weight and type of fabric, and was it cut on the correct grainline for the shape of the seam?
- If you used a fusible stabilizer, did it adhere correctly or have you done a sloppy job?
- Did the fabric surface change at all when a fusible interfacing was applied to the fabric?
- If you used a sew-in stabilizer, does it lay flat and appear "as one" with the fabric?

REVIEW CHECKLIST

- **Do** I understand how important a stabilizer is in structuring the garment shape?
- **Do** I understand that volume and fullness, by way of gathering, tucks, and scrunching the fabric, can structure the silhouette?
- **Do** I grasp the important concept that the fabric weight and drape guide me in the choice of stabilizer and where to place it?
- **Do** I understand the benefits of sampling first before applying the stabilizer to the garment?
- **Do** I understand that multiple samples may need to be tried before finally deciding on the best stabilizer?
- **Do** I understand that different weights and types of stabilizers can be applied to one garment for different purposes?
- **Do** I understand that it is the designer who needs to be educated about stabilizers? For this reason, I need to use stabilizers to know them.
- **Do** I understand that some fabrics have the natural ability to hold their shape and don't need stabilizers, and other fabrics don't structure well without a stabilizer being used?
- **Do** I understand that the weight of fabric and weight of stabilizer need to go hand in hand?
- **Do** I understand how to apply a sew-in and a fusible stabilizer?
- **Do** I understand that an interfacing can be used as an underlining, an interfacing, or a stabilizing tape?

Darts: Tapering to Fit the Garment

Darts and seams are the fitting essentials of clothing construction that provide the contouring necessary to take a flat piece of fabric and mold it to the shape of the body. It is important to understand the shape of a woman's body. Keep in mind that a garment needs to be well sculpted, fitting over each body curve—the bust, waist, and hips. A dart sewn in the wrong place creates shaping where it isn't needed and results in wrinkles or bulges in the garment.

To achieve a well-fitted garment, begin with the darts, and the seams will follow.

As simple as darts are, making them look perfectly smooth requires precise marking, stitching, pressing, and careful adjustment to the figure. Taking time to be accurate prevents off-center or misplaced darts. Before pressing the darts, check the fit of the garment. If the darts are misplaced or incorrectly sewn, the time to correct these issues is before you press creases into the garment.

Different methods of dart construction are outlined in this chapter. To choose the best one for your garment, begin with your fabric choice. Each dart construction needs to suit the fabric weight and the final look the designer wants to achieve. Darts are both functional, providing fit and shape, and decorative, adding design interest. Once again, begin with sampling so that each dart is beautifully stitched and tapered to fit each body curve.

STYLE I.D.

Here are some dart styles that illustrate what this chapter is about. Look at the variation of fitting that is achieved by the different use of darts. By

Style I.D.

the end of this chapter, you'll know where these darts are placed within the garment, and how they are stitched (Figure 4.1).

GATHER YOUR TOOLS

In any job the right equipment is essential, and fashion design is no different. Having the correct tools at your fingertips helps when stitching a garment. For the techniques in this chapter, you will need a tape measure, fabric marking pen, dressmaker transfer paper, tracing wheel, scissors, pins, seam ripper, hand sewing needle, thread to match the garment fabric, tailoring or pressing ham, and pressing cloth. Now you are ready to begin stitching darts.

NOW LET'S GET STARTED

Darts are the fitting tool of the fashion designer and are often overlooked in the initial design illustration. Darts require precise marking and stitching, and good pressing skills. It's important to check that the darts are evenly stitched in terms of both length and how they are aligned on the garment. For example, one bust dart shouldn't be longer or lower than the other.

What Is a Dart?

A **dart** is an amount of fabric taken from the flat garment to create shape. Darts are usually placed at the bust, hips, waist, shoulders, and neck and elbow to accent and fit the garment to

4.1A BUST DARTS   4.1B FRENCH DART   4.1C CONTOUR DARTS   4.1D SHOULDER AND ELBOW DARTS

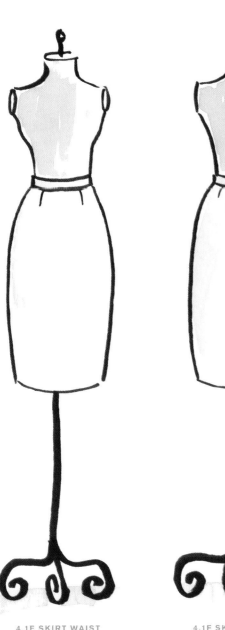

the body's curves. Darts can be used to create shape where there is none.

Darts are either **straight**, tapered darts, such as those used at the bust (Figure 4.1a), waist and hips (Figures 4.1e and 4.1f), shoulders and elbow (Figure 4.1d); or they are **shaped**, such as contour darts (Figure 4.1c), French darts (Figure 4.1b). A princess seam can also have a small bust dart when the seam itself is placed toward the side of the garment. The dart helps facilitate the shape necessary in the seam to fit over the curve of the bust.

Darts control the shape and silhouette of a garment, and a clear understanding of the correct size and position of darts within the garment and on the body is necessary for the darts to be successful. As shown in Figure 4.1, the number of darts and their position results in garments that differ in fit from loose to contoured. Decisions about the use of these features must be made by the designer to accomplish the desired fit in the garment. Too many design students illustrate their garments without indicating any apparent fitting. The structure must be planned in the design stages, carried through in the patternmaking, and finally, stitched into the garment. The

4.1E SKIRT WAIST DARTS–FRONT

4.1F SKIRT WAIST DARTS–BACK

4.1G PANT WAIST DARTS–FRONT

4.1H PANT WAIST DARTS–BACK

A)

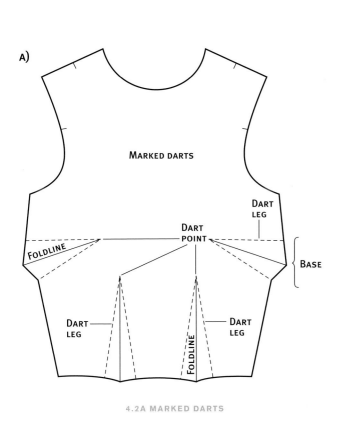

4.2A MARKED DARTS

B)

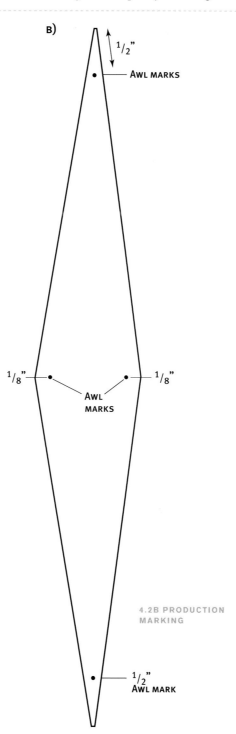

4.2B PRODUCTION MARKING

Darts begin as wedge shapes, as shown in Figure 4.2a, and consist of the base, the dart legs, the fold, and the dart point. The beginning of the dart is the *base*, which brings the fabric closer to the body. The **dart legs** are equal in length. The stitch line of the dart legs can be sewn curving in toward the tip of the dart point to provide better shaping, for example, at the waist to the hip. The *dart point*, or the end of the dart, releases the maximum fullness to contour over a body curve. The French dart can be slashed open to reduce bulk and allow the dart to lie flat and smooth (Figure 4.6).

Darts are marked differently in production. An **awl**, a pointed metal instrument, makes holes within the dart area. Stitching must be accurate (just outside the markings) to avoid having this marking show on the garment front (Figure 4.2b).

shape and silhouette will not happen by placing flat fabric on a shaped body. Remember to consider the shape of a woman's body, and the curves that need to be contoured. The darts must be compatible with the fabric, the fit of the garment on the body, and the shape and silhouette of the design. However—and this is very important—many design students go to the opposite extreme and overfit the garment, leaving little or no ease. This looks great on the dress form, but couldn't possibly be worn on a real body that moves and breathes! Fashion and function must meet.

✂ Before stitching darts, all pattern markings should have been transferred to the garment sections, directional staystitching completed. Sometimes darts can be stitched later in the stitching order.

● Mark the dart carefully and accurately.
● Place the pins perpendicular to the stitching line.

NOTE

A tailoring ham is a firm, rounded cushion shaped somewhat like a ham and covered with tightly woven fabric, sometimes with cotton on one side and wool on the other. It is used to mold the shaped areas that have curves. *Never* press the garment flat once the dart has been sewn—the shape will be pressed out!

- Begin stitching at the widest part of the dart (Figure 4.2a).
- Reduce the stitch length to 1.5 or 1.0 on the stitch length dial of the sewing machine when approximately 1 inch from the dart point, stitching off the fabric at the dart point (Figure 4.3a).
- *Do not* backstitch—the buildup of thread at the dart point will create an unfortunate dimple at the bust that no amount of pressing will remove.
- Always press the stitching line in the direction in which it was sewn—this is called **melding** the stitches (Figure 4.3b).
- Bust darts are pressed downward toward the hem of the garment using a tailoring ham; all other darts are pressed toward the center of the garment (Figure 4.9) or, if slashed, pressed open (Figure 4.7).

Where Is a Dart Placed?

Darts are used to shape and fit the garment to the body. Stitch a muslin of the garment to understand where the curves are to be fitted, or make a sample using the garment fabric. When using a fabric that has not been stitched before, always

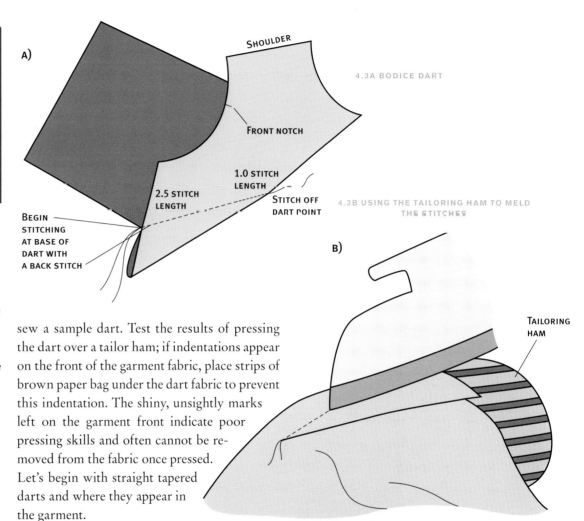

A)

SHOULDER

4.3A BODICE DART

FRONT NOTCH

1.0 STITCH LENGTH

2.5 STITCH LENGTH

STITCH OFF DART POINT

4.3B USING THE TAILORING HAM TO MELD THE STITCHES

BEGIN STITCHING AT BASE OF DART WITH A BACK STITCH

B)

TAILORING HAM

sew a sample dart. Test the results of pressing the dart over a tailor ham; if indentations appear on the front of the garment fabric, place strips of brown paper bag under the dart fabric to prevent this indentation. The shiny, unsightly marks left on the garment front indicate poor pressing skills and often cannot be removed from the fabric once pressed. Let's begin with straight tapered darts and where they appear in the garment.

The *bust dart*, as shown in Figure 4.2a, is located along the side seam of the garment front, and the **bust point** refers to the exact center of the bust, or the apex. A dart is never stitched to this mark; rather, the fullness resulting from the dart is referred to this area, allowing the garment to glide over the curve. The distance between the bust point

IMPORTANT

Darts are always pressed with the folded edge toward the center of the garment, or in the case of the bust darts, they are always pressed down toward the hem (Figure 4.9).

4.4A SHAPED DARTS

4.4B ASYMMETRICAL DARTS

and the end of the dart depends on the number of darts, the size and location of the darts, the garment design and fit, the bust size, and the designer's preference.

Symmetrical darts are the same on both sides of the garment, as shown in Figure 4.9 and all Style I.D. figures.

Asymmetrical darts cross the center front of the garment. Both darts originate at the side seam, although they are spaced apart. This location of the darts is decided at the patternmaking stage by the designer and uses the excess from a waist dart to form the lower dart (Figure 4.4b).

The **waist dart** (Figure 4.1e–f) is used on skirts, pants, and dresses, shaping the fabric in at the waist to allow for fullness at the hips. There are usually two darts on the front of the garment and two or four darts on the back of the garment. All darts can be divided into several smaller darts, providing the same fit, while also adding more surface design interest.

The **elbow dart** (Figure 4.1d) is shaped from the sleeve underarm seam toward the elbow. It functions to shape the sleeves on dresses, tailored jackets, and coats and also to allow room for movement on tight sleeves and for the arm to bend. One dart may be used, or several smaller darts. Some designs may not require the dart to be stitched; instead, they may ease the extra fullness from the dart into the seam allowance.

The **shoulder dart** (Figure 4.1d) is used to shape the garment over the curved area on the back of the garment between the armhole and the neckline. This prevents the collars of garments from standing away from the body and ensures that the neckline lies flat on the body rather than gaping.

The **neck dart** provides a close fit around the neck and can be used in place of a bust dart. If the bust dart is transferred to a different placement that still gives bust shape, it can be incorporated into the design of a garment.

The **contour dart** (see Figures 4.1c and 4.5a), also known as a fisheye or double-pointed dart, is often used at the waistline of a fitted dress, jacket, or coat without a waistline seam. The dart serves double-duty of shaping the garment in the bust and shaping the waist out in the hip area.

- Accurately transfer the dart markings to the fabric (see Figure 4.5a).
- With the correct sides of the fabric together, fold the dart along the central foldline, matching the markings; pin or handbaste (see Figure 4.5b). The handbasting keeps the longer dart from shifting while being stitched.
- Begin stitching the dart from the center of the dart to one end, then from the center of the dart to the other end.
- Backstitch a few stitches in the center for reinforcement in this stress area.
- In order for this dart to lie flat, and to prevent puckering, clip the dart in the center where the stitching began and where the reinforcement stitches have been sewn. Use the tips of very sharp scissors to take a short clip into the dart, being careful not to snip into the line of stitching.
- The garment is often lined to cover the clipping necessary for this dart to lie flat.

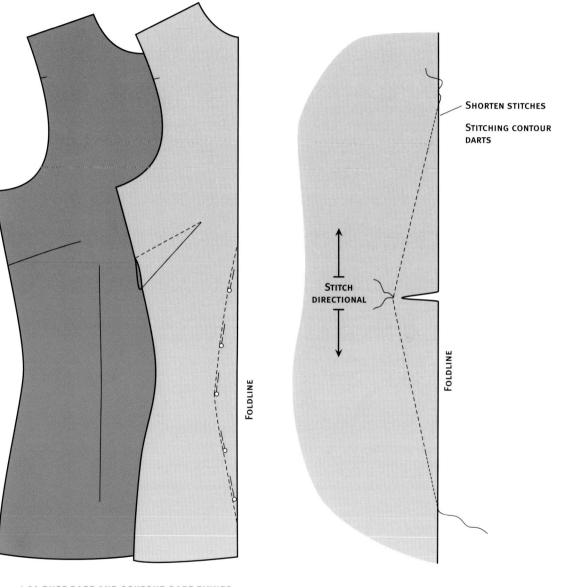

4.5A BUST DART AND CONTOUR DART PINNED, READY TO SEW

4.5B STITCHING THE CONTOUR DART

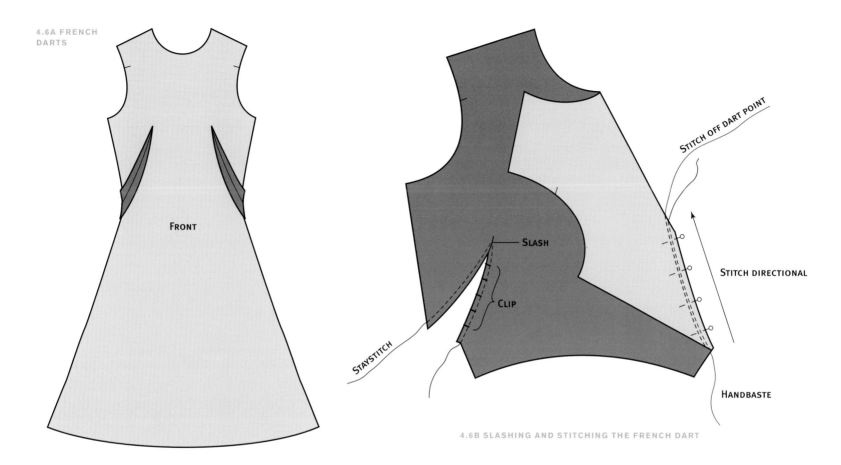

FRONT

STITCH OFF DART POINT

STITCH DIRECTIONAL

SLASH

CLIP

STAYSTITCH

HANDBASTE

4.6B SLASHING AND STITCHING THE FRENCH DART

The **French dart** (Figure 4.6a) is also called the curved dart, as it forms a curve extending from the side seam at the waist in a diagonal, curving line to the bustline. A French dart appears only on the front of a garment. Since it is much wider than a straight, tapered dart, the bulk must be cut out of the dart before it is stitched for the stitching lines to be perfectly aligned. The French dart gives wonderful shaping from the bust to the waist and can be fitted to contour the waist-to-bust area on the garment.

- Accurately transfer marking lines and stitching lines, and include any slash lines.
- Add seams to the cutaway dart, reducing bulk; consider in the sampling stage whether or not these edges should be finished, and if so, finish the edges before continuing.
- Staystitch and clip on the concave curve (see Figure 4.6b).
- With correct sides of the fabric together, match and pin the stitching lines.

- Handbaste inside the marked stitching lines (see Figure 4.6b).
- Stitch the dart from the widest edge to the point, changing to a short stitch length approximately 1 inch from the point, and sewing off to secure the end of the dart (see Figure 4.6b).
- Press the dart in the direction it was stitched, melding the stitches.
- Remove the handbasting stitches.
- Press open the dart.

Shaped Dart

Shaped darts are a lovely addition to a garment design, creating a functional fit as well as providing an interesting line detail to a garment. Shaped darts can be curved, as shown in Figures 4.4a and 4.7, or combined with an angular seam, as shown in Figure 4.8a–c. Accurately lining up the matchpoints and notches is the key to success in stitching an angled seam dart. Alternating on each side of the garment, the shaped darts start on the shoulder on one side of the garment, and begin at the waist on the other side of the garment. Directions for stitching the shaped dart in Figure 4.7 follow:

- Transfer the markings accurately and slash open the dart to within ½ inch of the point.
- Staystitch both sides of the darts just inside the seam allowance up to the beginning of the slash point (see Figure 4.7).
- Clip on concave curves only (see Figure 4.7).
- Pin carefully or handbaste, matching the notches.
- Stitch the dart beginning at the widest point.
- Press the stitched dart toward the center.

STITCHING TRICKY FABRICS

The fabric is the basis on which all decisions are made during clothing construction. The nature of the fabric, drape, and hand (whether stiff or soft) all contribute to the type of dart to be stitched. After these considerations, how the fabric will be supported (whether it's underlined or lined) also influences the placement and use of the correct dart in the garment.

Darts and the silhouette of the garment go hand in hand. To achieve the best look, the best fit, darts are a necessary part of design. All fabrics cannot be covered in one chapter, but the following tips will help student designers decide how to use darts in some specialty fabrics.

Matching Stripes, Plaids, Patterns, and Repeat Patterns

Do match plaids at the crosswise bars along center-front and center-back seams; side seams will only match from the dart down if there is a side seam dart (see Figure 2.16).

Do strategically place prominent repeats in appropriate pattern locations.

Do handbaste or pin the darts at the bust area to match the stripes.

> **IMPORTANT**
>
> It cannot be stated enough: it is important for the designer to press at each step of the way when stitching any garment construction, and this is essential with darts. It can be difficult or impossible to get back inside a garment after it is completed. *PRESS* as you sew!

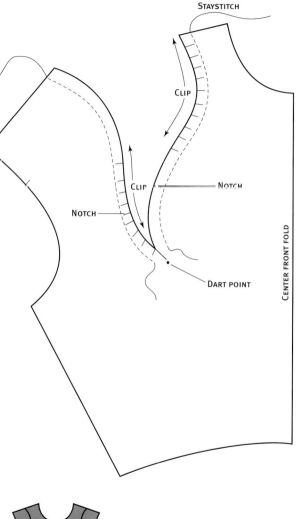

4.7 STITCHING THE SHAPED SHOULDER DART

- STITCH DART
- PRESS DART TOWARD C.F.

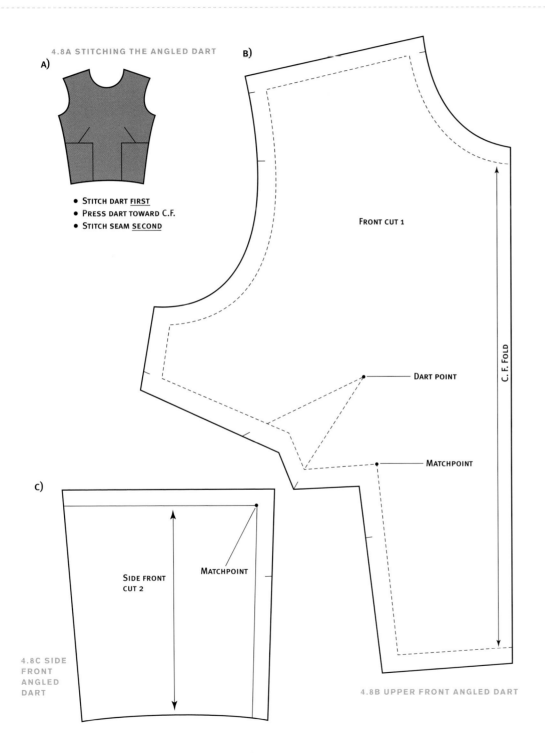

A)

• Stitch dart <u>first</u>
• Press dart toward C.F.
• Stitch seam <u>second</u>

B)

Front cut 1

C. F. Fold

Dart point

Matchpoint

C)

Side front cut 2

Matchpoint

Do place waist darts parallel to the fabric grain on plaids.

Do match waist darts in stripes or checks.

Don't try to match darts in plaids cut on the bias.

Don't place a large flower or obvious geometric repeat in the bust point area.

Don't try to match underarm bust darts, as matching these darts is impossible.

Sheer Fabrics

Do consider using gathers, pleats, tucks, or easing in place of darts.

Do use a double-stitched dart to reduce shadowing. Here's how:

• Mark the stitching lines.
• Stitch to the dart point.
• With the needle down in the fabric, raise the presser foot.
• Turn the dart around and stitch again, trim, and finish.

Do bobbin-stitch the dart, as follows:

• Handbaste the dart just inside the dart legs.
• Thread the machine as usual.
• Tie the bobbin thread and spool thread together.
• Gently pull the knot through the needle.
• Pull just enough of the bobbin thread up onto the spool of thread so the knot is on the spool.
• Stitch the dart, beginning at the point, not the widest part of the dart.

Don't try to overfit sheer fabric with too many darts.

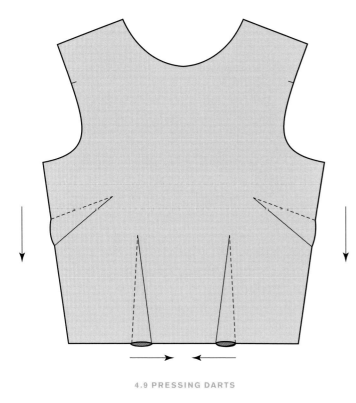

4.9 PRESSING DARTS

Lace

Do overlap the lace to create the dart, as follows:
- Use handbasting to mark the shape of the dart (Figure 4.10a).
- Cut around the curved edge of the lace motif (Figure 4.10b).
- Overlap the dart, matching basting stitches together.
- Hand stitch around the left edge of the dart (Figure 4.10c).
- Trim away lace underneath the dart.

Don't stitch a traditional dart in lace—it's too bulky and will show through to the front of the garment.

Satin

Do *sample* the dart on a scrap of fabric before stitching the dart on the garment; although we say this often, it can't be emphasized enough—the result will be much better!

Do tissue-stitch the dart to reduce the chances of imprinting the feed dogs or the dart on the surface of the satin.

Do consider that the type of dart should compliment the weight of the fabric. For example, if using a heavier weight of satin, it would be difficult to stitch a shaped dart that would lie flat and smooth.

Don't overpress satin—it can ruin the fabric.

Beaded Fabric

Do carefully consider where the dart placement will be on the garment, and place the dart where it will least interfere with the beading.

Do consider an alternative to a dart that works with the fabric.

Do remove as much of the beading as possible before attempting to stitch a dart.

Do handbaste the dart inside the dart legs.

Do only hand stitch the darts in beaded fabrics—the machine stitch tension will be terrible if stitching over beads!

Do baste the raw edges of the dart legs to the underlining to keep the dart flat, or, if not using underlining, invisibly stitch the dart legs to the garment.

Don't press directly on the dart—press only on the stitching of the dart legs.

Knits

Although knits don't usually need darts, some double knits and firm knits can be darted and used with great success.

Do use the "crooked straight" stitch, referenced in Chapter 6, when stitching the dart legs to avoid puckering (see Figure 6.44b).

Do consider dart alternatives in knits, as the stretch of the knit garment influences the fit.

Don't press the dart without strips of tissue or brown paper bag underneath.

Denim

Do reduce the bulk of the dart by cutting open and pressing flat whenever possible.

Do finish the edges of the dart with the flattest possible finish. Refer to Chapter 6 for suggestions.

Do topstitch darts in denim.

Do consider alternative dart options, such as style lines.

Don't overfit the garment with too many darts in heavier-weight denim.

Velvet

Do place and stitch the dart carefully—ripping out stitches in velvet leaves marks on the fabric surface.

Do steam and finger-press the dart—pressing directly on velvet crushes the nap and leaves shiny marks that cannot be removed.

Do use a needle board specifically designed to support the nap of the velvet when pressing the stitching line *only*.

4.10 LACE DART–STEPS

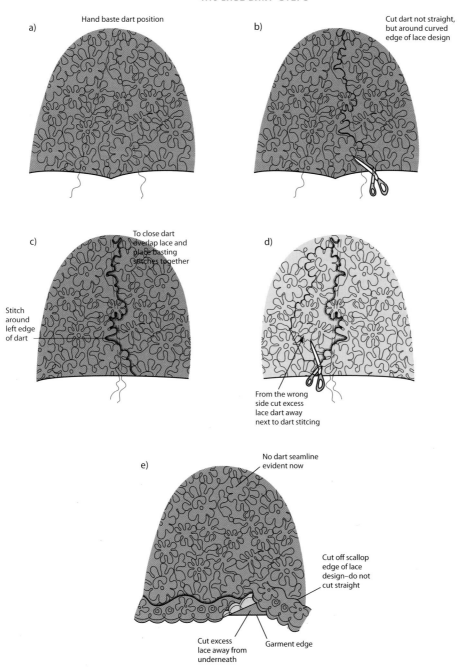

a)   Hand baste dart position

b)   Cut dart not straight, but around curved edge of lace design

c)   To close dart overlap lace and place basting stitches together

Stitch around left edge of dart

d)   From the wrong side cut excess lace dart away next to dart stitcing

e)   No dart seamline evident now

Cut off scallop edge of lace design–do not cut straight

Cut excess lace away from underneath

Garment edge

Do slash open the dart to reduce bulk in heavier-weight velvet, and invisibly catch stitch (see Figure 6.51b) the dart legs to the garment to keep the dart flat.

Do consider French darts.

Don't overfit the garment with too many darts—the beauty of velvet is the fabric itself.

Leather

Do consider the weight of the leather.

Do stitch the straight, tapered dart as previously mentioned, but finger-press and pound lightly to flatten (Figure 4.11a).

Do trim to ⅜ inch (Figure 4.11b) when stitching a wider dart, angling the dart legs at the point (Figure 4.11c) and pounding the dart legs flat. Finish by gluing with leather cement or topstitching.

Do use a lapped dart for narrow bust darts. (A lapped dart has the inside fabric of the dart cut away—leave ⅛ inch; then the two raw edges are joined together by lapping the raw edges over each other and topstitching.) Here's how:

- Cut along the upper dart stitching line to the dart point (Figure 4.12a).
- Apply glue to the underside of the cut dart.
- Lap the cut edge over the lower dart stitching line (Figure 4.12b).
- Place a small square of interfacing under the dart point.
- Topstitch along the cut edge (Figure 4.12c).
- Trim away excess leather on the wrong side.

Do use pintucks in place of darts on lightweight leather.

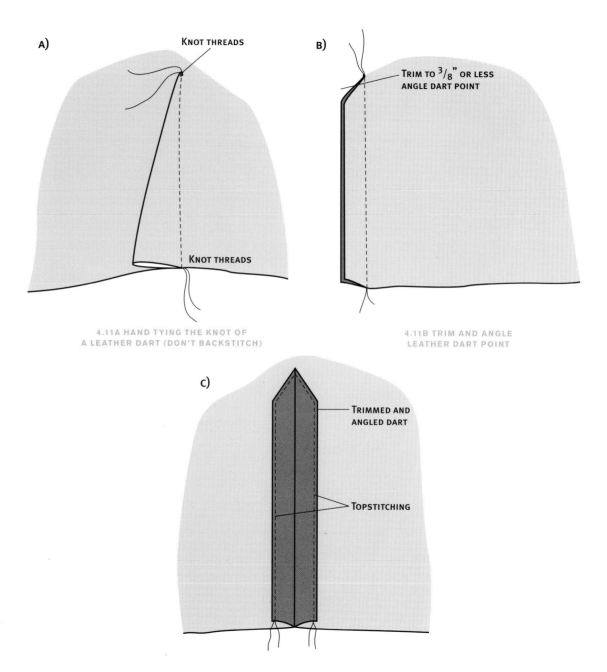

A) KNOT THREADS

KNOT THREADS

4.11A HAND TYING THE KNOT OF A LEATHER DART (DON'T BACKSTITCH)

B) TRIM TO ³/₈" OR LESS ANGLE DART POINT

4.11B TRIM AND ANGLE LEATHER DART POINT

C) TRIMMED AND ANGLED DART

TOPSTITCHING

4.11C TOPSTITCHING THE ANGLED LEATHER DART

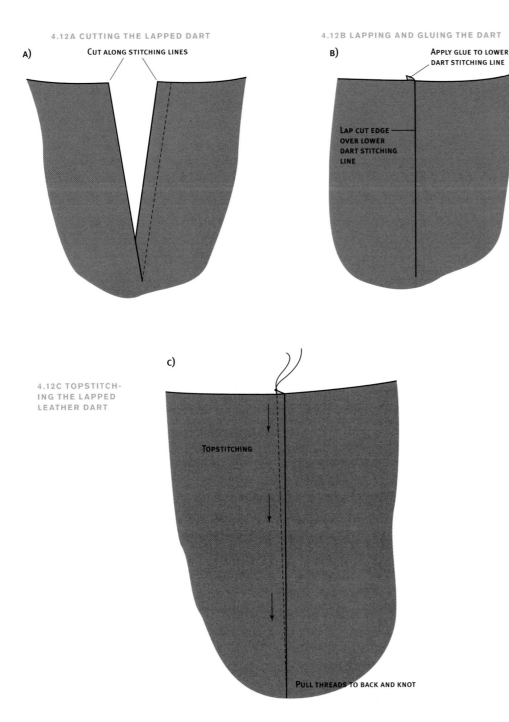

4.12A CUTTING THE LAPPED DART

A)

CUT ALONG STITCHING LINES

4.12B LAPPING AND GLUING THE DART

B)

APPLY GLUE TO LOWER DART STITCHING LINE

LAP CUT EDGE OVER LOWER DART STITCHING LINE

4.12C TOPSTITCHING THE LAPPED LEATHER DART

C)

TOPSTITCHING

PULL THREADS TO BACK AND KNOT

Don't leave the leather untrimmed for any style dart—the goal for the dart is to be smooth and flat.

Faux Fur

Do stitch darts on the stitching line and catch stitch the edges to the garment (see Figure 6.51b).

Do push the hairs of the fur out of the way of the stitching to reduce bulk in the seam.

Do use a toothbrush to pull out the hairs on the correct side of the garment after stitching.

Do use style lines in place of darts—the bulk of the fur prevents intricate shaping.

Don't sew darts in the traditional way on faux fur.

Heavyweight Fabric

Do slash open the center of the dart before stitching to reduce bulk.

Do press open, using lots of steam and a clapper to flatten the dart.

Do use handbasting to stitch the dart legs to the garment, to keep the dart legs flat.

Do trim, grade, and clip as necessary to produce a smooth flat dart.

TRANSFER YOUR KNOWLEDGE

Now that you know how to stitch darts, and have become more familiar with where darts are placed and why, take that knowledge and try one of the following techniques. Remember, always sample a new technique before applying it to a garment and allow plenty of time to do so. You never know where sampling will take you!

Dart Transformations—Gathers, Pleats, Tucks, Style Lines, and Cowls

Darts can be transferred with pattern alteration into other construction details such as tucks, gathers, shirring, pleats, and godets (the godets are stitched into the trimmed dart area) to produce fullness within the garment. Such dart transformations require careful planning if the designer is to avoid losing the basic shape of the garment. In woven fabrics, darts are needed to provide the shape of the garment; while in knits, the amount of stretch in the fabric and the cut of the design influence the fit.

A dart always works from a pivot point within the garment, but the space between the dart legs can be used to form shape in other ways. The excess space, or dart transformation, is always directed toward the pivot point and ends before reaching the pivot point. Darts would never, for example, be sewn to and through the bust point.

Identifying the creative elements of the design and knowing where and how the dart excess is used is a patternmaking principle. Transferring the dart to a different location should not affect the size or fit of the garment. The designer must decide if this suits the garment and maintains the original fit of the garment.

Gathers

Gathering the dart excess to create fullness in place of a dart is best used in softer, lightweight fabrics. For example, a darted bodice in an empire waist dress would look less tailored with the darts softly gathered at the bodice before being sewn to the lower garment section.

Pleats

A *pleat* is an unstitched, folded dart held securely along the joining seamline. Pleats arrange and distribute fullness in a garment and also add design interest. Although they are usually associated with skirts, they can be placed in pants, tops, jackets, or dresses. Pleats can fall in soft folds or be pressed into sharp creases. They can be narrow or wide depending on how much fabric is available from the dart. Not all fabrics are suitable for pleating, so it is important to choose the correct fabric and style of pleating for the garment being designed.

Some pleats to consider for dart replacement would be side or knife pleats or inverted pleats. The critical determination is the amount of dart ease that is available, which influences the size of the pleats—they may end up being very narrow, and not as effective as if the dart were sewn. Narrower pleats are more effective in smaller areas such as a bodice or a section of a bodice. Refer to Chapter 7 for detailed information on pleats.

Tucks

Tucks are narrow folds in the fabric and are used to control fullness and shape the garment. Tucks can be substituted for darts to give the garment a less fitted look. Tucks are usually formed on the outside of the garment but can be stitched on the inside as well. The designer decides on the most attractive placement of the tucks on the garment. The most frequently used tucks are blind tucks, spaced tucks, dart tucks/release tucks, and pin tucks. Refer to Chapter 7 for detailed information on tucks.

Blind tucks are tucks that meet. The foldline of one tuck touches the stitching line of the adjacent tuck so no spaces show between the tucks.

Spaced tucks are separated by space left between the foldline of one tuck and the stitching line of the next.

Dart Tucks

A dart tuck is a partially stitched, inverted dart. This type of tuck is used to add fullness to an area on the garment. The designer uses dart tucks as substitutes for darts when a softly shaped line is desired. These tucks are usually placed at the

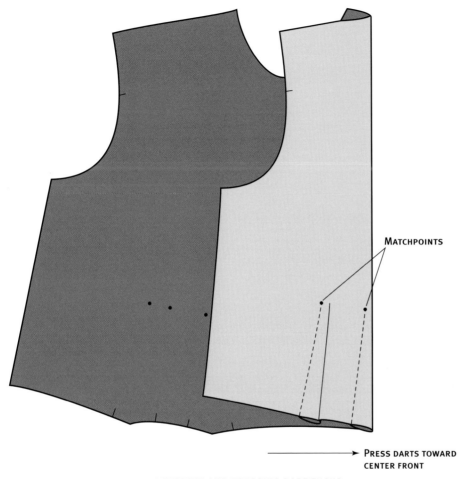

MATCHPOINTS

PRESS DARTS TOWARD
CENTER FRONT

4.13 STITCHING AND PRESSING DART TUCKS

and fit at the shoulder, sleeve cap, sleeve, cuff, or waist of a garment. The take up of the tucking where it ends and releases the fullness acts much like gathers or pleats, or replaces darts. Accurate marking and careful, even stitching produce beautiful pin tucks. Varying the length of the pin tucks controls the focus of the fullness. Refer to Chapter 7 for further details on pin tucks.

Style Lines: Princess Seam—Not a Dart!
Often, a princess seam is mistaken for a type of dart. Although the **princess seam** is a style line, it is formed by joining the inward and outward curves of a shoulder dart and a waist dart. The curved seam is shaped out over the bust, fitted in at the waist, and shaped out toward the hip. The back can also have princess seaming. Refer to Chapter 6 for more information.

Cowls
The bodice cowl is a transferred dart, and depends on the excess taken from the basic dart. The lower the depth of the cowl, the greater the amount of excess needed to produce the cowl. A high, relaxed cowl transfers some of the dart excess, while a cowl that falls between the neck and bust takes up to one-half of the waist dart excess. This is an application of dart manipulation. The designer must decide at the patternmaking stage what look is intended for the garment. Cowls can be in-one with the garment or be set-in to save fabric. Refer to Chapter 12 for detailed information on cowls. French darts used in place of waist darts are an effective combination with the cowl.

waistline or neck edge. They are stitched on the inside or outside of the garment.

Dart tucks or release tucks can be open at one end, or both ends, or the free end of the tuck may be stitched down to the garment across the bottom. Care must be taken to avoid stretching the off-grain stitching lines of the tuck

when they are pinned, stitched, and pressed (Figure 4.13).

Pin tucks are tiny tucks made by hand or machine by sewing a running stitch parallel and close to the edge of a fold in the fabric. Opened out flat, the stitched fold is pressed to one side. Used in multiple rows, pin tucks provide shape

TRANSFER YOUR KNOWLEDGE

Transferring your knowledge to changing dart locations and changing darts into other construction details requires time, accuracy, patience, and lots of sampling. Each time a technique is successful, it becomes easier to sample the next one. And in sewing and designing, there is always a "next one"!

STRETCH YOUR CREATIVITY

Stretching your creativity involves taking the stitching techniques learned in this chapter and applying them to designs in a more unique, nontraditional way. In other words, think creatively. When thinking creatively, however, always consider whether this is adding to the design or taking away from it. Remember, just because you can, doesn't mean you should!

- Add darts alternating from side to side of the correct side of a garment for fitting and visual effect (Figure 4.14a).
- Stitch an uneven number of darts on the outside of a neckline with contrasting thread (Figure 4.14b).
- Stitch darts into unevenly placed positions on each half of a dress (Figure 4.14c).
- Create asymmetrical darts across the front of a garment (see Figure 4.4b).

Stretch Your Creativity

4.14A ALTERNATING DARTS ON GARMENT SURFACE

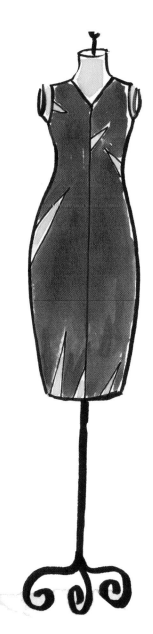

4.14B NECKLINE DARTS ON GARMENT SURFACE WITH FRENCH DARTS

4.14C UNEVENLY PLACED DARTS OF VARIOUS SIZES ON SURFACE OF GARMENT

STOP! WHAT DO I DO IF . . .

. . . my darts are puckered?

Check the stitch length for the fabric being stitched, handbaste the dart just inside the seam line, and stitch again.

. . . my dart legs don't match up?

Accurate measuring and trueing of the dart pattern will ensure even dart legs, but sometimes the fabric slips or the markings are difficult to transfer accurately on the fabric choice. Use handbasting to mark the dart legs and then carefully handbaste the dart legs together. Check the positioning before machine stitching—correct stitching begins with correct patternmaking. Perhaps the pattern wasn't correct.

. . . my darts are uneven on the garment?

Again, accurate measuring will ensure that the darts are positioned evenly on the garment. Remove the stitched darts, press to remove creases, reposition the pattern piece onto the garment section, and carefully mark the wrong side of the fabric. Handbasting the markings may turn out to be more accurate.

. . . I've cut open my dart and it is crooked?

Stitch a piece of fabric to the dart legs—either lightweight fusible interfacing (the fusible glue will stabilize the raw edges of the dart legs) or lining fabric—and redraw the darts, carefully checking the position. Baste first by hand to preserve the fragile edges, and if correct, then machine stitch.

. . . I've ripped out my dart and the previous stitch lines show!

Often, stitching leaves holes in the fabric once it's been removed. This is another reason to always sample your fabric and the technique to see what will happen if you have to rip out the stitches. Occasionally, steaming the wrong side of the area and using your nails to rub the holes results in some of the markings disappearing. If this is not enough, try fusing a small strip of lightweight interfacing over the section if it won't show through to the front of the garment. However, this still may not be enough to salvage the garment section and it may have to be recut and resewn. This is an experience that all designers and sewers have encountered!

SELF-CRITIQUE

Take a look at your finished garment and ask the crucial question, "Would I wear this garment or would I purchase this garment?" If the answer is "No," then ask yourself, why not?

If you would not wear your garment, it may be because you don't like the design, the proportions, the cut, or the fabric choice. However, when we ask students this question, an often-stated reason that would prevent them from wearing or purchasing their own garment is the quality of the stitching.

Then ask yourself the following questions to critique the quality of your dart stitching:

- Are the darts stitched evenly without any dimpling at the dart point?

- Are the bust darts pressed correctly (down toward the hem)?
- Are any press marks visible on the front of the garment?
- Are the darts of equal length and width?
- Do the darts look symmetrical—mirror image on both sides?
- If not, can the darts be successfully transferred into other shaping techniques, such as tucks, gathers, or pleats?
- This is an opportunity to stand back and assess your work. Don't wait until the end of the project to do this—do this throughout the entire stitching process.

REVIEW CHECKLIST

- Do the darts add fullness to the correct area on the garment?
- Do the darts add to the overall design?
- Are the tucks, gathers, pleats, or other shaping techniques maintaining the original garment shape and fit?
- Is the dart replacement technique in harmony with the style of the garment?

Darts are an important part of garment fit, silhouette, shape, and construction. They guide and control the finished look of the design on the body; without proper construction and placement, the design will not be successful. With repetition, and good sewing and pressing skills, darts will become an important part of your design creativity.

Pockets: Building a Handy Compartment

I n this chapter, we explain, illustrate, and sew pockets using the correct stitches, with suitable stabilizer and lining appropriate for the fabric and design. Many shapes, sizes, and types of pockets can be designed. When designing your garment, care should be taken to combine the pocket design appropriate for the style of the garment and the purpose of the pocket (functional design). You will need to determine if the pocket is part of the structure, just decorative, or a

functional part of the garment. The placement and size of the pocket are integral to the function and comfort of the garment. This chapter also addresses trims, braids, and piping as further options of the pocket. Yes, pockets can be a handy compartment, and with excellent stitching, they will certainly hold up to this function.

STYLE I.D.

Figure 5.1 shows several styles of pockets and how they can be used in design. Can you iden-

tify which ones could be used as functional design and which ones could be used as a decorative part of the garment?

GATHER YOUR TOOLS

These are the tools you will need to stitch pockets: machine needles appropriate for your fabric, such as size 12 or 14 for medium- to heavier-weight fabric, and size 9 or 11 for lighter-weight fabrics; scissors; matching thread; seam ripper; point turner; stabilizer; fabric marking pen; piping (premade or made to match or

KEY TERMS

Edgestitching
Flap
Patch Pocket
Single-Layer Pocket
Topstitched Pocket
Welt

NOTE

Functional design is expressed in a working pocket for practical use, and decorative design is expressed in a pocket that is not for use, but for decoration, beauty, and style.

Style I.D.

5.1B IN-SEAM SIDE POCKETS

5.1C INVISIBLY SEWN PATCH POCKET

5.1A IN-SEAM POCKET
WITH FLAP

5.1D SHAPED
POCKET FLAP

coordinate with the pocket); trim; zippers (contrasting, decorative, functional); and contrasting or decorative thread for topstitching.

NOW LET'S GET STARTED

Determine what pocket you are going to use for your design. Take into consideration what the purpose of this pocket will be—functional or decorative.

If the pocket is meant to be functional:

- Placement of the pocket at the correct position is paramount to the comfort of its use.
- Unevenly spaced pockets can jar the eye, detracting from the overall look of the garment.
- Are the pockets in proportion to the garment? Too large? Too small?
- Will the pocket stand up to repeated use where it is placed?
- If the fabric is delicate or might ravel, will adding a stabilizer or a lining create a pocket too expensive for the garment being produced or will the benefits outweigh the cost?
- Will a less time-consuming pocket application serve as well as a more involved type of pocket (patch pocket versus welt pocket)?

If the pocket is meant to be decorative:

- Does the pocket add important design detail that enhances the garment?
- Is the proportion of the decorative pocket in keeping with the overall theme of the garment?

- Time equals money in production; does the pocket take excessive time to produce?
- Will the cost of the trims, such as piping, ribbon, buttons, or topstitching, exceed the value of the garment?

Use of the pocket detail may be the selling point of a moderately priced garment, adding just the "designer" touch that prompts the sale of the garment. In higher price ranges, added details and beautiful execution of pockets is in keeping with luxurious fabrics and trims.

INTERFACING IN POCKETS AND FLAPS

When is interfacing used in pockets or flaps? (Refer to Chapter 3, "Introduction to Stabilizers.")

- To provide body to a loosely woven fabric.
- To provide support to an area that is clipped.
- To prevent seams from pulling out or apart.
- To prevent seam slippage.
- To provide a crisp edge that doesn't cave in.

Types of Interfacing to Use

Always drape both the interfacing and the fabric together to see whether the weight of the stabilizer works with the fabric being used.

- Try different weights of interfacing on the fabric for the desired effect.
- Determine how the fabric and interfacing interact before choosing the interfacing/stabilizer for your pocket or flap. (Refer to Chapter 3, "Introduction to Stabilizers.")

> **IMPORTANT**
>
> Placement of the pocket is critical to the overall success of the garment and the pocket. Carefully check that the pocket is not too close to the center front, or too close to the hem.

POCKET LININGS

Many fabric choices are available for use as lining. (Refer to Chapter 16, "Lining.") The lining must suit the garment fabric being used for a pocket. As the hand enters the pocket, the lining should allow easy entry.

- Outerwear garments have different requirements than a suit jacket or trouser pockets, which must have sturdy, hard-wearing pockets. Sturdy cotton twill stands up to daily use in suit jacket pockets and trousers.
- On a coat or an outerwear jacket, warmth is a factor; fleece or flannel would be good choices.
- If a very bulky fabric is being used for a pocket or a flap, a lightweight but firmly woven lining fabric is a suitable choice.
- Lined patch pockets require a lining fabric that reduces the bulk of the pocket, making the pocket easy to turn for application.
- White or light-colored pockets that are lined look best using a skin-colored lining that reduces the chance of shadowing, or the seams showing through to the front of the pocket.

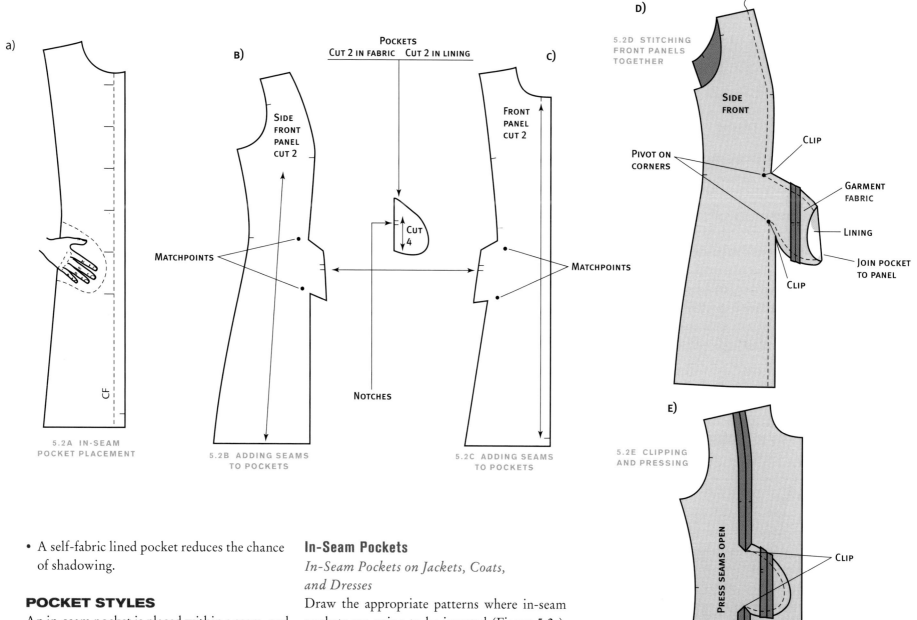

a)

5.2A IN-SEAM POCKET PLACEMENT

CF

B)

SIDE FRONT PANEL CUT 2

MATCHPOINTS

5.2B ADDING SEAMS TO POCKETS

POCKETS
Cut 2 in fabric   Cut 2 in lining

CUT 4

NOTCHES

C)

FRONT PANEL CUT 2

MATCHPOINTS

5.2C ADDING SEAMS TO POCKETS

D)

5.2D STITCHING FRONT PANELS TOGETHER

SIDE FRONT

PIVOT ON CORNERS

CLIP

GARMENT FABRIC

LINING

JOIN POCKET TO PANEL

CLIP

E)

5.2E CLIPPING AND PRESSING

PRESS SEAMS OPEN

CLIP

• A self-fabric lined pocket reduces the chance of shadowing.

POCKET STYLES

An in-seam pocket is placed within a seam, and if correctly sewn, is not easily seen. Smooth, flat, careful sewing results in this pocket following the seam line.

In-Seam Pockets

In-Seam Pockets on Jackets, Coats, and Dresses

Draw the appropriate patterns where in-seam pockets are going to be inserted (Figure 5.2a). Look in the mirror and place your hand where it would feel most comfortable entering a pocket. Mark with pins. The placement and size of the pocket opening *must* feel comfortable and not too tight! Transfer this marking to the pattern. This is part of functional design.

POCKET PLACEMENT

POCKET PATTERN

- Plot the pocket pattern. It would take a lot of fabric to cut both panels with the pockets cut all-in-one. This would not be cost-effective in production.
- An extension seam can be added to the panels and cut off the four pocket pieces. Moving the seam inward when the coat is worn, the self-fabric will be visible in the pocket opening and not the lining. Mark notches for pocket seam join. Cut off the pocket section and draw a parallel grainline for pocket placement (Figure 5.2b).

- For pockets to be warm and comfortable, the bottom layer (where your hand rests) needs to be cut from the original garment fabric. The pocket will wear better made in self-fabric. The other pocket section (that lies on top of this pocket) is best cut from lining. This will prevent the pockets from adding too much bulk. Mark pivot points—these markings are essential for the construction process. Add notches where pockets are joined to seam as shown in Figure 5.2b and c.

STITCHING IN-SEAM POCKETS

- Place the correct sides of fabric together and stitch the four pocket sections to each panel. The two fabric pockets will be stitched to the side-front panel, and the two lining pockets to the center-front panels. Press the pocket seams open (Figure 5.2d).
- Clip into the two corners of the side-front panels, leaving 1/8 inch of fabric intact. Press the coat with the pockets turned in toward the center front of the coat (Figure 5.2e).

In-Seam Pockets with Flaps —Jackets and Coats

When adding flaps to in-seam pockets on jackets or coats, the flaps are added before the pockets are stitched into the seam. See above.

- The flaps are the same length as the pocket opening. The width of the flap depends on the design of the garment—flaps can't be too narrow or they will disappear into the fabric,

nor can they be too wide, overwhelming the front of the garment. Consider starting at 2 inches wide plus seam allowances, and the length you measured for the pocket opening.
- Cut on the fold for each pocket flap and interface the flap to suit the fabric weight. Cut off both panel extensions when stitching flaps to inseam pockets. (Use full size pockets as shown in Figure 5.3d.)
- Fold each flap in half, with the correct sides together. Stitch around three sides, back-stitching at the beginning and end. Trim corners to reduce bulk and trim seam allowances. Turn and press (Figure 5.3a).
- When using a rounded edge flap, cut notches into the seam allowance to reduce bulk and to ensure smooth turning of the flap, as shown in Figure 5.3b.
- Place the flap on the correct side of the front panel, aligned to matchpoints, as shown in Figure 5.3c. Machine baste in place.
- Place the pockets over the flaps on both panels; stitch (Figure 5.3d). Press. Continue with construction of the pockets; clip into the corners. Turn the pockets to the inside; the flaps will be on the outside of the garment. Pin the flaps into place. Stitch-in-the-ditch by rolling the side seams back and stitching through all layers. Press a final time (Figure 5.3e).

In-Seam Pockets—Pants and Skirts

Cut the garment front pocket from lining fabric to reduce bulk, and the garment back pocket from the same fashion fabric as the garment, so that when your hand slides into the pocket,

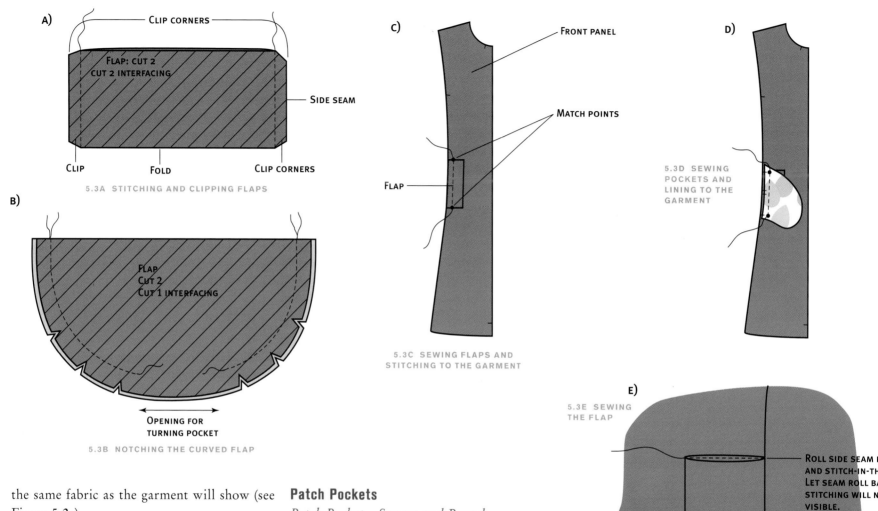

A)

CLIP CORNERS

FLAP: CUT 2
CUT 2 INTERFACING

SIDE SEAM

CLIP   FOLD   CLIP CORNERS

5.3A STITCHING AND CLIPPING FLAPS

B)

FLAP
CUT 2
CUT 1 INTERFACING

OPENING FOR
TURNING POCKET

5.3B NOTCHING THE CURVED FLAP

C)

FRONT PANEL

MATCH POINTS

FLAP

5.3C SEWING FLAPS AND
STITCHING TO THE GARMENT

D)

5.3D SEWING
POCKETS AND
LINING TO THE
GARMENT

E)

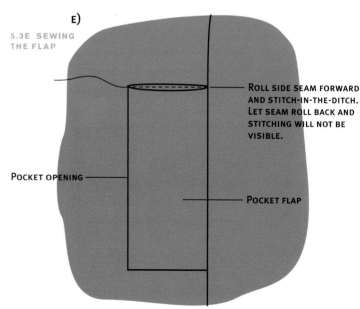

5.3E SEWING
THE FLAP

ROLL SIDE SEAM FORWARD
AND STITCH-IN-THE-DITCH.
LET SEAM ROLL BACK AND
STITCHING WILL NOT BE
VISIBLE.

POCKET OPENING

POCKET FLAP

the same fabric as the garment will show (see Figure 5.2c).

- With the correct sides of the fabric together, place the pockets on the front and back of the garment.
- Stitch the pockets to the garment extensions. Press. Clip as shown in Figure 5.4; press the seams. Turn the pockets toward center front, and press.

Patch Pockets

Patch Pocket—Square and Round, with Template

A **patch pocket** is used on tailored garments such as dresses, suits, sportswear, and casual garments. The patch pocket can have a self-fabric facing; can be unlined, interfaced, lined, or self-lined; and can be made in as many shapes as you can imagine. It can be functional or purely decorative. It also can have a flap, buttoned or

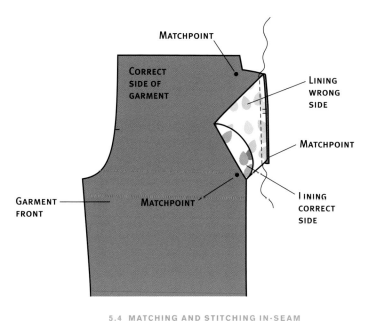

Labels on figure: MATCHPOINT, CORRECT SIDE OF GARMENT, LINING WRONG SIDE, MATCHPOINT, GARMENT FRONT, MATCHPOINT, LINING CORRECT SIDE

5.4 MATCHING AND STITCHING IN-SEAM POCKETS AND LINING

unbuttoned, plain or shaped. It can be zippered, or closed with Velcro, or with other types of closures such as frogs, buckles, straps, ribbons, cords, or whatever else complements the garment design. A patch pocket can have decorative piping to complement its edges, and its grainline can be changed to create a particular effect, such as on the bias or on the crossgrain with stripes or plaids. In fact, a patch pocket is only limited

IMPORTANT

Always create a sample pocket from the fabric you are using *before* applying the pocket to your garment.

by the type of fabric that is being used and the purpose for which the pocket is designed.

Patch Pocket with Self-Facing
This pocket is the simplest of all patch pockets.

- Cut out the pocket with either a squared or curved bottom edge.
- For a crisp edge, apply sew-in or fusible interfacing (see Chapter 3, "Introduction to Stabilizers") that is compatible with your fabric to the upper pocket edge.
- The upper edge of the self-fabric facing is serged or clean-finished (refer to Chapter 6, "Seams"), depending on your type of fabric. The self-facing is made by turning back the finished upper edge of the pocket along the foldline to the correct side of the pocket. Begin stitching a $1/2$-inch seam allowance at the top of the pocket and continue around to the other side of the pocket to establish the seamline, as shown in Figure 5.5a.
- After trimming the corners to reduce the bulk, turn back the facing to the wrong side of the fabric and lightly press.
- The stitching line provides an accurate marking for folding the seam allowances inside the pocket in preparation for sewing the pocket to the garment surface. For the rounded patch pocket, ease stitching gathers the curve of the pocket for smooth turning of the seam allowance (Figure 5.5b). Press.
- Change the stitch length and stitch as shown in Figure 5.5c.
- The matchpoints for the pocket placement

NOTE

Place the garment on a tailoring ham or seam roll. Match the markings on the garment for the placement of the pocket, and pin the pocket in place. Placing the garment on the curve of the tailoring ham or seam roll allows for the contour of the body, preventing the patch pockets from sticking out from the garment.

should be $1/8$ inch in from the finished edge of the pocket and $1/8$ inch down (Figure 2.4). In production, a machine drills holes into the garment for the pocket placement. It is important to place the pocket accurately so the holes don't show! Carefully edgestitch or topstitch the pocket in place, backstitching to secure the pocket (Figure 5.5d).

Because the patch pocket is on the surface of the garment, attention is drawn to its construction and stitching. Create a sample piece of the edgestitching or topstitching, using the same fabric as your pocket and the same thread you will be using. Try various stitch lengths to see which one best complements the pocket and garment design. This detail should enhance the overall look of the garment. You may wish to collect these samples in your workbook.

Invisibly Sewn Patch Pocket
—Machine Stitched
Medium to large patch pockets can be invisibly sewn to jackets or coats by machine. The pockets

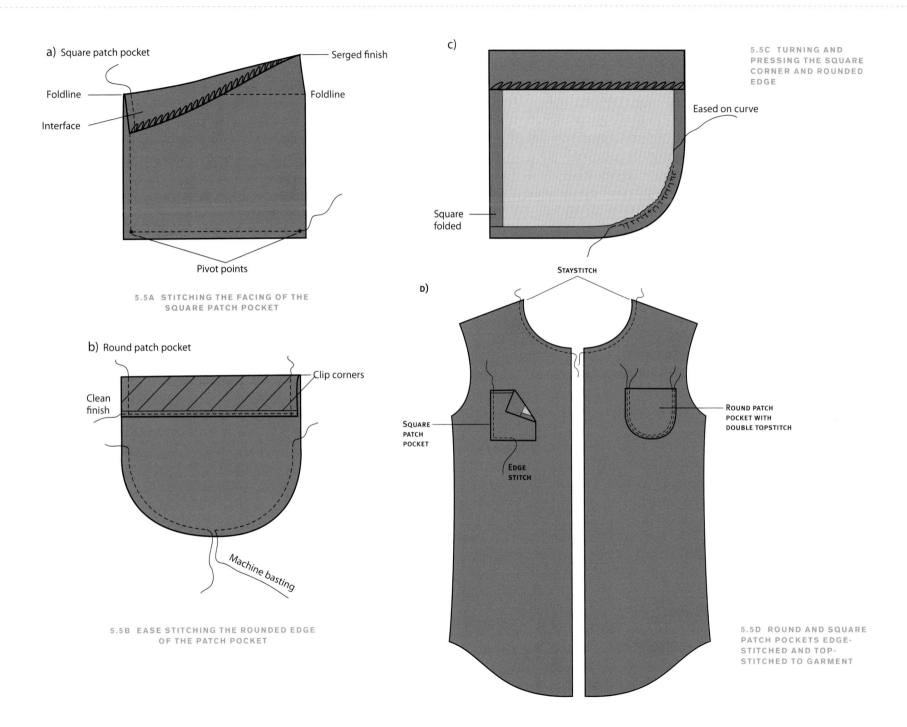

a) Square patch pocket

Serged finish

Foldline

Foldline

Interface

Pivot points

5.5A STITCHING THE FACING OF THE SQUARE PATCH POCKET

b) Round patch pocket

Clip corners

Clean finish

Machine basting

5.5B EASE STITCHING THE ROUNDED EDGE OF THE PATCH POCKET

c)

5.5C TURNING AND PRESSING THE SQUARE CORNER AND ROUNDED EDGE

Eased on curve

Square folded

STAYSTITCH

d)

SQUARE PATCH POCKET

EDGE STITCH

ROUND PATCH POCKET WITH DOUBLE TOPSTITCH

5.5D ROUND AND SQUARE PATCH POCKETS EDGE-STITCHED AND TOP-STITCHED TO GARMENT

can be applied straight or at an angle, as seen in Figure 5.1c. This takes some preparation and careful sewing, but the effort is worth the beautiful results.

- Using the curved patch pocket pattern, cut one each of fabric and of fusible interfacing. Fuse the interfacing to the pocket, and serge the raw edges or clean finish the top of the pocket. Stitch, then fold the facing to the wrong side of the fabric; press.
- Beginning at the top of the pocket, ease stitch a ½-inch seam allowance all around the pocket.
- Place a cardboard or oak tag template (a manila file folder is a good substitute) that is the finished size of the pocket within the pocket and press the seam allowances over the template. With your pressing cloth, press really well, holding the iron in place to create a sharp crease.
- Remove the template and trim the seam allowance to ¼ inch. If your fabric is loosely woven, serge these raw edges before trimming, as the serging will cut off approximately ¼ inch of the seam, or zigzag stitch over the raw edges for a cleaner finish before trimming to prevent the fabric from unraveling or the seam allowances from pulling out. Turn in edges to ease in the corners (Figure 5.5c).
- Using a single strand of contrasting thread, handbaste the pocket in place on the garment (Figure 5.6a).
- Using a contrasting thread color, set the

sewing machine for a wide zigzag stitch, just catching the stitch in the edge of the pressed pocket as you stitch all around the pocket (see Figure 5.6a).

- Remove basting stitches. Reaching inside the pocket, starting from the top of the pocket, backstitch then stitch with a straight stitch of 2.5 or 3.0 (depending on the thickness of your fabric), around the curve to the center of the bottom of the pocket. Repeat for other side of the pocket. Remove zigzag stitching (Figure 5.6b).
- Stitch in small sections, leaving the needle down in the fabric. Lift the presser foot to smooth the fabric to avoid catching the garment fabric in the pocket stitching.

Patch Pocket—Lined, Lined with Facing, and Self-Lined

Lined patch pockets add a finishing detail and also provide a clean finish to fabrics that are loosely woven. Using the lined-edge-to-edge method also reduces bulk and is an easy way to finish a pocket. This is an efficient way to finish a novelty shaped pocket. The key to a beautifully lined patch pocket of any shape is accurate sewing, precise clipping, and trimming.

- Match the lining fabric to the garment fabric. For each pocket, cut one pocket pattern of garment fabric and one pocket of lining fabric.
- Cut the lining pocket ⅛ inch smaller than the pocket to ensure the lining piece will not show on the correct side of the garment once the pocket has been turned.

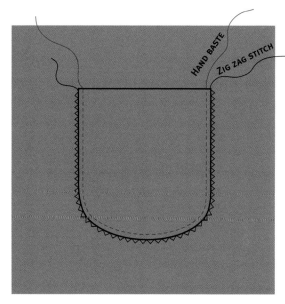

5.6A ZIGZAG STITCH AROUND PATCH POCKET EDGE

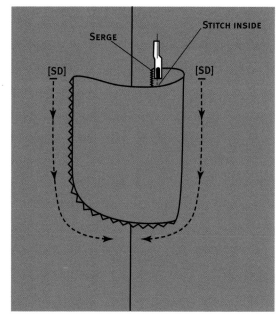

5.6B MACHINE STITCHING INSIDE THE PATCH POCKET FOR AN INVISIBLE FINISH

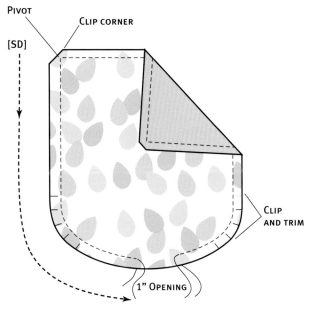

PIVOT
CLIP CORNER
[SD]
CLIP AND TRIM
1" OPENING

5.7 STITCHING THE LINED PATCH POCKET

• Match the lining pocket edges to the garment fabric edges and pin. With the correct sides of the fabric together, begin stitching at the center of the bottom of the pocket, up and across the top, pivoting at the opposite top corner, down to the center of the bottom, and leaving an opening of at least 1 inch or larger to turn the pockets to the correct side (Figure 5.7).
• Trim the corners to reduce bulk; trim the seam allowances to ¼ inch, clip and gently pull the pockets through the opening to the front. Using an awl or a point turner, carefully push out the corners of the pocket. The opening at the bottom of the pocket will be pulled to the inside. Press, making sure that

the lining is not visible on the front.
• Match up the pocket markings and pin the pocket to the garment. Topstitch or edge-stitch from the upper corner of the pocket, backstitching to reinforce, and continue to the opposite upper corner, backstitching again (Figure 5.5d).

Patch Pocket—Lined with a Self-Fabric Facing
A patch pocket with a self-fabric facing that is lined uses the same pocket pattern as the unlined patch pocket. The lining is sewn to the edge of the facing, so that as the hand enters the pocket, the garment fabric is visible, not the lining fabric.

• To create the lining pattern piece, fold over the facing on the pocket pattern. Trace the bottom area of the pocket, adding a ½-inch seam allowance to the upper edge of the lining piece.
• Sew the lining piece to the lower edge of the pocket facing, leaving an opening of 1 inch in the middle. Press the seams open (Figure 5.8a).
• With the correct sides of the lining and the pocket fabric together, stitch together both pieces, beginning at the top of the pocket facing and continuing around to the opposite side. Clip corners and trim seam allowances (Figure 5.8b).
• Carefully pull the pocket to the correct side through the opening in the middle of the facing seam allowance. Press. Slipstitch the 1-inch opening closed (Figure 5.8c).

• Match the pocket markings to the garment for pocket placement. Place over a seam roll or a tailoring ham, and pin the pocket in place.
• Edgestitch or topstitch the pocket to the garment.

Patch Pocket with Flap
A pocket with a flap is both decorative and functional. It can be decorative and made in any shape to repeat design details of the garment. Occasionally, details such as flaps may be added at the end of construction of a garment as a brilliant decorative design detail. A flap can be functional, acting as a covering of the pocket opening. When creating this pocket, be mindful of proportion. The flap should not overwhelm the pocket. Accurate marking of pocket placement is also important to ensure that both the pocket and flap line up evenly. Because it is applied to the surface of the garment, any detail out of order will be glaringly obvious and detract from the design. The stitching must be impeccable!

• To begin, determine the size of the pocket. The patch pocket will be sewn to the garment first (Figure 5.9a).
• The flap should extend beyond the sides of the pocket; at least ⅛ inch to ensure that the flap totally covers the pocket when sewn (Figure 5.9b). This may vary, however, depending on the weight of the garment fabric. If the fabric is very bulky or heavy, increase this measurement to accommodate the turning of the seam allowances of the flap. To further reduce bulk, consider using

A)

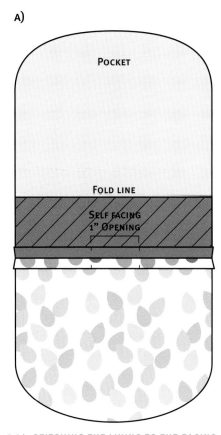

5.8A STITCHING THE LINING TO THE FACING

B)

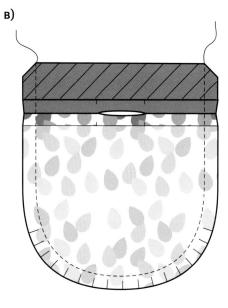

5.8B STITCHING A FACED LINING TO THE POCKET, CLIPPING, AND TRIMMING

C)

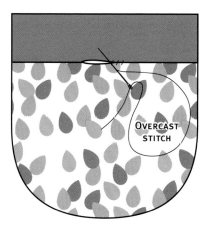

5.8C SLIPSTITCHING THE LINING TO THE FACING

lining fabric for the underlayer of the flap. Cut two pieces of fabric (or one piece of garment fabric and one piece of lining fabric if your fabric is bulky) for the determined flap shape and size.

- Interfacing the flaps helps to maintain the shape (refer to Chapter 3, "Interfacing and Other Stabilizers"); cut one piece of interfacing for each flap. With correct sides of the fabric together, stitch around three sides of

the flap, leaving the top open for turning. Clip corners of side seams to reduce bulk.

- Turn and press. Add any type of decorative stitching, such as topstitching, to the flap before continuing.
- Place the flap above the pocket, with the flap opening facing the top of the pocket. The flap should extend slightly beyond the sides of the pocket. Pin in place. Stitch along the seam allowance, clip the corners to reduce the bulk, and trim the seam allowance to $1/8$ inch (see Figure 5.9a). Fold the flap down, press, and topstitch the flap $1/4$ inch from the folded edge (see Figure 5.9b). This keeps the flap in a downward position, covering the top of the pocket.

Side-Front Slanted Pockets

Two different pattern pieces are used to create and sew this pocket: the side-front section, which is cut from the garment fabric, and the pocket section, which can be cut from lining fabric or garment fabric, depending on the weight of the fabric. Be creative—the shaping and the look of the garment are up to the designer. Begin with the pocket pieces:

- The pocket side-front section is cut from garment fabric and the under pocket from lining to reduce bulk.
- Stabilize the pocket edge (Figure 5.10a and Figure 3.13).
- Serge the outside edges of the pocket pieces.

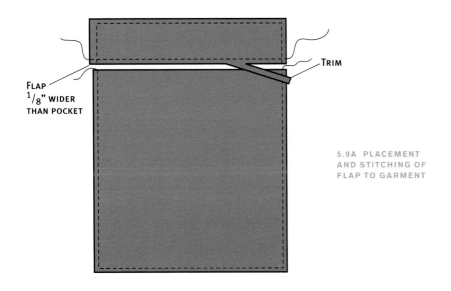

5.9A PLACEMENT
AND STITCHING OF
FLAP TO GARMENT

FLAP
$^1/_8$" WIDER
THAN POCKET

TRIM

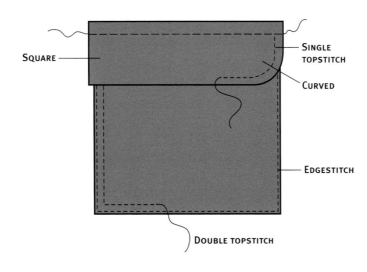

SQUARE

SINGLE
TOPSTITCH

CURVED

EDGESTITCH

DOUBLE TOPSTITCH

5.9B PLACEMENT AND STITCHING OF
FLAP TO GARMENT

• With the correct sides together, stitch the lining to the pocket edge using ¼-inch seam allowance. Press (Figure 5.10b).

• Press the seam allowances toward the pocket lining and understitch.

• Press the pocket on the front side using a pressing cloth; topstitch the pocket edge (Figure 5.10c).

• Place the side front onto the pocket section, matching waistline and hipline notches (Figure 5.10c).

• From the wrong side of the garment, stitch around the pocket pieces only, using a ½-inch seam allowance. Staystitch along the waist pocket area and where the pocket joins the side seam (Figure 5.10d). This keeps the pieces in place during construction. The pocket edges could be serged together as a final finishing to the seams.

Single-Layer Pockets

A **single-layer pocket** is a pocket that is **top-stitched** to the surface of the garment. Often found on casual garments of lightweight fabric, it is exactly what the name implies: a single layer of fabric cut into a pocket shape, finished on all sides with a side opening, and stitched to the surface of a garment. Functional or decorative, it can be in any shape that suits the design of your garment.

• Clean finish all the edges of the pocket. Ease stitch around the curves or corners of the pocket. Press under the seam allowances. Topstitch ¼ inch from the pressed edges. Edgestitch the pocket hand opening, pulling the thread to the wrong side of the pocket and tying a knot.

- Carefully place the pocket, aligning match-points on the pocket to the garment, and pin into place. Edgestitch the pocket to the garment, beginning at the upper opening of the pocket, pivoting at the top, continuing around the pocket to the opposite pocket opening. Backstitch at the beginning and end to reinforce the sewing. Press. A decorative thread could be used to draw attention to this detail, but keep in mind that a steady sewing hand must guide these stitches for a truly excellent result.

Outside Shaped Single-Layer Pocket—Topstitched

Similar to the patch pocket, an outside single-layer pocket can also extend up into the waistline, creating belt loops, or it can extend into the waistline, finished by the waistband or facing. Creating a casual look, it is constructed before being sewn onto the surface of the garment. Some fabrics may require stabilizing such as fusible interfacing (refer to Chapter 3, "Introduction to Stabilizers").

- A pocket pattern of any shape can be used for this application. One example is using the pocket pieces from the side-front slanted pocket application. The pocket can be curved, slanted, squared—whatever shape

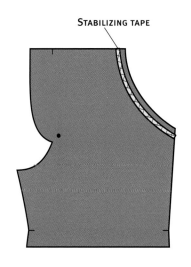

5.10A STABILIZING THE POCKET EDGE

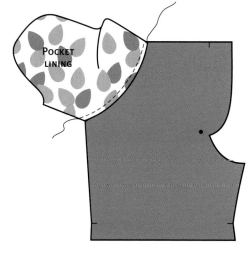

5.10B STITCHING POCKET AND UNDERSTITCHING

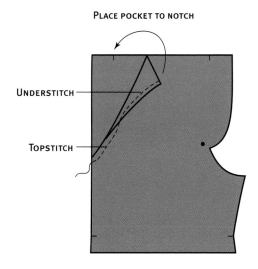

5.10C STITCHING THE SIDE-FRONT POCKETS

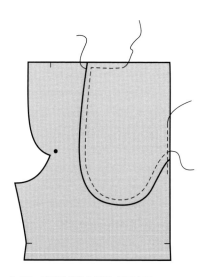

5.10D STITCHING THE SERGED EDGE OF THE POCKETS

and proportion suits the design of your garment. Be creative and have fun!

- Clean finish all the edges of the pocket if it will not show through the fabric to the correct side. Turn under the seam allowances; if the pocket edges are curved, stitch $1/8$ inch around the curves first, and then clip along the curve if necessary so the pocket lies flat. If the corners are squared, it may be necessary to clip into the corners to allow the seam allowances to lie flat and to reduce bulk. Press and use the stitching line as a guide.
- Accurately place the pocket on the garment, pin in place, and edgestitch. On linear-shaped pockets, stitch a second row of topstitching $1/4$ inch from the edgestitching. This provides additional support for the pocket (functional design) as well as decorative finishing.

Pleated, Gathered Pockets

To create pleated or gathered pockets, the finished size of the pocket must be determined before adding the amounts needed for the pleats or gathers. Proportion plays a very important part in this determination. A small pocket would not look good with a very large pleat taking up its entire surface, nor would a very large pocket look good with a few tiny gathers, looking more like wrinkles than gathers. The type of fabric being used will also dictate whether gathers or pleats will be used. Pleats generally look best on a square or rectangular-shaped pocket, while gathers look fullest on rounded shapes. Before you begin, consider:

- Is this pocket functional or decorative?
- Will the pockets be in proportion to the garment?
- Will this pocket enhance the design enough to justify the time and cost involved?
- Will this design detail prompt the customer to "have to have it"?

Pleated Pockets

Pleats are well recognized features of garments such as skirts or kilts, but they are a strong linear detail that can be applied elsewhere on garments such as at necklines, collars, cuffs, and yes, pockets. (Refer to Chapter 7, "Tucks and Pleats.") The functional part of the pleat is the extra fabric that adds volume in the pocket. The decorative aspect of a pleated pocket is the linear repetition, and whether the pleat is crisp or soft.

There are four basic pleat styles, which can be used singly or in a series: knife pleats, in which the folds go in one direction; box pleats, with two folds turned away from each other and under folds meeting in the center; inverted pleats, which are box pleats in reverse with folds turned toward each other and meeting; and accordion pleats. Accordion pleats would be the least likely pleat to be used in a pocket.

- For crisp folded edges on the pleats, edgestitch the front edges of the pleats. Leave the pleats unstitched for a softer look.
- Place strips of brown paper under each pleat to avoid ridging on the front of the fabric when pressing. Using a pressing cloth, press the pleat thoroughly. Baste across the top and

bottom of the pleats to hold in place while finishing construction of the pocket.

Gathered Pockets

Gathers are small, soft folds made by machine basting two rows of stitches within the seam allowance and pulling up the bobbin thread. Gathers complement a round-shaped pocket (see Figure 5.13). Refer to Chapter 6 (Figure 6.23) for more information on gathers.

Fabric choice is a major consideration in gathering the pocket into soft folds. Always sample your fabric using various stitch lengths to produce the softest folds. Avoid using fabric that produces stiff gathers that resemble folds, unless that is the desired effect.

Welt Pockets

Welt Pockets—Single, Double, with Flap

Welt pockets are not difficult, but they do require great accuracy in marking, and precision in cutting and stitching. A shorter stitch length helps control for accuracy when beginning and ending the stitching. Single welt pockets and welt pockets with flaps are considered variations of the double welt pocket. When flaps are added to the welt pocket, they are slipped under the upper welt and stitched after the welts have been stitched, but before the pocket bag is completed. The standard length of the welt pocket is 5 inches but can easily be made shorter or longer for comfort or design aesthetic. Careful marking of the pocket placement on the correct side of the garment begins this technique (Figure 5.11a).

PATTERN TIP FOR GATHERED POCKET IN FIGURE 5.13

- Slash and spread the pocket from the top marked notches to the bottom marked notches, cutting to, but not through, the notches to create the extra fabric needed for gathering. Doubling the width creates quite a bit of fullness, so create a sample to establish the look that complements the design of the garment. Draw a new pocket pattern piece, marking the seam allowances with notches.
- Sew a row of stitches within the ¹/₂-inch seam allowance at the top of the pocket, leaving the ¹/₂-inch side seam allowances unstitched. Pull up the bobbin thread to create the gathers (see Figure 6.23).
- Create a separate facing piece for the top of the pocket that matches the finished size and shape of the gathered pocket. This may be shaped, as the pocket may enlarge down the side seam as it accommodates the gathering. Clean finish the edge of the pocket facing with serging or the clean-edge seam treatment. Or, a narrow bias strip can be used to finish this edge (refer to Chapter 12, "Facings").

- Distribute the gathers evenly along the top of the pocket, tying the threads into knots to hold the gathering stitches.
- With the correct sides together, pin the facing piece to the top of the pocket and sew together using a ¹/₄-inch seam allowance, beginning at the bottom of the facing at the side seam, sewing to the top of the pocket, pivoting, sewing over to the opposite top of the pocket, pivoting, and continuing down the side seam. Clip corners, turn, and press. Turn under the remaining ¹/₂-inch seam allowance of the pocket, using an ease stitch to gather in the fullness at the curved lower edge, and press well. If the fabric is lightweight, a facing may shadow through. Use a piece of bias-cut fabric to finish the edge.
- Pin the pocket in place, "pin basting" the fullness of the pocket to avoid catching tucks or pleats of fabric at the edges, which creates an unprofessional appearance.
- Carefully match the pocket to the garment markings and pin in place. Stitch the pocket to the garment. Use care while pressing the stitched seam allowance to avoid pressing the gathers flat.

- First, measure the length of the finished welt pocket. Handbaste or mark the length clearly on the fabric of the garment, taking care that the other pockets are evenly placed as well. Nothing detracts more from welt pockets than being uneven!
- Reinforce the area behind the pocket. This may already be fully underlined with fus-ible or sew-in interfacing. Pink the edges to prevent ridging from appearing on the front of the fabric (Figure 5.11b).
- Cut two welts, 1½ inches wide by 8 inches long, from the garment fabric or contrasting fabric for each pocket. The welt can be cut on the same grainline as the garment, on the crosswise grain, or on the true bias. Fold the welts in half, interfacing at least half of the welt, and baste exactly ¼ inch from the fold (this will be the stitching guideline). Trim the edges of the welts to ¼ inch (Figure 5.11c). The width of the seam allowance and the welt must be equal for the welts to work.

- Place the welts on the garment fronts with the raw edges of the welts meeting in the middle of the pocket marking. Handbaste or pin in place. Check with a ruler that the stitching lines of the welts are exactly ½ inch apart (Figure 5.11d).
- Guided by the stitching lines on the welts, and using a small stitch length (2.5 or smaller, depending on your fabric), stitch the welts to the garment. Press.
- Slash the garment *only* down the middle of the stitching lines, cutting to within a ½ inch of the end placement lines. Cut diagonally into the corners, up to, but not through, the stitches (Figure 5.11e).
- Place a drop of liquid Fray Check in the corners to prevent fraying of loosely woven fabrics. Test the Fray Check on a scrap of your fabric before applying it to the welts or your garment.
- Carefully pull the welts through to the

IMPORTANT

Begin and end exactly at the placement lines; backstitch a few stitches to secure, or the pocket will end up uneven from the correct side.

A)

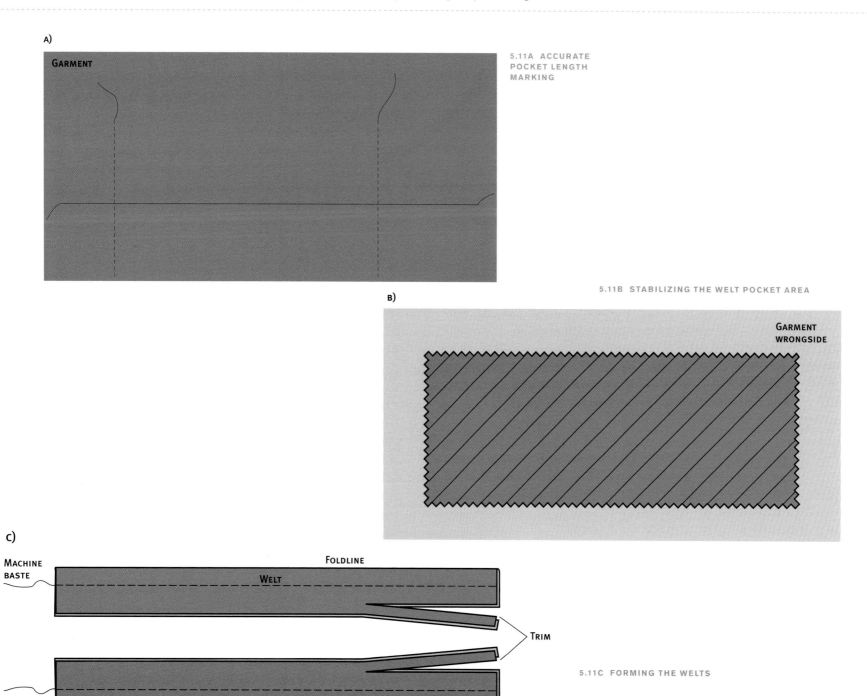

GARMENT

5.11A ACCURATE
POCKET LENGTH
MARKING

5.11B STABILIZING THE WELT POCKET AREA

B)

GARMENT
WRONGSIDE

C)

MACHINE
BASTE

FOLDLINE

WELT

TRIM

5.11C FORMING THE WELTS

D)

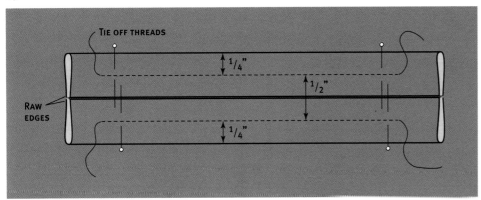

5.11D ACCURATE PLACEMENT OF WELTS AND HANDBASTING

E)

5.11E SLASHING THE WELT OPENING

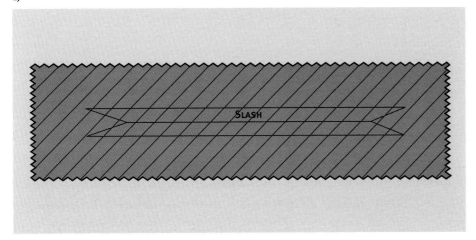

5.11F HANDBASTING THE WELTS TOGETHER

F)

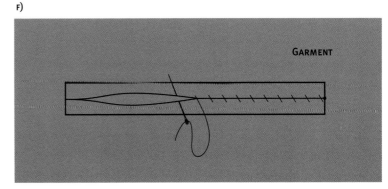

back of the garment. From the front of the garment, arrange the welts so that they are straight and even. Using silk thread or Sil-amide, baste the welts together (Figure 5.11f).

- If any puckers occur in the corners, turn the welts back to the outside and clip further into the corners, releasing the pulls or puckers.

To make the pockets:

- Cut two pocket pieces: one of garment fabric, and one of lining.
- Place the garment fabric pocket piece against the upper welt; stitch along the previous stitching lines. Stitch the lining to the bottom welt.

- With the correct side of the garment facing you, turn it back, exposing the small triangles from the slashing. Machine stitch through the triangles several times to secure (Figure 5.11g), and continue stitching the pocket pieces together to the top of the other side (Figure 5.11h). Trim the excess fabric, leaving a ¾-inch seam allowance.

Piped Pockets

To avoid confusion, sometimes the welt pockets are referred to as piped pockets. Premade piping of fabric matching or contrasting with the garment can be used as the welts for the double welt pocket. Or, cording can be placed within the welts, forming a "piping." The construction

G)

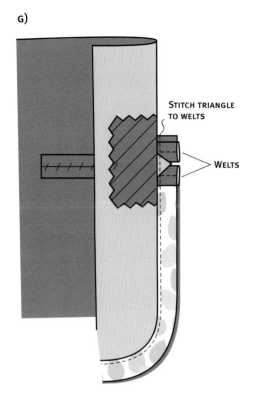

STITCH TRIANGLE
TO WELTS

WELTS

5.11G SECURING THE TRIANGULAR ENDS
OF THE SLASH POCKET OPENING,
AND STITCHING THE POCKET

H)

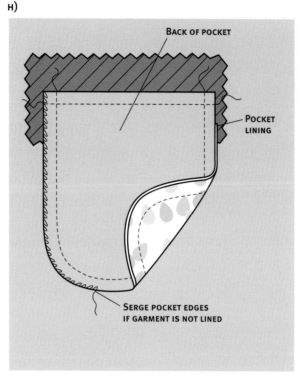

BACK OF POCKET

POCKET
LINING

SERGE POCKET EDGES
IF GARMENT IS NOT LINED

5.11H SECURING THE TRIANGULAR ENDS
OF THE SLASH POCKET OPEN

is the same, but the cording, which is the same length as the welt, is placed within the welts as they are positioned on the garment front, and before the triangles left from slashing are sewn and reinforced. Any excess cording is trimmed away before the triangles are stitched to reduce bulk. The cording produces a rounded effect of the welts.

Begin with wider-than-needed strips of bias when making piping. It's easier to work with and to cut off the unneeded width after the piping is sewn.

Pockets with Zippers

Pockets with zippers can be both functional and decorative. Because of the wide variety of zippers available, these pockets are useful on sportswear but can be applied to other garments as well. On pockets, a 5- or 7-inch zipper works well.

- Extend this pattern to a length that is comfortable for the hand to fit into from the side or the top, and that is in proportion to the garment you are making. Separate the pattern into three pieces: the upper pocket, the lower pocket, and the lining, which can be made from flannel or fleece for warmth. This pocket is constructed before placement on the garment and topstitching.

- With the correct sides of the upper pocket together, place the zipper in between the two layers and stitch with a ¼-inch seam allowance (Figure 5.12a). The zipper teeth will be facing the correct side of the fabric and the zipper stop must be included in this length. Turn the upper pocket to the correct side and press, edgestitching along the fold, near the teeth (Figure 5.12b).

- With the correct sides of the lower pocket together, place the other side of the zipper tape in between the two layers and stitch again, at ¼-inch seam allowance. Turn the lower pocket to the correct side, press, and then edgestitch along the fold near the teeth of the zipper (Figure 5.12b).

- With the teeth of the zipper showing on the correct side of the pocket, place the correct side of the lining piece against it. Carefully stitch around the entire pocket using a ¼-inch seam allowance; avoid stitching through the zipper, which could break the needle. Clip the corners to reduce bulk; make a slash through the lining near the bottom just large enough to pull the pocket through. The slash opening can be fused closed with a piece of fusible interfacing or hand stitched together (Figure 5.12c).

- Place the pocket on the garment, matching markings for placement. Edgestitch the pocket, leaving an opening on the side or the top, large enough for easy hand entry. Backstitch to reinforce this opening, and stitch again ¼ inch away from the first stitching (Figure 5.12d).

Pocket with Exposed Zipper

Popular on sportswear and novelty-shaped pockets alike, the exposed zipper is inserted into a "window"-shaped opening in the pocket.

• Because the pocket is cut open, the entire shape of the pocket needs to be interfaced to control and prevent fraying. (Refer to Chapter 3, "Introduction to Stabilizers.") Mark the opening ¼ inch wide and ⅛ inch longer than the zipper being applied on the wrong side of the pocket. Stitch around the "window" using a short stitch of 1.5 or 2.0. Slash open the "window," clipping into the corners, but not through the stitching.

• Carefully turn the edges to the back of the pocket; press. Baste the turned-back edges to the pocket. (Same stitching method used in Figures 17.14 a and b.)

• Place the zipper under the "window." Baste in place or use a temporary adhesive basting tape (refer to Chapter 3, "Introduction to Stabilizers") to hold the zipper in place. Edgestitch around the opening, then stitch again ¼ inch away from the first row of stitching.

• Press under the seam allowances, place the pocket on the garment, and topstitch.

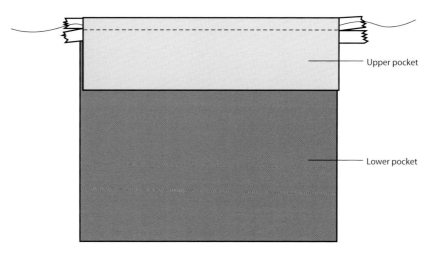

Upper pocket

Lower pocket

5.12A STITCHING THE ZIPPER TO THE UPPER POCKET

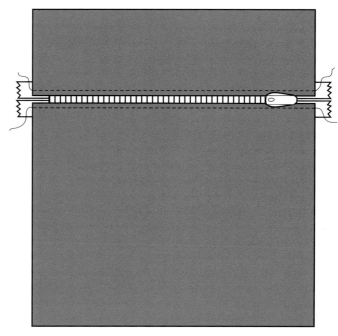

5.12B EDGESTITCHING THE ZIPPER TO THE LOWER POCKET

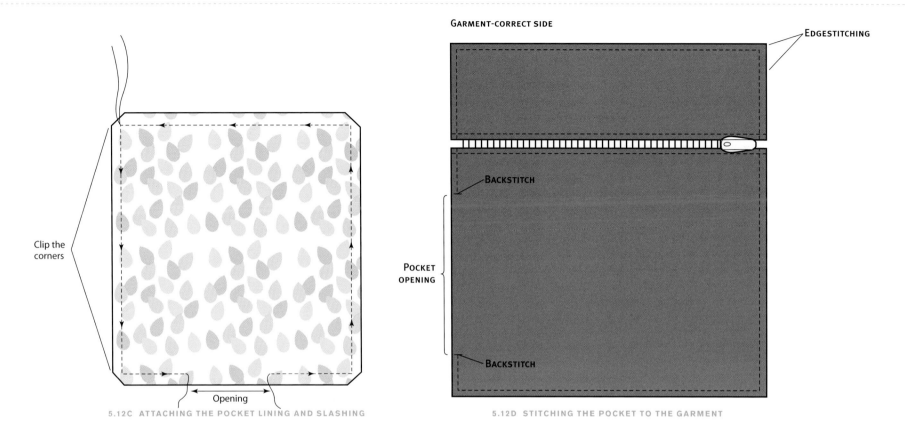

Clip the corners

Opening

5.12C ATTACHING THE POCKET LINING AND SLASHING

GARMENT-CORRECT SIDE

EDGESTITCHING

BACKSTITCH

POCKET OPENING

BACKSTITCH

5.12D STITCHING THE POCKET TO THE GARMENT

Pocket Flaps and Welts

The flap can be inserted into a welt or placed over a pocket. The difference between a flap and a welt is that a **flap** hangs down without any securing stitches, whereas a **welt** usually is placed facing upward and is stitched along its sides to the garment. The flap is functional, covering the top of a pocket. Both the flap and the welt can be used decoratively, stitched to the garment without a pocket underneath. They both can be made into any shape that complements the design of the garment or provides a contrasting detail to highlight the design.

- The *rectangular-shaped flap* is most commonly used.
- Interfacing is applied to half of the flap/welt, which is cut in the same direction as the garment surface. Fold in half, with correct sides together, and stitch the side seams together at ½-inch seam allowance. Clip the corners to reduce bulk, turn, and press (see Figure

5.3a). This flap/welt can also be made in two pieces, using lining fabric for the under flap to reduce bulk. Any decorative stitching on the flap/welt should be done before attaching the flap/welt to the garment.

- The flap is attached to the garment by matching the markings for placement. The flap is placed with the raw edges facing toward the hem. The raw edges can be clean finished by serging, or if the fabric is lightweight enough, the raw edges can be folded inside and basted closed.

- Stitch along the foldline through the flap seam allowances and garment.
- Fold the flap to the correct side of the garment; press. Topstitch ¼ inch from the folded, pressed edge, securing the flap to the garment.

The *rounded pocket flap*, as shown in Figure 5.3b, is constructed in two pieces, with an upper flap/welt of garment fabric and an under flap of garment fabric or lining fabric. Any novelty shaped flap/welt would be constructed the same way.

- Stabilize with interfacing.
- After stitching around the curve, cut notches up to, but not through the line of stitching. Trim the seam allowance to ¼ inch. Press, and turn the pocket to the correct side. The notching reduces the bulk around the curve, allowing the fabric to lie smoothly.
- Turn the pocket to the correct side and press. Any decorative stitching on the flap/welt would be done before attaching to the garment.
- Continue construction as above.

The *pointed flap/welt* can be centered or asymmetrical (off-center) for more interest. Constructed in two pieces, an upper flap/welt of garment or contrasting fabric, and an under flap/welt of matching fabric or lining, it follows the same steps as listed above, with the following exception:

- When stitching the side seams down to the point, pivot at the point and take two small, straight stitches across the point before pivoting again, and continuing up the opposite side.
- The two straight stitches at the point allow clipping, easing the turning point, and actually creating a sharper point. Use a point turner in this area, very carefully so as not to push the point turner through the point.

All pocket flap/welts can be topstitched. This stitching should be done to the welt *before* sewing it to the garment or pocket. Topstitching can be one or more rows of functional/decorative machine stitching through all the layers of the flap/welt. Topstitching is stitched from the correct side of the flap/welts, and sewn very carefully, parallel to the seam line. Topstitching is functional in that it holds the flap/welt flat. It is decorative as an accent of seam lines, and to emphasize the structural lines of the flap/welt. Thread can match or contrast. Specialty thread can be used, or two strands of needle thread. A steady hand directing the stitching and close attention to accuracy makes this detail an outstanding addition to the flap/welts or other areas of the garment.

Pocket flap/welts can be enhanced by piping, as explained in Chapter 6. Piping is a folded bias strip made in various widths of the same or contrasting fabric. It can be filled with cording to create a rounded shape, or it can be made without cording. Because the piping is made from bias, it's flexible, allowing it to be shaped (Figures 6.20 and 6.21). This decorative technique can be used to emphasize convex or concave curves, or scalloped edges, and to provide a design detail and point of interest to edges. Accurate sewing that maintains the width of the piping is absolutely necessary when drawing attention to lines and curves.

Piping can be premade or made to match the flap/welts. Insert the piping between the seam allowances, matching the raw edges of the piping to the raw edges of the flap/welts. Stitch the seam allowance using a zipper foot, which allows the needle to stitch closely to the sandwiched piping. The seam allowance can vary from narrow (¼ inch), which reduces bulk, to wider (½ inch or more) for easier application. *SEW, CLIP, PRESS.* The piping is now on the outside edges of the flap/welt.

BAR TACKS

Bar tacks are used to reinforce small areas of strain, such as at the upper edges of the pockets and elsewhere on garments. When made by a home sewing machine, a group of zigzag stitches overlap or touch one another or there is a special stitch for this technique. In industrial sewing, specialized machines produce this stitch. As a couture touch on tailored garments, this stitch is called the Arrowhead tack. Use topstitching thread, buttonhole twist thread, or two strands of needle thread to create this stitch by hand.

CLOSURES ON POCKETS

There are two basic categories of closures for pockets: functional and decorative. Functional closures are those elements that actually work, such as buttonholes, buttons/loops, zippers, tabs and buckles, and D-rings, to mention a few.

Decorative, nonworking closures add a design element to the garment when applied to the pocket or flap. Some examples include buttons applied over a stitched buttonhole that is not cut open, fabric frogs applied to the surface of the pocket, an unopened zipper stitched directly on the surface of the pocket, or loops applied along the upper edge of the pocket. (Refer to Chapter 17, "Closures.") As long as the decorative closures add appeal, and complement and work with the fabric weight and hand, have the courage to use something unique!

POCKETS IN TRICKY FABRICS
Stripes or Plaids

Changing direction when using stripes or plaids can add an exciting design element to the garment. When turning the direction of the grainline, consider how this element affects the look

IMPORTANT

Reinforce the area supporting the closures with stabilizer that is appropriate for the garment fabric.

of the garment and whether the cost of the additional fabric needed is justified when using bias. Bias pockets made from stripes or plaids require stabilizing; changing the lengthwise grainline to the crosswise grainline may produce some stretching. Stabilize the entire pocket, or use stay tape at the upper edge to prevent stretching.

Sheer Fabrics

Sheer fabrics fall into two categories: firmly woven, such as organdy, or softer, more drapable sheer, such as chiffon. When working with these fabrics, extra care must be taken in cutting and sewing (Figure 2.19). For greater accuracy in cutting and sewing, use tissue paper over and under the fabric.

Purchase a package of multicolored gift tissue and use a color that is similar to the fabric you are using, whether it is a solid or a print. The tissue tears away easily, but if tiny bits are left within the seam allowance, it will be less noticeable than white tissue paper.

A detail such as a pocket that is functional needs to be underlined. Pockets in sheer fabrics such as georgette or batiste can be underlined using another firm sheer fabric such as silk organza for support.

A decorative pocket such as a gathered pocket made from chiffon can be self-lined.

Always match the fabric to the use. A fabric can be made to work in a way for which it was not intended as a design statement. In order for it to look well made, it must complement and enhance the design, as well as be impeccably constructed.

Lace, Beaded, Velvet, and Satin Fabrics

These very special-care fabrics that require particular attention to careful handling can all be stitched as in-seam pockets. Because of the potential bulkiness of velvet and lace, a facing pocket paired with lining will reduce the bulk and produce a smooth, flat pocket. When using beaded fabrics for in-seam pockets, all of the beading should be removed from the surface of the pocket fabric before stitching. Satin fabrics will often show ridging on the surface of the garment if serging is used to finish seams; finish the seam edges of the pocket with sheer Seams Great for the flattest, smoothest finish.

Knits

Any type of pocket could conceivably be made in knit fabric, but the success of the pocket style depends on the weight and stretch of the knit. For example, you would not put a tailored, welt pocket into slinky knit—the stretch of the knit would completely prevent the finished pocket from interacting with the drape of the knit. Patch pockets are often found on stable knit garments that are heavier weight. In-seam pockets are most often used on skirts, dresses, and pants made from knit fabric.

Denim

All styles of pockets are fabulous in denim. Sample the style of pocket you want to use before placing it onto or into the garment.

Leather

Any style of pocket that can be made in fabric can also be made in leather. Welt pockets can be constructed as described earlier. Lighter weight skins of leather have some give and require stabilizing (only use low-temperature fusible) to prevent stretching. Test several weights and types of interfacing on sample pieces of leather to obtain a perfect match. (Refer to Chapter 3, "Introduction to Stabilizers.") Use stabilizer tape at the top edge of leather pockets to prevent the pocket opening from stretching. Use craft glue to position patch pockets on the surface of a leather garment.

TRANSFER YOUR KNOWLEDGE

This chapter has explained the many different types of pockets; the importance of accurate marking, cutting, and stitching; how to assemble and create both functional and decorative styles of pockets and flaps; and how pockets and flaps are used in design. Pockets are attention-getting elements and, for this reason, it is best to start out perfecting the easiest pocket, trying all the possible combinations that can be made of that pocket, and then moving on to another, more complex pocket.

- Let's say a garment design calls for tweed, and the welt of the pocket would look great in leather. You've never sewn with leather before, but you know how to accurately mark, carefully cut, evenly stitch, pivot, clip, trim, and stabilize patch pockets.
- Putting it all together by thinking of what you do know, you can begin to:
  – Stabilize the front of the garment.
  – Accurately mark the welt placement.
  – Straight stitch the welts from leather.

Knowing these techniques will get you started. Then, with the help of your instructor and by following the explanations of the welt pockets, you can learn to stitch the welt pocket in leather or another fabric, broadening your sewing skills. Given what you learned from stitching patch pockets and flaps, you will transfer that knowledge to other pocket designs and fabrics such as the welt pocket in leather.

The cutting, marking, and stitching you have learned in this chapter can also be transferred to the following design suggestions:

- Choose a detail from the print of the design fabric, such as a flower or a geometric design. Create a pocket from this detail.
- Mimic the lines of the fabric print on a shaped flap, and topstitch with a contrasting thread color from the print.
- Add piping to the edge of a one-piece flap pocket with a machine-stitched buttonhole.
- Bind the edges of a rounded, gathered pocket with bias binding on a single-layer pocket.

STRETCH YOUR CREATIVITY

As a creative person training to be a fashion designer, your willingness to experiment with new ideas is critical. Taking the basic patch pocket, flap, or shaped side pocket as a start, you can create many different versions as shown in Figure 5.13. Try some of the listed suggestions, have fun, and see where the design ends up!

- Layer several differently sized and shaped pocket flaps of different colors or textures, and so forth, but consider bulk and fabric weight at the top of the flap.
- Cut an asymmetrical flap that folds over at two different points.
- Create an unusual novelty pocket with wildly contrasting lining.
- Make a shaped welt pocket, such as a triangle or a curve.
- Turn the direction of the grainline of a welt pocket to achieve a different look in the design, using the same sewing techniques.
- Use decorative machine stitches to topstitch pocket flaps.
- Create a false piping by cutting the lining $1/4$ inch larger than the pocket, rolling it to the outside, and topstitching the pocket to the garment.
- Create a border of sheer organza gathered pockets to trim the neckline and hem of a linen dress—strictly decorative!
- Add a ruffle around the pocket; could be cut on bias with raw edges or a folded ruffle.
- Experiment with changing the direction of

5.13 VARIATIONS ON THE BASIC POCKET AND FLAP

PATCH POCKET ⟶ BECOMES

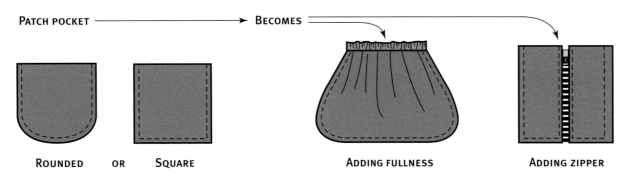

ROUNDED OR SQUARE

ADDING FULLNESS

ADDING ZIPPER

POCKET FLAP ⟶ BECOMES

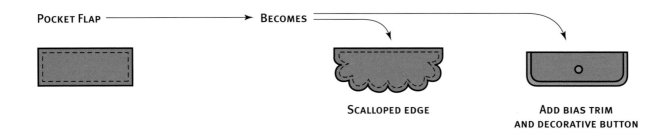

SCALLOPED EDGE

ADD BIAS TRIM
AND DECORATIVE BUTTON

SIDE POCKET ⟶ BECOMES

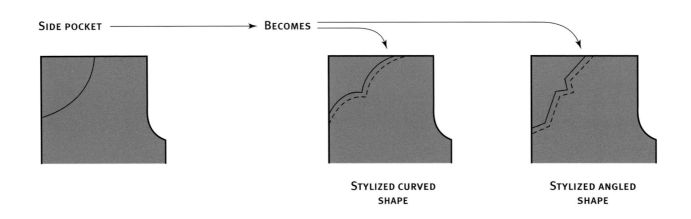

STYLIZED CURVED
SHAPE

STYLIZED ANGLED
SHAPE

the pockets in an asymmetrical design.

- Create a sheer, single-layer pocket with drape at top of the pocket; leave edges raw.
- Use two rows of topstitching to create "jeans" pockets. Create your own design, using unique thread.

STOP! WHAT DO I DO IF . . .

. . . the welt slashes are too big and extend beyond the markings?

If you have slashed too far, you can first try to adjust the stitching to extend beyond the slashing if it doesn't involve too many stitches. However, the welts will not be sewn at the same size, so you will also have to add stitches to the welts to attempt to match it all up. This is very difficult, but worth a try. This solution only has a chance of working if you have not already trimmed the excess length of the welts. Otherwise, you will have to cut longer welts and restitch.

. . . the patch pockets are unevenly sewn despite careful pinning?

Accurate placement of the patch pockets is essential. Using various marking supplies such as fabric marking pens, transfer paper with a tracing wheel, or stitch tracing on very difficult fabrics can help. In production, small drill holes are placed $1/8$ inch down from the top of the pocket placement and $1/8$ inch in from the side of the pocket placement. The pocket, if accurately placed, covers these holes. The solution to slipped, pinned pockets can be handbasting of the pocket or trying an adhesive basting tape to temporarily hold the pocket in place while stitching.

SELF-CRITIQUE

- Are the pockets cut on the correct grainlines?
- Are the pockets placed evenly—that is, are they symmetrical (unless in the design they are asymmetrical)?
- Are the pocket seam allowances turned smoothly—with no puckering or unnecessary, unintended gathering?
- Are the decorative elements such as buttons, trim, piping, or closures sewn on invisibly?
- Are the welts exactly even in width over the pocket opening?
- Is there any puckering at the corners where the welts have been turned?
- Do the flaps or shaped pockets lie flat, without bulk?

REVIEW CHECKLIST

What do patch pockets with all-in-one flaps and patch pockets with separate flaps have in common? Indicate what you don't understand, and ask your instructor for further help.

- They both can be lined to the edge with self-fabric, contrasting fabric, or lining.
- The flaps are stabilized.
- They both can be made into many unique shapes.
- They both can have functional closures.
- They both can have decorative applications to the pocket or flap.
- Depending on their size, they can be functional or decorative.

Look at your pockets and ask yourself:

- Is this pocket functional, and does it actually work?
- Does the pocket look like it belongs with the design?
- Does the pocket enhance the design enough to justify the time and cost involved?
- Will this pocket detail prompt the customer to "have to have it"?

With practice, patience, accuracy, and good sewing skills, pockets will become a favorite featured design element.

CHAPTER

Seams: Joining It All Together

Seams hold the garment together and give it shape. This aspect of structural design is on view in this chapter. Choosing the appropriate seam finish for the fabric and design is crucial if the garment is to look its very best. In this chapter many seam finishes are explained and illustrated to help guide student designers in their choices. We also offer ideas to extend the student's creativity.

Appropriate seam finishes for different fabric types, such as leather, knits, lace, velvet, and other fabric types, are discussed. The aim is for each student to be able to analyze the fabric and choose the best seam finish that compliments the fabric and design. Seam sampling before any project begins is essential to achieve this goal.

A garment takes form as multiple seams are stitched together until the garment is completed. When designers create collections, the question needs to be asked, "What makes one collection stand out from the others?" Giam-battista Valli, a designer who worked for Karl Lagerfeld, the Fendis, and Emanuel Ungaro, knew what he wanted before he went out on his own. The designer said, "I love to make the type of clothes that brings back the sound of scissors and are more about shape [seams] and cut than draping—clothes that are made of beautiful fabrics and are created by people working with patterns to produce a refined tailoring."[1] Giambattista knows the importance of seams and how they sculpture and shape fabric to the female form.

KEY TERMS

Closed Serged Seam
Enclosed Seam
Godet
Grading
Matchpoints
Open Serged Seam
Pivot
Safety Stitch
Seam Allowance
Serging
Staystitching
Stitch Directional
Stitch-in-the-Ditch
Structural Seam
Topstitching
Twin Needle Topstitching

135

Style I.D.

V-SHAPED
SEAM

EASED
SEAM

GATHERED
SEAM

CIRCULAR
SEAMS

INTERSECTING
SEAMS

PIPED
PRINCESS
SEAMS

ANGLED
TOPSTITCHED
SEAMS

6.1A BRA-TOP DRESS

6.1B CURVED SEAMED
DRESS

6.1C CHECK JACKET AND
HIGH-WAISTED PANTS

6.1D FLORAL SUMMER DRESS

STYLE I.D.

Take a look at the sketches of designs in this chapter in the Style I.D. (Figure 6.1) and observe all the seams that build shape into each garment. Make a list of all the different seams you see.

GATHER YOUR TOOLS

Thread, machine needles (variety of sizes and types), tape measure, seam gauge, pins, scissors, hand sewing needles, fabric markers, stabilizing tapes, and a good sense of humor are needed!

NOW LET'S GET STARTED

What Is a Seam?

The contour of a woman's form is shaped and curved. Seams (and darts) are essential to create the shape required for the garment to contour the bust, waist, and hips of the female form to flatter her figure. It is the designer's challenge to create seams to contour this curvaceous body shape (see Figure 2.7c).

Every seam has **seam allowance** to protect the stitches from pulling away from the seam (Figure 6.2). **Structural seams** such as the shoulder seam, side seam, and sleeve underarm seam help define the garment silhouette. Structural seams are also placed within the garment silhouette to shape the garment to the body. **Enclosed seams** are the edges of collars, some pockets, and waistline and cuff edges. These also help define the garment silhouette. The garment silhouette can also be defined with a folded edge rather than a seam. An illustration of this is the hem.

Seams can be vertical, horizontal, curved, round, or diagonal—a seam can be shaped in

any direction. Take a look at the Style I.D. in Figure 6.1. Can you find these shaped seams?

How Are Seams Created?

The sketch is the designer's guide to how the garment is going to look. After the designer determines the silhouette of the garment—defining the length, width, neckline and armhole shapes, sleeve length, and more—the silhouette becomes the framework within which to work.

The designer then plots the design lines, placing them within the silhouette in accordance with the sketch. Each line drawn represents a dart or a seam. The designer rearranges the lines until all the lines are aesthetically pleasing. The designer uses good eye judgment, looking for proportion, balance, repetition, and ultimately unity of design.

After the seamlines are plotted, **notches**, **matchpoints**, and grainlines are marked onto each pattern piece before they are separated. Seam allowance is added after the pattern pieces are separated. Pattern markings are an essential part of stitching accurate seams. (This concept was introduced in Chapter 2; see "It All Begins with the Pattern.") Cutting the pattern "on grain," following the pattern grainline, ensures that the seams will not look twisted when they are stitched. Even though pattern marking was discussed in Chapter 2, we cannot overemphasize the importance of this step in the design and construction of the garment.

When notches are snipped in the seams, matching the fabric pieces together is a smooth process. Time is not wasted trying to figure out which fabric piece goes where. Figure 6.3a illus-

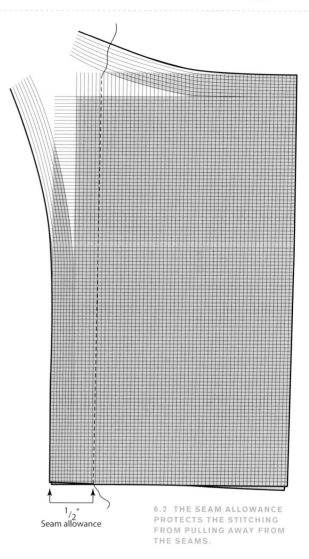

1/2″
Seam allowance

6.2 THE SEAM ALLOWANCE PROTECTS THE STITCHING FROM PULLING AWAY FROM THE SEAMS.

trates how the seams in the front of the bra-top dress (see Figure 6.1a) were stitched when the notches were matched together. Compare with Figure 6.3b. Observe how the same dress looks when notches were *not* snipped at the cutting stage. All the pieces were stitched together incorrectly and stretched to fit seams they didn't belong to. The seams will need to be seam ripped, pressed, and stitched again. This was a waste of precious time! By using pattern markings, success is guaranteed.

Choosing the Best Seam for Your Project

Let's recap what we learned in Chapter 2:

- Keep in mind there is always more than one method of stitching seams.
- To choose the appropriate seam finish for your project, you must *sample!*
- The best guide is the fabric itself—the type and weight.
- The seam finish is the designer's choice; for this reason, sound construction knowledge is important.
- The target customer and the price point of the garment can define the seam finish you choose. For example, a summer jacket could be made in cotton brocade. A Hong Kong finish could be used for the entire jacket (seams, facing, and hem edges). This would be labor intensive, and thus costly, but the completed jacket would look fabulous on the inside. On the other hand, the same fabric could be stitched together with a safety stitch. A safety stitch is a quick, cost-effective seam finish. A well-heeled shopper would purchase the first jacket at a store such as Saks Fifth Avenue; the customer on a budget would purchase the second jacket at a store such as Target or Old Navy. As you can see, identifying the target customer has an impact on the seam techniques that characterize particular collections.

LET'S PREPARE TO STITCH

Let's go over a few basic stitch tips before we begin. These tips, and much more, were discussed in Chapter 2, "Let's Stitch!"

- First thread the sewing machine.
- Check the bobbin tension.
- Use the correct needle size number.
- Adjust the stitch length dial to the appropriate stitch length for the fabric.
- With the tape measure around your neck or seam gauge by your side and pins at your fingertips, you are now ready to begin to stitch seams.
- Stitch a sample seam using two pieces of muslin or the fashion fabric you are using. *Do not* use a single layer of muslin, as this will not give an accurate stitch.

What Do I Do if My Stitches Are Not Quality Stitches?

- Check that the machine is threaded correctly.
- Check the bobbin tension.
- Try a different needle size.
- Try a new needle.
- Experiment with the machine tension.
- Check that you used two pieces of fabric for sampling.

> **IMPORTANT**
>
> High-quality fabrics are easier to stitch than those of poorer quality. Quality fabric, stitching, and finishing are what make one designer's work stand out from another's.

> **IMPORTANT**
>
> Check on both sides of the fabric that the stitch tension is correct. Figure 2.26b illustrates how the stitches look when the tension is correct. Do attend to this now—if your stitch tension is not correct, you cannot stitch quality stitches. Adjust the machine or bobbin tension accordingly.

- Sample again and again . . . with experience it will get easier.

After the fabric has been cut, and pattern markings applied, stabilizers such as an interfacing or an underlining are next in the stitching order. It must be noted that some seams need stabilizing to prevent them from stretching in the stitching process. Any fabric edges cut on the bias grain have the potential to stretch and may need a stabilizing tape (as an alternative to an underlining or an interfacing) to stabilize and reinforce a seam before it is stitched (Figure 3.8). How this is done is covered in Chapter 3, "Stabilizing Tapes." Refer to the stabilizing tape chart in Table 3.1.

After attending to the stabilizer, next in the stitching order is flat construction (such as darts, tucks, and any seams that must be stitched before the side seams are stitched together).

Seam Supports

A seam support is any aid that helps and supports you when stitching seams. Seam supports can vary: tape measure, seam gauge, pins, fabric markers, and handbasting all aid in accurate and

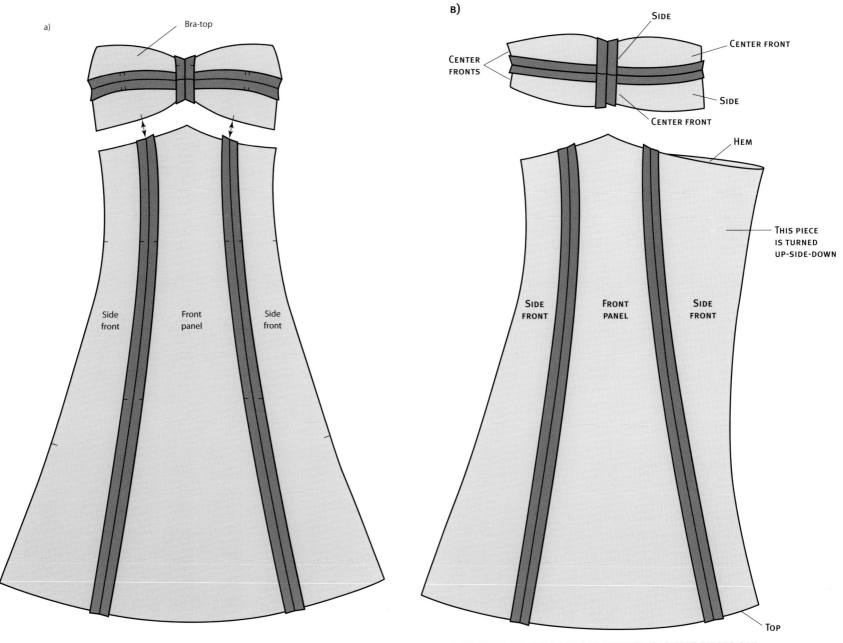

a)

Bra-top

Side front

Front panel

Side front

B)

CENTER FRONTS

SIDE

CENTER FRONT

SIDE

CENTER FRONT

HEM

THIS PIECE IS TURNED UP-SIDE-DOWN

SIDE FRONT

FRONT PANEL

SIDE FRONT

TOP

6.3A WHEN NOTCHES ARE SNIPPED, EACH GARMENT PIECE FITS PERFECTLY TOGETHER. THIS IS THE FRONT SECTION OF THE RED DRESS IN FIGURE 6.1A STITCHED PERFECTLY TOGETHER.

6.3B WHEN NOTCHES ARE NOT SNIPPED, GARMENT PIECES CAN BE TURNED UPSIDE DOWN AND STRETCHED TO FIT OTHER SEAMS AND ARE EASILY STITCHED TOGETHER WRONGLY.

parallel seam stitching. It is *important* to use them and not to skip this process! Students who skip this process usually end up having to undo their stitching and restitch.

Use the following seam supports:

- A tape measure placed around your neck aids you in measuring the seam allowance (Figure 1.1). Guessing the width is *not* good enough!
- A seam gauge also helps to measure accurate seam allowances (Figure 2.1).
- Following the needle plate on the machine can help in stitching the seam to the correct width. Figure 2.23 points to where the throat plate is located on the sewing machine. Some throat plates are marked (¼ inch, ½ inch, ¾ inch, and 1 inch) and some are not—if yours is not, then use your seam gauge to measure the seam allowance.
- Marking the stitching position on both *wrong* sides of the muslin will help new design students stitch seams parallel to the fabric edge. Marking the seamline will also help you remember the width of the seam allowance you are using. Figures 2.21c and d shows how this is done.
- Seam allowances are then secured with pins; however, don't overpin!

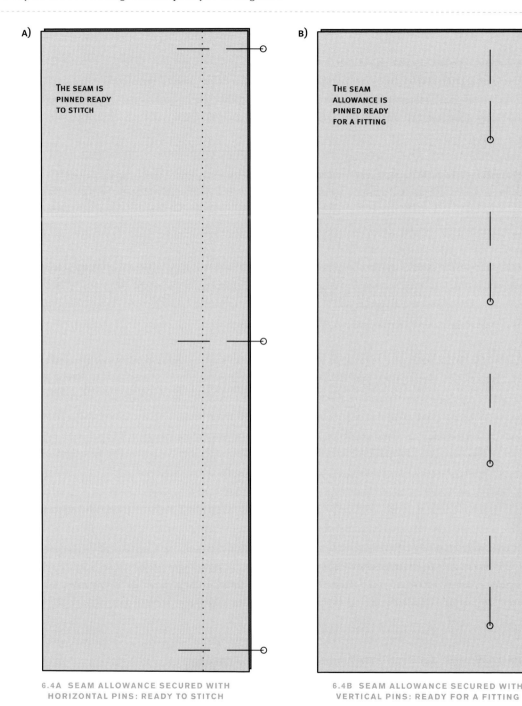

A) THE SEAM IS PINNED READY TO STITCH

B) THE SEAM ALLOWANCE IS PINNED READY FOR A FITTING

6.4A SEAM ALLOWANCE SECURED WITH HORIZONTAL PINS: READY TO STITCH

6.4B SEAM ALLOWANCE SECURED WITH VERTICAL PINS: READY FOR A FITTING

• Pins placed horizontally hold the seams together, ready to be stitched. Remove the pins as you approach them, as stitching over the pins can break the needle (Figure 6.4a).

• Pins placed vertically are used for fitting purposes. Pinning for fitting purposes requires more pins placed closer together (Figure 6.4b).

• Seams can be handbasted together, as illustrated in Figure 6.5. These are temporary hand stitches that help hold the seams together. They are removed after the seam is permanently stitched. Refer to the discussion of handbasting under "Sew-in Stabilizer" in Chapter 3.

• Seams can also be tissue stitched using strips of tissue paper (of the same type used for gift wrapping) in a color nearest to that of the fabric. Cut 2-inch-wide strips of tissue and place them under the seams to stabilize. Line up the tissue paper edge with the seam edge and stitch. Tear the tissue paper away after the seam is completed.

In production, machinists rarely use pins. Remember, a machinist is sewing all day long and we are not! With practice you too will use fewer and fewer pins as you become more experienced. Pins are a wonderful seam support but don't overuse them (such as pinning every inch).

Stitching the "Perfect" Seam

Let's begin by refreshing your memory of the stitching rhythm, *SEW, CLIP, PRESS,* that

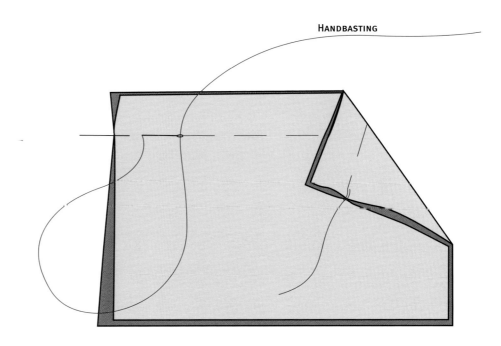

HANDBASTING

6.5 HANDBASTING HELPS TO HOLD THE SEAM IN PLACE.

was discussed in Chapter 2. Begin by using this stitching rhythm with your very first stitches. As you practice this method, you will find in time that it will become second nature. By following this method, you will achieve smooth, flat, perfect seams. Stitching a perfect seam also involves clipping the threads and pressing the seams. Take pride in your work.

It is very important to press each seam as you go. The care and respect given to the garment during construction is important. Overpressing can be disastrous. If all the pressing is left until the end, it can be hard to get back into the garment to press. For more information, refer to Chapter 2, "How to Press a Garment."

The student's aim should be to learn to stitch "perfect" seams.

A "perfect" seam is one that:

• Lies flat and smooth. After seams are stitched, they may look slightly puckered owing to the thread. This could indicate that the bobbin was wound too fast, tightening up the thread; then, as the seam was stitched, it wasn't able to relax. Pressing the seam in the direction in which it was stitched, and then pressing it open, "melds" the stitches into the fabric. Pressing helps seams lie smooth and flat and prepares the fabric to be stitched to the next fabric piece.

- Hangs "on grain" and does not look twisted when the garment is fit on the dress form.
- Does not look stretched, puckered, or wobbly from the correct side of the garment. Crooked or wobbly seam stitching needs to be seam ripped and restitched.

LET'S BEGIN TO STITCH
Staystitch

Staystitching is one single row of stitching stitched to one layer of fabric to reinforce and prevent seams from stretching and distorting in the stitching process. Any fabric can be staystitched to stabilize it—the main consideration isn't the type of fabric, but rather the grainline on which the seam is cut, or the angle of the seamline.

When angled seams are stitched together, the inside corner *must* be clipped into the pivot point or matchpoint before it can be stitched to another garment piece. The pivot point is the corner where the angle meets on the seamline. Look at Figure 6.6a to see the pivot point, and the position of the staystitching. Likewise, before curved or round seams can be stitched, the inward curve needs to be clipped to allow

the seam allowance to spread and open so it can be joined to another shaped fabric piece. Figure 6.6b illustrates this clearly. Any clipped seam has pressure at these points, and a staystitch acts as a fence, preventing the clipping from ripping, fraying, or splitting.

Staystitching also *must* be used for reinforcing angled and shaped neckline edges before a facing or lining is applied. Look at Figure 6.6b, c, and d to see where the staystitching is stitched on the scooped, round, and V necklines.

- If the garment is underlined, apply the staystitching after the underlining has been applied (see Figure 3.17).
- Stitch the staystitch $1/16$ inch inside the seamline.
- Use a small stitch length (2 is a good, general stitch length).
- Staystitch the neckline directionally; in this case, that means stitching from the shoulders to the center front of the neckline. Stitching directional does not distort or stretch the fabric (Figure 6.6b,c, and d).
- To reinforce corners, begin and end at a point 1 inch to either side of the corner (Figure 6.6a). Corners can also be stabilized with fusible or nonfusible interfacing for extra reinforcement. Also notice in this figure that a small piece of interfacing can also be used to reinforce the angled corner. It is important that the interfacing not shadow to the correct side, as this would distract from the overall appearance of the garment.

Stitch Directional

When stitching a seam, it is advisable to stitch from the top of the garment to the bottom of the garment. This approach, referred to as **stitching directional**, prevents the garment pieces from stretching when they are stitched together. By beginning the stitching from the top of the garment, if a *slight* discrepancy in seam lengths occurs, the extra length can be trimmed from the hem. In Figure 6.7a, the pant leg is stitched directional. Later in this chapter, in the section "Intersecting Seams," two pant legs will be stitched together around the crotch seam. The skirt in Figure 6.7b is also stitched directional.

Plain Seam

A plain seam is the most basic and least noticeable of all the seams. It is appropriate for just about any location on the garment, and suits most fabric types. Plain seams can be straight, curved, round, or angled and each will be discussed in this chapter. When a plain seam is stitched in the traditional way, the seam allowance is facing the inside of the garment, on the wrong side of the fabric. On the correct side of the garment, seams look smooth with clean lines. However, plain seams can also be topstitched, exposed, piped, boned, or embellished with trims. All of these ideas will be discussed in this chapter as we move forward. A plain seam is exposed or "deconstructed" when the seam allowance is unfinished and shows on the correct side of the garment. Exposed seams are popular in fashion today.

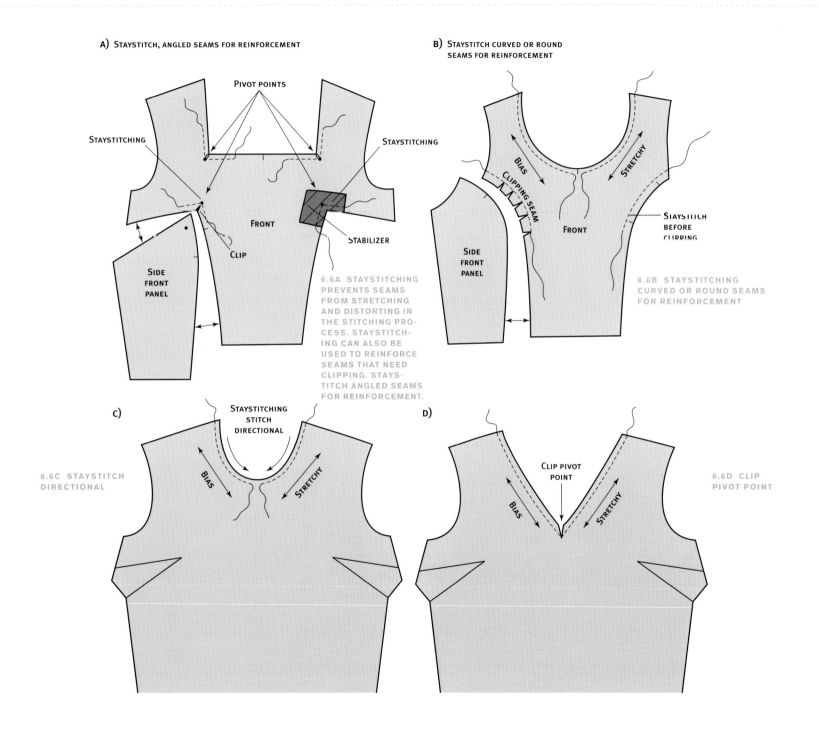

A) STAYSTITCH, ANGLED SEAMS FOR REINFORCEMENT

PIVOT POINTS

STAYSTITCHING

STAYSTITCHING

FRONT

CLIP

STABILIZER

SIDE FRONT PANEL

6.6A STAYSTITCHING PREVENTS SEAMS FROM STRETCHING AND DISTORTING IN THE STITCHING PROCESS. STAYSTITCHING CAN ALSO BE USED TO REINFORCE SEAMS THAT NEED CLIPPING. STAYSTITCH ANGLED SEAMS FOR REINFORCEMENT.

B) STAYSTITCH CURVED OR ROUND SEAMS FOR REINFORCEMENT

BIAS

CLIPPING SEAM

STRETCHY

FRONT

SIDE FRONT PANEL

STAYSTITCH BEFORE CLIPPING

6.6B STAYSTITCHING CURVED OR ROUND SEAMS FOR REINFORCEMENT

C)

STAYSTITCHING STITCH DIRECTIONAL

BIAS

STRETCHY

6.6C STAYSTITCH DIRECTIONAL

D)

CLIP PIVOT POINT

BIAS

STRETCHY

6.6D CLIP PIVOT POINT

6.7   STITCH DIRECTIONAL

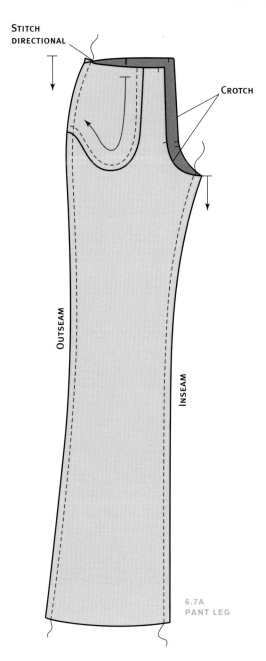

STITCH
DIRECTIONAL

CROTCH

OUTSEAM

INSEAM

6.7A
PANT LEG

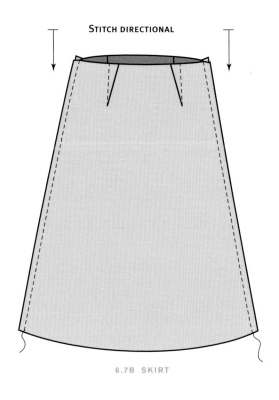

STITCH DIRECTIONAL

6.7B SKIRT

- Place the correct sides of two pieces of fabric together, matching both cut edges. Pin in place (see Figure 6.4a).
- Lay the fabric flat on the machine throat plate with the seam allowance to your right. Position the pressure foot at the fabric edge ready to stitch a ¼-inch, ½-inch, or ¾-inch plain seam. Refer to Chapter 2, "Seam Allowance."
- Hold both the top and bobbin threads behind the presser foot. As you begin to stitch, gently pull the threads to help the machine feed the fabric.
- Begin and end every seam with backstitches.

IMPORTANT

As you stitch, always keep your eyes open to what is happening under the seam as well as on top.

A backstitch secures the seams so they don't unravel during the construction process. To backstitch, stitch forward ¼ inch then back ¼ inch, then continue to stitch the entire seam and also end the seam with a backstitch. (Figure 6.8a shows the direction of the backstitching. Figure 6.8b shows how the seam actually looks when it is backstitched.)

- When the seam is stitched, the stitching should be parallel to the cut fabric edges.

Practice Makes Perfect

Don't be discouraged if your seam needs to be restitched—all beginners stitch crooked seams no matter how hard they try. Just take a deep breath and use your seam ripper (Figure 2.27), slowly and carefully, to undo each stitch. Be sure to remove all threads and press the seam flat again before restitching the seam.

Bias-Cut Seam

When stitching two bias-cut edges together, the fabric can be overstretched or puckered in the stitching process. For this reason, special attention is needed when stitching bias-cut seams. Place the color-matched tissue paper underneath the seam to stabilize and *slightly* stretch the seam as you stitch. Slightly stretching the

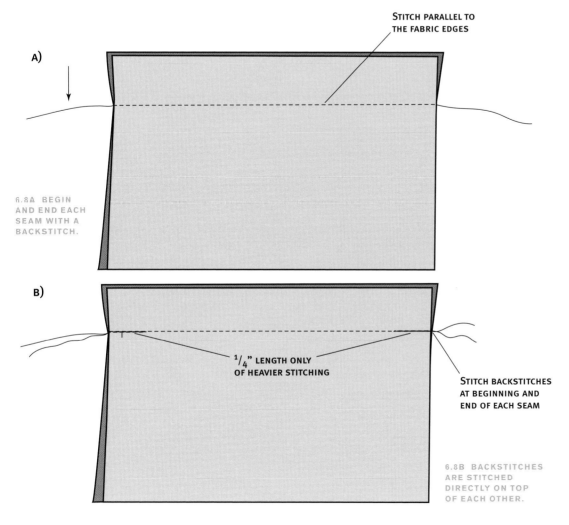

STITCH PARALLEL TO
THE FABRIC EDGES

A)

6.8A BEGIN
AND END EACH
SEAM WITH A
BACKSTITCH.

B)

¹/₄" LENGTH ONLY
OF HEAVIER STITCHING

STITCH BACKSTITCHES
AT BEGINNING AND
END OF EACH SEAM

6.8B BACKSTITCHES
ARE STITCHED
DIRECTLY ON TOP
OF EACH OTHER.

seams prevents the stitches from "popping" when the garment is worn. Notches are essential in bringing together bias-cut seams.

Bias/Straight Grain Seam

Any fabric cut on the bias has the potential to stretch. Fabric cut on the straight grain (verti-cal or crosswise) is stable. When stitching a bias grain to a straight grain, begin by plac-ing the correct sides together. Stitch the seam with the bias side facing up. As you stitch, don't stretch the bias piece; rather, ease it into the seam.

OPEN OR CLOSED SEAMS

Before structural seams are finished, decide whether your garment will have open or closed seams. This decision influences the way the seams are pressed. The designer makes the choice of seam finish, guided by the weight of fabric. The bulk of the seam also needs to be consid-ered. Let's consider a heavyweight fabric; an open seam would create less bulk. Next, consider a sheer lightweight fabric; a closed seam would not add bulk and would look less conspicuous, especially if the seam shadowed from the correct side of the fabric. Take a look at Figure 6.9a and b to see how to press open and closed seams.

SERGED SEAM FINISH

Structural seams are finished along the cut edges using a variety of methods. Seam fin-ishes add polish and quality to a garment and help the seams to stand up to constant wear and tear. Serged seams are the most common seam finish found in production. **Serging** is a profes-sional seam finish that prevents the seam edges from unraveling. A serger cuts and overcasts the fabric edges, as it stitches in one step. It's a *very fast* machine that stitches 1,500 stitches per minute. Sergers use between two and five cones of thread and no bobbin. Seams edges can be serged open or closed.

Open Serged Seam

Careful serging is required—an **open serged seam** is serged along each cut edge. Be careful not to serge any seam allowance off (Figure 6.10a).

Closed Serged Seam

When a seam is **serged closed,** both cut edges are serged together and pressed to one side (Figure 6.10b). A ½-inch seam can be serged closed or in lighter-weight or sheer fabrics, serged back to a ¼-inch width. A ¼-inch serged seam is used often in production as a more cost-effective alternative to stitching a French seam.

There are two choices as to when the seam is serged.

1. The seam edges can be finished first, before they are stitched; or
2. The seam edges can be finished after the seams are stitched together.

The design student should take time to consider whether to finish the seams first, before the seams are stitched, or after. While the garment is being developed, the fit is being perfected. Recutting, restitching, and more fitting continue until the style is exactly how you want

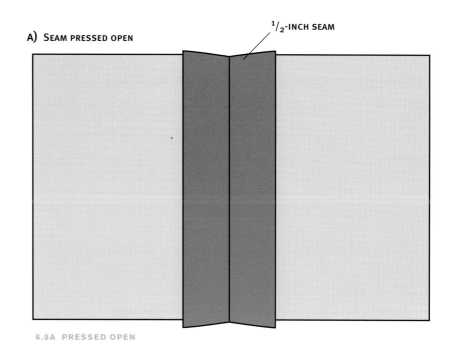

A) SEAM PRESSED OPEN

½-INCH SEAM

6.9A PRESSED OPEN

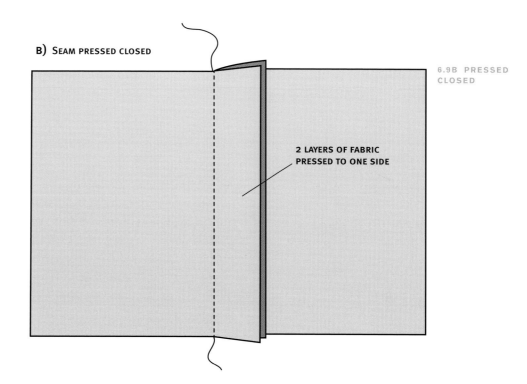

B) SEAM PRESSED CLOSED

6.9B PRESSED CLOSED

2 LAYERS OF FABRIC PRESSED TO ONE SIDE

it to look. So, to finish the seams first may be problematic. The decision is up to the design student and guided by the individual style being stitched. Consultation with your instructor will also help in making the best decision.

SAFETY STITCH

A **safety stitch** serves a dual purpose, by stitching the seamline and the edge finish simultaneously. A safety stitch is cost-effective in production, as it saves time, and time is money. It would not be used in haute couture but is used in cheaper lines of clothing. Four cones of thread are used for a safety stitch. Figure 6.11 illustrates a safety stitch.

SHAPED SEAMS

The secret to stitching shaped seams that lie perfectly flat is by making sure, before you begin, that notches are snipped, matchpoints marked, and staystitching and clipping attended to before joining the seam together.

Curved Seam/Princess Seam

Princess seams create a flattering seamline that contours the garment to the curves of a woman's body. A princess seam can be located on a top, blouse, dress, skirt, jacket, or coat, and be located on the front or the back of the garment. In tops, a princess seam can begin from the armhole or the shoulder seam. However, a princess seam can also start from other points, as illustrated in the dress in Figure 6.1a.

Princess seams are quite popular. Go back to Chapter 1 and look at the structural seams in each of the designs in Figures 1.4, 1.5, and 1.6.

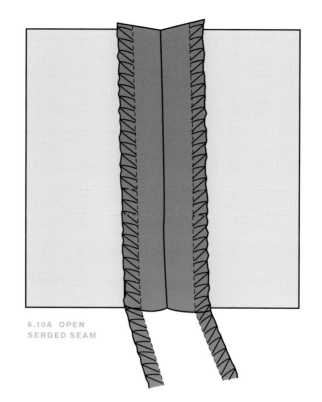

6.10A OPEN SERGED SEAM

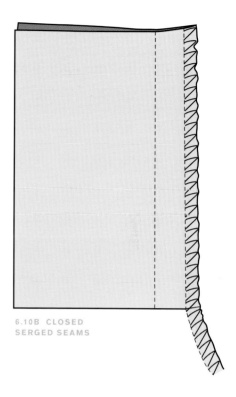

6.10B CLOSED SERGED SEAMS

The stitching order will be for a princess seam curved into the armhole. A curved princess seam into the armhole has one inward and one outward curved section that are stitched together (see Figure 6.6b).

- Staystitch the front panel beginning $1/2$ inch from the armhole edge, and stitch around the curved area. Notches should mark this section to be staystitched. Staystitch $1/16$ inch inside the seam allowance (Figure 6.12a).
- Clip into the seam allowance up to the staystitching (see Figure 6.12a). Observe that only the front panel is clipped.
- Place the correct sides of the side and center-front panels together, matching the notches. Pin

IMPORTANT

It is important that the seam be clipped right up to the staystitching, otherwise the two pieces of fabric will not fit accurately together (Figure 6.12a).

in place. You will notice how the clipping on the front panel allows the seam allowance to open so the seamline can then fit accurately together (see Figure 6.12a).

- With the clipped side facing up, stitch a $1/2$-inch seam starting from the armhole edge (see Figure 6.12a).

- Serge the seams closed and press the seam allowance toward the front panel (Figure 6.12b). Press all curved seams over a tailor's ham to shape the princess seam. Refer to Figure 4.3b. Even though a dart is being pressed in this illustration, the method is the same. Also refer to Chapter 2, "How to Press a Garment."

Circular Seam

The colorful dress in Figure 6.1b, in the Style I.D., is called "the Circular Dress." Can you see why this dress has this name?

- Staystitch the inward curve (concave) $1/16$ inch inside the seamline.
- Clip into the seam up to the staystitching at regular intervals around the seam—this is essential! The clipping allows the seam allowance to open up so the seams can be stitched together (Figure 6.13a).
- The more circular the seam, the closer the clipping needs to be.
- With correct sides together, with the clipped side facing up, pin the two seams together and stitch a $1/2$-inch seam (Figure 6.13b).
- Serge a closed seam and press the seam facing upward (with clipping underneath the seam).

Angled Seam

Look at the high-waisted pants in Figure 6.1c to see an angled seam. The angle becomes more prominent when fabrics in contrasting colors are used in the design. The angled seams also have been topstitched.

- Mark matchpoints—they are essential in stitching a successful angled seam (Figure 6.14a).
- Staystitch the corner $1/16$ inch inside the seam allowance for approximately $3/4$ inch on the angled corner. The staystitching reinforces the inward corner and keeps the fabric from pulling away from the seam. Clip into the corner up to the staystitching (Figure 6.14b).
- Place the correct sides of the fabric together. With the clipped side facing up, pin one seam down to the clipped corner. Don't pin the other side of the seam at this stage, as it needs to hang freely.
- Stitch a $1/2$-inch seam to the clipped corner; leave the needle down in the fabric, and *pivot* by swinging the fabric around 180 degrees. Notice how the clipped corner allows the fabric to open to complete the "perfect" angled seam. Stitch the remaining seam and end with a backstitch (Figure 6.14b and c).
- Serge the seams closed in two steps: serge one seam and then the other, and press the seam (Figure 6.14c).

V-Shaped Seam

This is a very popular style line in design and is often used on an empire line or shaped as a bra-cup. Refer back to the Style I.D., in Figure 6.1a, to view the V-shaped seam in the red dress. Notice that the bra section has a center-front seam. If there is *no* center-front seam, then staystitching is necessary for pivoting at the V shape (Figure 6.15a). Staystitching and clipping *are not* necessary when there is a center-front seam, as illustrated in Figure 6.15b.

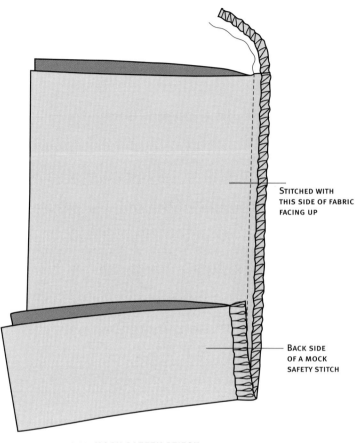

STITCHED WITH THIS SIDE OF FABRIC FACING UP

BACK SIDE OF A MOCK SAFETY STITCH

6.11 MOCK SAFETY STITCH

IMPORTANT

From the correct side of the fabric, no pleat or pucker should be evident at the corner when these instructions are followed.

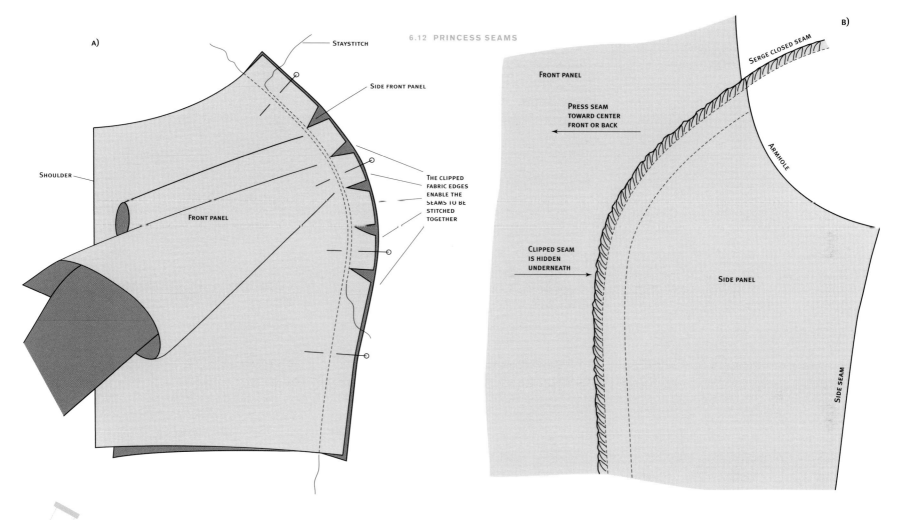

6.12 PRINCESS SEAMS

A)

STAYSTITCH

SIDE FRONT PANEL

SHOULDER

FRONT PANEL

THE CLIPPED FABRIC EDGES ENABLE THE SEAMS TO BE STITCHED TOGETHER

B)

FRONT PANEL

SERGE CLOSED SEAM

PRESS SEAM TOWARD CENTER FRONT OR BACK

ARMHOLE

CLIPPED SEAM IS HIDDEN UNDERNEATH

SIDE PANEL

SIDE SEAM

- Mark the matchpoints. If the design doesn't have a center-front seam, staystitch the center-front V and clip before stitching to the top section (see Figure 6.15a).
- If the design has a center-front seam, as in the dress in Figure 6.1, then stitch an open serged seam. Begin stitching from the top edge to the matchpoints. *Do not* stitch beyond this point into the seam allowance (Figure 6.15b).

- Whether there is a center-front seam or not, place the correct sides of the top and bottom sections together and stitch a ½-inch seam. When you get to the matchpoints, leave the machine needle down in the fabric and pivot on the corner. Swing the fabric down so the seam allowance opens, enabling the remaining stitching to be completed (see Figure 6.15a and b).
- Serge the seam closed (Figure 6.15b).

- Remember, always stitch a sample seam in your fashion fabric (not muslin) to help provide direction as to the best seam finish for use in your project.

PIPED SEAMS

A piping is a bias-cut piece of fabric wrapped around cording and inserted into a seam. Even though the piping is a decorative element, which

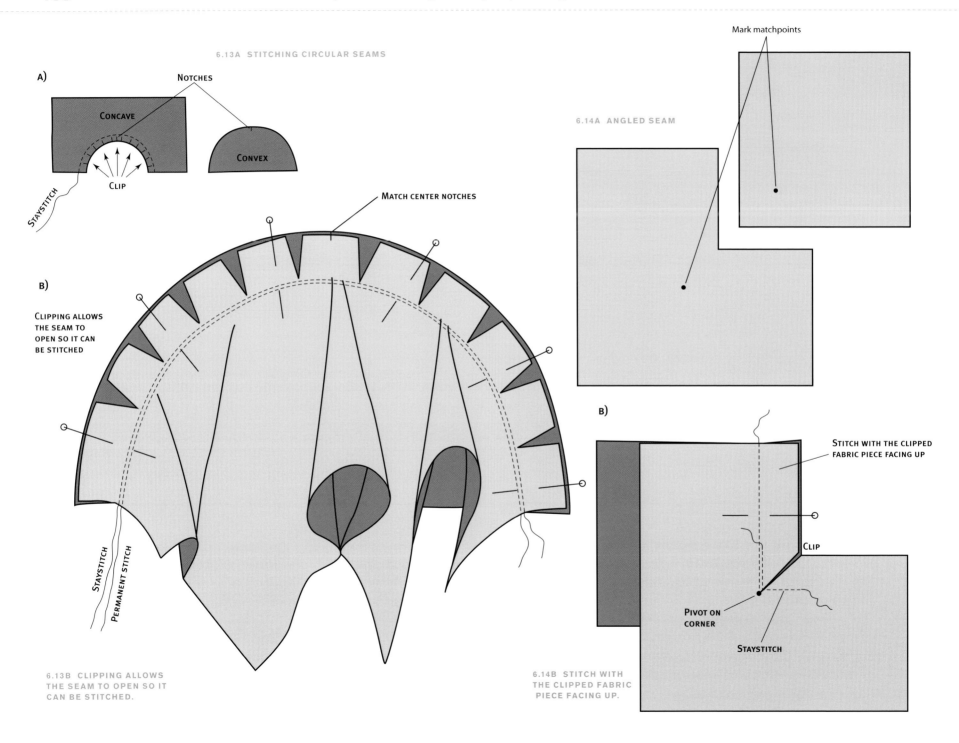

A)

NOTCHES

CONCAVE

CONVEX

CLIP

STAYSTITCH

B)

CLIPPING ALLOWS
THE SEAM TO
OPEN SO IT CAN
BE STITCHED

MATCH CENTER NOTCHES

STAYSTITCH

PERMANENT STITCH

6.13B CLIPPING ALLOWS
THE SEAM TO OPEN SO IT
CAN BE STITCHED.

Mark matchpoints

6.14A ANGLED SEAM

B)

STITCH WITH THE CLIPPED
FABRIC PIECE FACING UP

CLIP

PIVOT ON
CORNER

STAYSTITCH

6.14B STITCH WITH
THE CLIPPED FABRIC
PIECE FACING UP.

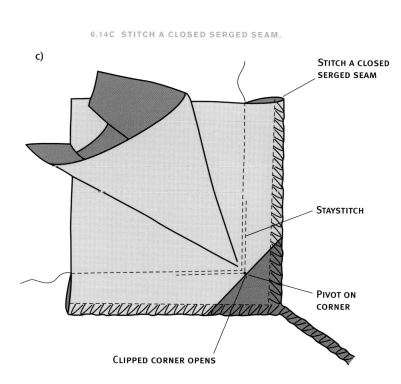

6.14C STITCH A CLOSED SERGED SEAM.

c)

STITCH A CLOSED
SERGED SEAM

STAYSTITCH

PIVOT ON
CORNER

CLIPPED CORNER OPENS

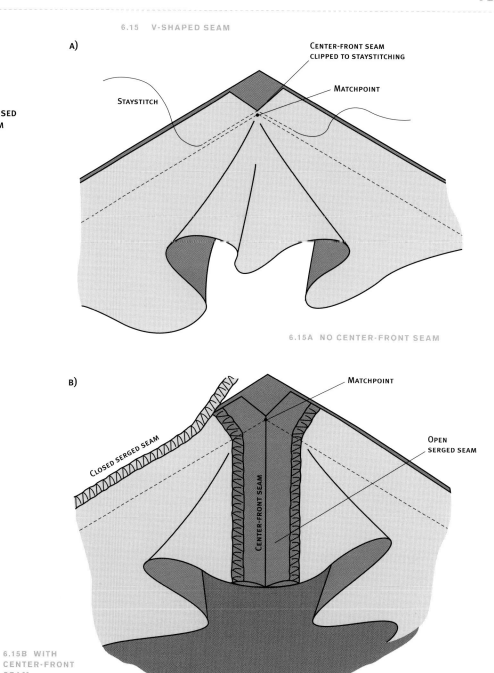

A)

CENTER-FRONT SEAM
CLIPPED TO STAYSTITCHING

MATCHPOINT

STAYSTITCH

6.15A NO CENTER-FRONT SEAM

B)

MATCHPOINT

CLOSED SERGED SEAM

OPEN
SERGED SEAM

CENTER-FRONT SEAM

6.15B WITH
CENTER-FRONT
SEAM

highlights a seam, it's still part of the structural design. Quality stitching is important so the piping lies flat and doesn't become twisted.

Piping can be manipulated around curves and angles and inserted into virtually any shaped seam. To view a piped princess seam, refer to Figure 6.1a in the Style I.D. Piping highlights the seams so they stand out as a feature in the design. Silk dupioni would be the perfect weight and an ideal choice for the piping in the bra-top dress in Figure 6.1a. Different sizes of cording are available. We've found that 1/8-inch cording is just right for piped seams.

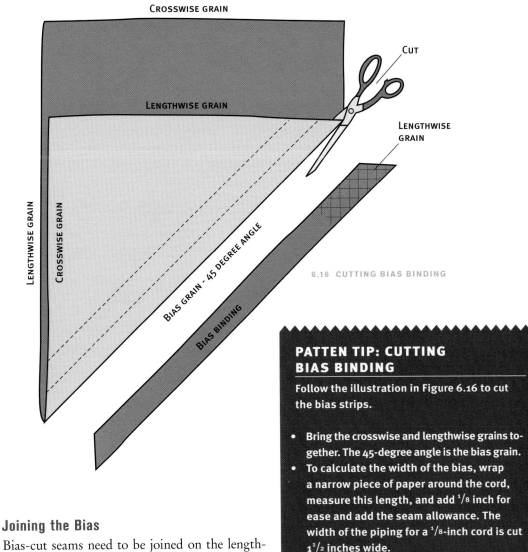

CROSSWISE GRAIN

LENGTHWISE GRAIN

CUT

LENGTHWISE GRAIN

LENGTHWISE GRAIN

CROSSWISE GRAIN

BIAS GRAIN - 45 DEGREE ANGLE

BIAS BINDING

6.16 CUTTING BIAS BINDING

Stitching the Piping

- Use a zipper foot for the entire stitching process (Figure 6.18a).
- Lay the cording so it is centered on the binding.
- Turn the top edge over the cording approximately $3/8$ inch for a clean-edge finish (see Figure 6.18a).
- Bring the two raw edges of the binding together, wrapping it around the cord. Stitch as closely as possible to the cord so it is a tight fit. Be careful not to twist the bias as you stitch (see Figure 6.18a).
- Place the piping to one side of the seam, matching the raw edges together. Pin the piping in place (Figure 6.18b).
- Stitch the piping to the seam, directly on top of the previous row of stitching. Don't stretch the piping as you stitch or it will pucker the seams (see Figure 6.18b).
- Turn the piped fabric over to the wrong side and match to the other seam edge, so that the correct sides are facing. The piping is now sandwiched between both fabric pieces. Stitch the seam directly over the previous stitches (Figure 6.18c).
- Now grade the seam and serge as a closed seam (Figure 6.18d).

Grading Seams

Grading refers to trimming the seam allowance to different levels to eliminate bulk. The amount of grading needed depends on the thickness of the seam.

Fabrics can be divided into those that are heavy, medium, or light in weight. Depending on the fabric weight and the type of seam

PATTEN TIP: CUTTING BIAS BINDING

Follow the illustration in Figure 6.16 to cut the bias strips.

- Bring the crosswise and lengthwise grains together. The 45-degree angle is the bias grain.
- To calculate the width of the bias, wrap a narrow piece of paper around the cord, measure this length, and add $1/8$ inch for ease and add the seam allowance. The width of the piping for a $1/8$-inch cord is cut $1^{1}/_{2}$ inches wide.
- Cut parallel strips on the same bias grain, as indicated in Figure 6.16, to get the required length.

Joining the Bias

Bias-cut seams need to be joined on the lengthwise grain. If seams are joined on the bias grain, they will stretch easily. Figure 6.17a and b illustrates how the seam is joined, pressed open, and trimmed.

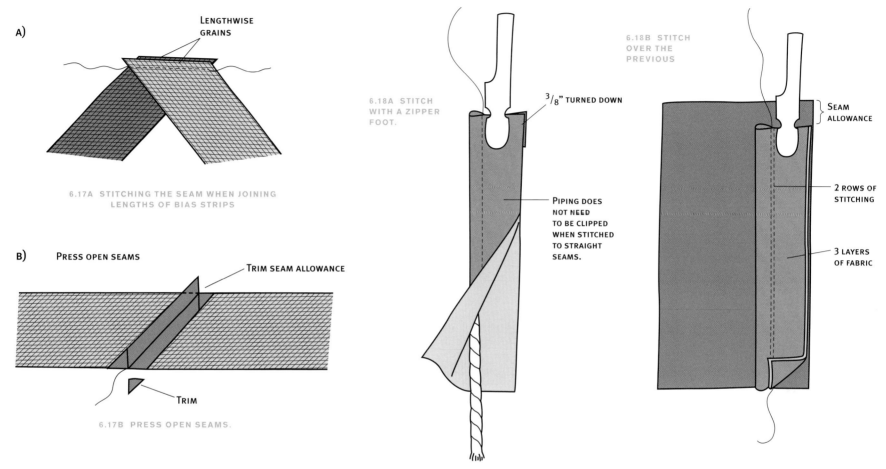

A)

LENGTHWISE
GRAINS

6.17A STITCHING THE SEAM WHEN JOINING
LENGTHS OF BIAS STRIPS

B)

PRESS OPEN SEAMS

TRIM SEAM ALLOWANCE

TRIM

6.17B PRESS OPEN SEAMS.

6.18A STITCH
WITH A ZIPPER
FOOT.

3/8" TURNED DOWN

PIPING DOES
NOT NEED
TO BE CLIPPED
WHEN STITCHED
TO STRAIGHT
SEAMS.

6.18B STITCH
OVER THE
PREVIOUS

SEAM
ALLOWANCE

2 ROWS OF
STITCHING

3 LAYERS
OF FABRIC

stitched, bulk will be more prevalent in some seams than in others. Bulk needs to be reduced from intersecting seams, collar corners, overlapping pleats, seam insertions, and any other thick seams. Figure 6.18d and other references throughout this book will help you understand how to reduce bulk.

- Figure 6.29a show how *bulk* is cut away from open seams that intersect.

- Figure 6.30 shows how closed serged seams are turned in opposite directions to reduce *bulk* when the seam intersects.
- Figure 6.34b shows how *excess fabric* is cut away from a flat-felled seam to reduce bulk.
- When a ¼-inch enclosed seam is stitched around facings, collars, cuffs, and pocket flaps, *bulk* can be less of a problem; however, grading is still needed in many cases (Figures 11.9 and 12.10a).

- *Bulk* is also reduced in hems to prevent ugly ridges from showing on the correct side of the fabric. (Refer to Figure 15.7.)

Piping can also be inserted into princess, circular, and angled seams. Notice that the piping is prepared differently for curved/circular and angled seams. The piping is prepared using the same stitches but they are clipped differently depending on the shape of the seam. Piping ap-

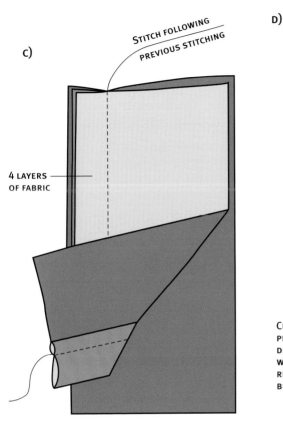

c)

STITCH FOLLOWING
PREVIOUS STITCHING

4 LAYERS
OF FABRIC

6.18C STITCHING THE SEAM

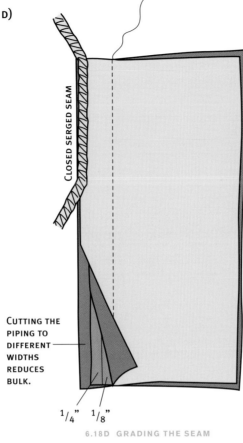

D)

CLOSED SERGED SEAM

CUTTING THE
PIPING TO
DIFFERENT
WIDTHS
REDUCES
BULK.

$^{1}/_{4}$" $^{1}/_{8}$"

6.18D GRADING THE SEAM

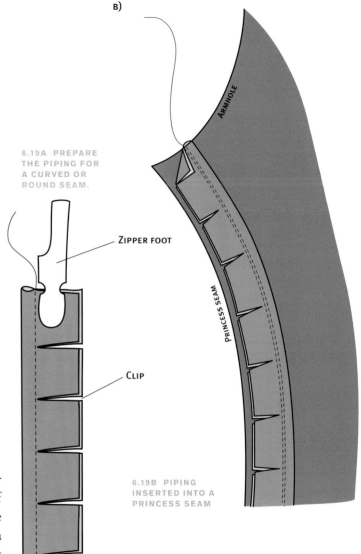

6.19A PREPARE
THE PIPING FOR
A CURVED OR
ROUND SEAM.

ZIPPER FOOT

CLIP

6.19B PIPING
INSERTED INTO A
PRINCESS SEAM

ARMHOLE

PRINCESS SEAM

plied to a curved or round seam is illustrated in Figures 6.19a and b, and 6.20. Piping applied to an angled seam is pictured in Figure 6.21a and b.

After piping is applied to any shaped seam, the seam is then stitched as described in the earlier section on "Shaped Seams."

EASED SEAM

An eased seam has a slight fullness on one side of the seam. An eased seam is most often used to create roundness or fullness. Examples of

eased seams include the sleeve cap (to fit over the shoulders) and waistline (used instead of darts to create shape over the hip or to create shape to fit over the bustline instead of using a bust dart). Refer to Chapter 14 for details about eased seams in sleeves.

- On the longer section, stitch one row of basting stitches, between the notches and $^{1}/_{16}$ inch inside the seamline (Figure 6.22a).

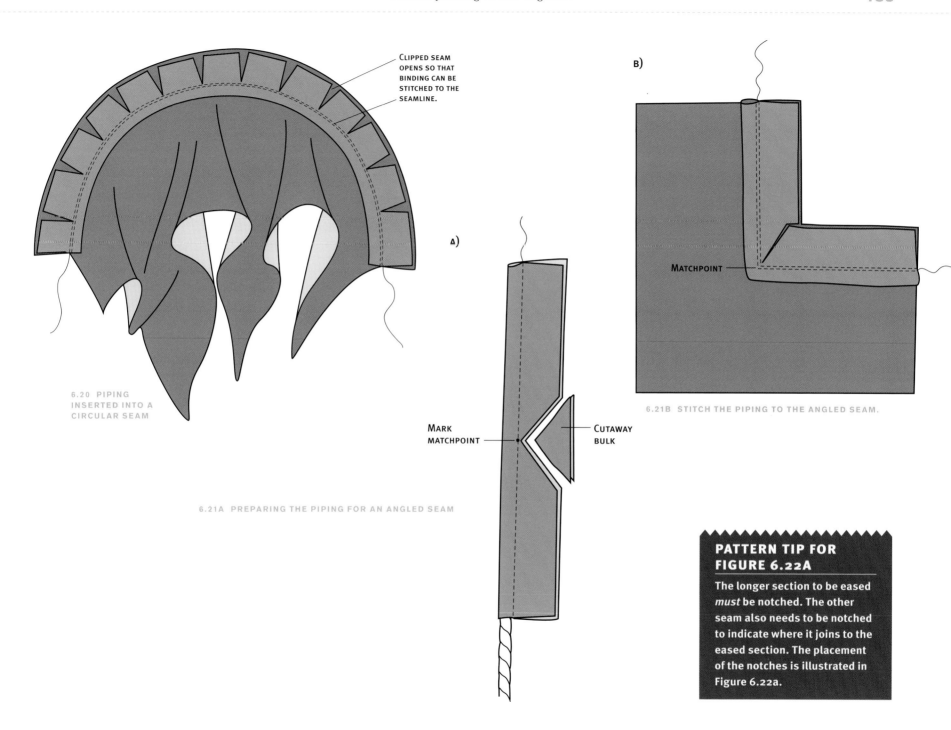

CLIPPED SEAM OPENS SO THAT BINDING CAN BE STITCHED TO THE SEAMLINE.

B)

6.20 PIPING INSERTED INTO A CIRCULAR SEAM

A)

MATCHPOINT

6.21B STITCH THE PIPING TO THE ANGLED SEAM.

MARK MATCHPOINT

CUTAWAY BULK

6.21A PREPARING THE PIPING FOR AN ANGLED SEAM

PATTERN TIP FOR FIGURE 6.22A

The longer section to be eased *must* be notched. The other seam also needs to be notched to indicate where it joins to the eased section. The placement of the notches is illustrated in Figure 6.22a.

A)

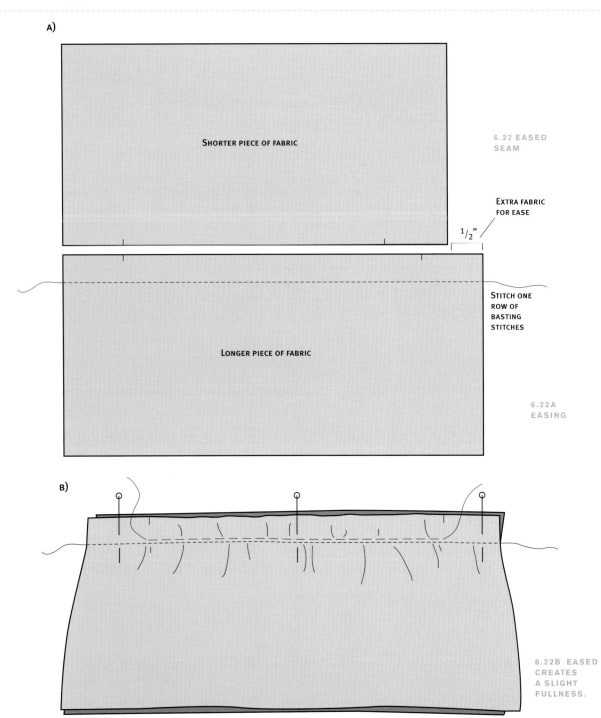

SHORTER PIECE OF FABRIC

6.22 EASED
SEAM

EXTRA FABRIC
FOR EASE

¹/₂"

STITCH ONE
ROW OF
BASTING
STITCHES

LONGER PIECE OF FABRIC

6.22A
EASING

B)

6.22B EASED
CREATES
A SLIGHT
FULLNESS.

- Pull the bobbin basting thread until easing is formed (a slight fullness).
- Place the correct sides of the fabric together. With the basting stitches facing up and evenly distributed, pin in place and stitch a ¹/₂-inch seam (Figure 6.22b).
- No puckers should be evident from the correct side in an eased seam.

GATHERED SEAM

One or both sides of a seam can be gathered. For a gathered seam to be successful, a light- to medium-weight fabric should be used—bulky fabrics do not gather as well. Refer back to the Style I.D. to see the floral summer dress in Figure 6.1d. Notice the gathered seam on the armholes. In the pattern drafting stage, the dart was transferred into fullness to provide shape in the bust area.

- Position two rows of gathering stitches within the seam allowance—one row is stitched just above the ¹/₂-inch seamline and the other row is stitched ¹/₄ inch above that one (Figure 6.23a).
- Take the two bobbin threads in your hand and *gently* pull them up until small puckers appear that are closely pushed together.
- Even out the gathering so it is evenly distributed (Figure 6.23b).
- Place the correct sides of the fabric together and pin in place so the gathered section fits the length of seam to which it is being stitched (Figure 6.23b).

- With the gathering facing up, stitch along the seamline with a straight stitch just below the basting stitches. The bottom row of basting stitches does not need to be removed, as it will not show (see Figure 6.23c).
- Serge the seam closed (see Figure 6.23c).

TOPSTITCHED SEAMS

Topstitching refers to rows of stitches that are stitched to the surface of the fabric on top of the seam. Topstitching makes a seam stronger, highlights the design lines, and helps the seam lie flat, as well as adding a decorative element to the garment. In Figure 6.1c, the angled seam on the high-waisted pants is topstitched—do you notice how your eyes are drawn to the seams?

Topstitching can be applied by machine or

6.23   GATHERED SEAM

A)

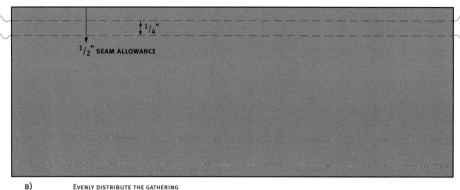

STITCH 2 ROWS OF MACHINE BASTING STITCHES

$1/4$"

$1/2$" SEAM ALLOWANCE

6.23A GATHERING: STITCH TWO ROWS OF BASTING STITCHES.

B)   EVENLY DISTRIBUTE THE GATHERING

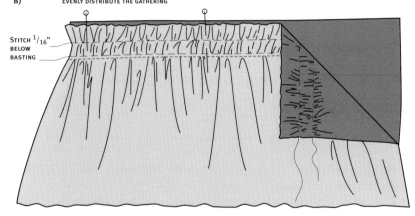

STITCH $1/16$" BELOW BASTING

6.23B EVENLY DISTRIBUTE THE GATHERING.

C)

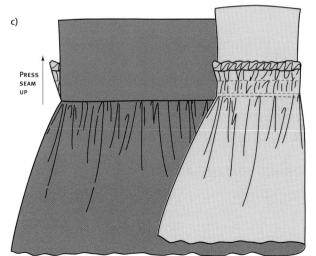

PRESS SEAM UP

6.23C PRESS SEAM UP.

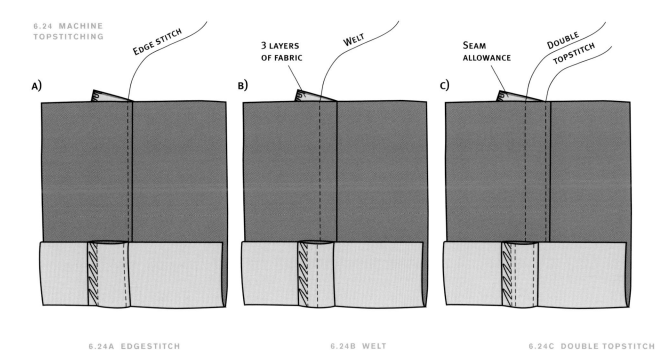

6.24 MACHINE TOPSTITCHING

A) EDGE STITCH

B) 3 LAYERS OF FABRIC / WELT

C) SEAM ALLOWANCE / DOUBLE TOPSTITCH

6.24A EDGESTITCH   6.24B WELT   6.24C DOUBLE TOPSTITCH

by hand to open or closed seams; however, because of the thickness of closed seams, it is more successful in the latter. The seam allowance in a closed seam acts as padding, enabling the topstitching to sink in, and slightly raising the section between the seamline and the topstitching.

Look at each of the topstitched seams in Figures 6.24. Observe how each seam has been stitched. Three layers of fabric (seam allowance and outer layer of fabric) nicely pad the topstitched seams. Notice the seam allowance is *not* graded. Topstitching can be one, two, or three rows of permanent stitches, zigzag stitches, or decorative stitches—the choice is yours!

- Each seam has been stitched with a $^1/_2$-inch closed serged seam (see Figure 6.10b).
- Increase the stitch length—the more layers of fabric there are, the longer the stitch length needs to be because the stitches sink into the fabric.
- Topstitching thread, single thread, or two strands of thread in matching or contrasting colors can be used for topstitching. Use a larger-sized needle for two strands and topstitching threads, as the needle eye will be larger and easier to thread.

Edgestitch

- With the correct side of the fabric facing up, stitch a row of topstitching $^1/_{16}$ inch away from the

seamline (Figure 6.24a). The name says it all—this is *edge* stitching!

Welt Seam

- With the correct side facing up, line up the presser foot so it butts up next to the seamline. Stitch $^1/_4$ inch away from the seamline. By keeping the presser foot butted up next to the seamline, the topstitching will be parallel for the entire distance (Figure 6.24b).

Double Topstitched Seam

- A double topstitch combines an edgestitch and a welt.
- With the correct side of the fabric facing up,

stitch a row of edgestitching (see Figure 6.24a).

- To stitch the next row of stitching, line up the presser foot next to the seamline and *not* to the edgestitching. Stitch the second row of topstitches for the entire distance so the two stitching rows are parallel to each other. The total width of the stitching from the seamline should be ¹/₄ inch (see Figure 6.24c).

Topstitching Shaped Seams

There is no limit to the use of topstitching on seams. Seams of all shapes can be topstitched; however, the more the seams are shaped, the more time and care will be needed when stitching.

Curved or Circular Seams

- When topstitching a circular seam, stitch in short bursts of approximately 1 inch at a time, then stop (with the machine needle down in the work), turn the fabric slightly, and continue to stitch. The circular seams in Figure 6.1b in the Style I.D. have been carefully topstitched.
- Alternatively, hand-walk the sewing machine. Figure 2.23 shows the location of the handwheel on the sewing machine. To hand-walk the machine, turn the wheel with your hand; this allows you to stitch very slowly and carefully. Your feet *don't* touch the pedal when you hand-walk the sewing machine.

Angled Seams

- Topstitching an angled seam is the same as stitching a seam—just pivot on the corner.

Look at the Style I.D. in Figure 6.1d. Do you see the angled topstitched seams?

Twin Needle Topstitching

A twin needle has two needles that sit side by side. **Twin needle topstitching** produces two "perfect" parallel rows of topstitching (Figure 6.25). Twin needle topstitching is ideal for knits as it allows the knit to stretch. Twin needles come in different sizes and widths—numbers such as 2.5 and 4.0 refer to the distance between each needle; numbers such as 75/80/90 refer to the needle sizes. Chapter 2, "Sewing Machine Needle Types," describes twin needles in detail.

On fine knits, tissue stitch if the twin needle stitching does not lie flat. Twin needle stitching can be used to topstitch woven fabrics, and it works well on denim. Hems can also be twin needle stitched. In this chapter, the section on "Stretch Seams" provides more information about stitching knit fabrics.

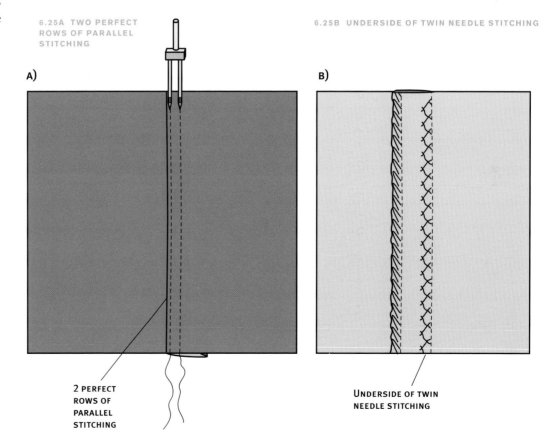

6.25A TWO PERFECT ROWS OF PARALLEL STITCHING

6.25B UNDERSIDE OF TWIN NEEDLE STITCHING

A)

B)

2 PERFECT ROWS OF PARALLEL STITCHING

UNDERSIDE OF TWIN NEEDLE STITCHING

A)

TIE OFF THREADS
AND BURY IN THE
SEAM ALLOWANCE

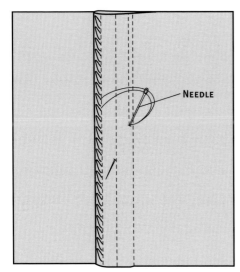

NEEDLE

B)

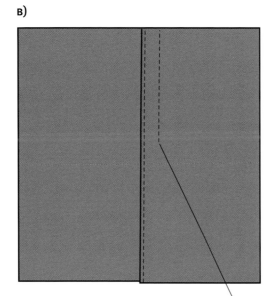

BEGIN STITCHING
HERE AGAIN

chine needle directly in the stitch hole where the previous topstitch broke (Figure 6.26b).

- Continue to stitch from this point to the end of the seam.
- From the correct side, the topstitching join will not be visible.

Hand Topstitching

When topstitching by hand, time and patience are required to produce nice-looking, even stitches. Outlined here are a saddle stitch and a pick stitch. These are not the only hand topstitches—designers can create their own variations of hand topstitching.

Purchase embroidery thread and a needle with an eye large enough to thread comfortably. Many varieties of embroidery floss are available: 100 percent cotton, 100 percent rayon, 100 percent linen, variegated, pearlized, and metallic, in a huge assortment of colors.

Saddle Stitch

- Saddle stitches are evenly spaced and stitched approximately ¼-inch long and ¼-inch apart. (Figure 6.27a).
- It is important that the stitches be placed parallel to the seamline.
- Hand stitch a sample first to experiment with the thread type, color, needle size, and width of topstitching.

Pickstitch

A pickstitch is a small stitch showing on the fabric surface with a longer stitch underneath (Figure 6.27b).

- Thread two strands of thread through the sewing machine; separate the threads just above the needle by hooking them apart before threading the two needles.
- To stitch, line up the presser foot to the seamline and carefully stitch. The two rows of stitches will be perfectly parallel to each other (Figure 6.25a).
- On the wrong side of the fabric, the stitches loop

over a central thread, forming a small zigzag. Any zigzag stitching motion is "ideal" for stitching knits and allows the seam to stretch (Figure 6.25b).

If Your Topstitching Thread Breaks . . .
Take heart, there is no need to rip out your topstitching and start again. The stitches can be joined together as follows:

- Pull the broken threads through to the wrong side, tie the threads together, and thread through a large-eyed needle. Bury the threads into the seam (Figure 6.26a).
- Begin topstitching again by placing the ma-

NOTES

Twin needle topstitching is difficult on angled corners; however, it can be stitched around princess and circular seams.

6.27 HAND TOPSTITCHING

> **NOTES**
> A saddle stitch or pick stitch can be top-stitched $^1/_{16}$ inch, $^1/_4$ inch, or $^1/_8$ inch away from the seamline—the choice is the designer's!

SANDWICHED SEAM

In a sandwiched seam, three layers of fabric are stitched together to make the seam. This seam is often used to stitch a yoke in a shirt, skirt, or blouse. It is a popular style line, especially in men's shirts. However, this does not exclude its use for women's wear. Observe the back yoke of the striped shirt in Figure 6.28a. Refer to Figure 6.28b to see how the two yoke pieces are placed on either side of the back shirt section, sandwiching them together. After the yoke seam is stitched, it is pressed and topstitched with an edgestitch, welt, or double topstitch (Figure 6.28c). Next, the front shoulder seams are stitched, as illustrated in Figure 6.28d. Do notice that the front bands and pocket were stitched to the fronts before the yoke was applied.

INTERSECTING SEAMS

Intersecting seams are two seams that are stitched together. This creates bulk at the seam juncture with so many layers of fabric concentrated in one area.

Open Intersecting Seams

To see where intersecting seams can be placed in the design, refer to the Style I.D. in Figure 6.1a. Notice the center-front bra-top seams. The

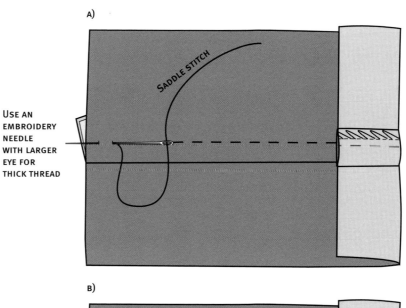

A)

USE AN
EMBROIDERY
NEEDLE
WITH LARGER
EYE FOR
THICK THREAD

SADDLE STITCH

6.27A SADDLE STITCH

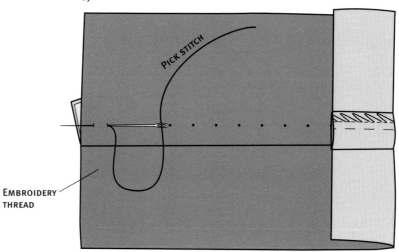

B)

PICK STITCH

EMBROIDERY
THREAD

6.27B PICK STITCH

a) Stripe shirt

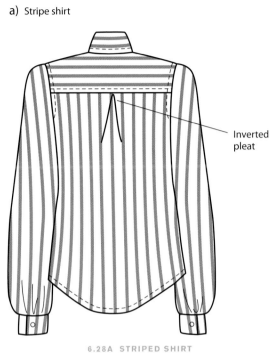

Inverted pleat

6.28A STRIPED SHIRT

two horizontal and vertical seams are intersecting seams. In Figure 6.1b, the position where the two black garment pieces meet on the empire waist also represents intersecting seams.

- Place the correct sides of both open serged seam sections together, matching the seamlines together. Pin together directly on the seam join.
- Stitch a ½-inch seam and only remove the pin as you near the seam join (Figure 6.29a).
- Clip all four corners diagonally from the seam allowance to remove bulk (see Figure 6.29a).
- Press the seam open, as illustrated in Figure 6.29b.

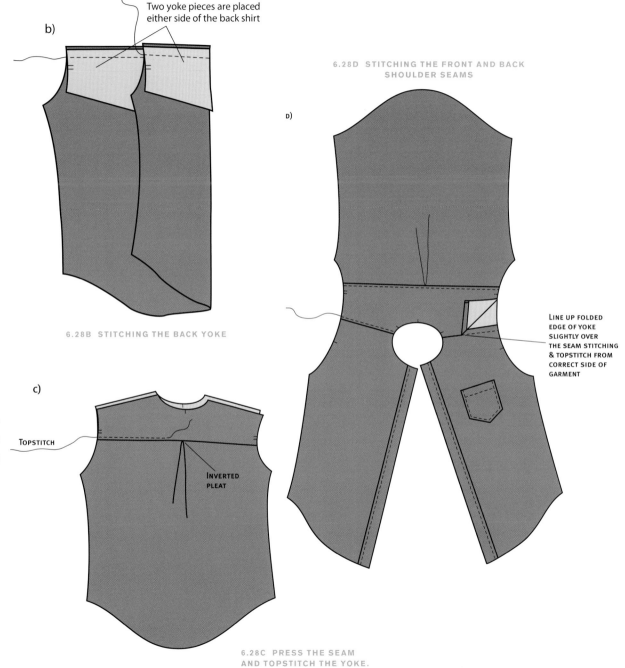

b)

Two yoke pieces are placed either side of the back shirt

6.28B STITCHING THE BACK YOKE

c)

TOPSTITCH

INVERTED PLEAT

6.28C PRESS THE SEAM AND TOPSTITCH THE YOKE.

6.28D STITCHING THE FRONT AND BACK SHOULDER SEAMS

D)

LINE UP FOLDED EDGE OF YOKE SLIGHTLY OVER THE SEAM STITCHING & TOPSTITCH FROM CORRECT SIDE OF GARMENT

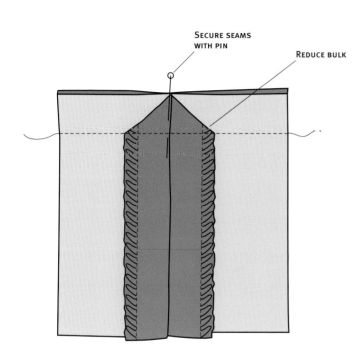

SECURE SEAMS
WITH PIN

REDUCE BULK

6.29A INTERSECTING SEAMS: OPEN SEAMS

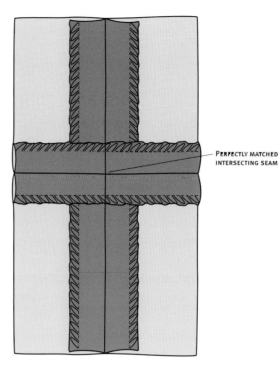

PERFECTLY MATCHED
INTERSECTING SEAM

6.29B PRESS THE SEAM OPEN.

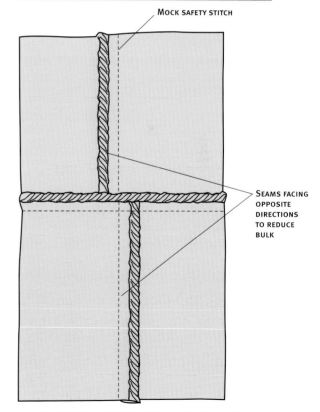

> **IMPORTANT**
>
> Both the *crotch* and the *underarm* intersecting seams are an exception to the rule—both intersecting seams are *not* pressed open nor are they clipped to reduce bulk. Because both intersecting seams have stress placed on them (at the intersecting seam position), the removal of bulk in this case may weaken the seam. For a sleeve underarm seam, the seam allowance is left to face up toward the shoulders. Likewise, the crotch seam allowance is directed up toward the waistline.

MOCK SAFETY STITCH

SEAMS FACING
OPPOSITE
DIRECTIONS
TO REDUCE
BULK

6.30 INTERSECTING SEAMS: CLOSED SEAMS

Closed Intersecting Seam

An intersecting seam can also be a closed seam. Figure 6.30 illustrates a closed *safety stitch* intersecting seam. Notice the direction of each seam—they are pressed in opposite directions to reduce bulk. Intersecting seams are also found on the underarms of tops, shirts, dresses, jackets, and coats, when a sleeve is set into the armhole (refer to Chapter 14).

Another intersecting seam that is common in clothing construction occurs where the inseams join together in the crotch seams. If you refer back to Figure 6.7a, which discussed directional stitching, you will see how the inseam and outseams of one pant leg were stitched. Now notice in Figure 6.31 how the crotch seam is stitched. One pant leg has been slipped inside the other so both wrong sides of the fabric are visible; this makes it easier to stitch the crotch. The crotch seam is then stitched from the front zipper matchpoints to the back waistline. Sometimes in the stitching order the zipper is applied first; however, in this pair of pants it is applied later in the stitching order.

OTHER SEAM FINISHES
Clean-Edge Finish

This seam finish has a folded stitched edge to finish the raw edges. Each side of the seam allowance will be ⅜ inch wide when it is finished. This seam finish is not suitable for heavyweight fabrics as it would be too bulky. A clean-edge finish is used more often for high-end garments.

- After a ¹/₂-inch seam is stitched, and pressed open, turn both fabric pieces to the left with the correct side of the fabric down on the machine plate, ready to stitch (Figure 6.32a).
- Fold ¹/₈ inch of the seam allowance back to the wrong side of the seam allowance and stitch ¹/₁₆ inch from the folded edge (Figure 6.32a).
- Repeat on the other side of the seam allowance to complete (Figure 6.32b).

Hong Kong Finish (or Bound Finish)

A Hong Kong finish encases both raw edges with a bias binding. Bias binding can be purchased or cut, as detailed below. The binding can be stitched to open or closed seams. For binding, it's important to use fabric of the appropriate weight, such as silk charmeuse, organza, or silk dupioni, as they don't add bulk to the seams. This seam finish is used in more expensive garments and is a wonderful finish to use on unlined jackets and coats. A Hong Kong finish is a recommended seam finish to use for a partial lining. This is discussed in Chapter 16, "Open Partial Lining."

NOTES

Seams Great, a sheer stabilizing tape, can also be used to bind the seam edges in fine and tricky fabrics, producing an excellent seam finish without showing a ridge on the correct side of the garment as serging would on open or closed bound seams. Seams Great is described in Chapter 3, "Stabilizing Tapes."

Cutting Bias Binding

For both closed and open Hong Kong seam finishes, cut bias binding to the required width and length. Refer to Figures 6.16 and 6.17 to see how to cut and join the bias binding. Use as few seam joins as possible.

Open Hong Kong Seam Finish

- Cut bias binding 1 inch wide and to the appropriate length. Place the correct sides of the seam and bias facing together with the cut edges lined up, and pin in place.
- Stitch the bias binding to the seam using a ¹/₄-inch seam allowance. It is important not to stretch the bias binding as you stitch, as this could pucker the seams (Figure 6.33a).
- The stitched seam allowance must not be wider than ¹/₄ inch. After stitching, turn the bias to the correct side and press the seamline.
- Wrap the binding around the raw seam edge and handbaste in place. The binding lies flat under the seam (Figure 6.33b).
- Any excess binding can be trimmed so it sits comfortably next to the seamline.

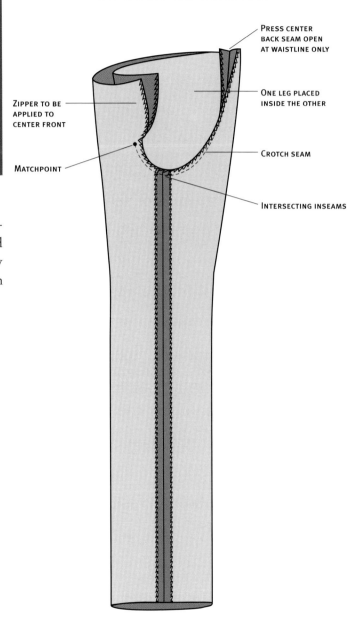

PRESS CENTER BACK SEAM OPEN AT WAISTLINE ONLY

ONE LEG PLACED INSIDE THE OTHER

ZIPPER TO BE APPLIED TO CENTER FRONT

CROTCH SEAM

MATCHPOINT

INTERSECTING INSEAMS

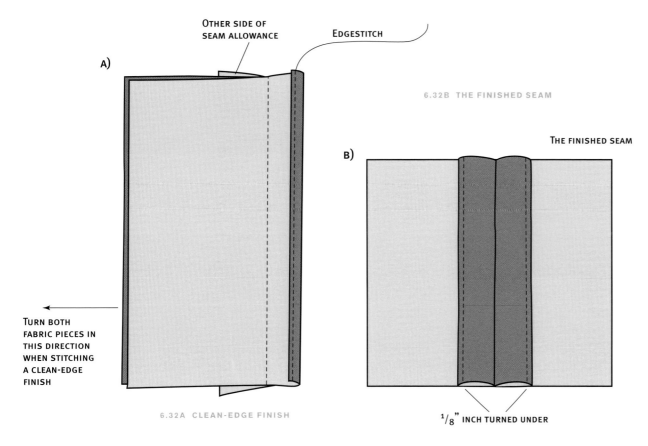

A)

OTHER SIDE OF SEAM ALLOWANCE

EDGESTITCH

6.32B THE FINISHED SEAM

THE FINISHED SEAM

B)

TURN BOTH FABRIC PIECES IN THIS DIRECTION WHEN STITCHING A CLEAN-EDGE FINISH

6.32A CLEAN-EDGE FINISH

$^1/_8$" INCH TURNED UNDER

- From the correct side, carefully stitch the binding by stitching-in-the-ditch (see Figure 6.33b), as described below.

Stitching-in-the-Ditch

Stitching-in-the-ditch is a technique used to secure and complete a Hong Kong finish. It is a row of stitches, stitched from the correct side of the fabric, and buried in the "seam well" or seamline. This makes the stitches *almost* invisible. Using a zipper foot allows the needle to get close

to the seam well and provides a better view of where the stitching goes. Stitching-in-the-ditch also secures facings and waistbands in place.

> **NOTES**
>
> A Hong Kong seam finish can also be stitched as a waistband finish, facing finish, armhole finish for set-in sleeves, or as a hem finish. Refer to each individual chapter for more information.

Closed Hong Kong Seam Finish

- For a closed Hong Kong finish, place the binding $^1/_4$ inch back from the $^1/_2$-inch seam edges. Pin the bias in position. Trim the seam allowance back to the binding cut edge (Figure 6.33c).
- Wrap the binding over the raw edges. Tuck under $^1/_4$ inch and butt the folded edge to the seamline but *not* over it. If the binding is too wide, it may need trimming. We definitely advise handbasting the binding in place, as bias can twist very easily (see Figure 6.33b).
- Using a hand needle, the binding can be slip-stitched to the seamline or carefully machine stitched as an edgestitch (Figure 6.33d). Refer to Figure 6.24a for edgestitching. Refer to Chapter 15 to see a slipstitch.

Flat-Felled Seam

A flat-felled seam has a clean finish on both sides of the garment (Figure 6.34a). It is often used in sportswear and commonly used in denim garments such as jeans, jackets, and men's and women's shirts. The side seam of the striped shirt in Figure 6.28a could be stitched with a flat-felled seam or a closed serged seam.

> **NOTES**
>
> A Hong Kong Finish can also be used to finish other edges, such as facings and waistbands. If you turn ahead to Chapter 16 (see Figure 16.25c and d), you will see how a Hong Kong finish has been applied to all the seams and edges of the partial lining of a coat.

A)

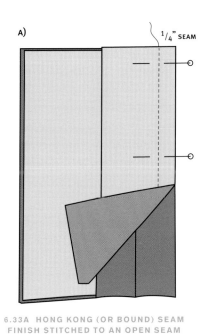

¼" SEAM

6.33A HONG KONG (OR BOUND) SEAM FINISH STITCHED TO AN OPEN SEAM

B)

WRAP THE BINDING AROUND THE SEAM & HANDBASTE IN PLACE

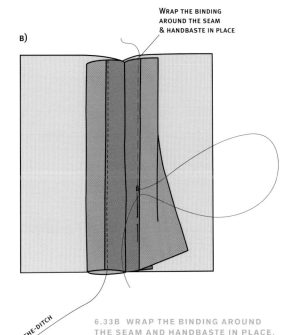

STITCH-IN-THE-DITCH

6.33B WRAP THE BINDING AROUND THE SEAM AND HANDBASTE IN PLACE.

> **IMPORTANT**
>
> The pressing is really important at this point. If the seam is not pressed properly, it will not look flat on completion. Make sure the seams are pressed symmetrically—that is, *both* sides are pressed toward the back or front.

6.33D COMPLETE STITCHING THE BINDING.

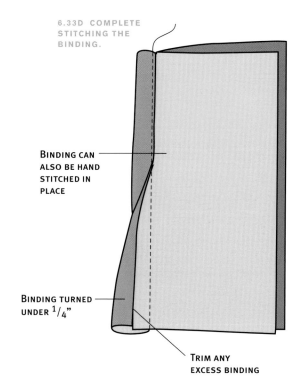

BINDING CAN ALSO BE HAND STITCHED IN PLACE

BINDING TURNED UNDER ¼"

TRIM ANY EXCESS BINDING

- Place the *wrong* sides of the garment together, secure with pins, and stitch a ½-inch plain seam. Press both seam allowances to one side (Figure 6.34b).
- Trim the bottom seam allowance back to ¼ inch (see Figure 6.34b).
- Fold the top seam allowance over ¼ inch and tuck it over the bottom seam allowance (Figure 6.34c).
- Handbaste the seam in place along the folded edge to secure the seam together (see Figure 6.34c).
- Edgestitch ¹/₁₆ inch back from the folded edge (see Figure 6.34c).
- Press and remove handbasting stitches.

6.33C HONG KONG (OR BOUND) SEAM FINISH STITCHED TO A CLOSED SEAM

CUT AWAY

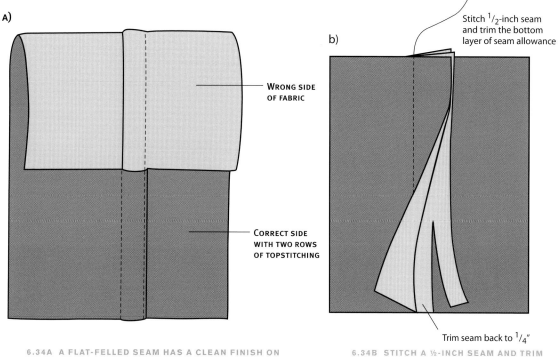

A)

WRONG SIDE OF FABRIC

CORRECT SIDE WITH TWO ROWS OF TOPSTITCHING

6.34A A FLAT-FELLED SEAM HAS A CLEAN FINISH ON BOTH SIDES OF THE GARMENT.

b)

Stitch ¹/₂-inch seam and trim the bottom layer of seam allowance

Trim seam back to ¹/₄"

6.34B STITCH A ½-INCH SEAM AND TRIM THE BOTTOM LAYER OF SEAM ALLOWANCE.

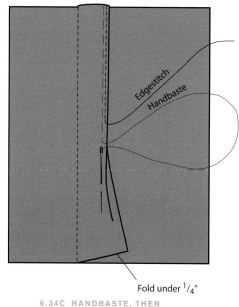

c) Handbaste then edgestitch the seam

Edgestitch

Handbaste

Fold under ¹/₄"

6.34C HANDBASTE, THEN EDGESTITCH THE SEAM.

NOTE

Contrasting thread also can be used but it *must* be used from the beginning when the first seam is stitched, as these stitches are visible—and don't forget to use the same stitch length for stitching the seam and the edgestitch.

French Seam

A French seam is a narrow enclosed seam that looks like a small, neat, tucked seam from the wrong side. This narrow seam is ideal to use for seams in sheer fabrics, as it only shows a small tuck (Figure 6.34a).

- To stitch, place the *wrong* sides of the fabric together and stitch a slightly *bigger* seam than ¼ inch—this means stitching slightly more than ¼ inch and slightly less than ³/₈ inch (Figure 6.35b).
- Trim the seam allowance back to ¹/₈ inch and press the seam to one side (see Figure 6.35b).
- Refold the fabric so the correct sides are facing. Stitch a slightly *smaller* seam than ¼ inch, and parallel to the seamline (Figure 6.35c). This row of stitching *must* enclose the raw edges inside encased in the seam.
- Press the seam to one side.

NOTE

French seams can be stitched on princess seams, but careful stitching is required as you stitch the second row of stitching around the curve. There is no need to clip the curved seam before stitching, as it will be cut back to ⅛ inch. If the princess seam has any easing, a French seam cannot be stitched. A hairline seam can be used instead. French seams cannot be stitched on circular seams or angled seams.

Hairline Seam

A hairline seam is a narrow, ¼-inch closed seam. It is an excellent finish for sheer fabrics, and a good

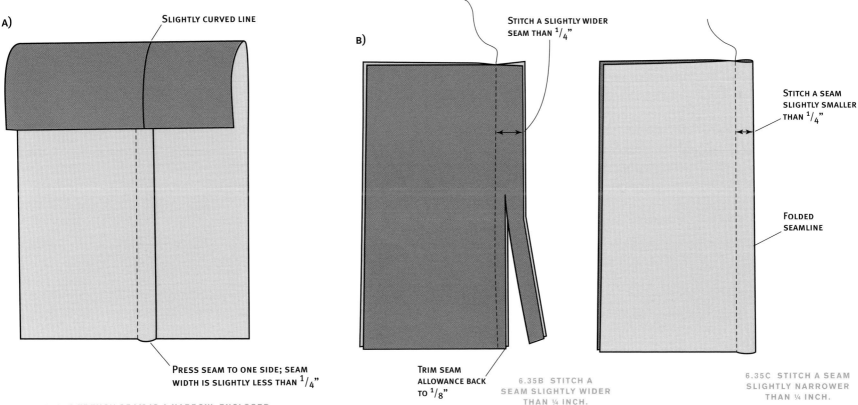

A)

SLIGHTLY CURVED LINE

PRESS SEAM TO ONE SIDE; SEAM
WIDTH IS SLIGHTLY LESS THAN $^1/_4$"

6.35A A FRENCH SEAM IS A NARROW, ENCLOSED
SEAM IDEAL FOR SHEER FABRICS.

B)

STITCH A SLIGHTLY WIDER
SEAM THAN $^1/_4$"

TRIM SEAM
ALLOWANCE BACK
TO $^1/_8$"

6.35B STITCH A
SEAM SLIGHTLY WIDER
THAN ¼ INCH.

STITCH A SEAM
SLIGHTLY SMALLER
THAN $^1/_4$"

FOLDED
SEAMLINE

6.35C STITCH A SEAM
SLIGHTLY NARROWER
THAN ¼ INCH.

alternative to stitching French seams on these fabrics. In production, hairline seams are also a less-expensive alternative to French seams.

• Follow Figure 6.36 to stitch a hairline seam. Some design schools may have industrial sewing machines that stitch a zigzag stitch. However, your home machine will definitely have a zigzag stitch.
• Place the correct sides of the fabric together, stitch a plain ½-inch seam, and press the seam to one side.

• Stitch a row of zigzag stitches $^1/_{16}$ inch away from the seamline. The zigzag stitch should be slightly wider than $^1/_8$ inch.
• Cut the excess seam allowance off, leaving $^1/_{16}$ inch beyond the zigzag stitches.
• The finished seam should be ¼ inch wide.

Slot Seam

A slot seam features two open tucks folded to the center. The tucked seams are stitched to an underlay, which can be cut from contrasting or self-fabric. The tucks can be butted together or

PATTERN TIP

• Cut the underlay 1¼ inches wide and to the length of the seam.
• If the tucks are separated (with underlay showing between tucks) then the underlay needs to be cut wider. Calculate the measurement to your specification.

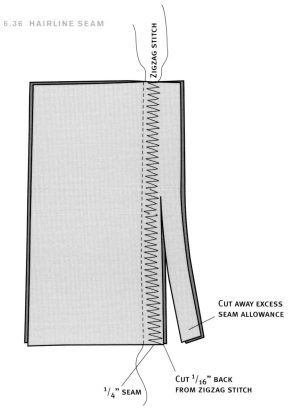

6.36 HAIRLINE SEAM

ZIGZAG STITCH

CUT AWAY EXCESS SEAM ALLOWANCE

CUT 1/16" BACK FROM ZIGZAG STITCH

1/4" SEAM

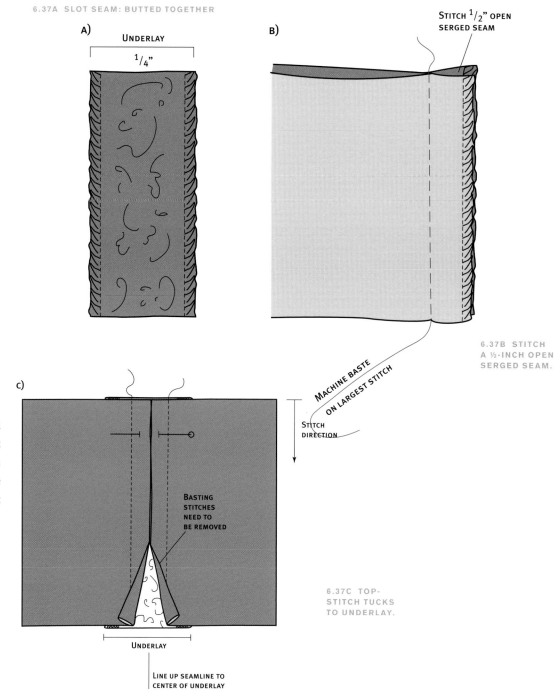

6.37A SLOT SEAM: BUTTED TOGETHER

A)

UNDERLAY

1/4"

B)

STITCH 1/2" OPEN SERGED SEAM

6.37B STITCH A 1/2-INCH OPEN SERGED SEAM.

MACHINE BASTE ON LARGEST STITCH

STITCH DIRECTION

c)

BASTING STITCHES NEED TO BE REMOVED

UNDERLAY

LINE UP SEAMLINE TO CENTER OF UNDERLAY

6.37C TOP-STITCH TUCKS TO UNDERLAY.

set apart, leaving a distance between each tuck and showing more of the underlay. Be sure that the underlay fabric is not too heavy, as bulk is being added when stitching these seams. The tucks and topstitching are not stitched to a set width. This decision is the to the designer.

- Serge edges of the underlay and garment separately (Figure 6.37a, b).
- With the correct sides of the fabric facing each other, stitch a ½-inch seam with a *large basting* stitch (see Figure 6.37b).

- Place the correct side of the underlay facing up. With the correct side of the garment facing up, match the seamline to the center of the underlay and pin in place (Figure 6.37c).
- Topstitch ¼ inch (don't forget to lengthen the stitch length) on either side of the seamline. Stitch directional so the stitching lies flat and not twisted. The topstitching should be parallel to the seamline (see Figure 6.37c).
- Carefully remove the basting stitches with the seam ripper and press.

SOME ESSENTIAL HAND STITCHES USED FOR STITCHING SEAMS

Although machine stitching is most often used to stitch seams, hand stitching also can be used. Garments that have hand-stitched seams will be expensive, and these garments are usually found in haute couture. Hand stitches can be used as permanent or temporary stitches, for gathering, easing, and topstitching. Hand stitching of any type adds cost to the garment because of the time it takes. Lace and beaded fabrics may need to be hand stitched in some areas because of the shape of the seam or because the fabric is so delicate.

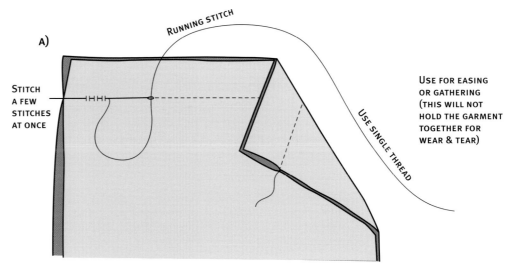

A)

RUNNING STITCH

STITCH A FEW STITCHES AT ONCE

USE SINGLE THREAD

USE FOR EASING OR GATHERING (THIS WILL NOT HOLD THE GARMENT TOGETHER FOR WEAR & TEAR)

6.38A RUNNING STITCH: USE FOR EASING OR GATHERING.

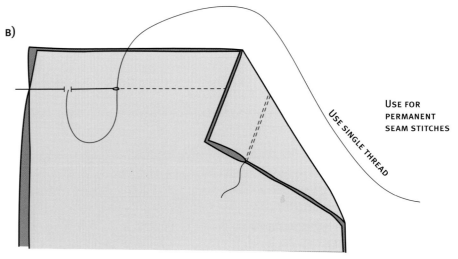

B)

USE SINGLE THREAD

USE FOR PERMANENT SEAM STITCHES

6.38B BACKSTITCH: USE FOR PERMANENT SEAM STITCHES.

C)

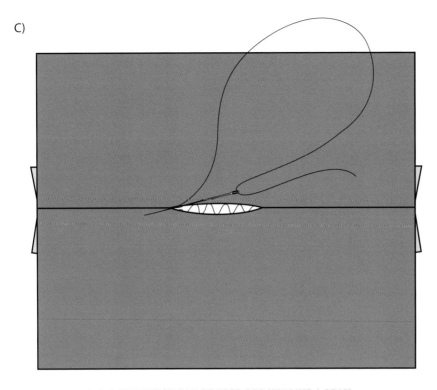

6.38C A SLIPSTITCH CAN BE USED FOR MENDING A SEAM.

Backstitch

A backstitch is a permanent hand stitch used to hand stitch almost any seam. It is a useful stitch for areas of the garment that would be difficult to machine stitch and is also useful when stitching darts in a beaded fabric.

After securing the thread, take a stitch back $1/16$ to $1/8$ inch through both layers of fabric to underneath and bring the needle back up for the same distance ($1/16$ to $1/8$ inch) forward from the previous stitch. Continue stitching to the end of the seam in this sequence (Figure 6.38b).

MORE ADVANCED SEAM STITCHING

Boning

What Is Boning?

Boning is used to stiffen and stabilize seams and to add structure to garments. It is flexible and will support the seams so the garment molds to the body. Boning supports and adds structure to a strapless garment so it sits firmly on the body. If you are not sure what a strapless garment looks like, turn to Figure 1.6 to view the elegant beaded strapless dress.

- Choose a hand needle that suits the fabric weight of your garment. Refer to Chapter 2, "Hand Sewing Needles." Always hand stitch with a single thread—not a double thread, except for closures.
- Cut the end of the thread on an angle, as it is easier to thread.
- Keep your thread lengths short—no longer than 22 inches; long threads get tangled and take longer to pull through the fabric.
- Make sure the stitches are not pulled too tight, creating puckers.
- Work from right to left. (Switch directions if left-handed.)

- At the beginning and end of a seam, secure the thread with several backstitches. Tying a knot does not always provide the security needed to hold the seam.

Running Stitch

A running stitch will not hold a seam together on a garment but can be used for gathering and easing by hand. A running stitch may be a better choice of stitch for gathering some delicate fabrics such as fine silk georgette. Take several small even stitches at once, weaving in and out of the fabric. Pull the thread through before taking a few more stitches (Figure 6.38a).

Boning can be purchased by the yard and comes in two forms:

1. Boning that is stitched directly to the seams: Purchase Euro Rigelene boning. It is flexible, woven, and made from polyester. The edges of the boning can be stitched to the seams. It is available ¼ inch and ³/₈ inch wide and is sold by the yard.
2. Boning in a casing: The boning is inserted into black or white cotton- or polyester-covered casing. After the casing is stitched to the seams, ¼-inch wide boning is inserted into the casing.

It is absolutely essential that strapless garments be stabilized with fusible or sew-in underlining before the seams and boning are stitched. Refer to Chapter 3, "How to Apply a Sew-in Underlining (or Interfacing)." Boning on its own, without interfacing, is not sufficient to structure a strapless gown. The stabilizer is crucial to the success of the garment—a stabilizer is needed that is both heavy enough to hold the garment and compatible with the fabric type

and weight. Before choosing your stabilizer, it is most *important* to read "How to Choose the Best Stabilizer for Your Project" in Chapter 3. We also encourage you to sample first to find the best stabilizer option.

For All Boned Seams

Garments that are boned don't need the seam edges finished; leave raw edges, as this reduces bulk and prevents ridges from forming on the correct side of the fabric. After stabilizing and stitching open pressed seams, the boning is stitched. In both of the following techniques, no stitching is visible on the correct side of the garment.

- Stitch ½-inch seams. If the seams are princess seams, refer to Figure 6.12.
- If a woven stabilizer has been used, trim the seam allowance back to the seamline (see Figure 3.18).
- Press the seams open.

Boning in Casing

- Remove the boning from the casing before stitching the casing onto the seams (Figure 6.39).
- Place the wrong side of the garment facing up. Lay the seam allowance flat with both garment pieces facing to the left (see Figure 6.39).
- Center the casing on the seam allowance and pin in place (see Figure 6.39).
- Stitch the casing to both edges of the seam allowance, stitching directly on top of the stitches used to form the casing (see Figure 6.39).
- Staystitch the bottom casing edge ¹/₁₆ inch inside

the seamline and trim the tape back to ¹/₈ inch to reduce bulk (see Figure 6.39).

- Slide the boning back into the casing and trim the top length so that there is ¹/₂-inch clearance—no boning should be in the seam allowance (Figure 6.40a).
- Staystitch the top casing ¹/₁₆ inch inside the seam allowance and trim back to ¹/₈ inch. Now the boning is held stable in the casing and cannot move.

Boning—No Casing

When this boning application is stitched, the garment from the correct side shows no evidence of the boning (other than giving structure and support). This is how the boning would have been applied in the gorgeous strapless dress in Figure 1.6.

Rigelene is stitched directly to the seam allowance as follows:

- Use a large needle size such as a leather needle.
- Place the wrong side of the garment facing up and lay the seam allowance open with both garment pieces facing to the left. This is the same stitching method illustrated in Figure 6.39, as the casing and boning are interchangeable.
- Center the boning on the seamline, positioning it ½ inch down from the top edge to clear the seam allowance. Boning cannot be included in any seam allowance. The sketch in Figure 6.39 also applies to stitching the boning directly to the seam allowance.
- Stitch the boning to both sides of the seam allowance. Stitch the boning ¹/₁₆ inch back from the boning edge to both sides of the seam allowances (Figure 6.39).

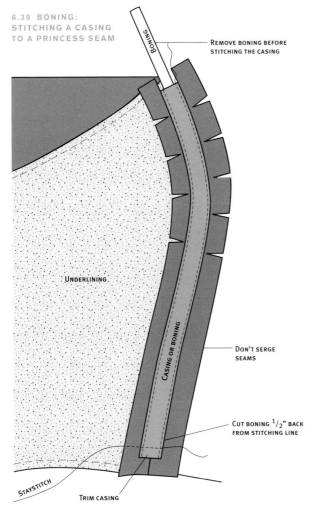

6.39 BONING: STITCHING A CASING TO A PRINCESS SEAM

BONING

REMOVE BONING BEFORE STITCHING THE CASING

UNDERLINING

CASING OR BONING

DON'T SERGE SEAMS

CUT BONING ¹/₂" BACK FROM STITCHING LINE

STAYSTITCH

TRIM CASING

NOTES

On princess seams, stitching the boning and the casing to the seam allowance will not interfere with the clipped seams laying flat or interfere with the fit of the garment.

Topstitched Boned Seams

For a different look, boning can be inserted into slots and topstitched. With this method, the boned seams are highlighted as a feature. The boning can be inserted into one or two slots. The seams are topstitched to form the slots, as seen in Figure 6.40.

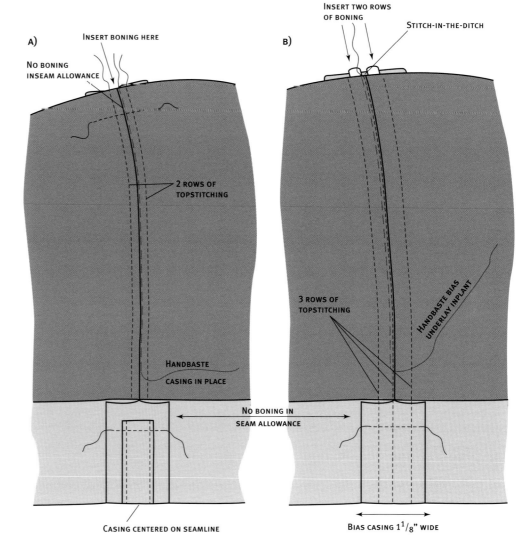

A)
NO BONING INSEAM ALLOWANCE
INSERT BONING HERE
2 ROWS OF TOPSTITCHING
HANDBASTE CASING IN PLACE
CASING CENTERED ON SEAMLINE

B)
INSERT TWO ROWS OF BONING
STITCH-IN-THE-DITCH
3 ROWS OF TOPSTITCHING
HANDBASTE BIAS UNDERLAY INPLANT
BIAS CASING 1¹/₈" WIDE

NO BONING IN SEAM ALLOWANCE

6.40A BONING INSERTED INTO SLOTS

6.40B INSERT TWO ROWS OF BONING. BIAS UNDERLAY.

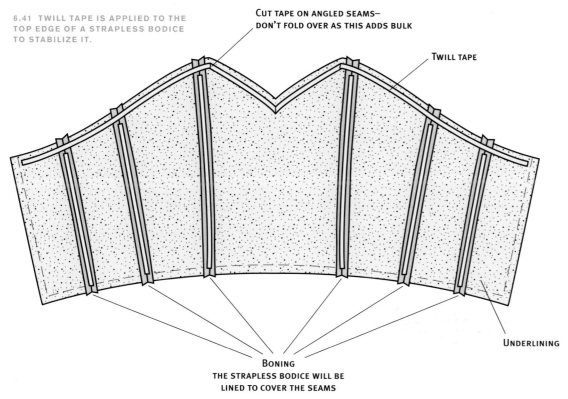

CUT TAPE ON ANGLED SEAMS—
DON'T FOLD OVER AS THIS ADDS BULK

TWILL TAPE

UNDERLINING

BONING
THE STRAPLESS BODICE WILL BE
LINED TO COVER THE SEAMS

One Slot

It is advisable to stitch a sample seam first to test stitch the width of the slot seam so the boning fits into the slot snugly (yet not too tightly).

- After the seams are stitched, center the boning casing (without boning) on the seamline of the wrong side of the fabric and pin in place.
- From the correct side, handbaste the casing (in-the-ditch) of the seamline so the handbasting holds the casing in place (see Figure 6.40a).
- From the correct side, follow the direction of handbasting and topstitch two rows of paral-

lel stitching to form the slot. Stitch approximately ⅛ inch on either side of the seamline (see Figure 6.40a).

- Slide the boning into the casing and staystitch the casing at each end, as illustrated in Figure 6.40a. Remove the handbasted stitches.

Two Slot

- Cut a *bias* strip 1⅛ inches wide and to the length of the seam to form the casing. The width and length of the casing must include seam allowances. The bias does not need to be serged when the garment is lined. The

serging only adds bulk. The underlay being bias-cut will mold beautifully to the curved seam.

- On the wrong side, center the bias underlay on the seamline and pin in place.
- From the correct side, handbaste the bias to the garment (in-the-ditch) in the seam line (see Figure 6.40b).
- From the correct side, stitch two rows of topstitching ¼ inch on either side of the seamline (see Figure 6.40b).
- Slide the boning into both slots and staystitch both ends, as explained earlier in "Boning with Casing" (see Figure 6.40b).

After the panels of the strapless bodice have been underlined, stitched, and boned, then twill tape needs to be applied to the top edge in one length so it is stabilized and does not stretch (Figure 6.41). Cut the tape to the angle of the top edge if it's shaped; don't fold the twill tape over, as this only adds bulk. The zipper is stitched next only if the garment is a top. If the garment is a dress, stitch the waistlines together next and then apply the zipper. The lining is stitched to the top edge of the strapless bodice and covers all the seams. Hand stitch the lining to the zipper tape. Refer to Chapter 16 (Figure 16.10).

Godets

Godets are V-shaped (triangular) pieces of fabric that are inset into a seam. A godet adds flare and fullness to the section where it is inserted. Godets can be stitched into skirts (see Figure 3.5) and dresses, as illustrated in Figure 6.42.

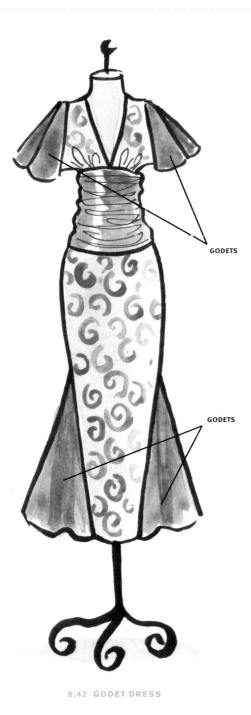

GODETS

GODETS

6.42 GODET DRESS

Inseam Godets

The first and most important part of stitching godets is to have matchpoints marked on the seams and the godets. Matchpoints are marked on both sides of the seams (Figure 6.43a). Another matchpoint is centered on the seamline of the godet, as illustrated in Figure 6.43b. Without marking these matchpoints, godets *cannot* be successfully stitched.

- Serge all seams, as open seams will be stitched. Also serge both sides of the godet but not the hem (see Figure 6.43). The hem will be serged in one stitching process after the godet is stitched.
- Place the correct sides of the garment together, stitch a ½-inch seam to the matchpoints, and end with a backstitch (see Figure 6.43a).
- Press the seam open to the matchpoints.
- Place the correct sides of the godet and one seam edge together and pin from the matchpoint to the hem (see Figure 6.43b).
- Begin stitching at the matchpoint. Lower the needle directly into the matchpoint and carefully stitch forward ¼ inch and back to secure the seam. Do not stitch further back than the matchpoint or the godet will *not* fit correctly! Continue stitching a ½-inch seam to the hem (see Figure 6.43b).
- Insert the other side of the godet into the other side seam by following the same stitching order.
- Press the godet and side seams together in one direction as indicated in Figure 6.43c. The seams *must* not be attached together at any point other than the seam stitching.

Stretch Seams

Knowing how to stitch stretch seams in knit fabrics is important to the designer. Knits can be fun to stitch! The stretch element in each knit differs; some knits are stable, while others are very stretchy. When seams are stitched in knit fabrics, they need to stretch to the stretch capacity of the fabric. For this reason, sample first before constructing your knit garment. This is essential so that stitches can be individualized for each knit.

Stable knits have minimal stretch and can be stitched using ½-inch seams pressed open. A straight stitch will "pop when stretched." Moderate to stretchy knits are best stitched with ¼-inch serged seams or a crooked straight stitch[2]. (Figure 6.44b zigzag width of .5 and stitch length of 2.5.)

Since knits don't ravel, seams generally don't need to be finished; however, a serged edge gives a more professional look and would be used in production. Some cut edges do curl, so a finish will give a better look to the garment.

Another useful stretch stitch is a three-stitch zigzag. It also has the same back-and-forth motion as the crooked straight stitch and serging, which allows the seam to stretch. This stitch is used to apply clear elastic to the seam allowance to stabilize seams. Look at Figure 6.44c to see this stitch. A wide zigzag stitch could also be used in its place. In production the elastic would be applied in one stitching process when the seams are serged together. At school, operating the serger to do this, without experience, can be a hard task.

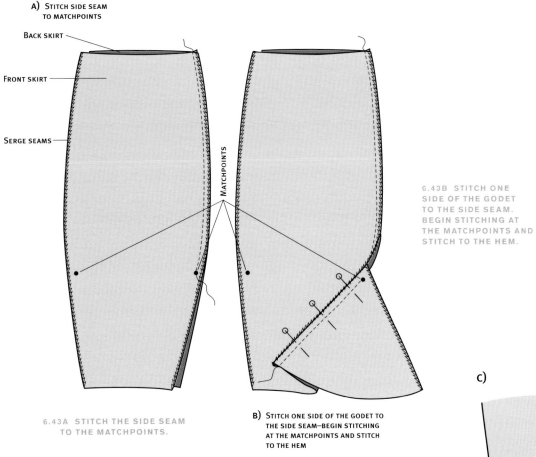

A) **STITCH SIDE SEAM TO MATCHPOINTS**

BACK SKIRT

FRONT SKIRT

SERGE SEAMS

MATCHPOINTS

6.43A STITCH THE SIDE SEAM TO THE MATCHPOINTS.

6.43B STITCH ONE SIDE OF THE GODET TO THE SIDE SEAM. BEGIN STITCHING AT THE MATCHPOINTS AND STITCH TO THE HEM.

B) **STITCH ONE SIDE OF THE GODET TO THE SIDE SEAM—BEGIN STITCHING AT THE MATCHPOINTS AND STITCH TO THE HEM**

Elastic can be applied in two ways:

1. Applied to straight seams to stabilize: Clear elastic or bias-cut Seams Great can be used to stabilize straight seams. Don't stretch the elastic when applying it to the seams (Figure 3.15 on shoulders).
2. Applied to edges so they cling to the body: When the elastic is applied to garment edges, it needs to be stretched as you stitch.

6.43C GODET STITCHED INTO THE SEAM AND PRESSED

Look at the jersey knit dress n Figure 6.45 to see all the seams and edges where the elastic has been applied. On average, the elastic length needs to be 1 to 1½ inches shorter than the seam length. However, we advise you sample first. Notice, also, that the edges are topstitched with twin needle stitching. Oh yes! This stitch also has that back-and-forth motion. Look at Figure 6.46 to see how the elastic is stretched as it is stitched to the neckline of the dress in this figure.

c)

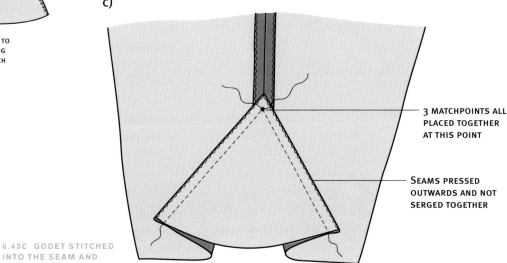

3 MATCHPOINTS ALL PLACED TOGETHER AT THIS POINT

SEAMS PRESSED OUTWARDS AND NOT SERGED TOGETHER

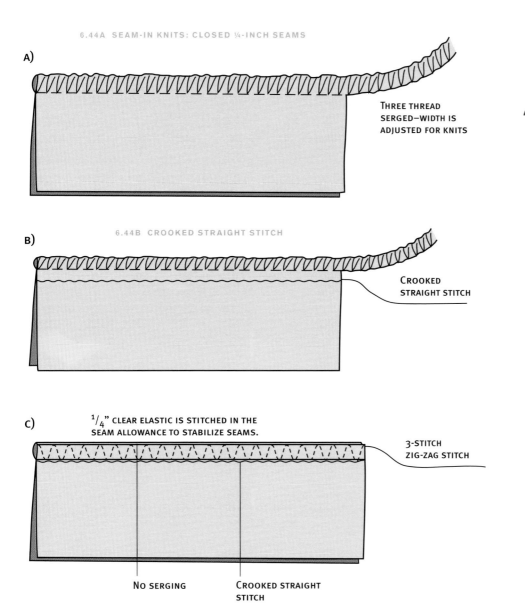

A)

THREE THREAD
SERGED—WIDTH IS
ADJUSTED FOR KNITS

B)

CROOKED
STRAIGHT STITCH

C)

$^1/_4$" CLEAR ELASTIC IS STITCHED IN THE
SEAM ALLOWANCE TO STABILIZE SEAMS.

3-STITCH
ZIG-ZAG STITCH

NO SERGING

CROOKED STRAIGHT
STITCH

6.44C CLEAR ELASTIC IS STITCHED IN THE SEAM ALLOWANCE TO STABILIZE SEAMS.

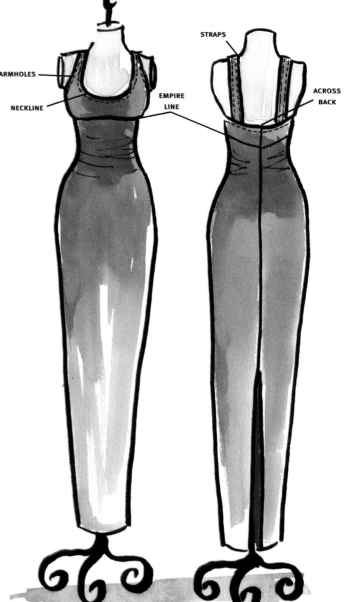

6.45 JERSEY KNIT DRESS. ELASTIC APPLIED TO THESE
EDGES SO THAT THE DRESS CLINGS TO THE BODY.

STRAPS

ARMHOLES

NECKLINE

EMPIRE
LINE

ACROSS
BACK

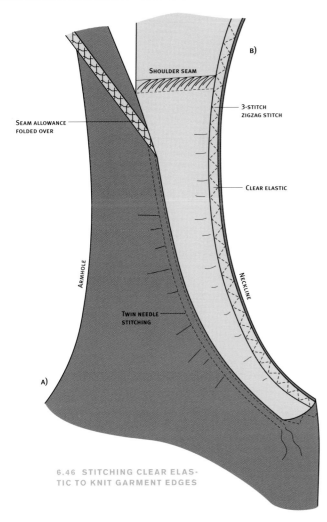

6.46 STITCHING CLEAR ELAS-
TIC TO KNIT GARMENT EDGES

STITCHING SEAMS IN TRICKY FABRICS
Matching Stripes, Plaids, Patterns, and Repeat Patterns

Refer to Chapter 2, "Tricky Fabrics—What They Are and How to Prepare to Use Them." Do read this section, in particular, "Matching Stripes, Plaids, Patterns, and Repeat Patterns." When stitching seams in stripes,

checks, plaids, or fabrics with repeat patterns, it is important to line up the seams perfectly so the patterns, stripes, and checks match when they are stitched. It would be helpful to take a look at Figures 2.15, 2.16, and 2.17, as they illustrate how to cut striped, checked, and one-way patterned fabrics. Garments with seams that don't match will probably be the ones discounted 50 percent at the end of the season. Such haphazard construction could leave a company with a reputation for producing poor-quality garments. The check jacket in Figure 6.1c, in the Style I.D. has perfectly matched seams—so perfect, in fact, you can't even see the seams!

Do cut stripes and plaids to match; if they are not cut to match, they cannot be stitched to match.
Do pin the seams at more regular intervals than usual to hold the stripes, checks, or plaid in place (Figure 6.47).
Do walk your machine over the pins (this is an exception to the rule—don't stitch over pins) if you feel the seams will be out of alignment if the pins are removed.
Don't use handbasting stitches because they will not hold stripes and checks in place as well as pins.

Sheer Fabrics
Do use a 60 or 70 machine needle for your project.
Do try tissue stitching the seams.
Do stitch ¼-inch narrow seams on sheer fabrics—French seams (see Figure 6.35), hairline

seams (see Figure 6.36), or closed ¼-inch narrow serged seams. Narrow seams show minimal shadowing from the correct side of the garment.
Do stitch ½-inch seams in sheer fabrics if the garment is lined. Press the seams open and cut the seam allowance back to a ¼ inch. The lining will cover the raw edges and the seams will not be noticeable, especially if they are not finished.

6.47 SEAMS IN STRIPES, PLAIDS, AND REPEAT
PATTERNS CAN ONLY BE STITCHED TO MATCH
WHEN THEY HAVE BEEN CUT TO MATCH.

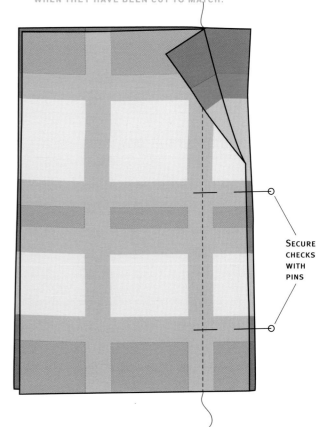

Lace

Do use a machine needle suitable for the weight of lace.

Do try tissue stitching the seams.

Do try an open or closed (the decision depends on the fabric weight) Hong Kong seam finish on unlined lace garments (see Figures 6.33). Bias binding can be cut from a nude sheer fabric such as silk organza to blend with the lace. It is important in lace that any seam finish looks as inconspicuous as possible.

Do stitch a ½-inch plain open seam (*not* serged) when the garment is lined. The seam allowance can be cut back to ¼ inch to eliminate any shadowing from the correct side.

Do consider overlaying the lace and hand stitching over a structured garment. Use good-quality lace such as guipure lace. To do this:

- Carefully cut off the scalloped border from the lace (Figure 6.48a).
- The lace is molded over the structured garment, as illustrated in Figure 6.48a.
- As the lace is molded, hand stitch the lace using a backstitch or overhand stitch (see Figure 6.38).
- Cut away the excess lace from underneath after each section is stitched (see Figure 6.48a).
- The scallop border can be appliquéd to any edge by hand stitching. After the scallop border is applied, cut the excess lace from underneath (Figure 6.48b).

When lace is stitched using this stitching technique there are *no* lace seams. The seams are still there underneath, in the garment, but the lace hides them. After the lace is applied in this way, the lace over the entire section will appear to be one piece of lace with no seam joins. Look at Figure 6.48b; can you see any seams? Even lace sleeves can be stitched in this way to eliminate armhole seams. As you can imagine, overlaying lace is labor intensive and adds to the cost of the garment. Although time consuming, this technique is well worth the time it takes.

Satin

Do tissue stitch the seams. Choose tissue that is nearest in color to that of the fabric. Tear the tissue paper away after the seam is completed.

Do stitch satin in a clean environment. Make sure your hands are clean, your space cleared, and your sewing machine area cleaned of any grease, because satin marks very easily.

Do mark matchpoints as lightly as possible—sample first to check that pattern markings will not show from the correct side of the fabric.

Do stitch directional.

Do hold the fabric taut when stitching to prevent puckered seams.

Do use fine needles instead of pins on fine satin fabrics, as pins may leave marks in the fabric.

Do finish seams as flat as possible in satin fabrics.

Do press satin fabrics with a pressing cloth of silk organza.

Do a test seam if you want a serged open seam. Press the seam open and, from the correct side of the fabric, look to see if the serging has left any ridges. If a ridge is noticeable, choose another seam finish or leave raw edges (the lining will cover them).

Don't forget to handbaste seams in delicate satins.

Beaded Fabric

Do try stitching the seams with tissue paper. Place it under the seams to stabilize the fabric while stitching. Choose tissue paper in a color that is a match to the fabric.

Do protect delicate beaded fabric when you are laying it out and cutting. Place a piece of pattern paper on the table to cover the entire surface, as delicate fabric snags easily.

Do clean your machine and the work area before you begin stitching, because beaded fabric is delicate and may snag easily.

Do remove all the beads from every seam allowance, seam edge, and darts before any seams are stitched. The sewing machine cannot stitch over beads on the fabric.

Do use a wooden block, covered with paper, as base for smashing the beads from the seam allowance. Place a sheer fabric (so you can see what you are doing) over the seams to protect the fabric. Carefully "smash" the beads with a hammer and remove them from all the seam allowances.

Do stitch the darts or difficult seams by hand using a backstitch. The sewing machine foot often gets in the way of the beads.

Do sample ½-inch plain seams pressed open, French seams, or ¼-inch closed serged seams. Find the seam that best suits the fabric.

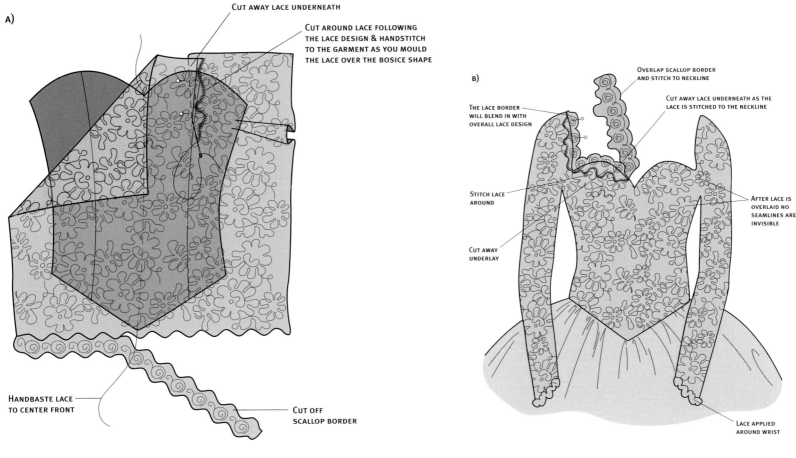

A)

CUT AWAY LACE UNDERNEATH

CUT AROUND LACE FOLLOWING
THE LACE DESIGN & HANDSTITCH
TO THE GARMENT AS YOU MOULD
THE LACE OVER THE BOSICE SHAPE

HANDBASTE LACE
TO CENTER FRONT

CUT OFF
SCALLOP BORDER

6.48A OVERLAY THE LACE BY MOLDING IT OVER THE
UNDERSTRUCTURE OF THE GARMENT.

B)

OVERLAP SCALLOP BORDER
AND STITCH TO NECKLINE

THE LACE BORDER
WILL BLEND IN WITH
OVERALL LACE DESIGN

CUT AWAY LACE UNDERNEATH AS THE
LACE IS STITCHED TO THE NECKLINE

STITCH LACE
AROUND

AFTER LACE IS
OVERLAID NO
SEAMLINES ARE
INVISIBLE

CUT AWAY
UNDERLAY

LACE APPLIED
AROUND WRIST

6.48B APPLIQUÉ LACE SCALLOP BORDER

Do sample a closed Hong Kong finish on unlined garments. The finished seam will be ¼ inch—it looks clean and neat (see Figure 6.33d). **Don't** overdesign beaded fabrics—keep the design lines simple, with as few seamlines as possible.

Don't finish the raw edges, if the fabric is lined. Leave the cut edges as this helps to prevent shadowing from the correct side.

Knits

Do use ¼-inch seam allowances for all knit seams.
Do insert a ballpoint needle in the appropriate size for the fabric weight.
Do use differential feed on your serger when stitching knit seams. Differential feed is two sets of feed dogs that oppose each other. This prevents the fabric from stretching out due to the high rate of sewing speed.

Do try a crooked straight stitch. This slightly zigzagged stitch works wonderfully well for the stretch seams needed on knit garments (see Figure 6.44b).
Do use a three-thread serger, as it works very well on most knit seams (see Figure 6.44a). Always check bulk, as serged seams may be too bulky in heavier knits.
Do stitch clear elastic (not stretched) to

shoulder seams to stabilize. Stitch clear elastic, slightly stretched, in the seam allowance and edges (using a three-stitch zigzag) to help low-cut garment edges cling to the body (see Figures 6.44c and 6.46).

Do use clear elastic pulled tightly as a method of gathering a length of knit into a ruffle.

Don't use permanent straight stitches for stitching seams in stretch knit fabric, as the stitches will "pop." Instead use a stretch stitch.

Denim

Do enjoy working with denim, as it's an easy fabric to work with, especially for a beginner.

Do topstitch denim garments. Denim loves to be topstitched—the use of topstitching is rarely overdone in denim—just look at your own jeans.

Don't line denim garments, as denim is a casual fabric for everyday wear.

Velvet

Do use the appropriate needle size for the velvet.

Do handbaste seams in pile fabrics before stitching. The underneath seam can easily creep up as you stitch, leaving one seam longer if the seam is not handbasted in place before stitching.

Do tissue stitch velvet using the color of tissue that most closely matches your fabric.

Do hold the fabric taut as you stitch.

Do stitch with the nap.

Do use a Velvaboard for pressing velvet fabric. Refer to Chapter 2, "Tricky Fabrics—What They Are and How to Prepare to Use Them."

Do flatten seams by holding the iron approximately 2 inches above the seam; give it a shot of steam, and stroke the seam in the direction of the pile to flatten the seams.

Do stitch ½-inch plain open seams in velvet.

Do design velvet garments simply, as velvet is a challenging fabric to work with.

Don't topstitch velvet—topstitch denim instead!

Don't place the iron directly on the velvet, as it will leave a shiny imprint of the iron and flatten the pile. (We *have* known students to press iron marks on the fabric purposely as a decorative surface finish!)

Don't stitch closed serged seams on velvet.

Don't serge the seams if the garment is lined.

Leather

Do stitch seams using a leather needle in the appropriate size for the weight of leather.

Do make the stitch length longer when stitching leather (approximately 7 to 9 stitches per inch).

Do tie the thread at the beginning and end of the seam.

Do reduce your speed for more accurate stitching. Seam ripping in leather results in permanent needle holes.

Do stitch directional.

Do lower the iron temperature and turn off the steam when pressing leather.

Do stitch ½-inch seams in leather and secure seams with leather cement. Use cotton Q-tips (purchased from the supermarket or pharmacy) to apply (Figure 6.49).

Do topstitch seams in leather—they don't need to be glued. Trim the seam allowance back to the topstitching.

Do grade bulky seams in leather

Do use a mallet and wallpaper roller to flatten the seams in leather.

Do stitch curved, angled, or circular seams in leather; clip seams, and barge open. Cut V shapes out of shaped seams to reduce bulk (Figure 5.3b).

Do stitch a lapped seam in leather (Figure 6.50). It's an ideal seam for use in leather, suede, vinyl, and plastic. A lapped seam uses only one seam allowance to eliminate bulk. To do so:

- Cut off the other ½-inch seam allowance from *one* seam; do this symmetrically on each side. Use a rotary cutter, as it cuts a smooth, even edge.
- Apply fabric glue (this is not permanent glue) to secure the seams together. Bring the seam edge (the edge with no seam allowance) and place it to the seamline of the other garment piece.
- Finger-press the two pieces together.
- Topstitch the lapped seam with a double topstitching.

Don't begin stitching seams with a backstitch, as it cuts into the leather.

Don't pin seams—instead secure seams with small binder clips.

Don't press leather without placing a brown paper over the leather as a surface protection.

Don't need to finish seams in leather—leather does not fray.

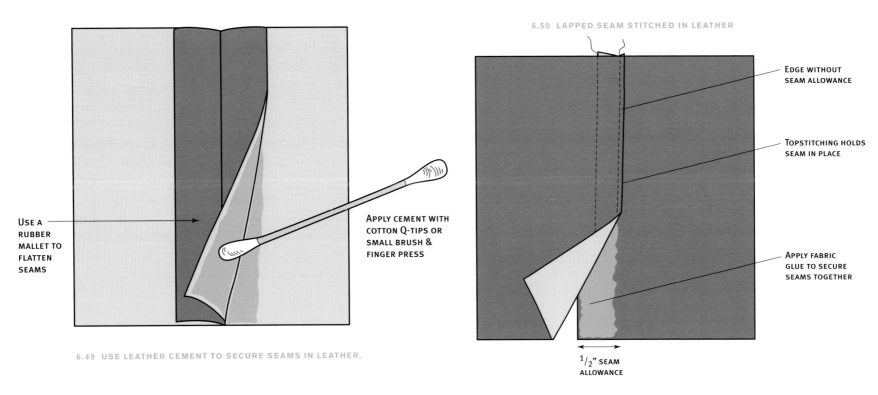

USE A RUBBER MALLET TO FLATTEN SEAMS

APPLY CEMENT WITH COTTON Q-TIPS OR SMALL BRUSH & FINGER PRESS

6.49 USE LEATHER CEMENT TO SECURE SEAMS IN LEATHER.

6.50 LAPPED SEAM STITCHED IN LEATHER

EDGE WITHOUT SEAM ALLOWANCE

TOPSTITCHING HOLDS SEAM IN PLACE

APPLY FABRIC GLUE TO SECURE SEAMS TOGETHER

¹/₂" SEAM ALLOWANCE

Faux Fur

Do design fur carefully, as intricate seamlines will not be noticed in fur.

Do trim away the fur from every seam allowance before stitching the seams. Trimming the fur from the seams reduces bulk and will help the seam to sit flat (Figure 6.51a). This also means trimming the fur from the seam allowance of collars, necklines, and front edges. After the seams are stitched, the seamlines will look inconspicuous. Finger-press the seams open and catchstitch the seam edges to the faux fur backing (Figure 6.51b). Refer to Chapter 15, "Catchstitch."

Do try turning the scissors on an angle to trim the fur.

Don't trim the fur off the hem allowance—it remains in place.

TRANSFER YOUR KNOWLEDGE

- If you know how to stitch curved, angled, and circular seams, you can stitch *any* shaped seams by transferring your knowledge.
- If you know how to stitch a closed Hong Kong finish, then you can stitch a bias binding around a pocket flap, shaped neckline, armhole, and collar or tab edges. Figure 6.33 shows this seam finish.
- If you know how to insert piping into a seam and you know how to stitch gathered seams, then you can combine these sewing tech-

niques and stitch a gathered piped seam. For this to be successful, the right fabric weight needs to be chosen so the seams are not too bulky.

- If you know how to stitch one in-seam godet, then you can stitch a godet within a godet.
- A slot seam can also be designed so the underlay is showing. The pattern would need to be adjusted and the underlay width cut wider to the specifications of the design. Then, don't butt the seams together, as indicated in Figure 6.37c; instead, leave a gap to show sheer lace. This would look fabulous down the center of a sleeve or stitched above the hemline.

STRETCH YOUR CREATIVITY

- Stitch beads to the seam instead of topstitching.
- Try stitching a panel insertion by stitching a layer of lace over the fabric using a zigzag stitch. After stitching, cut away the fabric to reveal the lace (Figure 6.52).
- Knowing how to stitch angles, curved, circular, and V-shaped seams is the student's ticket to being able to stitch *any* shaped seam! All you need is practice, imagination, and determination to create interesting seamlines.
- Stitch a lapped seam with a Hong Kong seam finish. The binding can then be diagonally stitched by hand, as illustrated in Figure 6.53.

- What about making a special garment for Valentine's Day? The topstitching says it all (Figure 6.54a)!
- Insert any trim into a seam (Figure 6.54b).
- Figure 6.55 illustrates how different seam techniques can be combined in one design. The seam techniques used are piped seams, slot seams, gathered seam, lace panel insertion, and appliquéd scallop border on the neckline and sleeve hem.

STOP! WHAT DO I DO IF . . .

. . . one seam ends up longer than the other?

Were notches used? If they weren't, this may be why one seam ended up longer than the other.

Any seam can grow in the stitching process without the guidance of notches. Did you stitch directional? Neglecting to stitch directional can result in one seam ending up longer than the other. Check your pattern—perhaps your seams were not equal in length. Seam rip the garment and compare the seam length with your pattern—perhaps it has not been cut correctly.

. . . my seam looks twisted? What did I do wrong?

Fabric pieces cut off grain will look twisted. Seams of unequal lengths can make the seam look twisted. If a shorter seam is stretched to fit a longer seam, then the seam will look twisted.

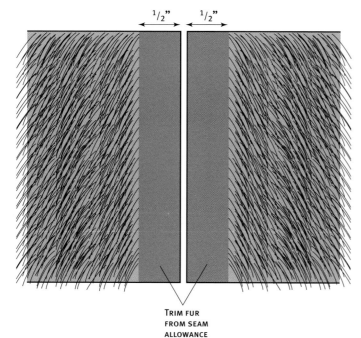

6.51A STITCHING SEAMS IN FUR: TRIM THE FUR FROM THE SEAM ALLOWANCES TO REDUCE BULK.

½" ½"

TRIM FUR FROM SEAM ALLOWANCE

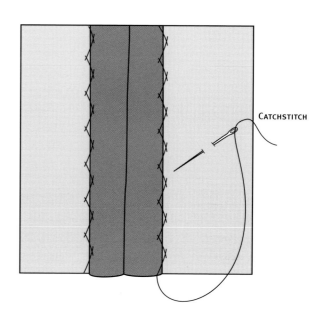

6.51B CATCHSTITCH SEAMS IN FUR TO HOLD FLAT

CATCHSTITCH

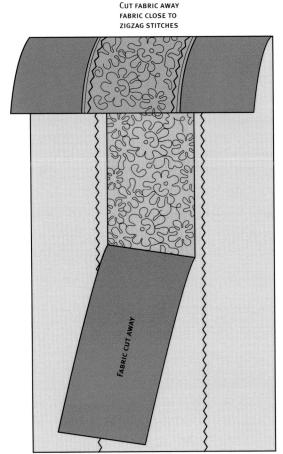

CUT FABRIC AWAY
FABRIC CLOSE TO
ZIGZAG STITCHES

FABRIC CUT AWAY

6.52 PANEL INSERTION

It sounds like a pattern problem, so readjust the pattern so the pattern seams are of equal length. Seam rip the seam, and press the seams so they lie flat. Then place the patterns back on top of the fabric and recut. Restitch the seam, making sure to pin the seam for support. Just an added

note—with notches, seams will line up perfectly and not look twisted!

. . . my seam ripples?

Did you sample the seam first to experiment with the fabric and to check the machine tension? Often students skip this step, as they think it will save time—no, it doesn't save time! Perhaps you have the incorrect needle size for the fabric weight? Seam rip the stitches and press the seams so they lie flat. You could try tissue stitching—this helps prevent the seams from puckering. Also, be sure to hold the fabric taut as you stitch, and remember to use a seam support, such as pins and handbasting, to help hold the seam in place.

. . . I have skipped stitches?

Here is list of things you can do:

- Check that you have used the correct needle size and type.
- Check the machine tension.
- Check the machine threading.
- Apply a new needle and sample again.
- Tissue stitch the seam, as this often improves the problem.

SELF-CRITIQUE

Take a look at your finished garment and ask the crucial question: "Would I wear this garment or would I purchase this garment?" If the answer is "No," then ask yourself, why not? It may be because you don't like the design, the proportions, or the fabric choice. However, when we ask stu-

6.53 LAPPED SEAM
WITH HONG KONG
SEAM FINISH

dents this question, many of them respond that it is the quality of stitching that would prevent them from wearing or purchasing their own garment. Ask yourself the following questions to critique your seam stitching:

- Did I use the correct number of stitches per inch to suit the fabric type and weight?
- Did I use the *SEW, CLIP, PRESS* method of stitching?
- Do the seams lie flat?
- Are the seams bulky?
- Is the seam finish appropriate for the fabric?
- Do the seams shadow from the correct side?
- Do the seams pucker and look twisted?
- Did I stitch enough samples to make an informed decision regarding the best seam technique to use?

A) CREATIVE TOPSTITCHING

DON'T GRADE THE SEAM—THE SEAM ALLOWANCE USED TO PAD THE STITCHES

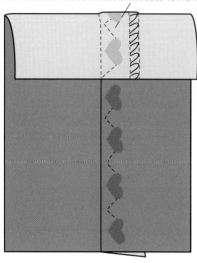

6.54A STRETCH YOUR CREATIVITY: CREATIVE TOPSTITCHING

B) INSERT ANY TRIM INTO A SEAM

DON'T FORGET TO GRADE THE SEAM ALLOWANCE

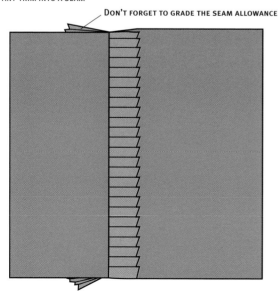

6.54B STRETCH YOUR CREATIVITY: INSERT ANY TRIM INTO A SEAM.

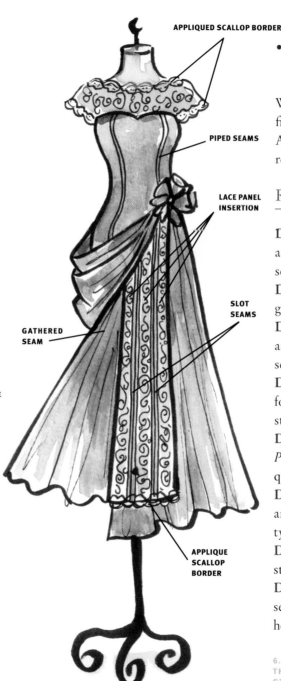

APPLIQUED SCALLOP BORDER

PIPED SEAMS

LACE PANEL INSERTION

SLOT SEAMS

GATHERED SEAM

APPLIQUE SCALLOP BORDER

6.55 STRETCH YOUR CREATIVITY: THE FOLLOWING SEAMS HAVE BEEN STITCHED IN ONE CREATIVE DESIGN.

• Did I continually fit my garment on the dress form as I stitched the seams together?

We suggest restitching a sample of any seam finishes that need to be improved or changed. Add the samples to your workbook for future reference.

REVIEW CHECKLIST

Do I understand the concept that fabric weight and drape should help me determine the best seam finish for my project?

Do I understand that cutting my fabric "on grain" will avoid twisted-looking seams?

Do I understand how pattern markings, such as notches and matchpoints, help me match my seams perfectly?

Do I know how important staystitching is for reinforcement and to prevent seams from stretching when I stitch?

Do I understand how using the *SEW, CLIP, PRESS* method of stitching helps me to stitch quality seams?

Do I understand that I need the correct type and size of machine needle to suit each fabric type and weight that I stitch?

Do I understand that the stitch length I use for stitching seams does matter?

Do I know the importance of stitching quality seams (part of structural design) as the seams hold the garment together?

Tucks and Pleats: Tailoring a Texture

Tucks and pleats are stitched folds of fabric used to take in fullness or to create shape in a garment. This is fashion meeting function. Tucks and pleats can be used decoratively on sleeves, blouses, dresses, and skirts (to take in a full skirt at the waist). Tucks and pleats can be crisply pressed or left unpressed as soft folds. The width of a tuck or pleat depends on the fabric weight and the desired design effect.

Tucks can be stitched as dart tucks, pin tucks, or corded tucks. Cross tucks add texture to the garment surface on lightweight fabric, and shell tucks can create a beautiful, delicate edge to fine fabrics.

Although there are many variations, all pleats are essentially different types of folds. Knife pleats are the most common pleat; they may face the same direction or be stitched in two directions, on either side of the center front and center back. Other types of pleats include box pleats, inverted pleats, and kick pleats. Accordion pleats are narrow knife pleats and

are the same width from top to bottom of the pleat, whereas sunburst pleats are narrower at the waist and graduate in size to the hem. Both of these pleats are most often found in evening wear and are usually pleated by a professional pleating service. Once the concept of pleats or tucks has been learned, the designer can add many variations of width and height to the garment successfully.

STYLE I.D.

Figure 7.1 illustrates some of the styles of tucks and pleats discussed in this chapter. Look at the

KEY TERMS

Accordion Pleat
Box Pleat
Corded Tuck
Cross Tuck
Dart Tuck
Inverted Pleat
Kick Pleat
Knife or Side Pleat
Overhand Tuck
Pin Tuck
Unpressed Pleat
Release Tuck
Shell Tuck
Sunburst Pleat

7.1A BLIND TUCK

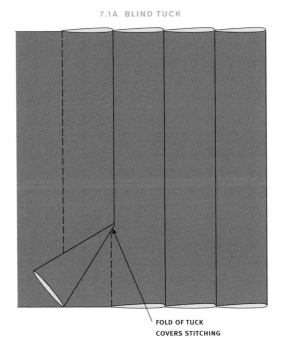

FOLD OF TUCK
COVERS STITCHING

7.1B CORDED TUCK

7.1C DART TUCKS OPEN AT ONE END

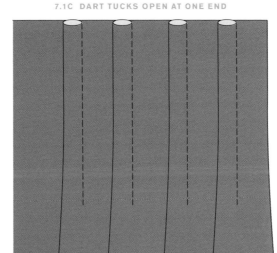

variation of each style. By the end of this chapter you will know how these techniques are stitched.

GATHER YOUR TOOLS

The tools needed to stitch pleats and tucks are: fabric marking pen; dressmaker tracing paper and wheel; pins; hand sewing needles; matching and contrasting thread; and pressing cloth. And don't forget your ruler and tape measure.

NOW LET'S GET STARTED

With your tools organized, you are now ready to begin the stitching process for pleats and tucks.

THREADS ARE PULLED
TO BACK AND KNOTTED

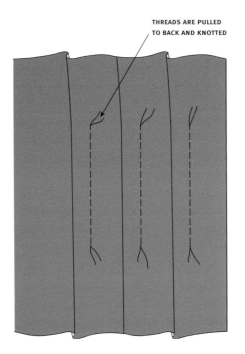

7.1D DART TUCKS OPEN AT BOTH ENDS

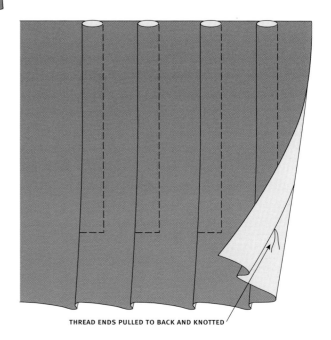

THREAD ENDS PULLED TO BACK AND KNOTTED

7.1E DART TUCK STITCHED ACROSS BOTTOM

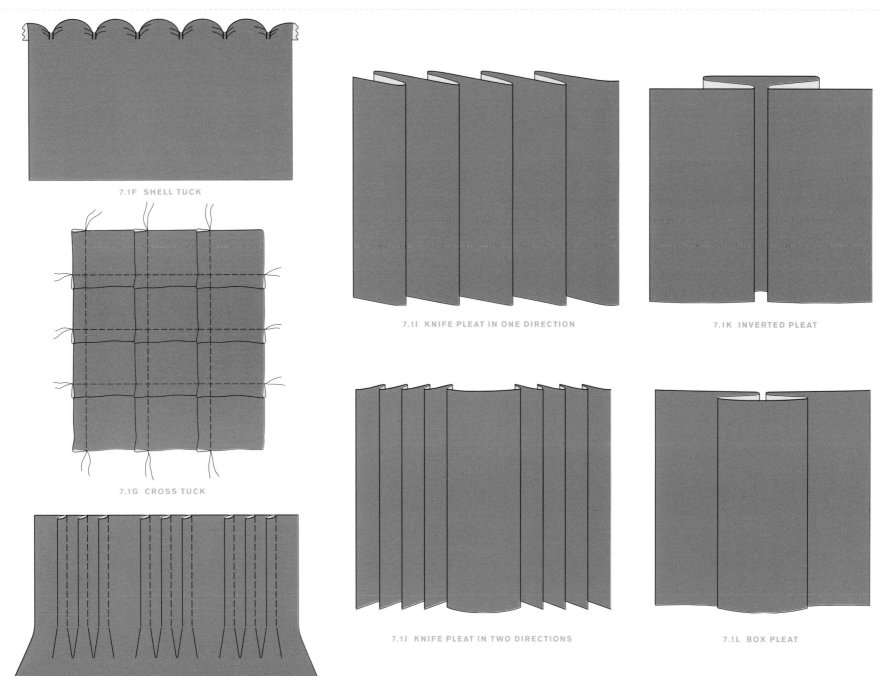

7.1F SHELL TUCK

7.1G CROSS TUCK

7.1H PIN TUCK

7.1I KNIFE PLEAT IN ONE DIRECTION

7.1J KNIFE PLEAT IN TWO DIRECTIONS

7.1K INVERTED PLEAT

7.1L BOX PLEAT

TUCKS

What Is a Tuck?

Tucks are folds of fabric stitched down either all or part of the way, such as release tucks. Tucks can be functional, used to shape the garment, as well as decorative. Tucks are usually folded on the lengthwise or crosswise grain to lie flat. Tucks stitched on the bias stretch easily. Each tuck is formed from two stitching lines that are matched together and stitched. The distance from the fold to the matching line determines the tuck's width. Tucks that meet or overlap slightly are called **blind tucks**

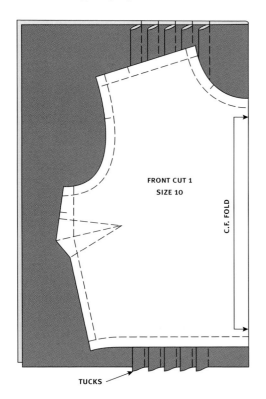

FRONT CUT 1
SIZE 10

C.F. FOLD

TUCKS

7.2 STITCHING TUCKS ON PLAIN FABRIC BEFORE PATTERN IS CUT

> **NOTE**
>
> Tucks can be stitched to the flat fabric before cutting out the garment. Stitch the tucks on the fabric, lay the pattern piece over the tucked area, then cut out the pattern piece (Figure 7.2).

(Figure 7.1a); tucks with predetermined space between them are spaced tucks, and a **pin tuck** is a very narrow tuck, as shown in Figure 7.1h, approximately ⅛ inch wide, or the designer's choice in conjunction with the weight of the fabric.

Light- to medium-weight fabrics are suitable for tucking, but design and print should be taken into consideration. Extra fabric is required when adding tucking to garments. To calculate the extra fabric needed, first establish the width and the number of tucks required. Double the width and multiply by the number of tucks. This amount must be added to the finished width of the garment pattern piece. *Example:* 10 tucks x ⅛ inch, doubled is 10 tucks x ¼ inch = 2½ inches of extra fabric that must be added to the pattern piece before cutting out and stitching the tucks.

- Establish the spacing between each tuck and the depth of the tuck.
- Notch the stitching lines for the tucks and the matchpoints (as shown in Figure 4.13) at the beginning and finish of each tuck.
- Using a disappearing fabric marker, mark the stitching lines on the correct side of the fabric for decorative tucks and on the wrong side of

the fabric for shaping tucks to ensure straight stitching.

- For delicate fabrics, handbaste the stitching lines.
- Stitch the tucks in the order shown in Figure 7.3.
- Begin with the center tuck, stitching downward.
- Next, complete the tucks on either side, stitching upward.
- Then move to the tucks on either side of those you've already done, stitching downward until complete.
- Switching the direction of stitching keeps the tucks straight and prevents puckering.
- Press each tuck individually as stitched, using a pressing cloth.
- Complete by pressing all the tucks in the desired direction.

Dart Tucks

Dart tucks are darts that are not stitched to a point; they are stitched the same length or shorter as the dart, but are left to open into full-

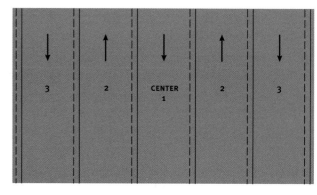

7.3 STITCHING ORDER OF TUCKS

7.4A DART TUCK

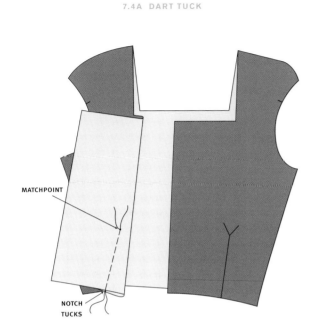

MATCHPOINT

NOTCH
TUCKS

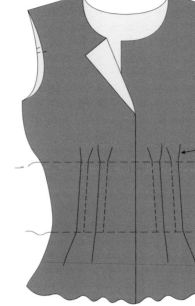

NOTE

When pressing a dart tuck, take extra care to press the tuck only, not the fabric folds released at the end of the tuck.

THREADS ARE PULLED
TO BACK AND KNOTTED

USE BASTING STITCHES
AS A GUIDE WHEN
STITCHING TUCKS

7.4C DART TUCKS ENDING ON AN EVEN LINE

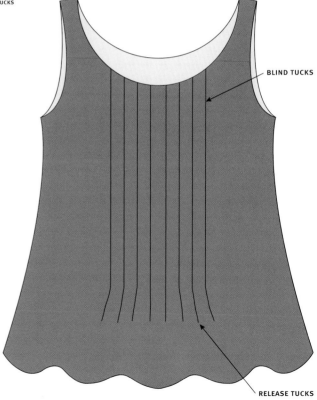

BLIND TUCKS

RELEASE TUCKS

7.5 BLIND TUCKS

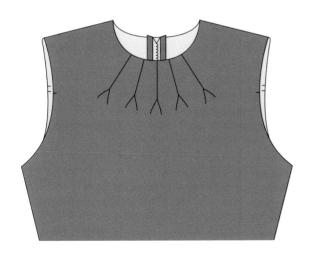

7.4B DART TUCKS FORMED ON WRONG SIDE OF FABRIC

ness (Figure 7.4a). Dart tucks can be stitched on the surface of the garment, providing decorative interest, or on the inside of the garment (Figure 7.4b). Rows of dart tucks can be stitched to end on an even line (Figure 7.4c), or stitched at an angle (Figure 7.4b). One dart at the bust or waist can be divided into several small dart tucks with the released fullness directed toward the curve it's covering.

Blind Tuck

Blind tucks (Figure 7.4b) are placed close enough together so that they meet, with no visible spaces

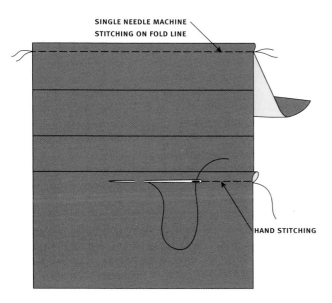

SINGLE NEEDLE MACHINE STITCHING ON FOLD LINE

HAND STITCHING

7.6A PIN TUCKS: HAND AND MACHINE STITCHING

between them (Figure 7.1a). The foldline of the tuck meets the stitching line of the next tuck. The tucks can all go in one direction or they can be pressed to each side of a center-front or center-back seam or opening (Figure 7.5).

Pin Tucks

Pin tucks (see Figure 7.1h) are a very beautiful detail on light- to medium-weight fabrics. Often associated with heirloom sewing, pin tucks can be machine stitched or hand sewn (Figure 7.6a); placed on sleeve caps, fronts, and backs of garments, or at the waist, cuff, pockets, or collars; or used in place of darts. In short, pin tucks can be stitched anywhere the designer wants to add textural interest. Pin tucks can also be used to control fullness when their ends are released into the garment.

Each tuck may be spaced to create a variety of designs. Machine stitching close to the folded edge of the pin tuck is what creates the beauty of this technique (see Figure 7.6a). A pin-tuck foot, available for home sewing machines, aids in the machine stitching. The use of a twin needle also creates wonderful pin tucks through the adjustment of the upper needle tension, which is easy to do on home sewing machines (Figure 7.6b). Excellent straight stitching with a steady hand is essential for the pin tucks to turn out prop-

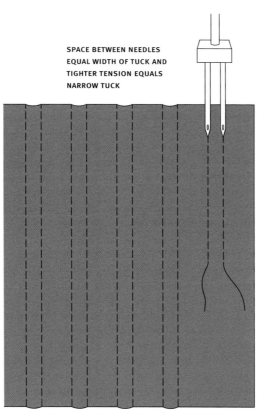

SPACE BETWEEN NEEDLES EQUAL WIDTH OF TUCK AND TIGHTER TENSION EQUALS NARROW TUCK

7.6B PIN TUCKS, DOUBLE NEEDLE

NOTE

When planning pin tucks, keep in mind that a 2-inch dart equals eight ¹/₄-inch pin tucks; a 1-inch dart equals four ¹/₄-inch pin tucks.

erly. The height of the pin tucks can be varied to create even more textural interest and control of the fullness.

To produce pin tucks on a home sewing machine, use a combination of a pin-tuck foot, the right thread, and the correct needle tension. The pin-tuck foot has multiple grooves that pull up the fabric into a consistent ridge while other grooves allow the foot to ride over the previous tucks. The right weight of thread affects the height of the tuck and the color of the thread changes the appearance of the tuck.

Follow these steps to replace a bodice waist dart with pin tucks:

How to Replace a Dart with Pin Tucks

- Fold the dart closed, and measure the bodice width (Figure 7.7a).
- Open the dart and cut a sample piece of garment fabric the same measurement as the bodice with the dart open (Figure 7.7b).
- Mark the dart center line (see Figure 7.7b).
- Begin to stitch pin tucks in parallel rows on either side of the dart center line until the sample is the same width as the bodice with the dart closed (Figure 7.7c).
- Count the number of pin tucks needed to replace the dart. Fewer rows are needed with

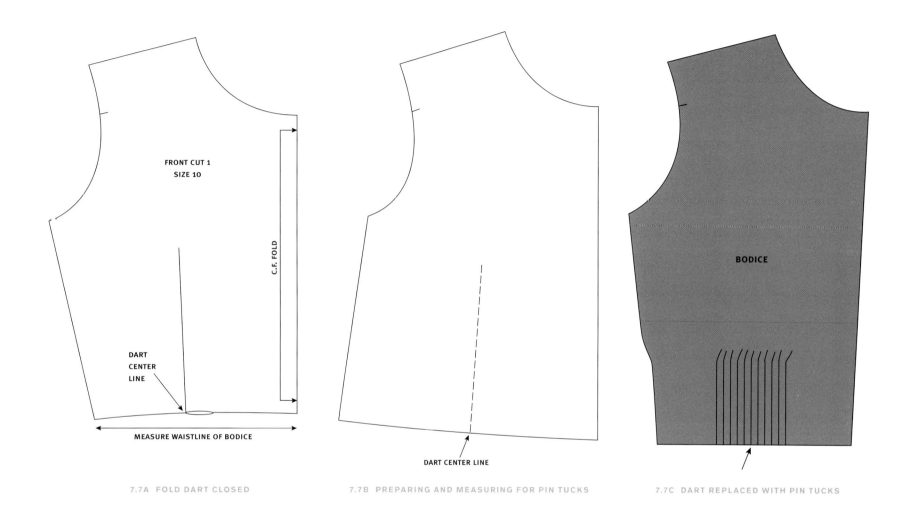

7.7A FOLD DART CLOSED   7.7B PREPARING AND MEASURING FOR PIN TUCKS   7.7C DART REPLACED WITH PIN TUCKS

larger pin tucks; more rows with smaller tucks.

- Don't pin tuck the entire height of the dart—this affects the side shaping. Pin tuck half the length of the dart to create a softer look.
- Pin tuck the waistline of a garment to replace darts and edges of the sleeves to control and direct the cuff fullness (Figure 7.7c).

Corded Tucks

Corded tucks are produced on firm fabric by placing piping cord inside the foldline of the tuck, matching the stitch line, and using a zipper foot to machine stitch along the stitching lines. The piping cord gives a raised, stuffed look to the tuck, which can be determined by the size of the cord and the depth of the tuck.

Corded tucks add firmness to the garment, and the fabric choice influences just how much firmness can successfully be added to the garment before it becomes too stiff. Use of cording that is too thick could result in unattractive tucks. Remember, just because you can, doesn't mean you should.

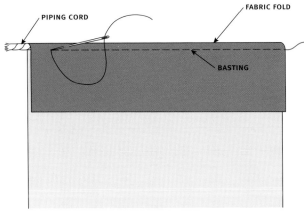

7.8A CORDED TUCKS

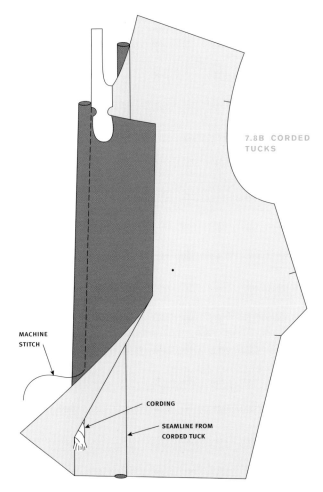

7.8B CORDED TUCKS

To stitch corded tucks:

- Choose a piping cord that is suitable for the width of the tuck.
- Fold the tuck, matching the stitching lines.
- Lay the piping cord inside the fold, and handbaste through the two layers of fabric to enclose the cord (Figure 7.8a).
- Use a zipper foot to machine stitch close to the cord along the basting line (Figure 7.8b).
- Avoid catching the cord in the machine stitching.
- Remove the basting stitches.
- Trim ends of the cord even with the garment seamline if being stitched to another garment section.

Cross Tucks

Cross tucks are a decorative arrangement of rows of tucks made crosswise and lengthwise on the fabric. These tucks can be absolutely beautiful on sheer fabrics, creating a graphic design that can be enhanced further by the choice of thread color used to stitch the tucks. Careful matching of the horizontal tucks to the previously stitched vertical tucks results in perfectly aligned stitching lines. Once you have gotten the spacing organized, the stitching can go along quite quickly. Consider tucking a plain piece of fabric first, then placing the pattern piece over it.

- Mark, baste, stitch, and press all the vertical (lengthwise) tucks in one direction (Figure 7.9).
- Next, mark, baste, stitch, and press the horizontal (crosswise) tucks, checking that the

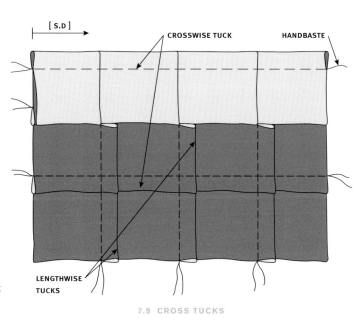

7.9 CROSS TUCKS

vertical tucks are going in the correct direction (see Figure 7.9).

- Press, making sure that all the tucks are going in the correct direction.

Shell Tucks

Shell tucks are decorative tucks formed by hand or machine stitching, so they can be very narrow or wide, depending on the look the designer desires and the fabric being used. Shell tucks are very effective in a soft fabric and are textured looking when used in a medium-weight fabric. When hand stitching the shell tuck:

- Mark the tuck stitching lines with fabric marker, but do not press flat; the shell should be rounded and gathered looking.
- Baste the narrow tucks and stitch by hand using a small running stitch or by machine

using a 2.0 stitch length (refer to Chapter 6, Figure 6.38a, for details).

- Stitch several overstitches over the fold at determined intervals to produce the scallops for the shell tuck (Figure 7.10).
- If the tucks are stitched by machine, the hand-stitching thread will have to be carried within the fold of the tuck from shell to shell.
- Shell tucks add textural interest when they are inserted into seams.

Overhand Tucks

A narrow, decorative tuck called an **overhand tuck** is produced on curved lines using very accurate hand stitching and measuring. This detail is a subtle addition to a garment and requires patience, control of the thread, and a very strong desire to create a curved teeny-tiny tuck! Completion of more than one tuck requires a serious allotment of time, so take that into con-

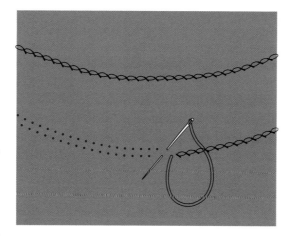

7.11A HAND-STITCHED OVERHAND TUCK

sideration when planning to use this technique. Curved lines appear in many places within a garment, and the decision about where this tuck would be most effectively placed is the designer's choice.

- Begin with accurate marking of two lines for each curved tuck on the garment; use a fabric marker or handbasting—sample the marker on your fabric first (Figure 7.11a).
- Also mark the distance between each stitch with a dot.
- Using a double strand of thread, pull the needle and thread from the wrong side of the garment to begin stitching at the top of the marked stitching line (Figure 7.11a).
- Take an overhand stitch approximately 1/8 inch from where the thread was brought up and match a dot on the opposite side of the stitching line (see Figure 7.11a).

> **NOTE**
>
> A very narrow zigzag machine stitch set at 1.0 stitch length and 1.3 width stitched along the folded stitching lines of this tuck produces a flatter, shallower, curved tuck. Stitching very carefully, the zigzag stitch must swing off the edge of the fold (Figure 7.11b).

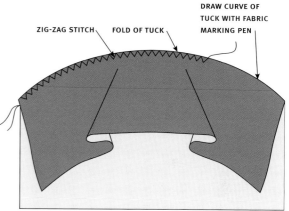

DRAW CURVE OF TUCK WITH FABRIC MARKING PEN

ZIG-ZAG STITCH   FOLD OF TUCK

7.11B MACHINE-STITCHED OVERHAND TUCK

- Continue stitching along the marked lines, pinching the narrow tuck between your fingers while stitching—hand stitching allows the formation of a very curved tuck.
- Keep the thread taut—the tuck should stand up from the surface.
- Press alongside the stitching on either side of the tuck, leaving the stitched tuck upright to create textural interest.
- A contrasting thread will highlight the tuck.

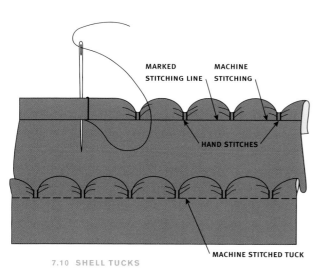

MARKED STITCHING LINE   MACHINE STITCHING

HAND STITCHES

MACHINE STITCHED TUCK

7.10 SHELL TUCKS

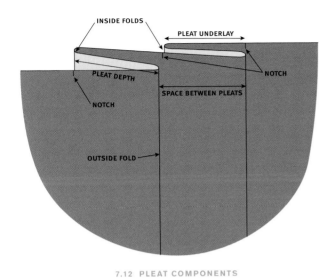

7.12 PLEAT COMPONENTS

Tucks add visual interest and also function as shape-makers. It is of the utmost importance when stitching tucks that they be measured accurately and be absolutely straight and even when stitched. When drawing attention to details such as any of these tucks, they must be executed with excellence.

PLEATS
What Are Pleats?

Pleats are folds of fabric used to control or add fullness in a garment. They can be stitched and left **unpressed,** forming soft folds in the garment. Or, they can be crisply pressed down the entire length of the pleat, to form a sharp edge. Although differentiated by names that describe their particular use or appearance, pleats comprise two basic types: **side pleats** (also known as **knife pleats** when they are crisply pressed), and **box pleats.** When a box pleat is made wrong

side out, it is called an **inverted pleat.** When it is short and inserted in the lower edge of a skirt, it is called a **kick pleat.** Pleats are spaced across the fabric, or in small groups, and are usually folded to their full depth. **Sunburst pleats,** which are narrow side pleats that are wider at the bottom than at the top, are made on a perfect circle of fabric. **Accordion pleats** are made the same way but may be formed on the straight grain of the fabric. These types of pleats are often used in evening gowns made in chiffon or crepe. Because of the difficulty of forming these pleats evenly, sending the fabric out to a professional pleating service provides the best result.

In production, it is more cost-effective to send the fabric to a company that specializes in pleating than it is to have it done in-house. The manufacturer provides the hip and waist measurements and the length of the finished pleated garment for all graded sizes.

There are three components to forming pleats (Figure 7.12):

1. The *pleat depth,* equal to the distance from the outside fold of the pleat to the inside fold of the pleat;
2. The *pleat underlay,* which is two times the pleat depth; and
3. The *pleat spacing,* which is the amount between the pleats.

Marking Knife Pleats on the Fabric
• Begin the pleat series with the seam allowance (Figure 7.13).

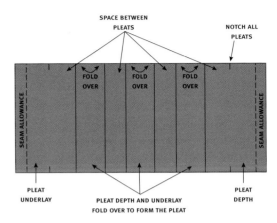

7.13 MARKING KNIFE PLEATS

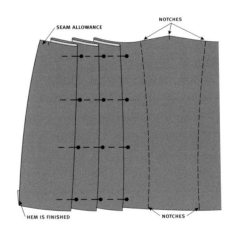

7.14 MARKING KNIFE PLEATS

• Next, mark the pleat underlay with notches (Figure 7.13).
• The space between the pleat follows.
• The pleat depth and underlay are next, folding over to form the pleat (Figures 7.13 and 7.14).
• Repeat this marking to the hip measurement ending with the pleat depth and seam allowance.

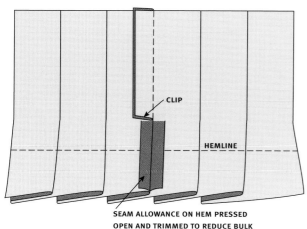

7.15A SEAMS IN PLEATS

CLIP

HEMLINE

SEAM ALLOWANCE ON HEM PRESSED
OPEN AND TRIMMED TO REDUCE BULK

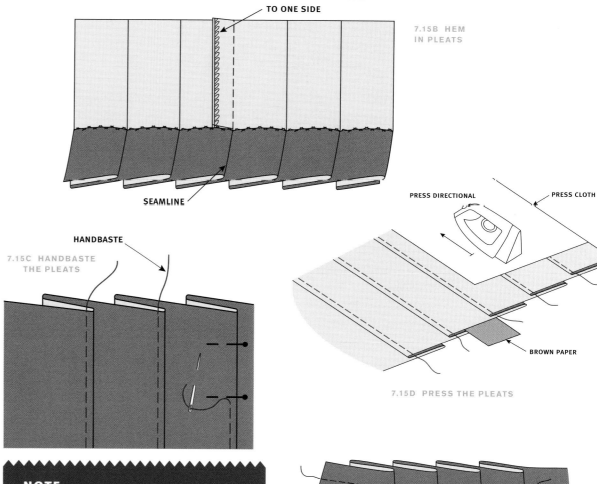

SERGED SEAM PRESSED
TO ONE SIDE

7.15B HEM
IN PLEATS

SEAMLINE

HANDBASTE

7.15C HANDBASTE
THE PLEATS

PRESS DIRECTIONAL

PRESS CLOTH

BROWN PAPER

7.15D PRESS THE PLEATS

- Handbaste each pleat through all layers.
- The seam is hidden in the center fold of the pleat.

Adjusting Pleats to the Waistline

Pleats are formed to fit the circumference of the hip measurement. In order for the pleated garment to fit at the waist, the pleats have to be adjusted (Figure 7.14).

To adjust the pleats to fit the waistline:

- Find the difference between the waist and hip measurements.
- Divide the difference by two times the number of pleats (each pleat has two sides). The resulting measurement represents the

NOTE

When a skirt or dress is hung from a yoke, a straight piece of fabric can be pressed parallel into pleats to match the bottom measurement of the garment piece. This can also be inserted into a part of the garment such as a section of the sleeve. In straight pleating, the fabric is set just the same at the top and the bottom. The pleats can be box pleats, side pleats, or inverted pleats.

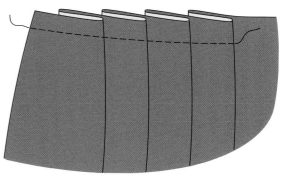

7.15E STAYSTITCH PLEATS

extra amount each pleat will take up to fit the waist.

- Measure this amount from each side of the pleat as shown in Figure 7.14.
- Blend a curved line, which becomes the new stitching line, from each mark to approximately 4½ inches below the waist as shown in Figure 7.14.

7.16 TOPSTITCHING PRESSED PLEATS

- Pleats can be topstitched at varying lengths below the waist (Figure 7.15c).

- Notch the pleats at upper edge and pin the corresponding positions to the hem (Figure 7.13).
- Insert side zipper (Figure 7.16).
- Join the seams (flat application—not stitched in-the-round).
- Trim the seam allowances to reduce bulk and mark the hemline (Figure 7.15a).
- Hem the pleats (Figure 7.15b).
- Mark the foldlines and the placement lines accordingly, and pin (see Figure 7.14).
- Handbaste the pleats along the folds; remove pins (Figure 7.15c).
- Press the pleats lightly in the direction they will face (Figure 7.15d).
- Staystitch the pleats across the upper edge (Figure 7.15e).
- Join the last seams (stitch in-the-round).
- Hand stitch the last section of hem and press.

Pressing the Pleats
- With the wrong side up, place strips of brown paper or tissue under each pleat to prevent an imprint of the pleat on the correct side of the garment (Figure 7.15d).
- Press, using a pressing cloth to set the pleats.
- For synthetic fabrics only, mix a solution of 1 part vinegar to 9 parts water for use in set-

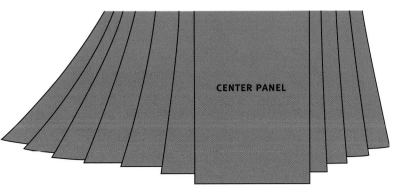

7.17 KNIFE PLEATS IN TWO DIRECTIONS

ting the pleats. Dampen a pressing cloth with the mixture and press through it to set the pleats for increased stability—always sample on a scrap of fabric.
- Turn to the correct side and steam the pleats, using a pressing cloth.
- Allow the pleats to dry on the ironing board before moving.
- Topstitch the pleats if desired (Figure 7.16).

Side Pleats/Knife Pleats

The most common form of pleats, the side pleat is formed with a single foldline and a single placement line. When folded and positioned, all side pleats face the same direction (Figure 7.1i). A sharply pressed, narrow side pleat is known

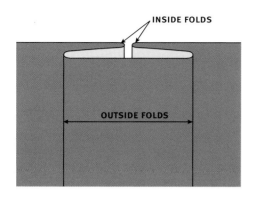

7.18 BOX PLEAT

as a knife pleat and is constructed the same way. The Perfect Pleater, developed by Clothilde, is an arrangement of folded canvas and cardboard that resembles closed window blinds. It comes in different configurations and sizes for use in constructing knife pleats and box pleats on fabric of any length and up to 27 inches wide. The size of the pleats can be varied by skipping any number of the canvas folds. Asymmetrical pleating patterns can be created in the same way. Some fabrics may require professional pleating to heat-set the narrow pleats.

- If there is a seam beneath a side pleat, do not press the seam open, but press to one side (see Figure 7.15a).
- Side pleats can be graduated in size, with deeper pleats at the top of an all-pleated skirt to allow it to fit smoothly at the hips and waistline.
- Pleats can be topstitched ¼ inch in from each pleat fold from waistline to hipline (Figure 7.16).

Knife Pleats in Two Directions

Formed in two separate sets, each set faces in the opposite direction from the other, on either side of the center front and center back (Figure 7.17).

Box Pleats

In box pleats, the two front folds of each pleat face away from one another (Figure 7.18). The back folds face each other on the wrong side and may meet centrally, although this is not essential. A box pleat may be unpressed, pressed in place, or partially stitched. Box pleats can be grouped or designed to form a panel.

Inverted Pleats

Inverted pleats are the reverse side of box pleats (Figure 7.19a). The two side pleats are folded to meet each other on the correct side of the garment. The pleat can be edgestitched along the foldline (Figure 7.19b). Inverted pleats are found in many areas of garments: in the front and back seams of skirts; as one or two pleats set below a shirt yoke (see Figure 6.28c), at the princess line seam; in gored skirt seams to increase the width of the garment; in sportswear garments to provide room for arm movement; and at the center back of coats and jackets, providing sitting ease. They also can be placed at the center front or center back of garments designed for maternity wear.

Kick Pleats

Kick pleats are used to give fullness to a skirt at the knee for walking and ease of movement—

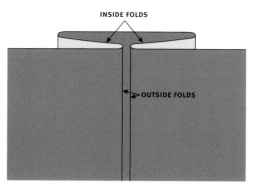

7.19A INVERTED PLEAT

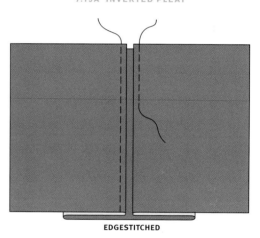

EDGESTITCHED

7.19B INVERTED PLEAT

this is functional design, while retaining a smooth, unpleated hipline. Some skirts have kick pleats in the front or back; others have them in the front *and* back; and there are skirts with kick pleats at the side seams. An unstitched kick pleat is folded back and becomes a vent. (Refer to Figure 15.30a.)

Single Kick Pleat

A single kick pleat adds width at the hem.

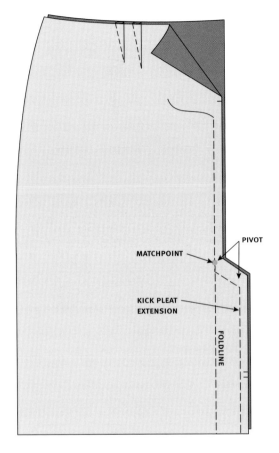

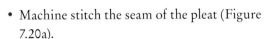

7.20A STITCH CB KICK PLEAT SEAM

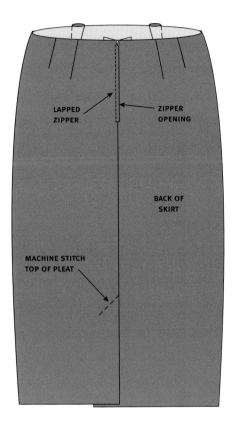

7.20B SECURING PLEAT TO GARMENT

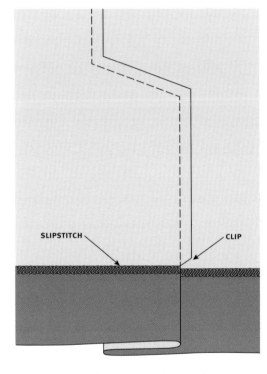

7.20C HEMMED KICK PLEAT

- Machine stitch the seam of the pleat (Figure 7.20a).
- At this point, the zipper is inserted and side seams are stitched.
- Pin the fold of the pleat so that it lies along the seamline (Figure 7.20b).
- Machine stitch across the top of the pleat to keep it securely in place (Figure 7.20b).
- Pull thread ends to the wrong side of the skirt and tie knots.

- Clip the seam allowance of the pleat where it meets the hem so the seam can move freely (Figure 7.20c).
- Press open the seam allowance of the pleat to lie flat within the hem (Figure 7.15a).

Set-in Kick Pleats (with Underlay)

Set-in kick pleats look like inverted pleats at the bottom. A separate piece or underlay is cut for the back of the pleat. To make the single pleat:

- Cut pleat, underlay and skirt with pleat extension (Figure 7.21a and b).
- Transfer all the markings and matchpoints carefully.
- Stitch down the seam of the skirt as far as the seam extensions to matchpoints (see Figure 7.21a).
- Pin and baste the underlay to each side of the seam extensions and machine stitch in place; begin stitching at the matchpoint of each

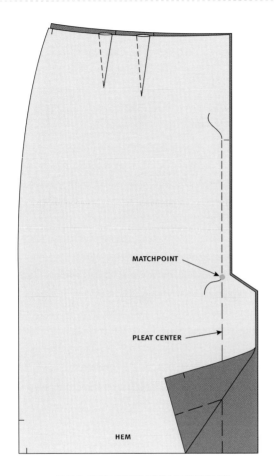

7.21A KICK PLEAT WITH EXTENSION

7.21B UNDERLAY BASTED TO PLEAT

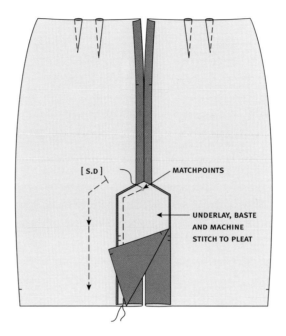

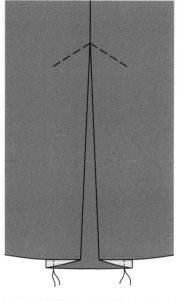

7.21C STITCHED PLEAT WITH UNDERLAY

side of the underlay, and stitch to the bottom (Figure 7.21b).

- The inverted pleat, meets in the center of the underlay; machine stitch across the pleat from the correct side of the garment (Figure 7.21c).
- Bring thread ends to the wrong side of the garment and knot.
- Finish hem as for the single kick pleat (see Figure 7.20c).

Underlay Cut-in-One

Kick pleats without a separate underlay are planned at the patternmaking stage and are cut in one with the seam, as an extension. The amount of the extension determines the width of the kick pleat, which can be a single kick pleat (Figure 7.22a) or a double kick pleat (Figure 7.22b). Accurate marking of the depth and foldlines of the double kick pleat is critical to the finished look of this pleat.

STITCHING TRICKY FABRICS
Matching Stripes, Plaids, Patterns and Repeat Patterns

Do use the lines of an even plaid (vertical and horizontal lines symmetrical on each side of the dominant bars) as a guideline for pleating.

Do match the bars of an uneven plaid at the seamline of a center front or center back seam to keep the plaid in a continuous pattern when the pleats are formed.

Do use stripes (which can be even or uneven vertically or horizontally) to determine the depth of a pleat or tuck.

Do purchase extra yardage to match plaids and crosswise stripes.

Do handbaste seams to match bars and prevent slippage when stitching seams.

7.22A INVERTED DOUBLE KICK PLEAT WITHOUT UNDERLAY

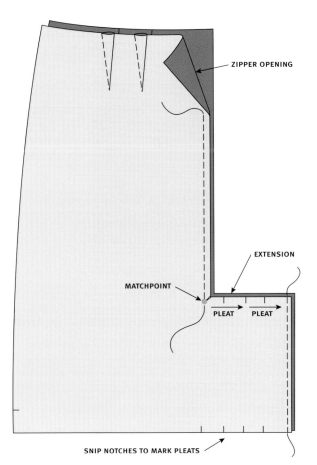

7.22A INVERTED DOUBLE KICK PLEAT WITHOUT UNDERLAY

ZIPPER OPENING

EXTENSION

MATCHPOINT

PLEAT   PLEAT

SNIP NOTCHES TO MARK PLEATS

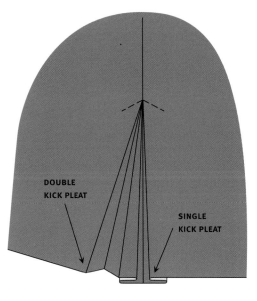

DOUBLE
KICK PLEAT

SINGLE
KICK PLEAT

7.22B INVERTED DOUBLE AND SINGLE KICK PLEAT
WITHOUT UNDERLAY CUT-IN-ONE

Do stitch the pleats in a thread color that matches the most dominant color of the plaid. **Don't** waste your time sewing plaids if they are not matched!

Sheer Fabric

Do use soft, released pleats on drapable sheers.

Do use pin tucks on crisp sheers.

Do use professionally pleated accordion or sunburst pleats on sheers in evening wear.

Do use an underlining to support sheer fabrics when pleating.

Don't use all-cotton fabric—it doesn't hold the shape of knife or box pleats.

Lace

Typically lace is not pleated unless it is very lightweight.

Do edgestitch the pleat on lightweight lace to keep the shape of the pleat.

Do use lots of steam and the appropriate temperature to press pleats in lace with a high percentage of polyester—the higher the amount

of polyester, the better the pleats will hold.

Do match the motifs of the lace when planning pleats.

Don't use heavily embellished lace for pleating—the pleats won't hold.

Satin

Do use a professional pleating service to prepleat fabric, for example, when using a large amount of fabric for bridesmaids' gowns.

Do use lots of steam and the appropriate temperature setting when pressing pleats.

Do use tissue or brown paper strips under pleats to avoid marking an impression on the fabric.

Do use medium- to heavyweight satin to hold the pleat shape.

Beaded Fabric

Don't pleat beaded fabric—the beading prevents the fabric from being folded or pressed into a pleat.

Knits

Do *sample* the knit to see if the desired pleat result occurs.

Do use soft unpressed pleats in cotton/Lycra-blend fabric.

Don't attempt to pleat knits in general—trying to re-pleat the fabric each time it is washed is never successful.

Denim

Do preshrink denim twice before pleating.

Do be absolutely on grain or the pleats will not press flat and stay flat.

Stretch Your Creativity

7.23A OPEN-ENDED
STITCHED TUCKS

7.23B BLIND TUCKS

7.23C CORDED TUCK
PATCHES INSERTION

7.23D STITCHED CLOSED
INVERTED PLEATS INTO
KNIT DRESS

7.23E RELEASED
BOX PLEATS

Do use a denim needle, which has an acute point and a strong shaft for stitching through multiple layers of tightly woven, dense fabrics.
Do trim pleat seam allowances to reduce bulk.
Do topstitch pleats to hold them in place.
Do use pressed or unpressed pleats.
Don't put pleats or tucks in heavyweight denim.

Velvet

Do use soft, unpressed, released pleats in velvet.
Don't press velvet to create pleats—the nap will be crushed.

Faux Fur

Don't even think about trying to pleat faux fur!

Heavyweight Fabric

Do use massive amounts of steam, a wooden clapper, and lots of pressing muscle to achieve pleating in heavyweight fabrics.
Do trim seam allowances of pleats to reduce bulk.
Do use a partial lining approximately 1 inch longer than the hipline area and cut from lining fabric to hide all the cut edges (Refer to Chapter 16, Style I.D., Figure 16.25a.)
Do use brown paper bag strips underneath the pleats to avoid leaving an impression.
Do match the pleat to the weight of the fabric: small knife pleats will not be effective in heavyweight coat fabric.
Don't try to force bulky fabrics into pleats—it doesn't work!

TRANSFER YOUR KNOWLEDGE

Now that you know the basic types of tucks and pleats, transfer your knowledge by trying the following:

- Stitch the ease of a sleeve cap into tucks or pintucks.
- Use the darts from the front and back of a skirt and stitch pin tucks of the same or varying lengths all around the garment in place of the darts.
- Pin tuck a patch pocket.
- Stitch a ¼-inch shell tuck of fabric and use as a trim inserted between the facing and the garment edge.
- Create tucks on a strip of fabric and use as a trim or inserted between the facing and the garment edge.
- Create pleated trim; insert around the neckline edge and center front of a garment.
- Insert a knife pleat into the princess line seams of a skirt or dress.
- Attach a pleated section of fabric to the bottom of a straight skirt or a sleeve hem.
- Alternate the types of pleats within one garment such as a skirt.

STRETCH YOUR CREATIVITY

Take the techniques learned in this chapter and apply them to design in a creative, nontraditional way. Tucks and pleats can be used all over a garment, so think outside the box.

- Stitch large, open-ended tucks all over the surface of a garment (Figure 7.23a).

- Blind tuck the entire skirt of a garment and repeat on one third of the sleeves (Figure 7.23b).
- Create corded tuck patches, and stitch together to create an insert in a knit garment (Figure 7.23c).
- Create shaping in a skirt by using inverted pleats that are stitched closed at the top and bottom of the pleat. Add tulle to hold shape (Figure 7.23d).
- Pleat a skirt with box pleats that are released above the waistline and staystitched at the waistline (Figure 7.23e).

STOP! WHAT DO I DO IF . . .

. . . I've stitched my pin tucks and they are crooked?

Accurate marking and stitching are key to beautiful pin tucks. If the garment has not yet been sewn together, use a seam ripper to remove the crooked pin tucks, check the marking, press and restitch. If too many pin tucks are crooked, the entire garment section may have to be redone.

. . . I've replaced my darts with tucks and don't like the way they look on the garment?

If the garment has been stitched together, rip out the stitches of the seam where the tucks have been placed. Press and carefully mark the position of the dart, and then stitch the dart and the seam allowance.

. . . the pleats on my completed garment are not full enough to balance the garment?

The pleat depth is decided at the patternmaking stage. A sample of how your fabric looked pleated and how much fabric was needed to create a good pleat would have revealed such a deficiency before your garment was pleated and pressed. If you have followed the *SEW, CLIP, PRESS* directions we have offered in every chapter, then it will be difficult or impossible to remove pleating from the fabric. If somehow the pressed pleat marks could be removed from the fabric, fewer pleats could be formed by joining two pleat allowances together, allowing more depth per pleat. Otherwise, another section of the garment will have to be cut.

SELF-CRITIQUE

Take a look at your finished garment and ask the crucial question, "Would I wear this garment or would I purchase this garment?" If the answer is "No," then ask yourself, why not?

If you would not wear your garment, it may be because you don't like the design, proportions, cut, or fabric choice. However, often it is the poor quality of the stitching that discourages wearing or purchasing the garment. Stand back and assess your work throughout the stitching process. Ask yourself the following questions to critique your tucks and pleats stitching:

- Are my tucks stitched evenly?
- If using a double needle, is the stitch tension evenly balanced?

- If the tucks are replacing a dart, do I have the correct fitting to replace the darts?
- Is the cording for the corded tuck the appropriate thickness for the fabric?
- Is the stitching even and straight?
- Are the cross tucks pucker-free?
- Are the overhand stitches spaced evenly and is the hand stitching tension even?
- Does the stitching follow the curve?
- Have I used enough pleat depth to create a generous pleat?
- Have the pleats been handbasted and pressed well?
- Have the pleats been pressed in the correct direction?
- Is the hemming of the pleats bulk-free?
- Do the pleats lie flat?
- If topstitched, are the stitches the correct stitch length?
- Is the topstitching straight?
- Does the thread color of the topstitching match or contrast nicely with the fabric?

REVIEW CHECKLIST

Keep improving on your stitching techniques, and perhaps do some more sampling. Enlist the help of your instructor, too.

- Do I understand the difference between a tuck and a pleat?
- Do I understand how to accurately mark the stitching lines of a tuck or a pleat?
- Do I understand why the grainline is important when creating tucks and pleats?
- Do I understand how to use a double needle to create a pin tuck?
- Do I understand the three components of a pleat?
- Do I understand how to determine how much fabric I need when adding pleats or tucks?
- Do I understand how to space the pleats or tucks?
- Do I understand the difference between a box pleat and an inverted pleat?
- Do I understand the concept of adding the extension in patternmaking for the kick pleat?
- Do I understand the underlay of a pleat?
- Do I understand the necessity of clipping and trimming the seams of pleats before hemming?

The fashion designer needs an excellent knowledge of clothing construction. Measuring, stitching, and pressing tucks and pleats are important design elements. Remember, designing, patternmaking, and construction are closely linked together.

Zippers: Fastening Your Way into the Garment

Zippers are part of structural design and must physically work well in all garments. There are many different ways to apply a zipper into the garment. It is easier to insert a zipper into a garment while it is still flat and not sewn together. Some zipper applications are invisible, giving a seamlike finish; other zippers can have larger teeth in contrasting metals and become the focal point in the design of the garment.

Function must meet form, which means they must go hand in hand. You can put any zipper in a garment, anywhere, but should you? Contrast is exciting, but does it suit the garment? A technically correct zipper can be an absolute disaster if not placed properly. Form and function must collaborate, without disparity.

After practicing the methods in this chapter, insertion of the challenging fly-front zipper will become second nature. This technique and others will enable the student designer to achieve the look he or she desires in the garment. This chapter explains zipper applications for different fabric choices and designs.

STYLE I.D.

Figure 8.1 illustrates the basic types of zippers—all-purpose, invisible, and separating—and their applications.

GATHER YOUR TOOLS

The following supplies will ensure that zipper applications go smoothly: basting thread (such as Silamide), hand sewing needle, beeswax, temporary double-sided adhesive basting tape (such

KEY TERMS

All-Purpose Zipper
Bottom Stop
Centered Zipper
Cord
Exposed Teeth
Invisible Zipper
Invisible Zipper Foot
Lapped Zipper
Pull Tab
Separating Zipper
Tape
Tape Ends
Top Stop
Zipper Coils
Zipper Foot
Zipper Teeth

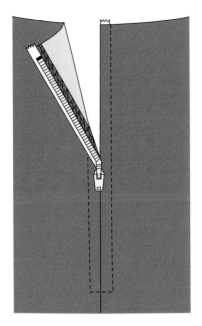

8.1A ALL-PURPOSE ZIPPER: CENTERED

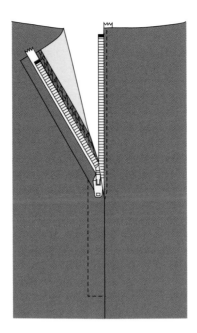

8.1B ALL-PURPOSE ZIPPER: LAPPED

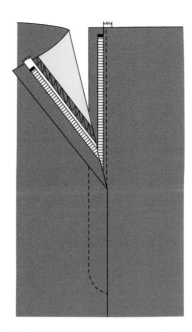

8.1C ALL-PURPOSE ZIPPER: FLY-FRONT

as Wash-a-Way Wonder Tape), pins, pressing cloth, fabric marking pen, scissors, **zipper foot,** and invisible **zipper foot.**

Zipper Feet

A "regular" zipper foot is used for all-purpose and separating zippers. This foot can be adjustable or, for computerized home sewing machines, a fixed foot is used on either side of the zipper by adjusting the needle position. Industrial sewing machines use single toe-hinged or rigid zipper feet that have an opening on either the left or right side of each foot. A special foot is used for invisible zippers and can be purchased to fit most home sewing machines.

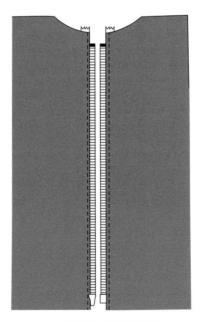

8.1D SEPARATING ZIPPER

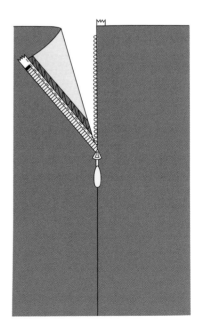

8.1E INVISIBLE ZIPPER

Think Ahead—Order Now

Many supplies are no longer readily available at the local fabric store. Chain fabric stores might not have an extensive color or size selection of zippers. Once you have decided that a zipper is part of the design, purchasing the appropriate zipper is just as important as selecting the correct fabric. Begin the research to find the correct zipper and order it as soon as possible. (Check the "Where to Buy" appendix at the back of this book.)

NOW LET'S GET STARTED

Answering these questions will help you determine the type and application of zipper to use:

- What type of garment is being sewn?
- What is the garment being used for?
- Is it washable or dry-clean only?
- What type of fabric is being used?
- Will the weight of the zipper match the weight of the fabric?
- Is the fabric a sheer?
- How will the zipper function in the garment?
- Will the zipper hold up to use in the garment?
- Will it be easy or difficult to apply the zipper in the garment?
- Will the application of the zipper add to the design or distract?
- Is the application of the zipper in keeping with current fashion?

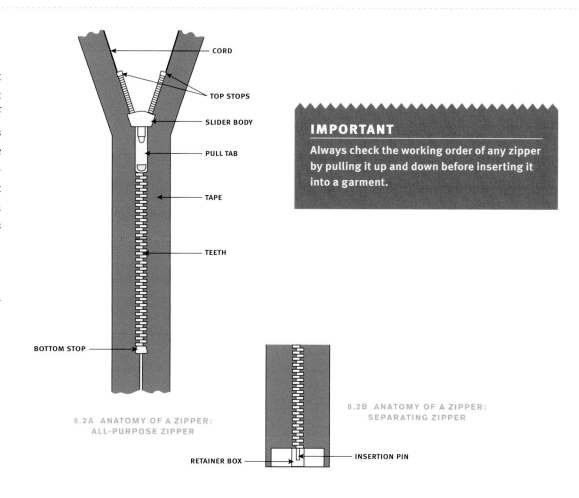

CORD
TOP STOPS
SLIDER BODY
PULL TAB
TAPE
TEETH
BOTTOM STOP

8.2A ANATOMY OF A ZIPPER:
ALL-PURPOSE ZIPPER

8.2B ANATOMY OF A ZIPPER:
SEPARATING ZIPPER

RETAINER BOX
INSERTION PIN

> **IMPORTANT**
>
> Always check the working order of any zipper by pulling it up and down before inserting it into a garment.

WHAT IS A ZIPPER?

An **all-purpose zipper,** as shown in Figure 8.2a, is one type of closure that completely fastens by means of interlocking **teeth** or **coils**, which are attached to the cord of the zipper tape as shown in Figure 8.2a. The teeth can be metal or plastic, or the coils can be a nylon or polyester strand twisted into a spiral. The numbers 3, 4, 5, 8, or 10 refer to the weight of the coils or teeth, with the lowest number being the light-est weight. Metal teeth are strong and sturdy, somewhat inflexible, and are designed to stand up to heavy use. Think of jeans zippers, men's trousers, upholstery zippers, and zippers used in purse-making. The lighter weight, flexible, nylon or polyester all-purpose zippers or invisible zippers can be used almost anywhere.

A **pull tab** is a common zipper closure that can be decorative or functional. **Top** and **bottom stops** keep it from being pulled off of the zipper.

The fabric **tape** attached to the zipper coils or teeth is usually made of polyester, preventing the possibility of shrinkage when the tape is stitched to the garment without preshrinking it first. A **separating zipper** has an insertion pin at the bottom of the zipper with a reinforced retainer box (Figure 8.2b).

Specialty zippers of unusual lengths and for specific uses are available. If a really long zipper is needed, zipper by the yard can be used. The coils are wound onto a reel, and the slides are spaced throughout, to accommodate any length that might be needed. A bar tack, sewn into place before cutting at the bottom of the chosen length, prevents it from coming apart. Zippers can also be purchased in their components (the coils or teeth, the pulls, decorative or functional pulls) and put together to reach the desired length. High-fashion color mixes, choices of metal finishes for metal teeth zippers, rhinestones, crystals, and colored plastic teeth, plus replacement parts for fixing zippers, are also available and easily obtained from sewing supply resources on the Internet. (Refer to the "Where to Buy" appendix at the back of this book.)

Zipper Sizes

Zippers come in many sizes, beginning as small as 2 inches and ranging up to 100 yards when purchased on a reel. In manufacturing, zippers can be ordered to specific sizes, in specific colors for particular garments, which is why they are not available to the retail sewing market. Special-order sizes are available for use in home decorating, upholstery, camping equipment, and sports

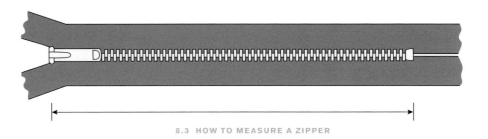

8.3 HOW TO MEASURE A ZIPPER

gear. The most commonly used sizes are those used in garments: skirts and pants use 7- to 9-inch lengths, dresses use 20 to 24 inches, and jackets, 18 to 24 inches. Coats use longer zippers according to the finished length of the garment. While these are general suggestions, a zipper of any size can be used to accommodate an opening in the garment and adjusted to fit. Accurate measuring is key to determining the best size to use. Using a measuring tape, lay the all-purpose zipper flat, pressing it if it is wrinkled from packaging. Identify the top of the slider, and measure down to the tip of the bottom stop; the resulting measurement is the size of the zipper (Figure 8.3). The zipper **tape ends** at the top and bottom are measured separately, and are not taken into consideration in length or the placement of the zipper on the garment.

Shortening Zippers

A zipper can be shortened, if the correct size is not available.

- Most zippers can be shortened from either the top or the bottom; however, separating zippers must always be shortened from the top.
- To shorten from the bottom of the zipper,

measure and mark the new length. Whipstitch or bar tack by machine across the teeth or coils to form a new bottom stop. Cut the zipper ½ inch below the stitching, and insert the zipper as usual.

- To shorten the zipper from the top, measure and mark the new length. Open the zipper, keeping the slider at least 1 inch below the mark. Whipstitch new top stops over the teeth or coils on both the left and right sides of the zipper (Figure 8.19).
- The zipper can be shortened from the top by having the waistband or facing become the top stop. Simply insert the zipper with the extra length at the top. Open the zipper and attach the waistband or facing, stitching over the teeth or coils; trim the excess zipper tape above the stitching and encase the cut ends in the waistband or facing.

Metal teeth used in jeans zippers can be removed (with difficulty) using needle nose wire clippers or a tool that can be purchased specifically for this process. Once the teeth have been removed from the tape, the tape can be trimmed or placed within the seam allowance of the garment where it is being inserted (Figure 8.24).

ZIPPER TYPES

There are three basic types of zippers: the open-top, all-purpose zipper; the invisible zipper; and the separating zipper. Let's begin with the all-purpose zipper.

All-Purpose Zipper

Sometimes called a conventional zipper, an all-purpose zipper is closed at the bottom. When used in a placket application, the zipper is closed at the top as well, usually with handbasting. When the zipper is closed at both ends, it is most often used on the underarm seam of dresses. It can be used in pockets for functional or decorative design as well. An all-purpose zipper is most common on skirt or neckline openings and trousers, slacks, and pants.

The weight of the zipper refers to the coils or teeth, whether they are polyester, nylon, or metal. In specialty zippers, such as those set with Swarovski crystals, the surrounding fabric must be able to support the weight of the zipper, either through an interfaced facing or the weight of the fabric itself.

The length and color of the zipper are other important decisions. Does the length allow easy access into and out of the garment? Do the length

NOTE

It's important to choose the correct zipper that matches the weight of the fabric and that suits the purpose for which the zipper is being used.

and application of the zipper suit the style of the garment? If a longer zipper is needed, will the area into which it is being put support it? Does the zipper match the color of the garment, and if not, does the application cover the zipper? Making these decisions before inserting the zipper leads to a successful application and gives a professional-looking finish to the garment.

All-Purpose Zipper Applications

The most common types of application of all-purpose zippers are centered (see Figure 8.1a), lapped (see Figure 8.1b), fly-front (see Figure 8.1c), mock fly-front, and **exposed teeth** (Figure 8.1d), shown as a separating exposed zipper. The all-purpose zipper is inserted underneath the seam allowance folds that cover the zipper, or into a slash opening, with the teeth exposed.

It is a good idea to test sample a zipper application, especially if the garment fabric is difficult, has an obvious repeat, or if stabilizing may be needed. Always sample a new technique before applying it to the garment.

A good steam pressing of the zipper tape removes any wrinkles resulting from packaging, and eliminates the possibility of any shrinkage of the tape if it's made of cotton. There is nothing worse than a puckered zipper in a garment! Let's begin with the centered zipper application.

Centered Zipper Application

The **centered zipper** is usually found on moderately priced garments and can be applied to

IMPORTANT

A $^3/_4$-inch seam allowance is used when applying centered, lapped, or invisible zippers (see Figure 2.8b). Before beginning any zipper application, a stabilizer is applied to the seam allowance area if needed. The seam is usually finished (if the garment will not be lined), basted together, and pressed open.

the center back of skirts, pants, or dresses. It also can be found stitched up from sleeve edges into the sleeve, or in home decorating products. With careful measuring of the seam allowance and evenly sewn basting, this zipper application is a crisp finishing detail. Stitching must be straight and even. All zippers can be handbasted in place, and for some specialty fabrics, handbasting the zipper is the only way to secure the zipper prior to sewing. The use of an adhesive basting tape to hold the zipper in place while sewing it into the garment eliminates the puckering that can occur in some fabrics when pinned, especially when the zipper is long (Figure 8.4). This is a fast way to hold the zipper in place, and most double-sided adhesive basting tapes are washed or dry-cleaned away. It is important to test a sample of your fabric with the adhesive basting tape to make sure it doesn't show through the fabric or leave a mark. In production, an experienced machinist would not use any type of basting. It would not be cost-effective to add this step to the manufacturing process.

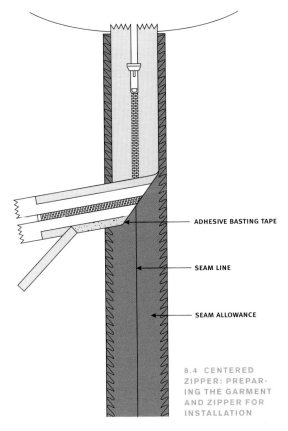

ADHESIVE BASTING TAPE

SEAM LINE

SEAM ALLOWANCE

8.4 CENTERED ZIPPER: PREPARING THE GARMENT AND ZIPPER FOR INSTALLATION

When the garment is being finished with a facing, the top stop of the zipper is placed ½ inch below the waist or neckline seam. When the garment is being finished with a waistband, place it directly below the seamline.

- Stitch seam with basting stitches (5.0 S/L) from upper garment edge to notch; change stitch length to permanent stitch (2.5 S/L); backstitch and stitch to hem; backstitch; press.

- Remove the paper from the basting tape, and place the zipper with the coils facedown onto the seam allowance of the garment. Finger-press into place (Figure 8.4).
- From the correct side of the garment, use a fabric marking pen or handbaste ¼ inch from the center of the coils seam to indicate the stitching line. The laps of the seam allowance have to be deep enough to cover the zipper coils from the front once the temporary basting stitches are removed from the seam. If the fabric being used in the garment is bulky, the laps may have to be made larger, perhaps ³⁄₈ inch to cover the zipper and to allow for the turning of the fabric of the lap.

- Using a zipper foot, begin stitching at the top of the zipper, using a stitch length that is compatible with your fabric and zipper weight. This may have to be adjusted to avoid puckering the fabric. Stitch to the bottom of the zipper. Pivot, and stitch across the bottom of the zipper. Pivot again, and continue to stitch to the top of the zipper (Figure 8.5).

NOTE

Stitch in the same direction on both sides of the zipper if you have problematic fabric, or are matching a repeat pattern in the fabric, a plaid, or a stripe.

IMPORTANT

Do not attempt to rip out the stitches without cutting them every 3 or 4 inches! The zipper laps could be ripped by the thread—a disaster that can only be remedied by removing the zipper and trying to move the laps over (something that usually is not successful in the center back of a garment)!

- Press, using pressing cloth.
- Using the seam ripper (Figure 2.27), remove the basting stitches from the center of the seam by cutting into the stitching every 3 or 4 inches and carefully pulling out the basting stitches (Figure 6.5).

Centered Zipper Welt Insertion

This type of zipper installation is found on sportswear, such as parkas, snowsuits, boating jackets, hoods of coats and jackets, leather, suede, or vinyl. It is closed on both ends, and sewn much like a double welt, with the seam edges centered on the zipper and stitched ¼ inch to ½ inch parallel to the finished seamline. This type of zipper installation can be really creative when other fabrics or trims are used for the laps/welts.

Center-Back Waist Finishing

On pants and skirts, a designer has many options for finishing the waistline. A popular way to finish this area is with a waistband, in all its variations, or using a facing. The waistband can

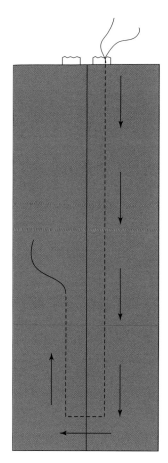

8.5 SEWING THE CENTERED ZIPPER

be of any width, is usually interfaced, is sewn to the garment at the waistline seam allowance, and has some type of closure. The facing is a shaped piece of fabric that is interfaced, sewn to the garment at the waistline seam allowance, and has a hook-and-eye type closure hand sewn at the top of the zipper opening to hold the garment together while the zipper is being closed. Also refer to Chapter 9, "Waistbands," or Chapter 12, "Facings," for details.

Lapped Zipper

The **lapped zipper** is stitched in between two sides of the garment, one side at a time. The overlap forms from the left side of the garment, and completely covers the zipper, so it's possible to use a zipper that doesn't match the color of the garment. The lapped zipper is placed at the center-back opening of dresses, skirts, and pants, and the lap faces from left to right. Sometimes called the placket zipper when used on the side seam of garments, the lap of the zipper faces from the front toward the back. A lapped zipper can be used with a waistband or a facing. Refer to Chapter 9, "Waistbands," and Chapter 12, "Facings."

- Prepare the zipper opening (as previously described).
- Apply basting tape to the upper side of the zipper tape on the right-hand side of the zipper. Extend the right-hand seam allowance $1/8$ inch, placing the zipper coil-side down. Remove the paper and finger-press the zipper onto the seam allowance.
- Turn the zipper over, faceup, forming a fold in the seam allowance. Bring the $1/8$-inch fold close to, but not over, the zipper coil. Stitch along the edge of the fold through all layers (Figure 8.6).
- Turn the garment to the right side. Smooth the fabric as flat as possible over the remaining unstitched zipper tape. Apply basting tape to the zipper tape, then finger-press in place to the seam allowance.
- From the correct side of the garment, begin stitching at the bottom, taking several stitches

across the zipper, pivoting, and continuing to stitch up to the top of the garment (Figure 8.7). Backstitch carefully or pull the threads to the back and hand knot.
- Press.
- Continue with the waistband or facing finishing.

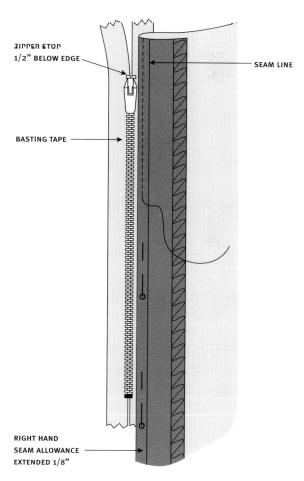

8.6 LAPPED ZIPPER: STITCHING THE RIGHT-HAND SIDE

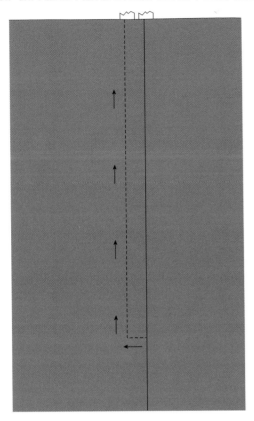

Lapped Side-Seam Waist Zipper Insertion

An all-purpose zipper is applied to a garment side seam that is closed at both ends. This type of application is most often used in garments that are fitted at the waistline when an opening extending into the neckline would detract from the design (see Figure 2.11). The zipper in these applications extends 7 inches below the waistline and up to the underarm. An invisible zipper can also be applied this way.

• Follow the steps for a lapped zipper.

NOTE

A longer zipper length can be used and shortened. Most zippers can be shortened from either the top or the bottom; however, separating zippers must always be shortened from the top. Refer to the section on "Shortening Zippers" earlier in this chapter.

• A placket zipper in a side seam is basted across the top of the zipper as well as being closed at the bottom of the zipper. To hold the lap in place, it is stitched at the top and the bottom of the zipper.

• Stitch the first side down to the bottom, pivot, stitch across the zipper, pivot, stitch up to the top of the zipper, and stitch across the top of the zipper, meeting the beginning of the stitching (Figure 8.8).

Fly-Front Zipper

Considered to be the most challenging of all zipper applications for students, the fly-front zipper relies on accurate marking as well as good sewing skills. A regular all-purpose zipper is used for pants or skirts, while metal zippers that have an auto lock under the tabs to prevent the zipper from opening are used with jeans and men's trousers. Molded plastic sportswear zippers are used on some jackets, coats, or rain and snow gear.

There are two methods of fly-front zipper application. One method involves cutting the facings all-in-one with the garment; this is sometimes called the "mock" fly-front (Figure

8.9a). The second method involves applying a separate zipper facing. Zippers for women can be inserted right over left, mainly for business wear, or left over right for jeans and casual wear. This is the designer's choice. The directions that follow illustrate the facing cut in one piece with the pants, and right over left closure.

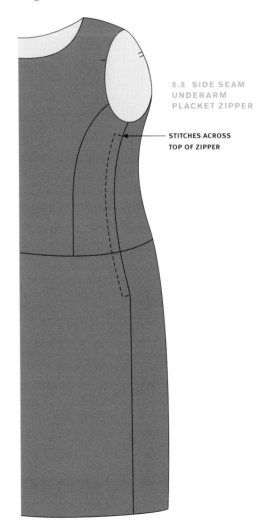

8.8 SIDE SEAM UNDERARM PLACKET ZIPPER

STITCHES ACROSS TOP OF ZIPPER

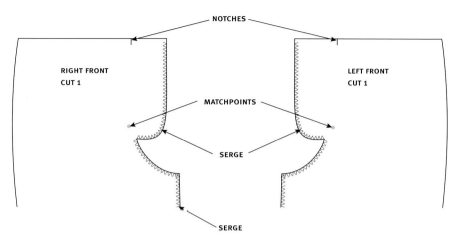

NOTCHES

RIGHT FRONT
CUT 1

LEFT FRONT
CUT 1

MATCHPOINTS

SERGE

SERGE

8.9A FLY-FRONT PATTERN WITH CUT ALL-IN-ONE FACINGS

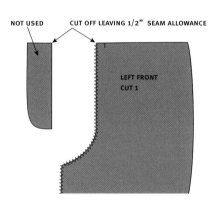

NOT USED

CUT OFF LEAVING 1/2" SEAM ALLOWANCE

LEFT FRONT
CUT 1

**8.9B FLY-FRONT ZIPPER INSERTION:
LEFT FRONT**

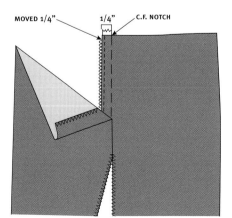

MOVED 1/4"

1/4"

C.F. NOTCH

**8.9C FLY-FRONT ZIPPER INSERTION:
LEFT FRONT**

**8.9D PINNING
THE CENTER
FRONT**

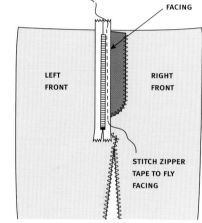

FACING

LEFT
FRONT

RIGHT
FRONT

**8.9E FLY-FRONT
ZIPPER: SEWING
THE RIGHT FRONT
FACING TO THE
ZIPPER**

STITCH ZIPPER
TAPE TO FLY
FACING

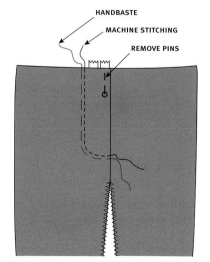

HANDBASTE

MACHINE STITCHING

REMOVE PINS

**8.9F BASTING/
STITCHING THE
RIGHT FLY-FRONT
TOPSTITCHING**

Fly-Front Facing Cut in One Piece

Interfacing can be applied to the front facing to stabilize lightweight fabrics.

- Cut off the left front fly extension, leaving ¹/₂-inch seam allowance all round. Serge the crotch and edges of the facings (see Figure 8.9b).
- Use a zipper foot for the following procedures.
- With the pants facing you, pin the zipper ¹/₂ inch down from the waistline edge to the left front. Move the center front seamline over ¹/₄ inch away from the stitching line. Stitch as close to the zipper edge as possible—approximately ¹/₁₆ inch. Press the center-front foldline on the right side, from the waistline notch to join at the crotch (see Figure 8.9c).
- Pin the center fronts together, matching the waistline notches. Do not remove the center-front pins until after topstitching of the fly-front is completed (see Figure 8.9d).
- Turn the garment to the wrong side. Pin the zipper tape to the right front facing, making sure that it lies flat. Stitch the zipper to the facing only, stitching as close to the zipper teeth as possible. Do not cut off the excess zipper length (see Figure 8.9e).

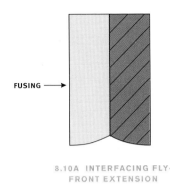

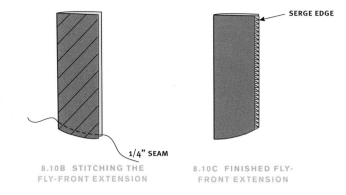

FUSING

1/4" SEAM

SERGE EDGE

8.10A INTERFACING FLY-FRONT EXTENSION

8.10B STITCHING THE FLY-FRONT EXTENSION

8.10C FINISHED FLY-FRONT EXTENSION

- Turn the garment to the correct side. On the right front, handbaste the position of the fly-front top stitching. Begin stitching from the waistline and curve the stitching into the crotch join, ending in a backstitch to reinforce this stress point. The fly-front can be double topstitched at this point in matching or contrasting threads. The center-front pins can now be removed (see Figure 8.9f).

Fly-Front Zipper with Separate Extension

- Stabilize one half of the extension (Figure 8.10a).
- Place the correct sides together. Stitch a ¼-inch seam allowance, slightly curving the lower edge (see Figure 8.10b). Turn to the correct side and press. Baste the raw edges together and serge (see Figure 8.10c). Do not serge at top waistline edge of the facing.
- With the garment turned to the correct side and facing up, place the extension on the right side of the garment under the zipper and lining up from the waist edge. Pin in place. Stitch over the previous stitching, as closely as possible, down to the bottom

end of the zipper. Cut off the excess zipper length, if necessary (see Figure 8.11).

- Turn the garment to the wrong side and stitch together both the bottom edges of the fly-front facing and the extension. Stitch approximately ¹/₂ inch in length, back and forth, to hold the area securely (see Figure 8.12).

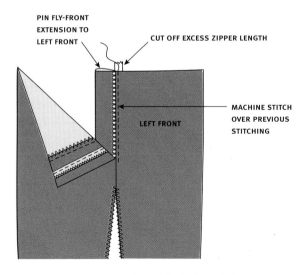

PIN FLY-FRONT EXTENSION TO LEFT FRONT

CUT OFF EXCESS ZIPPER LENGTH

LEFT FRONT

MACHINE STITCH OVER PREVIOUS STITCHING

8.11 STITCHING THE FLY-FRONT EXTENSION: CUTTING EXCESS ZIPPER LENGTH

PATTERN TIP

The fly-front facing needs to be wide enough to cover the topstitching. This decision needs to be made at the beginning when pattern drafting. Don't forget to add ½-inch seam allowance.

8.12 STITCHING THE FLY-FRONT FACING TO THE EXTENSION

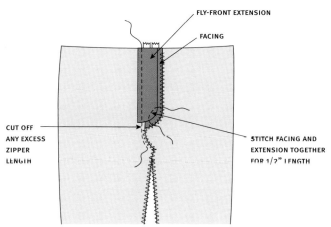

FLY-FRONT EXTENSION

FACING

CUT OFF ANY EXCESS ZIPPER LENGTH

STITCH FACING AND EXTENSION TOGETHER FOR 1/2" LENGTH

Fly-Front Closure

There are many different designs for fly-front closure and this is always the designer's choice. The following closures are for skirts and pants. A variety of sew-on, hook-and-bar closures are available in various widths and either black or silver to blend with the fabric used. Since these closures are not visible, they don't need to be matched to the fabric.

Applying a Hidden Button and Buttonhole to a Waistband

A button and buttonhole can be applied to the waistband for a stronger closure. The waistband holds much better with a button and buttonhole closure, which is essential to functional design. When a button is used for the waistband as well as the hook-and-bar closure, an extension needs to be added onto the waistband pattern. Refer to Chapter 9, "Waistbands."

> **NOTE**
> Finishing details are what set extraordinary garments apart from the ordinary. Take time to perfect hand sewing techniques while doing a sample. Practice, sample, practice!

- Choose a small, flat button, 1/2 inch to 5/8 inch in size.
- On the left-hand side of the waistband, sew a buttonhole horizontally, in the middle of the width of the waistband. The buttonhole should be the correct length to fit the button and

should be placed approximately 1/2 inch in from the edge of the waistband. Placing center fronts together, mark the position for the button.
- On the top waistband, on the wrong side, sew the button without the stitches showing on the correct side of the waistband (see Figure 8.13). Yes, this can be done!

Applying a Sew-on Hook and Bar to a Waistband

The hooks and bars are strong and flat, so the hook cannot be easily seen, nor will it slide off the bar.

- Position the hook on the underside of the

8.13 APPLYING A HIDDEN BUTTON AND BUTTONHOLE TO FLY-FRONT WAISTBAND

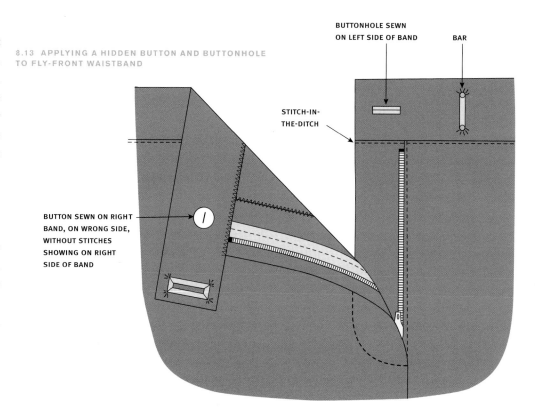

BUTTONHOLE SEWN ON LEFT SIDE OF BAND   BAR

STITCH-IN-THE-DITCH

BUTTON SEWN ON RIGHT BAND, ON WRONG SIDE, WITHOUT STITCHES SHOWING ON RIGHT SIDE OF BAND

overlap, 1/8 inch back from the edge. Secure by stitching over the holes, around the opening. Hook the bar in place and stitch to secure. How is the hook held in place? Use a very small piece of the double-sided adhesive basting tape to get the first stitches started (see Figure 8.13).

• Place the button in the buttonhole, and position the bar in line with the hook.

There are many ways to finish the fly-front. This is the designer's choice! Refer to Chapter 17, "Closures" (see Figure 17.2).

Exposed Zippers

On garments where there is no seam, an exposed zipper is applied to a slash opening, and reinforced with a stay of either interfacing or firmly woven lining fabric. Typically inserted at a neckline and used on knit fabrics, an exposed zipper can also be used on the pockets of garments, or anywhere else the designer chooses, from the hem up. Think of mock turtleneck sweaters, polar fleece sports garments, cell phone pockets on jackets, and more. This type of zipper application can be both functional and decorative. When a metal or plastic molded zipper is used, the amount of tape exposed becomes a focal point of a garment. A specialty zipper such as one made of Swarovski crystal, rhinestones, or a Riri zipper with multicolored metal teeth adds a strong design element to a garment. Thanks to the Internet, zippers previously only available to manufacturers are more readily available to designers.

Prepare the area for the zipper. Choosing the correct stabilizer is of utmost importance. Refer to Chapter 3, "Introduction to Stabilizers," to guide this decision.

• When sewn to the garment, the stay facing creates a finished edge that is stable after it is slashed. The facing should be approximately 3 inches wide and 2 inches longer than the length of the zipper (see Figure 8.14a). With the correct sides of the fabric together, mark the center of the facing; baste to the garment. The opening should only be wide enough to expose the zipper teeth, approximately 1/4 inch to 3/8 inch wide (see Figure 8.14a). The width of the opening depends on how much zipper tape is going to be shown.

• Begin stitching the facing to the garment, about 1/8 inch from the center marking. Stitch to the bottom of the stay, pivot, stitch across the bottom, pivot again, and continue stitching up to the top. Slash the opening along the center marking. Clip into the lower corners (see Figure 8.14b).

• Turn the facing to the wrong side of the garment and press carefully so that the facing does not show through to the front and the corners form clean, right angles.

• Place the zipper underneath the opening, and handbaste the garment to the zipper tape along the teeth (Figure 8.15).

• Lift the garment to expose the bottom of the zipper and, using a zipper foot, stitch the triangular piece of the stay to the zipper (Figure 8.16).

• Turn the garment to the wrong side and expose the original sewing line. Stitch zipper to the garment from the bottom to the top; stitch the other side the same way (Figure 8.17).

• Remove the handbasting that held the zipper along the teeth. Press.

• As a finishing detail, the opening can be topstitched if appropriate to the garment and the design. Refer to Chapter 6, "Seams," for details on topstitching.

When inserting an exposed zipper into a flat area such as a pocket:

• Reinforce the area with the appropriate interfacing for the fabric.

• Mark stitching lines appropriate to the size of the exposed area for the zipper being used. Stitch along these lines, using a short stitch length.

• Slash the opening down the center, and clip into the corners.

• Turn the slashed edges to the back side and press.

• Carefully edgestitch around the pressed edges (Figure 8.18a).

• Place the zipper into position, making sure the zipper stop is included in the exposed length; stitch 1/8 inch from the previous line of edgestitching to secure the zipper to the fabric (Figure 8.18b).

An exposed zipper can also be inserted without the topstitching showing on the front of the garment. For example, when a small, coiled, plastic zipper that is lightweight and flexible is used at the neckline or in a turtleneck, topstitching it into place may make it too stiff. It is important that the stay be compatible with the fabric and large enough to support the area into which the

8.14B EXPOSED ZIPPER: BASTING STAY FACING
TO THE GARMENT

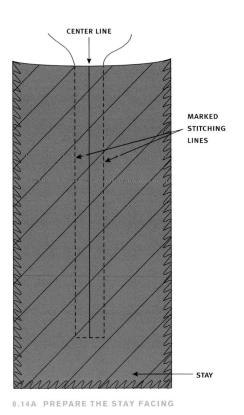

8.14A PREPARE THE STAY FACING

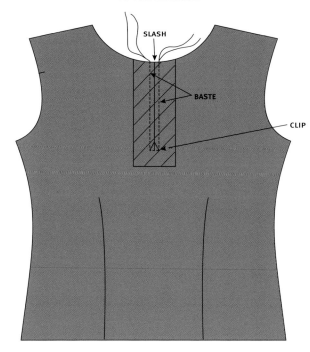

8.14B EXPOSED ZIPPER: BASTING STAY FACING
TO THE GARMENT

NOTE

This type of zipper insertion requires excellent, straight stitching. Sample and practice on the garment fabric to ensure stitching skills that hold up to the attention this application receives. Uneven, poor-quality stitching draws negative attention to this technique.

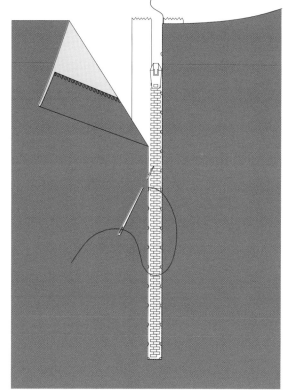

8.15 EXPOSED ZIPPER: BASTING THE ZIPPER TO
THE GARMENT OPENING

zipper is being stitched. A stay at least 3 inches wide and at least 2 inches longer than the zipper should be sufficient.

- Prepare the facing, the stitching lines, and the center of the opening. With correct sides of the fabrics together, stitch along the marked lines using a short stitch length. Slash and clip into the corners at the bottom of the opening.
- Turn the facing to the back side; press. Allow

the facing to roll a little to the underside so that the facing does not show through to the front.
- Handbaste the correct side of the fabric to the zipper tape along the teeth of the zipper, using a small slipstitch.
- Lift the bottom of the garment and stitch the bottom of the facing to the zipper.
- Flip back one side of the garment, exposing the zipper tape, and stitch the zipper to the facing.
- Repeat for the other side (Figure 8.17).

8.16 EXPOSED ZIPPER: STITCHING THE TRIANGULAR PIECE OF STAY TO THE ZIPPER

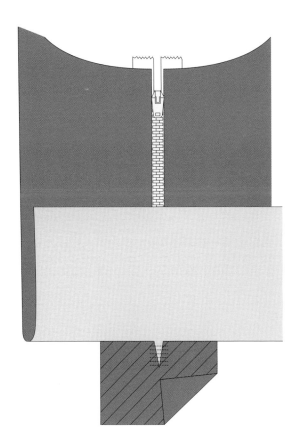

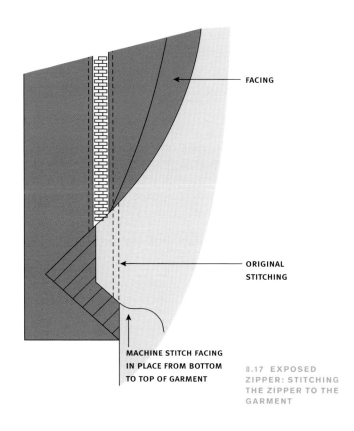

FACING

ORIGINAL STITCHING

MACHINE STITCH FACING IN PLACE FROM BOTTOM TO TOP OF GARMENT

8.17 EXPOSED ZIPPER: STITCHING THE ZIPPER TO THE GARMENT

Invisible Zipper

The invisible zipper is the most versatile, suitable for almost any garment or fabric. It is also available as a separating zipper, and as a lightweight mesh, suitable for fine fabrics as well as lingerie. (See Where to Buy section in this text.) The zipper closure produces a "seamlike" finish and the zipper itself is invisible! The only part of the zipper that should show is the pull. Match the pull color to your fabric; if it is not available, the pull can be "colored" to match the fabric using nail polish or paint if needed.

To insert an invisible zipper:

- Purchase a zipper at least 1 ½ inches longer than the finished length. This will ensure that the final zipper opens to the correct length. (When the zipper is stitched into the garment, the zipper foot will touch the pull, preventing you from sewing all the way to the end.) Any excess length beyond 1½ inches can be removed after the zipper is inserted (Figure 8.19).
- Serge the seam edges before the zipper is inserted (see Figure 8.20 on page 222).
- Open the zipper and, on the wrong side, press the coils flat so that the two woven

8.18A EDGESTITCHING THE OPENING FOR THE EXPOSED TEETH ZIPPER

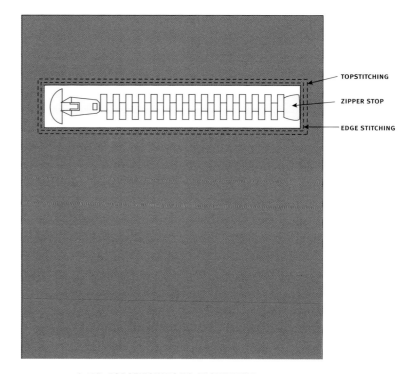

8.18B TOPSTITCHING TO SECURE THE EXPOSED TEETH ZIPPER

NOTE

Unlike other zippers, the invisible zipper is applied to the opening edges using flat application construction before the seam is stitched. This enables the student to work with a flat, flexible area. The facings are applied after the zipper is sewn in place. If the garment requires a special construction, the zipper can be inserted with the seam sewn from 2 inches below the opening, and then the final 2-inch segment rejoined with the zipper stitching.

rows in the zipper tape show. Use a synthetic setting on the iron. Do not close the zipper after pressing, as it will cause the coils to become rounded again. Attach the zipper foot to the machine. Specialty feet for the invisible zipper are available for all sewing machines. The right and left zipper feet on the industrial sewing machines are very narrow and have openings in the foot that allow the needle to stitch very close to the coils.

• Place the front side of the zipper so it faces the correct side of the fabric surface. Working on

the left side of the garment, pin or use adhesive basting tape to hold the right side of the zipper to the left side of the garment. Position the zipper stop $1/2$ inch above the cut edge of the fabric. Place the coils on the seamline (Figure 8.21). The edge of the zipper tape should face the edge of the garment.

• Slowly stitch the zipper into the garment by sewing close to the pressed flat coils. If the stitches catch on the coils, the zipper will not pull up. Stitch closer to the coils if the fabric is lightweight, and a little bit farther away

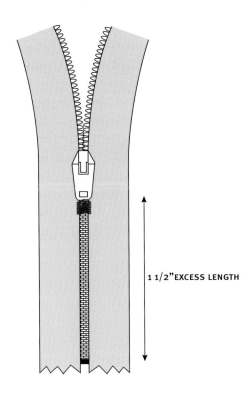

8.19 SHORTENING THE INVISIBLE ZIPPER

1 1/2"EXCESS LENGTH

from the coils if the fabric is thick. If the stitches are too far away from the coils, the zipper tape will show on the right side of the garment, and this does not look very good! Stitch until the zipper foot touches the pull tab and carefully backstitch (Figure 8.21).

• To stitch the remainder of the zipper, place the right side of the zipper down on the right side of the garment, on top of the correct side of the fabric. Pin or use adhesive basting tape to position the zipper. Stitch slowly, avoiding

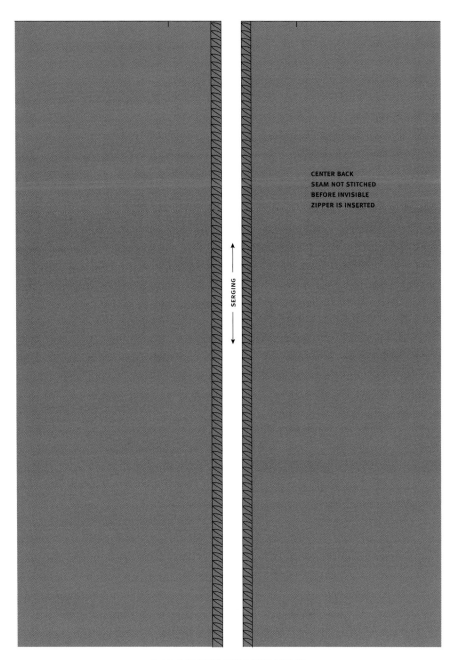

CENTER BACK
SEAM NOT STITCHED
BEFORE INVISIBLE
ZIPPER IS INSERTED

SERGING

8.20 SERGING THE SEAM EDGES

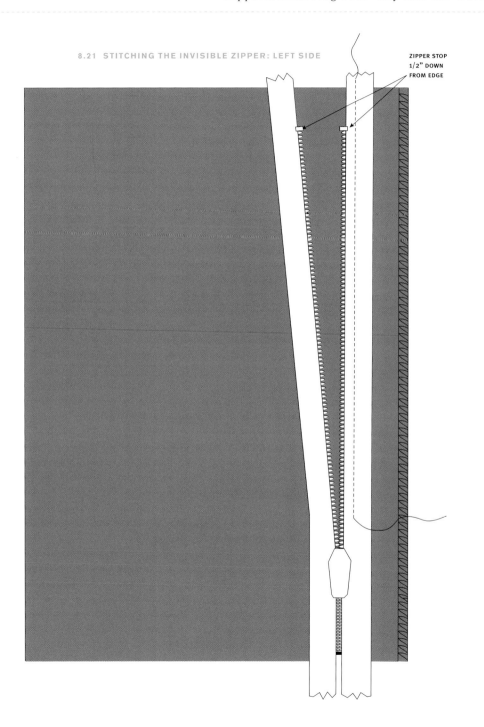

8.21 STITCHING THE INVISIBLE ZIPPER: LEFT SIDE

ZIPPER STOP
1/2" DOWN
FROM EDGE

stitching into the coils, keeping the stitching straight. Stop stitching when the zipper foot touches the zipper pull. Backstitch.

IMPORTANT

The zipper must be aligned parallel to the seam allowance. If this is not done, the zipper will look crooked and uneven, and not "invisible" at all! Mark the seam allowance if necessary to keep it even.

- Turn the garment to the wrong side. Close the zipper, and pull the end of the zipper out of the way (Figure 8.22).

NOTE

Remember to backstitch at the beginning of the stitching.

- Stitch the center-back seam closed, starting at the end of the previous zipper stitching. Continue stitching to the end. Matching up the stitching from the end of the zipper is the key to eliminating the puckering that almost always occurs if you sew the seam first, and then insert the zipper (see Figure 8.22).
- To secure the zipper, keep it flat, and prevent it from popping out of the seam, stitch the ends of the zipper tape to the seam allowances only (Figure 8.23).

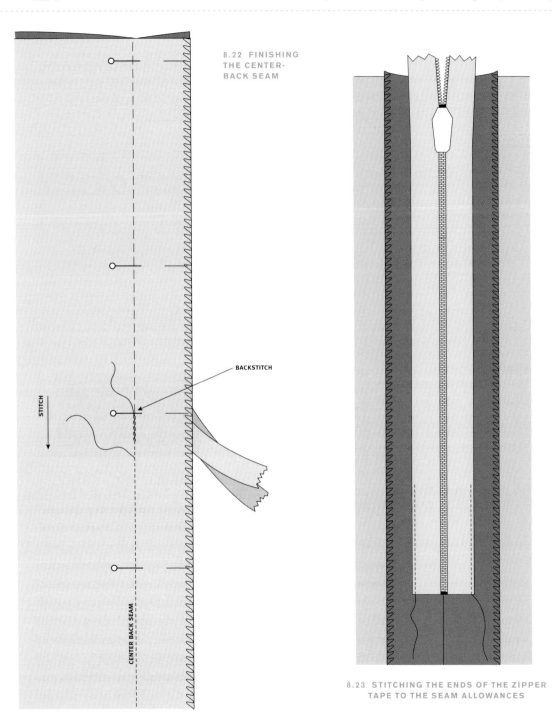

8.22 FINISHING THE CENTER-BACK SEAM

BACKSTITCH

STITCH

CENTER BACK SEAM

8.23 STITCHING THE ENDS OF THE ZIPPER TAPE TO THE SEAM ALLOWANCES

- Gently steam and finger-press the closed zipper from the correct side. *Do not* press this zipper flat—the idea is for it to look rolled.

Invisible Separating Zipper

The invisible zipper is available as a separating zipper in limited lengths and colors. Due to the weight of the coils and tape, it would be used on sweaters or jackets. It more closely resembles the separating zipper category. The installation of the zipper, however, follows the directions for invisible zippers, without finishing the seam at the bottom of the zipper. The bottom of the invisible zipper should be positioned at the marked hemline or finish.

Separating Zipper

The separating zipper is often seen on sweaters, jackets, and sportswear. Two-way separating zippers are found in fleece garments, sportswear, snowsuits, and skiwear, where the ability to release half of the zipper for wearing ease is valued. This reduces the strain on a zipper and also reduces the number of broken zippers. The two-way separating zipper has two zipper pulls and can also be used in pockets, splitting the zipper in half, and using one half for each pocket. This is helpful when matching zipper colors and styles. The separating zipper can be inserted as a centered, lapped, or exposed application. The garment edge where the zipper is applied can be finished in several ways, including facings, bindings, and decorative techniques. Refer to Chapter 12, "Facings," for more details.

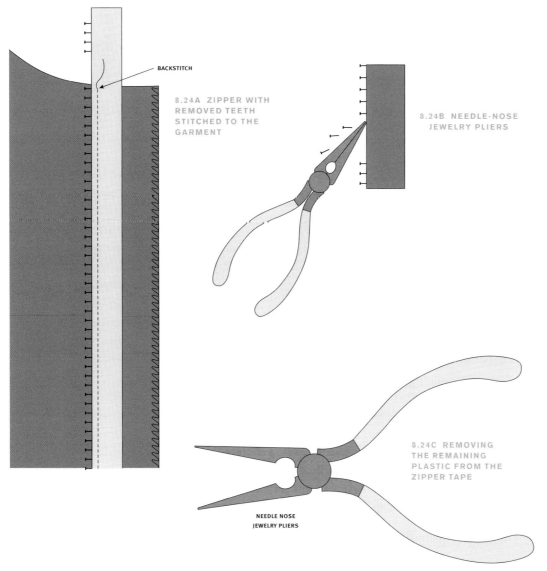

BACKSTITCH

8.24A ZIPPER WITH
REMOVED TEETH
STITCHED TO THE
GARMENT

8.24B NEEDLE-NOSE
JEWELRY PLIERS

8.24C REMOVING
THE REMAINING
PLASTIC FROM THE
ZIPPER TAPE

NEEDLE NOSE
JEWELRY PLIERS

> **NOTE**
> The zipper is always shortened from the top.

look lost, whereas the plastic molded teeth of a sportswear zipper or the metal teeth of a jeans or trouser zipper more closely match the weight of the leather while still providing contrast. Separating zippers come in many colors, but not all colors are available, so use a close match or use a completely contrasting color to provide a strong design element.

Shortening a Separating Zipper

Because separating zippers are only available in limited sizes, they often end up being too short or too long. To avoid this dilemma, purchase a zipper that is longer than the opening of the garment—4 inches is usually enough additional length.

- Sew the zipper in place, extending the excess length above the top opening. Backstitch to secure the stitching (Figure 8.24a).
- Unzip the zipper.
- Cut off approximately 1 inch of plastic teeth above the backstitch. Cut off only the plastic portion of the zipper teeth that extends beyond the zipper tape (Figure 8.24a). Use wire cutters such as Fiskar diagonal cutters, which have short, pointed blades, or needle-nose jewelry pliers, which will also work (Figure 8.24b). "Regular" tool wire cutters are too big to cut off the teeth one at a time.

The zipper application should match the garment's overall design. Is it adding to the design or detracting from it? Some students do not match the type of zipper to the type of fabric and style of garment being made, using a sport-weight separating zipper with plastic teeth in the back of a satin or silk garment. This is not a design statement as much as it is a technical error. When striving for an unusual contrast, the zipper and the garment must still share a harmonious relationship: a flexible, small, coiled zipper sewn into a leather garment with exposed coils would

- Use the points of the cutters to "tweeze" the remaining plastic part that is still on the zipper tape (Figure 8.24c). The result will be a smooth, toothless section of zipper tape.
- Cut off the excess zipper tape *above* the 1-inch section of "toothless" tape.
- To create the zipper stop, fold the smooth "toothless" zipper tape back onto itself, or bar tack the zipper by hand or machine (Figure 8.19).

The zipper is easiest to insert before facings or collars are applied to the garment or hems are finished.

Centered Separating Zipper
- Determine if the seam allowances need to be stabilized before beginning the zipper application. Refer to Chapter 3, "Introduction to Stabilizers" (Figure 8.25a).
- Finish the seam edges, if a facing will not cover the zipper. Or stitch a Hong Kong finish. Refer to Chapter 6, "Seams," for detailed instructions.
- Machine baste the seam where the zipper will be applied, for example, the center front of a jacket or sweater (Figure 8.25a).

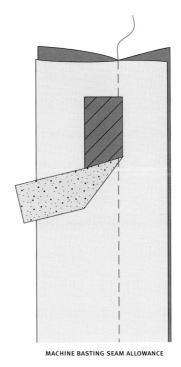

MACHINE BASTING SEAM ALLOWANCE

8.25A POSITIONING AND HAND-BASTING THE SEAM

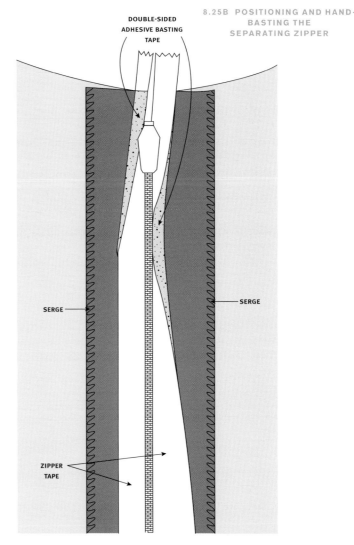

DOUBLE-SIDED ADHESIVE BASTING TAPE

8.25B POSITIONING AND HAND-BASTING THE SEPARATING ZIPPER

SERGE

SERGE

ZIPPER TAPE

- Press open the seam allowances.
- Center the teeth of the zipper over the seam, and handbaste to seam allowances or use adhesive basting tape to position the zipper.
- Turn under the tape ends of the zipper at an angle to avoid the zipper teeth. Topstitch each side of the zipper, 1/4 inch to 3/8 inch (for a

zipper with larger-size teeth and bulkier fabrics) from the basted center seam (Figure 8.25b).
- Press and fold the facings and hems, catching the edge of each in the machine stitching of the zipper (Figure 8.26). Do not backstitch; leave long thread tails, pull them to the back

of the fabric, and knot off. Carefully remove the basting threads from the center seam.

- Or, turn up the hems, slipstitching in place at an angle to avoid the zipper teeth; then finish the hem with a slipstitch or machine stitch. Refer to Chapter 15, "Hems," and Chapter 12, "Facings."

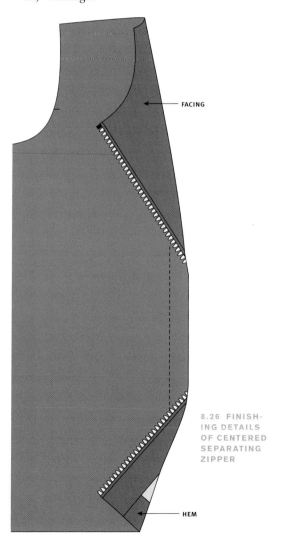

8.26 FINISH-ING DETAILS OF CENTERED SEPARATING ZIPPER

FACING

HEM

Lapped Separating Zipper

A lapped zipper insertion follows the same steps, whether you are sewing an all-purpose zipper or a separating zipper, except the bottom is open, and there is finishing at the top and bottom such as facings and hems. Because the top and bottom are both open, it is an easier application. Refer to the lapped zipper application illustrations in Figures 8.6 and 8.7.

- Finish the garment with appropriate facings, hems, or bindings, folding the facing or hem edges at an angle to keep them free of the zipper teeth, but allowing them to be caught in the machine stitching.
- Stitch the hems or facings to the garment to complete.

Hand-Stitching Zippers

Also referred to as a hand-picked zipper, a zipper inserted by hand is beautiful as well as practical. Heavily embellished fabrics and delicate fabrics benefit from this couture touch. Because this technique highlights the handwork, the stitching and spacing must be even and accurate. Either a centered application or a lapped application adds luxurious detail to the garment.

- Stabilize the zipper area (Figure 8.25a). On delicate or heavily embellished fabrics, consider using strips of silk organza. This prevents rippling and any distortion that could occur from handling the fabric while stitching. Sample several choices of stabilizers and interfacing to see what works best

with the fabric being used. Refer to Chapter 3, "Introduction to Stabilizers."

- Position the zipper at the top of the right-hand garment side opening, centering the folded edge of the lap over the zipper (Figure 8.27). Pin the closed zipper to the garment from the correct side of the garment. Use very fine pins for this step to avoid marking the fabric with holes. If the zipper is being placed in an area of the garment that receives a lot of stress, overlap the laps of the opening a mere $1/16$ of an inch more so the teeth of the zipper remain covered. Handbaste the zipper in place.
- It is most pleasing to the eye when the spacing of the stitches measures the same amount in from the edge of the lap as the stitches are apart. Refer to Chapter 6, "Seams" (see Figure 6.27b), for further details on the hand-picked stitch. If this is an unfamiliar stitch, sample, sample, sample!
- Unzip the zipper. Begin stitching the zipper

at the top of the tape. A very small amount of thread should show on the surface of the garment (Figure 8.27).

- Stitch to the end of the opening. *Do not stitch across the bottom of the zipper.* This causes puckering and pulling.
- Begin stitching the left side of the zipper opening at the bottom of the zipper, continuing up to the top. By stitching in two different directions, occasional mismatching may occur when reaching the top of the zipper opening. If this does occur and it is slight ($1/16$ inch or less, without producing visible distortion), it can be adjusted in the finishing facing or waistband. However, if it is visibly

distorted, the stitching must be removed and redone.

STITCHING TRICKY FABRICS
Inserting Zippers in Plaids, Checks, Repeat Patterns, and Horizontal Stripes

When constructing a garment of one of the above-mentioned fabrics, keep in mind that extra care and attention must be paid to the layout before cutting out the garment. It's very unattractive to see checks, stripes, or plaids that don't match, and as you are the designer, there is no reason to let this happen.

When inserting a zipper, there are two important steps to matching plaids, checks, repeats, or stripes: careful basting, and accurate marking. There is no shortcut! The placement of a zipper into one of these fabrics interrupts the movement of the fabric, so great care must be taken to ensure that the pattern matches exactly on both sides of the zipper, allowing the eye to continue across the garment. The directions that follow are for an invisible zipper, which is the least conspicuous application for a busy fabric.

Do press the invisible zipper flat. Handbaste the zipper to the left side of the garment.
Do stitch the zipper in place, close to the coils to avoid any tape showing on the front of the garment.
Do lay the left side of the zipper onto the right side of the garment, matching up the elements. Mark each matchpoint on the zipper tape (Figure 8.28).
Do place the unsewn right-hand zipper onto

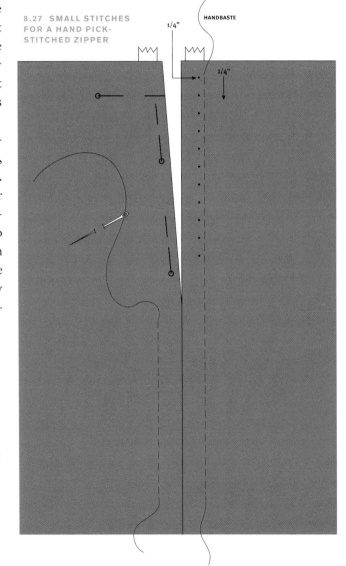

8.27 SMALL STITCHES FOR A HAND PICK-STITCHED ZIPPER

1/4"

HANDBASTE

1/4"

the right garment side. Handbaste, matching each marked matchpoint. The basting controls the fabric and any slippage that may occur while stitching. Pull the zipper up before stitching to check if the pattern matches. **Do** stitch the right side of the zipper (Figure 8.29). Close the zipper and see the amazing results of matched elements across the garment!

Bias

The key to working with bias is for the fabric to be perfectly "on grain" to establish the true bias. A center-back invisible zipper is the most versatile application; however, the garment design may not include a center-back seam. Zippers in side seams should be sampled, as it is more difficult to get them to lay flat.

When inserting a zipper into bias-cut seams, try one of the following methods.

Method 1: Stabilized Seam Allowances
- Cut the seam allowances 1½ inches wide to allow for accurate sewing. It's very difficult to hold the bias fabric taut with a tiny seam allowance. A fabric cut on the bias doesn't always stretch the same amount in every fabric. Refer to Chapter 6, "Seams."

> **NOTE**
> Always purchase a similar fabric to test in bias, or purchase additional yardage of the garment fabric. If pretested in muslin, reduce the seam allowances to ³/₄ inch.

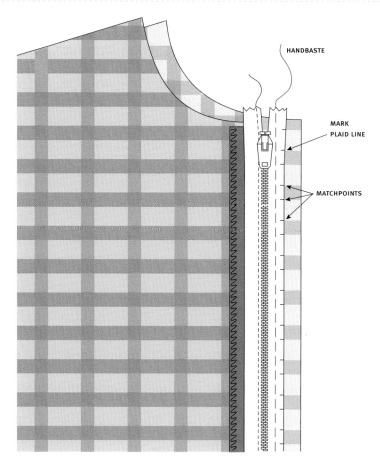

HANDBASTE

MARK PLAID LINE

MATCHPOINTS

8.28 BASTING ZIPPER MATCHPOINTS TO PLAID LINES

- Stabilize the area with either silk organza cut on the straight grain and hand sewn in, or a very lightweight fusible interfacing. Refer to Chapter 3, "Introduction to Stabilizers."
- Clearly mark the stitching line for the zipper; bias always appears narrower.
- Handbaste the zipper into place.
- Stitch several inches, stop with the needle down into the fabric, and lift the zipper foot to allow the fabric to settle and maintain the grain.

- Drop the zipper foot back into place and continue stitching to complete the seam, stretching the bias approximately ¼ inch for a 7-inch zipper (the specific amount may differ depending on your fabric choice) as you sew to avoid puckered seams.
- Remove the excess stabilizer and seam allowances if needed.
- Hand sewing the zipper into place is an alternative to consider when working with lightweight fabrics.

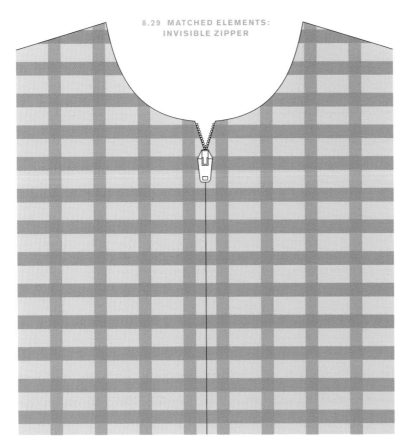

is very slippery, organza is very slippery, and this combination can cause the fabric to bunch up, making pleats and creating stitching havoc!

• Open the zipper. Using a narrow, open, slightly zigged zigzag stitch, stitch the stabilizer and seam allowance to the zipper tape. This provides greater stability of the zipper in a stressed area as well as neatly finishing the seam allowances on a sheer fabric. After stitching, trim away any excess organza and seam allowance.

Sheers

Fabrics such as chiffon, silk, gauze, organza, and voile are often found in evening wear dresses, skirts, or palazzo pants where zippers are traditionally used. Even the lightest-weight zipper can be too heavy for some of these fabrics, causing sagging, so it is important to sample the zipper application first before proceeding to the garment. Always choose the lightest-weight zipper available, such as a mesh lingerie zipper. Removing the stitches from these delicate fabrics is practically impossible without ruining the fabric. Keep in mind the following:

• Will the garment be underlined or lined? If so, the zipper can be sewn to the underlining or lining, leaving the outer layer free.
• Is this a stress area? Stabilize the seam the zipper will be put into; refer to Chapter 3, "Introduction to Stabilizers." Try several samples for the best result.

Method 2: Stabilized Seam Allowances on the Bias

When inserting a zipper into bias-cut fabric, cut the stabilizer on the bias as well, and gently stretch it an inch of the length of the zipper opening as you stitch.

• Mark the zipper length 1 inch shorter on the stabilizer.
• Cut a strip of silk organza on the bias, approximately 3 inches wide and an extra 3 inches longer than the zipper opening. Skin-

colored organza blends well with many sheer fabrics and is less noticeable than white.

• Handbaste the silk organza to the garment fabric, stretching it taut to reduce puckering in the seam.
• Baste the zipper to the silk organza, again stretching it taut to fit the opening.
• Machine stitch, close to the teeth to avoid any tape showing on the front of the garment. Stop frequently, with the needle down in the fabric, to adjust the bias strip of silk organza, keeping it flat and pucker-free. Bias

- Invisible zippers and both lapped and centered zippers can be used in these fabrics, depending on the location of the zipper on the garment.
- Hand sewing an invisible zipper provides more flexibility and a softer zipper.
- Consider alternative closures for sheers such as hooks and eyes, or loops and buttons. Refer to Chapter 17, "Closures."

Satin

On bridal wear, buttons with premade elastic loops are the closure of choice. Using a zipper in combination with the buttons and thread loops offers a very secure closure on a long opening of a bridal gown. The zipper application must be right the first time it is inserted, due to the stitching marks left behind when stitches are removed.

Do use lightweight coil zippers—the best choice.

Do hand stitch the zipper on special-occasion garments.

Do use a lapped zipper on the back of a wedding dress or ball gown. Create the look of buttons and loops by sewing the buttons closely to the edge of the zipper stitching.

Do machine-stitch zippers on satin that is used for daytime garments, or garments that are washable.

Do use a fine machine needle to sew the zipper into the garment to prevent snagging the surface of the satin and to avoid skipped stitches.

NOTE

The weight of the lace and the embellishment on lace determine the correct zipper application, and several samples may be required. When working with costly specialty fabrics, it's worth the time and the effort to make sure that the application chosen is the most appropriate.

Lace

Do use a lapped zipper application for laces with raised surfaces or beading.

Do use an invisible zipper for flatter laces that can easily accommodate the turn that occurs when the zipper is closed.

Do use other closures such as hooks and eyes, or buttons with elastic loops, if the lace is to be a separate layer and not lined or underlined.

Do use a hand-picked zipper as an elegant finish for the garment (see Figure 8.27).

Do consider that lace can have repeats, in other words, motifs or design elements that occur regularly throughout the fabric. When inserting a zipper, care should be taken to match these elements. Refer to "Inserting Zippers in Plaids, Checks, Repeat Patterns, and Horizontal Stripes," earlier in this chapter, for marking directions to match these elements.

Do stabilize the zipper opening with silk organza or tulle; use tulle with very small holes, such as bridal tulle, which comes in a wide assortment of colors.

Do handbaste the zipper in place before stitching.

Do hand sew a lapped or centered zipper into a garment of lace that has raised designs with cords or ribbon on the surface. This prevents snagging that could occur if the zipper were sewn by machine. The invisible zipper will go in smoothly if the lace is not too thick or bulky.

Sequined Fabrics

Do insert a zipper by hand. Both the lapped and invisible zipper can be used in sequined fabric.

Do use the plain fabric borders on either side of the sequined area for the seam allowance into which the zipper will be inserted.

Do remove some of the sequins in the zipper seam allowance.

Do stabilize the zipper area, using a sew-in stabilizer.

Do handbaste the invisible zipper into place. Sew the zipper in by hand, backstitching (see Figure 6.38b) and making sure that the zipper does not pull the sequins into the roll of the zipper, which would prevent them from lying flat. Careful hand sewing of the zipper allows the stitches to rest in between the sequins without distortion.

Don't use heat and moisture from steam; it may discolor metal sequins or melt plastic sequins.

Beaded Fabrics

Beaded fabrics can have intricate allover designs, or motifs that are scattered across the fabric.

Do insert a hand-picked zipper in beaded fabrics.

Do insert an invisible zipper if the beading is not too dense. Here's how:

- Remove the beading from the seam allowances by using an upholstery hammer or pliers to smash the beads. Wear safety goggles.
- Using a zipper foot, staystitch along the seam allowances from which the beads have been removed. This helps to hold the beading threads in place and prevents the beading from coming loose.
- Stabilize the area with tulle or silk organza, and hand sew.
- Handbaste the zipper into place. When using an invisible zipper, close the zipper to check that the zipper tape is not showing on the front of the fabric.
- Sew the zipper into place, using the hand backstitch.

Velvet

When inserting a zipper in velvet, it is of the utmost importance to avoid crushing the nap by pressing. Stitches must be of the correct size and evenly sewn. If seams are ripped out, holes and unsightly marks are left behind. A zipper in

IMPORTANT

A velvet board is a pressing tool for fabrics with nap or pile. It has short wires embedded into a flexible or rigid base, and these wires keep the nap or pile from becoming crushed when pressing. This is the *only* way to press velvet without ruining it. Regular pressing will crush the pile and leave shiny marks, called glazing, which cannot be removed. Lightweight fusible interfacing can be applied to velvet when using the velvet board, using a very light touch of the iron to hold the fusible in place.

velvet is a one time opportunity! The best zipper to apply to velvet is the invisible zipper—velvet does not topstitch well.

Do stabilize the area in which the zipper will be inserted. Refer to Chapter 3, "Introduction to Stabilizers," for more information.

Do allow for larger seam allowances at the zipper insertion. A larger seam allowance is easier to work with when sewing a tricky fabric.

Do serge or clean finish the edges of the seam allowances before applying the zipper. Even if the garment will be lined, it will be easier to sew the zipper in without messy raw edges.

Do handbaste the zipper in place; this will keep the zipper from slipping off the velvet as it is stitched. Pins can leave marks on the fabric.

Do allow a smidge more for the nap of the velvet to turn once the zipper is complete.

Do stitch close to the teeth to eliminate any of the tape showing through to the garment front.

Do lengthen the stitch length to 3.0 to avoid buckling and slippage that can occur when using smaller stitches on fabrics with nap or bulk.

- Stitch slowly and, leaving the needle down in the fabric, occasionally lift the presser foot to allow the garment to settle. This avoids any puckering or slipping, and gives better control of the stitching.

Do place the garment facedown, flat on a velvet board. Lightly apply the iron to the stitched zipper tape to set the stitches. *Do not press the zipper!* Even with a velvet board for pressing, marks can be left on the front of the garment if too much pressure is applied, or if the iron is too hot.

Knits

Zippers are used occasionally in knits.

Do stabilize the zipper area with a narrow strip of fusible interfacing or tape suitable for the fabric being used. Refer to Chapter 3, "Introduction to Stabilizers," for suggestions.

Do cut the strips to fit the seam allowances, approximately ½ inch. *Sample* this first to be sure the interfacing you are using does not leave a ridge on the correct side of the fabric.

Do use invisible zippers; they are the most flexible choice due to their lightweight coils.

Do use a hand-picked zipper on double knit garments for a very nice finish.

Denim

The fly-front zipper application, using a metal, self-locking zipper, is designed for trousers or jeans. A metal zipper is generally used for jeans, and can be shortened to fit the opening of the garment, as previously discussed. Internet sources have specially sized zippers for jeans, and many online sources offer special-order sizes, some as small as 2 inches. See the "Where to Buy" appendix at the back of this book. If the garment is trouser jeans or a skirt, a lapped or invisible zipper will work as well.

Do use a fly front, lapped, or invisible zipper if the garment is trouser jeans or a skirt.

Do use a hammer (that's right, a hammer!) to reduce bulk in seams or hems. This compresses the fibers, and makes it easier to sew through.

Do consider serging seams, then topstitching to reduce bulk. Refer to Chapter 6, "Seams."

Do leave enough room between stitching on the tape and the coils of an invisible zipper so that the denim will have enough space to turn when the zipper is closed. Twill weave is very firm, even in lightweight denim, and needs a smidge more of space to curl around the coils, but not so much that the tape shows on the front of the garment.

Do avoid sewing too close to the teeth, or through the teeth, as the zipper will not close. Instead it will pull apart, looking broken, and will have to be resewn.

Leather, Faux Leather, and Ultrasuede

Invisible, slot, lapped, and decorative zippers work well on leather. The invisible, fly, lapped, slot, and exposed zipper applications can be used in faux suede, matching the zipper weight and function to the garment. Since fraying does not occur in these fabrics, topstitching and edgestitching are used with great success in zipper applications. Both conventional and flat method zipper applications work on these fabrics.

Leather

Do stabilize leather. Refer to Chapter 3, "Introduction to Stabilizers."

Do use fusible twill tape in calfskin when inserting an invisible zipper in the center-back seam of a skirt.

Do use a strip of suitable interfacing to provide a base on which to insert the zipper on heavier leathers.

Do protect the leather when applying fusible stabilizers with an iron by using brown paper bag strips and no steam.

Do use the correct size and type of needle to prevent skipped stitches. Always sample different sizes of needles using the smallest size that gives the best results in stitch quality.

Do use double-sided adhesive tape to hold the zipper in place while stitching, or use Steam-a-Seam fusible fabric iron-ons, especially if the garment is being lined.

Do use craft glue to hold seam allowances in place before inserting slot and lapped zipper applications. Pound with a hammer to flatten the seam allowances. Baste the zipper in place with double-sided adhesive tape; topstitch the zipper.

Do use an X-Acto knife or rotary cutter to cut out the rectangular opening for exposed zippers up to $1/2$ inch wide and the length of the zipper. Use glue or double-sided adhesive tape to hold the zipper in place. Edgestitch.

Do use Teflon zipper feet, available from The Sewing Emporium, as well as adhesive-backed Teflon sheets (which can be cut to size to fit the bottom of a standard zipper foot) for easier zipper application on leather or suede.

Don't backstitch on leather or Ultrasuede—ties knots.

Ultrasuede

Ultrasuede (faux suede) has the expensive look of real suede without the disadvantages. It is water resistant; doesn't stiffen if it gets wet; and is lightweight, wrinkle resistant, and colorfast.

NOTE

The weight of the denim will determine whether to use a zipper application other than the fly-front, such as an invisible zipper. As always, if you haven't tried a particular application in denim before, *sample*. Sampling will also reveal whether stitch marks will be left if you have to rip out any stitches that are not perfect, as in topstitching.

NOTE

Both leather and Ultrasuede are a onetime sewing fabric, which means that any stitches removed will leave marks.

It doesn't fray, and the raw edge can be used as the finish. It can also be pressed on the wrong side using a pressing cloth and a steam iron set on the synthetic setting. Faux suede garments look especially well-made when topstitching and edgestitching are used to enhance them.

Do use a "with a nap" layout.

Do avoid garments that require easing—Ultrasuede does not ease well.

Do machine wash and dry—the more it's washed and dried, the softer it becomes.

Do use a suitable stabilizer in the seam allowance area of the zipper to prevent a puckered look to the stitching. Refer to Chapter 3, "Introduction to Stabilizers."

Do avoid ripping out stitches, which would leave holes in this fabric. Careful stitching is required for successful zipper applications in Ultrasuede.

Do use center, lapped, or exposed zippers for the best result in Ultrasuede.

Don't use side seam zippers in Ultrasuede— they do not lie flat.

Faux Fur

Because faux furs are bulky, an exposed zipper, a lapped zipper, or a centered zipper set into contrasting fabric bands (plackets), such as leather, suede, faux suede, or ribbing, creates a flat area for the zipper to be inserted and also complements the fur. With very long-haired faux furs, consider using an alternative type of closure. Refer to Chapter 17, "Closures."

Remove the faux fur from the seam allowances before inserting the zipper. Use a razor, a fabric shaver, or an X-Acto knife. This process takes time and is messy! Also try long bladed, very sharp embroidery scissors, holding them at an angle while cutting away the pile in the direction of the nap. Trim away any excess pile that is not cut away at first, trimming very close to the backing without cutting through it. Be careful of how much of the pile is removed; if too much is trimmed, the edge may look too blunt and the pile may not lie flat at the edge of the placket. Either method removes the pile while it reduces bulk, and allows easier, accurate stitching of the zipper. Refer to Chapter 6, "Seams."

Do stabilize the zipper area when the backing is made of knit. Refer to Chapter 3, "Introduction to Stabilizers."

Do determine how much of the zipper tape will be exposed before basting the zipper into place.

Do allow for more space between the teeth of the zipper and the longer pile of the fur.

• Stitch slowly, keeping the pile of the fur away from the teeth of the zipper.

• Use a seam ripper or an awl, placed flat, to hold the pile out of the way while stitching.

Creating a band of leather, suede, or the faux versions of leather or suede provides the option of an exposed zipper, a lapped zipper, or a centered zipper. The raw edges of these fabrics do not need to be finished and create a neat, tai-

lored finish to the inside of the zipper. Excellent, straight stitching highlights this technique.

• Determine the width of the band. This could be a design element that is both functional and decorative; the decision is up to the design student.

• The flat method of construction uses two pieces of leather/suede for each side of the zipper. The zipper is inserted into the raw edges, and topstitched to the zipper tape and the trimmed seam allowance of the fur.

Another method of zipper application is the lapped or centered zipper with band or placket. Prepare the seam allowance area by trimming away the fur.

• Determine the width of the placket. Cut two strips the same width for each side of the zipper. If using faux suede, stabilize one half of each strip that will be on the top of the garment. This prevents stretching of the placket while stitching through all the layers. If possible, also loosen the presser foot tension to accommodate all the layers.

• When using faux suede, baste the two pieces together down the center of the strips. When the basting stitches are removed, they will not be visible on the surface of the faux suede.

• Place the edge of the garment inside the basted placket pieces. Using double-sided adhesive tape on top of the zipper tape, place the zipper under the center of the plackets. Finger-press in place on the wrong side of the garment.

- Carefully pin the placket through all the layers from the correct side of the garment.
- Using a zipper foot, edgestitch the band nearest the garment. Lengthen the stitch length to 3.0, and sew slowly and evenly to the bottom of the zipper. The pile of the fur will cover this edge.
- Move over 1/8 inch to 1/4 inch and stitch another row, catching the zipper tape in this line of stitching.
- Repeat for the other side.

TRANSFER YOUR KNOWLEDGE

In this chapter you have learned about zippers. This chapter has explained:

- The many different types of zippers;
- Installation techniques;
- The importance of accurate marking, basting, edgestitching, and topstitching;
- How to choose the correct zipper for the fabric being used;
- The functional and decorative uses of zippers; and
- How to effectively use zippers in specialty fabrics.

Zippers can be attention-getting elements of a design, and it is best to perfect the techniques necessary for a flawless zipper before tackling more difficult techniques such as working with a bias-cut fabric, or specialty fabrics such as silk or satin.

When a student is adding a new element to the design, such as a zipper, it can be difficult to know which zipper to use, where to put it, and how to stitch the zipper into the garment.

Example

The garment design calls for a centered zipper to be placed in the center-back seam. As the designer, you prefer a smoother, more subtle opening, such as an invisible zipper. You've never attempted an invisible zipper before, but you know how to measure the opening for a zipper, accurately mark, handbaste, carefully cut, and evenly stitch. Transfer knowledge when you:

- Stabilize the seam allowances, if necessary;
- Accurately mark the opening;
- Press the zipper tape flat, removing any packaging wrinkles, and press open the coils;
- Baste the zipper to the seam allowance, one side at a time;
- Begin to stitch, close to the teeth, slowly and evenly.

Even though these are not techniques used in production, knowing these techniques will get you started. Then, with the help of your instructor and by following the explanations of the invisible zipper, you can learn to stitch the invisible zipper in place of the centered zipper. Once you have mastered the first invisible zipper, you will be able to transfer that knowledge to other garments and fabrics.

STRETCH YOUR CREATIVITY

- Stitch zippers of different sizes and colors all over the surface of a garment as a decorative element (Figure 8.30a).
- Place an invisible zipper opening asymmetrically.
- Use an upholstery zipper with metal teeth or zipper by the yard as both piping around the neckline of a jacket and as a working zipper (Figure 8.30b).
- Use separating zippers to join layers that can be unzipped and removed, such as a skirt (Figure 8.30c).
- Use decorative ribbon such as velvet, grosgrain, or embroidered trim to cover the centered zipper.
- Place an exposed zipper in a seam, such as a raglan (Figure 8.30d).
- Place an exposed zipper with metal teeth down the center of each sleeve.
- Use an exposed, metal teeth zipper down the entire center back of a garment.
- Use an exposed, metal teeth zipper with decorative pull on each entire side seam of a skirt.

STOP! WHAT DO I DO IF . . .

. . . there is puckering or pleating at the bottom of my invisible zipper?

Remove the stitching at the bottom of the zipper. Release enough of the sewing machine

Stretch Your Creativity

ZIPPER
AS PIPING

WORKING
ZIPPER

SEPARATING
ZIPPER

8.30A STRETCH YOUR CREATIVITY: SUGGESTIONS

8.30B STRETCH YOUR CREATIVITY: SUGGESTIONS

8.30C STRETCH YOUR CREATIVITY: SUGGESTIONS

8.30D STRETCH YOUR CREATIVITY: SUGGESTIONS

stitches to flatten the area. Using a backstitch, sew the seam by hand. Carefully press the seam allowance only.

. . . the stitching is uneven despite my best sewing?

There are many ways to mark the stitching line when sewing the zipper. The zipper tape often has woven lines to follow, or a fabric marking pen can be used to draw a line on the zipper tape. From the correct side of the fabric, a 1/2-inch-wide piece of temporary tape called Magic Tape by Scotch brand can be centered over the zipper and used as a guide for stitching. *Sample this tape first on a scrap piece of fabric.* This tape has a light amount of adhesive, which makes it easy to remove; however, it may not work well with some specialty fabrics.

. . . the zipper is stiff and it is difficult to open and close?

Try using a drop of Sewer's Aid on the teeth of the zipper, and open and close the zipper several times to help spread the liquid. Sewer's Aid is a liquid used on machine embroidery threads to prevent breakage and aid their passage through the tension discs of the sewing machine. Apply it carefully, so it doesn't run off the teeth and into the garment fabric. A little bit of this goes a long way.

. . . a zipper doesn't look good in my design?

Often the zipper cannot be removed without leaving unsightly stitch marks. Another area of the garment may not be available to redesign a different type of closure, or it may be too time-consuming or costly to use a new idea. Next time take time to plan the design, sample different techniques on the garment fabric, and realize that sometimes no matter how good the design looks, a detail in the end may not be the best look after all. Perfecting skills takes time and practice. Zippers challenge our sewing skills with every fabric that is used in the design of a garment. A perfectly sewn zipper is the result of patience and perseverance.

SELF-CRITIQUE

- Are the seams into which the zippers are inserted cut on the correct grainline?
- Are the stitch length and tension correct for the fabric type and weight?
- Is the thread color a good match?
- Is the stitching straight and even?
- Is there any puckering in the stitching or at the bottom of the zipper?
- Is the centered zipper actually evenly centered over the zipper teeth?
- Does the invisible zipper roll nicely over the coils without any zipper tape showing?
- Does the invisible zipper open smoothly and easily?
- Is the lap of the lapped zipper the same size from top to bottom, and does it cover the teeth of the zipper?
- Does the exposed zipper reveal an even amount of the teeth or the zipper tape on both sides?

REVIEW CHECKLIST

Do I understand what centered, lapped, invisible, and separating zippers have in common? Look at your zippers and ask yourself:

- Is this the correct weight of zipper for this garment?
- Does the centered, lapped, invisible, or separating zipper look like it belongs with the design?
- Is the stitching straight and evenly sewn?
- Is there any puckering?
- Does any of the zipper tape show after stitching invisible, centered, or lapped zippers?
- Are the teeth visible?
- Does the zipper enhance the overall design enough to justify the time and cost involved?

Waistbands: Planning the Horizontal Edge

The horizontal edge of a waistband can be straight or curved, depending on the position of the waistband. Waistbands sitting comfortably on the waistline are usually straight and cut in one piece. Waistbands sitting on the hips are curved and cut in two pieces. Waistbands can be designed in a variety of widths and styles. The underside of the curved waistbands can be cut from a variety of fabrics for a couture finish. A waistband can also be cut all-in-one with the

skirt or pant. The garment can be darted to contour the waistline, creating a high-waisted look. This style comes and goes in fashion trends.

The fabric is the basis on which all decisions are made for waistbands. The nature of the fabric, the drape, the hand (whether it is stiff or soft) all contribute to the type of waistband to be stitched. How the fabric will be stabilized or interfaced also influences the type of waistband to be constructed. Fabric and interfacing go hand in hand, and in waistbands it is essential to choose the correct type of support for the type of waistband being designed.

The waistband should be comfortable for the wearer—this is functional design. Waistbands, when they are worn, should not be too tight or too loose. The structure of the waistband is extremely important. It needs to have firmness so it doesn't cave in when it is worn. A properly constructed waistband is the first step toward lasting comfort, and what stabilizes the band is the key to a firm, smooth, professional finish. The final waistband, whatever its shape, width, or style, should blend in beautifully with the whole garment.

Style I.D.

9.1A STRAIGHT WAISTBAND
WITH APPLIED TIE

9.1B CONTOURED WAIST-
BAND WITH TOPSTITCHING
AT WAIST AND HEM

9.1C EXTENDED WAIST-
BAND WITH BELT LOOPS

9.1D ELASTIC CASING AT WAIST
WITH DRAWSTRING TIES

STYLE I.D.

The Style I.D. shows examples of commonly used waistbands and suggests creative styles (Figure 9.1).

GATHER YOUR TOOLS

For the techniques in this chapter, you will need waist-specific support, which includes tape measure interfacing and elastic; marking pen; scissors; pins; bodkin; hooks and bars; hooks and eyes; buttons; and appropriate needle and thread to match the garment. Think ahead—order now.

Before applying waistbands, darts should be sewn and pressed, seams sewn, and zippers applied.

NOW LET'S GET STARTED
What Is a Waistband?

A waistband is a band of fabric, usually fully interfaced, seamed to the waistline of skirts or pants and fastened to hold the garment firmly around the waist. Waistbands hold the garment in the proper position on the body. Ease is determined by the designer at the patternmaking stage of construction. The waistband must match the skirt at the waistline. A waistband can be both functional and decorative. In its functional use, a waistband finishes the edge of a garment and provides support on the body. In its decorative use, the style and eye appeal of the garment are enhanced. The waistband can open at the center front, center back, or side seam, or follow the lines of a princess seam (Figure 17.2).

The Three Types of Waistbands

Waistbands fall into three categories: straight, curved, and extended. The waistband should fit the waist snugly yet comfortably. The designer may be tempted to cinch the waist to create a slimmer look, but this usually has the opposite effect and forces the stomach to bulge out. This garment would be uncomfortable to wear.

It is best to base the waistband on the waist measurement and the amount of wearing ease preferred by the designer. The length of the waistband should equal the waist measurement plus ease and, if using an underlap or overlap, at least an additional 1 inch. The **underlap** is the **extension** of the waistband on the center-back edge or the left side if the garment opens in the front. The underlap is a place to sew garment fasteners. The **overlap** (Figure 17.2b) can be extended with a shaped end as a decorative detail.

The waistband is stitched to the garment after the zipper is inserted (if using one) and the seams have been completed.

Straight Waistbands—One Piece

Most straight waistbands are cut in one piece with a foldline in the middle. Straight waistbands can be wide or narrow but on average are cut 2 inches wide.

To calculate the waistband, measure as indicated in Figure 9.2a.

> **NOTE**
>
> It is important to determine the proper stabilizer for the waistband being constructed. Sample several choices of stabilizers to determine the interfacing that best suits the fabric.

- To wear better and stay in shape, the waistband should be interfaced.
- Select a weight of interfacing that will not overpower the fabric, yet will provide body and support to the waistband. Refer to Chapter 3, "Introduction to Stabilizers," for further information.
- For full support, interface the entire waistband with fusible interfacing; or, cut the interfacing the same width as the waistband with a row of machine stitching below the foldline on the facing half, to prevent the interfacing from shifting when using sew-in interfacing.
- Or, use slotted waistband interfacing, specifically designed for waistbands.

- Stitch the straight waistband to the waistline seam by matching the notched edges (Figure 9.2b).
- The unnotched edge is folded under on the seam allowance, edge pressed, and trimmed to reduce bulk at the waistline before finishing by hand slipstitching or stitching-in-the-ditch (see Figure 9.2b).
- The unnotched edged can also be serge finished to further reduce bulk.

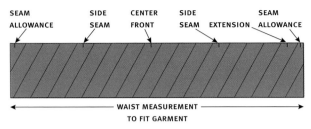

SEAM ALLOWANCE   SIDE SEAM   CENTER FRONT   SIDE SEAM   EXTENSION   SEAM ALLOWANCE

WAIST MEASUREMENT TO FIT GARMENT

9.2A STRAIGHT WAISTBAND: CALCULATION

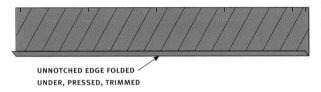

UNNOTCHED EDGE FOLDED UNDER, PRESSED, TRIMMED

9.2B STRAIGHT WAISTBAND: FOLDED, PRESSED, AND TRIMMED

Hand-Finished Application

To attach a waistband without edgestitching or topstitching, follow the direction for applying the straight waistband, except:

- Pin baste and stitch the correct side of the waistband to the correct side of the garment waistline (Figure 9.3a).
- Stitch the right extension from the notch to the top of the waistband; stitch the right side waistband (Figure 9.3a).
- Turn the waistband to the inside of the garment and slipstitch the folded, pressed edge of the waistband to the seamline.
- Slipstitch the open edges of the underlap together (Figure 9.3b).
- Complete the waistband with your closure of choice (Figure 9.3b).

Topstitched Application

Attaching the waistband by topstitching changes the order of the application. Topstitching is meant to be seen, so the stitch length is usually extended to 3.0 or more. Often a contrasting thread type or color can be used to highlight this stitching, which is done from the correct side of the garment. This is entirely the designer's choice. This type of stitching must be straight, even, and without obvious starts and stops. If this skill has not been mastered, consider using edgestitching in place of topstitching.

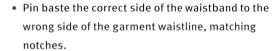

- Pin baste the correct side of the waistband to the wrong side of the garment waistline, matching notches.
- Double-check that the waistband will actually be turned to the correct side by folding the waistband over the seam edge to the correct side of the garment.
- Also check that the extension is on the correct end (Figure 9.4a).
- Stitch the waistband to the waistline.
- Trim, grade, and clip the seam allowances.
- Press the seam allowance flat; then press the seam allowances up into the waistband (Figure 9.4b).
- Fold the waistband ends so the correct sides are together; stitch the left side from the notch to the top of the waistband; stitch the right side. Trim the corners (Figure 9.4b).
- Flip the waistband to the correct side of the garment (Figure 9.4c).

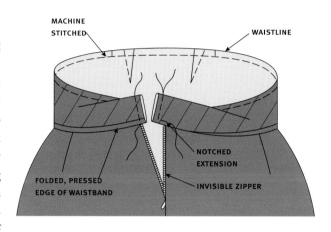

MACHINE STITCHED   WAISTLINE

FOLDED, PRESSED EDGE OF WAISTBAND

NOTCHED EXTENSION

INVISIBLE ZIPPER

9.3A HAND-FINISHED WAISTBAND APPLICATION

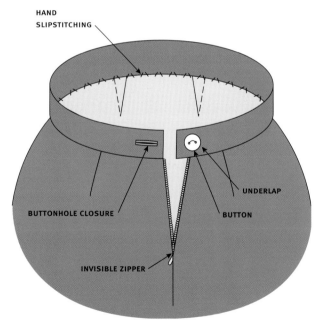

HAND SLIPSTITCHING

BUTTONHOLE CLOSURE

UNDERLAP

BUTTON

INVISIBLE ZIPPER

9.3B HAND-FINISHED WAISTBAND APPLICATION

NOTE

If the folded waistband edge ripples or appears too big, the ends of the waistband may not have matched perfectly when stitching. Remove the stitching, and adjust the amount needed to remove the rippling. It may not be much, so don't take in the ends too much! Take time to measure the amount, using your tape measure or your seam gauge.

- Place the folded, pressed edge of the waistband slightly over the waistline stitching, just enough to be caught in the topstitching.
- *Do not* stretch this edge when pressing or it will not lie flat when topstitched.
- Pin baste the folded edge to the seamline.
- From the correct side of the waistband, topstitch the folded edge to the waistline (see Figure 9.4c).
- With the needle down in the fabric, lift the presser foot, pivot, and continue topstitching the waistband, extension, and top of the waistband (see Figure 9.4c).
- Complete the waistband with appropriate fasteners for the garment. Refer to Chapter 17, "Closures."

Straight Waistbands—Two Piece

A straight waistband is cut in two pieces when the waistband is a decorative shape. Eliminate bulk by using a lighter-weight fabric for the waistband facing, and for comfort if the fabric is heavily textured or itchy. A lining fabric may

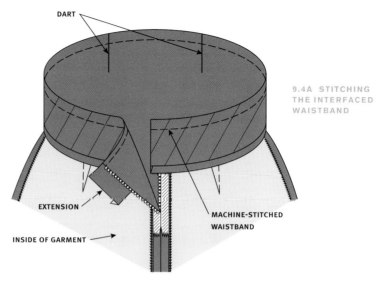

9.4 TOPSTITCHED STRAIGHT WAISTBAND APPLICATION

9.4A STITCHING THE INTERFACED WAISTBAND

DART

EXTENSION

MACHINE-STITCHED WAISTBAND

INSIDE OF GARMENT

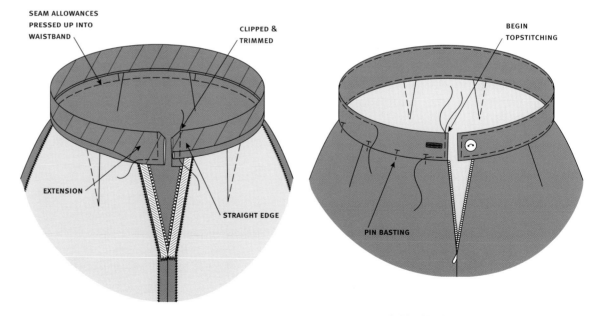

SEAM ALLOWANCES PRESSED UP INTO WAISTBAND

CLIPPED & TRIMMED

BEGIN TOPSTITCHING

EXTENSION

STRAIGHT EDGE

PIN BASTING

9.4B STITCH THE EXTENSION AND STRAIGHT EDGE OF THE WAISTBAND

9.4C TOPSTITCH THE WAISTBAND

be used instead for the underband of the waistband. Accurate sewing and careful clipping,
trimming, and grading contribute to the success
of this type of waistband.

- Determine the finished waistband length, including the extension.
- Remove seam allowances from fusible interfacing
  before applying to the waistband to reduce bulk
  in the seam allowances (Figure 9.5a).
- Stitch the upper and under waistbands together
  along the top edge; press, and understitch
  (Figure 9.5b).
- Pin baste the upper waistband to the correct side
  of the waistline; stitch (see Figure 9.5c).
- Trim and grade the seam allowance; press toward
  the waistband.
- Stitch the ends of the upper waistband to the
  ends of the under waistband, trim ends, and turn
  waistband correct side out.
- Secure the under waistband to the waistline
  seam using any of the previously mentioned techniques: whipstitch by hand, stitch-in-the-ditch,
  topstitch, or edgestitch.
- Complete the waistband with the appropriate
  closure.

Bias Binding at Waist

The waistline can be finished by using bias binding to provide a narrow edge finish. Decide if
this will be contrasting fabric or the same fabric
used for the garment. The technique described
here is effective for single or double binding.
Refer to Chapter 6 and Chapter 12 for details
about how to create bias strips for this finish
(see Figure 6.16 and Figure 12.26).

- Apply zipper, sew darts, and seams before
  stitching bias onto waistline.
- Stitch twill tape around waistline to stabilize
  the waistline. Refer to Chapter 3, "Introduction to Stabilizers."
- Leave a ½-inch seam allowance at either end
  of the binding (Figure 9.6a).
- The seam allowance for stitching is the finished required width of the binding.
- Press the seam up into the binding after
  stitching.
- Turn each end of the seam allowance in
  toward the binding, and turn the remaining
  bias over to the back, encasing all the raw
  edges.
- Finish the binding by hand slipstitching
  the edge of the bias binding to the machine
  stitches at the waistline (Figure 9.6b) or by
  machine stitching-in-the-ditch from the correct side of the garment (Figure 9.6c).
- For heavier, bulky fabrics such as denim or
  wool, serge one edge of the binding (Figure
  9.6d).

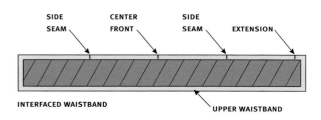

9.5A TWO-PIECE STRAIGHT WAISTBAND

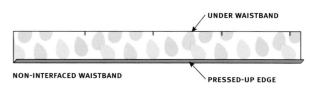

9.5B TWO-PIECE STRAIGHT WAISTBAND

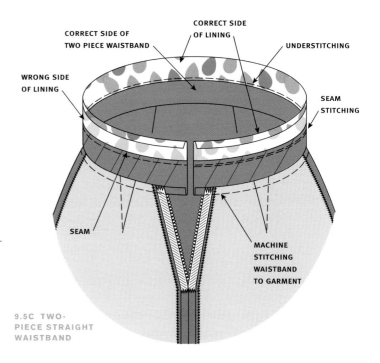

9.5C TWO-
PIECE STRAIGHT
WAISTBAND

9.6 BIAS BINDING WAIST FINISH

9.6A APPLY THE BIAS TO THE WAISTLINE

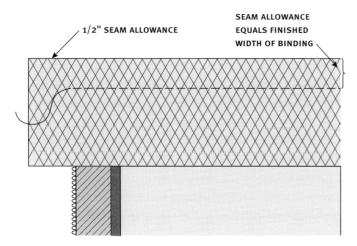

1/2" SEAM ALLOWANCE

SEAM ALLOWANCE EQUALS FINISHED WIDTH OF BINDING

9.6B BIAS BINDING AT WAIST: SLIPSTITCH

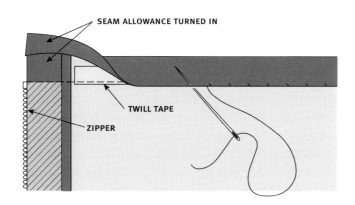

SEAM ALLOWANCE TURNED IN

TWILL TAPE

ZIPPER

9.6C BIAS BINDING AT WAIST: STITCH-IN-THE-DITCH

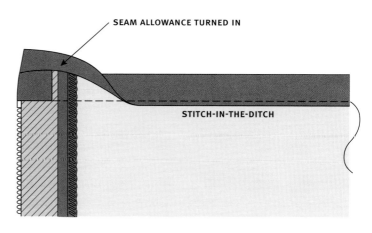

SEAM ALLOWANCE TURNED IN

STITCH-IN-THE-DITCH

9.6D BIAS BINDING AT WAIST: SERGED FINISH

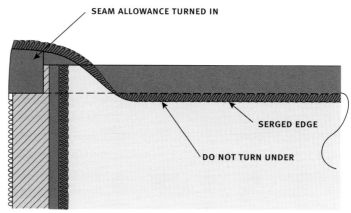

SEAM ALLOWANCE TURNED IN

SERGED EDGE

DO NOT TURN UNDER

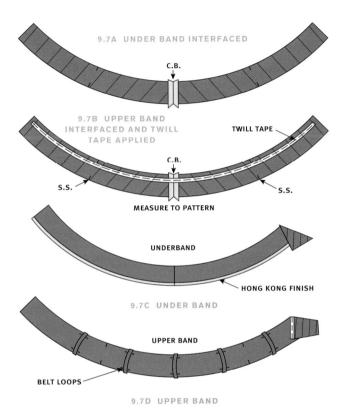

9.7A UNDER BAND INTERFACED

C.B.

9.7B UPPER BAND
INTERFACED AND TWILL
TAPE APPLIED

TWILL TAPE

C.B.

S.S.   S.S.

MEASURE TO PATTERN

UNDERBAND

HONG KONG FINISH

9.7C UNDER BAND

UPPER BAND

BELT LOOPS

9.7D UPPER BAND

- Turn the binding over, encasing the raw edges.
- Leave the serged edge flat—do not turn under.
- Stitch-in-the-ditch from the correct side of the garment (Figure 9.6d).

Curved or Contoured Waistbands

A **contoured waistband** consists of identical pattern pieces: two waistbands and two pieces of interfacing, shaped to coincide with the contour of the rib cage or upper hip. Belt loops are often a feature of this waistband, and the designer determines the width and the number of loops. Refer to the section in this chapter "Belt Loops and Thread Carriers" for more information. When the designer plans this waistband, the fabric's ability to retain shape and the type of interfacing needed to support the shape need to work together. When waistbands extend above the waistline, very firm interfacing, staystitching, and twill tape are needed to provide stability, while the weight of the interfacing is completely dependent on the weight of the fabric. Take time to sample different weights and types of interfacing when constructing this type of waistband. Refer to Chapter 3 for further information on appropriate stabilizers. No matter what the shape, it is the same stitching order as shown in Figure 9.5).

- Fuse interfacing to upper and under waistbands, matching all notches.
- Join upper and under bands at center-back seams (Figure 9.7a and b).
- On the wrong side of the upper waistband, sew twill tape around the top edge of the band, using slightly less than ¼-inch seam allowance, being careful not to stretch the band when stitching (see Figure 9.7b).
- Finish the under waistband using the Hong Kong finish (Figure 9.7c) or a serged finish.

- If you have decided to use belt loops, position the belt loops on the upper waistband; baste the loops at top and bottom to the waistband (Figure 9.7d).
- Attach the upper band to the garment using the allotted seam allowance, matching all notches.
- With the correct sides of the band facing each other, stitch using a ¼-inch seam allowance around the top edge of the band; understitch the top of the waistband and stitch each end of the waistband. (This may differ depending on the design, as seen in Figure 9.4.)
- Clip the corners, turn, and press.
- On the wrong side of the garment, pin the waistband in place.
- From the correct side of the garment, stitch-in-the-ditch to attach the under waistband.
- Press, using a tailor's ham to shape the curve of the waistband—*do not stretch the waistband when pressing.*
- Complete the waistband with the appropriate closure. (Refer to Figure 8.13.)

Waistline Stay

A **waistline stay** in a strapless dress or a gown helps keep the waistline from stretching and relieves stress and strain on the closure. Zippered waistlines close more easily if they are stayed. Grosgrain ribbon makes an excellent stay.

- Cut a piece of grosgrain ribbon equal to the waistline plus 2 inches.
- Finish each end by folding back 1 inch.
- Turn under again ½ inch from the fold, and edgestitch down to the stay.

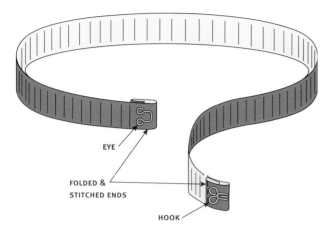

EYE

FOLDED &
STITCHED ENDS

HOOK

HAND STITCHED

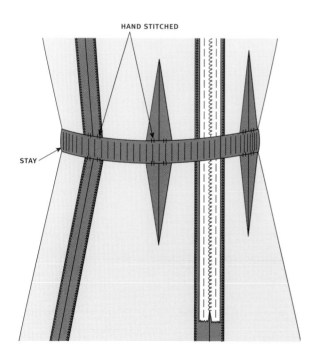

STAY

- Sew hooks on one end of the ribbon stay and round eyes on the other (Figure 9.8a).
- Position the ribbon on the waistline with the ends meeting at the zipper.
- Fasteners should face the zipper tape.
- Machine stitch the stay to the waistline seam allowance.
- Or, whipstitch the stay to the side seams and darts if there isn't a waistline seam.
- Leave the stay free for 2 inches on either side of the zipper to provide necessary room to close the hooks and eyes (Figure 9.8b).

Extended Waistbands

A waistband can also be cut all-in-one with skirt or pants and darted to provide contour, but this is a style that comes and goes in fashion. A more familiar and commonly used style of waistband that is cut-in-one with the garment is the **foldover elastic waistband**.

The **cut-in-one-with-the garment waistband** is an extension of the garment. The shape at the top of the waistband must be equal in width to the area of the body it will meet. The facing of the extended waistband must also match the upper edge of the extended waistband. All of these requirements must be addressed by the designer at the patternmaking stage. Careful, accurate stitching of the seams results in the extended waistband width fitting the body width when complete.

Darted, Extended Waistband

- Stitch, slash open, and press the darts (Figure 9.9a).

- Interface the facing; if using a lining, leave the facing edge unfinished (Figure 9.9b).
- Twill tape can be added to stabilize the upper edge of the extended waistline.
- Install the zipper.
- Stitch the facing to extended waistline upper edge, press the seam allowances, and understitch (Figure 9.9c).
- Turn the facing inside the garment; press.
- If using a lining, stitch the completed skirt lining to the lower edge of the facing (Figure 9.9d).
- Whipstitch the facing/lining seam to darts and side seams, and stitch the lining around the zipper. Look ahead to chapter 16, Figure 16.12a.
- Or, secure the ends of the facing to the zipper tape, seam allowances, and darts if not using a lining.
- Hand stitch a hook and eye to the top edge above the zipper (Figure 17.31).

Elastic Waistband

All elastic waistbands fall into two categories—elastic inserted into a **stitched-down casing** (Figure 9.10c) and elastic sewn directly to the fabric. It is of utmost importance that the waistband be able to slide over the hips as well as be comfortable at the waist—this is where fashion meets function. The ideal of the elastic waistband is comfort; the width of the elastic contributes to the comfort and is the choice of the designer. Nonroll elastic is the best choice for this waistband to avoid rolling, crushing, or curling. Good-quality elastic retains its shape and recovery.

A **bodkin** (Figure 9.11a) is a handy and reliable tool used to thread the elastic through

9.9 HIGH-WAISTED SKIRT

9.9A STITCH AND CLIP THE DARTS AND WAISTBAND

PRESS DARTS OPEN

WAISTLINE CLIP

CLIP

CLIP

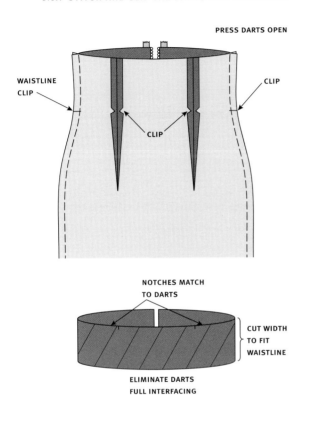

NOTCHES MATCH TO DARTS

CUT WIDTH TO FIT WAISTLINE

ELIMINATE DARTS FULL INTERFACING

9.9B PREPARING THE FACING

TWILL TAPE

INTERFACING LINING

9.9C STITCHING THE FACING TO THE SKIRT

LINING

LINING JOINED TO SKIRT

FACING

UNDER-STITCHING

DARTS

SKIRT

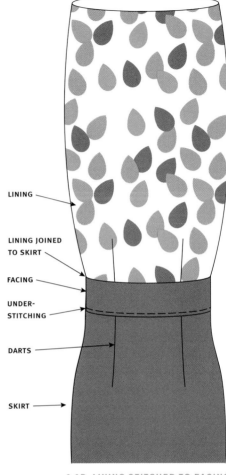

9.9D LINING STITCHED TO FACING

the **casings,** whether the casing is at the waist, wrist, or ankle. However, the width of the bodkin prevents it from being used in casings narrower than ⅜ inch. A large safety pin can be used as well, if a bodkin is not available, but often springs open during the threading process, usually in the middle! Then the entire length of elastic has to be pulled back out, and the threading begun again. In addition to the

inconvenience of restarting the threading, a pin is nearly impossible to close while inside the casing, and the pin point can damage the fabric, rip a small hole, or become entangled so that the casing has to be ripped out and resewn. Use whatever fits safely into the casing.

Follow the directions below for the style that best suits the skirt and pant fabric. Elastic waistbands can be:

- Cut all-in-one and invisible on the surface of the garment (Figure 9.10a).
- Cut separately and joined to the garment (Figure 9.10b).
- Topstitched, with one row of elastic inserted into the casing (Figure 9.10c).

9.10A INVISIBLE CASING

9.10B JOINED CASING

9.10C TOPSTITCHED CASING

9.10D MULTIPLE ROWS OF ELASTIC CASINGS

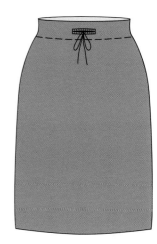

9.10E CASING WITH DRAW-STRING CORD/ELASTIC

- Several rows of topstitching in which several rows of narrow elastic have been inserted (Figure 9.10d).
- A drawstring with elastic attached to ties inserted through a buttonhole stitched on the correct side of the garment (Figure 9.10e). (Also see note on page 365.)

Topstitched Casing

- Cut the determined length of elastic equal to the measurement of the waist, less 2 to 4 inches. This depends on the width, the amount of stretch in the elastic being used, the quality of the elastic, and the comfort factor.
- Add 1 inch for overlapping and stitching the elastic together.
- The casing width should be the width of the elastic and the seam allowance, plus $\frac{1}{8}$ inch.

- To stitch both sides of the casing, add a total of $\frac{1}{4}$ inch, using $\frac{1}{8}$ inch at the top and $\frac{1}{8}$ inch at the bottom of the casing for stitching.
- Fold over the amount allotted for the casing, turn under the raw edge $\frac{1}{4}$ inch, and handbaste the casing in place (Figure 9.11a).
- If the fabric is bulky, consider serging the edge of the casing instead of folding it under.
- Begin stitching the casing on a seamline at the center back or side seam.
- Stitch around the waistline, leaving a 2-inch opening (see Figure 9.11a).
- Using a bodkin, feed the elastic through the opening (see Figure 9.11a).
- Pull both ends of the elastic out of the casing and overlap (by placing one side over the other, *not* stitched as a seam) and stitch a square to secure the elastic edges (Figure 9.11b).

- Slipstitch the opening closed, then topstitch to complete the casing.

Casing with Several Rows of Topstitching

A wider size of elastic is usually used for this technique, in which the casing is formed and stitched, and the elastic is pulled through. Several evenly spaced rows of topstitching secure the elastic to the garment, creating a look of individual rows of elastic. This works well with an elastic that recovers its stretch after being stitched. Sample to make sure the elastic returns to its original size. Cut the elastic approximately 1 inch smaller, as it will stretch with multiple rows of stitching. If this does not work in the sample, choose another type of elastic, or a different technique.

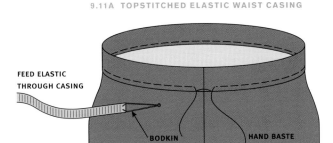

9.11A TOPSTITCHED ELASTIC WAIST CASING

FEED ELASTIC
THROUGH CASING

BODKIN   HAND BASTE

SEAMLINE

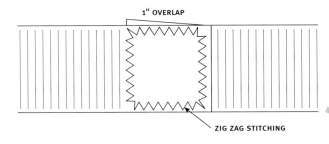

1" OVERLAP

ZIG ZAG STITCHING

9.11B TOPSTITCHED ELASTIC WAIST CASING

Casing with Multiple Rows of Narrow Elastic

Once the total width of the waistband has been determined, divide it into the number of rows for the narrow elastic to be inserted into, plus ⅛ inch (see Figure 9.10d).

• Stitch each row evenly, beginning at the center back or side seam, leaving an opening of approximately 2 inches to pull the elastic through.

• Thread the elastic through each row, securing the ends by overlapping them and stitching a square.

• Close each opening with hand slipstitching and then machine topstitching.

Casing with Cords or Elastic and Cords

A casing with cording is constructed as follows without the addition of the elastic. The designer can also add a narrow width of elastic sewn to each end of the ties. The elastic is equal to three-quarters of the total waist measurement. After the ties are stitched to the ends of the elastic, they are pulled through stitched buttonholes to resemble a drawstring waist (see Figure 9.10e).

• Prepare the ties: use bias strips or straight grain strips (as shown in Figure 9.16) to make the ties, or use purchased cording or trim.

• The ties should be long enough to pull the elastic to control the waistband size and to tie closed and not show.

• Stitch the ties to the ends of the elastic (Figure 9.12a).

• Stabilize the buttonhole areas before stitching (Figure 9.12b).

• Mark and stitch the buttonholes on the front of the garment before folding over and stitching the casing for the elastic (see Figure 9.12b).

• Using a bodkin, thread the elastic and attached ties through the buttonholes.

• Distribute the casing fullness along the elastic before stitching-in-the-ditch at the side seam.

• Tie knots in the ends of the ties, hand slipstitch the ends closed, or push the tie ends in with a point (of scissors or seam ripper)—if the ties are bias, the ends will stay pushed in (Figure 9.12c).

Invisible Casing

In an **invisible casing** (Figure 9.10a), elastic is stitched to the edge of the waistline, turned to the inside of the garment, and then stitched at the side seams. For this type of elastic finish, the look must have a smooth fit. This method avoids the look of an elastic casing while retaining the comfort of the elastic waist and does not show any topstitching from the correct side. It is important that the fabric have enough stretch to slide over the hips if no other type of opening will be used.

• Stitch the side seams of the skirt.

• Deduct 1 to 2 inches from the total waist measurement and cut the elastic this length, without any seam allowance. Take into consideration the width of the elastic, and very important, the quality of elastic being used.

• The elastic will stretch as it is stitched to the waist edge.

• Form a circle with the elastic by butting the elastic ends together and stitching a *wide* zigzag/short length, or stitch a three-stitch zigzag (Figure 9.13a).

• Divide the elastic and waistline into quarters (Figure 9.13b).

• Place the elastic on the wrong side of the garment, matching the elastic join to the center back or side seam.

9.12A ELASTIC WAIST CASING WITH CORDS AND BUTTONHOLES

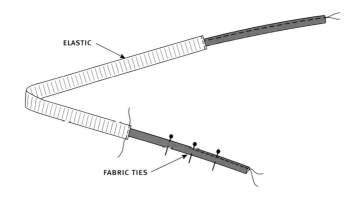

ELASTIC

FABRIC TIES

9.12A ELASTIC WAIST CASING WITH CORDS AND BUTTONHOLES

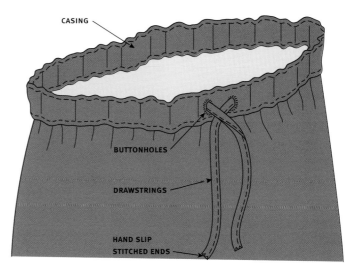

CASING

BUTTONHOLES

DRAWSTRINGS

HAND SLIP
STITCHED ENDS

9.12C ELASTIC WAIST
CASING WITH CORDS
AND BUTTONHOLES

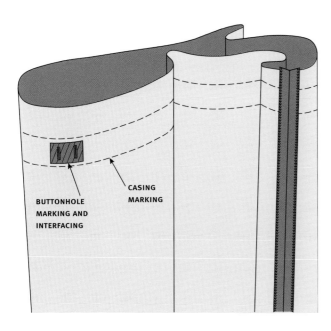

BUTTONHOLE
MARKING AND
INTERFACING

CASING
MARKING

9.12B ELASTIC WAIST CASING WITH CORDS
AND BUTTONHOLES

- Pin the elastic and the garment waistline together.
- With the elastic on the wrong side of the garment facing up, stitch the elastic to the outer edge of the waistline, stretching the elastic to fit the waistline edge (Figure 9.13b).
- Use a medium zigzag stitch or serger, but do not cut the elastic off with the serger.

- Stitch another row of zigzag stitches to secure the inner elastic edge to the garment (see Figure 9.13b).
- Turn the elastic to the inside of the garment and secure the elastic by stitching-in-the-

ditch in every vertical seamline from the correct side of the garment (Figure 9.13c).

Joined Elastic Casing

While this waistband looks the same as a conventional waistband that requires a zipper, the **joined elastic casing** is really a pull-on waist finish that works on both knits and stretch wovens.

- Cut a firm, nonroll elastic 1 inch wide and equal in length to the waist measurement.
- Lap the ends over ½ inch and stitch, forming a circle.
- Divide into fourths, marking the divisions, avoiding the lapped, stitched section.

9.13 INVISIBLE ELASTIC CASING

9.13A STITCHING THE ELASTIC TOGETHER

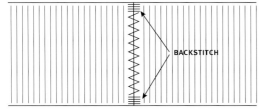

BACKSTITCH

ELASTIC BUTTED TOGETHER

PINS DIVIDE WAISTLINE
INTO QUARTERS

ELASTIC JOIN
ON SEAMLINE

2 ROWS OF
ZIGZAG STITCHING

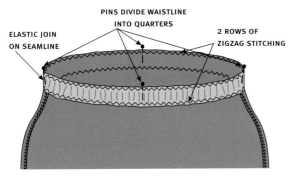

9.13B ZIGZAG STITCH THE ELASTIC TO THE WAISTLINE

STITCH IN THE DITCH

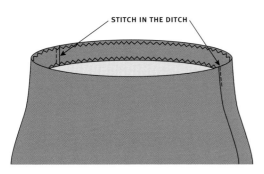

9.13C FINISH THE INVISIBLE
ELASTIC CASING

- Stitch the ends of the fabric waistband, and press the seam open so it's stitched in-the-round.

NOTE
- Check the fit of the waistband on the body or dress form to be sure it goes over the hips.

- Pin the waistband to the garment, right sides together, and match the notches of the garment and waistband; stitch (Figure 9.14a).
- Pin and match the quarter divisions of the elastic to the waistband side seams, center front, and center back (Figure 9.14b).
- Zigzag stitch the elastic to the garment seam allowance, stretching the elastic to fit the garment, while keeping the lower edge of the elastic butted up to the waistband seamline (see Figure 9.14b). Serge finish the other edge.
- Fold the waistband tightly over the elastic; pin in place (Figure 9.14c).
- Stitch-in-the-ditch from the correct side of the garment (Figure 9.14d).

Belt Loops and Thread Carriers

Loops are needed to hold a belt in the desired position on the garment. They are usually placed at the side seams on dresses or a coat. On pants or a skirt, the loops create a more slimming look when removed from the side seams and placed 2 to 3 inches on either side of the center front and center back waistband. This measurement depends on waist size and style of waistband. They should be long enough for the belt to fit through easily. Loops can be made from fabric strips or thread.

Thread Carriers

Thread carriers are narrow and inconspicuous. They are most suitable for dresses, tops, and coats where little or no strain will be exerted on the carrier.

CONSTRUCTING THE THREAD CARRIERS

To make a thread carrier, select a matching color of thread of buttonhole twist or use several strands of regular machine thread.

- Determine the length of the carrier and add ½ inch for ease.
- Place a pin indicating the beginning and end points on the garment (Figure 9.15a).
- If the carrier extends over a waistline seam, center the carrier (Figure 9.15a).
- Begin the carrier on the correct side of the garment, by attaching the thread on the wrong side of the garment first, taking several backstitches at one end.
- Sew back and forth, by hand, from one end marking to the other, until there are several strands of thread, making sure the strands are all equal lengths—these threads form the core of the finished carrier (see Figure 9.15a).
- Work a **blanket stitch** over the core strands, keeping the stitches close together. Form the blanket stitch around the threads by inserting the tip of the needle between the thread strands and the garment. Hold the thread from the previous stitch in back of the point of the needle. Pull the needle up and out, drawing the thread close around the thread strands (Figure 9.15b).

9.14 JOINED ELASTIC CASING

9.14A POSITIONING THE ENCASED ELASTIC WAISTBAND

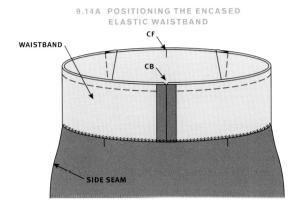

9.14C PINNING THE WAISTBAND

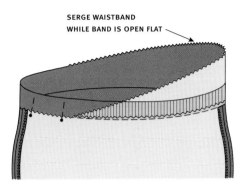

SERGE WAISTBAND WHILE BAND IS OPEN FLAT

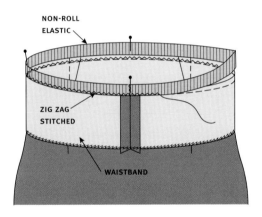

9.14B STITCHING AND SERGING THE WAISTBAND

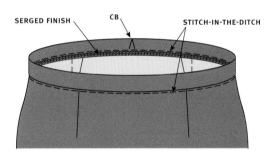

9.14D FINISHING THE WAISTBAND

- Continue this stitch until all the strands have been covered.

For a sturdier version of the thread carrier, combine eight or more strands of sewing thread with zigzag stitching.

- Determine the length of the carrier, cut the strands of thread to that length—it's much

easier to precut the lengths of thread rather than struggle with one long piece.

- Smooth out the sewing thread strands, pressing them, if necessary, to lie flat.
- Holding the threads taut, place under the pressure foot of the machine, and begin to stitch a narrow zigzag stitch (1.0 width, .5 length) over all the strands (Figure 9.15c).

- Continue stitching until the entire length is sewn.
- There will be some thread at the top and at the bottom of this length that will not be covered by stitching due to the space needed to begin the stitching and to allow for knotting off at the bottom of the length.
- Use a large-eyed tapestry needle and thread the carrier through the eye (Figure 9.15c).
- Knot one end of the sewn strands.
- Place a pin marking the beginning and end of the carrier on the garment (Figure 9.15a).
- From the inside of the garment, push the threaded needle through to the front of the garment at one of the pin markings.
- Push the needle through the other marking to the inside of the garment, knot off the sewn strands, and cut.
- Repeat for each carrier position.

Belt Loops

Belt loops can be made from the same fabric as the garment, or they can be made in contrasting fabric, such as leather on tweed. However, bulk needs to be considered.

CONSTRUCTING THE BELT LOOPS
- Calculate the length of fabric that is needed for all the belt loops being made.
- The length of the belt loop is the width of the belt plus ½ inch ease and an additional 1 inch for two seam allowances.
- Count the total number of belt loops needed. Example: 6 multiply by the measurement of 1

belt loop with ease included (2 inches); total length = 12 inches.
- The width of the belt loop depends on the method used to stitch the loops.
- If the fabric is not too heavy, cut the strip four times as wide as the finished size to add some body to the belt loop.
- Fold the strip in fourths with the raw edges on the inside (Figure 9.16a).
- Edgestitch down the length of the strip through all layers; edgestitch the other side, forming two rows of stitching (Figure 9.16b).

Fusible webbing applied to lightweight fabrics does not need to be edgestitched and can be used to make a belt loop.

- Cut the belt loop strip twice the width of the finished carrier plus ¼ inch, using the selvage for one long edge.
- Cut the webbing strip the same width as the finished width of the belt loop.
- Place the webbing on the wrong side of the folded belt loop strip fabric, slightly off center and closer to the cut raw edge.
- Fuse the raw edge of the fabric over the fusible web (Figure 9.17a).
- Next fuse the selvage edge down, just covering the raw edge (Figure 9.17b).
- No stitching is necessary; the fusible web holds the edges together.

APPLYING THE BELT LOOP

Once the belt loop strip is stitched, cut it into individual loops. The ends of the loops are fin-

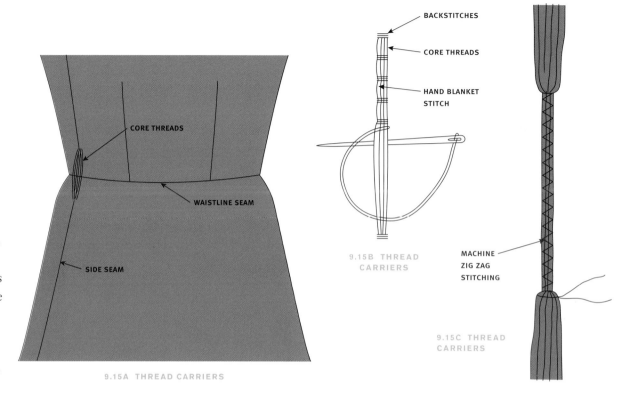

9.15A THREAD CARRIERS

9.15B THREAD CARRIERS

9.15C THREAD CARRIERS

ished when they are attached to the garment. The method of applying the loop will depend on the location of the loop on the garment and the stage of construction of the garment.

If the loop is at a side seam or the interior of the garment:

- Pin mark the placement lines on the garment.
- Place one end of the carrier on the bottom pin mark.
- The seam allowance of the end should be extending up, with the correct side of the loop placed on the correct side of the garment (Figure 9.18a).

- Stitch the loop to the garment (see Figure 9.18a).
- Flip the loop up to the top placement mark, turn under the raw end and, lifting the loop to the side, machine stitch or topstitch the end to the garment (Figure 9.18b).

If the waistband is already stitched to the garment:

- Fold the belt loop ends under and topstitch them to the top and bottom of the waistband through all fabric thicknesses (Figure 9.19).
- This works well for a waistband that is already topstitched.

If the waistband has not been stitched to the waistline, the belt loops can be stitched to the waistband or included in the waistline seam.

- Place the ½-inch seamline of the belt loop end on the foldline of the waistband (Figure 9.20a).
- The end will extend into the waistband.
- Stitch the belt loop to the waistband with the correct sides together.

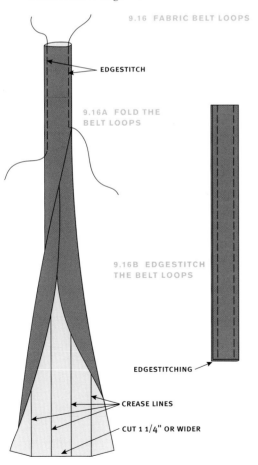

9.16 FABRIC BELT LOOPS

EDGESTITCH

9.16A FOLD THE BELT LOOPS

9.16B EDGESTITCH THE BELT LOOPS

EDGESTITCHING

CREASE LINES

CUT 1 1/4" OR WIDER

- Place the belt loop down and stitch the other end to the lower edge of the waistband—this end of the belt loop will be stitched into the waistline seam. Note: Belt loops in Figure 9.20b are stitched to the two piece waistband before stitching to the garment.

STITCHING TRICKY FABRICS

All fabrics cannot be covered in one chapter, but the following suggestions will assist the designer in deciding what type of waistband to construct for the fabric being used.

Matching Stripes, Plaids, Patterns, and Repeat Patterns

Do consider placing stripes or plaids on the bias as a contrast to the garment.

Do consider using a solid color for the waistband that contrasts with the stripe, plaid, or repeat pattern of the garment.

Don't spend time attempting to match the entire waistband to the garment.

Sheer Fabric

Do underline the sheer fabric to avoid showing the interfacing used.

Do consider using an alternative finish, such as bias binding, to finish the waistline.

Do use a contrasting fabric or ribbon for the waistband.

Don't design a waistband that requires heavy stabilizing or is intricately shaped.

Lace

Do use a lining fabric for the facing side of a

9.17A FUSIBLE WEBBING BELT LOOPS

9.17B FUSIBLE WEBBING BELT LOOPS

RAW EDGE

RAW EDGE FOLDED IN

SELVAGE

FUSIBLE WEB

waistband made of lace.

Do use a contrasting fabric such as taffeta or satin as a narrow bias binding at the waistline in place of a waistband.

Do use a coordinating fabric, such as satin or taffeta, paired with lace as the waistband.

Don't use lace on both sides of the waistband—many laces have intricate, raised details that would be scratchy and uncomfortable against the skin.

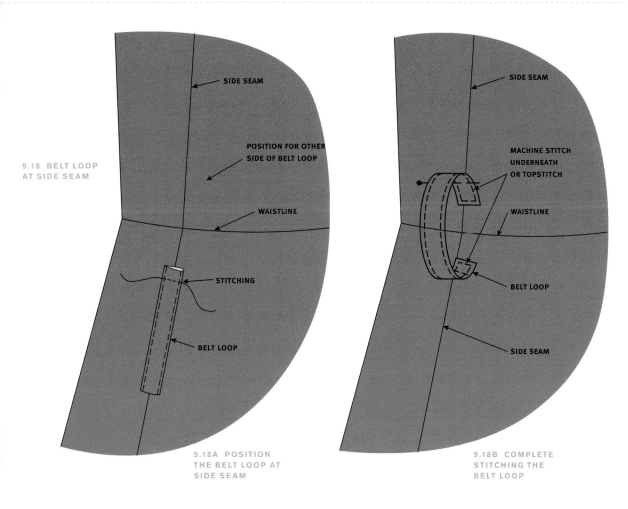

9.18 BELT LOOP AT SIDE SEAM

SIDE SEAM

POSITION FOR OTHER SIDE OF BELT LOOP

WAISTLINE

STITCHING

BELT LOOP

9.18A POSITION THE BELT LOOP AT SIDE SEAM

SIDE SEAM

MACHINE STITCH UNDERNEATH OR TOPSTITCH

WAISTLINE

BELT LOOP

SIDE SEAM

9.18B COMPLETE STITCHING THE BELT LOOP

Don't use topstitching as a finish for the waist-band on lighter-weight satins.

Beaded Fabric

Do use a contrasting fabric such as satin or taffeta for the waistband.

Do use a contrasting fabric as a bias binding in place of the waistband.

Do use the flattest finish possible at the waist to reduce bulk.

Don't use the beaded fabric for both sides of the waistband—beaded fabric is uncomfortable against the skin.

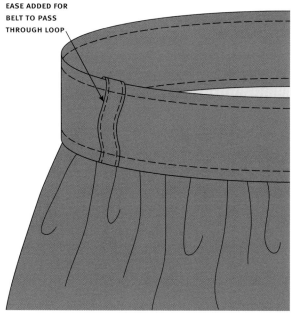

EASE ADDED FOR BELT TO PASS THROUGH LOOP

9.19 TOPSTITCHED BELT LOOPS ON A STITCHED WAISTBAND

Satin

Do choose the interfacing carefully when using satin as the waistband.

Do mark the fabric as little as possible to avoid "bleed-through."

Do cut the waistband, using the "with nap" direction.

Do test a sample seam for slippage, which often occurs at stress points such as the waist-

band. Refer to Chapter 3, "Introduction to Stabilizers."

Do pin only in the seam allowances.

Do handbaste the waistband with silk thread to avoid marring the surface of the satin.

Do use silk thread to hand slipstitch the waist-band to the inside of the garment.

Do use new machine sewing needles to avoid "pulled" threads when stitching.

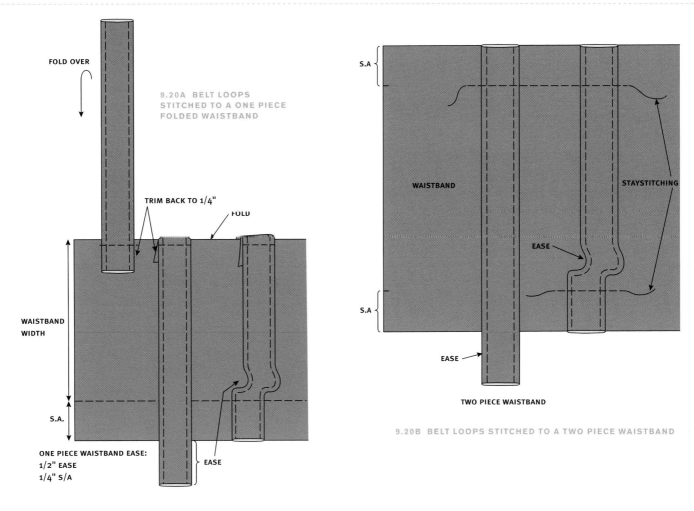

FOLD OVER

9.20A BELT LOOPS STITCHED TO A ONE PIECE FOLDED WAISTBAND

TRIM BACK TO 1/4"

FOLD

WAISTBAND WIDTH

S.A.

ONE PIECE WAISTBAND EASE:
1/2" EASE
1/4" S/A

EASE

S.A

WAISTBAND

STAYSTITCHING

EASE

S.A

EASE

TWO PIECE WAISTBAND

9.20B BELT LOOPS STITCHED TO A TWO PIECE WAISTBAND

Knits

Do construct a one-piece, stabilized waistband and apply to the knit garment with a zipper opening—the stabilizer must take the stretch element out of the knit so it doesn't stretch.

Do use an encased elastic waistband without a zipper opening.

Do use a foldover, cut-in-one waistband with elastic.

Do use only nonroll elastic to support the waistband.

Don't overstabilize the waistband with a too-stiff stabilizer.

Denim

Do use a one-piece waistband, interfaced on one-half only to reduce bulk.

Do trim seam allowances of interfacing before fusing to reduce bulk.

Do use bias binding to finish the waistline.

Do cut binding for single bias only. Refer to Chapter 12, "Facings," for further information on bias bindings.

Do serge one edge of the binding, rather than turning under a clean finish edge.

Do turn binding over to the inside of the garment, encasing raw edges.

Do leave the serged edge flat, not turned

under, and stitch-in-the ditch from the correct side of the garment.

Do trim and grade the seam allowances to reduce bulk.

Do use topstitching to complete the waistband.

Don't hand stitch the waistband to the garment—it won't be sturdy enough.

Velvet

Do use a two-piece waistband.

Do follow a "with nap" layout.

Do use a lining fabric for the waistband facing to reduce bulk.

Do use a contrasting fabric for a one-piece waistband, and interface appropriately.

Don't use topstitching to finish the waistband.

Leather

Leather garments can be constructed with one-piece tailored waistbands or faced waistbands.

Do interface the waistband (because leather does stretch) with "low heat fuse" interfacing.

Do add an additional layer of stabilizer in the area where the closures, such as bound buttonholes or hooks and eyes, will be sewn.

Do use a thread shank and a backing button when attaching the button to the waistband.

Do use leather cement to glue the leather in place, followed by topstitching where appropriate.

Do sample glue on your leather to be sure it doesn't bleed through to the front.

Do sample topstitching before using this stitch on the leather garment—stitch holes cannot be removed.

Don't use pins to secure the leather—use binder clips (Figure 14.19).

Don't press leather with a high temperature or use steam.

Don't store leather folded—the resulting creases may not come out.

Faux Fur

It's hard to imagine that a designer would make a waistband out of faux fur, but you never know!

Do preshrink the faux fur, if washable—check the bolt label for directions.

Do stabilize faux fur using a sew-in stabilizer—the backing of the fur can be made of knit or woven.

Do remove the fur from the seam allowances.

Do tape the pattern pieces to the faux fur, carefully transferring the markings.

Do use a size 14 or 16 needle and lengthen the stitches to 8 to 10 per inch.

Do loosen the tension and pressure.

Do stitch in the direction of the nap.

Do steam the pile side of the faux fur, and pound the seams and edges to reduce bulk.

Don't apply an iron directly on the faux fur.

Heavyweight Fabric

Do choose the flattest waistband treatment for the garment.

Do use lining or contrasting fabric for the under waistband.

Do use the appropriate interfacing for the fabric weight.

Do remove the seam allowances of the interfacing before applying, to reduce bulk.

Do trim and grade the seam allowances accurately.

Do use a pressing cloth.

Don't apply the iron directly onto the fabric—press marks may appear on the face of the garment.

TRANSFER YOUR KNOWLEDGE

• Once the designer has correctly interfaced and stitched the waistband, this knowledge can be applied to cuffs and collars. Think of the waistband as an upside-down cuff or collar.

• The knowledge gained from forming the waistband can be transferred to creating unusual shapes that repeat elements of the style or fabric of the garment such as a waistband, cuff, or collar.

• The designer can transfer the knowledge gained from stitching a waistband to stitching shaped bands applied to the center fronts of garments or at hemlines.

STRETCH YOUR CREATIVITY

Stretching your creativity involves taking the stitching techniques learned in this chapter and applying them to the design in a more creative, nontraditional way. In other words, think outside the box. When thinking outside the box, however, always consider whether this is adding to the design or taking away from it. Remember, just because you can, doesn't mean you should.

• A waistband can become an exciting area of interest. An unusually shaped waistband can repeat an element of the fabric such as scallops or a geometric shape along the upper edge (Figure 9.21a). If meeting at the center front, it can have mirror image, shaped edges (Figure 9.21b).

- The waistband can be asymmetrical (Figure 9.21b and c).
- Bias grainline can be used effectively when working with plaids, but must be well stabilized to prevent stretching out of shape.
- Embellishments, such as grommets, studs, or embroidery, can be applied to the waistband to create a focal point.
- A waistband can mimic a belt with tabs and buttons (see Figure 9.21c).
- Belt loops can be made from a variety of materials, but they must be able to function as the carrier of a belt. Experiment with materials such as leather, braided yarn, felted wool, or canvas, fraying the edges of the loops reinforced with staystitching, embellishing the loops, or using two layers of ribbon fused together. *As always,* the details must be in harmony with the design.

STOP! WHAT DO I DO IF . . .
. . . my waistband is too long?

First, assess how much "too long" it is. The length can be adjusted before stitching the waistband to the garment. Check the measurements again, matching all pattern markings to see where the waistband went astray. Reduce and cut the amount from one end of the waistband, and redraw the markings to match.

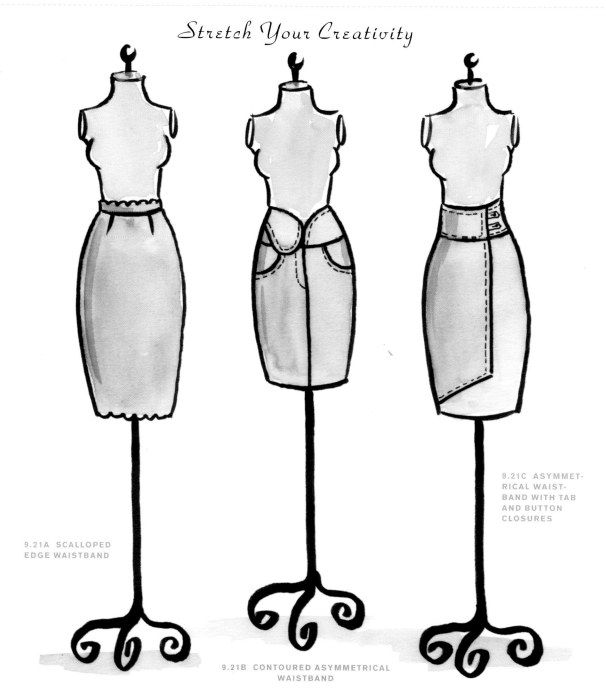

Stretch Your Creativity

9.21A SCALLOPED EDGE WAISTBAND

9.21B CONTOURED ASYMMETRICAL WAISTBAND

9.21C ASYMMETRICAL WAISTBAND WITH TAB AND BUTTON CLOSURES

. . . my waistband is too short?

If the waistband is sewn together at the center back seam, such as in a contoured waistband, cut at the side seams and add an equal amount to both sides. Don't forget to add seam allowances to the pieces you are adding! If this doesn't look good and will be very visible in an unattractive way, recut another waistband after checking that your measurements are correct. If the waistband is cut in one piece and fabric is limited, try cutting it apart at the side seams and adding the additional amount needed. If that doesn't look good, or if there isn't enough fabric for the waistband to be cut out again, use another contrasting fabric.

. . . my belt loops are crooked?

If the loops have been stitched into place unevenly, release the loops from the points where they are stitched, and remeasure them evenly before stitching again. If the loops have been cut unevenly, the crooked loops will have to be ripped out and realigned.

SELF-CRITIQUE

Take a look at your finished garment and ask the crucial question, "Would I wear this garment or would I purchase this garment?" If the answer is "No," ask yourself, why not? Then ask yourself the following questions to critique the quality of your waistband construction stitching:

- Is my waistband appropriately interfaced?
- Does it fit the garment correctly?

- Is it stitched evenly to the garment?
- Does the style of the waistband complement the garment?
- Is the visible stitching, such as topstitching or edgestitching, even on the waistband?
- Is the waistband stitched evenly at the center back or side seam?
- Does it cover the zipper?
- Is the extension facing the right direction?
- Is the closure for the waistband the correct style for the garment (button/buttonhole, hook/bar, hook/eye)?
- Are the closures correctly stitched?
- Is the stitch-in-the-ditch actually stitched-in-the-ditch and not all over the waistband?
- Are the belt loops evenly spaced?
- Are the belt loops correctly sewn?
- Can the belt easily go through the carriers?
- If using thread carriers, are they sturdy enough to stand up to use?

REVIEW CHECKLIST

- Does the waistband match the waistline of the garment?
- Is the waistband in proportion to the style of the garment?
- When using a decoratively shaped waistband, is the waistband stitched, trimmed, graded, and clipped to lie flat, without bulk?
- Is the waistband appropriately interfaced and stabilized?
- Is the edgestitching or topstitching of the waistband straight and even?

- Is the stitching-in-the-ditch actually in the "ditch" of the seam well?
- Are the belt loops the correct length to allow a belt to pass through?
- Are the belt loops securely stitched to the garment and waistband?
- Is the elastic for the waistband securely stitched within the casing?
- Are the elastic waistbands completed in such a way that they do not twist?
- Is the casing of the elastic waistband stitched evenly?
- Does the casing of the elastic waistband lie flat and smooth, and is it bulk-free?
- Are the ties of the elastic drawstring waistband neatly stitched and finished?
- Is the buttonhole of the drawstring waistband reinforced?
- Is the buttonhole of the drawstring waistband sewn evenly, and is it the correct size for the ties to slide through?
- Is the encased elastic waistband divided and stitched evenly, preventing twisting of the elastic or the garment?

A waistband is an important part of garment construction, providing support to hold a garment to the body and finishing the edge of the garment. It is functional and can also be decorative, becoming an area for design possibilities. As with all other sections of the garment, with repetition and good sewing skills, the waistbands you create will provide support and finish for a well-designed garment.

Ruffles and Flounces: Feminine and Flirty

Ruffles and flounces fabricate a soft, delicate texture to the surface of the garment. The way ruffles and flounces are cut and stitched, and the fabric used, determines how these elements look in the final design. It is important for the design student to understand that ruffles and flounces are different from each other.

This chapter opens with the Style I.D., which distinguishes ruffles and flounces. Knowing how

to classify each begins with the sketch. They are then defined by the way they are cut and stitched. The fabric weight also influences how ruffles or flounces drape. Tips will be given in this chapter to cover all these aspects of ruffles and flounces.

With an understanding of the differences between ruffles and flounces, and by experimenting with the sewing techniques in this chapter, an expert knowledge will be gained while you are in design school of how to design, cut, and stitch ruffles and flounces.

STYLE I.D.

The three dresses in Figure 10.1 show how ruffles and flounces look stitched to similar styles of dresses. Let's begin with Figure 10.1a. A ruffle is stitched to the neckline, sleeve, and hem edges. Take note of how different the ruffles look from flounces when sketched.

Figure 10.1b has a flounce stitched to the same neckline, sleeve edge, and hem edge as Figure 10.1a. However, they look different. Can you see a difference in how ruffles and flounces drape? Then in Figure 10.1c, we see a gathered flounce,

KEY TERMS

Closed Ruffle or Flounce
Edge Application
Faced Flounce
Faced Ruffle
Flat Application
Flounce
Fluted Ruffle
Mock Seam
Open and Closed Flounces
Open Ruffle or Flounce
Ruffle
Seam Application
Stitched In-the-Round
Surface Application

which has more fullness than a flounce that is not gathered. Can you see that the hem edge is now more curly and wavy? Let's read on to find out why ruffles and flounces drape so differently.

GATHER YOUR TOOLS

You'll need machine needles—60/08 (most likely the fabric you are working with will be sheer and lightweight so these needles will be the appropriate size), scissors, thread, seam ripper (always essential), tape measure, and trims such as lace for adding delicate edges to ruffles and flounces.

NOW LET'S GET STARTED

With the equipment at your fingertips and tape measure around your neck, you are ready to stitch ruffles and flounces. Quality construction begins with the correct patterns. If you are not sure how ruffles and flounces are cut, then read on to learn how to do this. With this understanding, make the appropriate pattern and begin sampling before making any final choices as to the sewing techniques to use.

The Differences between Ruffles and Flounces

It all begins with the way ruffles and flounces are cut. Yes, this is the main reason they drape differently—it has to do with shape. This helps explain why the three dresses in the Style I.D. look distinctly individual.

Ruffles are cut as a straight piece of fabric and a **flounce** is cut circular, as Figures 10.2a and 10.2b indicate. A ruffle can be cut on any

Style I.D.

10.1A RUFFLES

10.1B FLOUNCES

10.1C GATHERED FLOUNCES

grainline: lengthwise, crosswise (both straight grains), or bias grain. A bias grain ruffle will drape quite differently from a ruffle cut on the lengthwise or crosswise grains. Because a flounce is circular, it is cut on all three grainlines, as you can see in Figure 10.2b; this is why flounces drape so beautifully.

10.2A RUFFLES CAN BE CUT ON BIAS OR STRAIGHT GRAIN.

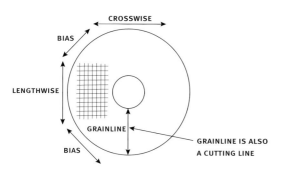

10.2B FLOUNCES ARE CUT ON ALL GRAINLINES.

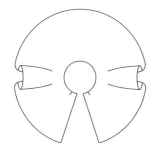

10.2C THE GRAINLINE IS ALSO CUT SO FLOUNCES CAN OPEN AND BE JOINED TO OTHER FLOUNCES OR JOINED INTO SEAMS.

Ruffles *must* be gathered, otherwise they are *not* ruffles! This construction is what makes a ruffle a ruffle, as is evident in the first dress illustrated in Figure 10.1a, in the Style I.D. Flounces do not need to be gathered; however, they can be gathered to add some extra fullness. Figure 10.1b illustrates a dress similar to the one in Figure 10.1a; however, flounces have been substituted for ruffles. Figure 10.1c illustrates the identical dress stitched with gathered flounces. Can you see the difference in each?

The grainline on the pattern indicates the direction of how ruffles and flounces are cut. Bias grain ruffles look fabulous made in lightweight fabrics such as chiffon or silk georgette and can have lots of gathering. Ruffles can also be cut on the lengthwise or crosswise grains (straight grains) of the fabric (see Figure 10.2a). When ruffles are bias cut, the benefit is—no hem stitching—bias does not fray. However, they can be finished if you prefer. And, P.S., good luck! Bias cutting does take more yardage, and this adds to the overall expense of the garment—yet it may be worth it!

The flounce grainline is placed on the vertical grain of the fabric, and this is also a cutting line. This line needs to be slit so the inner circle of the flounce can be cut (Figure 10.2c). The slit then becomes a seamline. Do you see the notches at the top edge of the flounce to indicate a seam?

The outside circular edge of the flounce is larger than the inside circle edge, as you observe in Figures 10.2b and c. To stitch a flounce, the inner circular edge is straightened and stitched to the garment. The outer circular

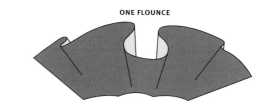

ONE FLOUNCE

10.3A WHEN THE INSIDE CIRCLE OF THE FLOUNCE IS STRAIGHTENED, THE OUTSIDE EDGE FORMS FOLDS.

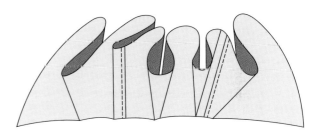

10.3B THREE FLOUNCES STITCHED TOGETHER

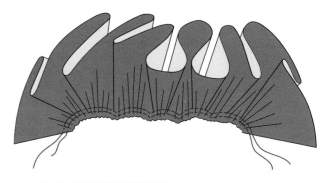

10.3C FLOUNCES STITCHED TOGETHER AND GATHERED

edge then forms soft folds (curls). This is what gives fullness to a flounce, as illustrated in Figure 10.3a. As many flounces as you like can then be joined together; the more circles that are stitched together, the more fullness is added (Figure 10.3b).

As previously discussed, flounces can also be gathered, as Figure 10.3c illustrates. However, the fabric needs to be the right weight and drape for this to be successful in design. Too much fullness may turn into bulk and this could spoil the design!

Successful Ruffles and Flounces Begin with the Correct Fabric Weight

The fabric weight will affect how ruffles and flounces look in your design. Play with the fabric while you are at the fabric store. Take the fabric in your hands; scrunch it up into the desired fullness; hold to the body to observe the softness and how it drapes. Notice the designer doing just that in Figure 3.4. Sampling is also essential so you can fine-tune the look you want to achieve.

Silk chiffon, silk georgette, and lightweight silk satin would all be ideal fabric choices for ruffles and flounces. Silk organza would also be ideal; it creates a stiffer ruffle or flounce and stands away from the garment. Ruffles and flounces cut in heavyweight fabric would look bulky and may be a disappointment. Ruffles cut on the bias will drape more softly than ruffles cut on the lengthwise and crosswise grains.

One important thing to be aware of when choosing fabric for flounces: Both sides of the fabric will show, so choose a fabric you will be happy to show on the wrong side, as well as the correct side. Take another look at the dresses in Figure 10.1b and c to see how the flounces flip and curl around the hemline, showing both sides of the fabric.

When making the muslin for ruffles and flounces, it is important to use a similar fabric weight (and not 100% cotton muslin fabric) so you can see exactly how they will drape in your final garment.

Quality Stitching Begins with Accurate Patterns

Before making any patterns for ruffles or flounces, take an accurate measurement of the total length of the section to which the ruffle or flounce will be stitched. *Do not* measure the cut fabric edges, as the fabric can easily stretch in the measuring process. Measure the pattern edge only, and take note of this measurement. Then draft the ruffle and flounce pattern to fit this measurement.

Ruffles

The length of the ruffle to be gathered needs to be calculated correctly—it can be two, three, or four or more times longer than the finished ruffle length, and then gathered to fit the seam it is stitched to. As a helpful guide, gather up your fabric, pin-mark the length, and then let it loose—use this as your guide for the final pattern length for ruffles.

Ruffles are best cut in one long strip if possible; however, this may not be the most economical way for the design student to cut them. Lengths of fabric can be joined to make one long ruffle, but keep the joins to a minimum. The width of ruffles is the designer's choice and can be ½ inch, 1 inch, 2 inches, 3 inches, 6 inches, or wider. The fullness in the ruffles is also the

designer's choice; however, the final length is driven by the fabric weight and drape.

Flounces

The smaller the inner circle of a flounce, the more fluted the edges of the flounce will appear. For example, a flounce stitched to the hem of a skirt will need a larger inner circle than a flounce stitched to the wrist. The inner circle length must be the same measurement as the seam length it is joined to. When a larger inner circle is straightened and stitched, it will not flute as much as the smaller inner circle of a flounce. However, as an alternative, several smaller flounces can be stitched together to get the required seam length; this will result in more folds and curls and give a fuller look. However, it will involve more stitching and will be far more time-consuming (Figure 10.3b).

LET'S STITCH RUFFLES AND FLOUNCES

After your ruffles and flounces are cut, the first step in the stitching order is to stitch any seam joins on the ruffle/flounce before stitching it to the garment. Although you may have to stitch together some seams, the ruffle/flounce may still need to be left open and not stitched circular. If this is the case, it is classified as an **"open" ruffle** or **flounce**. Figures 10.4a and b illustrate how this type of ruffle or flounce would look. In a **"closed" ruffle** or **flounce,** the seams for the entire ruffle/flounce are stitched together so they are circular, as Figures 10.4c and 10.4d illustrate.

If the fabric you are using is of medium weight, you can stitch the seams open or closed, then serge the edges. For sheer fabrics, stitch French seams, as they look inconspicuous, or stitch narrow ¼-inch closed serged seams. The seams will not be noticeable after they are stitched to the garment. Make sure you follow the *SEW, CLIP, PRESS* method of stitching— even when stitching ruffles and flounces! Refer to Chapter 6, "Open Serged Seam," "Closed Serged Seam," and "French Seam."

You may be asking, "How do I know if I need to stitch my ruffle/flounce 'open' or 'closed'?" Basically the decision is driven by the design, and also by the cost. Some stitching methods are quicker and more cost-effective than others in production. The stitching order also determines whether to stitch ruffles and flounces open or closed. Ruffles and flounces can be applied to the garment using the flat application method or by stitching in-the-round; both stitching methods are discussed next.

Flat Application and Stitched In-the-Round

Flat application refers to stitching the ruffles and flounces to the garment while the garment lies flat. When ruffles and flounces are **stitched in-the-round,** both the ruffle/flounce and the garment are stitched circular and the pieces are then stitched together. Either method can be used when stitching ruffles and flounces; the choice of which to use will be directed partly by design and partly by preference. Refer to Figure 10.5 to see how a flounce would be stitched to the edge of a short sleeve using each method.

The stitching order is slightly different in each method. In Figure 10.5a the hem is stitched *after* the underarm seam is stitched; in Figure 10.5b, the hem is stitched *before* the flounce is joined to the sleeve. Both methods are viable; however, when stitched in-the-round, the flounce tends to sit flatter on the intersecting seam join.

When ruffles and flounces are stitched to the surface of the garment, and not stitched into a seam, then flat application is the method to follow; this means the ruffles/flounces will be stitched as open ruffles and flounces.

In this chapter, as each ruffle and flounce is stitched to the garment, advice will be given as to which method to use. Sometimes it will be very clear which method to choose. Other times, you may need to discuss the decision with your instructor. As you continue to grow in your stitching skills, these decisions will become second nature.

STITCHING THE HEMS

After the seams are joined, the hems need to be completed next, before ruffles and flounces can be stitched to the garment. There are many hem finishes from which to choose; however, the hem finish *must* suit the fabric weight. You will notice in this section that different hem stitches are recommended for ruffles and flounces. The shape of the hem indicates which hem stitch to use. Not all hem stitches work well on circular hem shapes, so we recommend you *sample* first!

Choose a thread color to match for your fabric, as the stitches are noticeable. However,

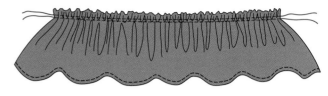

10.4A OPEN RUFFLE

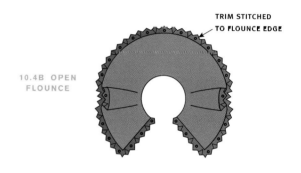

TRIM STITCHED TO FLOUNCE EDGE

10.4B OPEN FLOUNCE

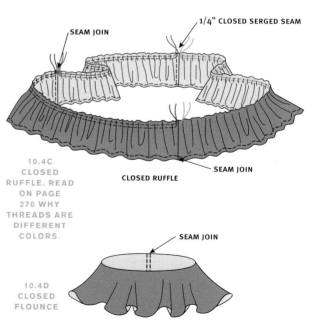

SEAM JOIN

1/4" CLOSED SERGED SEAM

10.4C CLOSED RUFFLE. READ ON PAGE 270 WHY THREADS ARE DIFFERENT COLORS.

SEAM JOIN

CLOSED RUFFLE

SEAM JOIN

10.4D CLOSED FLOUNCE

CLOSED FLOUNCE

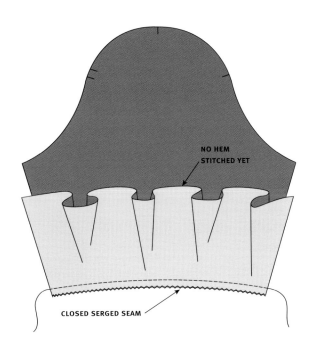

10.5A FLAT APPLICATION: THE FLOUNCE IS STITCHED
TO THE SLEEVE EDGE WHILE THE SLEEVE LIES FLAT.

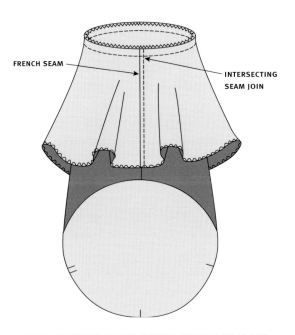

10.5B STITCHED IN-THE-ROUND: THE FLOUNCE AND
SLEEVE ARE BOTH STITCHED IN-THE-ROUND AND THEN
STITCHED TOGETHER.

a contrasting thread may add a visual interest and this is a viable choice as well. Here are the choices for hem finishes. All these finishes are outlined in more detail in Chapter 15.

Raw Edge (Excellent for Bias-Cut Ruffles)

The raw edge on a bias-cut ruffle works well, as bias grain does not fray. Bear in mind, the cut edges do not stay sharp; they get slightly "roughed" after they are worn. Can you imagine how much stitching time you would save not having to stitch the hems (Figure 10.6a)! Leaving your flounce with raw edges is not recommended since flounces are cut on all grain-lines. Lengthwise and crossgrain fibers fray easily and will pull away from the edges of the flounce. Refer back to Figure 10.2b to see how flounces are cut.

Narrow, Rolled, Machine-Stitched Hem (Excellent Hem Finish for Ruffles and Flounces)

This is a neat hem finish and gives a professional finish to ruffle and flounce edges. A machine-stitched rolled hem is more time-consuming to stitch around a full circular flounce. However, it is achievable following the three-step stitching technique in Figure 15.24a–c. Stitching the hem on bias grain is easy, as it has some give, but the straight and crossgrains have no flexibility as you stitch around the curve.

In Figures 10.6b, c, and d, all ruffles are cut as one single layer of fabric. Each has a machine-stitched rolled hem; however, you will observe that each is stitched to different degrees. How the ruffle hem is stitched is directed by how the ruffle is stitched to the garment. For example, the ruffle in Figure 10.6b has only one hem edgestitched—this is because the other three edges are going to be inserted into a seam and therefore don't need hem stitches. In Figure 10.6c, three sides of the ruffle have been hem stitched—this is because only the top edge of the ruffle is going to be inserted into the seam. In Figure 10.6d, the entire ruffle has been hem stitched—this is because the ruffle is going to be stitched to the surface of the garment and all the hems need to be stitched first.

Faced (Folded Edge) (for Ruffles and Flounces)

Ruffles can be a **faced ruffle**; this means two layers of fabric are folded together and become one—the folded edge is then the hem and the two top fabric edges will be gathered as one. A folded ruffle will be bulkier when stitched into a

seam, as this takes three layers of fabric (two for the ruffles and one for the garment seam). When you use this method, the choice of fabric weight is important so it doesn't create too much bulk. Figure 10.6e illustrates a faced ruffle. Notice the bottom foldline gives a clean finish to the edge of the ruffle (Figure 13.1c), and no hem stitching is needed. Press a crease line in the hem of a faced ruffle before it is gathered.

If a faced ruffle is going to be stitched as an open ruffle, then fold the correct sides of the fabric together and stitch a ¼-inch seam at both ends. Clip the corners to reduce bulk, turn the flounce to the correct side, and press and sharpen the corners with a point turner.

Flounces can also be a **faced flounce**; however, since they are round, they cannot be folded in the same way as a faced ruffle. No topstitching will be visible around the hem edge of a faced flounce, as the flounce is lined in self-fabric or a lightweight lining and has a clean finish, just as the ruffle does.

Cut two flounces (from the same pattern) in self-fabric or self-fabric and a lining (Figure 10.7a). Silk organza is an ideal choice to use as a lining, as it reduces bulk; however, it will give more shape and structure to a flounce. In fact, a faced flounce, overall, will look more structured than a flounce cut in a single layer of fabric.

A contrasting colored or patterned lining may add an interesting effect in the design, especially if the lining is patterned and the flounce fabric is sheer. A variety of other lightweight linings that could be used are listed in Chapter

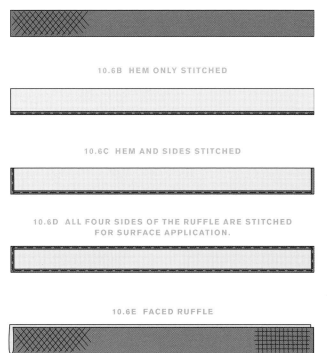

10.6A BIAS CUT: RAW EDGES

10.6B HEM ONLY STITCHED

10.6C HEM AND SIDES STITCHED

10.6D ALL FOUR SIDES OF THE RUFFLE ARE STITCHED FOR SURFACE APPLICATION.

10.6E FACED RUFFLE

FOLDLINE IS HEM EDGE

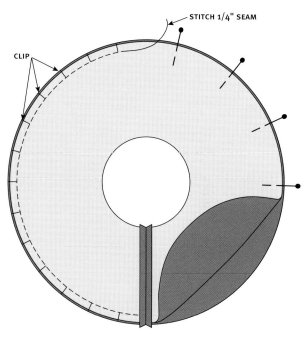

10.7A FACED FLOUNCE

STITCH 1/4" SEAM

CLIP

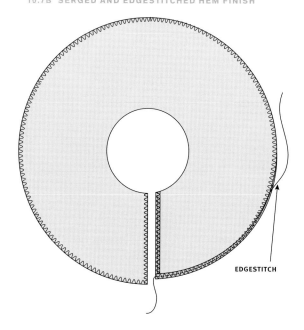

10.7B SERGED AND EDGESTITCHED HEM FINISH

EDGESTITCH

16, in "Lightweight Lining." Do take a look at these other options.

To stitch the faced flounce, refer to Figure 10.7a. Begin by placing the two flounces together with correct sides facing together and pin in place. Stitch a ¼-inch seam around the outer edge, then clip up to the seam stitching and press the seam open before turning. This can be challenging to do, so use the method recommended in the following chapter for pressing around a curved collar edge using the end of the sleeve board. This is illustrated in Figure 11.5b. After the flounce seam is pressed open, turn the flounce to the correct side and press again. The two inner circles are then handbasted together, ready for application.

Serged Hems (for Ruffles and Flounces)

The following three serged hem stitches will all work beautifully as hem finishes for both ruffles and flounces. Each method will look neat and not bulky. We highly recommend using a serged edge finish for flounces. The serger is easy to manage, especially when stitching around circles.

The *serged and edge-stitched hem* finish begins by serging around the hem of the ruffle or flounce. The hem edge is then turned back to the wrong side of the fabric and edgestitched. In Figure 10.7b you can see how the hem edge has been serged and turned over *and* edgestitched. When completed, press the hem.

The *lettuce edge* is a fabulous hem finish for ruffles and flounces. It is a tiny rolled hem, as Figure 15.25 illustrates. Two methods of stitching the lettuce edge are outlined in this figure, so refer to them and match the hem finish to your fabric type.

A *serged rolled hem,* stitched on the serger, is an excellent choice for hem finishes on ruffles and flounces, especially in finer fabrics. The stitch is much like a satin stitch, but very narrow and fine. You would see this on commercially produced napkins, place mats, tablecloths, and, yes, some hems. The rolled edge is often serged with woolly nylon to provide flexibility and softness.

Trim as a Hem Finish (for Ruffles and Flounces)

Trims in the form of lace or some other types of trims can be stitched to ruffles and flounces as an alternative hem finish. Trims can be stitched to "open" or "closed" ruffles and flounces. A trim wider than approximately ½ inch may need to be ease stitched or gathered first before being applied to a flounce, otherwise it may pull tightly around the curved edges and look unsightly.

Trims can be topstitched to serged ruffle or flounce edges and applied with a straight or zigzag stitch—a zigzag stitch often blends

> **NOTE**
> Be careful as you stitch ruffles and flounces—the gathered fabric edge can easily get caught in the seam as you stitch. Keep your eyes open to what is happening underneath, in between, and on the surface of the fabric.

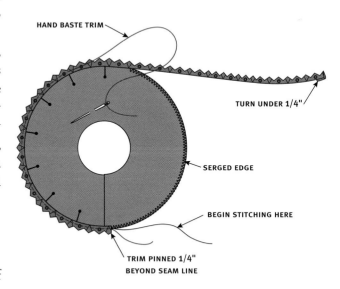

HAND BASTE TRIM

TURN UNDER 1/4"

SERGED EDGE

BEGIN STITCHING HERE

TRIM PINNED 1/4"
BEYOND SEAM LINE

better with textured lace and other trims. Serge the hem edge first, and then pin and handbaste the trim in place. Figure 10.8 illustrates how a trim is applied to the flounce edge—use the same method for applying a trim to a ruffle. Notice in the illustration that the trim is first pinned ¼ inch beyond the seamline. After pinning around the entire circle, the other end of the trim is turned over ¼ inch; this end of the trim will overlap the other side of the trim to give a clean finish.

Notice in Figure 10.4b that the trim has been stitched to the edge of an open flounce. In this case, the trim needs a mitered corner when applied around an angled edge. Fold the trim over (diagonally on the corner) and secure it with a pin until it fits snugly with the angle of the ruffle or flounce. Then hand stitch in place to secure the corner before machine stitching the trim in place.

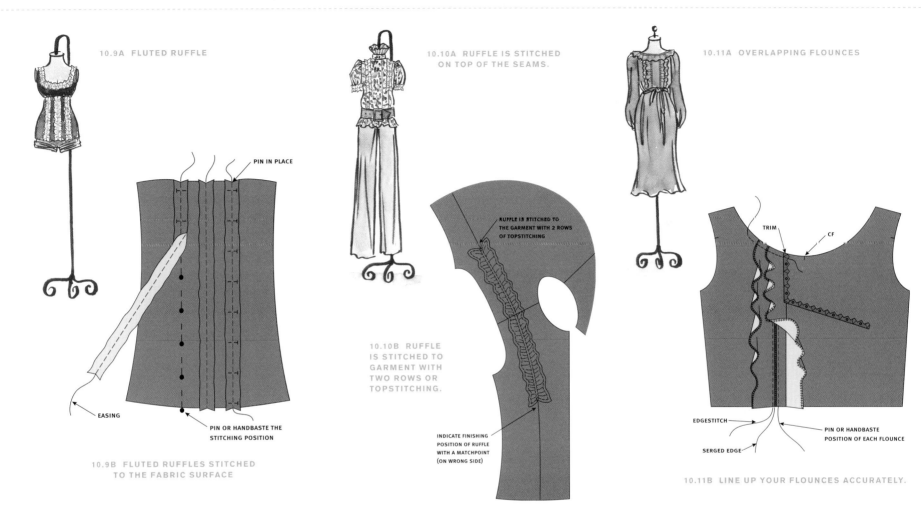

10.9A FLUTED RUFFLE

10.10A RUFFLE IS STITCHED
ON TOP OF THE SEAMS.

10.11A OVERLAPPING FLOUNCES

PIN IN PLACE

RUFFLE IS STITCHED TO
THE GARMENT WITH 2 ROWS
OF TOPSTITCHING

TRIM   CF

EASING

PIN OR HANDBASTE THE
STITCHING POSITION

10.10B RUFFLE
IS STITCHED
TO GARMENT WITH
TWO ROWS OR
TOPSTITCHING.

INDICATE FINISHING
POSITION OF RUFFLE
WITH A MATCHPOINT
(ON WRONG SIDE)

EDGESTITCH

SERGED EDGE

PIN OR HANDBASTE
POSITION OF EACH FLOUNCE

10.9B FLUTED RUFFLES STITCHED
TO THE FABRIC SURFACE

10.11B LINE UP YOUR FLOUNCES ACCURATELY.

Three ways of stitching ruffles and flounces to garments will be explained in the following sections. These three methods are surface application, seam application, and edge application. Sketches of dresses, blouses, and skirts will illustrate each stitching method as a guide so you will know how to apply each to your own garments.

SURFACE APPLICATION

Surface application refers to ruffles and flounces stitched to the surface of the garment and not stitched into a seam or a garment edge. Figures 10.9, 10.10, and 10.11 illustrate designs of ruffles and flounces stitched to the fabric surface. Before ruffles are stitched to the surface of the garment, the hems must to be stitched first and then gathered or fluted next.

Gathering a seam was illustrated in Figure 6.23. You will notice that two rows of basting stitches are applied within the ½-inch seam allowance. The seam can be trimmed back to ¼ inch wide or serged. Do note that when gathering very long ruffles or flounces, it is best to stitch the basting stitches in shorter sections. Each section has been color coded in red, blue, and green basting stitches in Figure 10.4c. When basting stitches are applied to one long section, you run the risk of the stitches breaking as you pull up the gathers. Stitching shorter lengths will prevent this from happening.

Fluted ruffles are narrow strips of fabric that are bias cut and left with raw edges; the raw edges add to their lightness, so don't hem stitch these ruffles. The narrow strips of bias-cut fabric will not fray; however, the cut edges will become slightly roughed. This softening adds to the overall look. Several rows of fluted ruffles can be stitched to the surface of the garment to create an elegant texture, as you can see in Figure 10.9a.

One row of basting stitches is stitched to the center of each bias strip. Refer to "Eased Seam," in Chapter 6, and look at Figure 6.22 to see how easy it is to flute ruffles with an ease stitch. Gently pull up the bobbin thread into easing until a soft wave appears. When the basting stitches are pulled into easing, it creates a fluted effect down both sides of the ruffle.

Once the fluted ruffles are prepared, it is now time to pin-mark and handbaste the fabric to indicate the stitching position for each ruffle. Lay the wrong side of fluted ruffles onto the correct side of the fabric following the basting stitches, as illustrated in Figure 10.9b. Stitch the fluted ruffles directly on top of the basting stitches, attaching them to the fabric surface. Fluted ruffles can also be stitched to the fabric surface using a zigzag stitch if you prefer. When stitching directly on top of an ease stitch, *no* puckers should be evident! (The same technique is used for stitching a sleeve into an armhole).

Tips for Stitching Ruffles and Flounces to the Surface of the Fabric

- Avoid placing seam joins on ruffles and flounces when they are being stitched to the front of the garment. However, if a seam join cannot be avoided (due to limited fabric) then position the seam on the shoulders.
- Always make sure the gathering is evenly distributed.
- Stitch the hem finish to best suit your fabric type and weight. For ruffles and flounces, the sections of hem stitching needed are design driven. Your options are outlined in Figures 10.6a, b, c, d, and Figures 10.7 and 10.8.
- Pin and handbaste the position for each ruffle or flounce before they are stitched in place. This can only be achieved by measuring accurately, with your tape measure, the distance between each ruffle or flounce.
- Ruffles are then stitched to the fabric surface using a straight stitch. Stitch directly on top of all basting stitches. If one row of basting

> **NOTE**
>
> It must be noted that gathering normally involves stitching *two* rows of basting stitches. However, there is an exception to this—ruffles stitched to the *fabric surface only* can be gathered with one row of basting stitches and then topstitched to the fabric surface with one row of stitches. One row of stitching can look less cluttered and is aesthetically pleasing to the eye.

stitches is stitched to gather the ruffle, then topstitch with one row of straight stitches; if two rows of basting stitches are stitched to father the ruffle, then two rows of topstitching will be used to stitch the ruffle to the fabric surface, and so on. Notice in this design that the ruffle has all four sides stitched with a hem finish (see Figure 10.10b).
- Lay each ruffle on the fabric surface (with both correct sides of fabric facing up). Ruffles can be stitched directly on top of a seam, as Figure 10.10b indicates. It is far quicker in production to stitch ruffles this way, using the seamline as your guide, since measuring the placement can be quite time-consuming.
- If several rows of flounces are part of the design, as in the dress in Figure 10.11a, the inner circle of the flounces is serged first. Then the outer edge of the circle only is hem stitched. If gathered ruffles were applied instead of flounces, then the edge would need to be serged *after* it had been gathered (this reduces bulk and flattens the seam

10.12A POSITION THE RUFFLES TO THE CENTER OF EACH TUCK.

10.12A POSITION THE RUFFLES TO THE CENTER OF EACH TUCK.

10.12B STITCH THE TUCK.

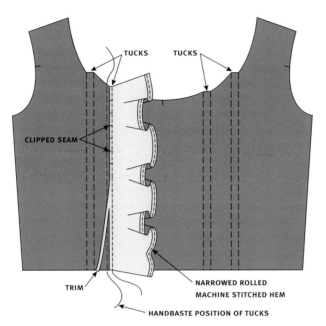

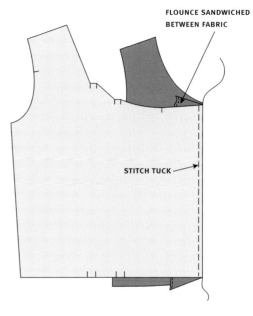

edge). Each flounce is then positioned as indicated in Figure 10.11b. Notice that the serged seams are hidden by overlapping the flounces. The trim covers the raw edge of the first flounce. If the fabric was sheer, the seam allowances would shadow, detracting from the look of the garment. A better option would be to insert the flounces into a seam or to stitch using a mock seam, as explained in the following section. If the ruffle is stitched to the bottom edge of the garment waistline, then place it at the seam edge; this is how it has been done in Figure 10.11b. If you want the ruffle to stand freely (and not be attached to the seam or hem), then position the ruffle on the finished seamline or hemline.

Mock Seam (Flounces Only—Ruffles Will Be Too Bulky to Stitch with a Mock Seam)

PATTERN TIP

The pattern will need a slight adjustment to allow for the tuck. Cut and spread the pattern, adding ½-inch to allow for each tuck, as indicated in Figure 10.12a. If this extra amount is not allowed for, the garment will be too tight for the customer to wear.

Another way to stitch the flounces in the dress in Figure 10.11a is to enclose the flounces in a mock seam. A **mock seam** is not the traditional seam—it is a seam that is formed by stitching a

tuck, as you can see in Figure 10.12b. A mock seam encloses the raw edge of the flounce, and the tuck creates a clean finish on the wrong side of the fabric.

- Lay the front of the garment flat on the table surface with the correct side facing up (see Figure 10.12a).
- Pin and handbaste the stitching position exactly where the flounce is to be positioned onto the garment (see Figure 10.12a). Do this by using your tape measure (which still should be around your neck!).
- Lay the correct side of the flounce to the correct side of the fabric with the flounce hem edge toward center front (see Figure 10.12a). If the

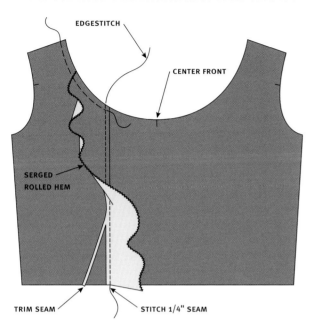

EDGESTITCH

CENTER FRONT

SERGED ROLLED HEM

TRIM SEAM

STITCH 1/4" SEAM

inside circle does not open up sufficiently, a stay-stitch can be sewn ¼ inch back from the raw edge and the seams clipped.

- Pin and handbaste the flounce in place and stitch the flounce to the garment using a ¼-inch seam allowance.
- Trim the seam allowance back to ⅛ inch, using appliqué scissors (as shown in Figure 15.25a). Be careful not to cut the garment by mistake (see Figure 10.12a)!
- Turn the garment to the wrong side and press the seam carefully—using only the tip of the iron (you do not want to crush the flounce).
- Fold both correct sides of the fabric back to-gether; the flounce raw edge is now sandwiched between the two layers (Figure 10.12b).

- Stitch a ¼-inch tuck. This is the ½ inch that was added to the pattern beforehand (see Figure 10.12b).
- Press the tuck toward center front.

Edgestitch (Flounces Only—Ruffles Will Be Too Bulky)

The flounces on the front of the dress in Figure 10.11a could also be topstitched with an edge-stitch. With this method, there is no need to serge the inner circle of the flounce, as it will be hidden. Notice in Figure 10.13 that when the flounce is stitched, the correct sides of the flounce and garment face each other, with the hem edge of the flounce facing toward the center front of the garment. The flounce is then stitched with a ¼-inch seam allowance and trimmed back to *a scant* ⅛ inch to reduce bulk. Next, the flounce is turned back toward the armhole, and the seam is pressed with the tip of the iron (you don't want to crease the flounce). Finally, the seam is edgestitched *slightly wider* than ⅛ inch back from the seamline, as illustrated in Figure 10.13. The edgestitching will enclose the raw edges and hold the flounce in place. Stitching can be tricky, as the flounce seam edge must be covered after it is stitched.

SEAM APPLICATION

Seam application implies that ruffles and flounces are inserted into a seam. They can be stitched into any seam as long as it suits the style and the fabric weight. Inserting ruffles and flounces into a seam can be done by flat application or by stitching in-the-round. Both methods are illustrated in Figure

10.5. Which method you use depends on your design and production method. If the flounce was stitched to the sleeve edge while the sleeve is laid flat (Figure 10.5a), then the hem would be stitched after the underarm seams were stitched. If the sleeve was stitched in-the-round, then the hem of the flounce would be finished first (Figure 10.5b).

The blouse in Figure 10.14a has ruffles in-serted into the front seams. How this is stitched will be outlined in the following stitching order. Flounces could also be inserted into the blouse seams instead. Notice that the ruffle has been hem stitched on three sides, as illustrated in Figure 10.6c. This has been completed before the ruffle is inserted into the seam.

- Place the correct side of the garment section flat on the table (Figure 10.14b).
- Place the correct side of the ruffle or flounce directly on top of the section to which it is being stitched, with the correct sides of the fabric facing together. Notice that the hem edge of the ruffle is facing toward the center front. Match any seam joins; notice in Figure 10.14b that the shoulder and ruffle seams are placed directly together. This needs to be planned in the patternmaking stage.
- Pin and handbaste the ruffle in place. Position the ruffle on the hemline so the ruffle can be flipped back and the hem turned up (see Figure 10.14b).
- Place the other garment section on top of the ruffle with the correct side facing down—the ruffle is now sandwiched between both front pieces (Figure 10.14c).

10.14A RUFFLES INSERTED INTO THE FRONT SEAM OF A BLOUSE

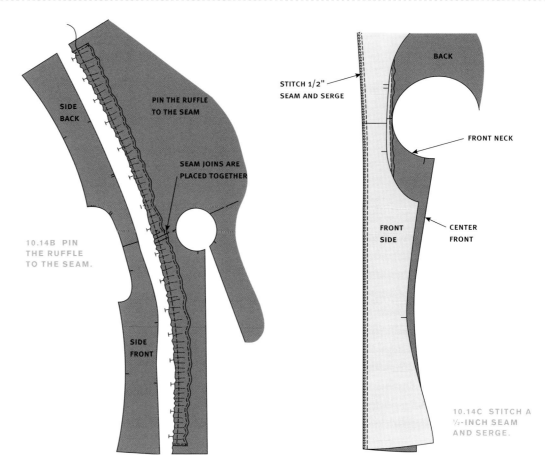

10.14A RUFFLES INSERTED INTO THE FRONT SEAM OF A BLOUSE

SIDE BACK

PIN THE RUFFLE TO THE SEAM

SEAM JOINS ARE PLACED TOGETHER

10.14B PIN THE RUFFLE TO THE SEAM.

SIDE FRONT

STITCH 1/2" SEAM AND SERGE

BACK

FRONT NECK

FRONT SIDE

CENTER FRONT

10.14C STITCH A ½-INCH SEAM AND SERGE.

- Stitch all three pieces together, using a ½-inch seam allowance, and serge a closed seam as illustrated in Figure 10.14c.
- Gently press the seam join only—the ruffle or flounce can be pressed when the garment is completed.
- From the correct side of the garment, the seam can be edgestitched to hold the seam allowance flat and perfectly in place. Edgestitching is illustrated in Figure 10.13. Although this figure illustrates edgestitching on a flounce, a ruffle is edgestitched in exactly the same way.

EDGE APPLICATION

Ruffles and flounces can be stitched as an **edge application** to any garment edge, for example, the neckline, sleeve edge, wrist edge, armhole edge, or hem edge. They can be stitched using either method: flat application or stitched in-the-round. Ruffles and flounces in these designs are interchangeable; flounces can be replaced with ruffles and vice versa. The method you use is driven by the stitching order that best suits your design. Both methods are outlined in this section.

Stabilizing Neck and Armhole Edges

When a ruffle or flounce is applied to a neckline or armhole, the garment edge needs to be staystitched first to prevent it from stretching in the stitching process. Staystitching is outlined in Chapter 6, "Staystitch," and illustrated in Figure 6.6. Stabilizing tape can also be used to stabilize edges and this is outlined in Chapter 3, "Stabilizing Tapes." Also refer to Figure 3.15. If you use a stabilizing tape, use a lightweight, sheer tape cut on the bias grain.

Your flounces may also need staystitching because they can easily stretch and become longer than the seam length they are being stitched to. If they have stretched, then stitch one row of basting stitches around the inner circle of each flounce, just inside the seam allowance, gently pull the easing to shorten the length, and steam-press to reduce the fullness.

Flat Application

Figure 10.15 illustrates how ruffles are stitched to a shirt while it lies flat. Leave your ruffles/flounces open and don't stitch them closed. Notice that the hem of the ruffle is not stitched yet (except for the center back section near the button extension).

- Make sure in each section that the gathering is evenly distributed before you stitch the ruffles in place.
- The correct side of the ruffles and fabric are facing together. Line up the seam edges and pin in place (Figure 10.15a).

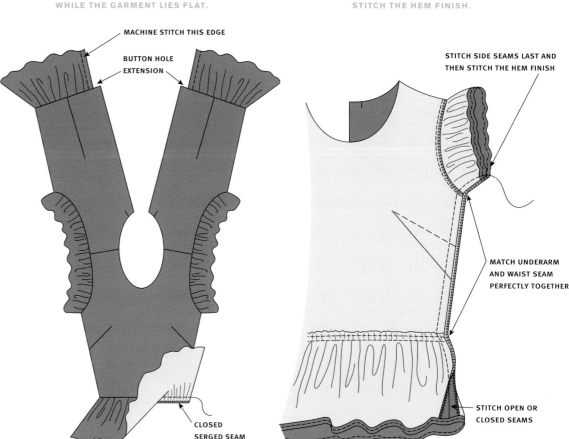

10.15A THE RUFFLES ARE STITCHED TO THE EDGES WHILE THE GARMENT LIES FLAT.

MACHINE STITCH THIS EDGE

BUTTON HOLE EXTENSION

CLOSED SERGED SEAM

10.15B STITCH THE SIDE SEAMS AND THEN STITCH THE HEM FINISH.

STITCH SIDE SEAMS LAST AND THEN STITCH THE HEM FINISH

MATCH UNDERARM AND WAIST SEAM PERFECTLY TOGETHER

STITCH OPEN OR CLOSED SEAMS

- Stitch and serge a ½-inch open or closed seam, as illustrated in Figure 10.15a.
- If you want an edge-stitched seam, then this must be completed now before the side seams are stitched together.
- To stitch the side seams, place the correct side together. Match intersecting underarm and waist seams together; if they don't match perfectly, it will draw attention to poor-quality stitching (Figure 10.15b).

- The hem is stitched last; notice that the side seams have been pressed open before stitching (see Figure 10.15b).

Stitched In-the-Round

All seams need to be stitched—that is, the garment and the ruffle/flounce all stitched in-the-round. The hem is stitched next and then it is gathered. When gathering, stitch in shorter sections; this prevents the thread from breaking when you pull up the gathers (see Figure 10.4c).

Next, the correct side of the ruffle/flounce is placed to the correct side of the skirt, and the seam edges pinned together.

Ruffle and flounce seam joins do not need to match up exactly with the garment seams. This can be very difficult to do. When placing ruffle/flounce seam joins to the garment seam, the seams should be positioned symmetrically,

10.16 EDGE APPLICATION: THE RUFFLE AND SKIRT ARE BOTH STITCHED IN-THE-ROUND AND THEN STITCHED TOGETHER.

so they look balanced on both sides of the garment, as this is pleasing to the eye. This is how the ruffle has been lined up to the skirt in Figure 10.16.

The seam is then stitched with ½-inch seam and, to reduce bulk, serged back to ¼ inch. In the skirt in Figure 10.16, the seam has been edgestitched to hold it in place; however, this is the designer's choice.

Stitched and Flipped

This method only applies to ruffles and flounces stitched around the neckline. A ruffle or flounce is stitched from the wrong side of the garment, then flipped to the correct side. With this constructional method, the ruffle or flounce will not sit flat around the neckline but will roll over and stand away from it. Try to cut the ruffle/flounce in one piece, and avoid shoulder seams. Although the flounce in Figure 10.1b could be stitched and flipped, this is not a couture stitching method. The price point of the garment may direct the stitching method when applying a flounce. Refer to "Bias Binding Edge Finish" in the upcoming section.

- Stitch the ruffle/flounce closed (stitched in-the-round) and finish the hem.

- Place the garment with the wrong side facing out. Position the ruffle/flounce on top of the garment around the neckline, also with the wrong side facing out, and pin in place.
- Stitch the ruffle/flounce to the garment with the ruffle/flounce facing up (Figure 10.17a).
- Stitch a ¼-inch serged seam (Figure 10.17b). (A ½-inch seam allowance will be too wide, preventing the ruffle/flounce from rolling over.)
- From the wrong side of the fabric, edgestitch around the neckline with the seam allowance turned toward the correct side of the fabric. The edgestitching will hold the seam allowance back when the ruffle/flounce is flipped over to the correct side of the garment. The edgestitching will also ensure that the seam is not visible from the correct side (see Figure 10.17b).
- Flip the ruffle/flounce to the correct side.

Bias Binding Edge Finish

A couture finish that cannot be ignored, because it is so ideal, is bias binding. It can be applied as an edge finish when ruffles and flounces have been stitched to the edges of the garment. It is a neat, narrow finish and does not ever shadow. Turn back to the Style I.D. and note that the necklines on the dresses in Figure 10.1a and 10.1c have both been finished with bias binding. Also refer to Figure 12.28, which illustrates how single or double bias binding is stitched.

HOW TO PRESS
Pressing Tips

Decide whether to press from the correct side or the wrong side of the fabric—you can only

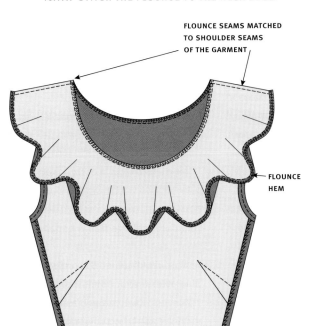

FLOUNCE SEAMS MATCHED
TO SHOULDER SEAMS
OF THE GARMENT

FLOUNCE
HEM

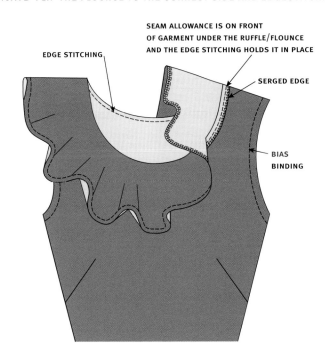

EDGE STITCHING

SEAM ALLOWANCE IS ON FRONT
OF GARMENT UNDER THE RUFFLE/FLOUNCE
AND THE EDGE STITCHING HOLDS IT IN PLACE

SERGED EDGE

BIAS
BINDING

determine this by test pressing first. Some fabrics need a pressing cloth to protect them—always have one on hand. Because it is transparent, a square of silk organza makes an excellent pressing cloth—it helps to see what is happening underneath the pressing cloth!

Ruffles

Figure 10.18 shows the garment slipped over the end of the ironing board with the iron placed at your right. To press, move the iron carefully, sliding it up into the folds. Lift the iron and repeat the action as you move the garment around the ironing board. Do not place the iron directly onto the gathering, as this will crush the folds.

Flounces

Lay the flounces out on the ironing board in a circular shape. Press around each flounce, spreading the flounce out as you move around the circle. Make sure you don't crease the flounces as you press.

STITCHING RUFFLES AND FLOUNCES IN TRICKY FABRICS
Matching Stripes, Plaids, Patterns, and Repeat Patterns

Do match checks and stripes on ruffle seam joins, as mismatches would be noticeable.

Do consider cutting striped ruffles in a direction opposite to that of the garment. For example, cut the ruffle on the horizontal stripe if the garment is cut on the vertical stripe.

Do cut multiple flounces in checks and stripes, matching in the seam joins to the line of the check or stripe (Figure 10.2b).

Don't worry about matching ruffles and flounces in checks and stripes when stitching them to the garment surface, inseams, or to edges; trying to do this would drive you crazy!

Sheer Fabric

Do use a 60 or 70 machine needle for your project.

Do stitch ruffles and flounces (and gathered flounces) in sheer fabrics such as chiffon and silk georgette; they will look fabulous!

Do sample the hem finish, as sheer fabrics are tricky to stitch.

Do stitch several layers of ruffles and flounces in sheer fabrics

Do stitch serged hem edges (various types of serged hems have been explained in this chapter).

Do stitch fluted ruffles in sheer fabrics, as they add a soft, light touch to a garment.

Lace

Do use a machine needle suitable for the weight of lace.

Do stitch ruffles and flounces only in lightweight lace with serged hem edges.

Do sample first to see if the lace fabric weight suits your design and the stitching method you use.

Don't stitch ruffles and flounces in heavyweight lace, as they will not drape well.

Satin

Do use ruffles and flounces in your design when using a lightweight silk satin such as silk charmeuse.

Do stitch flounces in heavyweight satin to the hem of a bridal or evening gown to create an interesting hem edge and attract attention. The skirt can be underlined, and structured with tulle to hold the shape.

Beaded Fabric

Do realize how time-consuming it would be to stitch ruffles and flounces in beaded fabric—read on to find out why.

Do refer to Chapter 6, "Stitching Seams in Tricky Fabrics," to find out what is involved in removing the beads from seams and hems before you stitch ruffles and flounces to the seams. We are not saying don't do it, but just want you to be forewarned.

Knits

Do insert a ballpoint needle in the appropriate size for the fabric weight.

Do use lightweight knit fabric so your ruffles and flounces will drape beautifully.

Do consider leaving raw edges on your ruffles and flounces; as knits don't fray, this saves a lot of time, especially in production.

Do stitch serged rolled hem finishes or lettuce edge (Figure 15.25) on ruffles and flounces.

Don't use stretch stitches when stitching hems of ruffles and flounces in knits, but do use them when inserting ruffles or flounces into seams. In Chapter 6, the section "Stretch Seams" explains which stitches to use in knits.

Don't use ruffles and flounces in your design if your knit is heavyweight.

Denim

Do sample first to check that the denim weight can be gathered if using ruffles.

Do realize that both sides of the fabric show when flounces drape on your garment. This

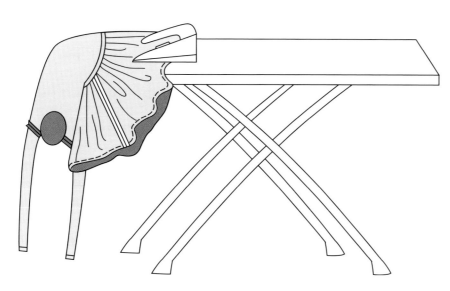

10.18 PRESSING RUFFLES AND FLOUNCES

may be an advantage or disadvantage in denim, depending on your taste.

Do use lightweight denim for ruffles and flounces. Stitch a serged hem edge, turn, and edgestitch, as this hem finish suits denim fabric.

Velvet

Do use the appropriate needle size for the velvet.

Do stitch faced flounces in velvet, as topstitching does not look as good; a clean finish suits velvet fabric.

Do hold the fabric taut as you stitch.

Do use a Velvaboard for pressing velvet fabric. Refer to Chapter 2, "Tricky Fabrics— What They Are and How to Prepare to Use Them."

Do design velvet garments simply, as velvet is a challenging fabric to work with.

Don't topstitch ruffles and flounces to the fabric surface in velvet.

Leather

Do stitch ruffles and flounces in soft leathers such as suede pigskin or deerskin.

Do use a leather needle in the appropriate size for the weight of leather.

Do refer to Chapter 6, "Stitching Seams in Tricky Fabrics," for tips on how to stitch ruffles and flounces in leather.

Do cut decorative edges with your rotary cutter on leather ruffles and flounces.

Don't worry about finishing leather hems, as leather does not fray like woven fabric.

Faux Fur

Don't stitch ruffles and flounces in faux fur, as it will look too thick and bulky.

TRANSFER YOUR KNOWLEDGE

The cutting and stitching of ruffles and flounces that you have learned in this chapter can be transferred to various designs:

- A gathered skirt is a longer version of a ruffle (Figure 10.14a).
- A circular skirt is a longer version of a flounce (Figure 15.1c).
- A handkerchief hemline is a squared flounce and could be used as a hem or sleeve edge.
- A tutu (worn by ballerinas) is made from rows and rows of tulle ruffles.
- A peplum is a flounce stitched to the waistline of the jacket (Figure 16.26c).

Here are a few suggestions for transferring your knowledge of ruffles and flounces:

- Narrow single or faced ruffles can be inserted around collar, cuffs, pockets, pocket flaps, and garment edges.
- Ruffles and flounces stitched to pants have not been discussed in this chapter, but we can't leave them out! Transfer your knowledge and stitch flounces into vertical seams

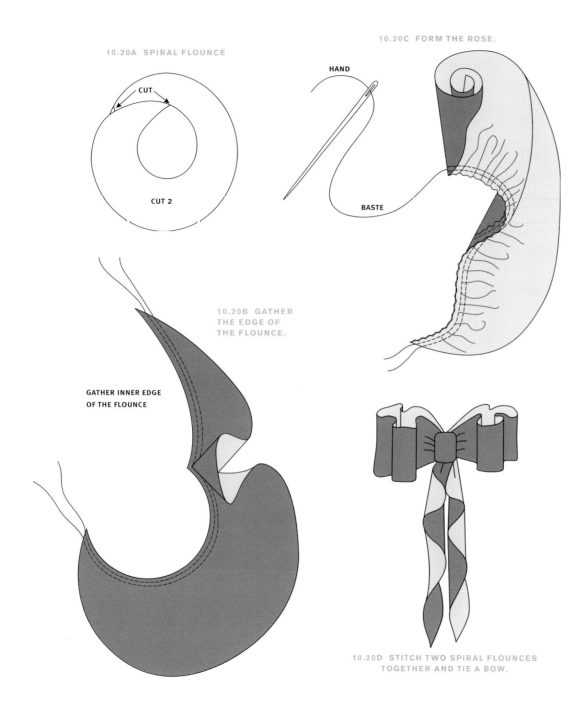

10.20A SPIRAL FLOUNCE

CUT

CUT 2

HAND

BASTE

10.20C FORM THE ROSE.

10.20B GATHER
THE EDGE OF
THE FLOUNCE.

GATHER INNER EDGE
OF THE FLOUNCE

10.20D STITCH TWO SPIRAL FLOUNCES
TOGETHER AND TIE A BOW.

on a pair of evening pants. Combine the pants with a gorgeous tailored evening jacket and a soft ruffled shirt. This stunning ensemble in Figure 10.19 would see you attending the Oscars!

STRETCH YOUR CREATIVITY

If you are a creative person and training to be a fashion designer, then you should be experimenting with new ideas to see where they take you in design. You will find that some new ideas work, and some don't work. However, it is often at these times, when our ideas don't work, that we end up finding a new and even more creative idea.

Listed here are some creative ways of using ruffles and flounces. You will probably be able to add to this list yourself. So stretch your creativity and have some fun by trying some of these new ideas.

- Try cutting a faced ruffle (on straight grain or bias grain—both produce different looks) to the required length before it is gathered. Gather each side of the ruffle separately and stuff the ruffle with polyester fill to form a rounded ruffle. Pin and handbaste the gathered edges together. Stitch it to your hem, sleeve edge, or neckline. Silk dupioni is an ideal fabric to use for the stuffed ruffle and illustrated in Figure 3.22a.
- Try making a rose from a faced spiral flounce. Look at the shape of the flounce in

Stretch Your Creativity

10.21A EVENING DRESS WITH LAYERS OF RUFFLES AND FLOWERS

LAYERS OF RUFFLES

FLOUNCE FLOWERS

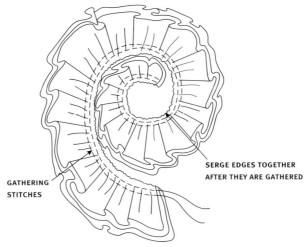

10.21B SEVERAL LAYERS OF BIAS RUFFLES OR FLOUNCES STITCHED TOGETHER AND GATHERED

GATHERING STITCHES

SERGE EDGES TOGETHER AFTER THEY ARE GATHERED

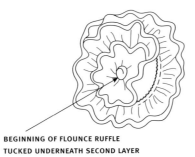

10.21C FORM THE FLOWERS.

BEGINNING OF FLOUNCE RUFFLE TUCKED UNDERNEATH SECOND LAYER

Figure 10.20a. The flounce is basted (Figure 10.20b). Gather then stitch the edge as you manipulate the shape into a rosebud (Figure 10.20c). Leave your thread hanging, and stitch a single rose or groups of roses to your garment to add a heavenly touch.

- Try stitching two spiral flounces together to form a beautiful bow as shown in Figure 10.20c. Experiment with different edge finishes.
- Try stitching several layers of bias ruffles or flounces into flowers. The flowers can be stitched to the hemline of a glamorous evening dress. Figure 10.21a shows how delicate flowers look stitched to the hem and waistline of an evening dress. The instructions are illustrated in Figures 10.21b and c.

STOP! WHAT DO I DO IF . . .

. . . my ruffle and flounce is too long for my seam?

You can stitch one row of basting stitches to your flounce edge, gently pull up easing, and steam-press the edge. This will shrink the flounce length beautifully. As for the ruffle, you can pull up more gathering to shorten the length. If it's too bulky with more gathers, then cut off some of the ruffle length and join the ruffle seam again. Check that the length is correct before reapplying to your seam.

. . . I don't like the ruffle I have stitched to my neckline?

Carefully seam rip the ruffle from the neck edge. Carefully press the neck edge and stitch a staystitch if it has not already been stitched. This will stabilize the neckline; it is now ready for an alternative neck finish. If your garment has not been fully stitched, you have several options: if your garment has been fully stitched, then you could add a collar or stitch a bias binding neck finish, or you could add a facing as well. A design is always in development, until the last stitch—but remember next time to make a muslin to define the style earlier.

. . . I serged a chunk out of the outside edge of my flounce?

Oh dear—how frustrating! If the flounce has been stitched to the garment, then carefully remove it with a seam ripper. It is best to recut your flounce again, plus a couple of extra flounces to practice serging circles. Sit at the serger, relax, and take your time to carefully serge your samples before serging final flounces. Remember, too, that mistakes are learning opportunities.

. . . I'm concerned because I used raw edges around my flounces and now the fabric is fraying?

Flounces are cut on all three grainlines, and the sections cut on the lengthwise and crosswise grains will fray (Figure 10.2b). If you still want the raw edges, stitch a row of permanent stitches ¼ inch inside the outer circle, which will prevent the edges from fraying. Other than that, you will need to stitch a hem finish. Have you thought of stitching a trim around the edge or serging a lettuce edge?

. . . I stitched two ruffles to my hem and it looks too thick and bulky?

Carefully seam rip the ruffles from the garment edge and try less gathering. Or remove a layer of ruffle or find an alternative fabric weight that is more suitable for your ruffles, then recut and restitch. This time, sample first to be sure that the fabric weight is suitable. As an alternative, you could stitch a flounce instead of the ruffle. Since your flounce does not need to be gathered, it won't look as bulky. You can also cut your flounce as a three-quarter circle instead of a full circle, which will reduce bulk.

SELF-CRITIQUE

Take the time to observe your ruffles and flounces, paying particular attention to the following:

- Did I use the *SEW, CLIP, PRESS* method of stitching as I stitched my ruffles and flounces?
- How do my ruffles and flounces drape? Did I cut them correctly?
- Are my ruffles and flounces stitched in parallel rows to the surface of my garment, or do they look wobbly?
- Are my flounces stitched using quality stitching, or do they look puckered?
- Does the hem stitching look professional or do I need more practice to perfect it?
- Did I use a hem finish that was suited to stitching around a circular flounce?
- Did I sample enough ruffles and flounces to get a clear direction for the stitching methods I was going to use?

Review Checklist

- What are the differences between ruffles and flounces?
- Do I understand that fabric weight and drape make a huge difference in how ruffles and flounces look in design?
- Do I understand that the grain on which I cut my ruffles can change the way they drape?
- Do I understand that ruffles have to be gathered but flounces don't?
- Do I understand that the design drives the stitching method I choose (flat application or stitched in-the-round) when applying ruffles and flounces to the garment?
- Do I understand that different hem finishes suit ruffles and flounces because of the way they're shaped?
- Do I understand how to flute a ruffle?
- What did I find difficult about stitching ruffles and flounces?

11

Collars: Silhouetting the Neck

A collar is stitched around the neckline of the garment, drawing attention to the upper body, as well as creating a focal point on the garment. Collars come in different styles, shapes, and sizes. Collars can be large or small, wide or narrow, stiff or soft. They can be V-shaped, square, or round, and stitched high or low on the neckline—designers can create collars in almost any shape. An important aspect of collars is that they *must* fit to the size of the neckline.

Collars can sit flat on the garment to mirror the neckline shape; stand up, hugging the neckline; or roll over onto the shoulders. Collars can also be symmetrical or asymmetrical, and can be detachable, which gives customers the option of wearing a collar or not.

Collars come in a wide variety of styles, from the small and dainty Peter Pan collar to a generously sized shawl or notched lapel collar. Most collars need a stabilizer; the type of stabilizer used will depend on the fabric used and the desired structure the designer wants to create. The possibilities of collar designs can be surprising and this is one area in which the designer can show creativity. Ruffles, pleats, or fabric embellishments can be stitched into the collar seam or to the surface of the collar to create different looks.

This chapter teaches and illustrates how to construct collars, which require precise stitching. The Style I.D. sets out the collars that will be discussed in this chapter. Take a look at each collar in Figure 11.1 and learn the name of each different style. Other collar designs will be illustrated in "Stretch Your Creativity" to show how different shapes and sizes can be created from basically the same collar structures.

Style I.D.

11.1A MANDARIN COLLAR
(STAND-UP COLLAR)

11.1B PETER PAN
COLLAR (SIT-FLAT
COLLAR)

11.1C SHIRT
COLLAR (ROLL-OVER
COLLAR)

11.1D CONVERTIBLE
COLLAR (ROLL-OVER
COLLAR)

11.1E NOTCHED
LAPEL COLLAR
(ROLL-OVER COLLAR)

11.1F SHAWL COLLAR AND
BIAS/ROLL COLLAR

STYLE I.D.

The stitching order for the collar designs in the Style I.D. (Figure 11.1) is outlined in this chapter. Each collar illustrated in the Style I.D. falls into one of the following three categories—sit-flat, stand-up, or roll-over collar.

Get to know the key terms used for collars. Each style of collar has its own style name. Understanding each term will help to communicate when stitching collars in the classroom.

GATHER YOUR TOOLS

The tools needed to stitch collars are the same tools needed for general stitching of garments: stabilizer, tape measure, thread, point turner, awl, scissors, hand stitching needles, tailor's ham, sleeve board, and pressing cloth. It is especially important to have a *point turner* and the *pressing equipment,* as they are integral to stitching and perfecting collars. If you don't have these tools yet, then purchase them *now!*

NOW LET'S GET STARTED

This chapter gives students an opportunity to further their design knowledge by learning how to stitch collars. Knowing how to stitch garments empowers the designer in design possibilities. Knowing how to stitch one collar will give you the ability to transfer this knowledge to the stitching of other collar designs in different shapes and sizes. Before stitching collars, let's define what a collar is and point out some of the important features of the collar.

What Is a Collar?

A **collar** is made from one straight piece of fabric (bias/roll collar) or two shaped pieces of fabric (mandarin, Peter Pan, shirt, convertible, notched, tailored, and shawl collars) that are stitched together around the outer edges. The collar is then turned, clipped, and pressed. The inner collar edge is the collar neckline. The collar neckline is stitched to the garment neckline (Figure 11.3).

The size of the collar neckline is determined by the garment neckline; they need to be of equal length. The outer collar edge and the collar neckline are shaped differently depending on the style of collar. The rounder the collar edge is, the farther it sits away from the neckline. Each category of collar—stand-up, sit-flat, and roll-over—is shaped differently. Notice the shape of each collar in Figure 11.2.

How the collar is stitched and how it fits to the garment neckline is an important part of functional design. The collar needs to fit comfortably around the neck and not feel tight! Chapter 1 discusses this aspect of functional design that is the designer's responsibility. Refer to Figures 1.4, 1.5, 1.6, and 1.7 to read comments that apply to functional design. Functional design is important, as the collar needs to close easily; complicated collar closures may prevent a garment from selling.

Collars can open on the front or back of the garment or be stitched-in-the-round, as in the case of a knit fabric when the collar stretches to fit over one's head. How the collar opens and closes is part of the garment closure, which is discussed in Chapter 17.

Collars offer an exciting opportunity for the designer, as many weird and wonderful shapes can be created. For creative collar ideas, refer to "Stretch Your Creativity."

It must be noted that adding a collar to any garment will add to the production cost. After you have made a collar, you will certainly understand the time it takes to make the pattern and stitch the collar. The stabilizer used and the stitching method also have an impact on the cost of the garment.

Features of a Collar

All collars need a **collar stand**. The collar stand is the height to which the collar stands up. It must be pointed out that *all* collars *must* have a collar stand; however, the height of the stand can differ. The height of the stand affects how high the collar sits on the back neck. Observe the different heights of the collar stands in Figure 11.2. The collar stand supports the collar and enables it to roll over. Some collars such as the mandarin collar, illustrated in Figure 11.2b, are constructed with only a collar stand and not the roll-over section.

The top edge of the collar stand, where the collar rolls over, is called the **roll line**. Observe the roll line on each of the collars in Figure 11.2a, c, d, e, and f. Notice the shirt collar in Figure 11.2d combines two collars that are stitched together. The seamline where the collar stand joins the mandarin collar section then becomes the roll line.

When stitching two collar pieces together, one collar is called the **upper collar** and the other collar, the **under collar**. This is discussed in "Upper and Under Collar Patterns" later.

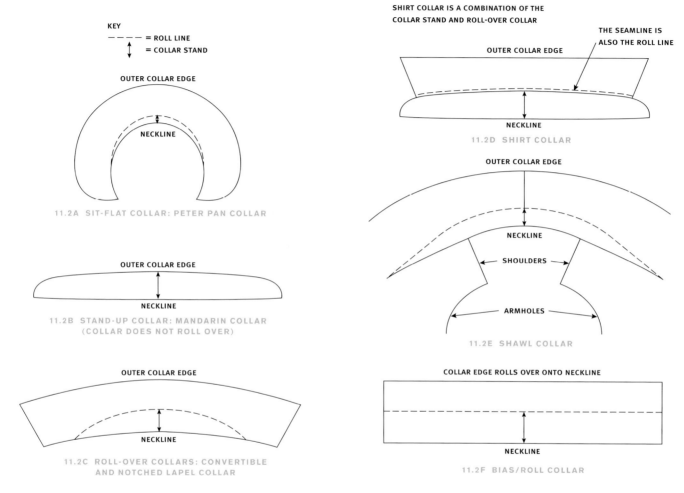

11.2 IMPORTANT FEATURES OF A COLLAR

KEY

— — — = ROLL LINE

↕ = COLLAR STAND

OUTER COLLAR EDGE

NECKLINE

11.2A SIT-FLAT COLLAR: PETER PAN COLLAR

OUTER COLLAR EDGE

NECKLINE

11.2B STAND-UP COLLAR: MANDARIN COLLAR
(COLLAR DOES NOT ROLL OVER)

OUTER COLLAR EDGE

NECKLINE

11.2C ROLL-OVER COLLARS: CONVERTIBLE
AND NOTCHED LAPEL COLLAR

SHIRT COLLAR IS A COMBINATION OF THE
COLLAR STAND AND ROLL-OVER COLLAR

THE SEAMLINE IS
ALSO THE ROLL LINE

OUTER COLLAR EDGE

NECKLINE

11.2D SHIRT COLLAR

OUTER COLLAR EDGE

NECKLINE

SHOULDERS

ARMHOLES

11.2E SHAWL COLLAR

COLLAR EDGE ROLLS OVER ONTO NECKLINE

NECKLINE

11.2F BIAS/ROLL COLLAR

TYPES OF COLLARS

Refer to Figure 11.2 and take a look at the collar styles for each category. Each collar is also illustrated in the Style I.D. in Figure 11.1. Each type of collar is descriptive of how the collar sits on the garment.

Stand-up Collars

A **stand-up collar** after it is stitched to the neckline stands up around the neck. An example of this style of collar is the mandarin collar illustrated in Figure 11.1a. The front collar edge can be square, round, or angled. The collar can

meet edge-to-edge or it can have an extension so it can be buttoned closed. All stand-up collars need to be stabilized to different degrees to add structure and support, otherwise they cannot stand up!

Sit-Flat Collars

Collars that **sit flat** around the neckline have a collar shape that is almost identical to the garment shape. Even though the collar may look flat, it isn't exactly flat (Figure 11.2a). A small collar stand is incorporated in the collar pattern to enable the collar to roll to the correct side of the garment after it is stitched. The Peter Pan collar in Figure 11.1b illustrates a collar that sits flat. These collars don't usually need stabilizers.

Roll-Over Collars

When a **roll-over collar** is stitched to the neckline, it stands up for a certain height (this depends on the amount of stand added to the pattern), then the collar rolls over onto the garment. The outer edge of the collar is wider than the garment neckline, and this enables the collar to sit away from the neckline. The Style I.D. illustrates five roll-over collars (see Figure 11.1c, d, e, and f); can you name each of them?

Correct stitching begins with correct patternmaking. Collars require meticulous and exacting stitching, especially when getting both sides of the collar to look the same. A badly stitched collar can spoil the look of a beautiful garment, so take the time to stitch carefully and precisely.

STITCHING COLLARS BEGINS WITH CORRECT PATTERNS
Upper and Under Collar Patterns

Upper and under collar patterns are needed to stitch successful collars. When two pieces of fabric are placed together and rolled over, the

PATTERN TIP

Neckline Measurement

No matter what shape the neckline is, the garment neckline *must* be measured first to get an accurate collar length. Since the collar is going to be stitched to the garment neckline, the collar and neckline lengths must be *exactly* equal. This measurement is crucial for stitching an accurate collar. If the collar is too small or too large for the garment neckline, the collar will *never* sit well and could look misshapen.

For a collar to fit the neckline accurately, take your tape measure and measure the front and back bodice neckline. Jot down the front and back neck measurements. The position of the collar needs to be defined before you measure the neckline. This is indicated on the designer's sketch. Collars can overlap and button together, as Figure 11.1a demonstrates. Collars can also meet directly together on the center front or back as Figures 11.1b and c illustrate. Collars don't have to button or meet on the center front of the neckline; they can be placed anywhere between the center-front neck and the shoulders—this is the designer's choice. Notice that the convertible collar in Figure 11.1d doesn't meet at the center front—it shows a gap. It is important when pattern marking to notch the placement of the collar on the neckline.

When drafting the pattern, be sure to indicate all the notches that are needed to stitch the collar neckline to the garment neckline; these notches will ensure accurate stitching:

- Garment neckline—starting position of the collar, center front and center back, and the shoulder position of the garment.
- Collar neckline—center back, center front (if there is an extension), and the shoulders. Figure 11.3 illustrates where all the notches are snipped in the garment and collar necklines. Snipping notches in these positions ensures that the collar is perfectly aligned on the garment and will never look twisted when the garment is worn.

top piece becomes smaller than the underneath piece. This is exactly what happens when two collar pieces are stitched together and rolled over. The upper collar becomes smaller than the under collar. To counteract this, two different collar patterns are needed—one larger than the other. The upper collar pattern is cut wider so when the two collars are stitched together they are perfectly aligned. The under collar being slightly smaller holds the seamline slightly underneath the upper collar after it is stitched.

When the collar rolls over, the collar seamline is not visible when the garment is worn. Snip two notches on the center back of the under collar, as this helps to differentiate between upper and under collars (Figures 11.4b and c).

An *average* amount added to the center back width of the upper collar is ⅛ inch and ¹⁄₁₆ inch on the collar corners. It must be emphasized that this is an *average measurement* only (Figures 11.4b–f). The weight of the fabric will affect the amount of extra width that must be

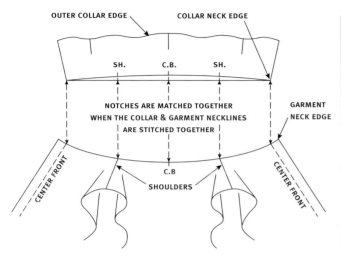

11.3 WHEN THE GARMENT AND COLLAR NECKLINES ARE NOTCHED, THEY WILL STITCH TOGETHER PERFECTLY.

added. For example, a heavyweight fabric may need more width added to the upper collar than a sheer lightweight fabric. To ascertain how much larger the upper collar should be, take two pieces (cut the same size) of your actual collar fabric in your hand and roll the two pieces over together. Measure the difference between the two pieces when rolled.

Only roll-over and sit-flat collars need upper and under collars. Even though sit-flat collars do sit flat around the neckline, they also *roll over* onto the garment. Stand-up collars *do not* need upper and under collars and can be cut with the same pattern, as illustrated in Figure 11.4a.

A reminder will appear under the heading "Pattern Tip" to make sure you begin with upper and under collars. Use Figure 11.4 as a reference for making upper and under collar patterns. Label the patterns—"Under Collar" and "Upper

Collar"—as illustrated. Also note the number of collar pieces to be cut for each pattern.

The breakpoint is also an important pattern marking. Notice in Figure 4.4e and f that the breakpoint has been notched. The **breakpoint** is the point on the collar where it begins to fold back. The first buttonhole is stitched horizontally at the breakpoint. Can you see this in the jacket in Figure 11.1e in the Style I.D.?

STITCHING THE COLLAR TO THE NECKLINE

When collars are stitched to the neckline, they can be stitched with or without a neck facing. Whether the collar is worn open or closed is the deciding factor. The style of garment and how it will be worn gives direction as to which approach to choose. For example, a shirt with a mandarin collar *would not* need a neck facing; however, a mandarin collar stitched to a jacket or coat *would definitely* need a front only or front and back facing, as the garment needs to hang open as well as closed.

No Neck Facing

When a collar is stitched with **no neck facing**, the collar is designed to remain closed rather

than be worn open; therefore, a facing is not required. One exception to this is a shirt collar designed to be worn open or closed. Because the shirt collar sits high on the neckline, the narrow band on the collar is sufficient and the wrong side of the fabric does not show when the collar opens (see Figure 11.1c).

Front Neck Facing Only or Front/ Back Neck Facings

Garments with collars that are going to be worn open and closed *must* be stitched with a **front neck facing** or **front and back neck facings**. When the garment is worn open, the facing is often visible. Stitching facings are especially important for jackets and coats that are worn open and closed. Both jackets in the Style I.D.

IMPORTANT

When any facing is applied to the neckline, the collar is stitched to the garment first and then the facing applied.

---

in Figure 11.1e and f have lapel collars, and the lapel collar that is showing is the facing (which is the upper collar).

GET THE STABILIZER RIGHT!

A stabilizer is an essential ingredient in a collar. However, having said this, not all collars need a stabilizer! Adding a stabilizer to the collar helps the collar retain its shape. It also adds support, strength, stability, and body to the collar so it can be stand-up or roll-over. The stabilizer must be able to support the style of collar and the fabric weight. For example, you will need

---

PATTERN TIP

If you have already made your patterns, do check them again, because the garment and collar neckline measurements *must* be equal lengths to experience a smooth stitching process for collars. If they are not equal, adjust the pattern now before you stitch, as it would be impossible to stitch a collar correctly! Also, check to be sure you have snipped notches in the collar and garment neckline patterns so the collar and garment necklines can be perfectly aligned together. Refer to Figure 11.3.

---

a very different weight of stabilizer for a large stand-up collar made in wool tweed compared with a stabilizer for a sheer silk georgette collar. Even if the collars were the same style, the stabilizer would need to be a different type and weight. It is essential in collars that all elements work together: design, fabric, and stabilizer. In Chapter 3, it was recommended that the weight of your stabilizer be similar in weight to that of the fabric for your garment. This is a good starting point; however, when constructing collars, there are a few other important considerations.

Analyze the Design

The first tip when choosing the stabilizer for the collar is to analyze the collar shape you want to create. Decide on how structured you want the collar to look—soft, medium, or firm—and find the stabilizer that will give you this structure. Many times the stabilizer needs to be heavier in weight than what you would choose for stabilizing a cuff or a facing. This may be because the collar is wide and stands up. It is possible to stabilize the upper and under collars with interfacing and then add another layer of canvas to the entire upper collar in the back section only, to give it more structure. The stabilizer for the collar does not need to be the same stabilizer used for an underlining, waistband, or facings. It is a *separate entity* in itself, so treat it that way. The important thing about stabilizing collars is—use whatever works! Reread Chapter 3, "How to Choose the Best Stabilizer for Your Project," if you need more guidance on choosing the best stabilizer for your collar.

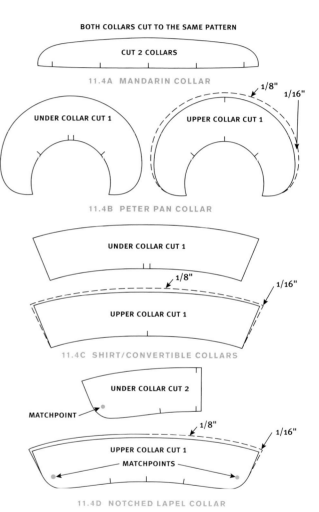

BOTH COLLARS CUT TO THE SAME PATTERN

CUT 2 COLLARS

11.4A MANDARIN COLLAR

UNDER COLLAR CUT 1   UPPER COLLAR CUT 1

1/8"   1/16"

11.4B PETER PAN COLLAR

UNDER COLLAR CUT 1

1/8"   1/16"

UPPER COLLAR CUT 1

11.4C SHIRT/CONVERTIBLE COLLARS

UNDER COLLAR CUT 2

MATCHPOINT

1/8"   1/16"

UPPER COLLAR CUT 1
MATCHPOINTS

11.4D NOTCHED LAPEL COLLAR

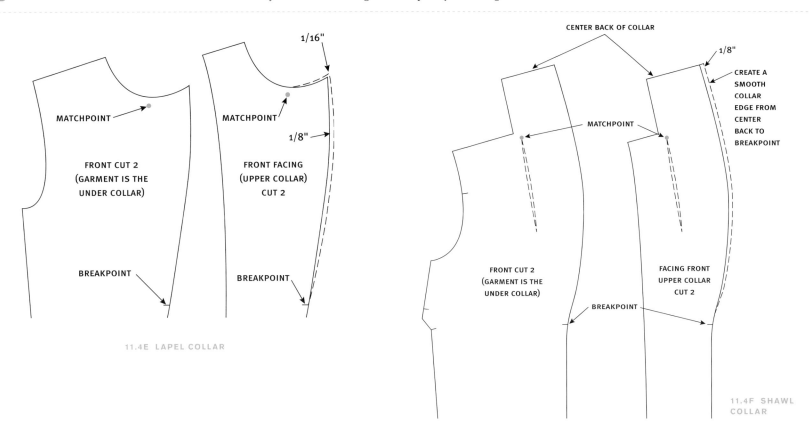

11.4E LAPEL COLLAR

11.4F SHAWL COLLAR

Before collars are applied to the neckline, the following stitching should be completed on the garment—underlining, darts, pockets, shoulder seams (leave side seams open), tucks and pleats, center-back zipper, waistband, ruffles, and flounces. The stitching order may differ, as each style has its own requirements; the main point is to have all the stitching completed on the front and back of the garment and the shoulder seams joined; then you are ready to apply the collar.

Collars can have different shapes—there is no "right" collar shape. So don't think you can't use the instruction for stitching a round collar when the collar you are stitching has a pointed shape. For ex-

ample, you may be stitching the notched lapel collar illustrated in Figure 11.1f. Notice it has a pointed collar shape; however, the collar and lapel could

both be rounded and you will find this would not interfere with the stitching order.

COLLARS STITCHED WITH NO NECK FACING
Peter Pan Collar (Sit-Flat Collar)
A Peter Pan collar sits flat and has rounded front collar edges; however, the designer can change

> **PATTERN TIP**
>
> Make upper and under collars as illustrated in Figure 11.4b. As mentioned previously, sit-flat collars do roll over even though they sit flat on the garment, so upper and under collars patterns are still necessary. Do snip notches in garment and collar necklines as well as the center back of the collar outer edges (see Figure 11.3).

> **NOTE**
>
> When a collar needs stabilizing on one side only, always stabilize the *upper collar* rather than the under collar.

IMPORTANT

Collars hold their shape better when a stabilizer is applied to *both upper and under collars*. A stabilizer will also prevent a seam image from showing on the correct side of the collar when pressed. There can be an exception to this advice; a flat collar may not need stabilizing on the upper and under collars. Adding stabilizer to a flat collar would prevent it from sitting flat and cause it to look too bulky. A sheer flat collar may not need stabilizing at all. When deciding on a stabilizer to use for upper and under collars, choose a *lighter weight* so the two stabilizers together will equal the weight of one stabilizer.

the outer collar edge to any shape. Figure 11.1b illustrates a traditional Peter Pan collar. In this text, the Peter Pan collar will be stitched with a bias binding neck finish. This would be the preferred way to finish the neck edge, which reduces bulk. Chapter 12 also discusses a bias binding as an alternative edge finish instead of stitching a facing; refer to "Bias Bindings" there.

STABILIZING THE COLLAR

- Apply the stabilizer to the *upper collar* only if needed. Silk organza may be a good stabilizer for flat collars.

Stitching the Collar

- Place correct sides of the upper and under collars together; match all notches, and pin around the outer collar edge. Don't be concerned that the under collar is smaller around the outer edge than the upper collar—still match both collar edges together—they will sit perfectly when the collar has been stitched, clipped, and turned (Figure 11.5a).

- With the under collar facing up, stitch a ¼-inch seam allowance around the outer collar edges; begin stitching from the center back, stitching directionally toward the front; overlap the stitches at the back by ½ inch (see Figure 11.5a). The under collar will need to be stretched slightly as you stitch—this is how it is meant to be stitched, so don't worry!

- Press the stitches while the collar lies flat, and then press the collar seams open; this will take time, so don't rush this step! Figure 11.5b illustrates the curved front collar section placed over the end of the sleeve board to press the seam open.

- Check that the collar shapes are mirror images of each other. The neckline edge can be trimmed if uneven; however, if the collar shape is uneven, it must be restitched so they look identical. If the collars are uneven, it *will* be noticeable (Figure 11.5d).

- Grade the *under collar* seam back to ⅛ inch and understitch. After understitching, the upper collar seam allowance can also be carefully trimmed back to ⅛ inch (Figure 11.5c).

- Pin and handbaste both collar neckline edges together, matching the notches so the collar is perfectly aligned.

Stitching the Collar to the Neckline

- Staystitch the garment neckline.

- Lay the collar onto the correct side of the garment neckline; place the collar notches to the garment neckline and pin and machine baste the collar to the garment (Figure 11.5e).

- Cut one bias strip (binding) approximately 1 inch wide and longer than the length of the neckline; press a ¼-inch seam allowance along one side to the wrong side of the fabric (see Figure 11.5e). To review how to cut and join bias binding, refer to Figures 6.16 and 6.17.

- Turn the front facing back at the notched position so the correct sides of the facing and garment are together (see Figure 11.5e).

- Pin the bias binding around the neckline; begin by placing the bias on the center-front notch. Stitch a ¼-inch seam allowance. The following steps are really important, as bulk *must* be reduced. Grade the neckline seam; begin by cutting the bias seam allowance back to ⅛ inch and then grade the collar seam allowance. Leave the garment seam allowance at ¼ inch and then clip into the neck seam allowance so it will spread when turned and stitched in place (see Figure 11.5e).

- Understitch the bias binding.

- Turn the bias toward the garment and handbaste in place; manipulate the bias with your hands so it is laying flat around the curved neckline shape. Remember, bias is stretchy! Handbaste the binding in place and press before stitching (Figure 11.5f).

- Edgestitch the bias to the garment; begin and end with a backstitch. Begin stitching at the garment front opening, just catching the facing, and stitch all the way around, catching the facing on the other side. Don't stitch beyond this point, otherwise the stitching will show from the correct side of the garment on the front. The stitching should be visible only when the collar is lifted (see Figure 11.5f).
- Clip the threads and press the collar.

Bias/Roll Collar (Roll-Over Collar)

A bias/roll collar adds a delicate, graceful touch to a garment. Since the collar is bias-cut, it rolls over beautifully and sits perfectly around the neck. This style of collar is cut double the final height of the stand so when the collar rolls over there are four layers of fabric sitting together (see Figure 11.2f). For this reason the fabric *must* be lightweight. It looks most delicate made in sheer fabrics or in satin silk charmeuse.

A bias/roll collar can sit high, hugging the neckline, or be stitched low to a scooped neckline. Either way, it is an elegant collar suited especially to blouses; however, this does not limit its use in design. Notice in Figure 11.1e, in the Style I.D., how the bias/roll silk georgette collar

NOTE

This collar must have an opening if it is high on the neckline; collars that are lower on the neck can slip over the head. This is part of functional design.

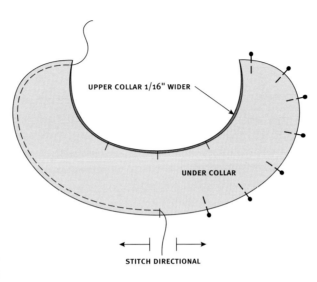

11.5A PIN AND STITCH THE UPPER AND UNDER COLLARS TOGETHER.

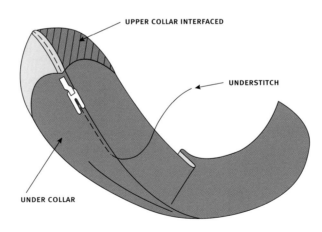

11.5C UNDERSTITCHING THE COLLAR

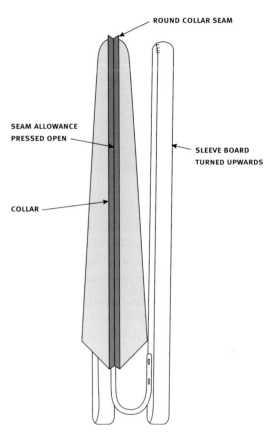

11.5B PRESSING A ROUND SEAM

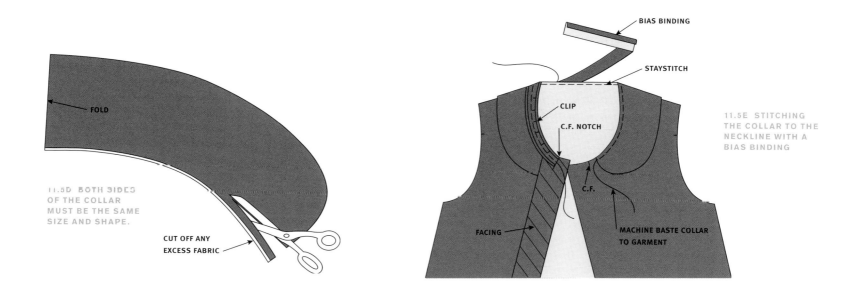

11.5D BOTH SIDES OF THE COLLAR MUST BE THE SAME SIZE AND SHAPE.

CUT OFF ANY EXCESS FABRIC

FOLD

BIAS BINDING

STAYSTITCH

CLIP

C.F. NOTCH

C.F.

FACING

MACHINE BASTE COLLAR TO GARMENT

11.5E STITCHING THE COLLAR TO THE NECKLINE WITH A BIAS BINDING

drapes perfectly around the neckline and compliments the tailored suit.

A bias/roll collar can also have a tie incorporated in the front that can be tied in a soft bow. How to stitch the tie ends will also be outlined in this section.

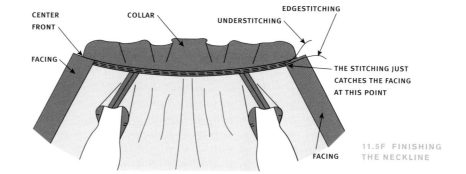

CENTER FRONT

FACING

COLLAR

UNDERSTITCHING

EDGESTITCHING

THE STITCHING JUST CATCHES THE FACING AT THIS POINT

FACING

11.5F FINISHING THE NECKLINE

STITCHING THE COLLAR

- Do *not* stabilize bias/roll collars.
- Press a ¼-inch seam allowance to the wrong side of the fabric along one collar neck edge (Figure 11.6a). This neck edge still *must* be notched!
- Fold the collar in half with the correct sides facing together; don't be tempted to press this foldline.

Stitch a ¼-inch seam at each end of the collar. Stitch directional from the collar neck edge to the foldline. At the collar neck edge, the seam allowance must still be folded back while the other seam allowance lies flat (see Figure 11.6a).

- Press the stitches flat, then press the seam

PATTERN TIP

Notching the garment and collar necklines will always provide a smoother stitching experience (see Figure 11.3).

allowance open, clip the collar corners, and turn the collar to the correct side. Use a point turner to square the corners and press.

Stitching the Collar to the Neckline

- Apply the stabilizer to the front facing. Stay-stitch the garment neckline and stitch the garment shoulders together; leave the garment lying flat *without* the side seams joined (Figure 11.6b).

- Fold the front facing back at the notched position so the correct sides are facing together; stitch across the width of the extension only, clip into the seam allowance at the notch up to the stitching, clip corners, turn and press the facing to the wrong side of the garment (see Figure 11.6b).

- Place the correct sides of the collar and garment necklines together, matching all notches. Begin by placing the collar edges to both sides of the front protruding clipped seam allowance (done in the previous step). Pin the collar to the neckline, matching all notches. Stitch a ¼-inch neckline seam allowance; then stitch the neck seam from the collar side. The neckline seam does not need grading since bias/rolls collars should be stitched in lightweight fabrics. Carefully press the seam allowance up into the collar (Figure 11.6b and c).

PATTERN TIP

A tie can be added to each end of the bias/roll collar. This collar is illustrated in Figure 11.7a and can be used in designing a blouse, shirt, or dress. The bias/roll tie collar can be stitched to a round or V–shaped, high or low neckline. The beginning of the tie *must* be stitched to the neckline 1 inch back from center garment line; this "gap" allows room for tying the bow.

- The collar can be finished in one of two ways: stitched-in-the-ditch from the correct side, or hand stitched from the wrong side. Both are illustrated in Figure 11.6c. To stitch-in-the-ditch, place the collar foldline slightly over the seamline, align the neckline notches together, and handbaste in place. This is important, as a bias collar can easily stretch and look twisted if it is not aligned correctly. Stitch-in-the-ditch from the correct side; hand stitch by placing the foldline to the seamline; and using an overhand stitch, stitch into every neckline stitch (see Figure 11.6).

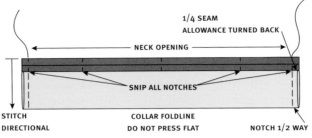

1/4 SEAM ALLOWANCE TURNED BACK
NECK OPENING
SNIP ALL NOTCHES
STITCH DIRECTIONAL
COLLAR FOLDLINE DO NOT PRESS FLAT
NOTCH 1/2 WAY

11.6A STITCHING THE COLLAR

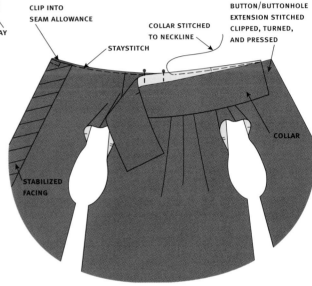

CLIP INTO SEAM ALLOWANCE
COLLAR STITCHED TO NECKLINE
STAYSTITCH
BUTTON/BUTTONHOLE EXTENSION STITCHED CLIPPED, TURNED, AND PRESSED
COLLAR
STABILIZED FACING

11.6B PREPARE THE GARMENT NECKLINE AND STITCH THE COLLAR TO THE NECKLINE.

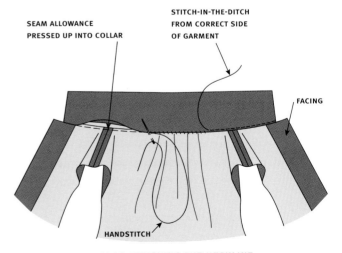

SEAM ALLOWANCE PRESSED UP INTO COLLAR
STITCH-IN-THE-DITCH FROM CORRECT SIDE OF GARMENT
FACING
HANDSTITCH

11.6C FINISHING THE NECKLINE

Bias/Roll Tie Collar (Roll-Over Collar)

STITCHING THE TIE COLLAR

- Do *not* stabilize a bias/roll collar that ties. Press a ¼-inch seam allowance to the wrong side along one neck edge of the collar.
- Fold the collar with the correct sides facing together, and stitch a ¼-inch seam allowance to both ends of the tie. First press the stitches flat and the seam allowance open; clip the curved seam, turn, and press the tie.
- Don't press the foldline of the roll collar, as this looks nicer rolling softly. These steps are illustrated in Figure 11.7b.

Stitching the Collar to the Neckline

To stitch the collar to the neckline, follow the same stitching order for Figure 11.6c. Figure 11.7c illustrates how the front facing is stitched to a V-neckline, incorporating a gap to allow a space for the collar to tie. Notice in Figure 11.7c how a gap is stitched (shown on the left-hand side of the garment between clips), and how it looks when it is finished (illustrated on the right-hand side of the garment).

Mandarin Collar (Stand-up Collar)

This collar was traditionally part of the design for Chinese mandarin robes. A mandarin collar usually has a curved edge that meets at center front; it can also be extended and buttoned, as illustrated in Figure 11.1a.

STABILIZING THE COLLAR

- Apply the interfacing to the wrong side of both collars.

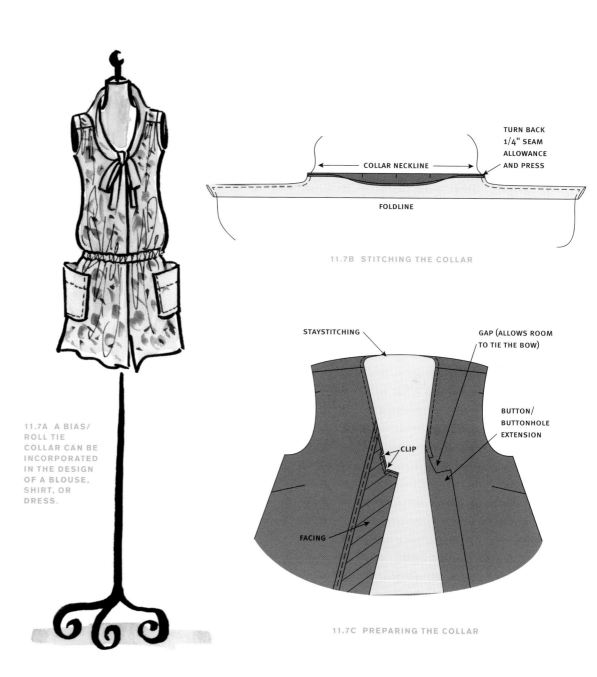

11.7A A BIAS/ROLL TIE COLLAR CAN BE INCORPORATED IN THE DESIGN OF A BLOUSE, SHIRT, OR DRESS.

11.7B STITCHING THE COLLAR

11.7C PREPARING THE COLLAR

PATTERN TIP

Both sides of the mandarin collar are cut to the *same size*. This is indicated in Figure 11.4a. Since the collar stands up, upper and under collars do not need to be cut. However, having said this, eventually you will see in the stitching order that upper and under collars are formed as you stitch.

Stitching the Collar

- Press the seam allowance of one neck edge of the collar to the wrong side; this collar is now the *under collar* (Figure 11.8a).
- Place the correct sides of both collars' outer edges together; match the front collar edges and center-back notches together, and pin in between these points. With the under collar facing up, stitch a ¼-inch seam allowance around the collar edges; make sure the under collar seam allowance is still folded back as it was pressed, and that the upper collar seam allowance is lying flat (see Figure 11.8a).
- Press the stitches flat, and then press the seam open. Place the curved collar shape over the end of the sleeve board to press the seam open (see Figure 11.5b).
- Turn the collar to the correct side and press flat; make sure the seamline is centered and does not roll toward the correct side.

- Don't clip the front curved shape. Instead, trim the seam back to ⅛ inch; trim and grade the rest of the seam allowance if bulk needs to be reduced (see Figure 11.8a). On sheer fabrics, trim the entire seam allowance back to ⅛ inch; seam allowances shadow through to the correct side of sheer fabric.

Stitching the Collar to the Neckline

- Staystitch the garment neckline just inside the seam allowance; clip into the seam allowance, if necessary, to help the collar fit the garment neckline.
- Place the correct side of the upper collar to the correct side of the neckline; pin all notches together. It is crucial that the front collar and neckline edges be aligned perfectly together; if the collar is positioned too far back or forward, the collar will not turn out correctly. If the collar and neckline do not fit together, then a pattern adjustment is needed. Refer to "STOP! What Do I Do If . . ." later in this chapter, or ask your instructor for help. Stitch a ¼-inch neckline seam; begin and end with a backstitch (see Figure 11.8b).
- From the inside of the garment, pin the folded collar neck edge just over the seamline. Make sure the front corner seam allowances are tucked underneath; they can be bulky, so trim if needed. Pin and handbaste the under collar stand in place. The collar can

be finished with an edgestitch, stitched-in-the-ditch, or slipstitched closed. Figure 11.8c illustrates all three options.

Shirt Collar (Roll-Over Collar)

A shirt collar is traditionally used on men's and women's shirts. Although the collar proportions, amount of spread (distance from each collar point), and shape (pointed, round, or squared) can differ, basically another separate collar is stitched to a mandarin collar to form the shirt collar. The seamline where the collars join becomes the collar roll line (see Figure 11.2d). Notice in Figure 11.1c that the stand-up section of the shirt collar is the same as the mandarin collar in Figure 11.1a.

STABILIZING THE COLLAR

- It is preferable to interface all collar pieces; however, interfacing can be applied to just one side of the shirt collar and collar stand; if all the collar pieces are interfaced, use a lighter-weight interfacing (Figure 11.9a).

Stitching the Collar

- Place the correct sides of upper and under shirt collars together. With the wrong side of the under collar facing up, pin the center backs and collar points of the outer collar edges together. Even though the under collar is smaller, pin all the points exactly together (Figure 11.9a).

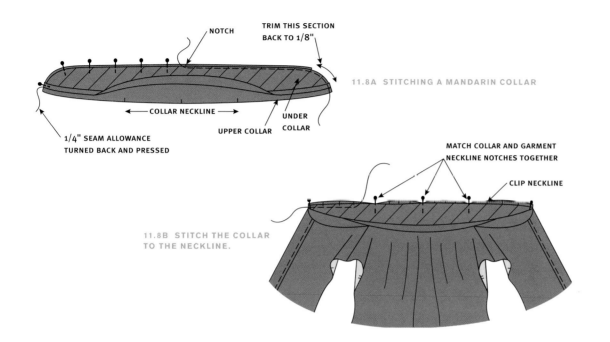

11.8A STITCHING A MANDARIN COLLAR

NOTCH

TRIM THIS SECTION BACK TO 1/8"

COLLAR NECKLINE

UPPER COLLAR

UNDER COLLAR

1/4" SEAM ALLOWANCE TURNED BACK AND PRESSED

MATCH COLLAR AND GARMENT NECKLINE NOTCHES TOGETHER

CLIP NECKLINE

11.8B STITCH THE COLLAR TO THE NECKLINE.

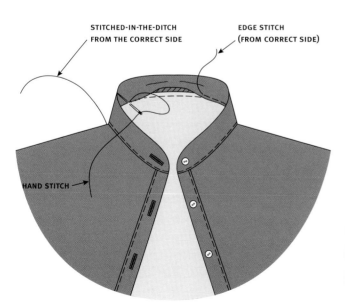

11.8C FINISHING THE COLLAR—THREE OPTIONS

STITCHED-IN-THE-DITCH FROM THE CORRECT SIDE

EDGE STITCH (FROM CORRECT SIDE)

HAND STITCH

- Begin from the neck edge and continue directional stitching to the center back. With the under collar facing up, stitch a ¼-inch seam allowance. Stretch the under collar slightly as you stitch—don't let this worry you, as this is how it is meant to be stitched. Stop ½ inch back from the collar point, reduce the stitch length, and stitch a little farther up, finishing a fraction back from the collar point seam allowance. Leave the needle down in the collar, pivot, and stitch two small stitches across the collar point (the two stitches should measure in total less than ⅛ inch); leave the needle down, pivot again, and stitch the remaining collar seam, finishing at the center back (Figure 11.9b).

PATTERN TIP

Make upper and under collars as illustrated for the shirt/convertible collars in Figure 11.4c. You will notice that the stand for the shirt collar (using the mandarin collar pattern) does not need upper and under collars patterns (see Figure 11.4a). Mark all neckline and collar notches (see Figure 11.3). Place two notches on the center back of the shirt collar to indicate the under collar; this differentiates the under collar from upper collar. Also notch the position where the shirt collar attaches to the collar stand. If the shirt collar is not aligned correctly, the collar won't button correctly at the center front, which ultimately affects how the garment functions and how it sells.

IMPORTANT

The two small stitches across the corner ensure beautiful collar points; stitching to the points without stitching across the point results in corners that bulge and do not look perfectly angled.

- Clip the collar corners to reduce bulk, and grade any thick seams (see Figure 11.9b).
- Press the stitches flat, and press the collar seams open; use the point of the iron so as not to press creases into the collar (Figure 11.9c).
- Turn the collar to the correct side; use a point turner or an awl to sharpen the collar points. From the correct side of the collar, you can use the point of the pin to *gently* pull out the tip of the collar corners. *Never* use your seam ripper to do this!

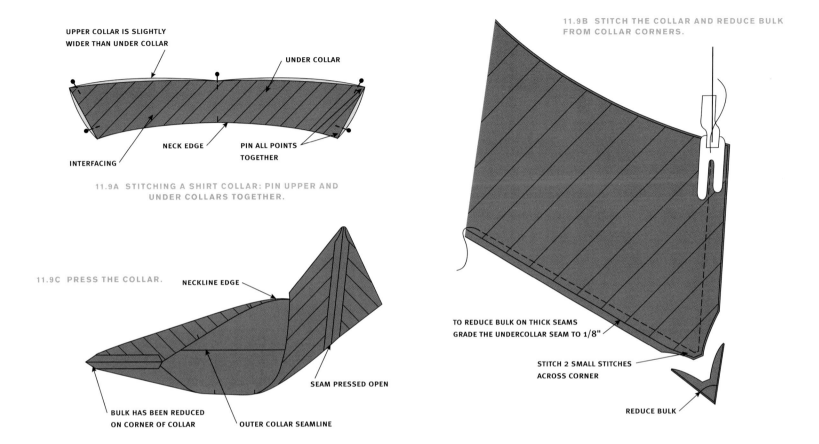

UPPER COLLAR IS SLIGHTLY
WIDER THAN UNDER COLLAR

UNDER COLLAR

NECK EDGE

PIN ALL POINTS
TOGETHER

INTERFACING

**11.9A STITCHING A SHIRT COLLAR: PIN UPPER AND
UNDER COLLARS TOGETHER.**

**11.9B STITCH THE COLLAR AND REDUCE BULK
FROM COLLAR CORNERS.**

TO REDUCE BULK ON THICK SEAMS
GRADE THE UNDERCOLLAR SEAM TO 1/8"

STITCH 2 SMALL STITCHES
ACROSS CORNER

REDUCE BULK

11.9C PRESS THE COLLAR.

NECKLINE EDGE

SEAM PRESSED OPEN

BULK HAS BEEN REDUCED
ON CORNER OF COLLAR

OUTER COLLAR SEAMLINE

- Take time to press the collar; this is impor-tant to the success of the collar. Since the under collar was cut slightly smaller, the collar seamline will sit *slightly* back toward the under collar; this ensures that when the collar rolls over, the seamline is not visible.
- Fold the collar points together and cut off any excess width at the neckline if they are not a mirror image. Even though the collar shape shown in Figure 11.5d is round, the process is the same for every collar shape.
- Place the upper shirt collar section onto one collar stand with the upper collar facing up, and pin together; position each end of the shirt collar to the snipped notches and pin. Machine baste the collars together, just inside the seam allowance; hold the collars taut as you stitch (Figure 11.9d).
- Press a ¼-inch seam allowance on the other collar stand to the wrong side—this is now the *under collar,* and the other collar is now the *upper collar* (Figure 11.9e).
- Turn the collar over and place the under collar stand over the roll-over shirt collar so it is sandwiched between the collar stands. Pin the collar edges together and stitch a ¼-inch seam allowance around the collar stand; make sure the under collar seam allowance remains turned back with the other seam al-lowance lying flat (see Figure 11.9e).
- Press the seam allowance open around the *front curved section* of the collar stand, as Figure 11.5b illustrates. Trim the curved seam allowance back to ⅛ inch—don't clip into the seam allowance, as it does not sit as well when finished. Grade the four layers of

11.9D STITCH THE TWO COLLAR SECTIONS TOGETHER TO FORM THE SHIRT COLLAR.

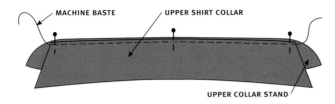

MACHINE BASTE

UPPER SHIRT COLLAR

UPPER COLLAR STAND

11.9E SANDWICH THE COLLAR BETWEEN COLLAR STANDS AND STITCH TOGETHER.

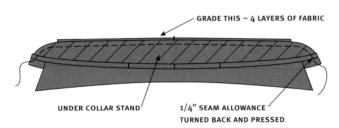

GRADE THIS – 4 LAYERS OF FABRIC

UNDER COLLAR STAND

1/4" SEAM ALLOWANCE TURNED BACK AND PRESSED

4TH LAYER OF FABRIC
3RD LAYER OF FABRIC GRADE
2ND LAYER OF FABRIC GRADE
1ST LAYER OF FABRIC

SEAM LINE

TRIM SEAM ALLOWANCE TO 1/8" AROUND THE CURVE

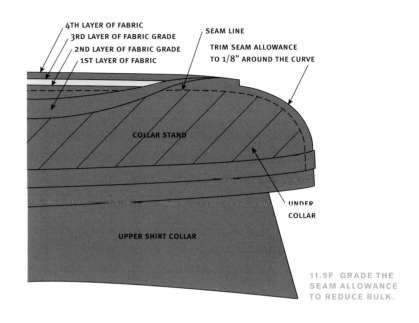

COLLAR STAND

UNDER COLLAR

UPPER SHIRT COLLAR

11.9F GRADE THE SEAM ALLOWANCE TO REDUCE BULK.

PLACE FRONT EDGES TOGETHER

UNDER COLLAR

UPPER COLLAR

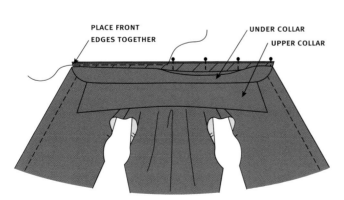

11.9G PIN AND STITCH THE COLLAR NECKLINE TO THE GARMENT NECKLINE.

HANDBASTE COLLAR

TOP STITCHING

BEGIN STITCHING AT CENTER BACK

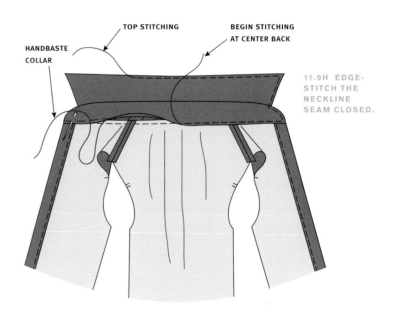

11.9H EDGE-STITCH THE NECKLINE SEAM CLOSED.

collar seam allowance along the collar seam to reduce bulk, and press the collar when completed (Figure 11.9f). The graded seam can also be understitched.

Stitching the Collar to the Neckline

- Staystitch the garment neckline just inside the seam allowance.
- Pin the collar and garment neckline edges together; place front edges exactly together, then pin the center back and shoulder seams to the collar notches. With the under collar stand facing up, stitch a ¼-inch neckline seam; begin and end with a backstitch and clip the threads (Figure 11.9g).
- From the inside of the garment, press the neckline seam allowance up into the collar stand; then pin the folded collar edge to the seamline. Make sure the front collar corner seam allowances are tucked underneath; they can be bulky, so trim if needed. Pin and handbaste in place (Figure 11.9h).
- Edgestitch the under collar from one front edge to the other. If the entire collar edge is stitched as illustrated in Figure 11.9h, then begin stitching from the center-back seam and continue stitching around the collar edge.
- Clip all threads and press the collar.

COLLARS STITCHED WITH FRONT NECK FACING ONLY
Convertible Collar (Roll-Over Collar)

A convertible collar is another type of shirt collar, but it is a different shape from the tra-

ditional man's shirt collar and does not have a collar stand. A convertible collar is constructed with a front neck facing so the collar can be worn open or closed; this is why it is referred to as *convertible*. This design gives the customer versatility in how the collar is worn. Figure 11.1d illustrates the collar buttoned closed.

Stabilizing the Collar

- Apply interfacing to both collars and facings (Figure 11.10a).

Stitching the Collar

- Place the correct sides of the collar together. Match the center back notches and collar points together and, even though the top collar will be slightly larger, pin them exactly together (Figure 11.10a). With the under collar facing up, stitch across the outer collar edges only; hold the collars taut as you stitch a ¼-inch seam allowance. (The under collar will need to be slightly stretched as you stitch; don't worry—this *is* correct!)
- Press the stitches flat and the seam allowance open; grade the *under collar seam only* if bulk needs to be reduced. Figure 11.9f illustrates how to grade the seam allowance.
- Understitch the collar by turning the seam allowance toward the under collar neck edge (see Figure 11.10a).
- Fold the correct sides of the collar together along the first stitching line. Pin both shorter collar edges together, and stitch a ¼-inch seam from the under collar. Stitch directional

from the foldline to the neckline; begin and end with a backstitch (Figure 11.10b).
- Clip the collar corners to reduce bulk (see Figure 11.9b).
- Turn the collar to the correct side and use a point turner or awl to sharpen the collar corners and press the collar.
- Machine baste the neck edges of both front collars together from the front edge of the collar to the shoulder notch (Figure 11.10c).
- Clip into the collar seam allowance at the shoulder position for the *whole* ¼-inch width. The position of the clipping is important to the collar stitching correctly from this point on. Press the upper collar ¼-inch seam allowance back to the wrong side (see Figure 11.10c).

Stitching the Collar to the Neckline

- Staystitch the garment neckline just inside the seam allowance (Figure 11.10c).
- Clip into the shoulder seam allowance for the *whole* ¼-inch width (Figure 11.10c).
- Pin the under collar to the garment neckline. Position the collar to the garment notches

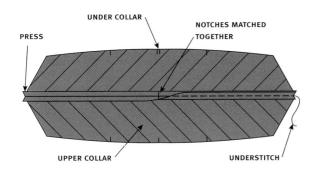

11.10A STITCHING THE CONVERTIBLE COLLAR

PRESS

UNDER COLLAR

NOTCHES MATCHED
TOGETHER

UPPER COLLAR

UNDERSTITCH

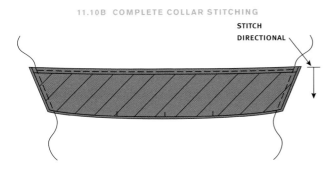

11.10B COMPLETE COLLAR STITCHING

STITCH
DIRECTIONAL

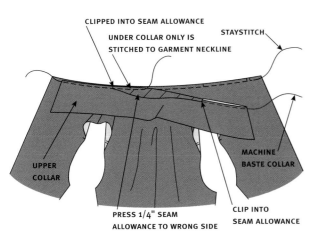

11.10C STITCH THE COLLAR TO THE NECKLINE.

CLIPPED INTO SEAM ALLOWANCE

UNDER COLLAR ONLY IS
STITCHED TO GARMENT NECKLINE

STAYSTITCH

UPPER
COLLAR

MACHINE
BASTE COLLAR

PRESS 1/4" SEAM
ALLOWANCE TO WRONG SIDE

CLIP INTO
SEAM ALLOWANCE

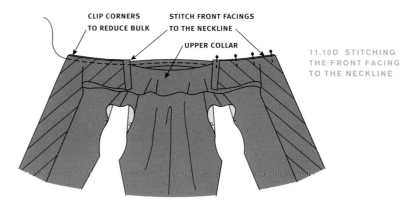

CLIP CORNERS
TO REDUCE BULK

STITCH FRONT FACINGS
TO THE NECKLINE

UPPER COLLAR

**11.10D STITCHING
THE FRONT FACING
TO THE NECKLINE**

for the collar placement, and then match the clipped shoulder position on the collar to the garment shoulder seam. Lift the upper collar out of the way, and pin the garment and under collar necklines together. Stitch a ¼-inch neckline seam. Stitch directional from the front edge to center back, then repeat the process on the other side (see Figure 11.10c).

Stitching the Front Facing to the Neckline
- Press the shoulder seam allowance of the facing to the wrong side.
- Fold the front facing back so the correct sides are facing together, and pin the front necklines together to the shoulder seams. Stitch a ¼-inch seam allowance from the front neckline to the shoulder seams; begin and end with a backstitch (Figure 11.10d). Leave the facing seam allowance at ¼ inch and grade the garment and collar seam allowance to

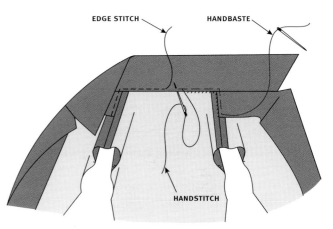

EDGE STITCH

HANDBASTE

HANDSTITCH

11.10E CLOSING THE BACK COLLAR

reduce bulk. Refer to Figure 11.9f to see how to grade the seam allowance.
- Turn the collar to the correct side and press.
- Place the foldline of the upper collar and shoulder facing slightly over the seamline; pin and handbaste in place. From the correct side, stitch-in-the-ditch to secure the collar and facing edges in place (Figure 11.10e) or use an overhand stitch.

Shawl Collar (Roll-Over Collar)

A shawl collar has a lapel on the front section of the garment that is cut all-in-one with the back collar (Figure 11.4f). Varying shapes can be designed for shawl collars. The design in Figure 11.1e illustrates a narrow shawl collar on a wrap jacket. The collar can be designed in a contrasting color or fabric as this figure illustrates.

Stabilizing the Collar

How the shawl collar is stabilized does depend on the fabric weight. It is advised to stabilize both sides of the collar for jackets and coats. This means underlining the garment as the garment and collar are cut all-in-one. However, for a blouse or dress you may only want to stabilize the facing.

Preparing the Collars

Complete the following stitching on the garment and facing. The stitching is identical for both. Figures 11.11a and b illustrate the following stitching:

NOTES

Press the seam allowance back ¼ inch if the garment is not going to have a back neck facing. A shawl collar can be stitched with or without a back neck facing. Figure 11.11b illustrates the back neck seam allowance pressed back.

- Staystitch the back neck; pivot on the shoulder/neckline corner, and staystitch ¾ inch in length on the shoulder seam.
- Stitch the front darts and press. (The darts help to shape the collar.)
- Stitch the center-back seams together, and press open.
- Clip into the corners at the matchpoints (the staystitching reinforces the corners). See Figure 11.11a.

Stitching the Collar

- Pin the necklines together, placing the center-back collar to the center-back garment neckline and the shoulder/neckline matchpoints together. Stitch directional using a

NOTES

If the garment will have a back neck facing, then stitch the collar to the facing just as you have stitched the previous step in Figure 11.11c. Note that a shawl collar can be stitched with or without a back neck facing—this is the designer's choice.

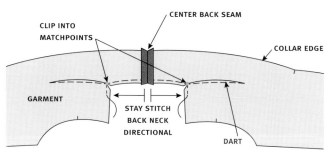

11.11A PREPARING THE FACING AND GARMENT: GARMENT

CLIP INTO MATCHPOINTS • CENTER BACK SEAM • COLLAR EDGE • GARMENT • STAY STITCH BACK NECK DIRECTIONAL • DART

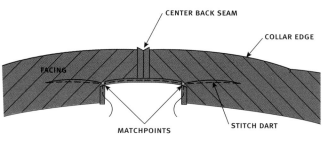

CENTER BACK SEAM • COLLAR EDGE • FACING • MATCHPOINTS • STITCH DART

11.11B FACING

¼-inch seam allowance on the neckline and ½-inch on the shoulder seams. Stitch from the center-back seam to the shoulder matchpoints, pivot on the corner, and stitch ½-inch shoulder seams (Figure 11.11c).

- Press the shoulder and neckline seams closed when there is no back neck facing applied. Press the seams open when a back neck facing is stitched to the front facing. Figure 11.11d illustrates the seams pressed open and closed.
- Pin the collar edges together. Clip into any seam allowance that needs to open to make it possible to stitch the seam lines together. Stitch directional. Begin stitching a ¼-inch seam from the center back and down toward the front of the collar to the hem.

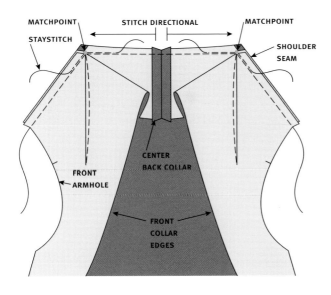

MATCHPOINT

STITCH DIRECTIONAL

MATCHPOINT

STAYSTITCH

SHOULDER SEAM

CENTER BACK COLLAR

FRONT ARMHOLE

FRONT COLLAR EDGES

11.11C STITCHING SHOULDER AND NECKLINE SEAMS

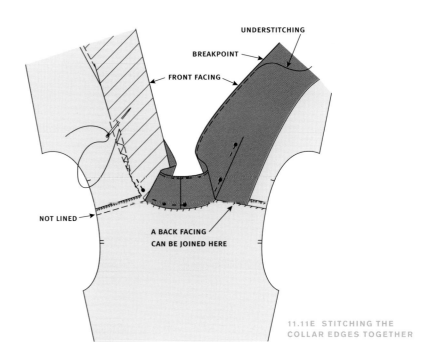

UNDERSTITCHING

BREAKPOINT

FRONT FACING

NOT LINED

A BACK FACING CAN BE JOINED HERE

11.11E STITCHING THE COLLAR EDGES TOGETHER

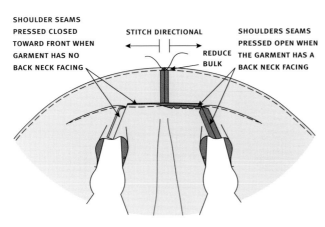

SHOULDER SEAMS PRESSED CLOSED TOWARD FRONT WHEN GARMENT HAS NO BACK NECK FACING

STITCH DIRECTIONAL

REDUCE BULK

SHOULDERS SEAMS PRESSED OPEN WHEN THE GARMENT HAS A BACK NECK FACING

11.11D CLOSING THE BACK NECK WITH NO BACK FACING

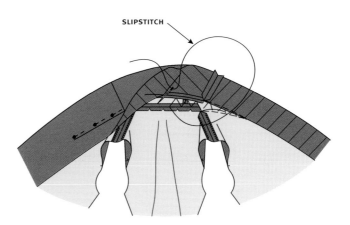

SLIPSTITCH

11.11F CLOSING THE SHAWL COLLAR WITH A BACK NECK FACING

- Always reduce bulk on intersecting seams; this is the case for the center-back seam join in Figure 11.11d. To see how this is done, refer back to Figure 6.29a.
- Press the stitches flat, and then press the collar seam open. Since the collar edge is curved, place the garment over a tailor's ham to press curved seams open, as illustrated for curved darts in Figure 4.3b.
- To grade the seam allowance, cut the garment seam allowance back to ⅛ inch and understitch the seam; finish understitching 1½ inches back from the breakpoint. (Remember that the breakpoint is the point where the collar folds back.) If the understitching goes beyond this point, it will be visible when the collar rolls over. For understitching collars, refer back to Figure 11.5c.
- Turn the collar to the correct side and press.
- To close the back collar without a facing, pin the foldline of the under collar to the seamline, and also pin the darts together. Using an overhand stitch, hand stitch into every neckline stitch to secure the collar in place. Turn back the facing and hand stitch the darts lightly together, using a slipstitch. Also slipstitch the folded edge of the facing to the shoulder seam (Figure 11.11e). A slipstitch is illustrated in Figure 15.9.

- For a shawl collar with a back neck facing, press the back garment and collar neck seam allowances open. Pin the open seams together on the seamline. Begin slipstitching from one dart, and hand stitch across the back neck to the other dart, as illustrated in Figure 11.11f.
- If there is no lining to be attached, make sure the facing edges are finished and hand stitched to the garment shoulder seams.

COLLARS STITCHED WITH FRONT AND BACK NECK FACINGS
Notched Lapel Collar (Roll-Over Collar)

A notched lapel collar is mainly used on tailored jackets and coats. Refer to Figure 11.1e, in the Style I.D., to see this popular collar style. The

lapel is the front section that folds back to form a revere. The notched section of the collar is the "L" shape, formed when the collar is stitched to the lapel. The position of the notch and the shape is the designer's choice—both can be round rather than pointed, or one can be round and the other pointed—there are no rules! If the garment is underlined, this should be applied to the cut fabric pieces before any stitching takes place. Refer to Chapter 3, "Underlining—Fully Covering the Fabric."

- Apply the stabilizer (fusible or sew-in) to the upper and under collars and facing.
- Join the shoulder seams of the facing and the garment together (Figure 11.12a).
- Staystitch the neckline of the garment and facing to the matchpoints (see Figure 11.12a).
- Stitch the center-back seam of the under collars, and press open.

- Stitch the under collar to the garment neckline and the upper collar to the facing. Place the correct sides together, and pin the matchpoints of the lapel and collar together; position the collar shoulder notches to the garment shoulder seams. Stitch directional, using a ¼-inch seam allowance. Begin stitching from the matchpoints (begin with a backstitch) and stitch to the center-back seam. Repeat on the other side (Figure 11.12b).

- Press both neckline seams open; clip the garment and facing necklines so the seam can open and lie flat, if needed (Figure 11.12c).
- To stitch the notched section of the collar, place the upper and under collar matchpoints *directly* together. To stitch the following steps, stitch directional, from the matchpoint to the center back of the collar. Position the machine needle down in the fabric at the matchpoints, stitch forward and back (this is the backstitch), and stitch to the center-back collar. Repeat on the other side; overlap the stitches on the center back by 1/2 inch (see Figure 11.12c).
- Place the garment and facing lapel matchpoints together. Position the machine needle down in the fabric directly on the matchpoints. Backstitch forward to the corner of the lapel, pivot and stitch down the front of the garment. Repeat on the other side (see Figure 11.12c). On pointed collars, use the same stitching technique illustrated in Figure 11.9b. Stitch two small stitches across the corner of the collar to achieve beautiful collar points.

- Use the same principle outlined in Figure 11.5d to make sure the collar and lapel shapes on both sides are mirror images. If they are not exactly the same, then restitch the collar points so they mirror each other.
- Reduce bulk on the collar and lapel corners (see Figure 11.9b). Press the seams flat and then press open; turn the collar to the correct side of the fabric, and sharpen the corners with a point turner or awl.
- To help hold the collar in place, lightly slipstitch the center-back seams together (the stitches *must* be invisible from the correct side).
- To close the collar, slipstitch the collar seams together. This must be done from the point of the lapel seam to the other side, as illustrated in Figure 11.12d.

STITCHING COLLARS IN TRICKY FABRICS
Sheer Fabric

Do use the correct machine needle size when stitching collars in sheer fabrics.

Do use self-fabric to stabilize sheer collars. Silk organza is also an excellent stabilizer to use on sheer fabrics.

Do cut all collar seam allowances back to ⅛ inch so they are even. On sheer fabric, the seam allowance is visible from the face of the garment.

Do be careful when designing collars in sheer fabrics; consider how many seams are in the collar, as they will be noticeable. For example, a sheer shawl collar would have fewer seams than a notched lapel collar.

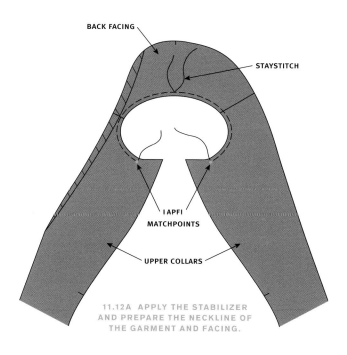

11.12A APPLY THE STABILIZER AND PREPARE THE NECKLINE OF THE GARMENT AND FACING.

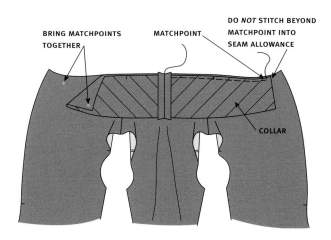

11.12B STITCH THE UNDER COLLAR TO THE GARMENT. STITCH THE UPPER COLLAR TO THE FACING.

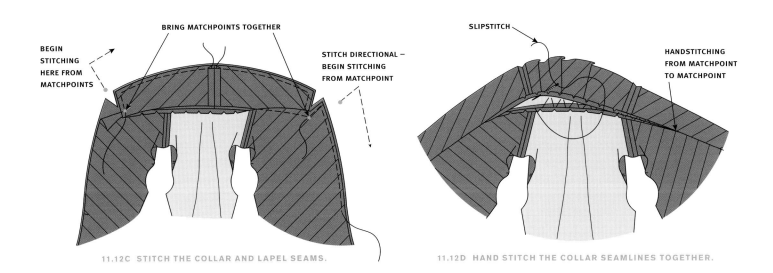

11.12C STITCH THE COLLAR AND LAPEL SEAMS.

11.12D HAND STITCH THE COLLAR SEAMLINES TOGETHER.

Do consider stitching several single layers of roll-over collars in lightweight sheer silk organza to create the shirt collar illustrated in Figure 11.13a. Three or four layers of single sheer collars will not create bulk but will create a fabulous textured look. Before the collars are inserted into the collar stand, stitch a hem finish around the outer edge of each collar. Instructions for doing this are outlined in Chapter 15.

Don't use a fusible interfacing on sheer collars—use a sew-in. The glue on fusibles may seep through on the face of the collar.

Lace

Do stitch collars in lace, but use a stabilizer to complement the lace; silk organza and netting are perfect stabilizers for lace.

Do consider stitching organza or satin silk collar and cuffs to a lace shirt as contrast.

Do cut lace scallop borders or motifs and appliqué them to collar edges

Don't stitch collars in heavy lace.

Don't topstitch lace collars.

Satin

Do use a sew-in stabilizer in the collar, as fusible interfacing can change the look of the fabric surface.

Do stitch collars in satin; however, match the fabric weight to the collar design.

Do be careful topstitching satin collars; there are no rules here, but sample first to see if you like the look.

Do use the correct machine needle size when stitching collars in satin; the wrong size or a blunt needle will cause little pulls to appear in the collar and spoil the look of the entire garment.

Beaded Fabric

Do smash all beads from the seam allowances, as stitching over the beads will break the needle.

Do use an interfacing that suits the fabric weight.

Do consider using a contrasting fabric such as silk georgette, organza, or satin silk charmeuse for collars to complement the beaded fabric.

Don't stitch complicated collars in beaded fabric.

Knits

Do use a stable interfacing that takes away the stretch element on the knit, as collars that have a closure don't need to stretch.

Don't stabilize a roll collar that stretches over the head, and make sure the collar fits over the head comfortably—this is how fashion meets function!

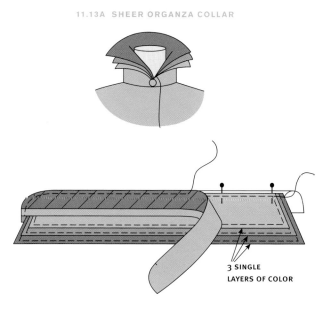

3 SINGLE
LAYERS OF COLOR

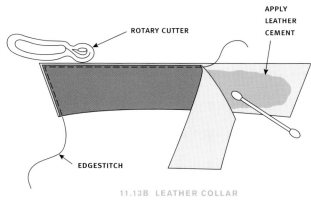

APPLY
LEATHER
CEMENT

ROTARY CUTTER

EDGESTITCH

Denim

Do stitch all kinds of collars in denim; be aware that some denim may not need to be stabilized because of the weight, yet other denim weights will need stabilizing, so sample first.

Do topstitch collars in denim; use double thread or topstitching thread in self or contrasting colors. Denim *loves* to be topstitched!

Velvet

Do be careful when stitching collars in velvet. Velvet is difficult to stitch and press, and collars need a lot of pressing to look fabulous.

Do choose simple styles of collars, such as mandarin or convertible, that do not require as much stitching and pressing as a notched lapel collar.

Do use a sew-in stabilizer; napped fabrics such as velvet are affected by pressing, and a fusible interfacing will iron-mark and squash the pile.

Don't place collar patterns on velvet fabric in both directions; since velvet is a napped fabric, always cut collars in one direction.

Leather

Do make collars in leather. They can be stitched, clipped, and turned.

Do topstitch around the outer collar edges, as they will not press very well.

Do use a leather sewing machine needle to stitch leather.

Do some sample stitching first on the collar corners to see if bulk is a problem.

Do reduce bulk in heavier-weight leather by securing two collar pieces together with leather cement. Apply between the collars and, with a rubber mallet, pound the collars to fasten them together; then edgestitch the collars. Cut the collar edges with a rotary cutter so the edges are perfectly aligned (see Figure 11.13b).

Do stabilize collars in leather; protect the surface with paper, and press low-heat fusible interfacing with a dry iron.

Don't try a soft roll collar in leather, as it won't roll. This collar needs to be bias cut, and leather does not have a grainline in the same way fabric does.

Faux Fur

Do stitch collars in faux fur, as they are so warm and snug for winter jackets and coats.

Do consider fur on the upper collar and use a lightweight fabric such as a satin silk or a lining fabric as the under collar, as both will reduce bulk.

Do use a sew-in stabilizer to suit the weight of fur.

Do trim all the fur from all collar and neckline seam allowances to reduce bulk. If this is not done, the collar will not stitch well (Figure 6.51a).

Do catchstitch by hand any open seams in fur, as fur does not press well. Refer to Figure 6.51b to see how this is done.

Don't ignore the bulk that is created when stitching seams in fur; it is important to reduce any bulk on collar corners.

Heavyweight Fabric

Do choose the collar style carefully in heavyweight fabrics; these fabrics stitch really well when the collars are generous, oversize, and stitched to jackets and coats.

Don't stitch small, dainty collars in heavyweight fabric.

TRANSFER YOUR KNOWLEDGE

The designer can have fun designing different collar shapes. Draping collars on the form is an ideal way of creating a new look in collars. No matter what the shape of collar, transfer your cutting and stitching knowledge. Here are some ways to transfer your knowledge:

• Collars can be topstitched by machine or by hand. Take a look at some of the stitches that can be used to topstitch. Figures 6.24, 6.27, and 6.54a picture some different options. Figure 11.14a illustrates a machine topstitch and a hand pick stitch, highlighting the edge of the notched lapel collar.

• The same collar in Figure 11.14a can also have bias loops inserted into the collar seam as a decorative finish. The stitching order for bias loops is outlined in Chapter 17, "Bias Loops."

• Stitch a bias binding around a collar edge. Use the same stitching technique for applying the Hong Kong finish in Figure 6.33d. The collar would draw all the attention if a patterned, contrasting bias binding was used. As this figure illustrates, the binding can be machine or hand stitched in place.

• A ruffle can be inserted in the collar seam, as illustrated in Figure 11.14b. Ruffles can be cut double (on the fold) or as a single layer. (In a single ruffle, the hem needs to be stitched before insertion. For more information, refer to Chapter 10.) To insert a ruffle in the collar seam:
  • Machine baste the ruffle to the upper collar edge; push a lot more gathered ruffle into the collar corners so the ruffle has room to span out around the corner of the collar without looking tight after the collar is stitched and turned.

• Place the under collar over the upper collar so the ruffle is sandwiched in between. With the upper collar facing up, stitch a ¼-inch seam allowance; stitch directly on top of the previous machine basting stitches.

• Reduce bulk by grading the collar seam; press and turn the collar and stitch to the neckline. Notice that the ruffle is part of the neckline collar measurement in Figure 11.14b. Make sure the width of the ruffle is taken off the length of the neckline in the collar pattern.

• Stitch a bias/tie collar to the wrist of a blouse or dress. Transfer your knowledge by following the same instructions. You will need to stitch a darted placket in the wrist first before applying the cuff. Stitch as illustrated in Figures 11.7a and b. This cuff stitched to a gathered wrist (with a placket) will look sensational! Refer to Chapter 13 for additional details.

• In Figure 11.14c, a bias trim has been stitched to the surface of the collar before the collar is stitched to the neckline. Notice the bias has been pleated on the corners of the collar. This is an excellent way to turn the bias on an angled corner—in fact, the entire bias strip could be pleated all the way around the collar edge if the designer chooses. Remember, a bias cut does not fray, so the edges can be left raw.

• Insert piping into a collar seam just the same way it has been inserted into a curved, circu-lar, or angled seam in Figures 6.19, 6.20, and 6.21. Choose the binding technique that suits the shape of the collar edge and transfer your knowledge.

STRETCH YOUR CREATIVITY

Designing new and interesting collars offers an avenue for expressing creativity, especially when making jackets and coats. Collars can be the focus of the garment, and an attention stop-per when an unusual collar design is worn, es-pecially when it is well made.

The following list gives some ideas for how to be creative with collars. The list is not exhaus-tive, but it offers many possibilities. Add your own ideas to this list:

• Combine two types of collars. The coat collar in Figure 11.15a is a combination stand-up and roll-over collar.

• A bias-cut roll collar can be cut longer than the neckline; both collar edges can be pleated at random (not evenly) and stitched to the gar-ment neckline. How this collar looks in design is illustrated in Figure 11.15b. The choice of fabric weight is important; a fabric that is too heavy will look too bulky in this design.

• The collar in Figure 11.15c is a variation of the notched lapel collar. Notice that the lapel has been cut and spread in the patternmaking stage to allow for gathering. Because of this, the lapel cannot be cut all-in-one with the front section of the jacket. The lapel is a separate collar piece that is stitched to the neckline. Notice that the lapel overlaps the collar.

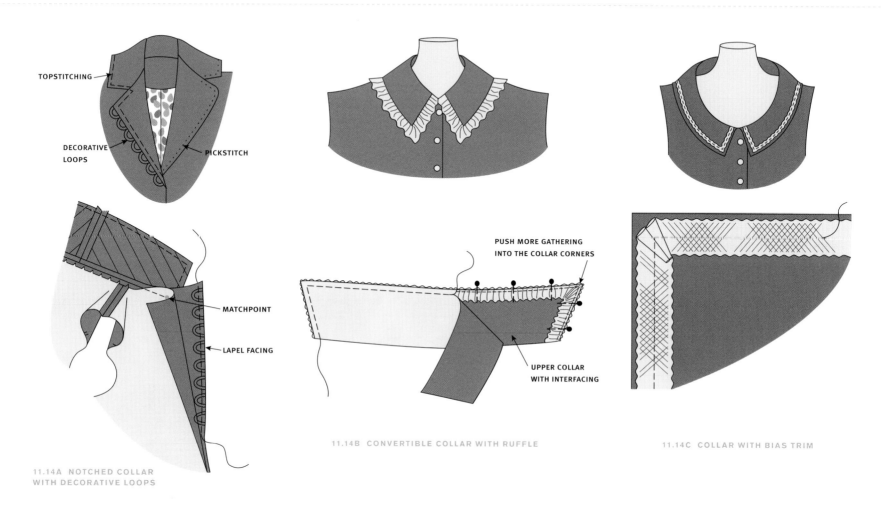

TOPSTITCHING

DECORATIVE
LOOPS

PICKSTITCH

MATCHPOINT

LAPEL FACING

**11.14A NOTCHED COLLAR
WITH DECORATIVE LOOPS**

PUSH MORE GATHERING
INTO THE COLLAR CORNERS

UPPER COLLAR
WITH INTERFACING

11.14B CONVERTIBLE COLLAR WITH RUFFLE

11.14C COLLAR WITH BIAS TRIM

- The collar stitched to the warm winter jacket in Figure 11.15d is a roll-over collar that has been cut wider and then padded with light-weight polyester fiber, which does not add weight. (It is the same fiber used to stuff toys and cushions.) The final weight of a coat is important because a coat or jacket that is too heavy to carry or wear is not *functional* and may prevent a garment from selling.

STOP! WHAT DO I DO IF . . .
. . . my collar shape is uneven and not a mirror image on both sides of the collar?

If the collar is already stitched to the neckline, carefully take off the larger side of the collar; press it flat, and trim and restitch the collar to mirror the smaller shape on the other side. Then stitch the collar back onto the neckline.

. . . my collar is too tight around the neckline and it won't button up?

Carefully take the collar off the neckline. Recut the garment neckline lower all the way around the neck edge. Cutting the neckline ⅛ inch lower all the way around could add another inch more in length. The neckline could also be lowered in the front only. Measure the new neck measurement and make a new collar

Stretch Your Creativity

11.15A COMBINATION OF STAND-UP AND ROLL-OVER COLLARS

11.15C VARIATION OF NOTCHED LAPEL COLLAR

11.15B VARIATION OF BIAS/ROLL COLLAR

11.15D VARIATION OF SHAWL COLLAR

> ⊵⊵⊵⊵⊵⊵⊵⊵⊵⊵⊵⊵⊵⊵
>
> **IMPORTANT**
>
> It's important to make all adjustments in small increments to begin with, as taking a huge chunk from the shoulder seams would throw the fit of the neckline off.

pattern to fit the new neck measurement. Restitch the new collar and stitch onto the garment neckline. In the end you will be pleased you made the effort to make a new collar, as you will now have a functional collar rather than a dysfunctional collar!

. . . my collar stabilizer is too heavy?

If you have enough fabric, then recut and restitch another collar and apply a lighter-weight stabilizer to both sides of the collar. Sample first to get the correct weight! If you have no more fabric, then try to remove the stabilizer from one side of the collar. This could be difficult if you used a fusible stabilizer. Sew-in stabilizers can be cut away from the seamline. If you are unable to purchase more fabric, perhaps purchase another fabric to complement the style and look of your garment. Then use this as an opportunity to learn to sample your stabilizer first next time!

. . . I don't like the collar style on my garment? Can I change the collar design?

Yes, you can! However, this will be difficult if the buttonholes have been stitched to the front of the garment. Discuss the available options with your instructor. If it is possible, do some sketches so you have plenty of ideas to choose from. The important thing is that the new collar design you choose *must* be the same neck measurement as the garment neckline. Make a muslin first to see if you like the shape and size of the new collar. Then off you go to stitch your new collar and apply it to the neckline.

SELF-CRITIQUE

This is the time to stand back and take a detailed look at your collar. Ask yourself the question: "Am I happy with the way my collar sits when I place my garment on the form?"

Ask yourself the following questions to critique your collar:

- Does the collar sit well on the form; does the collar stand up, sit flat, or roll over as you would like it to?
- Does the stabilizer hold the collar to the desired structure?

- Do the seams look bulky because they were not graded to reduce bulk?
- Does the collar fit comfortably around the neck, not feeling too tight? Do you think you have combined function and fashion together with the collar design and fit?
- Does the collar seamline roll slightly back to the under collar, or does it show? Did you use upper and under collar pattern pieces?
- Is the topstitching on the collar parallel to the collar seamline?
- When you stand back and view the overall garment, does the collar blend with the overall design or does bad collar stitching detract from the overall design?
- Did you stitch enough samples to make an informed decision regarding the best stabilizer and seam finish for the collar?

REVIEW CHECKLIST

- Do I understand the three types of collars: sit-flat, stand-up, and roll-over?

- Do I understand that all collars need a collar stand to be a collar? Do I understand that collar stands can be different heights?
- Do I understand the importance of beginning with correct patterns, with both the garment and collar necklines the same length and notched so they can be accurately stitched together?
- Do I understand that correct patterns set me up to achieve correct stitching?
- Do I understand that the stabilizer needs to be a lighter weight when it is applied to both sides of the collar?
- Do I understand the importance of having upper and under collars, and do I understand the difference they make?
- Do I understand that staystitching prevents the neckline from stretching in the stitching process?
- In what ways can I improve on my collar stitching in the future?

Facings: Encasing Unfinished Edges

Facings, when properly sewn, will professionally finish the raw edges on necklines with or without collars, the center fronts of jackets, blouses, and sleeveless garments. Hemlines on a wrist cuff, a skirt, or pants can also be finished and supported by a facing. Specially shaped edges provide an exciting area for design—for example, scallops, which can only be finished by using a facing.

Facings are both decorative and functional and fit into three general categories: shaped, extended/self, and bias. In this chapter, we develop the techniques for applying facings with correct interfacing support and finishing methods, ensuring that the inside of the facing is as beautifully encased and finished as the outside of the garment.

STYLE I.D.

Here are some neckline styles that illustrate what this chapter is about. Look at the variation of facings and by the end of this chapter you will know how these techniques are stitched.

The Style I.D. has examples of commonly faced areas, as shown in the "Little Black Dress," and is a suggestion of basic styles (Figure 12.1).

GATHER YOUR TOOLS

For the techniques in this chapter you will need interfacing, marking pen, dressmaker transfer paper, tracing wheel, scissors, rotary cutter and mat, appropriate needle and thread, cording for piping or 2-ply nylon plastic canvas yarn.

KEY TERMS

All-in-one
All-in-one Facing
Armhole Facing
Bands
Bias Facing
Concealed Placket
Cowl
Decorative Facing
Extended/Self-Facing
Functional Facing
Keyhole Facing
Narrow Bias Facing
Neckline Facing
Placket
Shaped Facing
Slashed Facing
Waistline Facing

Style I.D.

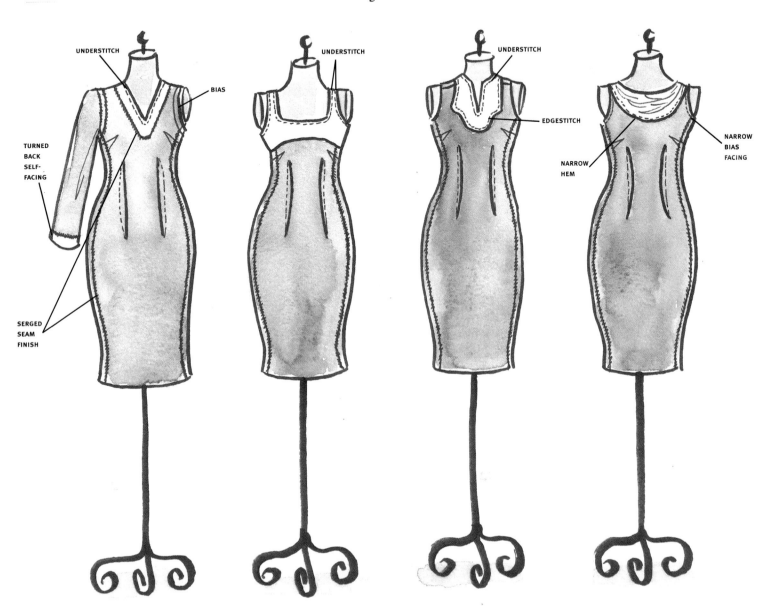

12.1A SHAPED FACING
V-NECK AND BIAS

12.1B ALL-IN-ONE

12.1C SLASH

12.1D COWL BIAS

Think Ahead—Order Now

Oftentimes chain fabric stores do not have an extensive selection of interfacings, stabilizers, silk organza, knit ribbing, or piping and trims. Once you decide what type of facing is part of the design, purchase the appropriate supplies, selecting the correct fabric, and order as soon as possible. Refer to Chapter 3, "Introduction to Stabilizers," for a list of fusible and sew-in options and the "Where to Buy" section of this text.

Before applying facings, all flat construction that can be completed should be:

- Darts should be sewn and pressed, and zipper application and pockets completed.
- If collars, ruffles, or other trims are part of the design, they should be basted in place in the seam before the facing is positioned and stitched.
- Whether or not the shoulder or side seams have been sewn at this stage depends on the type of facing that is being applied, and should follow the steps for that particular technique.

NOW LET'S GET STARTED
What Is a Facing?

A facing can be both functional and decorative. A **functional facing** is a piece of fabric that is attached to the raw edge of some part of a garment in order to finish that edge. It is turned to the inside of the garment. Depending on the shape of the area where it's applied and the weight of the fabric, the facing may need to be cut ⅛ inch smaller or wider, to prevent it from rolling to the front of the garment. A facing should not be visible on the correct side of the garment.

Facings are used in areas such as necklines, armholes of sleeveless dresses, and openings at the garment front or back. Hems can also be faced, and need to be in the case of an unusual shape. Refer to Chapter 15, Figure 15.1a, a coat-dress with a shaped hem.

Facings also provide support for the area being finished, and choosing the appropriate stabilizer for the fabric and the garment area being faced is of the utmost importance. Refer to Chapter 3, "Introduction to Stabilizers." The facing should lie flat; a bulky, rippling edge is not attractive!

Several steps contribute to the success of a facing: grading the seam allowance to reduce bulk; clipping into curves; trimming away excess seam allowance; and, *very important, understitching* the facing to the seam allowance to prevent it from rolling to the outside of the garment. Design students often omit this step to save time, resulting in a facing that keeps rolling to the front of the garment—an unfortunate detail that speaks of novice sewing skills. Don't worry, with practice your work will achieve professional quality.

A **decorative facing** is a piece of fabric that is attached to the raw edge of a garment to finish that edge, but turned to the correct side of the garment, functioning as a trim as well as a facing. Facings that will be turned to the outside of the garment should be cut about ⅛ inch to ¼ inch larger at the outer edge of the facing to allow for the turn of the fabric at the seamline. The weight, bulk, and texture of the fabric for the decorative facing should be considered when determining how much larger to make the facing. Excellent trimming and grading of the seam allowances also contribute to the flat turning of the decorative facing.

All facings should have beautifully finished edges when not attached to a lining. The edge finishes should contribute to the flatness of the facing. Several choices to consider are zigzag stitched, serged, clean finished, or a Hong Kong finish, or using the interfacing to "face" the facing. Sample these types of finishes in the fabric of the garment to determine which is the most suitable. Refer to Chapter 6, "Seams," for additional information.

> **NOTE**
>
> When pressing, a ridge sometimes occurs on the front of the garment from the seam finish if it is too bulky for the fabric, or from serger threads if that is the seam finish used. Using strips of brown paper bag between the facing edge and the garment reduces this effect. If this ridge continues to appear on the garment front, consider using a different edge finish that is flatter and smoother.

The Three Major Types of Facings: Shaped, Extended/Self-Facing, and Bias

What type of facing goes where? Which facing to use depends on the style and design of the garment, the purpose and use of the garment, how the garment will be cared for, the type and

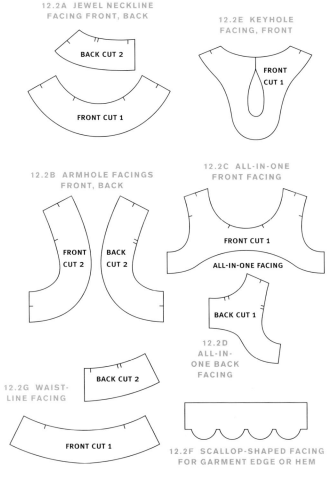

12.2A JEWEL NECKLINE FACING FRONT, BACK

BACK CUT 2

FRONT CUT 1

12.2B ARMHOLE FACINGS FRONT, BACK

FRONT CUT 2

BACK CUT 2

12.2G WAIST-LINE FACING

BACK CUT 2

FRONT CUT 1

12.2E KEYHOLE FACING, FRONT

FRONT CUT 1

12.2C ALL-IN-ONE FRONT FACING

FRONT CUT 1

ALL-IN-ONE FACING

BACK CUT 1

12.2D ALL-IN-ONE BACK FACING

12.2F SCALLOP-SHAPED FACING FOR GARMENT EDGE OR HEM

12.2b), and the combination facing called all-in-one, which is a one-piece facing for the neckline and armhole (Figure 12.2c and d). A keyhole/slashed neckline facing (Figure 12.2e) has a slit at the neckline, often in a contrasting color. Bias may continue around the neckline to finish it, or sometimes a collar is added. A shaped hem such as scallops (Figure 12.2f), or any other shape, would also be faced and the facing piece would match the shape of the hem, such as the sleeve shown in Figure 12.3b. The waistline of skirts and pants can be finished with a shaped facing (Figure 12.2g).

Extended/self-facings are facings cut in one piece with the garment. The edges are cut on the straight grain, and the facing is folded back to the inside of the garment (Figure 12.3a). The extended facing could be turned to the correct side of the garment to utilize a contrasting reverse side of the fabric; however, the stabilizer then has to be applied to the correct side of the garment. It is critical to transfer the markings and to interface appropriately for the type of closure that will be used. Extended facings are used at fronts and backs of garments. Plackets lap over each other and are extensions of the garment that allow for the placement of buttonholes, snaps, or other closures (Figure 12.4a). Plackets are found on sleeves with cuffs and center fronts of polo-style shirts or blouses. (See Chapter 13 for additional styles of plackets.) Jackets use concealed plackets in one or two-piece styles (Figure 12.4b).

Bias facings are flexible and easily shaped. The bias facing can be pressed to match the shape of the area it is being applied to by indi-cating the bias on the pattern piece. Bias facing can be used to replace bulky fabric or fabric that would be irritable against the skin. Using bias is particularly useful when working with sheers, where a wider facing would be too visible. Bias can be applied to any edge, and the student designer can determine what width best suits the garment. Bias can become the focal point of a garment when it is turned to the front and additional trimmings, such as raw edge trims, cording, piping, or braiding, are added. This is one of Chanel's stylistic signatures.

A cowl is a neckline finish that is self-faced (Figure 12.3c). It is cut on the bias and drapes back onto itself. The entire garment piece can be cut on the bias, such as the front of a blouse, or a section can be cut on the bias to create the cowl and inserted into a garment such as in a dress.

Stitching the Facings

Before stitching most facings to the garment, the facing pieces must be sewn together; appropriate stabilizer must be applied, whether it is fusible or sewn in; and the edges must be finished.

- Transfer all the markings to the facing pieces and stabilizer.
- *Staystitch* the edge of the seam allowance that will join the garment (Figure 12.5a). Check the cut edge of the facing with the pattern piece to be sure that the edge matches the original measurements.
- Match the seamline notches of the facings carefully. Smooth, continuous edges are especially important in the curved areas of the facing.

weight of the garment fabric, and the construction methods being used. The garment dictates the type of facing to use: a sleeveless garment uses an all-in-one facing, whereas a garment with sleeves uses a neckline facing at the neck only.

Shaped facings (Figure 12.2) match the area they are being sewn to, such as necklines (Figure 12.2a), sleeveless armholes (Figure

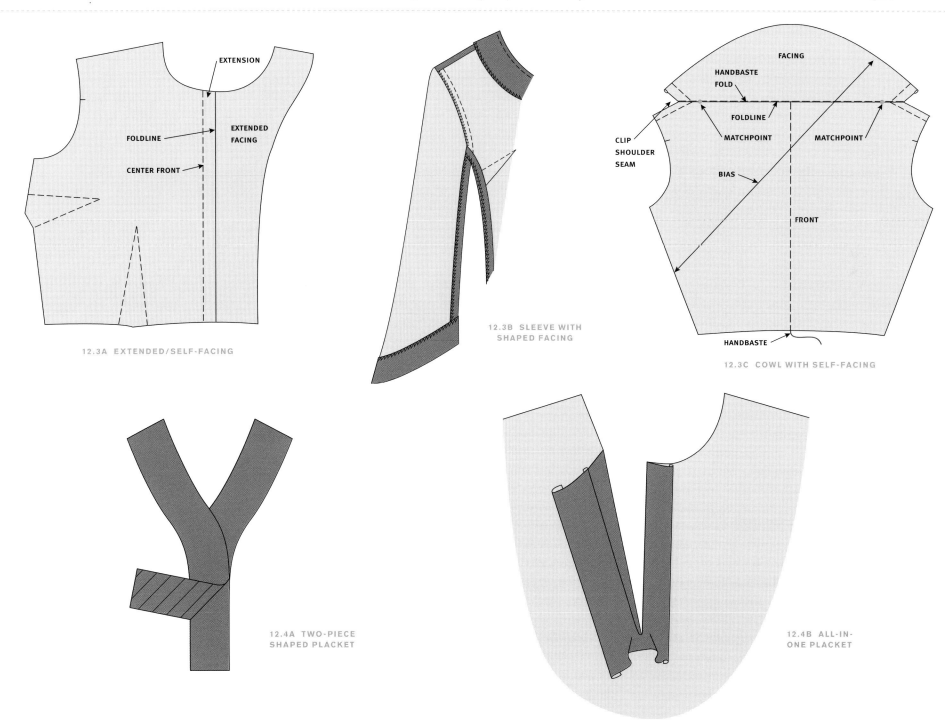

12.3A EXTENDED/SELF-FACING

EXTENSION
EXTENDED FACING
FOLDLINE
CENTER FRONT

12.3B SLEEVE WITH SHAPED FACING

12.3C COWL WITH SELF-FACING

FACING
HANDBASTE FOLD
FOLDLINE
MATCHPOINT
MATCHPOINT
CLIP SHOULDER SEAM
BIAS
FRONT
HANDBASTE

12.4A TWO-PIECE SHAPED PLACKET

12.4B ALL-IN-ONE PLACKET

- Sew the facing seam allowances together; press. Sew the seam allowances of the fusible interfacing together; finger-press open. Trim seam allowances to ¼ inch (Figure 12.5a). If using a sew-in stabilizer, carefully trim away the seam allowance after it has been stitched to the facing. Refer to Chapter 3, "Introduction to Stabilizers." The method as shown in Figure 3.20 would be more cost-effective in production.
- Using a pressing cloth, fuse the stabilizer to the facings.
- Finish the edge of the facings with an appropriate finish (Figure 12.5b).

Finishing Off Facings

Facings finish off the edges of garments; however, the facings themselves must also be finished. The garment should always look as good on the inside as it does on the outside. There are many ways to finish the edges of the facings. Also refer to Chapter 6, "Seams," for further details.

Edge Finishes

The garment fabric being used in the design is the first consideration in how to finish the facing, followed by how it was stabilized. The goal of

> **IMPORTANT**
>
> *Sample* all of the choices available for finishing the facing edge in order to find the best one. Lumpy, ridged facings detract from the finished look of the garment.

the facing is to be flat and smooth, so whatever finish is chosen, it must enable this goal.

- If the fabric is firmly woven but bulky, simply cut the edge, and stitch a straight stitch ¼ inch from the edge.
- Edgestitching the facing edge is suitable for lighter-weight fabrics; however, the straight stitching of this technique is somewhat difficult along curved edges if not carefully sewn.
- If the garment is not lined, use the elegant Hong Kong finish to complete the edges of any exposed facings or seams.
- A luxurious, contrasting fabric can add a touch of interest to the inside of the garment when using the Hong Kong finish. (Refer to Chapter 6, "Seams," and Figures 6.33a and b. The Hong Kong finish has been used to finish the edges of a partially lined coat in Figures 16.25c and d.)
- Bias-cut fabric does not ravel—thus no finishing is required on the edges—but it can be edgestitched, serged, or have a Hong Kong finish.
- Using a serger neatly cuts off the raw edges of the facing while finishing the edge with thread. Careful control of the facing as the curved edges are guided under the presser foot and blade is needed for a professional finish.

"Facing" the Facing with Fusible Interfacing

When using fusible interfacing for the facing, try this method of "facing" the facing, which produces a smooth, flat finished edge:

12.5A TRIM SEAM ALLOWANCES.

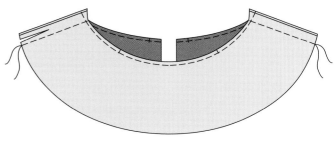

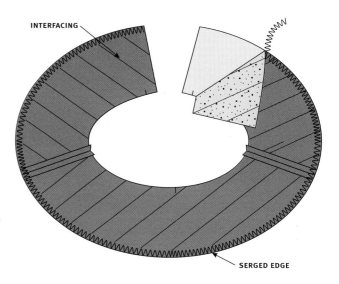

INTERFACING

SERGED EDGE

12.5B SERGED FACING WITH FINISH

- Prepare the facing, sew the pieces together, prepare the fusible interfacing, and sew the pieces together, as discussed above.
- With the correct sides together, sew the fusible interfacing to the facing at the outer, curved edge, using a ⅛-inch seam allowance. Sew carefully and evenly to create a smooth, even edge. The bumpy (resin) side of the

fusible interfacing will be faceup (Figure 12.6).

- Turn the facing and interfacing into each other, and press the ⅛-inch seam allowance only, fusing together the facing and the interfacing at the seam allowance only.
- Smooth the fusible interfacing over the wrong side of the facing; the fusible interfacing will extend beyond the upper edge by approximately ⅛ inch. Trim away any excess beyond that (see Figure 12.6).
- Using a pressing cloth, fuse the interfacing to the facing, using a lift-and-press motion that does not move the fusible interfacing. Be sure that no lumps or bumps of fusible interfacing are formed while pressing.

Finishing Facings with Linings
Facings finished with linings are not treated with an edge finish. Instead, they are sewn to the lining as detailed in Chapter 16, Figure 16.12.

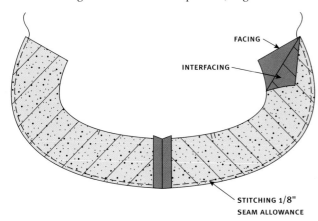

Securing Facings to the Garment

There are three ways to secure facings to the garment—understitching, topstitching, and stitching-in-the-ditch, described below.

Understitching
This technique is used to keep facings from rolling out to the front of the garment. It also gives a firm edge on which to turn and press the facing, preventing any of the facing from being visible from the front of the garment. A crisp edge, without any stitching or facing showing, is the hallmark of fine sewing.

- When the facing is sewn to the garment, the seam allowances are clipped to allow the sewn edge to spread to match the shape of the garment (Figure 12.7).
- Clip approximately every ½ inch; if the fabric is very bulky, clip more often, such as every ¼ inch.
- Press the seam allowances toward the facing.
- Sew the seam allowances to the facing approximately ⅛ inch from the seam.
- Turn the garment right side up and stitch slowly (see Figure 12.7).
- Turn the facing to the inside of the garment. Roll the seam slightly to the facing side, and press.
- Whipstitch the facings to the seam allowances, being careful to stitch only through the seam allowance fabric and the facing (Figure 12.7).

Topstitching
Topstitching is a technique that can be used to

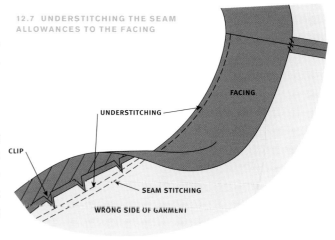

hold the facing to the garment in place of understitching, or to hold a decorative, shaped facing turned to the front of the garment. The use of this stitching technique depends completely on the fabric and style of the garment. Topstitching can be an important design element in itself, and requires careful, accurate stitching to be successful, as shown in Figure 4.1a. It is a design element that calls attention to the area where it is sewn, so if straight stitching has not been mastered, save this technique for later design work. Refer to Chapter 6, "Seams," for more information on stitching angled, curved, and circular topstitched seams.

Stitch-in-the-Ditch
Stitching-in-the-ditch is a technique used to secure facings and hold edge finishes such as bindings in place, as shown in Figure 9.6c. A zipper foot allows the needle to get close to the seam well and provides an easier view of where the stitching is going.

Shoulder or side seam stitching-in-the-ditch requires that the facing and the garment line up exactly at the seam. If they don't, because of inaccurate sewing, using this method will result in twisted facings with unattractive pull lines on the front of the garment.

- Secure the facing to the garment by stitching by machine, through both at the seamlines (Figure 12.8).
- The stitching must be done exactly in the front seamline if this method is to be invisible.

SHAPED FACINGS

The facing that finishes the edges of garments must match the shape of the area of the garment to which it is being stitched and also be

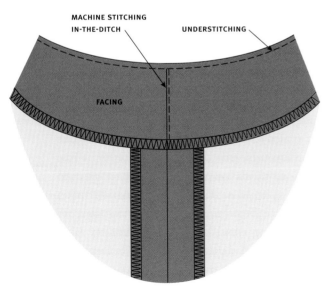

12.8 STITCHING-IN-THE-DITCH

cut on the same grain. The width of the facing is determined by the type of opening or edge of the garment, usually 2 inches wide plus seam allowances, but this can vary depending on the garment and fabric. On very narrow shoulder straps, an all-in-one facing can be as small as ½ inch. The student designer can best determine the width that is needed to support the area being faced, remembering that the facing is meant to be *invisible* when turned to the inside of the garment. A decorative facing can be of any size or shape when turned to the outside of the garment, becoming an important design element.

The facing pieces can be cut from the garment fabric, depending on the weight of the fabric, or from lining fabric.

Stitching the Facing to the Neckline

When the facing is finishing the edge of a skirt, pants, dress, or jacket, the zipper is usually installed before the facing is applied (Figure 12.9).

- With the correct sides together, match the notches of the facing to the neckline and the shoulder seams; pin.
- Stitch the facing to the neckline.
- Press the seam allowance, melding the stitches.
- Trim and grade the seam allowance, leaving the edge next to the garment the longest.
- Clip into the curved areas up to ⅛ inch from the seamline, allowing the curved areas to spread when the facing is turned.
- Trim diagonally across any corners in the seam allowance to reduce bulk.

12.9 SEWING THE FACING TO THE NECKLINE

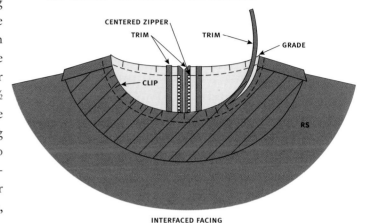

CENTERED ZIPPER · TRIM · TRIM · GRADE · CLIP · RS · INTERFACED FACING

- Understitch the seam allowances to the facing.
- Turn the facing to the inside of the garment; press.
- Turn under and slipstitch the center-back edges of the facing to the zipper tape (see figure 12.14d).
- Secure the facing edges at the shoulder seams with whipstitch or stitch-in-the-ditch.

Stitching the Facing to the Armhole

The shoulder seams of the garment are stitched before the **armhole facings** are applied. The steps are the same as those listed above, except:

- The facing can be sewn in the flat method of construction; that is, the side seam is left unstitched and the facing is stitched to the garment while the side seams are still open (Figure 12.10a).
- After the facing has been stitched, the side seams and the facing are stitched in one continuous seam (Figure 12.10b).

12.10A SIDE SEAMS FLAT APPLICATION

12.10B FACING UNDERSTITCHED

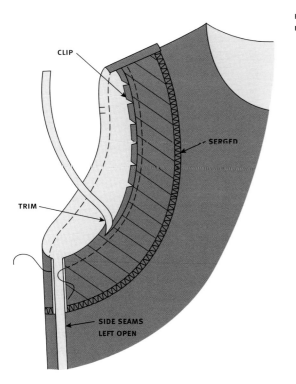

CLIP

SERGED

TRIM

SIDE SEAMS
LEFT OPEN

FACING
UNDERSTITCHED

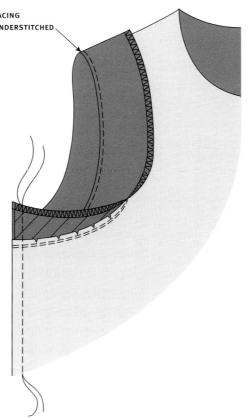

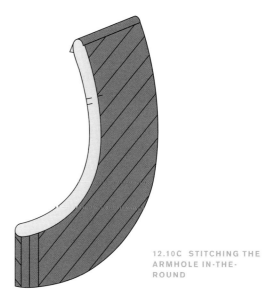

12.10C STITCHING THE
ARMHOLE IN-THE-
ROUND

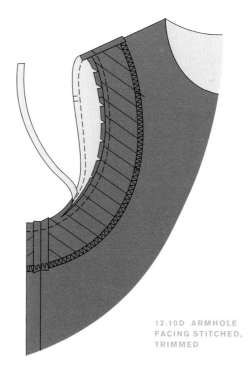

12.10D ARMHOLE
FACING STITCHED,
TRIMMED

- Or, the garment and the facings are both stitched at the shoulder and side seams (Figure 12.10c) and the facing is stitched to the garment in-the-round (Figure 12.10d).

All-in-One-Facing or Combination Facing

This facing is used to finish the neckline and armhole edges at the same time. The **all-in-one facing** is used in areas of garments where separate facings would overlap and be bulky.

It's usually used for sundresses or other sleeveless, low-cut garments and may be used for high necklines as well. This facing is turned to the inside of the garment by pulling it through the shoulder seams, which are left unstitched for this purpose.

- Apply interfacing to facing (Figure 12.11b).
- Stitch the underarm seams of the garment. Press open (Figure 12.11a).

- Do the same for the facing (Figure 12.11b).
- Trim the seam allowances of the armhole facing edges ⅛ inch so the facing is smaller in width. This ensures that the facing rolls to the inside after stitching and does not show on the front of the garment (Figure 12.11b).
- The shoulder seams are left unstitched (see Figures 12.11a and b).
- Fold back the shoulder seams of the facing; press (Figure 12.12a).
- Stitch the facing to the garment with correct sides together. Begin and end the stitching ½ inch from the ends of the shoulder seams. This must be accurate! Match the garment edges to fit the smaller, trimmed facing edges (Figure 12.12a).
- Trim and grade the seam allowance, leaving the edge next to the garment the longest; clip the curve (see Figure 12.12a).
- Press the seams open, then press the seam allowances toward the facing.
- Understitch the facing to the seam allowances as far as the presser foot will go up into the curves. This can actually be accomplished, but it takes careful sewing and patience (Figure 12.12b).
- Turn the facing to the inside of the garment by pulling the ends of the shoulder seams

down between the facing and the garment. Neckline and underarm sections of the facing will automatically turn in to the wrong side (see Figure 12.12b).
- Stitch the garment shoulder seams.
- Trim the seam allowance to ¼ inch and trim the ends of the seam away on the diagonal; press (see Figure 12.13a).
- Whipstitch at the shoulder seam, or stitch-in-the-ditch (Figure 12.13b).

Waistlines

Faced waistlines are finished with an edge that rests on the natural waistline. The **waistline facing** may be a shaped facing of an average finished width of 2 inches that corresponds with the shape of the waistline. Grosgrain ribbon, also known as Petersham, can be used to face and finish the waistline.

- Staystitch the waistline edge to prevent stretching (Figure 12.14a), and/or stitch twill tape over the waistline seam to prevent it from stretching (Figure 12.14b). Using twill tape at the waistline produces a firmer edge than just staystitching.

- Stabilize the facings (Figure 12.14a).
- Stitch the facing pieces together; press seams open.
- Finish the edges of the facings appropriately, unless a lining is being attached (see Figure 12.14a).

- Staystitch the garment waistline (Figure 12.14a).
- With the correct sides together, pin the facings to the garment edge, matching notches and side seams (see Figure 12.14b).
- Press the seam flat directionally, as stitched.
- Trim, grade, and clip the seam allowances.
- Press the seam allowance toward the facing and understitch (Figure 12.14c).
- Turn the facing to the inside of the garment, rolling the seam slightly to the inside, and press.
- Tack the edge of the facing down at the seams and darts.
- Turn under the ends of the facing and slipstitch to the zipper tape, keeping the edges of the facing free of the zipper coils (Figure 12.14d).

Facings for Sleeves

A self-fabric, turned-back facing (also known as a hem). A shaped facing also produces a plain, finished edge, whether it's cut all-in-one or it's a separate piece (see Figure 12.3b). In general, sleeve finishes are easier to sew before the sleeve has been stitched to the garment.

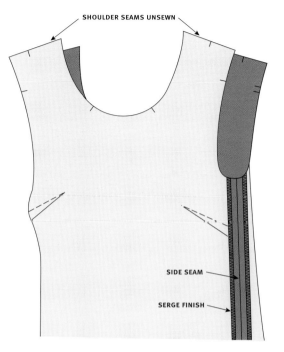

SHOULDER SEAMS UNSEWN

SIDE SEAM

SERGE FINISH

12.11A STITCHING THE GARMENT UNDERARM SEAM

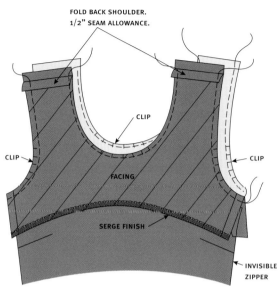

FOLD BACK SHOULDER.
1/2" SEAM ALLOWANCE.

CLIP

CLIP

CLIP

FACING

SERGE FINISH

INVISIBLE ZIPPER

12.12A MATCH THE TRIMMED FACING EDGES TO THE GARMENT EDGES.

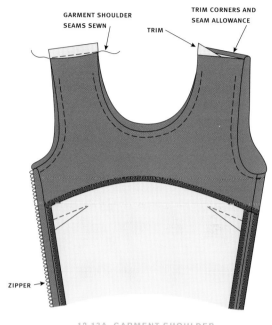

GARMENT SHOULDER SEAMS SEWN

TRIM CORNERS AND SEAM ALLOWANCE

TRIM

ZIPPER

12.13A GARMENT SHOULDER SEAMS SEWN

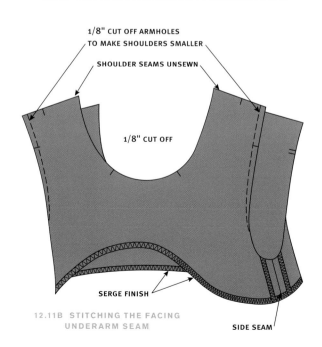

1/8" CUT OFF ARMHOLES TO MAKE SHOULDERS SMALLER

SHOULDER SEAMS UNSEWN

1/8" CUT OFF

SERGE FINISH

SIDE SEAM

12.11B STITCHING THE FACING UNDERARM SEAM

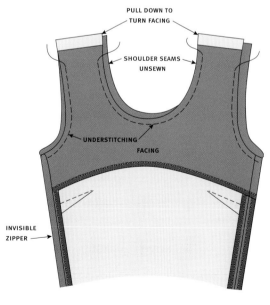

PULL DOWN TO TURN FACING

SHOULDER SEAMS UNSEWN

UNDERSTITCHING

FACING

INVISIBLE ZIPPER

12.12B PULLING THE SHOULDER SEAMS THROUGH

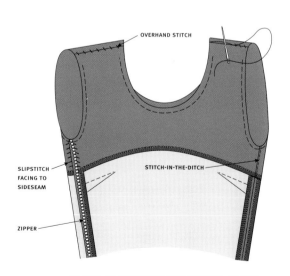

OVERHAND STITCH

SLIPSTITCH FACING TO SIDESEAM

STITCH-IN-THE-DITCH

ZIPPER

12.13B WHIPSTITCH THE FACING AT THE SHOULDER SEAM, OR STITCH-IN-THE-DITCH AT SHOULDER SEAMS AND SIDE SEAMS.

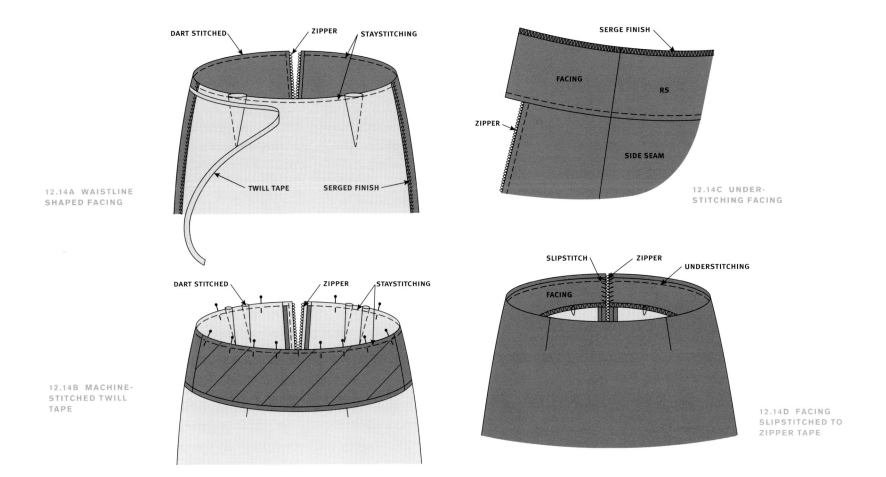

12.14A WAISTLINE
SHAPED FACING

12.14B MACHINE-
STITCHED TWILL
TAPE

12.14C UNDER-
STITCHING FACING

12.14D FACING
SLIPSTITCHED TO
ZIPPER TAPE

Decorative Shaped Facings Turned to the Outside

Facings turned to the outside of the garment still function as facings; however, this technique provides the designer with a multitude of decorative opportunities. When used in this manner, the facing becomes an important design element, limited only by the designer's imagination. A decorative facing can be made from contrasting fabric, such as suede or leather on tweed, or satin on denim. It can be made from faux fur, the reverse side of the garment fabric—the list is endless. The steps used to apply the shaped facing to the outside of the garment are the same as those listed above, but keep in mind that they are stitched the opposite way.

- A facing turned to the outside of the garment should be cut slightly larger (⅛ to ¼ inch) to allow for turning it over the seam allow-ances, especially with fabrics that are of a different weight or texture than the garment.
- When using a heavier fabric than the garment itself, the type of interfacing being used to support this area needs to be considered. Refer to Chapter 3, "Introduction to Stabilizers."
- The edges of the facing are finished and stitched to the garment.
- The facing area provides endless opportunities

for embellishment such as piping, braid, trim, ruffles, and more.

- The shape of the facing can mimic an element of the fabric if it is a print, or it can introduce another shape that becomes the focal point of the garment.

KEYHOLE AND SLASHED OPENINGS

The neckline is a key fitting area of a garment. A properly fitted natural neckline should lie flat and smooth at the base of the neck, without pulling, gaping, or riding back on the neck. The **neckline facing** should duplicate the shape of the garment opening and lie flat and smooth after stitching. The directions for three types of neckline facing treatments follow: keyhole openings, slash, and plackets.

Keyhole Facing

A **keyhole facing** is a neckline opening that allows the garment to fit close to the neck yet still be pulled over the head. A self-fabric bias loop, as shown in Figure 17.19, or thread chain

> **NOTE**
>
> A thread chain is easily made by sewing over four to six strands of matching sewing thread with a zigzag stitch, as shown in Figure 9.15c. Simply hold the strands of thread taut while guiding them under the presser foot, allowing the zigzag stitching to catch all the threads. Adjust the length to form a loop to fit the button.

and button typically close this opening. The designer can place a keyhole opening on the front or back of a garment. Keyhole openings are sometimes used decoratively on sleeves as well.

- Transfer all markings onto the stabilized front and back facing pieces, and notch the center front of the garment where the facing will be sewn.
- Staystitch the opening on the back facing.
- Stitch the bias loop together, and place the loop along the previous stitching line; stitch (Figure 12.15a).
- Stitch the garment front and back shoulders together and press.
- Stitch the front facing to the back facing at the shoulder seams; press.
- Clean finish the edges of the facings. With the correct sides together, pin the facing to the garment, matching the notches at shoulder seams, center fronts, and center backs.
- Begin stitching at the shoulder seam, stitching along the back neck, and sewing over the previous staystitching on the keyhole around the neckline to the starting point at the shoulder.
- Trim, grade, and clip the keyhole and neckline curve (Figure 12.15b).
- Understitch the facing to the seam allowance; turn the facing to the inside of the garment; press.
- Edgestitch around the keyhole; sew a button at the neckline opposite the loop.
- Secure the facings at the shoulder seams by machine stitching-in-the-ditch or hand tacking.

Slashed Facing

A **slashed facing** is a finished opening in a garment section that can be functional, decorative, or both. When the facing is turned to the inside of the garment, it is functional. When the facing is made of a contrasting fabric or grainline and is turned to the outside of the garment, it is functional and decorative. A slashed facing is used on sleeves and necklines where no seam is planned;

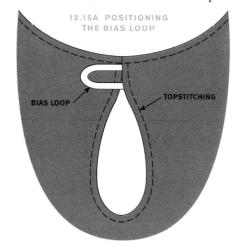

12.15A POSITIONING THE BIAS LOOP

BIAS LOOP　　TOPSTITCHING

12.15B KEYHOLE FACING: STITCHING THE OPENING IN THE FACING

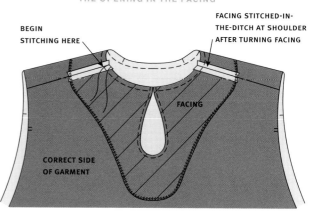

BEGIN STITCHING HERE

FACING STITCHED-IN-THE-DITCH AT SHOULDER AFTER TURNING FACING

FACING

CORRECT SIDE OF GARMENT

on garment edges that meet rather than overlap; on lower hem edges of blouses, skirts, and shorts to allow ease; up from hemlines for a split; or as a decorative design detail. The facing lies flat against the garment section and can be topstitched to add a design element. The functional slashed opening facing is stitched as follows.

- Mark the stitching and slash lines on the wrong side of the garment and the facing (Figure 12.16a).
- Stitch the garment sections together at the shoulder seams.
- Stitch the front and back facings together at the shoulder seam.
- Clean finish the edges of the facings.
- With the correct sides together, match the notches and pin the neckline edges of the garment and facings (see Figure 12.16a).
- Beginning at a shoulder seam, stitch the neckline seam edge to the slash lines; pivot and shorten the stitch length to 1.5.
- Stitch down to the point of the slash lines, pivot, sew two stitches across to the opposite side of the slash lines, pivot, and continue stitching up to the neckline seam edge, around to the starting point.

NOTE
Taking two stitches across the bottom of the slash point helps to turn a crisp point and keep the facing flat below the point.

NOTE
Understitching may not be possible in the slash area.

- Slash the neckline open between the stitching, trim the corners at the neckline, and clip into the corners at the bottom pivot points.
- Place a pin at the point to keep from cutting through the stitching.
- Trim, grade, and clip the neckline seam allowance; turn the facing to the inside of the garment; press.
- Understitch the facing to the seam allowances as shown in Figure 12.16b.
- Whipstitch the edges of the facing at the shoulder seams, or stitch-in-the-ditch by machine (see Figure 12.16b).

Decorative Slashed Opening
A decorative variation of the slashed neckline opening places the facing on the correct side of the garment. The facing is cut from a contrasting fabric or, if the fabric is a stripe or a plaid, the facing can be cut to run in the opposite direction or diagonal to the garment fabric.

- The stitching order follows the same order as for the slashed opening above.
- Turn the facing to the correct side of the garment and understitch as far as possible; press.
- Edgestitch the pressed outside edge of the facing to the garment (Figure 12.17), using a matching or contrasting thread.

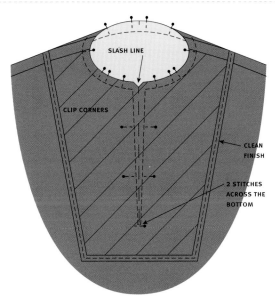

12.16A SLASHED OPENING FACING: FACING WITH CLEAN FINISHED EDGESTITCHED TO GARMENT

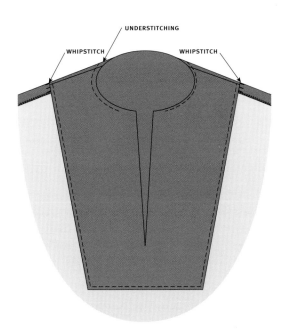

12.16B FACING SLASHED, TURNED

Placket

A **placket** is a finished opening in a garment section. Plackets are used on front or back neckline openings instead of a zipper. A placket can be made of two finished strips of equal width applied to a garment opening of any length (see Figure 12.4a). The two strips overlap, and the top strip is visible on the correct side of the garment. The same result can be achieved using an all-in-one facing, as described in Figure 12.4b. A concealed front placket can be constructed from this method as well, and is used in high-end garments at the center front, or on the back. This is especially effective when matching plaids, stripes, or print patterns when a visible closure would interrupt the design. At the neckline, the placket can be sewn with or without closures and with or without collars. A placket can be both functional, by providing a finish to an opening, and decorative, enhancing the garment opening with contrasting color, fabric, or shape. Plackets are found on sleeves and at neck openings, as well as on skirts, pants, or shorts. Refer to Chapter 13, Figure 13.4, for detailed sleeve information.

All-in-One Placket

- Use fabrics that don't ravel, or finish the seam edges before construction of this method.
- Prepare facing and interfacing; transfer all markings to facing and mark the center front of the garment (Figure 12.18a).
- Press each side edge of the facing under ½ inch.
- With the correct sides together, pin the facing to the garment front, matching the neck edges and the center-front placement line on the facing and garment.
- Using a short stitch length, 2.0 or 1.5, begin stitching at the top of the neckline along the marked stitching lines for the slash (see Figure 12.18a). Stitch to the point, pivot, stitch two stitches across the bottom, pivot, and stitch up to the neckline (Figure 12.18a).
- Cut down the center of the slash and into the corners (see Figure 12.18a).
- Turn the facing to the wrong side of the garment (Figure 12.18b).
- Press, rolling the seam slightly to the inside.

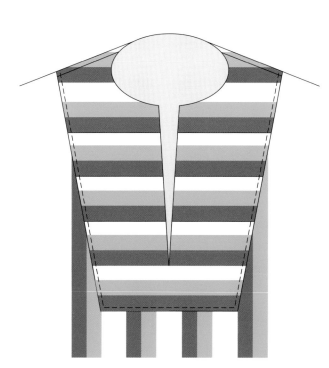

12.17 DECORATIVE SLASHED FACING

NOTE

A band becomes a placket when two bands are stitched together at one end to create an overlap. The other end of each band is left unsewn, as an opening into the garment section. The decision as to how the end of the band is finished is up to the designer. Some typical finishes are facings, collars, shaping, and sewing the end closed, or using bias binding to finish the entire neckline.

- Fold and press the facings so that center fronts match and each facing is 1 inch wide (Figure 12.18c).
- Edgestitch along the pressed edge of the facing on the inside of the right-hand facing only (see Figure 12.18c).
- Position the neck edge finish, such as in Figures 11.5e and f; stitch.
- Fold the facing extensions, with correct sides together, over the neck edge finish, and stitch in place (see Figure 12.18c).
- Turn the facings to the inside of the garment and press.
- Edgestitch the left-hand side of the facing, catching the pressed edge on the underside, or stitch-in-the-ditch.
- Place the faced front in the overlapped position, and press.
- From the correct side of the garment, stitch through all the layers on the lower end, forming a square to hold the ends of the facing in place.
- Lift the front of the garment and trim the facing ends to ½ inch.

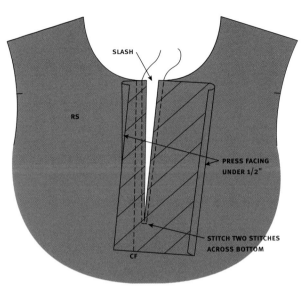

12.18A FACING SEWN AND SLASHED

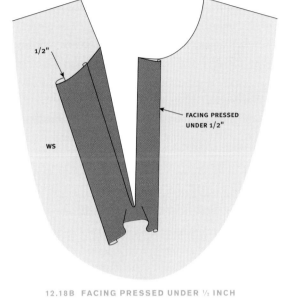

12.18B FACING PRESSED UNDER ½ INCH

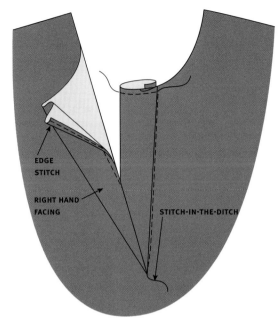

12.18C FACING TURNED BACK TO INSIDE

NOTE

The buttonholes are machine stitched vertically on the shirt placket or band, as shown in Figure 11.1c.

• Stitch or serge the placket tabs together very carefully (Figure 12.18d)—you don't want to accidentally catch the garment front in the serger or cut a hole in the fabric!

Concealed Front Placket

A **concealed placket** is actually a double-folded extended interfaced facing on the right side of

the garment front. Machine buttonholes are stitched to the extension before folding the facing and the underlay to the wrong side of the garment. The buttonholes are concealed behind the fold, which is held in place with stitching.

• Mark and stitch the buttonholes on the extended facing as shown in Figure 12.19a.
• Fold back the extended facing once, and stitch at the neckline and the hem; clip, turn, and press.
• Stitch the shoulder seams together, place and stitch the neckline facings (Figure 12.19a).
• Clip, understitch, and press.

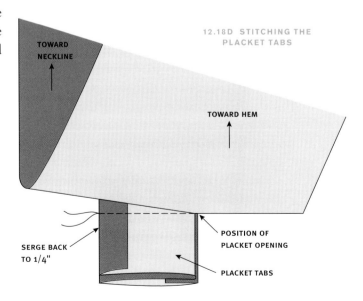

12.18D STITCHING THE PLACKET TABS

NOTE

Do not press the foldline of the facing until after it has been stitched to the garment.

- Fold the neckline facing to the wrong side of the garment.
- Turn and press the fold at the center front edge (Figure 12.19b).
- Baste the concealed placket down the middle of the facing; machine stitch through all layers (see Figure 12.19b), which secures the facing and hem.
- Press the facing section with buttonholes over to the center front.
- Invisibly slipstitch the facing edges to the neckline (see Figure 12.19b).
- Hand tack the sections of the facing at the buttonholes to the garment front to reduce stress and keep the facing flat.

EXTENDED/SELF-FACING

An extended/self-facing is cut in one piece with the garment and folded back to create the facing. It is used instead of a seam for edges cut on the straight-of-grain. The foldline reduces bulk at the center front or back. This type of facing is found on blouses, jackets, and garments without collars.

- Stabilize the facing area of the garment (Figure 12.20a).
- Transfer the markings at the center-front or -back foldlines.

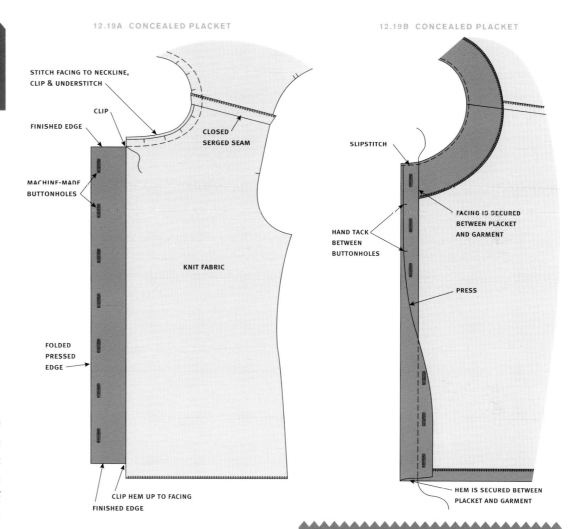

12.19A CONCEALED PLACKET

STITCH FACING TO NECKLINE, CLIP & UNDERSTITCH

CLIP

FINISHED EDGE

CLOSED SERGED SEAM

MACHINE-MADE BUTTONHOLES

KNIT FABRIC

FOLDED PRESSED EDGE

CLIP HEM UP TO FACING

FINISHED EDGE

12.19B CONCEALED PLACKET

SLIPSTITCH

FACING IS SECURED BETWEEN PLACKET AND GARMENT

HAND TACK BETWEEN BUTTONHOLES

PRESS

HEM IS SECURED BETWEEN PLACKET AND GARMENT

- Attach additional facing sections such as the back neck facing before stitching the facing to the garment.
- Clean finish or serge the facing edges.
- Bound buttonholes should be stitched in the front of the garment before the facing is turned back. Machine-made buttonholes are stitched after the facing is in place.

IMPORTANT

Crisp edges, sufficient support, and flat, smooth facings are details that strongly contribute to the success of a garment. Refer to Chapter 3, "Introduction to Stabilizers," to determine the correct weight and support for the facing. *Sample first!*

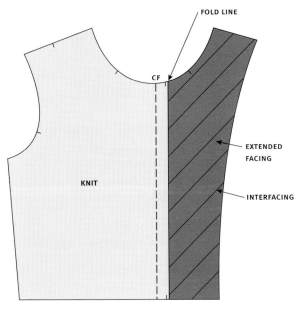

12.20A **STABILIZING AN EXTENDED FACING**

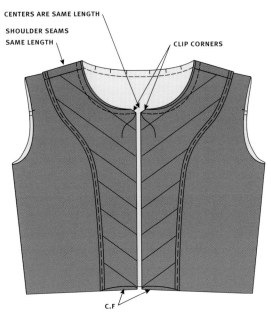

12.20B **MATCHING THE UPPER EDGES OF AN EXTENDED FACING**

IMPORTANT

Sloppiness in seaming an extended facing is very noticeable on the outside of the garment; it is easy to see if one neckline edge is longer than the other. Take time to be accurate.

- Before clipping the neckline corner, turn the facing to the wrong side of the garment and check that the front edges are exactly the same length from the top corner edge to the bottom edge (Figure 12.20b).
- Check that the distance from the shoulder seam to the front corner point is the same on both sides (see Figure 12.20b).
- Turn the facing to the correct side of the garment along the foldline.
- Stitch the neck seamline, trim the corners, grade the seam allowances, and clip along the curves.
- Understitch the seam allowances to the shaped back neckline facing between the shoulder seams and as far toward the center front as the presser foot will fit (Figure 12.7).
- Press; consider topstitching the edges in matching or contrasting thread.

Two-Piece Facing for Garment without a Collar

A garment without a collar can be faced in several ways. An extended/self-facing can be used or a separate two-piece facing can be constructed. Each method uses the original pattern piece to create the facings.

Two-Piece Facing

The facing is constructed in separate pieces when:

- The fabric yardage is more economical in production.
- A contrasting fabric will be used as a design detail or some type of trim or piping will be sewn to the garment edges. In each case, separate facing pieces would need to be drafted for the center-front and center-back neck facings.
- The facings are turned to the front as a decorative detail, such as using a contrasting color or texture of fabric. Additional trims or piping can also be added to the edges.

Garments with collars, and tailored jacket facings with notched collars, are covered in detail in Chapter 11, "Collars."

NOTE

Bound buttonholes **must be completed before the facing is applied. To create a functional buttonhole opening in the facing, a small window within the facing is created that is durable, flat, and smooth. The shape of this window is determined by the size of the buttonhole, and the type of button that will be put through the buttonhole. Bound buttonholes are covered in detail in Chapter 17, "Closures" (Figure 17.13).**

Cowl Necklines

Cowls are folds created by allowing fabric to fall at desired depths. The decision of how much drape, how deep the folds are, is made at the pattern drafting stage and is entirely up to the designer. The amount of drape is further influenced by the fabric being used. Cowls are in between two categories: bias, because they must be cut on the true bias in order to drape properly, and extended facings, because the facing is cut in one with the cowl.

A cowl can appear in many places within a garment; typically, it falls from the shoulder at the neckline, an armhole, or from the waist of dresses, gowns, blouses, pants, jackets, and coats. Cowls are most often cut in one with the garment; however, they can be cut separately as a fabric-saving decision and set into an area of the garment. Although placing a seam in this area of drape may seem stiff, remember this is a fabric-driven decision. Refer to Chapter 6, "Seams," for details on stitching a bias seam allowance to a straight grain seam allowance.

Constructing a separate cowl stay controls the drape of the front of the garment at the neckline. A cowl stay looks like a facing but is applied to the wrong side of the garment similar to an underlining. Because of the time and cost of the extra fabric used to construct the stay, it is used in higher-quality garments. As a substitute, a drapery weight or a bead can be attached at the point of the cowl facing to facilitate the drape, particularly at a neckline. Soft, loosely woven fabrics such as crepe, silk, gauze, rayon, satin, and some knits work best for this application.

- Establish the true bias on the fabric and mark the fold with chalk or a thread line.
- To prevent the fabric from slipping as the pattern is traced and cut, pin it to tissue paper or pattern paper. Refer to Chapter 2, "Getting Prepared," and Figure 2.19 for another view of this method.
- Place the pattern onto the fabric and transfer markings and matchpoints (Figure 12.21).
- Mark the foldline of the cowl facing with hand-basting, as shown in Figure 12.3c.
- Add a 1-inch seam allowance to allow for adjustments.

- Bias stretches as it relaxes, and the amount of stretch varies with the choice of the fabric; after cutting, compare the fabric pieces with the pattern pieces (Figure 12.21).
- If adding a stay, stitch the stay to the front and back of the garment pieces.
- Finish the edge of the cowl facing before constructing the garment.
- Baste the folds that create the cowl to avoid the folds slipping when stitching.
- Stitch the shoulder seams, clipping to the matchpoint to allow front shoulder to pivot when stitching (Figure 12.3c). Press seams open and hand stitch to shoulder seams.

BANDS

Bands are used as a finish for the edge of garment sections, as an extension of a garment edge such as on a hemline of jacket, blouse, sleeve, skirt, or pants, or applied as decoration on the face of a garment. Bands can be constructed from woven fabrics on the straight grain or bias, from grosgrain ribbon and nonwoven materials such as leather and Ultrasuede. Knit-ribbed bands purchased by the yard, in prepackaged amounts, tubular knits cut to a specific width, or knit yardage can be used to finish necklines, armholes, sleeves, and waistlines on knit or woven garments. Knit bands are stretched to match the garment edge during application. Knit bands can be both a decorative detail and a functional detail when used, for example, in a windbreaker cuff attached to a sleeve. The width of the band is determined by its location on the garment, the overall garment style, and the designer's preference.

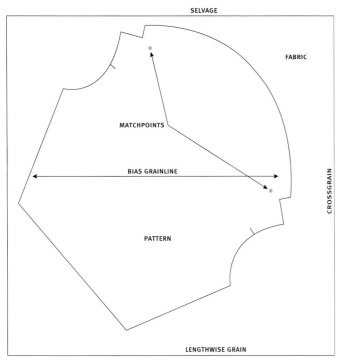

12.21 CUTTING THE BIAS COWL

Bands can be applied using topstitching, edgestitching, or stitching-in-the-ditch. The first step is to determine the desired width of the band.

- The location of the band on the garment suggests the appropriate width. For example, a band might be 4 inches wide on the wrist, but 1½ inches on a neckline or center front.
- The type of closure at the center front or center back will also determine the width needed.

- Determine the type of stabilizer that will best support the band and function. Refer to Chapter 3, "Introduction to Stabilizers."
- Without stabilizing, the bands of woven fabric will appear limp and detract from the finished look. However, a stabilizer is not needed for knit bands because they need to be able to stretch.
- Additional trims or piping added to the band should be basted to the band before application to the garment.

Shaped Edge-Stitched Two-Piece Band

Bands placed at curved neck areas are sewn from two pieces (Figure 12.22a). The front neckline band/front edge band and the shaped back neck band are stitched together at the shoulder seam before stitching it to the garment.

- Stabilize the upper band section.
- Press under ¼ inch on the outer edge of the upper band section; baste.
- With the correct sides together, pin the front band to the back neck band section and stitch (Figure 12.22b).
- Trim, clip, and press the seam allowances (see Figure 12.22b).
- Turn the band to the correct side; press.
- Turn the garment hem back and stitch.
- Pin the wrong side of the band section to the correct side of the garment.
- Stitch the seam and trim.
- Press the seam allowance toward the band.

- Stitch the band hem, turn, and press (Figure 12.22c).
- Pin the basted edge of the band over the seam line; baste (Figure 12.22c).
- Edgestitch close to both the inner and outer edges of the band (see Figure 12.22c).

Stitch-in-the-Ditch One-Piece Band

- Place the correct sides of the band and garment fabric together, leaving the underside of the band approximately ⅛ inch longer on the underside of the band; serge finish (Figure 12.23).
- Pin the stabilized side of the band to the garment.
- Stitch; turn the band to the inside of the garment and press.
- From the correct side of the garment, stitch-in-the-ditch next to the pressed seamline of the band as closely as possible (Figure 12.23).
- Stop often, with the needle down in the fabric, to check that all layers are being caught in the stitching.

Leather and Ultrasuede Bands

Leather and Ultrasuede need no additional finishing to be applied to the edges of garments. Both materials are suitable for shaped or straight-cut bands.

- Determine the width of the trim to be used on the garment.
- If using leather or Ultrasuede, use a ruler and rotary cutter to cleanly and evenly cut the

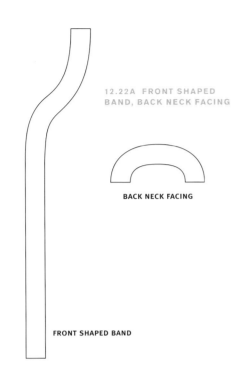

12.22A FRONT SHAPED BAND, BACK NECK FACING

BACK NECK FACING

FRONT SHAPED BAND

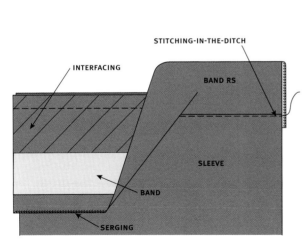

INTERFACING

STITCHING-IN-THE-DITCH

BAND RS

SLEEVE

BAND

SERGING

12.23 STITCH-IN-THE-DITCH BAND

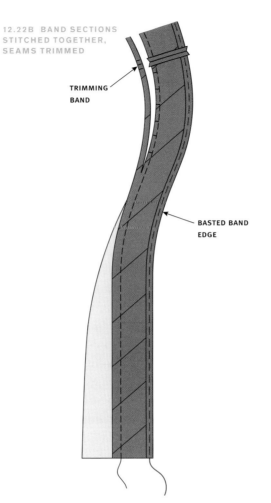

12.22B BAND SECTIONS STITCHED TOGETHER, SEAMS TRIMMED

TRIMMING BAND

BASTED BAND EDGE

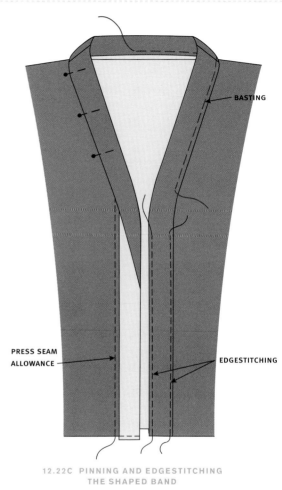

BASTING

PRESS SEAM ALLOWANCE

EDGESTITCHING

12.22C PINNING AND EDGESTITCHING THE SHAPED BAND

strips, which can be folded in half, or applied as two separate pieces.

- Refer to Chapter 3, "Introduction to Stabilizers," for the appropriate stabilizer for leather.
- Apply the stabilizer to the wrong side of one band (Figure 12.24a).
- With the wrong sides together, sew the edges together along one side to create the band (see Figure 12.24a).

- Slide the garment edge into the band.
- Sample pinning the bands on a scrap of leather or Ultrasuede; if holes are made, secure in place using a temporary adhesive tape (Figure 12.24b).
- Edgestitch slowly and carefully to avoid pleating or tucking of the band.

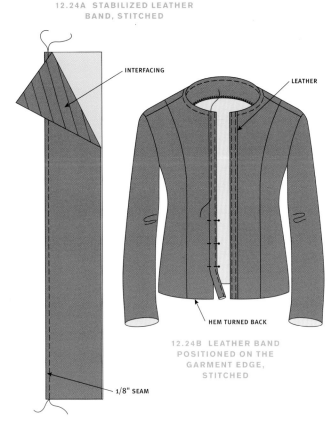

INTERFACING

LEATHER

HEM TURNED BACK

1/8" SEAM

12.24B LEATHER BAND
POSITIONED ON THE
GARMENT EDGE,
STITCHED

Rib Knit Bands at Necklines and Armholes

Knit bands applied to the neckline or armhole are strips of ribbing cut slightly less in length than the neckline or armhole itself. Check the recovery of the rib knit; after stretching, it should return to its original length. The best rib knits to use for curved areas are those with 50 to 100 percent stretch. A 1-inch-wide finished rib knit band is typical for a crew neckline, while a 2½-inch

finished width is typical for a mock turtleneck. This is the designer's decision. To determine the length of ribbing to cut for the neckline:

- The shoulder seams for the front and back should be sewn together. Fold the garment in half.
- Measure the neckline along the seamline, standing the tape on its side for accuracy.
- Double this amount for the total neck edge measurement.
- The length of the ribbing for a crew neck or mock turtleneck should be two-thirds of the garment neck seamline plus ½ inch for seam allowance.
- To determine two-thirds of the neck measurement, divide the total neck measurement by 3 and then multiply the answer by 2. Cut the band in paper and fold into three equal parts. *Example:* using a 21-inch neck measurement, 21 ÷ 3 = 7. Next, 7 × 2 = 14, + ½ inch for seam allowance. The total length of the ribbing would be 14½ inches.

Apply the Ribbing to the Garment Edge

- The seam allowance at the garment edge is ¼ inch.
- Sew the ends of the ribbing together, using a ¼-inch seam allowance, forming a circle (Figure 12.25a).
- Finger-press the seam allowance open, and with wrong sides together, fold the ribbing in half lengthwise, matching the cut edges together (Figure 12.25b).

- Divide the circle of ribbing into fourths and pin-mark the quarter divisions (see Figure 12.25b). The seamline becomes the center back.
- Divide the garment edge into fourths and pin-mark the divisions.
- Match the ribbing and garment pin-marks together; pin (Figure 12.25c).
- Stitch the ribbing to the garment edge (with a stretch stitch) with the ribbing faceup, stretching the ribbing to match the quarter divisions (see Figure 12.25c).
- Press the seam allowances toward the garment.

Finish the Stitched Ribbing Edge

To finish the stitched ribbing edge, try one of the following:

- Serge the ribbing and seam allowance together carefully; avoid catching the garment into the serging.
- Double stitch by sewing a second row of stitching ⅛ inch from the previous stitching, stretching all layers while sewing.
- Topstitch with a twin needle straddling the seam allowance, and stretching all layers while sewing.

BIAS FACING

Narrow bias facings are excellent for use in curved areas in place of shaped facings. They are usually narrower than the traditional facings and are inconspicuous on sheer fabrics. Bias used as a facing is both functional and decorative. In its functional purpose, it encases and finishes raw edges, stretching to fit the area it is being sewn

NOTE

The ribbing band seam matched to another seam is more aesthetically pleasing.

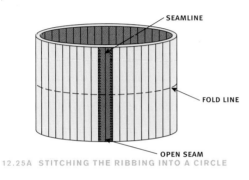

SEAMLINE

FOLD LINE

OPEN SEAM

12.25A STITCHING THE RIBBING INTO A CIRCLE

SEAM

12.25B LENGTHWISE FOLD OF RIBBING

12.25C DIVIDING, MATCHING, AND SEWING RIBBING TO THE GARMENT EDGE

to, such as curves at a neckline or armhole. As a decorative technique, bias can provide a contrasting edge finish as a binding or Hong Kong finish, be manipulated as a surface embellishment, as well as become piping, cording, or raw edge ruffles. Bias-cut fabric does not ravel and can reduce bulk and eliminate the need for edge finishes. A **bias facing** can be finished by hand sewing, topstitching, or stitching-in-the-ditch.

Bias strips cut from the garment fabric provide an exact match, ensuring that the bias facing will not be noticeable. There are other advantages to making bias strips from the garment fabric: the designer determines the width of the bias strip; only a small amount of the garment fabric is required to make a generous amount of bias yardage; and any yardage not used for the current design can be utilized in later designs. Bias strips can be cut and sewn together individually or they can be configured to be continuous strips.

Making the Bias Strips for Facings

A bias facing must always be cut on the true bias. A true bias is the 45-degree angle of a square. Refer to Chapter 2, "Getting Prepared" and Figure 2.2. Even though cutting fabric on the "near bias" would save fabric, never do this because the bias facing will not lie flat.

- First determine the total width of the bias strip, including seam allowances. When applying the bias facing, a seam allowance of ¼ inch is usually standard.
- *Example:* using a 1-inch bias facing, you will need ¼-inch seam allowance to sew to the

garment edge, and another ¼ inch to turn under the raw edge; 1 + ¼ + ¼ = 1½-inch-wide bias strip. This is a good width to use, but the key to successful bias trim is to *sample!*

- The width is up to the designer to determine in conjunction with the fabric choice, but cutting 2-inch-wide bias strips allows a little bit of extra fabric when working with slippery or difficult fabrics, and allows for turning the facing edge to the inside.
- Determine the total length of the bias needed for the facings, which should equal the length of the edge to be faced, plus 2 inches for finishing off the ends.
- *Example:* the total of the armhole opening from side seam around to side seam is 17¼ inches plus 2 inches for finishing; 17¼ + 2 = 19¼ inches.
- Always try to use a piece of fabric large enough to cut the bias strips in one length. However, some piecing of strips may be necessary when using a smaller piece of fabric.

There are two methods of creating bias strips: the cut-and-piece method and the continuous-strip method. The *cut-and-piece method* is best if only a short piece or pieces of bias are to be used, or if only small pieces or scraps of fabric are available to make bias strips. Refer to Chapter 6, Figure 6.17, for directions on this method. The *continuous-strip* method is the preferred method for cutting lots of bias strips, but requires a large piece of fabric.

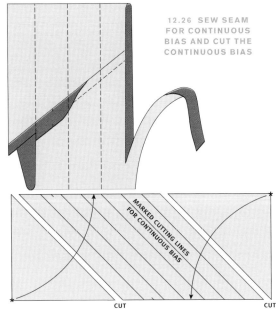

12.26 SEW SEAM FOR CONTINUOUS BIAS AND CUT THE CONTINUOUS BIAS

MARKED CUTTING LINES FOR CONTINUOUS BIAS

CUT   CUT

FOLD THIS CORNER* TO MATCH
EDGE TO ESTABLISH TRUE BIAS;
PRESS AND CUT OFF

- Using half yard of 45 inch wide fabric determine the true bias, as previously described.
- Cut off the triangle formed at the side.
- Measure and mark the cutting lines the total desired width.
- Trim off the triangle left at the other end, making another true bias cut edge.
- Pin baste the lengthwise ends (straight grainline) correct sides together, letting one width of bias extend over at the end (see Figure 12.26).
- Match corresponding cutting lines, being careful to place a pin at each of these points exactly.
- Stitch a ¼-inch seam, creating a continuous round of bias fabric.
- If the tube of bias is very narrow, press the seam open using a sleeve board.

- Begin cutting the strip at one extending end, following the marked cutting lines for uniform width of bias strips (Figure 12.26).

Applying the Bias Facing

Bias facings can be very narrow and provide an inconspicuous finish to a garment edge. Only bias-cut fabric can be contoured to go around curves. Press the bias facing to match the shape of the edge to which it is being stitched. Shrink the inner edge of the bias strip, and stretch the outer edge to match the garment's wider outside edge. In Figure 12.27a, a flounce is added to the neckline edge and is finished with a bias strip pressed to match the neckline and flounce curve. The correct side of the flounce is placed against the wrong side of the garment and handbasted. The bias facing is stitched over the raw edges of the neckline and then turned to the correct side and edgestitched (Figure 12.27b). When the flounce is turned to the correct side of the garment, the edgestitching remains unseen under the flounce. Refer to Chapter 11, "Collars," for directions on how to finish the neckline for a collar using bias strips (see Figure 11.5f). To stitch bias facings to an angled edge, miter the corners as discussed in Chapter 15, Figure 15.23.

In Figures 12.27c and d the bias is applied to a plain round neckline.

- With the wrong sides together, press the bias binding in half lengthwise.
- Open the strip, and fold each lengthwise edge to form seam allowances, leaving one edge about ⅛ inch longer than the other.

- Place the correct side of the bias strip to the correct side of the garment; pin. Leave ½ inch seam allowance beyond the edge (Figure 12.27c).
- Stitch in place, stretching the bias strip the slightest amount to produce a smoother appearance to the finished edge (Figure 12.27c).
- Trim and clip the seam allowance, then press (see Figure 12.27c).
- Understitch the bias strip to the seam allowance; press the seam allowance toward the bias facing. This creates a sharp line to turn the bias facing into the garment.
- Turn the bias to the inside of the garment.
- In production, the bias facing strip is machine edgestitched, creating a topstitched look on the front of the garment (Figure 12.27d).
- Because bias does not ravel, a seam edge finish is not necessary. However, the edge is often finished with serging, or turned under and then edgestitched.

Finish the Bias Facings
To complete the facings, consider one of the following finishes:

- Clean finish the edge of the facing and stitch-in-the-ditch (Figure 12.8) at the seam-

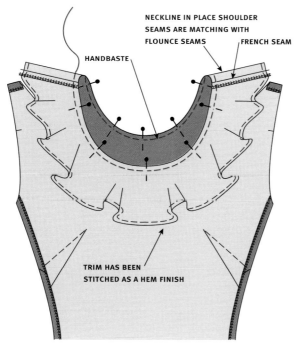

HANDBASTE

NECKLINE IN PLACE SHOULDER
SEAMS ARE MATCHING WITH
FLOUNCE SEAMS

FRENCH SEAM

TRIM HAS BEEN
STITCHED AS A HEM FINISH

12.27A RUFFLE HANDBASTED TO NECKLINE

**12.27B STITCHED AND
TURNED BIAS FACING**

WHEN RUFLE TURNS
OVER TO CORRECT SIDE
IT HIDES THE FACING

BIAS FACING

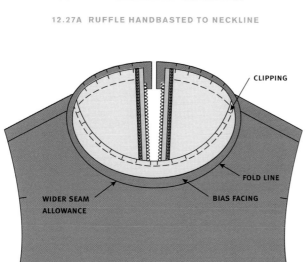

CLIPPING

FOLD LINE

BIAS FACING

WIDER SEAM
ALLOWANCE

12.27C TOPSTITCHING THE BIAS

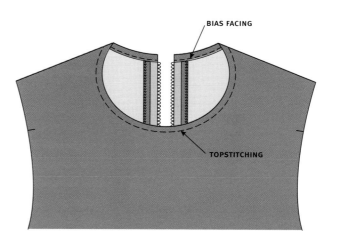

BIAS FACING

TOPSTITCHING

12.27D SEWING, TRIMMING, AND CLIPPING THE BIAS FACING

lines to hold the facings to the inside of the garment.

- Use a decorative machine stitch through the facing and garment layers to secure the facing to the garment.

BIAS BINDINGS

Bias binding covers both sides of an edge, whereas bias facing is visible on only one side, usually the inside of the garment. Bindings can be applied to garment edges that are also faced to provide more support to the garment, while highlighting an edge. The facing is basted to the wrong side of the garment, and the bias binding is stitched over both the facing and the garment edge. Bias bindings are necessary for curved edges, but can also be applied to straight edges. Straight grain bindings can be applied only to straight grain edges.

A twin needle can be used to stitch bias facings in place. It produces two rows of evenly spaced stitching at one time. The stitching on

IMPORTANT

Always create a sample of the bias binding on the fabric being used. Before cutting large amounts of bias, use a small piece of bias to determine if the width you plan to use for bias will be wide enough to cover the edges. Keep in mind that the width of the seam allowance determines the finished width of the bias binding. This is particularly important if the fabric is limited. On bulky fabrics, the width of the bias may need to be increased in order to lie flat; on sheer or fine fabrics, it may need to be narrower.

the face of the garment appears as two rows of stitching, while the bobbin side produces a zigzag stitch. Carefully match the bobbin thread to make this stitching less visible.

Single Bias Binding

- Trim away the garment seam allowance.
- The width of the bindings should allow for double turning of the fabric, so that the edge of the garment slides in between the two folded edges of the binding (Figure 12.28a).
- The width of the binding that slides to the back of the garment edge should be slightly larger, approximately ⅛ inch, to allow the machine stitching to catch the edge of the binding underneath.
- Handbaste the bias binding in place through all layers.
- Using a zipper foot, stitch closely and slowly on the folded edge of the binding, stopping frequently with the needle down in the fabric, to check that both sides of the bias binding are being caught in the machine stitching.

Double Bias Binding (French Binding)

Double bias binding or, as it is sometimes called, French binding, is a good finish for sheer or transparent fabrics.

- Cut a true bias binding 1¾-inch wide and the desired length.
- Fold the bias binding in half lengthwise and baste or press the folded edges.

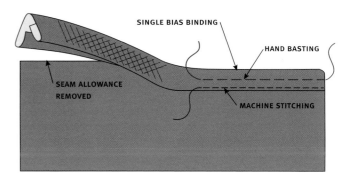

12.28A SINGLE BIAS BINDING

SINGLE BIAS BINDING

HAND BASTING

SEAM ALLOWANCE REMOVED

MACHINE STITCHING

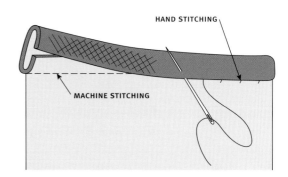

HAND STITCHING

MACHINE STITCHING

12.28B DOUBLE BIAS OR FRENCH BINDING

- Place the binding on the correct side of the garment with the unfinished edges parallel to the edge of the garment (Figure 12.28b).
- Stitch the edges in a narrow seam allowance this width, the finished binding width.
- Turn the folded edge of the binding to the inside of the garment.
- Invisibly hand stitch the folded edge to the seam allowance stitching (see Figure 12.28b).
- This same method can also be used with a single layer of bias.

Finish Binding Ends at an Opening

To finish the ends of the binding, follow these steps:

- Always allow extra length for the binding at a garment edge.
- Stop handbasting the binding in place approximately 2 inches from the garment opening.
- Unfold the binding, and place the correct sides together.
- Stitch a seam in the ends of the binding at a point 1/16 inch from the edge of the garment (Figure 12.29).
- Trim the binding seam allowance to 1/4 inch.
- Turn the binding right side out, and refold the binding.
- Finish basting before machine stitching-in-the-ditch.

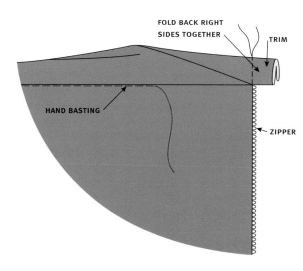

FOLD BACK RIGHT
SIDES TOGETHER

TRIM

HAND BASTING

ZIPPER

12.29 FINISHING BINDING ENDS

HOW TO JOIN THE FACING TO THE LINING

The facing can be attached to a lining with machine stitching. Refer to Chapter 16, Figure 16.12, for detailed instructions and follow the stitching order.

OTHER EDGE FINISHES
Raw Edge

Deconstructed edges are another way to finish the edge of a garment. Although they may look unplanned, in order to provide support for the edge, they must be well thought out.

- Sample—unless using bias-cut fabric, raw edges can look messy in fabrics such as polyester, which is nearly impossible to unravel nicely, as the grain changes direction across the shaped garment edge. Straight grain unravels nicely.
- A row of straight stitching sewn close to the edge reinforces the area and prevents the fabric from continuing to unravel.
- Stabilize the stitching line with twill tape or a strip of fusible interfacing before sewing.
- Use an awl or seam ripper to gently separate the fibers, to avoid pulls in the fabric.

Bias

Although bias doesn't unravel, it can be coaxed to fray. Separate the fibers with an awl or seam ripper, or use a firm toothbrush to fluff the edges of the bias-cut strips.

Using Two Strips of Bias-Cut Fabric

- Heavier-weight fabrics such as wool, linen, tweed, or boucle benefit from using two strips of bias-cut fabric.
- Hem the garment, unless the raw edge is also treated with bias strips. When turning a corner, be sure to miter the corner as shown in Figure 15.23.
- Cut the strips from matching or contrasting fabric 1 inch or wider.
- Allow twice as much length as needed.
- Place the garment between the bias cut strips.
- Stitch two rows of stitching 1/8 inch apart, down the middle of the strips, making sure to stitch through all three layers (Figure 12.30).
- Brush or comb through the fibers to fray the edges.

STITCHING FACINGS IN TRICKY FABRICS
Matching Stripes, Plaids, Patterns, and Repeat Patterns

Do place the facing pattern pieces on the fabric to match the same check or stripe as the garment is cut on.

Do use a contrasting fabric that complements the garment if the pattern of the fabric is too difficult to match.

Do use a different scale of the print from the garment fabric, another print, or a check with stripes, etc., as a contrast.

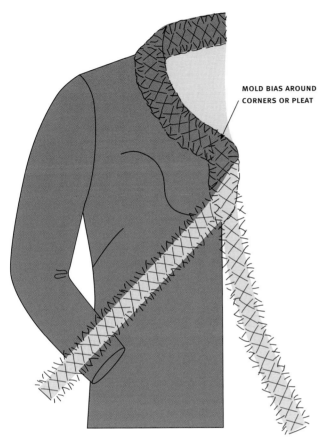

MOLD BIAS AROUND
CORNERS OR PLEAT

12.30 DOUBLE BIAS STRIP STITCHED TO THE RAW
EDGE OF THE GARMENT

Sheer Fabric

Do use a narrow, lightweight facing when sewing fabrics with a soft hand or drape, such as chiffon or silk. Otherwise, the facing may shadow from the correct side. The facing must be perfectly parallel to the edge to look good.
Do use bias facings as an elegant, functional way to finish the edges.

Do use bias bindings as an edge finish for sheers.
Do use a self-fabric double fold, turned-back facing at the center front/center back of a sheer garment.
Do sample the type of closure for the garment on this double fold facing before proceeding with the garment.
Do try additional stabilizing for this facing such as silk organza; several layers can be used to provide more structure; refer to Chapter 3, "Introduction to Stabilizers."
Don't use a stabilizer that changes the hand of the sheer fabric.

Lace

Do use narrow bias facings on lace.
Do use a scalloped appliqué edge finish, as outlined in Chapter 6, Figure 6.48b.
Do use piping, inserted between the garment edge and the facing, to provide additional support to fragile lace garment edges.
Don't use wide, shaped facings cut from the lace, which is bulky.

Satin

One wrong choice in stabilizer or interfacing for the facing can ruin the entire look of a satin garment. If it is too stiff, the facing sticks out under the garment, creating odd, angular pulls of fabric. If it is too soft, the area being faced collapses from the weight of the garment fabric. If the facing is not appropriately attached to the garment and under-stitched, the facing rolls out to the front of the garment, or the stitching is visible and mars the surface of the garment.

Do sample, and then choose the most unobtrusive facing for the area of the garment that will support the area while remaining flat and smooth.
Do place strips of brown paper bag under the edge of the facing to avoid leaving press marks on the correct side of the garment.
Do use a Seams Great Hong Kong finish as an edge treatment on satin facings if they will be visible when the garment is complete.
Don't hand stitch the facings to the garment, unless it's at the seams only.
Don't press satin directly on its surface.

Beaded Fabric

Do remove the beading from the seam allowances in order to stitch the garment sections together.
Do cut facings from fabric such as silk organza or silk charmeuse in a matching or contrasting color if the beaded garment is a firmly woven fabric.
Do underline sheer beaded fabrics (refer to Chapter 3, Figure 3.16) to support the weight of the embellishment.
Do line edge-to-edge, eliminating the need for facings.
Do use narrow piping between the facing and garment edges to provide additional support.
Don't use the beaded fabric itself as facing.

Knits

Using facings on knits may seem to be a contradiction in terms. Facings imply structure, whereas knits imply stretch. Shaped, extended, or bias facings can be applied to knits, but the amount of stretch must be considered when choosing the type of facing and stabilizer to use. Ribbing, plackets, and keyhole/slash neckline facings are also used to finish knit garments. Figure 3.11 shows the interfacing pattern grainline turned to stable direction.

Do stitch a shaped facing, appropriately stabilized, to any area of a knit garment requiring a stable edge; however, other edge finishes may be better, so sample first.

Do use a twin needle to stitch turned edges on stretchy knits (see Figure 6.46).

Do secure the facing by stitching-in-the-ditch at the seams to avoid any visible stitching or pulling on the front of the garment (see Figure 12.8).

Do use a keyhole/slash neckline facing in knits.

Do use an extended facing on knits at center front/center back areas of a garment such as a dress, structured top, or jacket with buttonholes. Refer to Chapter 3 for the correct stabilizer.

Do use bias-cut woven fabric on stable knits as an appropriate facing on a sleeveless garment or a neckline that must be large enough to pull over the head without an additional opening, or as a contrast at a neckline with a collar, such as a polo shirt.

Denim

Do stitch shaped facings, extended facings, and bias-cut fabric facings.

Do apply bands to the center front of jean jackets, to provide both finishing and support for closures.

Do sample several different interfacings on the denim being used to find the correct weight.

Do clip, trim, and grade the seam allowance to reduce the bulk.

Do edge finish the denim facing in the flattest way possible.

Do topstitch the facings to keep them inside the garment.

Velvet

The nap and bulk of velvet make it less desirable to use inside a garment as a shaped facing or an extended facing in areas of the garment such as the neckline, armhole, center front, or center back, where the nap would be crushed by wear. As a decorative facing on the outside of the garment, velvet must be placed carefully, taking into consideration the stress and wear of the area to which it's sewn. The nap of velvet, which changes color with direction, and its crushability, rule out using the bias-cut facing as well.

Do use a sew-in interfacing.

Do stabilize the outer edge of the facing with a straight stitch sewn ¼ inch from the edge, and use this line of stitching as a guide when attaching the lining.

Do clip, grade, and trim carefully.

Do use a shorter stitch length of 1.5 to reinforce corners of garments.

Do adjust the presser foot, as velvet slips and stretches during stitching.

Do use a pressing cloth to cover the nap of velvet while steaming—water drips leave marks on velvet.

Don't press directly onto velvet—iron marks never come out.

Don't topstitch on velvet—needle marks remain visible if stitching must be ripped out.

Heavyweight Fabric

The key to constructing a flat facing when using heavyweight fabrics is the reduction of bulk. The garment fabric may have to be used to complement the design, such as in turned-back lapels.

Do carefully select the interfacing and stabilizer being used.

Do clip, trim, and grade the seam allowances as closely as possible without creating ridges.

Do understitch whenever possible, as far as possible.

Do clip the roll line seam allowance where it ends to enable easier turning of the lapel on jackets and coats.

Do use lots of steam and a wooden clapper to pound the seams as flat as possible.

Do consider using a contrasting fabric if the garment fabric proves to be too stiff or bulky to use as the facing after sampling. A contrasting fabric that is less bulky also adds a decorative finish to the facing areas inside the garment.

Do sample several interfacings and stabilizers with the contrasting fabric to provide the support in the facing that complements the garment.

Do use lining fabric to construct the facing if the facing isn't visible on the garment front.

Don't use the garment fabric if it's too scratchy or bulky.

TRANSFER YOUR KNOWLEDGE

- After a designer has sewn a shaped facing successfully, the same process can be applied to the decorative facing that is turned to the outside of the garment, an area that is full of possibilities.
- The knowledge gained from cutting and sewing bias strips for bias facings can be transferred to creating bias trim, bias piping, and stitching for any garment area.
- Once a placket has been sewn to the neckline of a garment, the knowledge of this application can be applied to the plackets at the cuffs of garments.
- The designer can transfer the knowledge of sewing an extended facing to create a decorative extended facing on the outside of the garment, particularly when the reverse side of a fabric is an interesting contrast.

STRETCH YOUR CREATIVITY

- The fabric used for the garment is a bold floral print. To create a contrasting facing that becomes a focal point of the garment,

trace around the edge of a motif and use that design line as the edge of the facing in a solid, contrasting color (Figure 12.31a).
- The faced area is topstitched in many rows on the correct side of the garment, highlighting the shaped area (Figure 12.31b).
- The straight or slashed keyhole neckline can be changed to mimic any shape that highlights other design elements in a garment: curves, diamonds, triangles, and more (Figure 12.31c).
- Multiple rows of bias binding can be applied to garment edges or sections, highlighting or contrasting the garment fabric (Figure 12.31d).
- Facing can be used for entire shaped sections of a garment that hang free from the body of the garment (Figure 12.31e). Or, consider using the facing at the shaped edge only.

STOP! WHAT DO I DO IF . . .

. . . the facing is finished and has been stitched to the waistline, but after looking at the garment, I want to add a lining?

Stitch a row of straight stitching along the seamline of the lining. With the correct sides together, pin the lining to the facing. Clip, if necessary, so the lining lies flat on the facing. Use the stitching line of the lining and the upper edge of the serger threads on the facing as a guide, and stitch together; press. Understitch the lining to the facing, and press. To finish the hem of the lining, hand or machine stitch as shown in Figure 16.12.

. . . pleating and puckers occurred when I applied bias bindings, leather, or fabric bands?

Remove the stitches in the pleated or tucked area. You'll need to recut the binding, because the holes from the needle will show once the stitches have been removed. Reduce the pressure on the presser foot, and lengthen the stitch length. Sample temporary adhesive tape to hold the binding in place and reduce the distortion of pinning. Leave long threads to pull through to the back of the garment to hand knot. Bury the threads under the binding by pulling them into the binding with a needle, extending the thread, clipping it, and releasing it so that the thread goes under the binding.

. . . my facings look uneven and I've already clipped, trimmed, and understitched?

This problem is especially critical at center fronts and center backs of garments, where it is very noticeable if the edges do not match. Remove the stitching in the uneven area, plus a little bit more before and after the uneven area. Move the stitching line slightly into the garment area to balance the unevenness. Carefully redraw the stitching line with a fabric marker. Handbaste the changed stitching line, and turn the facing to check the result before machine stitching. Once you're satisfied with the result, machine stitch the new line.

. . . my facing looks too heavy; can I remove it and use another edge finish?

Yes, bias binding or a narrow bias facing could

Stretch Your Creativity

12.31A BOLD FLORAL PRINT

12.31B MULTIPLE TOP

12.31C KEYHOLE
VARIATION IN
KNIT DRESS

12.31D MULTIPLE ROWS OF BIAS AS EDGING

12.31E SHAPED, FACED
GARMENT SECTIONS

be used. Remove the facing, carefully ripping the stitches. Press the seam allowance flat; if it has been clipped to the line of stitching, the new line of stitching will have to be moved slightly out. Stitch the new edge finish and press, melding the stitches.

SELF-CRITIQUE

- Do the facings lie smoothly and without puckering?
- Is the area being faced supported by the interfacing used on the facing?
- Is the understitching stitched close to the seam, and is it evenly stitched?
- Is the correct facing type being used in the correct area of the garment?
- Have clipping, trimming, and grading been consistent?
- Is the topstitching stitched evenly?

- Are any hand stitches showing on the front of the garment?
- If the facings are decorative, do they add to the overall success of the design?
- If piping is inserted between the facing and the garment, is it stitched close to the garment edge?
- Do the center fronts or center backs of a garment match in length at the center?

REVIEW CHECKLIST

- Does the shape of the facing match the same shape of the garment it is sewn to?
- Does the grainline of the facing match the grainline of the garment it is sewn to?
- Is the facing width appropriate in weight and design for the garment?
- Are the stabilizer and interfacing the appropriate weight to provide support to the faced areas of the garment?
- Have clipping, trimming, and understitching been consistently done throughout the faced areas of the garment?
- Does the facing lie flat and smooth, and is it bulk-free?
- Is the stitching that joins the facing to the garment sewn evenly, without distortion?
- Is the facing secured to the garment in an appropriate technique for the garment?
- Does the decorative, outside facing lie flat, without twisting or pulling, and is it stitched in a way that complements the style of the garment design?
- Are bias facings cut on the true bias in order to lie flat?
- Is the combination, all-in-one facing used in areas where separate facings would overlap?

13

Cuffs and Other Wrist Finishes: Encircling the Wrist

Every detail in design matters! Even though cuffs and other wrist finishes are a small detail on the sleeve, they are no less important than pockets, seams, zippers, or collars. Cuffs and other wrist finishes draw attention to the wrist. The finish can be purely decorative or perform a function such as providing ease of wear and warmth.

Many cuff designs are outlined in this chapter, including straight and contoured cuffs and a

French cuff. Check out the other cuff options as well and perhaps you will feel inspired to stitch them on your designs. Also think of other creative wrist finishes. By transferring your knowledge, and with help from an instructor, you will be able to stitch your own ideas.

Other wrist finishes can add interest and excitement to the sleeve. Various elastic wrist finishes are also covered, along with bias binding wrist finishes, all of which are in fashion today.

The Style I.D includes ideas to get you thinking about cuffs and other wrist finishes in design. We hope that you will feel excited about

the design possibilities as you learn to stitch cuffs and other wrist finishes. Stitching new aspects of a garment should empower students to embrace more design possibilities; we hope this will be your experience.

STYLE I.D.

The Style I.D. illustrates two different cuff designs and two other wrist finishes that are presented in this chapter. Additional wrist finishes not illustrated in the Style I.D. are also covered.

The striped shirt in Figure 13.1a was shown in Figure 6.28a, except this shows the front view.

KEY TERMS

Contoured Cuff

Cuff

Edge-to-Edge Cuff

Full Interfacing

Gathered Wrist

Half Interfacing

Notched-Extension Cuff

One-Piece Cuff

Open Cuff

Placket

Slit

Tucked Wrist

Two-Piece Cuff

Wrist Finish

Style I.D.

13.1A STRIPED SHIRT
WITH CUFF BANDS

13.1B JACKET WITH
CONTOURED CUFFS

13.1C SHEER PRINT TOP
WITH SHIRRING ELASTIC

13.1D RUFFLED SILK
GEORGETTE BLOUSE

The cuff band is a simple cuff, and a popular cuff style that is regularly in production.

The cuff in Figure 13.1b is a contoured cuff with ruffles inserted around the bottom and side edges. The contrasting ruffle highlights the cuffs and complements the ruffled collar on the jacket.

Figure 13.1c has shirring elastic stitched as a wrist finish to add a soft delicate touch to the sheer print top. The shirring elastic is repeated around the neckline; both finishes employ the same stitching technique.

There are three components to the ensemble in Figure 13.1d; the ruffled blouse, soft, gathered, and made in silk georgette with a bias binding wrist finish; the blouse is paired with jeans; and, to finish this outfit, a midriff bustier cinches the waist.

Though all these wrist finishes are different, they have one thing in common—they are all functional. The placket opens the cuff to allow the hand to enter, then closes with buttons to secure the cuff in place. The shirring elastic stretches and enlarges the wrist for the hand to enter. The bias binding ties and unties for easy access. All wrist treatments should be functional and feel comfortable around the wrist: not too tight and not too loose.

GATHER YOUR TOOLS

You'll need the following tools: tape measure, pins, needles, thread, interfacing, point turner, buttons, buttonhole cutter, sleeve board, and, of course, your seam ripper and thread clippers.

NOW LET'S GET STARTED

Cuffs take time to stitch, as they are very detailed. However, the stitching time is worth the effort, as cuffs add a valuable detail to any garment. Cuffs can be categorized as open or closed.

What Is a Cuff?

A **cuff** is a separate piece of fabric stitched to the wrist or to a short, three-quarter-length (or another length between short and long). The bottom edge of the long sleeve is called the wrist. Figure 13.2 illustrates an open and a closed cuff stitched to the wrist.

Cuffs encircle the wrist and can be different styles, shapes, and sizes. For example, a cuff can be a straight cuff band, a contoured cuff, or a French cuff, which turns back on itself. Two of these cuffs are illustrated in the Style I.D. Cuff bands are narrower than contoured cuffs,

> **PATTERN TIP**
>
> All open cuffs must have an extension included in the overall length of the cuff. The extension is the base to which the buttons are stitched. Notice in Figure 13.3 how the position of the extension is marked with notches, which are then snipped in the fabric when the cuffs are cut. The notches are an important pattern marking to guide the student when stitching the notched cuff. Figure 13.3 illustrates three notched cuffs: a two-piece cuff (Figure 13.3a), one-piece cuff (Figure 13.3b), and a contoured cuff (Figure 13.3c).

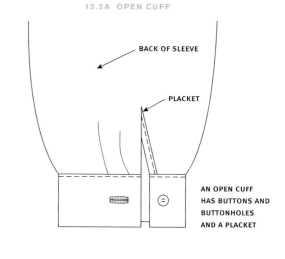

13.2A OPEN CUFF

BACK OF SLEEVE

PLACKET

AN OPEN CUFF HAS BUTTONS AND BUTTONHOLES AND A PLACKET

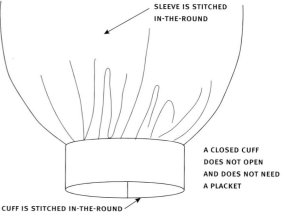

SLEEVE IS STITCHED IN-THE-ROUND

A CLOSED CUFF DOES NOT OPEN AND DOES NOT NEED A PLACKET

CUFF IS STITCHED IN-THE-ROUND

13.2B CLOSED CUFF

as you have observed. A contoured cuff begins from the wrist and extends up the arm for the width chosen by the designer.

Open or Closed Cuffs

Cuffs can be stitched to the wrist so they open (with buttons and buttonholes), or stitched

13.3A TWO-PIECE CUFF

13.3A TWO-PIECE CUFF

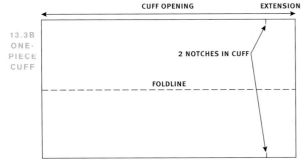

13.3B ONE-PIECE CUFF

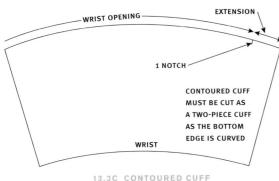

13.3C CONTOURED CUFF

to the wrist in the round, in which case they don't open.

Open cuffs button and unbutton, allowing the hand to enter through the wrist opening (Figure 13.2a). The opening is for practical reasons: to provide ease and comfort when wear- ing the garment. Open cuffs *must* have a **placket** stitched to the back of the sleeve to enable the cuff to open. Figure 13.2 illustrates the position of the placket. The placket is stitched into a **slit,** which is cut in the back of the sleeve up from the wrist.

Closed cuffs are cut in one length and then the two ends are stitched together in a seam and pressed open. The cuff is then stitched in-the- round and stitched to the sleeve, which is also stitched in-the-round. The cuff and sleeve un- derarm seams are placed directly together, so they line up (Figure 13.2b).

One-Piece and Two-Piece Cuffs

Open cuffs can be cut as a **one-piece cuff** or **two-piece cuff.** A one-piece cuff has the bottom seamline replaced with a foldline (Figure 13.3b). A two-piece cuff has a seam along the bottom edge. A two-piece cuff can be cut as a straight or contoured cuff (see Figure 13.3a and c).

A **contoured cuff** is a shaped cuff that cannot be cut on the fold. The reason why a contoured cuff is shaped is because it is cut wider than a straight cuff. (A straight cuff cannot be cut wider than approximately 3 inches.) If the designer wants a cuff wider than this measurement, then the cuff needs to be contoured to the shape of the arm. A con- toured cuff is shaped on the bottom and top edges, and longer on the top edge than the bottom edge. The bottom edge of the cuff fits around the wrist. This is indicated in Figure 13.3c. Any cuff that is shaped *must* be cut as a two-piece cuff.

The Placket

Any sleeve stitched to an open cuff needs a **placket** stitched in the sleeve up from the wrist. The posi- tion of the placket is important—it is placed at the back of the sleeve in line with the elbow. To see the position of the placket, refer to Figure 13.4.

There are three main styles of plackets ex- plained in this chapter: continuous placket, shirt-sleeve placket, and darted placket. All are illustrated in Figure 13.4 and Figure 13.6a.

Before the cuffs are stitched in place, the wrist is tucked or gathered on the sleeve edge. The gathers and tucks create a pleasing sleeve silhouette, rounding at the wrist to contour the arm. Stitching the tucks and gathers will be dis- cussed later in the chapter. If you look at Figure 13.4, you will clearly see tucks and gathers on the wrists of the sleeves.

MAKE SURE THE CUFF FITS COMFORTABLY

Slip the tape measure around your hand to get an accurate measurement for the cuff. The tape measure does not go around the wrist but around the *hand.* This measurement is the length of the

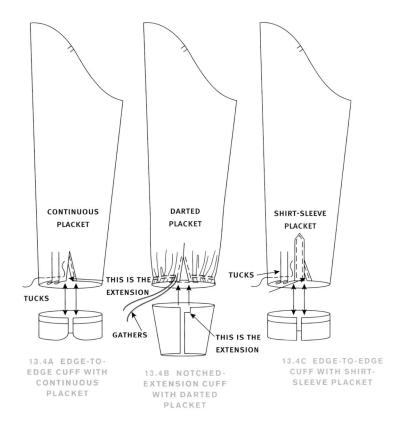

13.4A EDGE-TO-EDGE CUFF WITH CONTINUOUS PLACKET

13.4B NOTCHED-EXTENSION CUFF WITH DARTED PLACKET

13.4C EDGE-TO-EDGE CUFF WITH SHIRT-SLEEVE PLACKET

and not overtake the design; rather, it should blend and look aesthetically pleasing to the eye. It can be challenging for the design student to experiment with different wrist finishes. Always sample and experiment with your own ideas.

- When choosing a cuff finish, it is imperative that the wrist finish suit the fabric weight, texture, and sheerness. Play with the fabric—tuck and gather a small section to observe the

13.5A ONE-PIECE CUFF WITH FULL INTERFACING

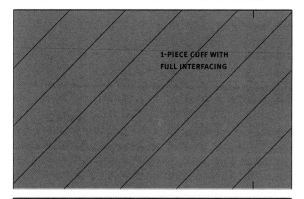

1-PIECE CUFF WITH FULL INTERFACING

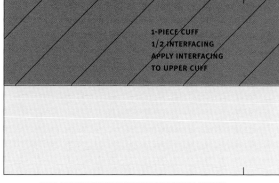

1-PIECE CUFF 1/2 INTERFACING APPLY INTERFACING TO UPPER CUFF

THIS MEASUREMENT INCLUDES THE WRIST LENGTH, EXTENSION & SEAM ALLOWANCE

13.5B ONE-PIECE CUFF WITH HALF INTERFACING

IMPORTANT

It is the designer's responsibility to make sure that the garment parts work. We emphasize functional design. Whether the cuff is open or closed, it needs to fit comfortably, not too tight and not too loose, with adequate room for the hand to enter.

wrist opening on the cuff. For open cuffs, the extension and seam allowances are added to this measurement. Figure 13.5 indicates the total length of the cuff, including the extension and seam allowances.

A closed cuff does not need an extension; however, the cuff does need an extra 1 inch of ease added to the length so the cuff slides comfortably over the hand.

HOW TO CHOOSE THE APPROPRIATE WRIST FINISH

Choosing the appropriate wrist finish for a garment is an important decision. The wrist finish needs to complement the overall design weight and drape of the fabric. This is a very practical exercise.

- Comfort is important—the way the wrist opens and closes is the practical side of functional design. This is so important when considering your target customer. Even though French cuffs look fabulous (see Figure 13.14c), a busy mom or the elderly may not have the physical ability or time to mange a closure such as this.
- The designer is usually limited by a budget! Cuffs and other wrist finishes are a small detail on the overall garment but can consume a lot of construction time. For example, in production the cost of stitching the placket and cuff may add too much to the overall cost of the garment.
- Trends in cuffs may direct the designer in choosing one style over another. For example, if you want to include a shirt in your collection, you may choose a straight, simple cuff over a French cuff.

STABILIZING CUFFS

Cuffs can be stabilized with **full interfacing**, which means both sides of the cuff are interfaced (Figure 13.5a). Cuffs can also be interfaced with **half interfacing**. Half interfacing is applied to the top side of the cuff only (Figure 13.5b).

The fabric directs the amount of interfacing that is needed to support the cuff. So sample both full and half interfacings in a variety of types and weights, and then make the final choice. Interfacing helps shape the cuff and support but-

tons and buttonholes as the closure. Apply the interfacing now before stitching the cuff.

As a general guide, if the fabric is heavyweight, use half interfacing. If the fabric is lighter, it may benefit from a full interfacing. A contoured cuff is best stabilized on both cuff pieces, as it needs more structure to enable it to sit on the wrist/arm. Even though Figure 13.5 illustrates interfacing applied to a straight cuff, the principle is the same whether the cuff is straight or contoured.

LET'S STITCH

Correct stitching always begins with correct patterns. Check that your notches have been snipped and the stabilizer applied to your cuffs. With this preparation attended to, have your tape measure around your neck, pins, scissors, and seam gauge by your side, and now you are ready to stitch cuffs.

OPEN CUFFS

Open cuffs have a placket stitched from the wrist up into the sleeve. A slit is cut into the sleeve, and the placket is stitched into the slit. It is the placket that enables the cuff to open. Buttons and buttonholes are stitched to the cuff to aid in opening and closing the cuff. Here is the general stitching order for stitching open cuffs to the sleeves:

FLAT APPLICATION

Stitch the placket into the wrist while the sleeve is flat. Then stitch the tucks and secure with a staystitch while the sleeve lies flat (Figure 13.6a). The

underarm seams are then stitched together before the cuffs are stitched to the wrist (Figure 13.6b).

STITCHED IN-THE-ROUND

Stitch the placket into the wrist while the sleeve is flat. If the wrist is gathered, then stitch the underarm seams next. Then stitch the basting stitches for gathers after the sleeve is stitched in-the-round (Figure 13.6b).

PLACKETS

Each placket has a particular way of being stitched. In preparation for stitching the placket, cut the slit in the sleeve to the length marked on the pattern.

Continuous Placket

If you look around the stores, you will notice that the continuous placket is one of the most popular plackets in sleeves. A separate binding is stitched to enclose both raw edges of the split. The cuff will be stitched edge-to-edge with the placket, so no notched extension is needed. It is a functional and practical placket opening to use for shirts and blouses.

> **PATTERN TIP**
>
> Cut the placket binding 1½ inches wide and twice the length of the slit plus an extra inch to account for the seam allowance.

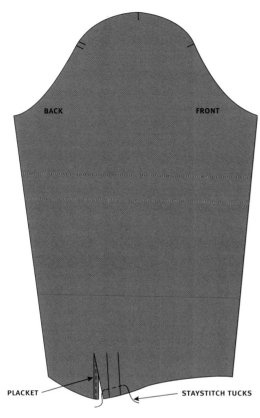

13.6A SLEEVES FLAT APPLICATION

13.6B STITCHED IN-THE-ROUND

- Press both sides of the binding seam allowance ¼ inch over to the wrong side of the fabric. Fold the binding in half again and press (Figure 13.7a).
- Unfold one side of the binding, and place the correct sides of the slit and binding together. Pin together at the wrist with a ¼-inch seam allowance. Taper the end of the slit so a ¹⁄₁₆-inch seam allowance is lined up with the ¼-inch seam allowance on the binding (Figure 13.7b).

- Use small stitches (approximately 2.0 stitch length) and begin stitching a ¼-inch seam allowance, ending with a scant ¹⁄₁₆ inch at the end of the slit; leave the machine needle down in your work. Notice the slit seam edge is now on an angle—don't worry, it's meant to look like this (Figure 13.7c).
- Pivot on this point by swinging the other side of the slit back so it is in line with the rest of the stitching; stitch the remaining placket to the other side of the slit in the same way (see Figure 13.7c).

- Press the seam allowance toward the center of the binding (Figure 13.7d).
- Place the binding foldline just covering the seam; pin or handbaste in place, then edgestitch the binding in place to form the placket, as illustrated in Figure 13.7d.
- Fold the correct sides of the binding together; stitch diagonally across the placket to hold it in place (Figure 13.7e).
- Fold the binding back on the tucked side, so it is hidden, and staystitch the placket in place (Figure 13.7f).

Shirt-Sleeve Placket

The shirt-sleeve placket is mainly seen on men's shirts. It may look complicated to stitch but it's simple once you get the hang of it! It is stitched using two separate placket pieces—one small and one large. Take your time to perfect this placket, as it's a classy look for shirts in women's wear. No interfacing is necessary in the placket, but do mark the matchpoints—they are important to the success of this placket.

The length of the small placket must equal the length of the slit plus ⅜ inch for the seam allowance (Figure 13.8a). On the large placket (Figure 13.8c), mark matchpoints equal to the length of the slit. Extra length is added beyond this on the large placket, and this part is topstitched to complete the shirt-sleeve placket.

13.7A PREPARE THE BINDING.

13.7B STITCH THE PLACKET TO THE SLIT.

13.7C STITCH THE ¼-INCH SEAM ALLOWANCE.

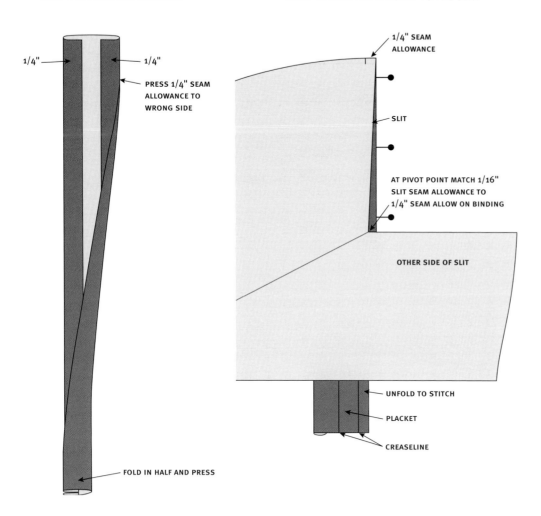

1/4"

1/4"

PRESS 1/4" SEAM
ALLOWANCE TO
WRONG SIDE

FOLD IN HALF AND PRESS

1/4" SEAM
ALLOWANCE

SLIT

AT PIVOT POINT MATCH 1/16"
SLIT SEAM ALLOWANCE TO
1/4" SEAM ALLOW ON BINDING

OTHER SIDE OF SLIT

UNFOLD TO STITCH

PLACKET

CREASELINE

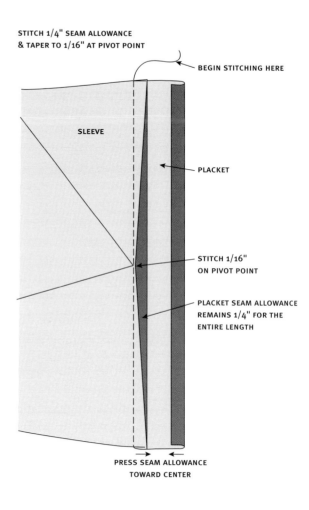

STITCH 1/4" SEAM ALLOWANCE
& TAPER TO 1/16" AT PIVOT POINT

BEGIN STITCHING HERE

SLEEVE

PLACKET

STITCH 1/16"
ON PIVOT POINT

PLACKET SEAM ALLOWANCE
REMAINS 1/4" FOR THE
ENTIRE LENGTH

PRESS SEAM ALLOWANCE
TOWARD CENTER

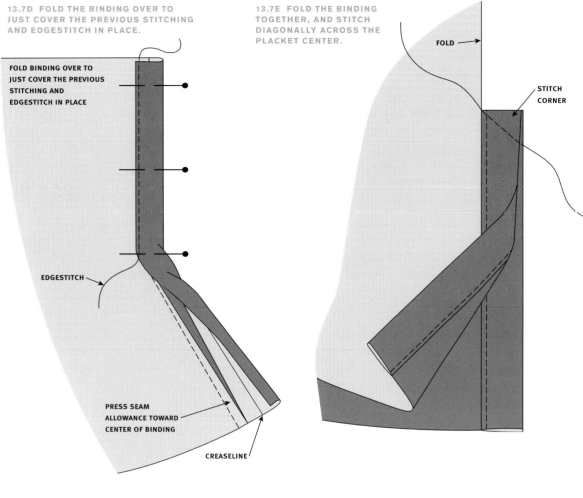

13.7D FOLD THE BINDING OVER TO JUST COVER THE PREVIOUS STITCHING AND EDGESTITCH IN PLACE.

FOLD BINDING OVER TO JUST COVER THE PREVIOUS STITCHING AND EDGESTITCH IN PLACE

EDGESTITCH

PRESS SEAM ALLOWANCE TOWARD CENTER OF BINDING

CREASELINE

13.7E FOLD THE BINDING TOGETHER, AND STITCH DIAGONALLY ACROSS THE PLACKET CENTER.

FOLD

STITCH CORNER

BACK SLEEVE

FRONT SLEEVE

PRESS CREASELINE

STAYSTITCH

13.7F FOLD THE BINDING BACK ON THE TUCKED SIDE AND STAYSTITCH IN PLACE.

FOLD PLACKET BACK

TUCK 1   TUCK 2

IMPORTANT

In preparation for stitching the placket, at the top of the slit, cut a V-shape on both sides of the placket, as illustrated in Figure 13.8a. The V cut becomes the seam allowance, ¼ inch on either side of the slit for the placket to be stitched.

Small Placket

- Press ¼-inch seam allowance to the wrong side on both sides of small placket. Fold the placket in half again, and press (Figure 13.8a).
- Wrap the small placket binding around the slit to enclose it; this is the side closest to the back underarm. Pin or handbaste in place (see Figure 13.8a).
- Edgestitch the binding, starting from the wrist and finishing at the top of the slit. This should leave ⅜ inch for the seam allowance. Press the small placket piece (see Figure 13.8a).

Lay the sleeve on a flat surface with the wrong side facing up. Fold the back sections of the sleeve over so the correct side is facing up. Staystitch the binding and the V-shaped sections together across the top. Don't be alarmed—the seam allowance is now showing on the correct side (Figure 13.8b).

Large Placket Piece

- Fold the correct sides of the large placket together. Stitch a ¼-inch seam around the edge, beginning from the matchpoints and pivoting on the angle; finish stitching with a backstitch on the foldline.

- Clip the corners and turn the placket to the correct side. Use a point turner to sharpen the point (Figure 13.8c).
- Press the remaining seam allowance to the wrong side (see Figure 13.8c).
- With the correct side facing up, wrap the large placket piece around the other side of the slit. Line the large placket matchpoints to the horizontal staystitching on the small placket. Make sure that the seam allowance is fully covered by the large placket piece; pin and handbaste in place (Figure 13.8d).
- Edgestitch the large placket using approximately a 2.0 stitch length. Begin stitching from the wrist, and stitch following the shape of the placket, pivoting on each corner. Finish stitching with a backstitch (this should be at the matchpoint position) (Figure 13.8e).
- Press the placket in place.

Notice that the small placket seam allowance is now hidden behind the topstitched large placket. An X can be stitched within the square as well; just continue stitching on from where the other topstitching left off (see Figure 13.13b).

Darted Placket

This is a very quick and easy method to stitch a placket. Both sides of a darted placket are topstitched. At the top of the placket, a dart is stitched to bring both sides of the slits together. This placket is especially cost-effective in production, as it is the fastest and easiest of all the plackets to stitch.

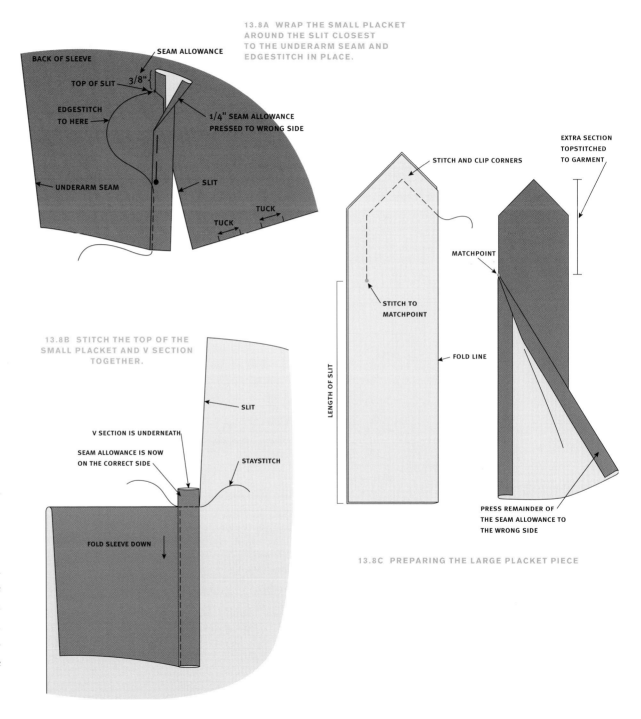

13.8A WRAP THE SMALL PLACKET AROUND THE SLIT CLOSEST TO THE UNDERARM SEAM AND EDGESTITCH IN PLACE.

13.8B STITCH THE TOP OF THE SMALL PLACKET AND V SECTION TOGETHER.

13.8C PREPARING THE LARGE PLACKET PIECE

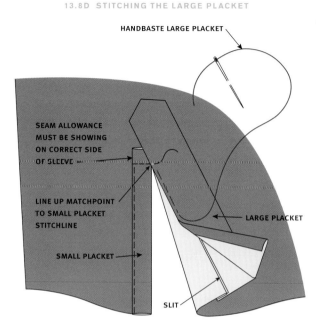

13.8D STITCHING THE LARGE PLACKET

HANDBASTE LARGE PLACKET

SEAM ALLOWANCE MUST BE SHOWING ON CORRECT SIDE OF SLEEVE

LINE UP MATCHPOINT TO SMALL PLACKET STITCHLINE

LARGE PLACKET

SMALL PLACKET

SLIT

13.8E TOPSTITCH THE LARGE PLACKET.

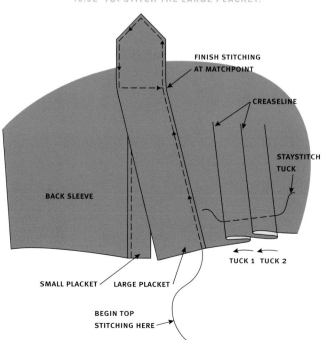

FINISH STITCHING AT MATCHPOINT

CREASELINE

STAYSTITCH TUCK

BACK SLEEVE

TUCK 1   TUCK 2

SMALL PLACKET   LARGE PLACKET

BEGIN TOP STITCHING HERE

- Press ⅛ inch to the wrong side on both sides of the slit. Fold another ⅛ inch over and machine stitch both sides close to the folded edge; stitch directionally from wrist up to the top (Figure 13.9a). The top of the slit should now look like a ∩ shape.
- Fold the correct sides of the placket together so they are lined up together. Stitch a short curved dart approximately 1½ inches in length. Always stitch darts from the widest to the narrowest point (Figure 13.9b).
- Press the dart to one side, and notice that both sides of the placket are now sitting together (Figure 13.9c).

Once the placket has been completed, the wrists are prepared, then stitched to the cuff. There are two styles in which to stitch the wrist; one method is tucked and the other method is gathered. The style of cuff will direct the choice of wrist finish.

PREPARING THE WRIST

Look back at Figure 13.4 to see the difference between gathers and tucks. At the pattern drafting stage, fullness is added into the wrist for both gathering and tucks. The extra fullness allows more room in the width of the sleeve so the arm can bend comfortably. Generally the darted plackets look aesthetically pleasing stitched to a **gathered wrist** (see Figure 13.4c). The continuous and shirt-sleeve plackets add a tailored finish when combined with the **tucked wrist** (see Figure 13.4a and b). A gathered wrist creates more fullness in the sleeve than the tucked

PATTERN TIP

Cut the slit an extra ½ inch longer to allow for the dart to be stitched.

wrist. Chapter 6, "Gathered Seam," explained how to stitch basting stitches so the wrist can be gathered. Figure 6.23 illustrates the steps involved. A tucked or gathered wrist is prepared before the cuffs are stitched.

Tucked Wrist

To stitch the tucks, the sleeves need to lay flat. This is the flat application method (see Figure 13.6a). Fold each tuck toward the placket, as illustrated in Figure 13.7f, and staystitch the tucks in place. Press a crease line a few inches up each tuck. Stitch and finish closed or open underarm seams after the tucks have been stitched.

Gathered Wrist

Before the wrist is gathered, the underarm seams *must* be stitched. Stitch the underarm seams; the sleeve is now in-the-round ready for the cuff to be applied (see Figure 13.4b). After the basting stitches are stitched, pull the threads into gathering to fit the wrist length. Evenly distribute the gathering.

TRIMS STITCHED TO THE CUFFS

A trim such as lace, ribbon, braid, or a ruffle can be stitched to the cuff to add glamour to the sleeve. The cuff in the Style I.D., Figure 13.1b, has a contrasting ruffle stitched to the cuff,

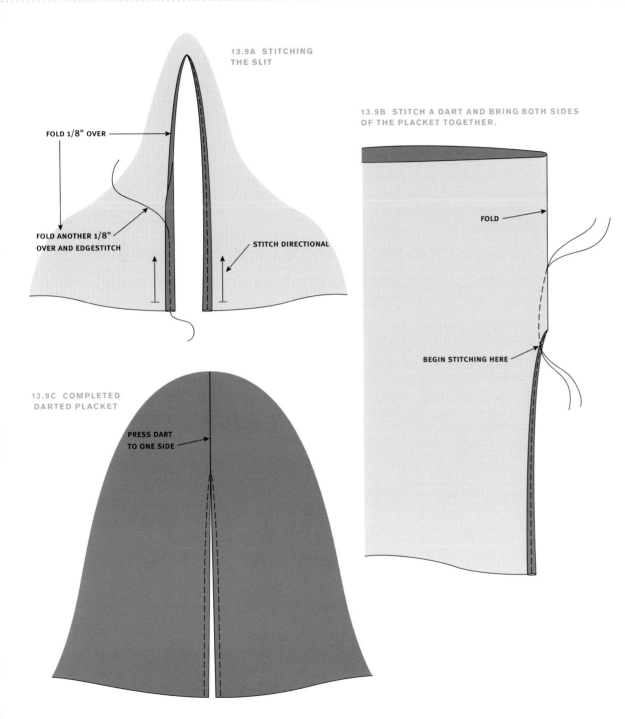

13.9A STITCHING THE SLIT

FOLD 1/8" OVER

FOLD ANOTHER 1/8"
OVER AND EDGESTITCH

STITCH DIRECTIONAL

**13.9B STITCH A DART AND BRING BOTH SIDES
OF THE PLACKET TOGETHER.**

FOLD

BEGIN STITCHING HERE

**13.9C COMPLETED
DARTED PLACKET**

PRESS DART
TO ONE SIDE

drawing attention to the cuff. This type of trim is stitched to the cuff, after the stabilizer is applied, and before the cuffs are stitched together. Figure 13.10 shows you how to position the ruffle around the seam edge of the contoured cuff for the jacket in Figure 13.1b.

- The trim is positioned on the *interfaced* cuff (see Figure 13.10).
- Finish the ruffle edges; how this is done depends on whether the ruffle is single or double. For a single ruffle, machine stitch a narrow rolled hem around the edges. For a double ruffle, fold and place the correct side of the fabric together. Stitch a ¼-inch seam on both ends of the ruffle. Clip the corners, turn, and press, and then gather the ruffle and evenly distribute the gathering.
- Pin and handbaste the ruffle in place. When pinning, push more gathers into the corners, as Figure 13.10 illustrates, so that the ruffle will span out when the cuff is turned to the correct side.
- Place the correct sides of the cuffs together and complete stitching the cuff.
- For more information on stitching ruffles, refer to Chapter 10.

STITCHING THE CUFFS

There are two different ways of stitching cuffs to the wrist. Cuffs can be stitched to the wrist **edge-to-edge** with the placket, as illustrated in Figure 13.4a and b, or stitched to the wrist with a **notched-extension cuff**, as illustrated in Figure 13.4c. Both cuffs *do* have an extension

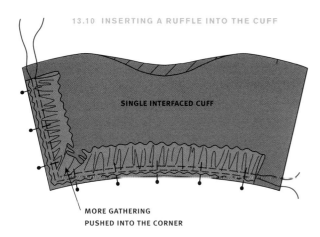

13.10 INSERTING A RUFFLE INTO THE CUFF

SINGLE INTERFACED CUFF

MORE GATHERING
PUSHED INTO THE CORNER

added into the cuff at the pattern drafting stage; however, the extensions are stitched differently.

Knowing which cuff to choose is guided purely by the style of placket used. Notice in Figure 13.4a and b that one side of the placket forms the extension. At the top of the placket, it tucks underneath the sleeve.

Then notice, in Figure 13.4c, the absence of an extension on the sleeve with the darted placket. When a darted placket is stitched, the extension is on the cuff rather than on the placket. Therefore, before the cuff can be stitched to a darted placket, an extension is stitched to the cuff first. The extension looks like a small step; can you see it in Figure 13.4c?

Both edge-to-edge and notched-extension cuffs will be outlined.

Edge-to-Edge Cuff
One-Piece/Two-Piece Cuff Band
An edge-to-edge cuff is the basic straight cuff. The striped shirt, illustrated in the Style I.D. in Figure 13.1a, has this exact cuff. It is often referred to as a band cuff. You will notice in Figure 13.4a and b that the bottom edge of the cuffs can be angled or curved. If you turn to Figure 13.2, you will see the placement for the button and buttonhole on an edge-to-edge cuff.

An edge-to-edge cuff is stitched to the entire length of the wrist. The wrist length includes the placket as well. You will notice that one side of the continuous placket in Figure 13.4a has been turned back before the cuff is stitched. How this is done will be explained in due course.

- Half interfacing or full interfacing is applied, depending on how structured you want the cuffs to be (Figure 13.5).
- On the one-piece cuff, fold the wrong sides together and press along the foldline; then open again.
- Along the top edge of the cuff, press a ½-inch seam allowance over to the wrong side (Figure 13.11a).
- Place the correct sides of the cuff together. With the seam allowance facing down, stitch a ½-inch

> **PATTERN TIP**
>
> The position of the extension needs be notched before stitching the cuff. Only with snipped notches can the cuff be stitched. Figure 13.3 shows where the notches are snipped when the cuffs are cut. Figure 13.12 also shows the notches snipped.

seam allowance down the sides and along the bottom edge of a two-piece cuff, and down the sides only of the one-piece cuff. The top edge of the cuff is left open; this section is stitched to the wrist (see Figure 13.11a).

- Trim the seam allowance back to ¼ inch, and trim the corners to reduce bulk.
- Turn the cuffs to the correct side; use a point turner to gently push the corners to sharpen the point.
- Figure 13.11b shows the edge-to-edge cuff finished, turned, and pressed, and ready to be stitched to the wrist.

Notched-Extension Cuff
One-Piece/Two-Piece/Contoured Cuffs

- Place the correct sides of the cuffs together with the interfaced cuff underneath (unless fully interfaced). On the upper cuff, on the side without the notched extension, fold a ½-inch seam allowance to the wrong side and pin in place (Figure 13.12a).
- Begin stitching the cuff at the notched extension. Start with a backstitch and stitch across the extension, pivot on the corner, and stitch the remainder of the cuff, following each cuff shape (see Figure 13.12a).
- At the notched extension, clip into the seam allowance, leaving ⅟₁₆ inch intact, and press the seam allowance down along the top edge of the cuff (Figure 13.12b).
- Trim the seam allowance back to ¼ inch, and trim the corners to reduce bulk (Figure 13.12a and b).

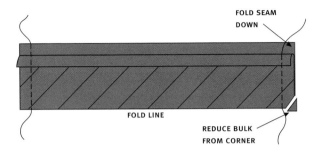

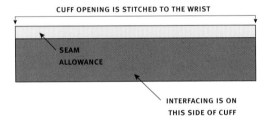

- Turn the cuffs to the correct side, and use a point turner to gently sharpen the corners.
- Press the cuffs. They are now ready to be stitched to the wrist. Figure 13.12c shows the notched-extension contour cuff stitched, turned, pressed, and ready to stitch to the wrist. Notice the seam allowance along the top edge is the opening that will be stitched to the wrist.

Mirror Imaging the Cuffs

This is an important step! After the cuff is completed and pressed, fold both sides of the cuff together—they should be exactly the same

IMPORTANT

Pressing the cuff is critical to cuffs looking absolutely fabulous. When the cuff is pressed, the seamlines should sit directly in the middle of the seam and not be pressed to one side more than the other.

shape and width; this is called *mirror imaging the cuffs*. Refer to Figure 11.5d to see how to mirror image a collar. Following the same idea, bring both sides of the cuffs exactly together. If the cuffs are not a mirror image, then seam rip one side and restitch so they match *perfectly* together. If the cuffs are not of equal width, it will throw off the buttoning. In clothing construction, every stitching detail matters and good-quality stitching is important.

Stitching Cuffs to the Wrist
Edge-to-Edge Cuff

Whether or not a continuous or shirt-sleeve placket is being stitched, the stitching order is exactly the same when it comes to stitching the cuff to the wrist.

- Turn the sleeve to the wrong side. Place the correct side of the cuff around the wrong side of the sleeve, matching the cuff and the wrist edges together. Pin in place (Figure 13.13a). Notice in this sketch that the outside edge of the cuff is curved—it is the designer's choice whether the cuff is straight, angled, or curved.
- Stitch a ½-inch seam allowance, and trim and grade the seam to reduce bulk (see Figure 13.13a).

- Working from the correct side, turn the seam allowance down into the cuff and place the folded edge just beyond the seamline (Figure 13.13b).
- Pin and handbaste the seam in place, as the

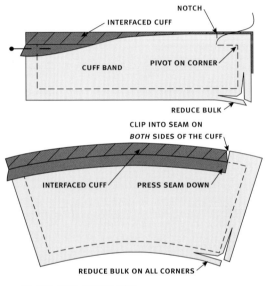

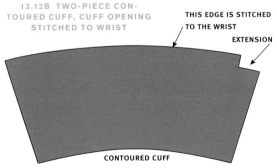

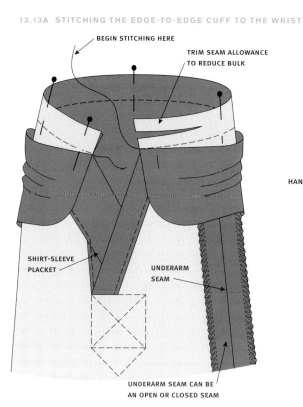

BEGIN STITCHING HERE

TRIM SEAM ALLOWANCE TO REDUCE BULK

SHIRT-SLEEVE PLACKET

UNDERARM SEAM

UNDERARM SEAM CAN BE AN OPEN OR CLOSED SEAM

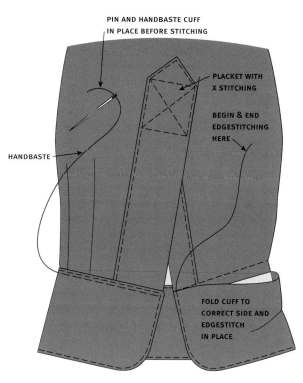

PIN AND HANDBASTE CUFF IN PLACE BEFORE STITCHING

PLACKET WITH X STITCHING

BEGIN & END EDGESTITCHING HERE

HANDBASTE

FOLD CUFF TO CORRECT SIDE AND EDGESTITCH IN PLACE

difference is that it is longer than the traditional shirt-sleeve placket. Follow the stitching order in Figure 13.8.

- Cut a two-piece cuff. Apply full interfacing to both sides of the cuff. This adds the structure needed to hold the turned-back section in place.
- Before stitching the cuff to the wrist, fold the small placket back to the wrong side of the sleeve and staystitch in place (Figure 13.14a).
- Stitch and finish the underarm seams before continuing—the sleeve is now stitched in-the-round and ready to be stitched to the cuff.
- To stitch the cuff to the wrist, follow the same stitching order as for the edge-to edge cuff outlined in Figure 13.13.
- After the cuff is stitched to the wrist, fold the bottom section of the cuff back to the correct side, placing it ⅛ inch beyond the seamline. Press a sharp crease along this edge (Figure 13.14c).
- Unfold the cuff and, with the tape measure, position the buttonholes, four in all, centered on the cuff and fold-back cuff. The buttonholes *must* be sitting directly together, in the middle of each cuff, when the cuff links secure them together (see Figure 13.14b).

seams can easily twist if not perfectly aligned. Pinning and handbasting ultimately save time.

- Edgestitch the top edge of the cuff from the correct side; begin stitching from the small placket; hold the cuff taut as you edgestitch to the other side of the placket and around the cuff edge if you desire (see Figure 13.13b).
- Press the cuffs.

French Cuff

This chapter is not complete without discussing the beautiful French cuff. It looks stylish yet

tailored, as half the cuff turns back and is fastened with cuff links. It is stitched as an edge-to-edge cuff.

PATTERN TIP

A placket for a French cuff is cut even longer than the shirt placket—with a finished length of approximately 5 inches.

- A French cuff has a shirt-sleeve placket that is stitched first before applying the cuff. The only

IMPORTANT

Pressing the French cuff is important to its success! The cuff needs to be *perfectly* pressed so the seamlines remain in the middle of the cuff, not rolling to one side. Take your time pressing the French cuff.

13.14A SHIRT-SLEEVE PLACKET FOR A FRENCH CUFF

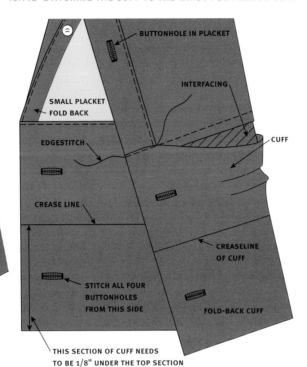

13.14B STITCHING THE CUFF TO THE WRIST FOR FRENCH CUFF

13.14C CLOSING THE FRENCH CUFF WITH CUFF LINKS

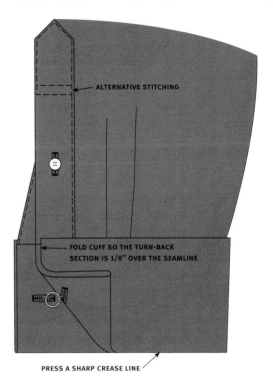

- Stitch the four buttonholes to the underneath side of the cuffs, as illustrated in Figure 13.14b.
- Also stitch a buttonhole to the placket from the correct side (see Figure 13.14b).
- Cuff links then secure the French cuffs together, as illustrated in Figure 13.14c. Cuff links can be purchased at the store, or you can be creative and make your own.

Notched-Extension Cuff

- Have the sleeve turned to the correct side. Wrap the cuff around the wrist, matching the edges together, evenly distributing the gathering (Figure 13.15a).
- Stitch the cuff and wrist together with a ½-inch seam allowance. Begin with a backstitch; start stitching from the extension around the wrist (see Figure 13.15a).

- Trim and grade the seam allowance to reduce bulk (refer to Figure 13.13a).
- To complete the cuff, turn the seam allowance down into the cuff. Position the folded edge of the under cuff to the seamline.
- Pin and handbaste the foldline in place, as the seams can easily twist if it is not *perfectly* in alignment. Pinning and handbasting ultimately save time.
- Close the cuff with a slipstitch or blindstitch.

Refer to Figure 15.9 to see these hand stitches. The cuff can also be machine stitched-in-the-ditch or topstitched as alternative finishes. If stitching-in-the-ditch, place the foldline just over the seamline (see Figure 13.15b).

Buttonhole and Button Placement

It is important that the buttonholes and buttons be positioned correctly on the cuffs. The designer needs to work out the size and number of buttons that will be used on the cuff. The width of the cuff should guide this decision. Generally cuff buttons are quite small.

- Position the buttonholes at least ½ inch to ⅝ inch in from the seamline, as Figure 13.16 illustrates. This will ensure that the buttonhole clears the thickness from the seam allowance when stitched. When buttonholes are stitched over the seam allowance, they will not be stitched properly.
- Place buttonholes an equal distance from each other.
- Pin the cuff closed, and pin-mark the button position. Refer to Chapter 17, Figure 17.11.

The following figures show a variation of how the cuffs can be buttoned:

- A straight cuff can button with one button, as illustrated in Figure 13.16.
- A straight cuff can also be buttoned with two smaller buttons when stitched to a shirt-sleeve placket *only*. This gives more flexibility for the tightness or looseness for the cuff. Don't

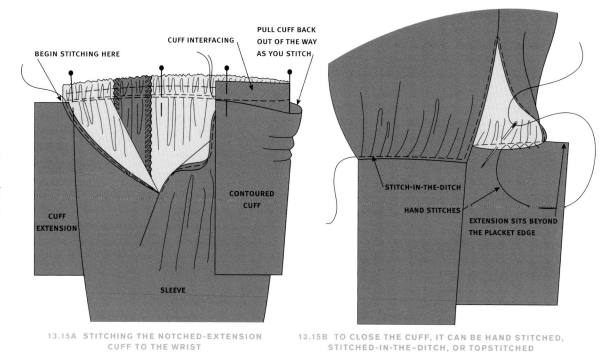

13.15A STITCHING THE NOTCHED-EXTENSION CUFF TO THE WRIST

13.15B TO CLOSE THE CUFF, IT CAN BE HAND STITCHED, STITCHED-IN-THE-DITCH, OR TOPSTITCHED

try this type of buttoning on a notched extension cuff, as it will never work (Figure 13.17).

- A contoured cuff with a ruffle inserted has three small buttons as its closure. Notice the position of each button and buttonhole. Whether there is a ruffle or not, the buttonhole/button placement is exactly the same (Figure 13.18).

CLOSED CUFFS

A closed cuff is one that doesn't open; it is simpler to stitch than an open cuff, as it doesn't need a placket. A closed cuff is stitched in-the-round to the bottom sleeve edge of a long or short sleeve. The cuff opening must allow enough room to comfortably slip over the hand

PATTERN TIP

As a general guide, closed cuffs need an extra inch added to the hand measurement for ease.

and not feel too tight—this is functional design. Closed cuffs are usually cut as a straight, one-piece cuff. A closed cuff is best cut as a straight one-piece cuff if it is being attached to the wrist (Figure 13.5). However, a contoured cuff will work, as long as the wrist measurement fits over the hand. How it fits depends solely on the measurements used. Stitch muslin first to test the proportions of your cuff design.

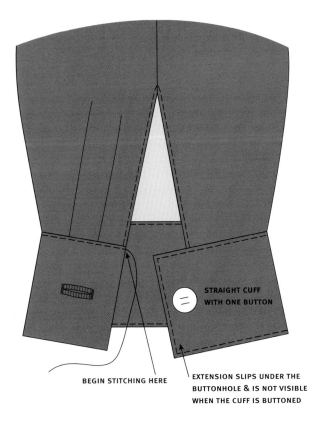

BEGIN STITCHING HERE

STRAIGHT CUFF
WITH ONE BUTTON

EXTENSION SLIPS UNDER THE
BUTTONHOLE & IS NOT VISIBLE
WHEN THE CUFF IS BUTTONED

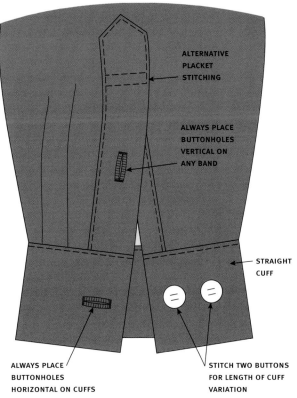

ALTERNATIVE
PLACKET
STITCHING

ALWAYS PLACE
BUTTONHOLES
VERTICAL ON
ANY BAND

STRAIGHT
CUFF

ALWAYS PLACE
BUTTONHOLES
HORIZONTAL ON CUFFS

STITCH TWO BUTTONS
FOR LENGTH OF CUFF
VARIATION

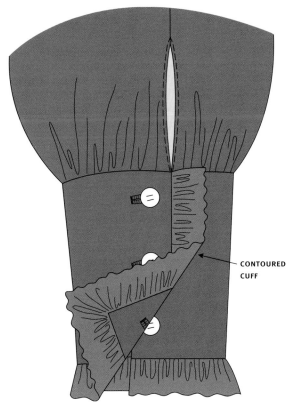

CONTOURED
CUFF

- Interface half the cuff (see Figure 13.5b).
- Fold the cuff in half with the wrong sides together, and press a crease line along the folded edge (Figure 13.19a).
- Along the top edge of the cuff (not interfaced), press ½-inch seam allowance to the wrong side (see Figure 13.19a).
- Open both the crease lines and refold the cuff, placing correct sides together. Stitch a ½-inch seam in the cuff, press the seam open, and

reduce bulk on the seams (see Figure 13.19a).
- Stitch and finish the underarm seams—the cuff and sleeve are both stitched in-the-round, ready to be joined together.
- Gather the wrist and turn the sleeve to the correct side. Place the sleeve inside the cuff with correct sides facing each other.
- Match the seamlines together; evenly distribute the gathering as the edges are pinned together. Stitch a ½-inch seam around the wrist;

trim the seam back to ¼ inch to eliminate bulk (Figure 13.19b).
- Turn the sleeve to the wrong side; turn the seam allowance down into the cuff. Line the other folded edge of the cuff to the seamline, and pin and handbaste in place (Figure 13.19c).
- Blindstitch or slipstitch the cuff in place (see Figure 13.19c)—it is too difficult to machine stitch a tight circle!

OTHER WRIST FINISHES

The popular wrist elastic casing is one of the wrist finishes outlined in this section. A bias binding wrist finish is also explained, along with shirring—all are popular wrist finishes today.

CASINGS

An elastic casing is a tunnel through which elastic, cord, or ribbon is threaded to tighten the wrist. This style of casing can be stitched to the wrist or any neckline edge or stitched into the waistline of a garment. These variations can be achieved by transferring your knowledge. The casing creates an eye-catching sleeve as soft gathers form around the wrist, which draws much attention to the wrist. The elastic casing stretches to allow the hand to comfortably enter the sleeve.

Edge Casing

This style of casing has a once-turned top-stitched hem on the edge of the wrist. The edge of the hem forms a slot for the elastic to enter; the elastic can be tightened at the wrist, which softly gathers the sleeve. This style of wrist finish looks marvelous made in soft, sheer fabrics.

PATTERN TIP

The width of the slot is defined by the width of the elastic. Decide on the elastic width, measure this, and add ¼-inch of ease and ¼-inch seam allowance. Add this total width below your wrist edge for the slot. The final width of the hem, when stitched, needs to be ⅛ inch wider than the elastic width.

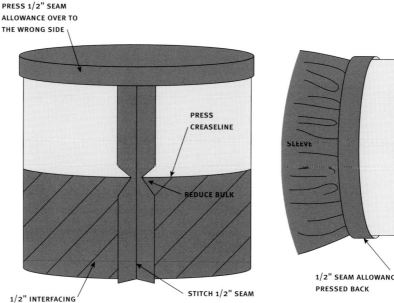

13.19A STITCHING A CLOSED CUFF

PRESS 1/2" SEAM ALLOWANCE OVER TO THE WRONG SIDE

PRESS CREASELINE

REDUCE BULK

1/2" INTERFACING

STITCH 1/2" SEAM

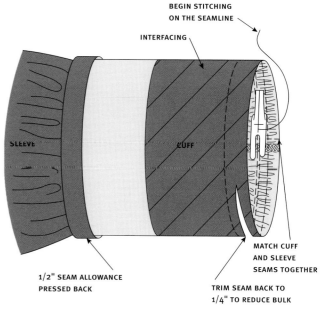

13.19B STITCHING THE CUFF TO THE WRIST

BEGIN STITCHING ON THE SEAMLINE

INTERFACING

SLEEVE

CUFF

1/2" SEAM ALLOWANCE PRESSED BACK

MATCH CUFF AND SLEEVE SEAMS TOGETHER

TRIM SEAM BACK TO 1/4" TO REDUCE BULK

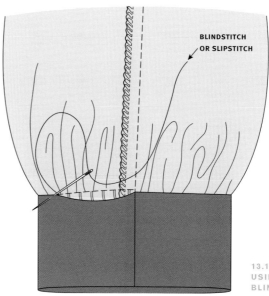

BLINDSTITCH OR SLIPSTITCH

13.19C THE CUFF IS CLOSED USING A SLIPSTITCH OR A BLINDSTITCH.

13.20A STITCH THE CASING AND SLIDE THE
ELASTIC THROUGH THE SLOT.

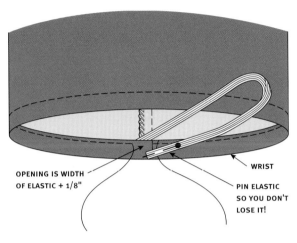

OPENING IS WIDTH
OF ELASTIC + 1/8"

WRIST

PIN ELASTIC
SO YOU DON'T
LOSE IT!

13.20B AFTER THE ELASTIC IS THROUGH THE CASING,
PULL BOTH ENDS OF THE ELASTIC OUT OF THE OPENING
AND ZIGZAG STITCH TOGETHER.

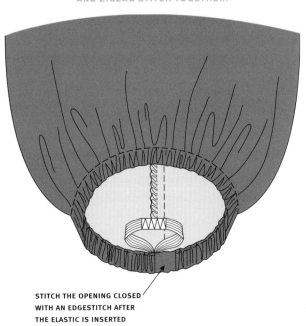

STITCH THE OPENING CLOSED
WITH AN EDGESTITCH AFTER
THE ELASTIC IS INSERTED

- Stitch and finish closed underarm seams; the sleeve is now stitched in-the-round. Press the seam to the left if right-handed or to the right if left-handed (see Figure 13.6b).
- Stitch a machine-stitched hem (see Figure 15.20). When the hem is stitched, leave an opening at the seam ⅛ inch wider than the elastic width. Begin and end the hem stitching with a backstitch (Figure 13.20a).
- Cut a comfortable elastic wrist length and add ½-inch seam allowance. Attach a safety pin to one end of the elastic and slide it through the casing, in the direction of the seam allowance (see Figure 13.20a).
- Pin the other end of the elastic to the casing so you don't lose it in the casing (see Figure 13.20a).
- Pull both ends of the elastic out of the casing opening as far as you can. Overlap the elastic ½ inch and zigzag stitch together (Figure 13.20b).
- To complete the casing, machine stitch the opening closed; begin and end with a backstitch (see Figure 13.20b).

Bias Casing

When a casing is stitched above the wrist, it needs a separate bias strip of fabric stitched for the casing. The position of the casing is the designer's choice. Figure 13.21a shows the casing a few inches above the wrist; however, this can be positioned at any level on the sleeve as long as it feels comfortable.

- Stitch and finish closed underarm seams. The sleeve is now stitched in-the-round (see Figure

13.21b). Machine stitch a narrow rolled hem or a lettuce edge finish. Refer to Chapter 15.
- Press both sides of the bias to the wrong side (Figure 13.21a).
- Turn the sleeve to the wrong side and slide it over a sleeve board. This makes it easier to measure; take your tape measure and measure the position of the casing up from the hem; pin and handbaste (see Figure 13.21a).
- Position the casing over the hand-basted stitches, beginning at the underarm seam. Pin the casing in place. At one end of the casing, fold ½ inch under to the wrong side (see Figure 13.21a).
- To finish the casing, fold the other bias edge under and butt it next to the other side of the casing. This leaves a small opening for threading the elastic (see Figure 13.21a).
- Edgestitch both sides of the casing, as illustrated in Figure 13.20a.
- Insert the elastic through the casing opening and stitch the elastic together as Figure 13.20b illustrates.
- After the elastic is inserted, close the opening with a few overhand stitches as Figure 13.21b illustrates.

BIAS BINDING WITH TIES

Any sleeve or other edge can be finished with bias binding. In fact, stitching a bias binding to an edge finish is a technique frequently used in clothing construction. By transferring your knowledge, a bias finish can be stitched to the neckline, armhole or sleeve edge, or the hemline.

PATTERN TIP

Measure the width of the elastic; add to this ¼ inch for ease and another ½ inch for seam allowance. *Example:* for ¼-inch-wide elastic, the bias casing would be 1½ inches wide. Allow plenty of length in the casing, as any excess can be cut off later. A store-purchased bias binding can be used; however, to cut your own from self-fabric will ensure a *perfect* match. Often the store bindings can feel scratchy next to the skin. Remember—this is where fashion must function.

Even though a binding with ties is discussed in this section, a bias binding can also be stitched to the wrist without ties.

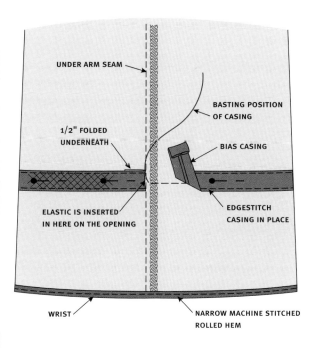

13.21A STITCHING THE CASING TO THE SLEEVE

UNDER ARM SEAM

1/2" FOLDED UNDERNEATH

BASTING POSITION OF CASING

BIAS CASING

EDGESTITCH CASING IN PLACE

ELASTIC IS INSERTED IN HERE ON THE OPENING

WRIST

NARROW MACHINE STITCHED ROLLED HEM

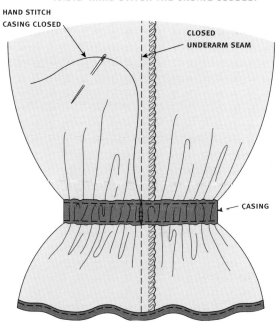

HAND STITCH CASING CLOSED

CLOSED UNDERARM SEAM

CASING

NOTE

A bias tie can be threaded through the casing and tied with a bow to add an extra touch of femininity. The tie is stitched to a shorter length of elastic (cut approximately 2 inches shorter than the wrist measurement). The ties are then zigzag stitched to each end of the elastic. A buttonhole is centered and stitched on the sleeve, in the position of the handbasting. This is done while the sleeve lies flat, before the underarm seams are stitched. Place a small square of sheer interfacing underneath the buttonhole before it is stitched to add stability. The stitching technique is the same when used in a wider waistband for skirts or pants, as shown in Figure 9.12.

- Stitch a darted placket (see Figure 13.22).
- Stitch and finish the underarm seams.
- Stitch two rows of basting stitches around the entire wrist for gathering.
- Pull the basting stitches into gathering to fit to the wrist measurement notched on the bias binding.
- Press a ¼-inch seam allowance to the wrong side along one edge of the bias binding (see Figure 13.22).
- Turn the sleeve to the correct side. Place the correct sides of the bias and wrist together and pin in place (see Figure 13.22.).
- Stitch a ¼-inch seam allowance from one placket edge to the other (see Figure 13.22).

PATTERN TIP

No seam allowance is added to the garment edge when a bias binding is applied. The width of finished bias binding is set by the width of the seam allowance. Whatever the width of the seam allowance, this becomes the finished binding width. In Figure 13.22, the seam allowance was ¼ inch. Consequently, the finished binding is ¼ inch as well.

For a finished ¼-inch binding, cut the bias 1¼ inches wide—this allows enough width for stitching, turning, and pressing the bias. Notch the wrist length on the binding. For functional design purposes, we suggest using a wrist measurement that allows the ties to be permanently tied so they don't need to be untied every time the garment is worn. Some people find it hard to tie a bow one-handed. Add approximately 9 inches to both ends for the ties.

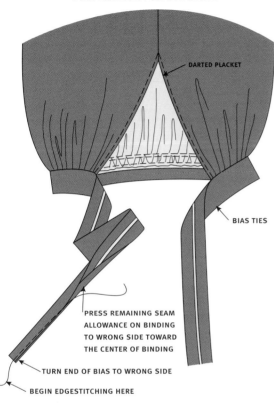

DARTED PLACKET

BIAS TIES

PRESS REMAINING SEAM
ALLOWANCE ON BINDING
TO WRONG SIDE TOWARD
THE CENTER OF BINDING

TURN END OF BIAS TO WRONG SIDE

BEGIN EDGESTITCHING HERE

- Working on the ironing board, press the remaining seam allowance on the ties to the center of the binding (see Figure 13.22).
- Press a ⅜-inch seam allowance to the wrong side on both ends of the ties.
- Fold the binding in half again and press, handbaste, and edgestitch the ties together and the binding in place around the wrist. Start stitching at one end of the tie; hold the thread taut as you stitch. Stitch to the other end of the tie;

take care that the seam allowance along the gathers is well hidden. Begin and end with a backstitch.

- Remove the handbasted stitches, press, and tie the binding in a bow.

SHIRRING ELASTIC

In the Style I.D., the sheer print top in Figure 13.1c has shirring elastic stitched around the wrists and neckline. Stitching several rows of shirring elastic creates a delicate, soft texture. Stitch as many rows of shirring elastic as you like. The more rows you stitch, the tighter and stretchier the wrist will become. Follow Figure 13.23 and carefully stitch the amount of rows you require of shirring elastic.

Hand wind the shirring elastic onto the bobbin—don't wind it too tight. Insert the bobbin and bring up the shirring elastic (through the bobbin tension) as you would if it were thread. Adjust the stitch length to a basting stitch length. Stitch the shirring elastic while the sleeve is flat—this is the flat application method. Using a tape measure, pin the position of the first stitching row. Then begin stitching from the underarm side seam—*don't* begin or end with a backstitch. As each row is stitched, the elastic will gather the fabric.

For each subsequent row of stitching, line up the edge of the machine foot with the previous row of stitching, as the stitching must look parallel. Stitch as many rows of elastic as you want. As each row of shirring elastic is stitched, stretch the fabric so it remains flat as you stitch.

SLEEVE VENT

To stitch a vent in the sleeve, you need to begin with a two-piece sleeve. The vent is positioned in the back of the arm, in line with the elbow. Sleeve vents need to be stitched with mitered corners, as illustrated in Figure 13.24a. Mitered corners are discussed in Chapter 15, "Mitered Corner" (see Figure 15.23).

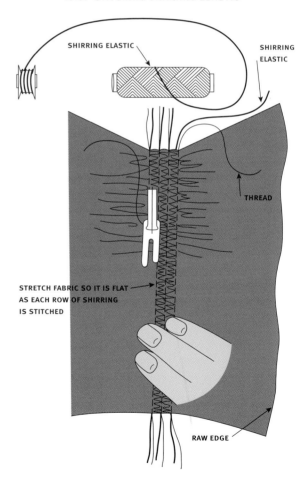

SHIRRING ELASTIC

SHIRRING ELASTIC

THREAD

STRETCH FABRIC SO IT IS FLAT
AS EACH ROW OF SHIRRING
IS STITCHED

RAW EDGE

The vent has buttons stitched to the sleeve surface; buttonholes do not need to be stitched, as a sleeve vent is purely decorative (Figure 13.24b). The stitching order is the same when stitching any vent, whether it's in a skirt, a dress, or a jacket hem. Refer to Chapter 15, "Vent" (see Figure 15.30).

On skirts, jackets, and dresses where the vent opens for functional purposes, the lining is stitched around the shape of the vent. On the sleeves, the vent does not need to open, so the lining can be stitched to the straight hem edge. Refer to Chapter 16 for more information. In particular, refer to Figure 16.19, as it illustrates how the lining is stitched to the sleeve hem.

There are many specialty fabrics that need extra special care when stitching. The Dos and Don'ts will help to guide you when stitching cuffs in tricky fabrics.

STITCHING CUFFS AND OTHER WRIST FINISHES IN TRICKY FABRICS
Stripes, Plaids, Patterns, and Repeat Patterns

Do cut cuffs in stripe or plaid fabric on a different grainline, such as the cross- or bias grains, to show contrast. The cuffs in the shirt in Figure 13.1a are cut in the opposite way to the body of the shirt for difference.

Do consider stitching a simple darted placket, because this style of placket does not involve matching. However, if the underarm seams are not cut to match, then the placket will not match either.

Do cut cuffs on an inconspicuous part of the fabric if the pattern is a repeat or a large bold print.

Do cut cuffs on the border (if the fabric has a border), as this really defines the cuffs in an exciting way.

Sheer Fabric

Do stitch sheer cuffs and collars to medium-weight shirts and blouses, as sheer fabrics show contrast.

Do be careful when choosing the interfacing for sheer cuffs (and collars), as interfacing can shadow through sheer fabric. Consider using self-fabric for interfacing sheer fabrics; then you know the color match will be perfect. For more information on stabilizers, refer to "Types of Stabilizers" in Chapter 3.

Do trim narrow seam allowances in sheer fabric neatly and parallel to the cuff seamline so they look as inconspicuous as possible; remember every seamline is visible in sheer fabrics.

Do stitch any style of placket in sheers, as bulk will never be an issue. Some advice here—do stitch a sample first to see which placket looks best in the fabric and design.

Do consider finishing cuffs with a couture hand stitch rather than topstitching with an edgestitch.

Do use a small stitch length (approximately 2.0) for topstitching sheer fabrics.

Do stitch shirring elastic as a wrist finish in sheers—it will look absolutely gorgeous!

Do stitch a bias binding wrist finish to sheer fabrics; binding edges in sheer fabric will not shadow in the same way that a facing will.

Do stitch gathered wrist finishes in sheer fabrics. Lots of fullness can be added in sheers, and this looks so delicate.

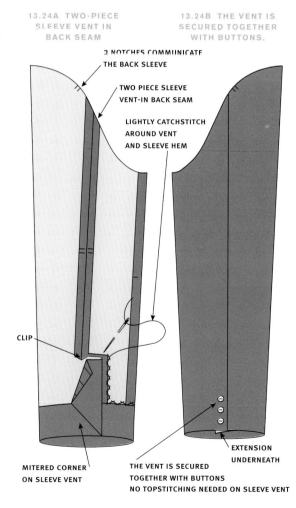

13.24A TWO-PIECE SLEEVE VENT IN BACK SEAM

13.24B THE VENT IS SECURED TOGETHER WITH BUTTONS.

2 NOTCHES COMMUNICATE THE BACK SLEEVE

TWO PIECE SLEEVE VENT-IN BACK SEAM

LIGHTLY CATCHSTITCH AROUND VENT AND SLEEVE HEM

CLIP

MITERED CORNER ON SLEEVE VENT

THE VENT IS SECURED TOGETHER WITH BUTTONS NO TOPSTITCHING NEEDED ON SLEEVE VENT

EXTENSION UNDERNEATH

Don't leave any loose threads inside cuffs made in sheer fabrics because they will be noticeable from the face of the fabric.

Lace

Do overlay a scallop edge around the wrist—this finish works beautifully in lace. Refer to "Stitching Seams in Tricky Fabrics" in Chapter 6.

Do stitch closed cuffs in lace fabric if you really want a cuff in lace.

Don't stitch bias binding finishes in most weights of lace, as it would become bulky. However, the bulk would depend on the weight of the lace fabric you use.

Don't stitch plackets and open cuffs in heavyweight lace, as the density of lace may be too difficult to work with. Consider using silk charmeuse for the placket, cuffs and collars, as it would combine very well with lace.

Satin

Do stitch cuffs in lightweight satin such as silk charmeuse. However, carefully choose the type and weight of interfacing. Silk organza may work well. Sample a seam first to see if any ridges are apparent from the correct side. If they are apparent, carefully grade the seams to reduce bulk.

Do consider finishing cuffs with a couture hand stitch rather than topstitching an edgestitch.

Don't stitch cuffs, casings, bindings, and shirring elastic in heavyweight satin fabrics; a better option is to hand stitch a neat hem.

Beaded Fabric

Do only stitch closed cuffs to beaded fabric, as plackets would not stitch well and a lot of work would be involved. Consider the time required—beads need to be smashed off all seams with a rubber mallet and beads may need to be restitched back onto the cuffs once they are stitched.

Do consider other wrist finishes in beaded fabrics; bias binding is an excellent option. However, do smash the beads off the seam allowance, and we suggest using a different fabric, without beads for the binding.

Don't try topstitching beaded cuffs—this *will not* work!

Don't stitch shirring to beaded fabric.

Knits

Do structure cuffs in knit fabrics with stable interfacing to take the stretch capacity out of the cuff. Fusi-Knit interfacing is excellent for stabilizing knit fabrics; place the cuff on the interfacing on the vertical grainline to stabilize it (see Figure 3.10).

Do stitch elastic wrist finishes on lightweight knit.

Don't use gathered wrist finishes in heavyweight knit fabrics.

Denim

Do stitch cuffs and plackets in denim; they also look great topstitched.

Do choose the type of placket carefully to best suit the fabric weight. A darted placket reduces any bulk; however, a shirt-sleeve placket will topstitch beautifully in denim. The fabric weight always needs to be considered when choosing the construction method.

Do topstitch denim cuffs with a longer stitch length, as stitches sink into several layers of thick fabric and do not show up.

Don't stitch bias binding, ties, and elastic finishes when the denim is medium to heavyweight. The wrist finish will look too thick and bulky, and bulky wrist finishes feel uncomfortable to wear.

Don't always interface denim cuffs. Some denim fabric already has the weight and stability without needing interfacing; however, sample first. If the cuffs are not interfaced, slip a small piece of interfacing under the buttonhole section *only*, so it does not stretch when the buttonhole is stitched and used.

Velvet

Do be careful if you are considering stitching cuffs in velvet fabric. Velvet needs as few seamlines as possible, as it is a *really* tricky fabric to stitch and press. We recommend choosing another wrist finish.

Do try a simple hand-stitched hem instead; this would be the perfect choice for a wrist finish in velvet.

Do hand stitch a trim to the wrist edge to add a special touch in velvet.

Do sample any gathered wrist finishes first before stitching the wrist. Shirring and other elastic finishes can look great stitched in lightweight velvet; however, their applicability can only be determined by sampling first.

Leather

Do stitch open cuffs in leather. The seam finish depends on the weight of the leather. Seams can be stitched, turned, and secured with leather cement or topstitched to hold them in place.

Do interface leather cuffs. If the leather does not need interfacing, slip a small square under the buttonhole section only, so the buttonhole does not stretch out of shape from use.

Do sample any placket finish in the leather first. The style of placket you choose depends on the weight of leather.

Do stitch a vent in leather.

Do be careful choosing gathered wrist finishes in leather. Use only lightweight leather, such as a very soft lambskin; however, it is a *must* to sample first.

Don't stitch plackets in heavyweight leather; in fact, don't stitch cuffs in heavyweight leather.

Faux Fur

Do stitch faux fur for the top side of your cuff. Since fur is thick, a lining needs to be stitched as the under cuff to reduce bulk.

Do stitch a simple turned-back hem as a wrist finish; hand stitch with a catchstitch. Refer to Figure 15.9 to see how to catchstitch.

Don't stitch plackets, gathered wrist finishes, or elastic wrist finishes to faux fur, as all these finishes are too thick and bulky.

Heavyweight Fabric

Don't stitch plackets and open cuffs in heavyweight fabric, as they would be bulky and uncomfortable. We recommend choosing another finish. However, if you do want to give it a go, sample first in your fabric choice to see how the cuff would look—there is nothing wrong with trying and gaining some experience from this exercise.

TRANSFER YOUR KNOWLEDGE

There are numerous other wrist finishes that could be explained in this chapter. All options cannot be covered here; however, by transferring your knowledge and by stretching your creativity, the knowledge you have gained will help you stitch other wrist finishes not outlined in this chapter.

- Any cuff or other wrist finish, such as a casing, bias binding, or shirring elastic, can be stitched to a short or three-quarter-length sleeve. Just transfer your knowledge and use the same stitching order—but do remember to measure the arm where the cuff is going to sit, as it will be larger than the wrist measurement. The soft pink, delicate dress in Figure 13.25 has short sleeves tucked to a closed cuff.

- A casing with elastic inserted can be stitched to any level on the sleeve as long as it feels comfortable. Try several rows, with two or three casings stitched around the level of the short sleeve, above the elbow, and at the wrist. This makes an interesting puffed sleeve design.

- A contoured cuff does not always need to be secured with buttons and buttonholes. How about stitching a row of bias loops instead, and using small pearl buttons for a glam look? Bias loops are outlined in Chapter 17, in the section "Bias Loops."

- In Figure 12.25 a rib band is stitched to the neck edge. Transfer your knowledge and stitch a rib band as cuff finish. Refer to "Rib Knit Bands at Necklines and Armholes" in Chapter 12.

- In Figure 13.1c the print sheer top has shirring elastic stitched around the wrist. How about stitching the same finish to a short or three-quarter sleeve or under the bust—or anywhere else the designer chooses to place it? Always make sure plenty of fullness is allowed in the pattern for gathering. Sample first to see how many extra inches are needed, as each fabric shirrs differently.

- Did you know that a notched cuff follows the same stitching order as a waistband? Transferring your knowledge, you would simply turn it upside down and stitch, using the same stitching order. Also take a quick look at Figure 15.33d to see an oversize contoured cuff stitched to the hem of the skirt. Do you also notice that the shirt-sleeve placket is stitched up from the hem on the skirt and in the neckline of the T-shirt in Figure 15.34b?

STRETCH YOUR CREATIVITY

The fold-back (or gauntlet cuff) is one of our favorite cuffs. It takes more time to stitch but is well worth the effort. We decided this chapter would not be complete without giving this cuff a mention. The skills you have gleaned so far in this chapter will be recognized as we teach you how to stitch this exotic cuff!

13.25 TRANSFER YOUR
KNOWLEDGE: STITCH AN
OPEN OR CLOSED CUFF
OR OTHER WRIST FINISH
TO A SHORT OR THREE-
QUARTER-LENGTH
SLEEVE. CLOSED CUFF
STITCHED TO A SHORT,
PUFFED SLEEVE.

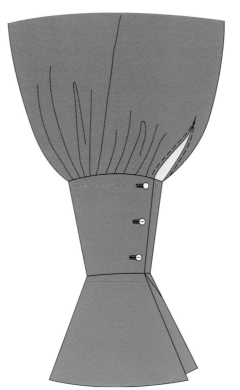

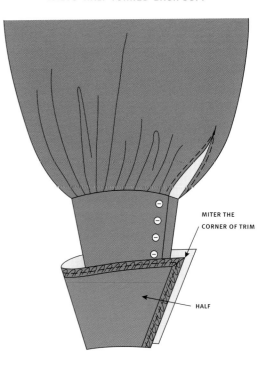

MITER THE
CORNER OF TRIM

HALF

13.26A WARM CHECK OVERCOAT WITH
FUR COLLAR AND CUFFS

First of all, it is a contoured cuff. It also has a separate contoured fold-back section stitched to the contoured cuff, which is folded back and elegantly stands away from the buttoned cuff.

The warm overcoat with fur collar and cuffs, illustrated in Figure 13.26a, has the fold-back cuff stitched to the wrists. A coat doesn't necessarily need a placket if the wrist opening is wide enough. Then the cuff would be stitched as a closed cuff. The fold-back section in the coat has been stitched in fur to mirror the collar, not only for beauty but also

for warmth. The collar can be turned up so you can snuggle into this coat. The cuffs turn down with the fur covering your hands to keep you warm on those freezing-cold winter days. This is also a great style for tall people, as the cuff can be turned down for those who have longer arms (Figure 13.26b). The cuff can also be turned back halfway and be stitched permanently. Hand stitch the under cuff only to the contoured cuff using double thread. Notice in Figure 13.26c that a trim has also been stitched around the edge of the cuff.

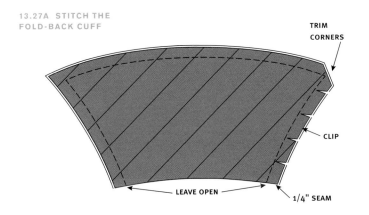

13.27A STITCH THE FOLD-BACK CUFF

TRIM CORNERS

CLIP

LEAVE OPEN

1/4" SEAM

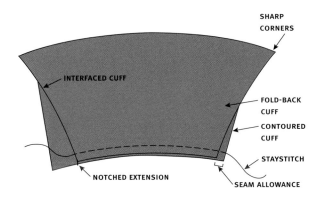

SHARP CORNERS

13.27B PLACE THE FOLD-BACK CUFF TO THE CONTOURED CUFF AND STAYSTITCH IN PLACE

INTERFACED CUFF

FOLD-BACK CUFF

CONTOURED CUFF

STAYSTITCH

NOTCHED EXTENSION

SEAM ALLOWANCE

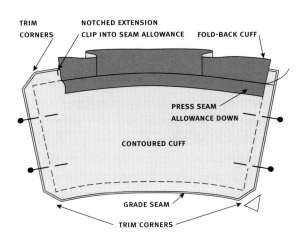

TRIM CORNERS

NOTCHED EXTENSION
CLIP INTO SEAM ALLOWANCE

FOLD-BACK CUFF

PRESS SEAM ALLOWANCE DOWN

CONTOURED CUFF

GRADE SEAM

TRIM CORNERS

13.27C PIN AND STITCH THE CONTOURED CUFFS TOGETHER; THE FOLD-BACK CUFF SECTION IS SAND-WICHED IN BETWEEN THE CONTOURED CUFF

Fold-Back Cuff or Gauntlet Cuff

- Interface the contoured cuff—we suggest interfacing one side only; however, this depends on the fabric weight.
- Interface *both sides* of the fold-back cuff. The interfacing should hold the structure so that

when the cuff turns back it will stay in place without flopping over. Refer to Chapter 3 for more information.

- Stitch the darted placket and underarm seams, and tuck or gather the wrist (see Figure 13.9).
- Take the two fold-back cuff pieces and place the correct sides together; stitch a ¼-inch seam around three sides, reduce bulk from the corners, and clip the curved seams. Notice the bottom edge is open (Figure 13.27a).
- Turn the cuff to the correct side and sharpen the corners with the point turner; press the cuff.
- Mirror image the turned-back cuff to check that both sides are equal widths.
- Place the turned-back cuff directly on top of the interfaced contoured cuff. Position from the notched extension to the seamline at the other end of the wrist. Staystitch in place (Figure 13.27b).
- Place the correct side of the other contoured cuff over the turned-back cuff. The fold-back cuff is now sandwiched between both contoured cuffs (Figure 13.27c).

- Pin the contoured cuffs together, following the illustration, and stitch the seam around the cuff (see Figure 13.27c). Be careful as you stitch—the turned-back section can easily get caught in the seam, so keep an eye on this!
- Clip into the seam up to the notched extension. Turn the seam allowance down and press (see Figure 13.27c).
- Grade the seam along the bottom edge to reduce bulk (Figure 11.9f), as there are four layers of fabric sitting together. Turn and press the cuff (see Figure 13.27c).
- Stitch the cuff to the wrist, following the stitching order for the notched-extension cuff.
- Stitch your choice of button and buttonholes in the cuff.

STOP! WHAT DO I DO IF . . .

. . . both sides of my cuff look different widths when they are buttoned together?

Carefully remove the cuff from the wrist at the end with the buttons stitched. Undo the cuff, turn to the inside, and readjust by pinning the width to match that of the other cuff. Restitch the width, and stitch the cuff back to the wrist. This is extra work, so next time be sure to check that the cuff is a mirror image at an earlier stage.

. . . my cuff is too tight?

If the cuff is too tight, there is no other option than to carefully remove the cuff using the seam ripper and stitch a new one to a larger measurement. Go back and measure the hand again, and make a new pattern. This time make sure you have an accurate measurement for the cuff, with ease included.

. . . my cuff is too big; what can I do to adjust it? I have already stitched the buttonhole!

Try stitching another button farther back from the first button (see Figure 13.17) to give the option of tightening the cuff. However, if this makes the placket and cuff look twisted, then try the following idea. Carefully take the cuff off the wrist from the button end, undo the cuff, and restitch to make it smaller. If the sleeve is gathered, then pull more gathering to shorten the cuff length to fit your new cuff length. If the sleeve is tucked, make the tucks larger or add another tuck to the wrist to reduce the wrist length. Reapply the cuff to the wrist.

. . . my cuff looks twisted?

When stitching the cuff closed with a machine-stitched edgestitch or a stitch-in-the-ditch, the cuff will twist easily if it was not pinned and handbasted first. Perhaps this step was skipped! Seam rip the stitching and realign the folded edge of the cuff—pin and handbaste in place before restitching.

SELF-CRITIQUE

To critique your wrist finish, ask the following questions about your wrist finish:

Cuffs

- Did I use the correct weight of interfacing for cuffs?
- Have I stitched the correct placket to suit the cuff?
- Do my cuffs mirror image each other? If not, why not?
- Do my cuffs lie flat, or do they look twisted?
- Is my edgestitching parallel to the seamline?
- Does the placket sit flat and smooth, and does it function properly?
- Have I stitched my buttonholes and buttons in the correct positions so my cuffs close properly?
- When the cuff is closed, is the wrist measurement comfortable?
- Are my buttonholes too tight, too loose, or just right?
- Did I stitch enough samples to make an informed decision regarding the best wrist finish for my fabric?
- Did I use quality thread for my stitching?
- Did I use the correct stitch length for permanent stitching and topstitching?

Elastic Finishes

- Is the elastic too tight, too loose, or just right?
- Is the elastic so tight in the casing it can't move freely?
- Is the shirring elastic stitched parallel to the hem?
- Does my wrist have enough fullness and gathering so the sleeve drapes beautifully?
- Did I sample sufficiently to make a wise decision as to the best wrist finish for my fabric?

REVIEW CHECKLIST

- Am I learning the important concept that the fabric weight guides me in the choice of wrist finish for my design?
- Do I understand how fashion and function *must* go hand in hand?
- Do I understand the concept that correct patterns are the foundation of correct stitching?
- Do I understand how crucial notches and other pattern markings are in setting myself up to successfully stitch the notched cuff?
- Do I understand the benefits of sampling first before stitching the garment?
- Do I understand the importance of having an accurate wrist measurement so my wrist finish is comfortable?
- Do I understand how important interfacing is to the structure of the cuffs?

CHAPTER

Sleeves: Rounding Off the Arm

leeves are an important aspect of garment silhouettes and can evolve from one era to
another. The opportunity for designs of the sleeve and the finish of the sleeve are endless.

Sleeves move with the body and need two holes: one for the arm to go into and another for
it to come out of. There are two categories of sleeves: a separate cut sleeve that is set into the
bodice, and a sleeve that is combined with all, or part, of the bodice. Set-in sleeves can be

designed to fit the armhole smoothly or with gathers. They can be designed to fit to the body or with exaggerated fullness and can be cut to any length from the upper arm to the wrist. The hemline of the sleeve can be finished in various ways, becoming an important focal point on the garment.

A sleeve with unsightly gathers and puckers or one that twists because proper grainlines were not maintained is a sign of inexperience, haste, or carelessness. We believe a perfectly set-in sleeve is a thing of beauty and can be achieved in all fabrics, with practice, patience, and a few good sewing tips.

In this chapter we explain and illustrate many variations of sleeves to extend the design student's construction knowledge. Add your samples to your workbook. Sewing sleeves can be a challenging process, so don't lose heart. Once experience and confidence in stitching have been gained, you will be able to stitch any sleeve perfectly!

STYLE I.D.

Often, sleeves are named for the area from which they are designed; for example, the cap sleeve is designed from the cap area of a complete sleeve

KEY TERMS

All-in-One Sleeve
Cap Sleeve
Dropped Shoulder Sleeve
Elbow Dart
Flat Insertion
Gathered Sleeve
Gusset (One-Piece)
Gusset (Two-Piece)
Kimono Sleeve
Raglan Shoulder Pad
Raglan Sleeve
Set-in Shoulder Pad
Set-in Sleeve, One Piece
Set-in Sleeve, Two Piece
Shirt Sleeve
Shoulder Pad
Sleeve Cap
Sleeve Ease
Sleeve Finish
Sleeve Head
Sleeve Hem

375

Style I.D.

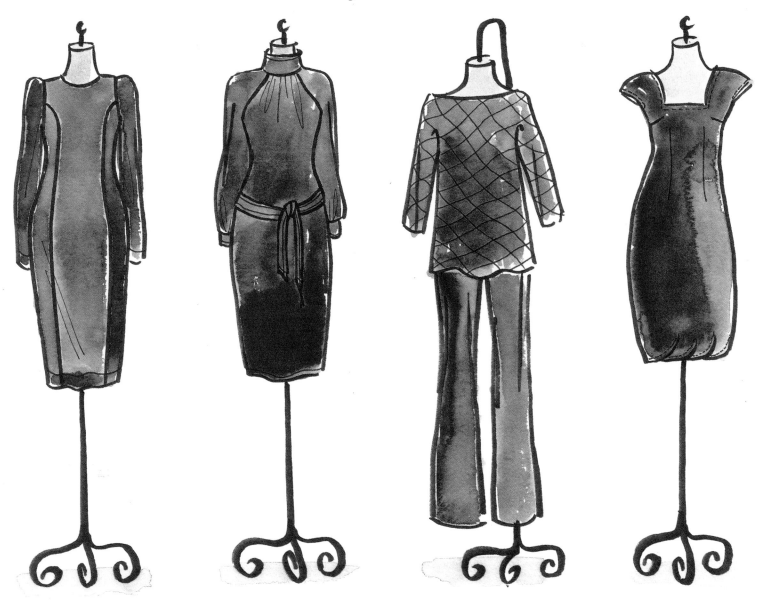

14.1A SET-IN   14.1B RAGLAN   14.1C KIMONO   14.1D CAP

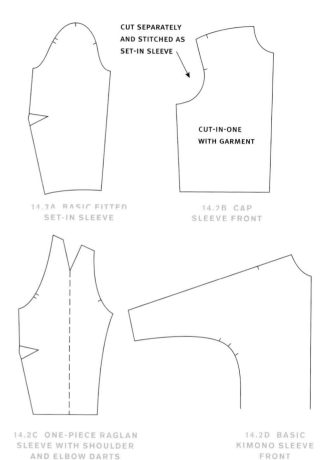

14.2A BASIC FITTED
SET-IN SLEEVE

CUT SEPARATELY
AND STITCHED AS
SET-IN SLEEVE

14.2B CAP
SLEEVE FRONT

CUT-IN-ONE
WITH GARMENT

14.2C ONE-PIECE RAGLAN
SLEEVE WITH SHOULDER
AND ELBOW DARTS

14.2D BASIC
KIMONO SLEEVE
FRONT

IMPORTANT

All good design comes from good patterns, which are developed from good slopers. Develop strong patternmaking skills to assist you in design!

and can be modified in endless ways. Look at the sleeve variations in the Style I.D.; by the end of this chapter, you will know how to stitch and insert these and many other styles of beautiful sleeves (Figure 14.1).

GATHER YOUR TOOLS

For the techniques in this chapter, you will need a tape measure, fabric marker, scissors, pins, threads, materials for sleeve heads, shoulder pads, and lots of patience! Think ahead—order now. Oftentimes chain fabric stores do not have an extensive selection of specific supplies needed for sleeves, such as a wide assortment of shoulder pads, or sleeve headers. Once you have decided what type of sleeve is part of the design, begin the research to find the correct supplies, and order them as soon as possible.

Before stitching set-in sleeves, the following steps in garment construction should be completed:

- The garment should be staystitched.
- Darts should be stitched and pressed.
- Side and shoulder seams should be stitched and pressed.
- Pockets should be stitched.

- The upper collar in jackets and coats should be stitched.
- Collars and facings in blouses and dresses should have been applied.
- Finish cuff and stitch to sleeve edge before sewing the sleeve into the garment.

NOW LET'S GET STARTED

The *Fairchild Dictionary of Fashion* defines sleeves as: "that part of an item of clothing that covers the arm."[1] As shown in Figure 14.2, sleeves can be fitted, set-in, cap, one- or two-piece raglan, or a variation of the kimono sleeve. The two most common categories of sleeves are **set-in sleeves** (Figure 14.2a), which join the bodice at the natural joint of the body where the arm meets the shoulder; and **all-in-one sleeves**, with no armhole (Figure 14.2d).

A well-fitted sleeve is one that hangs properly and fits the arm and shoulder smoothly; these aspects ensure the sleeve will be comfortable to wear. Stitching the sleeve into the armhole correctly is also part of achieving a well-fitted sleeve. However, this won't happen unless the pattern is correct—correct stitching begins with a correct pattern (Figure 14.3). This aspect of the sleeve must be attended to at the sloper stage of pattern-making. With the correct amount of ease in the sleeve, stitching the sleeve will also be a smooth stitching experience, not a dreaded stitching nightmare! *Ease*, as defined by the *Fairchild Dictionary of Fashion*, is "the process of joining a slightly larger garment piece to a smaller garment piece by evenly distributing the fullness along the seam where the pieces are joined."[2] As you

will see in Figure 14.4a, it is critical to the success of any sleeve to focus the ease where it is needed for smooth, pucker-free stitching.

Elements of a Sleeve and Their Proper Terminology

- **Sleeve cap** is the curved top of the sleeve from the front to the back (see Figure 14.3).
- **Sleeve ease** is the additional allowance of

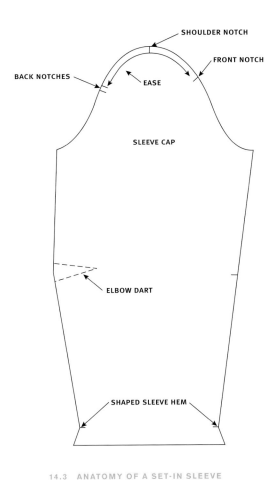

14.3 ANATOMY OF A SET-IN SLEEVE

fabric at the sleeve cap, biceps, elbow, and wrist to allow movement of the arm (see Figure 14.3).

- **Notches** are clips in the seam allowances, indicating the front of the sleeve (one notch), the back of the sleeve (two notches), and the center of the sleeve cap (a single notch), where the sleeve and shoulder meet (see Figure 14.3).

- **Sleeve head**, or heading, is a bias strip of various types of fabric used to fill out the sleeve cap. This is used in dress- and blouse-weight fabrics as well as in heavier coat or jacket fabrics (see Figure 14.5a).
- **Shoulder pads** are layers of padding made from materials such as cotton batting, felt, foam, or some of each. They support the shoulders of a garment for correct drape, and maintain and support the shoulder area of tailored garments (see Figure 14.16 and Figure 16.16).
- **Elbow dart** allows the arm to bend in a straight, fitted sleeve, and can be one or several smaller darts (see Figure 14.3).
- **Sleeve hems** are the finished lower edges of the sleeve, which can be turned to the inside of the sleeve, turned to the front of the sleeve as a decorative finish, or finished off with another technique such as bias binding or a cuff. The type of sleeve or hem finish used depends on the fabric, the style of the garment, the garment use, and the care of the garment (see Figure 14.3).
- **Sleeve finishes** refer to the various ways a sleeve can be completed, such as facings, openings in the seam, snaps, loops and buttons, zippers, and cuffs in all their myriad possibilities too numerous to mention here. Refer to Chapter 13, "Cuffs and Other Wrist Finishes," for detailed information on this important aspect of sleeve design.

Familiarity with the correct terminology in sewing assists the student in understanding the construction process, and is critical to good sewing at each step of the project. Our advice to students is to learn the correct term and use it!

SET-IN SLEEVES

The set-in sleeve is a classic sleeve, which can be constructed as one or two pieces. The cap of the sleeve is rounded to provide extra ease and comfort to fit over the shape of the shoulders (Figure 14.4a). In the pattern drafting stage, the shoulder area must be trued as shown in Figure 14.4b for a smooth armsyce. Most students find it difficult to shape and ease the cap smoothly, and often the problem stems from too much ease in the sleeve cap or choosing the wrong fabric. Unless

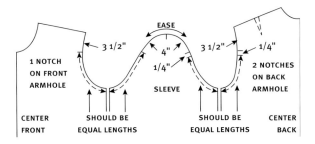

14.4A ESTABLISHING THE EASE

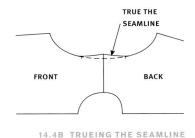

14.4B TRUEING THE SEAMLINE

fabric can be eased, either by machine basting or steam-pressing in the fullness, the sleeve will always be set-in with tiny pleats and gathers in the armhole seam. If this occurs repeatedly with the sample, consider another style of sleeve or a different fabric.

The set-in sleeve requires more time and sewing expertise but is worth the effort it takes for the end result: a beautiful, pucker-free sleeve that rounds off the shoulder. There are two ways to ease in the sleeve: using a bias strip of fabric or using the ease stitch to gather up the fullness. Both methods are effective and require practice to master. Over time, with patience, both of these methods produce beautiful results.

Method 1: Easing the Sleeve with a Bias Strip

A bias strip of self-fabric, nylon tricot, or lamb's wool 1½ inches wide and long enough to reach around the sleeve cap from notch to notch can be stitched to the seam allowance of the sleeve cap to gather in the ease. To ease the sleeve with a bias strip:

- Anchor the bias strip with a few machine stitches.
- Machine baste, stretching the strip firmly and evenly with the left hand and using the right hand to guide the sleeve cap beneath the presser foot; 1 to 2 inches are left at the end—do not stretch the strip for ½ inch on either side of the center notch cap (Figure 14.5a).
- Trim off the excess length when reaching the other notch; when the bias strip relaxes,

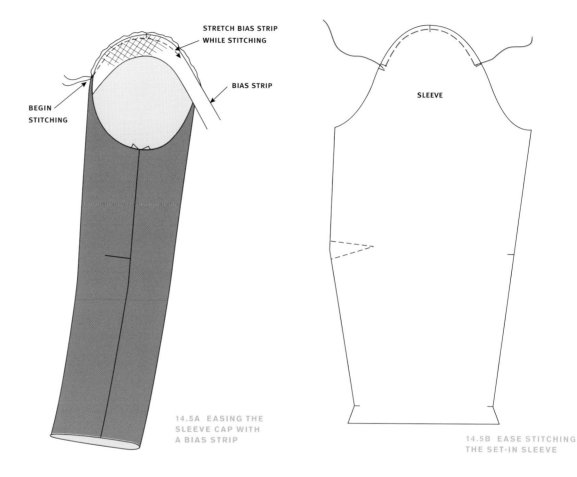

14.5A EASING THE SLEEVE CAP WITH A BIAS STRIP

14.5B EASE STITCHING THE SET-IN SLEEVE

the sleeve eases evenly—the sleeve cap should be dimple-free and the stitching line should be flat.
- Shrink out the excess fullness in the seam allowance (Figure 14.5d) by placing the sleeve cap over a tailor's ham; apply lots of steam to dampen, but use a dry iron to shrink out the fullness and flatten the seam allowance—*don't* press beyond the stitching line into the cap of the sleeve.

Method 2: Ease Stitching the Sleeve

The set-in sleeve is found in many styles of garments. Directions for ease stitching the sleeve cap begin the process of setting-in the sleeve. To sew the one-piece set-in sleeve:

- Prepare the sleeve: ease stitch the sleeve cap slightly inside the seamline (not outside!) between the notches (Figure 14.5b).

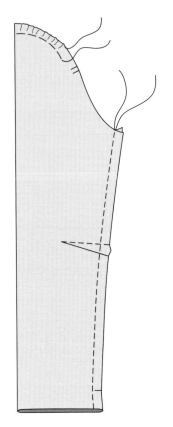

14.5C PULLING UP THE EASE STITCHING

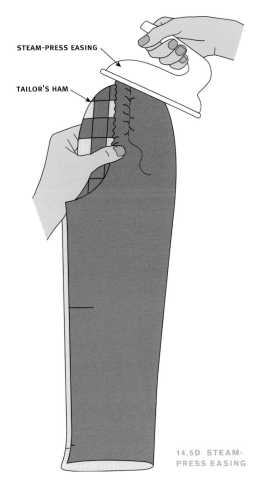

STEAM-PRESS EASING

TAILOR'S HAM

14.5D STEAM-PRESS EASING

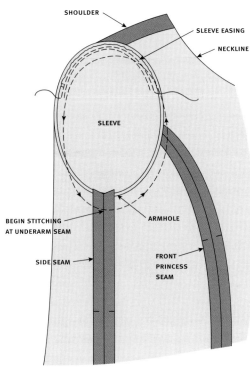

14.5E STITCHING THE SET-IN SLEEVE TO THE GARMENT

SHOULDER

SLEEVE EASING

NECKLINE

SLEEVE

BEGIN STITCHING AT UNDERARM SEAM

ARMHOLE

SIDE SEAM

FRONT PRINCESS SEAM

- Gently pull the basting stitches into easing on the sleeve cap (Figure 14.5c).
- Stitch and press the elbow dart or stitch the ease (see Figure 14.5c).
- Place the sleeve cap over a tailor's ham; hold both sides firmly at the notch points with one hand—pull taut (Figure 14.5d).
- Steam-press the sleeve cap with a steam iron to reduce the easing and to reshape the sleeve into a rounded shape to fit the curve of the shoul-

der (Figure 14.5d). Use your hands to mold the shape—this is where you get to develop heat-resistant fingers!
- Don't remove the sleeve until it has cooled down.
- Stitch the underarm seam and press open.
- Turn garment to the wrong side; have the sleeve turned to the correct side.
- Slip the sleeve into the armhole and match the underarm seams together; the correct sides are now facing together (Figure 14.5e).

- Pin key points together (see Figure 14.5e), as follows:
  - Shoulder seam to center of sleeve cap
  - Two back sleeve notches to armhole notches
  - One front sleeve notch to armhole notch
- Evenly distribute the ease between notches, and pin; if the ease has been properly determined in the patternmaking stage, the sleeve should fit easily into the armhole (see Figure 14.5e).
- Stitch the sleeve into the armhole with the sleeve

facing up, beginning at the underarm seam.

- The intersecting seams should be stitched with the seam allowances left up; don't trim or clip. Refer to Chapter 6, "Seams," for more information on stitching intersecting seams (Figure 6.29a).
- *No* puckers should be visible in the sleeve cap after stitching—if they are, use your seam ripper to remove the stitches and restitch the sleeve.

Two-Piece Set-in Sleeve

The two-piece set-in sleeve is found mostly in suits and coats. Both sections of the sleeve are shaped to produce a fitted sleeve with seams at the front and back armhole (Figure 14.6). The seams of the under sleeve and upper sleeve are stitched together before the sleeve is set into the garment. The sleeve is set into the garment following the same directions as for the one-piece set-in sleeve above.

Two-Piece Sleeve with Vent

Often two-piece sleeves are finished with vent openings at the lower edge (Figure 13.24). This type of finish has to be planned for during the sloper stage of patternmaking. To sew the two-piece sleeve with vent:

- On the upper sleeve, add 1½ inches for facing and hem.
- On the under sleeve, add 3 inches for the extension and facing and 1½ inches for the hem.
- Add ½-inch seam allowance on all pattern seams (Figure 14.7a).

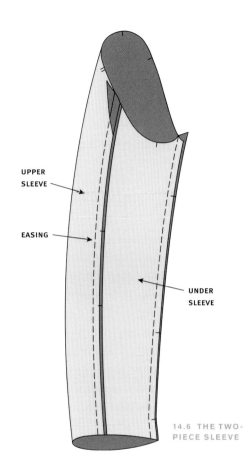

UPPER SLEEVE

EASING

UNDER SLEEVE

14.6 THE TWO-PIECE SLEEVE

- On the sleeve cap, fold back each seam allowance and cut the pattern using a mirror image of the sleeve shape.
- Fold the hem allowance back and cut the hem as a mirror image—this will ensure that when the seams and hems are stitched, the hem and facing will fit comfortably behind the wrist without pulling when the garment is worn (Figure 15.4).

- Mark all notches and matchpoints (Figure 14.7a).
- On the upper and under sleeves, fold the vent facing in and the hem up. Mark the position where the patterns intersect; open the pattern and connect these two points to stitch mitered corners. Add ¼-inch seam allowance (Figure 15.23a).
- Begin by stitching the back sleeve seam (Figure 14.7a). Lay the under sleeve with the correct side up; place the correct side of the upper sleeve on top, matching notches. Stitch the seam from the sleeve cap down to the matchpoint corner and clip into the matchpoint (Figure 14.7b).
- Press the seam open.
- Stitch the mitered corners; begin by folding over the diagonal seams with correct sides together, stitching from the ¼-inch seam allowance on the cut edge. Stitch through to the folded edge and clip the corner, finger-pressing the seam open. Turn using a point turner to get a sharp, right-angled corner; press (Figure 14.7b and Figure 15.23a).
- Hand stitch both facings of the vent to the garment using a catchstitch (Figure 14.7c).
- Stitch the front seam together and catchstitch the hem (see Figure 14.7c).
- The lining is stitched to the hem covering the entire sleeve hem. The lining does not need a vent nor does it need to be cut and stitched around the vent, as most vents are decorative rather than functional (Figure 14.7d and Figure 16.19).

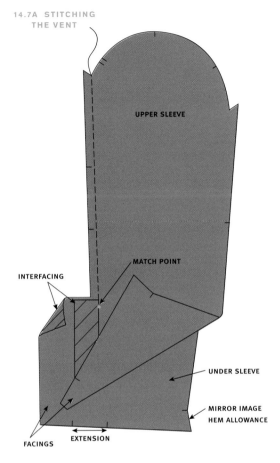

14.7A STITCHING THE VENT

UPPER SLEEVE

MATCH POINT

INTERFACING

UNDER SLEEVE

MIRROR IMAGE HEM ALLOWANCE

FACINGS

EXTENSION

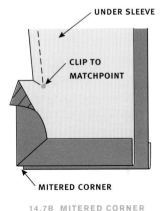

UNDER SLEEVE

CLIP TO MATCHPOINT

MITERED CORNER

14.7B MITERED CORNER

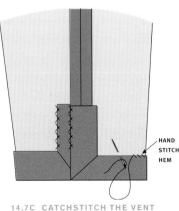

HAND STITCH HEM

14.7C CATCHSTITCH THE VENT

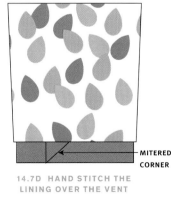

MITERED CORNER

14.7D HAND STITCH THE LINING OVER THE VENT

Gathered Sleeve

The **gathered** or puffed sleeve is a variation of the set-in sleeve (Figure 14.8a). Instead of easing in the fullness of the sleeve cap, this fullness is gathered in. Gathers are visible in the armhole seam, and the cap is puffy with plenty of fullness. At the patternmaking stage, this type of sleeve is slashed open and fullness is added into the sleeve cap in varying amounts per the designer's preferences. To gather the sleeve cap:

- Stitch two rows of basting stitches between the notches indicated on the sleeve (Figure 14.8b).
- Pull up the basting stitches, arranging the gathers near the cap of the sleeve; pin the sleeve to the armhole.
- *Do not* pull up the basting stitches after pinning the sleeve to the armhole—it gathers up the armhole seamline.
- Stitch slowly, beginning at the underarm

seam; stitch another row of stitches ⅛ inch from the seamline; trim away excess seam allowance, or serge the seam to finish the edges with the gathers underneath.
- With exaggerated gathering or for very soft fabrics, a sleeve header will support the fullness.
- Refer to Chapter 6, Figure 6.23, for further gathering information.

Shirt Sleeve

Shirt sleeves are a design feature of men's shirts, tailored blouses, shirtdresses, and casual styles with a dropped shoulder or armhole seam. This is a set-in sleeve that eliminates much of the frustration associated with set-in sleeves. The cap of the sleeve is shallow or flat. The sleeve is stitched into the armhole using **flat insertion**, which means it is stitched to the armhole before the side seams are stitched. The sleeve cannot be completely finished before stitching it to the garment. To stitch a sleeve using flat insertion:

- Stitch the yoke to the back shirt (Figure 14.9a).
- Pin or handbaste the sleeve cap to the armhole, correct sides together, matching notches and shoulder seam markings (Figure 14.9b).
- Stitch with the sleeve facing up, keeping the fabric taut.
- Press the seam, and finish the edges with serging (Figure 14.9c) or zigzag stitching; *or*, topstitch the seam allowances to the garment by pressing the seam toward the shoulder and topstitching the shoulder side of the armhole seam (Figure 14.9d). Refer to

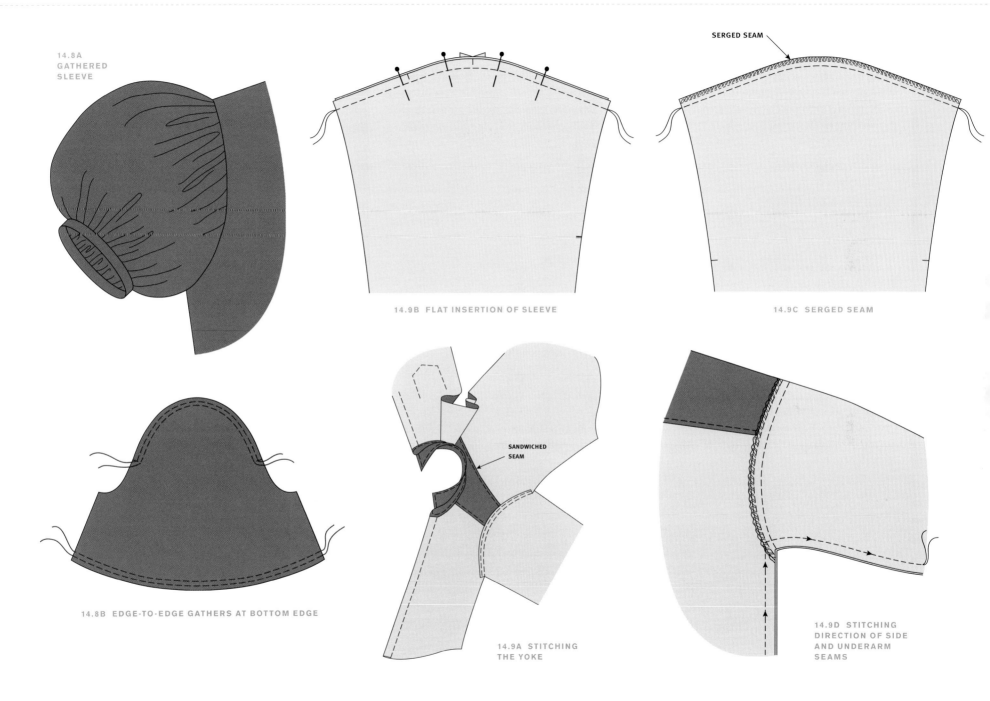

14.8A
GATHERED
SLEEVE

14.9B FLAT INSERTION OF SLEEVE

14.9C SERGED SEAM

SERGED SEAM

14.8B EDGE-TO-EDGE GATHERS AT BOTTOM EDGE

SANDWICHED
SEAM

14.9A STITCHING
THE YOKE

14.9D STITCHING
DIRECTION OF SIDE
AND UNDERARM
SEAMS

Chapter 6, "Seams," and Figure 6.28d for more information.

- Stitch the side seams in one continuous stitching, matching the armhole seamlines (Figure 14.9d); this seam can also be serged.
- Complete the sleeve.

Dropped Shoulder Sleeves

Dropped shoulders are created by a wider bodice that hangs off the shoulder onto the arm with a flattened sleeve cap that is joined in a seam. They are most attractive when loose fitting and made from fabric with drape. Blouses, dresses, and casual jackets or coats are good candidates for dropped shoulder sleeves. Part of the sleeve cap combines with the garment, covering the upper arm at different lengths. This can be extended or exaggerated as much as the designer desires. The garment can be developed with or without the lower sleeve. The lower sleeve can be attached to the garment at the extended cap. The sleeve can be of any length or style; the only consideration is that the top of the sleeve must be the same dimension as the extended cap.

Because there is no ease in this type of sleeve, follow these stitching directions:

- Stitch the side seams of the garment to the matchpoints, leaving the ½-inch seam allowance unstitched; backstitch. Press the seams open (Figure 14.10a).

- Stitch the side seams of the sleeve, leaving the ½-inch seam allowance unstitched; backstitch (Figure 14.10b). Press the seams open.
- With the correct sides together, match the sleeve to the garment at the notches and the underarm matchpoint; pin.
- Stitch, beginning at the underarm, with the garment up facing you; the stitching will actually be done in-the-round. Backstitch, and press.

Raglan Sleeves

The **raglan sleeve** gets it name from a loose overcoat named after an English general. This sleeve has long shaping at the top and is set into the garment before the underarm seam of the sleeve and garment is joined. The raglan sleeve is a versatile sleeve that can be used as the basis of many sleeve variations. The sleeve is cut from a separate pattern piece, and its seams, which extend diagonally from the neckline to the underarm, add a design detail to the garment. The sleeve does not have the traditional armhole seam, but retains the underarm of a set-in sleeve, as shown in Figure 14.11b. In a one-piece raglan sleeve, a dart at the shoulder gives some shaping to the shoulder area. In a two-piece raglan sleeve, the shaping at the shoulder comes from the shape of the seams.

For this sleeve, the side seams are stitched after the sleeve is sewn to the garment; however, an-

other option is to stitch the side seams of the garment and sleeve first, then sew the raglan sleeve to the garment (Figure 14.11b).

To insert a one-piece raglan sleeve with a dart:

- Stitch the dart or seam over the arm at the shoulder. Slash the dart open on the foldline and press; use a tailor's ham to shape this area (Figure 14.11a and Figure 14.3b).
- Pin the sleeve seams to the appropriate garment edges, correct sides together, carefully matching notches to ensure that the front of the sleeve will match the front of the garment.
- Stitch, trim, and then stitch again ⅛ inch from the first stitching between the notches (Figure 14.11b).

14.10A GARMENT SIDE
SEAM STITCHED

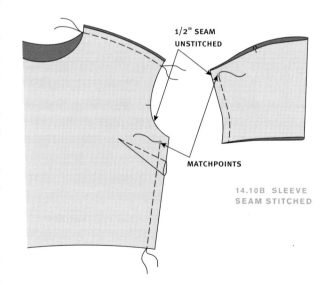

1/2" SEAM
UNSTITCHED

MATCHPOINTS

14.10B SLEEVE
SEAM STITCHED

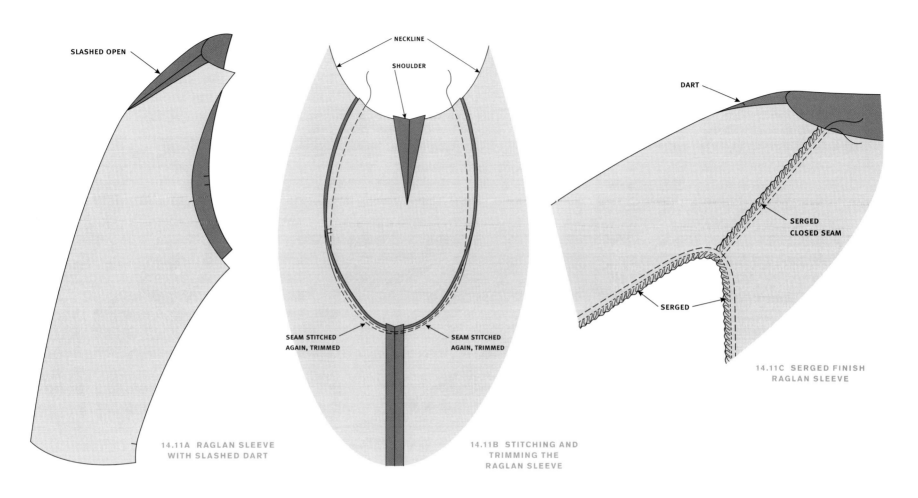

SLASHED OPEN

NECKLINE

SHOULDER

DART

SERGED
CLOSED SEAM

SERGED

SEAM STITCHED
AGAIN, TRIMMED

SEAM STITCHED
AGAIN, TRIMMED

**14.11A RAGLAN SLEEVE
WITH SLASHED DART**

**14.11B STITCHING AND
TRIMMING THE
RAGLAN SLEEVE**

**14.11C SERGED FINISH
RAGLAN SLEEVE**

- Press the seams flat as stitched (melding the stitches), then press open.
- Stitch the side seam and sleeve seam of the garment in one continuous plain seam; this seam can be serged closed after stitching to finish the seam edges (Figure 14.11c); or, if this seam is in a garment that will be lined, it can be left unfinished to be covered by the lining.

Two-Piece Raglan Sleeve
A two-piece raglan sleeve should be carefully marked to indicate the front and back.
- Match all notches and markings.
- Stitch each sleeve individually to the front and back; press the seams.
- Join the seam allowances along the shoulder seam in one continuous stitching; press—since this area is curved, press over a tailor's ham.
- Stitch the underarm seams.

SLEEVES CUT-IN-ONE WITH ALL OR PART OF THE GARMENT
Cap Sleeve

A true cap sleeve is created in the patternmaking stage of design development, and is drafted from the cap of a sleeve pattern. It is then sewn into the garment as a sleeve. It can be designed to conform to the arm or to stand away from the arm. When the cap sleeve is very short, it is lined to the edge (self-faced) (Figure 12.14a).

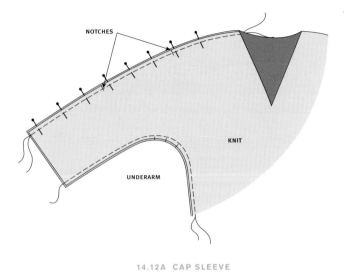

NOTCHES

KNIT

UNDERARM

14.12A CAP SLEEVE

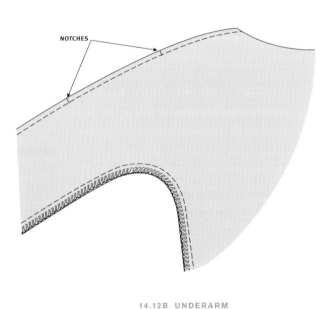

NOTCHES

14.12B UNDERARM

- Accurate marking of the matchpoint is critical for the proper setting of this sleeve.
- The cap sleeve is lined with its own fabric to the edge before being stitched to the garment.
- After the cap sleeve is stitched into the garment, use bias binding to finish off the underarm seam allowances and continue around the sleeve, finishing off the cap sleeve seam allowances at the same time.

> **NOTE**
>
> *Always* pivot corners with the needle in the fabric.

Sometimes the short-sleeved kimono sleeve is called a cap sleeve. It looks like an extension of the shoulder; it should not be fitted too closely or it will pull under the armhole. (Refer to the Style I.D., Figure 14.1d.)

Kimono Sleeve

The **kimono sleeve** is used in garments where a wide, loose sleeve is desirable. The sleeve is cut as part of the main body of the garment with half the sleeve on the front of the garment and the other half on the back of the garment. The pattern pieces resemble a T-shape, and there is no seamline around the armhole. The dolman sleeve is developed from the basic kimono sleeve. The underarm seam is reinforced to withstand the strain from arm movements. For extra ease and movement, a

one- or two-piece gusset is sewn in the underarm seam. To stitch a kimono sleeve without a gusset:

- Match notches and underarm curves of the front and back sleeves (Figure 14.12b).
- Pin the front sleeve to the back sleeve with the correct sides together.
- Stitch the shoulder/sleeves together; press.
- Stitch the underarm/side seams together; press.
- Reduce the stitch length; just inside the seam, stitch a second row of stitches in the seam allowance of the underarm curve for reinforcement for a very loose sleeve. Serge finish the edge of the seam allowances together if the garment will not be lined (Figure 14.12b).
- If the garment is lined press the seam allowances in the direction in which they were stitched, then press open. Because this seam is on the bias, it can be shaped with pressing.

One-Piece Gusset

The addition of a gusset to a sleeve provides extra ease and movement (Figure 14.13a). A **gusset** is a one-piece diamond or two triangles sewn to a slash in the underarm seam. Cutting these pieces on the bias gives the most ease and strength to the gusset. The diamond points of the gusset must end precisely in line with the underarm seamline and the slash points on the garment. If they don't, the sleeve will feel uncomfortable, be pulled slightly off center, and the sloppy gusset insertion will show when the arm is raised. To insert a one-piece diamond-shaped gusset in the sleeve underarm, edgestitch it to a finished opening. To begin:

- Transfer all matchpoints, slash, and stitching lines to the wrong side of the garment (Figure 14.13b) and the gusset (Figure 14.13c).
- Stitch a square of silk organza to the point on the wrong side of the fabric when sewing the reinforcement stitches (Figure 14.13b).
- Slash the opening for the gusset along the slash line, cutting up to ⅛ inch from the point; if the point is reinforced, cut through the reinforcement as well, then press it away from the garment, treating it like a seam allowance when stitching (Figure 14.13d).
- Stitch the side and underarm seams of the garment, ending precisely on the matchpoints of the slash opening edges of the slash opening; the opening will be similar to the shape of the gusset in each underarm area (Figure 14.13e).
- Position the gusset inside the sleeve under the opening with the correct side up.
- Match the finished underarm edges to the gusset stitching lines; pin and handbaste the gusset in place (Figure 14.13f).

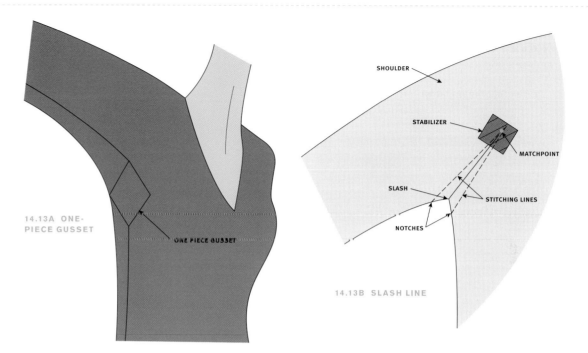

14.13A ONE-PIECE GUSSET

14.13B SLASH LINE

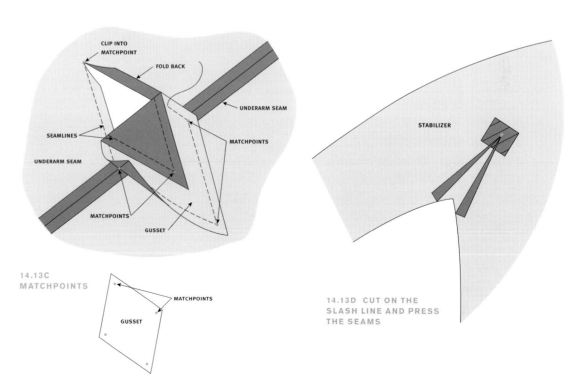

14.13C MATCHPOINTS

14.13D CUT ON THE SLASH LINE AND PRESS THE SEAMS

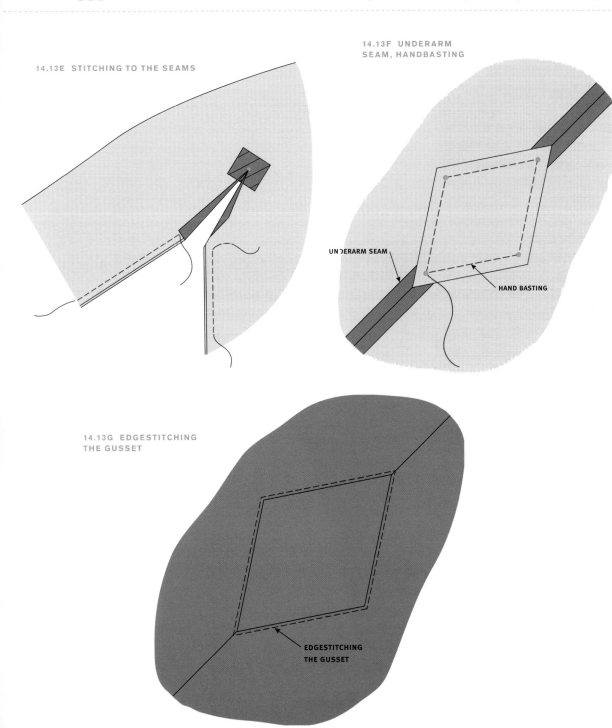

14.13E STITCHING TO THE SEAMS

14.13F UNDERARM SEAM, HANDBASTING

UNDERARM SEAM

HAND BASTING

14.13G EDGESTITCHING THE GUSSET

EDGESTITCHING THE GUSSET

• Edgestitch the garment edges to the gusset from the correct side of the garment (Figure 14.13g).

• Maneuvering the sleeve under the machine needle, especially if the sleeve is long, can be difficult when edgestitching; stitch carefully to keep the garment from bunching up and catching in the edgestitching.

• Or, machine stitch the gusset to the garment from the wrong side, aligning the match-points. The ½-inch seam allowance at the underarm seam must be left unstitched in order for the gusset to be machine stitched (Figure 14.13c).

Two-Piece Gusset

The two-piece gusset is easier to sew than a one-piece because the underarm seam is open when the gusset pieces are stitched to the slashed opening. This eliminates maneuvering around four corners (Figure 14.14a).

The finished two-piece gusset has a seam going down the center since one piece of the gusset is stitched to the front of the sleeve and the other is stitched to the back. Carefully marking the front and back pieces is a good safeguard against having to seam rip the wrong pieces. To stitch a two-piece gusset:

• Reinforce and stay the point of the slash opening in the garment as previously mentioned in the one-piece directions and shown in Figure 14.13b; cut the opening on the slash line to this point.

- Pin the front gusset triangle to the front slash, correct sides together, matching the matchpoints.
- Stitch the seam, reducing the stitch length at the point; pivot and continue to the end (Figure 14.14b).
- Stitch the back gusset to the back opening in the same manner.
- Press the gusset seam toward the garment; trim points and seam allowances (see Figure 14.14b).
- Pin the underarm seams with the correct sides together, precisely matching the beginning and ends of the gussets (Figure 14.14c).
- Stitch the underarm seam; press open (Figure 14.14d).

Dolman Sleeve

This sleeve is fitted at the wrist but cut with a very deep armhole. Dolman sleeves create a smooth line over the upper chest. The armhole section of the garment combines with the sleeve. The dolman sleeve and underarm seam can always be raised to create a closer fit while still maintaining the same bust and sleeve circumference.

- Stitch the shoulder/upper sleeve seam front and back together.
- Press after stitching.
- Stitch the underarm sleeve/side seams together; press.
- Continue with construction of the garment.

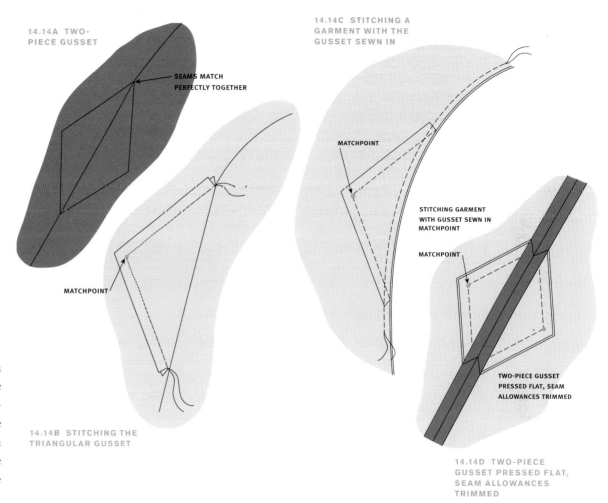

14.14A TWO-PIECE GUSSET

SEAMS MATCH PERFECTLY TOGETHER

MATCHPOINT

14.14B STITCHING THE TRIANGULAR GUSSET

14.14C STITCHING A GARMENT WITH THE GUSSET SEWN IN

MATCHPOINT

STITCHING GARMENT WITH GUSSET SEWN IN MATCHPOINT

MATCHPOINT

TWO-PIECE GUSSET PRESSED FLAT, SEAM ALLOWANCES TRIMMED

14.14D TWO-PIECE GUSSET PRESSED FLAT, SEAM ALLOWANCES TRIMMED

SLEEVE HEADS

Sleeve heads are strips of self-fabric bias cut organza, fabric, or batting that lift and support the gathered sleeve cap and enhance the sleeve's drape. The weight of the fabric or batting that is used to create the sleeve head depends entirely on the weight of the garment fabric. Inserting a shaped sleeve head is easy to do and eliminates the bulky seam allowances of traditional straight-cut heads. The sleeve head can be machine stitched 1/16 inch inside the sleeve cap seam allowance after the sleeve is set into the armhole (Figure 14.15).

- Cut the sleeve head in the shape of the sleeve cap for jackets or coats as shown in Figure 14.15a; for lightweight, sheer fabrics, cut as shown in Figure 14.15b.
- Center the head inside the sleeve cap with one long edge matched to the cap edge (Figure 14.15c).
- Pin and permanently hand stitch it to the cap seam allowance, close to the machine stitching—¼ inch apart and loose work best; or the sleeve head can be machine stitched ¹⁄₁₆ inch inside the sleeve cap seam allowance (see Figure 14.15c).
- Turn the seam allowance into the sleeve; the header will turn with it, supporting the cap.
- Continue with construction of the garment and/or lining.

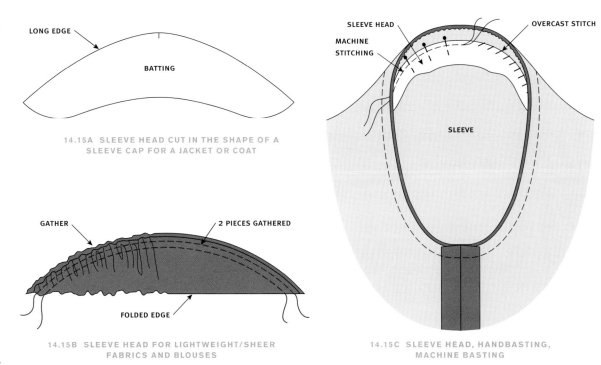

14.15A SLEEVE HEAD CUT IN THE SHAPE OF A SLEEVE CAP FOR A JACKET OR COAT

14.15B SLEEVE HEAD FOR LIGHTWEIGHT/SHEER FABRICS AND BLOUSES

14.15C SLEEVE HEAD, HANDBASTING, MACHINE BASTING

SHOULDER PADS

Shoulder pads are important for adding shape and structure to a garment, and they affect the way the garment fits, hangs, and looks on the body. Shoulder pads come and go in fashion, but a coat or jacket *always* looks better with a narrow, ¼-inch shoulder pad squaring the shoulders. Shoulder pads provide a well-made, finished-looking garment. There are two types of shoulder pads—those for set-in sleeves and those for raglan or dolman sleeves. Available in covered or uncovered forms, these pads come in many sizes and thicknesses from ¼ inch to 1½ inches.

A **set-in shoulder pad** has a long, straight edge that corresponds to a garment's sleeve seam, and its thickest part is along this edge. It creates a sharper line between the shoulder and the sleeve and gives a crisper, structured look.

Set-in pads (Figure 14.16a) that are specifically designed for jackets and coats are called tailor's shoulder pads and are generally larger in front than in back, in order to fill in the hollow of the chest below the shoulder. The sleeve edge of the tailor's pad is crescent-shaped to follow the shape of the top of the armhole. These pads have an extra layer of hair canvas or buckram covering the padding and are never covered with fabric because the garment's lining will cover the pad.

Smaller pads used in dresses and less tailored jackets are symmetrically balanced, front and back.

The **raglan shoulder pad** softly rounds off the point of the shoulder and helps fill in the area of the sleeve cap. Raglan shoulder pads (Figure 14.16b) are oval in shape, rounded at the shoulder edge, and slightly molded to fit over the shoulder point. The thickest part of the raglan pad is in the center of the pad.

Shoulder pads are made from a variety of materials, including cotton or polyester batting, and foam. They can be covered in lightweight lining fabric or tricot knit, or they can be purchased uncovered, to cover with fabric to coordinate with the garment.

Shoulder pads should never be visible from

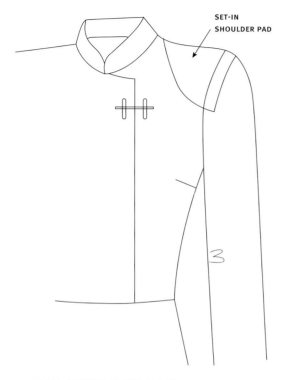

14.16A EXTENDED SET-IN PAD

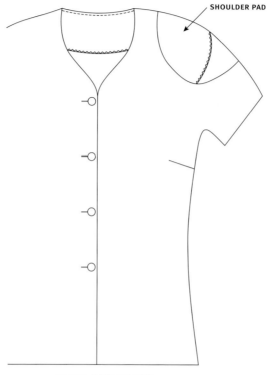

14.16B RAGLAN PAD

the outside of the garment. Most shoulder pads are made of graduated layers of batting, which prevent a visible ridge from forming. Shoulder pads improve the look of the garment and need to be positioned and inserted properly to be effective.

Inserting Shoulder Pads

A shoulder pad fits into a garment with its straight edge (for a set-in sleeve) or molded shoulder point (for a raglan sleeve) meeting the sleeve seam. Tailor's shoulder pads are matched to the outer edge of the seam allowance to extend slightly into the sleeve. The shoulder pad length is critical—it should cover the entire shoulder area, stopping about 1 inch from the neckline. If the shoulder pad is too long from the shoulder point to the neckline, trim it to fit and refinish the edge.

Set-in Shoulder Pads

- Pin the positioned shoulder pads in place from the correct side of the garment along the shoulder seam.
- Remove the garment from the dress form.
- Stitch each pad in place along the shoulder seam allowance using a catchstitch.
- Hand stitch each end of the pad in the sleeve seam allowance carefully, smoothing the pad to avoid pulling up or puckering the sleeve (Figure 14.17 and Figure 16.16, which shows the sleeve head and shoulder pad).

Raglan Shoulder Pads

- Position the shoulder pad over the ball of the shoulder on the dress form; pin in place from the correct side of the garment along the overarm seam or dart.
- Turn the garment to the inside and loosely catchstitch the shoulder pad to the overarm seam allowance or dart from the neck to the end of the shoulder.
- Catchstitch the shoulder pad beneath the neck facing.

Covering Shoulder Pads

If the garment is unlined, cover the shoulder pads with a lightweight fabric to coordinate with your garment, or Hong Kong–finished seams.

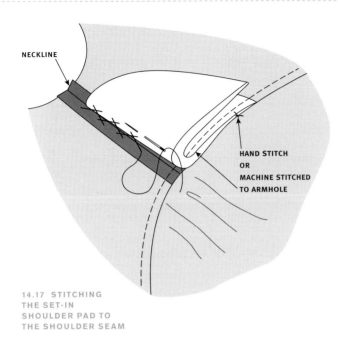

NECKLINE

HAND STITCH
OR
MACHINE STITCHED
TO ARMHOLE

14.17 STITCHING
THE SET-IN
SHOULDER PAD TO
THE SHOULDER SEAM

If there is a chance that the fabric would shadow through to the correct side of the garment, use a flesh-colored lining or tricot-knit fabric.

Set-in Shoulder Pads
- Cut two lining pieces, the same size as the pad, on the fold (Figure 14.18).
- Fold around the shoulder pad; pin in place.
- Serge, zigzag stitch, or bias bind the curved edge to maintain shaping (see Figure 14.18).

Raglan Shoulder Pads
- Cut a square of fabric large enough to fold over each pad.
- Place the pad on the fabric square and fold.
- Trace around the outside edge of the pad, allowing a 1-inch margin; cut along the outside of the marked line.

- To shape the covering, form and stitch a dart from the excess fabric on the underside of the pad covering.
- Refold the covering over the pad, with correct sides facing out; pin in place.
- Serge or zigzag stitch around the remaining edge; bias binding also makes a nice finish on unlined garments.

PRESSING THE SLEEVES

Even though we have stressed pressing as you sew in every chapter, we cannot say often enough how important it is to press the sleeve at each step of the construction. Pressing is almost as important to the sleeve as the stitching. Pressing is an art developed over time, based on experience with many types of fabrics. In all of our directions, pressing has been indicated at each step of the way, but additional emphasis is needed about the pressing of the sleeve.

- When steam-pressing the ease, do not press into the sleeve cap—press only the eased seam allowance.
- The seam allowance of the stitched armhole/sleeve *always* faces out toward the sleeve and *not* inward toward the neck.
- When pressing ease in a seam allowance such as at the side seam of a sleeve, steam the seam allowance and shrink the ease.
- *Never* press a crease down the center of a sleeve—always use a sleeve board to press the sleeve (Figure 2.31e). The only exception to this rule is a man's dress shirt or a tailored woman's shirt. If you are sewing at home

and do not have this piece of equipment, use a tightly rolled terry cloth bath towel in its place.
- *Do not* attempt to press the sleeve cap *without* a shaped pressing tool, such as a tailor's ham, underneath it—pressing is to aid in the shaping of this curved area, not to flatten it! (See Figure 14.5d.)
- Using lots of steam directed toward an area of the sleeve and smoothing it with your

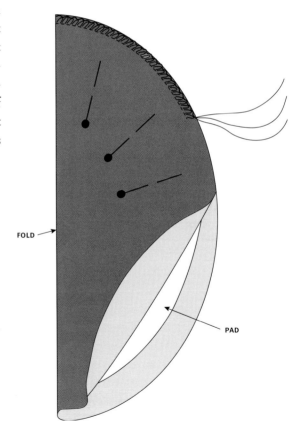

FOLD

PAD

14.18 COVERING SET-IN SHOULDER PADS

fingertips can be an effective way to get rid of small wrinkles in the upper sleeve.

- When working with lots of gathering, press into the gathers with the tip of the iron, taking care to avoid flattening the gathers.
- Finally, if the final pressing of your sleeve leaves something to be desired, consider taking the garment to a professional dry cleaner, which has pressing equipment specially designed for different areas of a garment. A good final press sets the shape of the garment.

STITCHING TRICKY FABRICS
Matching Stripes, Plaids, Patterns, and Repeat Patterns

Do use even plaids for easiest matching with set-in sleeves.

Do cut underarms of the sleeve on the same plaid for matching (Figure 2.16).

Do use the bias grainline for sleeves for a contrast that doesn't have to be matched.

Do match the front notch of a set-in sleeve to the notch on the garment bodice.

Do match front and back below the notch on the shoulder seams of kimono sleeves.

Do choose another fabric if the plaids cannot be successfully matched.

Don't try to match plaids on raglan sleeves—they won't match due to the slant of the seam.

Sheer Fabric

Do use serging to finish the seam allowances of sheer sleeves.

Do use tissue paper underneath the fabric when stitching to prevent slipping.

Do use very narrow bias bindings for finishing the sleeves at the hem or the armhole.

Do use a self-fabric or taffeta sleeve header in the sleeve cap to support gathers.

Do use self-fabric lining on the fold at the hem if the sleeve has a straight hem. This must be cut as a mirror image.

Don't leave regular seam allowances showing; always seam finish as narrow as possible.

Lace

Do use contrasting or flesh-colored underlining with lace sleeves to highlight the motifs of the lace.

Do use the self-edge of the lace, especially if there is a border for the hem of the sleeve (Figure 6.48).

Do use narrow French seams to finish seam allowances if the lace is not too heavy.

Do use a Hong Kong finish on heavier laces to finish the seam allowance; if the lace is underlined with a contrast fabric, finish the seam allowance edges with serging.

Do use tulle or taffeta for sleeve heads to support the cap of exaggerated, gathered lace sleeves.

Satin

Do use tissue paper underneath the satin when stitching to prevent the feed dogs from marring the surface.

Do pin only or handbaste within the seam allowances, as satin surfaces are easily marked by pins.

Do handbaste seams to avoid seam slippage.

Do avoid set-in sleeves on heavyweight satin—it can be difficult to ease in.

Do consider bias-cut sleeves.

Beaded Fabric

Do stitch kimono, raglan, or dropped shoulder sleeves—they're easiest to sew.

Do change the needle frequently, as beading can dull or burr the needle.

Do use two sleeve patterns, one for each side of the garment, and cut out the beaded sleeves from a single layer.

Do carefully match the front sleeve notch to the front bodice notch to match the beading pattern or repeat.

Knits

Do eliminate ease from the sleeve cap of knit sleeves—knits do not need easing.

Do use the flat insertion method for sleeves, using a ¼-inch seam allowance.

Do match the cap, the underarm points, and also halfway between the underarm and sleeve cap—this ensures even distribution of the knit sleeve.

Do stitch the armhole seam with the garment on top and the sleeve next to the sewing machine, gently manipulating the armhole to fit the sleeve.

Do stitch again ⅛ inch away from the first line of stitching.

Don't overstretch the armhole—this results in wavy seams.

Denim

Do construct any sleeve from denim, matching the weight of the denim to the style of the sleeve.

Do use covered shoulder pads in unlined denim jackets and coats.

Do topstitch around dropped shoulder armholes with the seam allowances toward the shoulder.

Don't use dolman or kimono sleeves in denim—the extra fabric in the sleeve may be too heavy.

Velvet

Do remember that velvet slips, and seams can pucker when setting in sleeves.

Do stitch the sleeves carefully—needle holes do not come out.

Do lift the presser foot every 4 inches or so to allow the fabric to relax when stitching around the curves of the sleeve—this also helps to eliminate any unwanted puckers.

Leather

Stitching sleeves in leather requires some pattern adjustment before beginning and additional supplies such as leather cement, small binder clips, a rubber mallet, and a specialty leather needle. As leather needles put holes into the leather, take care to match the needle size to the weight of the leather being stitched.

- Determine the amount of ease in the sleeve cap. A sleeve in leather can only take ¼ inch of easing on each side (½ inch total). If there is more than ½ inch ease, then fold out ⅛ inch of the extra ease across the sleeve cap (¼ inch total pattern). If there is still more ease left, take equal amounts off the sleeve underarm seam. Realign sleeve notches to armholes (Figure 14.19a).

- Stabilize front and back armholes (not including seam allowance) with bias tape or narrow cut tape (Figure 14.19b).

- Stitch the shoulder seams. Tie and clip threads to ¾ inch. Tuck the threads in between the garment and seam allowance. Use leather cement and flatten open seams using a mallet and roller (Figure 14.19f).

- Check the armhole shaping. Place the front and back pieces on a flat surface. The armholes across the shoulder line should be a smooth rounded curve. Reshape the shoulders if they come to a point (Figure 14.4b). If this line is not cut correctly, the sleeves will not sit right in the armhole.

- Stitch basting stitches (just inside the seam allowance) to the sleeves in four sections, as shown in Figure 14.19c:
  – From the center of the sleeve cap down either side to the notches (overlap the stitching by ¼ inch at the top)
  – From the notches down both sides to the underarms, finishing ½ inch back from the seam allowance

- Pull the basting stitches up into slight easing in all four sections. The sleeve cap should have more easing than the underarms. Clip threads back to approximately 3 inches in length (Figure 14.19d).

- Stitch the underarm seams of the sleeve (Figure 14.19d) and garment (Figure 14.19e), clip threads. Pull the threads up into the seam allowance and secure with leather cement.

- Place the sleeve to the garment, matching the following points:
  – Sleeve cap to shoulder
  – Notches to notches
  – Underarm seams together

- Secure each point with fabric craft glue and secure seam with binder clips (Figure 14.19f).

- Stitch the sleeves into the armholes, stitching just outside of the basting stitches. (Basting stitches should not show from the correct side of the sleeve—remember you cannot remove the stitches, as they leave holes in the leather.)

- Carefully clip Vs around the sleeve cap to eliminate bulk. Bring the Vs together and apply leather cement to the entire sleeve of the armhole. Flatten with a mallet.

- Cement the sleeve cap only (that is, the armhole and sleeve previously cemented) to the top of the shoulders. Place the sleeves over a tailor's ham. Mold the sleeve cap with your hands to create a rounded shape. Also use a mallet to flatten.

Whew! The leather sleeve is inserted into the garment; continue with construction.

Faux Fur

Do use raglan or dropped shoulder sleeves whenever possible with faux fur—they are the easiest to sew.

14.19A LEATHER SLEEVE PATTERN

1/8" FOLD OUT

SLEEVE PATTERN

14.19B SECURING SHOULDER SEAM WITH BINDER CLIPS

BIAS STABILIZING TAPE

14.19C BASTING STITCHES IN SECTIONS

EASING

NOTCH

NOTCH

SLEEVE
PULL UP EASING
FROM BOBBIN THREAD

14.19D PULLING UP EASE; STITCHING UNDERARM SEAM

BINDER CLIP

14.19E STITCH THE UNDERARM SEAM

PLACE THREADS UNDER SEAM

14.19F INSERTING THE SLEEVE

SHOULDER

SLEEVE

PLACE THREADS UNDER SEAM WHEN LEATHER CEMENT IS APPLIED

UNDERARM

Do trim away the fur from the seam allowances before stitching the sleeves to reduce bulk, or if the fur is short pile, stitch the seams together, then trim the fur away; use hair clippers or a razor.

Do place raw edges together and zigzag stitch together.

Heavyweight Fabric

Do use a catchstitch to hold seams in place in a raglan sleeve (Figure 6.51b).

Do use a damp wet cloth for extra steam if needed to press and flatten the seams.

TRANSFER YOUR KNOWLEDGE

Now that you know how to stitch sleeves, and have become more familiar with the different types of sleeves, take that knowledge and try one of the following techniques. Remember, always sample a new technique before applying it to a garment, and allow plenty of time to do so.

- Slash open the cap of the sleeve to add extravagant fullness to the cap of the sleeve; support the fullness with a sleeve header of taffeta.
- Cut a set-in sleeve on the bias grainline in both a plaid fabric and a nonplaid fabric; compare the fit.
- Combine two techniques on one sleeve: increase the ease at the sleeve cap and turn the ease into pin tucks or pleats, releasing the fullness toward the sleeve hem.
- Change the shape of the basic sleeve into a flare or direct the fullness of the sleeve toward the hem, making the hem of the sleeve the focus.
- Combine the front raglan sleeve with a different back, such as a kimono sleeve back.
- Change the depth of the dolman sleeve and add a gusset for better fit and ease.
- Add a slotted seam down the center of a set-in or raglan sleeve to reveal a contrasting fabric.
- Add tucks or inverted pleats to the center of a set-in sleeve to draw attention to the sleeve.
- Add a seam with piping inserted down the center of a set-in sleeve.

STRETCH YOUR CREATIVITY

Sleeves offer a myriad of design possibilities, so think outside the box when applying the sleeve techniques learned in this chapter.

- Slash the sleeve cap and add exaggerated pleats (Figure 14.20a).
- Apply beaded trim to the upper garment, extending from the neckline down the entire kimono sleeve (Figure 14.20b).
- Create self-fabric trim and apply over the dropped shoulder, continuing across the bodice (Figure 14.20c).

- In knit fabric, extend the raglan sleeve into the bodice, as shown in Figure 14.20d.

STOP! WHAT DO I DO IF . . .

. . . I've stitched my sleeve and there are unwanted, unsightly puckers!

Careful ease stitching and pin basting help to eliminate puckers as the sleeve is stitched into place. However, if these techniques do not prevent the puckers from forming, rip the stitches out of the section that is puckered, and press. If the fabric is difficult to ease, puckers are more likely to occur again, so handbaste the area that is puckered. The eased area may have to be extended around the entire sleeve to accommodate the excess amount in the sleeve cap. Check the stitch length and adjust it to a slightly smaller stitch length, then restitch. Also, check the amount of ease in the pattern, reducing the ease. Recut the sleeve and stitch into the armhole. Chalk this up to the learning experience!

. . . I've stitched a kimono sleeve and it really droops unattractively!

Adding a one- or two-piece gusset to the already stitched underarm area of the kimono sleeve will provide more fit and ease of movement. Adjusting the curve of the underarm area to a higher curve will also bring the sleeve closer to the body. Adjust this curve with basting stitches first *before* cutting away any of the underarm seam to see if it rectifies the dissatisfaction.

Stretch Your Creativity

14.20A SET-IN SLEEVE WITH EXAGGERATED PLEATS

14.20B KIMONO SLEEVE WITH BEADED TRIM

14.20C DROPPED SHOULDER WITH SELF-FABRIC TRIM

14.20D KNIT DRESS WITH RAGLAN SLEEVE

. . . I've added a one-piece gusset and the sleeve doesn't hang properly!

The key to inserting gussets is to be absolutely accurate in marking and stitching. Precision is paramount in this technique. Take out the gusset, and recut and re-mark a new one. Check the markings on the garment. Begin again. Learn from this experience, and always make a practice muslin in the same weight as the garment fabric. Remember, making a muslin does not necessarily mean using 100 percent cotton muslin. By using a similar weight for the muslin, you would see early on in the construction process how the sleeve would sit.

SELF-CRITIQUE

- Are my ease stitches evenly distributed on the marked area of the set-in sleeve?
- Are my set-in sleeves pucker-free?
- Do my set-in sleeves hang properly?
- Are the shoulder pads or sleeve headers visible from the outside of the sleeve?
- Do the shoulder pads or sleeve headers support the shoulder and sleeve cap?
- Is the pressing of my set-in sleeve smooth and wrinkle-free, adding to the shape rather than flattening it?

- Has the sleeve been pressed on a sleeve board, without a crease pressed down the center of the sleeve?
- When stitching the raglan sleeve, are the seams evenly sewn, pucker-free, and pressed without being visible on the outside of the garment?
- Has the proper sleeve support been inserted for the raglan sleeve?
- Does the two-piece sleeve hang properly with the correct shoulder support?
- If working with a specialty fabric, does the style of sleeve complement the design?

REVIEW CHECKLIST

- Do I understand the difference between a set-in sleeve and a cut-in-one sleeve?
- Do I understand the critical importance of accurate matchpoints, notches, and stitching in setting myself up for stitching the perfectly fitted sleeve?
- Do I understand that the amount of ease, so important to the setting in of sleeves, is determined at the patternmaking stage?

- Do I understand the significance of ease stitching, pinning, and basting to the successful pucker-free application of a sleeve?
- Do I understand the importance of choosing the correct combination of shoulder and sleeve cap support for the sleeve?
- Do I understand the difference the proper positioning of the shoulder pad makes to the support of the shoulder and sleeve?
- Do I understand how critical it is to correctly press along each step of the sleeve construction?
- Do I understand that the basic sleeve is just the beginning of sleeve design?
- Do I understand that changing the design of the sleeve and the hem finish of the sleeve offers unlimited design possibilities?

The fashion designer needs an excellent knowledge of clothing construction. Accurately marking, easing, pinning, and pressing sleeves are important steps of construction. Remember, designing, patternmaking, and construction are closely linked together and without good construction, there isn't good design. Learning to sew is a process, so keep sewing and never give up!

15

Hems: Defining the Length

The hem is one of the most noticeable aspects of a garment, as it defines the length. We have attended many student fashion shows and enjoyed them immensely. When each model appears on the catwalk wearing each glamorous garment, it is the hem that first hits the eye. If the hem has not been leveled and correctly stitched using a suitable hem technique for the fabric, it can spoil the entire look of the garment.

The process of stitching the hems is outlined in this chapter. Various hem finishes and hem stitches are explained, including invisible hand-stitched hems, machine-stitched hems, false hems, and other creative hem treatments.

This chapter outlines how to stitch both straight hems and shaped hems, such as curved, flared, circular, and angled hemlines. Knowing how to treat shaped hems is as important as knowing how to stitch straight hems.

The aim of this chapter is to discuss the options for hem finishes and hem stitches. The designer can customize the most suitable hem finish and stitch for each fabric type and individual garment.

STYLE I.D.

The Style I.D. illustrates different hemlines. With creativity, the designer can dream up an infinite number of shapes for hemlines.

The coatdress in Figure 15.1a has an asymmetrical hemline, which has been stitched with a false hem. Notice that one side of the hem (and collar) is scalloped and the other side has clean lines.

KEY TERMS
Hand-Stitched Hem
Hem
Hem Allowance
Hem Edge
Hem Finish
Hemline
Machine-Stitched Hem
Mirror Image
Mitered Corner
Pin-Mark
Shaped Hem
Skirt Marker
Smooth Hemline
Straight Hem

Style I.D.

15.1A COATDRESS

15.1B CUFFED PANT
AND SHORT JACKET

15.1C CIRCLE SKIRT
AND HALTER TOP

15.1D SUMMER PRINT
TOP AND JEANS

Figure 15.1b illustrates wool check pants with wide cuffs. Cuffs are not always the trend for the season; regardless, a designer needs to know how they are stitched. Notice the cute little jacket with the two front hem slits. Hem slits are often needed in garments for functional design purposes; other times they are purely decorative (which is the case in the jacket). Also notice that the sleeve hem has been stitched with cuffs. (If you turn back to Figures 1.4, 1.5, 1.6, and 1.7, the importance of functional design is discussed in full.)

The summer floral skirt in Figure 15.1c is circular, with a narrow, rolled, machine-stitched hem. This is the idyllic hem finish on full, floaty, circular hemlines.

The softly draped top in Figure 15.1d is paired with the jeans and has an angled hand-stitched hem.

As you can see, there is no standard hemline for garments—hems can be all shapes and sizes.

GATHER YOUR TOOLS

You'll need the following tools: skirt marker, chalk, pins, thread, machine and hand stitching needles, seam ripper, point turner, and a variety of hem tapes. With the tape measure around your neck, you are now ready to begin stitching hems.

NOW LET'S GET STARTED
What Is a Hem?

To help you understand each term associated with hems, look at Figure 15.2 and follow along as each term is defined.

A **hem** is an extra width of fabric added below the finished **hemline** at the pattern-drafting stage. This extra fabric is called the **hem allowance**. The border of the hem allowance is called the **hem edge**; this is the raw edge of the fabric. A hem is formed when the hem allowance is neatened with a **hem finish**. The hem is then turned back and stitched to the garment. The hem can be *hand stitched* or **machined stitched** to finish the hemline. The hemline is also the foldline; however, if a false hem is stitched to the hem edge, then the foldline is called a seamline.

The hemline is the folded edge that defines the length of the garment. Hems are added to blouses, shirts, shorts, pants, skirts, dresses, jackets, coats, and sleeves at the beginning when the pattern is plotted. A hem prevents garment edges from fraying and adds weight and support to the hemline as well as finishing the hem edge.

Defining the length is part of the silhouette of the garment; the silhouette or outline of the garment is one of the important design elements. The length of the garment is defined at the sketching stage of designing. There are many different hem lengths and shapes to choose from when designing collections. Hems can be straight, curved, circular, angled, or any other shape the designer chooses. The designer endeavors to cover a variety of hem lengths to appeal to the target customer.

Straight hems and **shaped hems** are stitched differently. The difference is slight yet important. A shaped hem cannot be folded back and stitched in the same way as a straight hem. But take heart, any shaped hem can be perfectly stitched into a beautiful hem!

HOW TO CHOOSE THE APPROPRIATE HEM

It can be difficult to choose which hem finish and hem stitch to use for each garment. We highly recommend beginning by sampling the hem in the same or similar fabric type as the garment. Then if one sample doesn't work, try another until you feel satisfied that the hem finish and stitches are "just right" for your project.

Choosing the appropriate hem finish and hem stitches for a garment is the first important decision when stitching the hem. How the final hem looks influences the success of the garment.

Here is a checklist with four helpful hints to consider:

1. The style and look you want to achieve. Whether the garment is for casual wear, day wear, business wear, or evening wear gives some direction as to the type of hem finish to use. For example, machine-stitched hems are used more often in casual garments such as active wear and sportswear. Hand-stitched hems can also be used for casual wear, and definitely used for business wear, evening wear, and high-end garments.

2. The weight, drape, and handle of the fabric. The type of hem must suit the fabric. For example, if the fabric you are working with

PATTERN TIP

Creating a Smooth Hemline
Before cutting the garment, every seamline must be perfectly matched together. Notches placed on the seamlines guide you in accurate stitching. Notches ensure that when the seam is stitched, the hem edges will match exactly together.

It is not only the seams that need to be perfectly matched together. The pattern also needs a smooth hemline; this is important to the success of the hemline.

How the pattern is shaped on the hemline affects how the hem sits when the garment is completed. Most students forget this

important step—so attend to this now before cutting the garment in fabric.

- To achieve a smooth hemline, butt the seamlines together.
- Observe the shape on the hemline at the seam junction. If the seam is pointing down, as it would for an A-line skirt (Figure 15.3a), or up in a V shape as it would for a pegged skirt (Figure 15.3b), then the hemline needs blending to create a smooth curved shape.
- It is not only the garment hemline that needs to be smooth but also the sleeve hemline.

NOTE

If pleats or a godet are inserted into the hemline, line up these patterns as well when creating a smooth hemline.

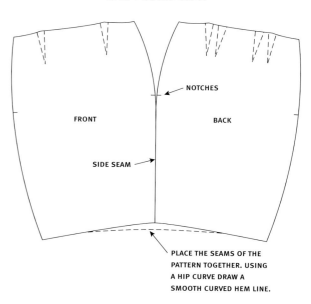

15.3A A-LINE SKIRT

NOTCHES
CENTER FRONT
CENTER BACK
SIDE SEAM
HEM EDGE
PLACE THE SEAMS OF THE PATTERN TOGETHER. USING A HIP CURVE DRAW A SMOOTH CURVED HEMLINE.

15.3B PEGGED SKIRT

NOTCHES
FRONT
BACK
SIDE SEAM
PLACE THE SEAMS OF THE PATTERN TOGETHER. USING A HIP CURVE DRAW A SMOOTH CURVED HEM LINE.

is sheer, then consider stitching a narrow rolled hem, because a wider hem allowance would shadow through to the correct side of the fabric. A narrow, rolled, hand- or machine-stitched hem would look the least obtrusive.

3. The price point. The chosen finish may need to reflect price constraints.
4. The big picture—time. This factor can also determine the hem finish. For example, whether you choose a hand-stitched rolled

hem or a machine-stitched rolled hem may depend on the time available; both would work well.

A SMOOTH, EVEN HEM BEGINS WITH THE CORRECT PATTERNS

A successful hem *always* begins with the correct patterns.

The Hem Allowance
The fabric and silhouette dictate the width of the hem allowance. Here are some pattern tips on how to decide on the width of hem allowance.

Table 15.1 is a guide that sets out some suggested hem allowances for different silhouettes and styles. Also look at Figure 2.9 to see the shape of each hemline referred to in the following pattern tips for hem allowances.

TABLE 15.1 HEM ALLOWANCES FOR DIFFERENT SILHOUETTES AND STYLES

Garment	Style/Silhouette	Hem Allowance	Hem Type
Skirt/Dress	Pegged	1½ inches	Hand stitch
	Pencil (straight)	1½ inches	Hand stitch
	A-line	1–1½ inches (eased)	Hand stitch
	Flared	1 inch (eased)	Hand stitch
	Circle	½ inch	Machine stitch narrow rolled hem
Pants	Straight	1½ inches	Hand stitch
	A-line	1–1½ inches (eased)	Hand stitch
	Flared	1 inch (eased)	Hand stitch
	Jeans	1–1½ inches	Machine stitch twice-turned
Blouse/Shirt	Straight	1 inch	Machine stitch
	A-line	½–1 inch (eased)	Machine stitch
	Flared	½ inch	Machine stitch narrow rolled hem
Jackets	Straight	1½ inches	Hand stitch
	A-line/Flared	1½ inches (eased)	Hand stitch
	Circular	1 inch (eased)	Hand stitch
	Jacket sleeve hem	1½ inches (as above)	Hand stitch
Coats	Straight	1½–2 inches	Hand stitch
	A-line/flared	1½ inches (eased)	Hand stitch
	Circular	1 inch (eased)	Hand stitch
	Sleeve hems (as above)	1½–2 inches	Hand stitch

PATTERN TIP

- *Straight hem:* The straighter the skirt, the wider the hem allowance can be.
- *A-line:* When the hemline starts to curve, reduce the hem allowance.
- *Flared:* The wider the hemline, the more the hem allowance will need to be decreased to reduce bulk.
- *Circular:* The wider and more circular the hemline, the more you should lessen the hem width and stitch a narrow hem.

garment hem edge and not add bulk. No matter what silhouette the garment has, this step is essential to the success of the hem.

How Is This Done?

Fold the pattern hem allowance back as if it is stitched in place. Make sure the hem allowance lies as flat as possible (this is more difficult when the hem is curved). Figure 15.4 shows how this is done to the hem of a pegged skirt and flared sleeve. Cut the hem allowance to exactly the same angle as the seam; this is the **mirror image**.

Why Is This Important?

In some styles, the silhouette narrows on the side seam, as it does for the pegged skirt in Figure 15.4a. If the hem allowance *is not* cut as a mirror image of the seamline, then the hem edge will not have enough length to turn back and sit *perfectly* flat when stitched. If this is not attended to at the patternmaking stage, the hem will look puckered from the correct side of the garment

NOTE

Some hems recommended for hand stitching can also be machine stitched as part of the design—this is the designer's choice.

Mirror-Image Hem Allowance

After the hem allowance is added to the pattern, it *must* be cut as a mirror image to the angle of the seamline. Cutting the hem allowance as mirror image ensures that when the hem allowance is turned back, it will lie flat behind the

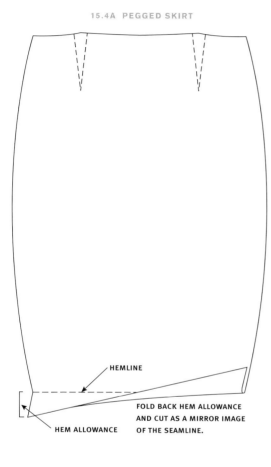

15.4A PEGGED SKIRT

HEMLINE

FOLD BACK HEM ALLOWANCE
AND CUT AS A MIRROR IMAGE
OF THE SEAMLINE.

HEM ALLOWANCE

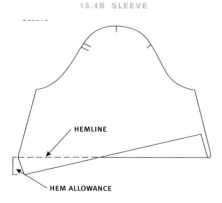

15.4B SLEEVE

HEMLINE

HEM ALLOWANCE

when turned back and stitched. An A-line or flared silhouette (widening gradually at the side seam) can also be cut as a mirror-image hem, as there will be too much fabric on the hem edge when turned back and stitched. Notice in Figure 15.4b that the same principle is followed for the sleeve hem allowance.

NOW LET'S PREPARE THE HEM
Leveling the Hem

It can never be assumed that creating a smooth hemline on the pattern is all that is needed to achieve a level hemline. Attending to the pattern is the first important step; however, after the garment is stitched, *leveling the hem* on a person or form must be attended to.

Hemlines are often cut on all three fabric grainlines: lengthwise, crosswise, and bias. This is especially so for a circular hemline. Each grainline drops at different levels on the hem edge. For this reason, the hem needs to be leveled.

Using a Skirt Marker

The hemline should sit parallel to the floor unless it is asymmetrical. To level the hem on skirts, dresses, and coats, we advise using a **skirt marker**. There are two types of skirt markers available to help level the hem: the pin-marker and the chalk marker.

Follow these tips for leveling the hem, and refer to Figure 15.5.

- After ascertaining the finished length of the hemline, add the hem allowance and **pin-**

> **NOTE**
>
> A circle skirt especially needs to be leveled on a form or on a person because of the different grainlines. If possible, allow a circle skirt to hang for at least a week or two to allow time for the bias grain to drop before leveling. When a circle skirt is left hanging from season to season, it will continue to drop and will need leveling again. To prevent this from happening, carefully fold the garment over the hanger from season to season.

mark this length, by placing a pin horizontally in the garment.

- Have the customer or fit model wear the garment. Ask her to stand on a table (if possible), otherwise you will need to crouch on the floor; this can be a backbreaking job for the designer.

- Always ask the customer to wear shoes that will be worn with the garment. The height of the shoe affects the finished length. The higher the shoes, the shorter the garment will look.

- Place the skirt marker on a flat surface and adjust the lever to the pin-mark.

- Move the skirt marker around the hem or ask your customer or model to turn slowly as you pin or chalk-mark the hem.

- When a fit model is not available, place the garment on a form and the form on the table. Move the skirt marker around the entire hem edge, and mark the length parallel to the floor. Lay the garment on a flat surface; trim the excess fabric off.

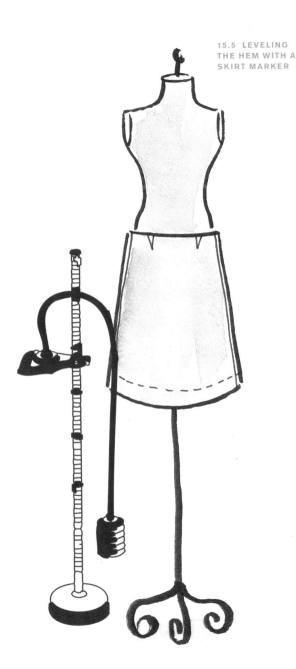

15.5 LEVELING THE HEM WITH A SKIRT MARKER

Without a Dress Form or Person

If a form or person is not available to level the hem, then it can be done on the workroom table as follows. This method is not as accurate as using the skirt marker but is better than not doing it at all. Follow Figure 15.6 to level the hem this way.

Skirt

- Fold the skirt in half with the center front on the fold. Place the garment flat on a table.
- Measure from waistline to hemline; move the tape measure around the skirt and pin-mark the skirt length.
- Add the hem allowance and cut away the excess fabric.

Dress

- On a dress, establish the waistline and pin-mark.
- Measure from the pin-mark to the hem, following the previous instructions for the "skirt."

LET'S STITCH

Each part of the hem also has its own stitching order. Following this order ensures successful construction of the hem.

- Have the garment fully stitched—the closure is next to be completed after the hem.
- Level the hem.
- Prepare the hem for the garment and lining.
- Attend to bulky seams.

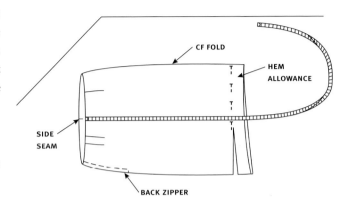

15.6 LEVELING THE HEM WITHOUT A DRESS FORM

- Stitch the hem finish.
- Pin the hem in place—don't press over the pins, as they may leave small hole marks in your garment.
- Handbaste hems in tricky fabrics such as sheers and beaded fabrics.
- Hem stitching—stitch the hem using the stitching method that best suits the fabric and design.
- Press the hem when it is completed—always use a pressing cloth!

BULKY SEAMS

When the hem is turned back on the seams, two layers of seam allowance sit together and can feel bulky. The bulk in the seams can show a ridge from the correct side of the fabric and spoil the look of the hem. Bulk can be cut away from open and closed seams using one of the following methods:

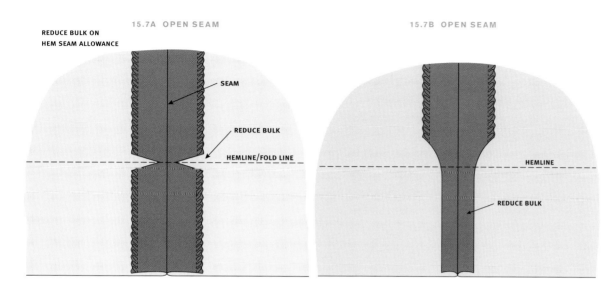

15.7A OPEN SEAM

REDUCE BULK ON
HEM SEAM ALLOWANCE

SEAM

REDUCE BULK

HEMLINE/FOLD LINE

15.7B OPEN SEAM

HEMLINE

REDUCE BULK

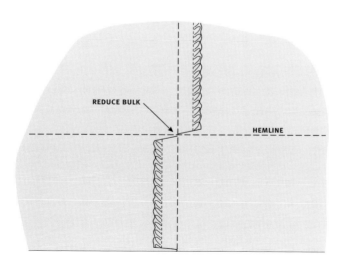

15.7C CLOSED SEAM

REDUCE BULK

HEMLINE

- Reduce bulk from the hemline, which is the foldline (Figure 15.7a).
- Reduce bulk on the hem seam allowance (Figure 15.7b).
- Reduce bulk by clipping into the seam allowance on the hemline, and turn the seam allowance in opposite directions (Figure 15.7c).

After bulk has been removed from the seams, it is time to apply a hem stabilizer if the garment needs be supported from the base up.

HEM STABILIZERS

PATTERN TIP

Place all the pattern seamlines together and draft a pattern for the hem stabilizer. If the garment is not lined, cut the hem stabilizer ¼ inch narrower than the hem allowance; then it will be hidden when the hem is turned and stitched in place. If the garment is lined, the hem stabilizer can be cut wider if the hemline requires more structure.

The hem is an important part of the silhouette and the overall structure of the garment. A hem stabilizer helps to support the garment silhouette to holds its shape. Many garments are enhanced by using a hem stabilizer; however, not all garments need them. Garments that do benefit from hem stabilizers are jackets and coats, irrespective of their length. The adorable little

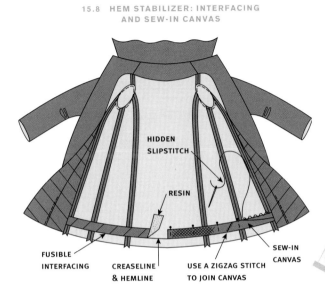

HIDDEN
SLIPSTITCH

RESIN

FUSIBLE
INTERFACING

CREASELINE
& HEMLINE

USE A ZIGZAG STITCH
TO JOIN CANVAS

SEW-IN
CANVAS

jacket in Figure 15.1b, in the Style I.D., has a hem stabilizer to help hold its shape.

Hems can be stabilized with a fusible or sew-in interfacing. Figure 15.8 illustrates both options; the sew-in interfacing in this case is bias-cut canvas. Care needs to be taken that the correct weight of stabilizer is used for the fabric weight and the desired structure. Refer to chapter 3, "How to Choose the Best Stabilizer for Your Project." For example, a lightweight fusible interfacing will lightly structure a hem. A sew-in canvas will add more body.

When a garment is underlined, a hem stabilizer is not usually needed, as the underlining takes its place, but there are exceptions to this rule. The coatdress in Figure 15.1a would be underlined but may also benefit from a hem stabilizer. Notice in Figure 15.8 that the coat is not

underlined; only the coat front and front facing (and collar) are interfaced, so adding a hem stabilizer in this case would be an advantage. This coat gets lined, so look ahead to Chapter 16. Always sample first to see if a ridge shows from the correct side of the fabric after the hem stabilizer has been applied.

Horsehair braid is another hem stabilizer used mainly for stabilizing hems in evening wear. The stitching method for applying horsehair braid is discussed in the section "Horsehair Braid," later in this chapter.

After stitching the hem finish, measure and fold the hem allowance to the wrong side and press a firm crease line, as shown in Figure 15.15 in the section "Preparing the Hem," later in this chapter.

Fusible Hem Stabilizer

Cut the interfacing in one long piece; if you don't have enough length, then pieces can be overlapped by ⅛ to ¼ inch and pressed in place along the crease line (which is the hemline).

Sew-in Bias-Cut Canvas

A sew-in canvas is an ideal hem stabilizer to use for tailored jackets and coats. It will be presumed that a jacket or coat with a canvas hem stabilizer will be lined. Bias-cut the canvas to the required length and approximately 3½ inches wide. If the canvas needs to be joined, butt the two pieces together on the straight grain and zigzag stitch together as illustrated on the right-hand side of the coat in Figure 15.8. Don't stitch a seam;

it will add bulk. Steam-press the canvas to the hemline shape.

If the crease for the hemline is hard to see, handbaste so it's visible. Line up the canvas on the crease; smooth and mold without stretching, and pin in place. Turn the canvas top edge back ½ inch and lightly hand stitch it to the garment using a hidden slipstitch. Finish the hem by hand, stitching the hem allowance to the canvas using a hidden slipstitch or catchstitch. Figure 15.9 illustrates both of these hand stitches.

There are a variety of hem finishes to choose from. The hem finish is applied to the hem edge, which is the raw cut edge of the fabric. Applying a hem finish prevents the garment from fraying and adds quality. Some hem finishes add bulk, while others shadow or show a ridge from the correct side of the fabric. The type of hem finish is an important decision. Take a look at Table 15.2 on page 430 for hem finishes for different fabrics.

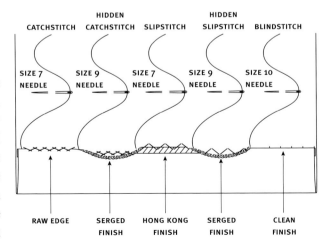

| HIDDEN | | | HIDDEN | |
| CATCHSTITCH | CATCHSTITCH | SLIPSTITCH | SLIPSTITCH | BLINDSTITCH |

| SIZE 7 | SIZE 9 | SIZE 7 | SIZE 9 | SIZE 10 |
| NEEDLE | NEEDLE | NEEDLE | NEEDLE | NEEDLE |

| RAW EDGE | SERGED FINISH | HONG KONG FINISH | SERGED FINISH | CLEAN FINISH |

NOTE

Serged hems can be hand stitched or machine stitched.

HEM FINISHES

The fabric gives the direction for the best hem finish. It may work out that the same seam and hem finishes can be used on one garment. As you learn to stitch hem finishes, many will be familiar to you—they are also seam finishes and were discussed in Chapter 6.

This section introduces you to hems by presenting an overview in Figure 15.9 of hem finishes, hand stitches, and hand stitching needles used to stitch hems. There are a variety of hem finishes to choose from, as you will see.

Fabric Edge as Hemline

A deconstructed raw edge can also be the hemline. This is a popular finish in design today. A raw-edged hemline can be left completely raw or a straight row of stitching can be stitched ¼ or ½ inch back from the hem edge to prevent fraying.

NOTE

Angled hems can also have a serged hem finish. This will be explained in the upcoming section "Mitered Corner."

Folded Edge as Hem Finish

A clean finish has a folded hem edge. The edge is then hand stitched to the garment using a blindstitch (Figure 15.9). This is an excellent hem finish for stitching hems in fine fabrics that are not bulky, such as voile, batiste, some fine silks, and other sheers. Any hem finish with a folded edge is best used for straight hems. A folded edge finish on curved and flared hems would only add bulk, as curved edges don't lie flat with a folded edge. If the hem was curved, an ease stitch would need to be stitched along the folded edge before folding the edge over, and this would make the hem bulky. In fine, sheer fabric, a serged finish will shadow to the correct side of the garment, and this could detract from a beautiful garment. Look at Figure 15.16 to see the hem edge pressed over ¼ inch to the wrong side of the fabric.

Serged Finish

A serged hem finish is stitched with a three-thread serger. Figure 15.9 illustrates serging used as a hem finish. The serger is quick and easy to use and neatly finishes the hem edge. A serged hem finish would be the most commonly used hem finish in production for straight, curved, flared, circular, or angled hems. Notice in Figure 15.10 that the serger has finished a curved hem.

Curved A-line and flared hems cannot be turned back in exactly the same way as straight hems. When the hem is straight, you only need to serge the hem edge before the hem allowance

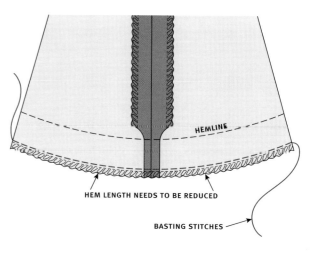

15.10A STITCH A ROW OF BASTING STITCHES TO THE HEM FINISH.

HEMLINE

HEM LENGTH NEEDS TO BE REDUCED

BASTING STITCHES

15.10B PULL UP BASTING STITCHES INTO EASING SO THE HEM SITS FLAT WHEN FOLDED BACK.

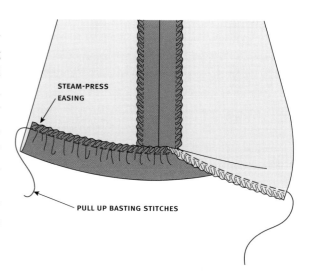

STEAM-PRESS EASING

PULL UP BASTING STITCHES

is turned back, ready to stitch to the garment (Figure 15.14). However, when a *curved* hem edge is turned back and stitched, it is wider than the garment to which it is being stitched. Some students think they can just fold little tucks along the hem edge to reduce the width and the hem will lie flat. *No*, this doesn't work! It only creates points on the hemline rather than creating a smooth curve.

After serging your hem finish, another stitching step is needed before completing the hem finish for curved A-line or flared hems. This extra stitching step will ensure a smooth, flat hem on your garment, and this will be evident as your garment is modeled on the catwalk.

- Notice that the hem width has been reduced to 1 inch (Figure 15.10a).
- Machine stitch one row of basting stitches along the bottom of the serged finish, approximately 4 to 6 inches on either side of the seamline. (The more flared the hemline is, the farther back you will need to stitch.) In some cases the entire hem edge may need to be basted and pulled up into easing (Figure 15.10a).
- After the hemline is prepared, pull the basting stitches into easing. When the hem is folded back, evenly distribute the easing until the hem lies flat. Don't pull the easing too tight or the hem will look wavy from the correct side. Steam-press the easing along the hem edge (Figure 15.10b).
- When completed, choose the hem stitch you want—a serged hem finish can be machine stitched or hand stitched.

Hong Kong Finish (or Bound Finish)

A Hong Kong finish encloses the raw edges with a bias-cut binding. After the binding is stitched, one edge lies flat underneath the hem to eliminate bulk (Figure 15.11). Store-purchased bias bindings are available in a variety of fibers and widths. You can also make your own binding using interesting contrasting fabrics, colors, and patterns, which is the case in Figure 15.11. When joining seams in the bias binding, make sure they are stitched on the lengthwise grain (see Figure 6.17).

It is important to use the correct weight of bias binding. A binding that is too heavy will add bulk to the hem and may show a ridge from the correct side after it is pressed. The stitching order for the Hong Kong hem finish is identical to that used when stitching a Hong Kong seam finish. Follow the stitching order in Figures 6.33a and b.

Curved A-line or flared hems can also have a Hong Kong finish. Bias is flexible so it will fit perfectly to a shaped hem edge. Prepare the hem edge with basting stitches, as Figure 15.10a illustrates; the only difference is, don't serge the hem edge—leave a raw edge. After the hem is eased and steam-pressed, as Figure 15.10b illustrates, the Hong Kong finish is then stitched to the *eased* hem edge in the same way it is stitched in Figure 15.11.

Seams Great

Seams Great is another variation of the Hong Kong finish. Seams Great was discussed in Chapter 3 as a stabilizing tape, and listed as a hem tape in your tool kit. As Chapter 3 points

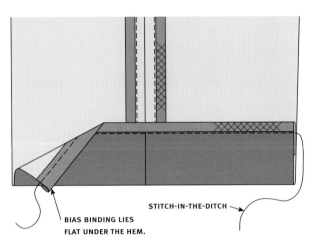

BIAS BINDING LIES
FLAT UNDER THE HEM.

STITCH-IN-THE-DITCH

out, Seams Great is made from tricot, which is lightweight, sheer, and not bulky. Due to its sheerness, it blends with most colors. It is ideal as a hem finish for lace and other sheer fabrics. Stitch *bias grain* Seams Great to straight or curved hem edges, and a *straight grain* Seams Great to straight hem edges. Refer to the "Where to Buy" section of this text.

You will find this an easy method—simply fold the Seams Great in half and wrap it around the hem edge, enclosing the raw edge. Hand-baste the binding in place to prevent twisting. Edgestitch the binding to the hem edge; be sure the fabric edge remains butted up to the foldline during the entire stitching process (Figure 15.12).

Hem Tape

Hem tape is an ideal hem finish to use on heavier-weight fabric, such as tweed, as it eliminates bulk. Stitching a hem tape as a hem finish is a

PATTERN TIP

Deduct the width of the hem tape from the total hem allowance and add ¼-inch seam allowance.

couture finish and also looks classy on luxury fabrics such as velvet and silk fabrics. Hem tape is available in nylon, lace, polyester, or rayon ribbon. It is available in a variety of colors and is approximately ½ inch to ¾ inch wide. A slip-stitch is the perfect hand stitch to use on this hem finish. How to slipstitch is explained in "Hand-Stitched Hems," later in this chapter.

Ribbon and lace hem tapes used as hem finishes are illustrated in Figure 15.13. Notice in Figure 15.13a how the hem tape is joined on the side seam by overlapping ¼ inch. Imagine how glamorous your bridal gown would look, with lace hem tape showing, when the garter was removed!

15.12 SEAMS GREAT IS AN IDEAL HEM FINISH ON SHEER FABRICS SUCH AS LACE.

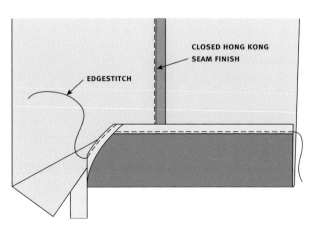

CLOSED HONG KONG
SEAM FINISH

EDGESTITCH

Whether you use lace or ribbon hem tape, the stitching order is identical. Notice the hem edge does not need to be serged. The hem tape is pinned or handbasted ¼ inch over the hem edge, as illustrated in Figure 15.13b. The tape is then edgestitched in place. Do not stretch the lace tape as you stitch, because it may pucker the hem.

Curved A-line or flared hems can also be finished with hem tape. Rayon tape is softer and easier to ease and steam-press into a curved shape than lace tape. First prepare the hem edge with basting stitches, as Figure 15.10a illustrates; the only difference is, don't serge the hem edge—leave a raw edge. The hem is then eased and steam-pressed. Figure 15.10b shows you how this is done. Next follow Figure 15.14 and stitch one row of machine basting stitches just inside one edge of the hem tape. Pull up the basting stitches into easing. The tape is now curved; steam-press the tape in this shape. Now edgestitch the tape to the curved hem edge, as Figure 15.14 illustrates.

PREPARING THE HEM

Let's recap what has been discussed about hems so far:

- The first step was to attend to the pattern; match the seams together, notch the seams, and draw a smooth hemline with minor hem allowances.
- The second step was to level the hem with a skirt marker.
- The next step is to prepare the hem after the hem finish is stitched.

15.13A LACE HEM TAPE

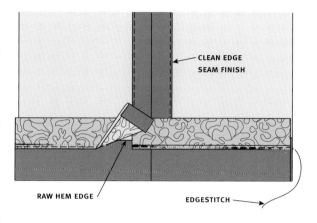

CLEAN EDGE
SEAM FINISH

RAW HEM EDGE

EDGESTITCH

15.13B RIBBON HEM TAPE

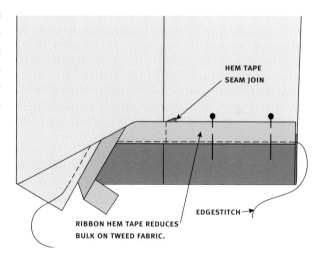

HEM TAPE
SEAM JOIN

EDGESTITCH

RIBBON HEM TAPE REDUCES
BULK ON TWEED FABRIC.

To prepare the hem, follow these helpful suggestions. Take your tape measure and accurately measure the width of hem allowance parallel from the hem edge up around the entire hem, and press in place (Figure 15.15a). Next pin the hem in place—pin *and* handbaste the hem in place on delicate fabrics (Figure 15.15b). No

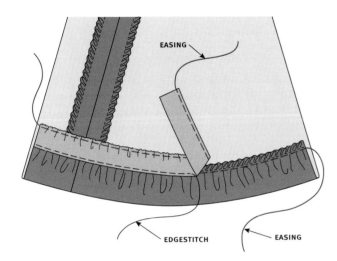

EASING

EDGESTITCH   EASING

matter what shape the hem is, these instructions are the same (except for a narrow rolled hem).

Hand-stitched hems look wonderful on any garment when they are well stitched. Hand-stitched hems are stitched with hand stitching needles and thread.

Hand stitches should not show from the correct side of the garment. Invisible hand-stitched hems do not draw attention; rather they should blend with the overall look of the garment. Hand stitching hems can take time and patience as you get the hang of the stitches. Some students love it and others don't. However, do persevere with it. The hem chart in Figure 15.9 gives an overview of the choice of hand stitches that can be used for stitching hems. Become familiar with these options for hand stitching hems.

HAND-STITCHED HEMS

Before beginning to hand stitch the hem, it is important to have the correct type and sizes of needles on hand. Using the correct needle makes all the difference in ensuring that the hem stitches look invisible from the correct side of the fabric.

Choosing the Correct Needle

To accomplish invisible hem stitching, the needles need to be the correct type and size. Needles need to be strong enough not to bend or break as you slip the needle through the fabric. So, choosing the correct hand needle type and size is important. Refer to Figure 2.22c to see the different needle sizes used for hand stitching. In needle sizing, the length and thickness of the needle denotes the size. The larger the needle size, the shorter and finer the needle will be.

- "Sharps" are good all-purpose needles and ideal to use for hems or other hand stitching. They have a sharp point, a round eye, and are of medium length. Select the needle according to the weight of the fabric. Notice in the hem chart in Figure 15.9 that the needles used for hand stitching hems are sizes 7, 9, and 10. (A good average size for invisible hem stitching is size 9.)
- Notice they are threaded with a single thread, ready to stitch hems. Embroidery needles, also known as "crewel" needles, are identical to sharps but have a longer eye, making it easier to thread multiple strands of threads.

Length of Thread

The length of the thread used to stitch is important. We see many students with thread so long that it tangles. We also see many students poised, ready to stitch their hem with double thread, thinking this will stitch *invisible* hem stitches!

Follow the checklist below so that you are prepared and ready with the correct needle and thread to hand stitch any hem.

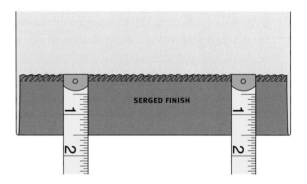

SERGED FINISH

15.15A PREPARE THE HEM: MEASURE THE HEM ALLOWANCE AND PRESS THE HEM.

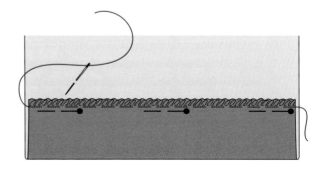

15.15B PIN THE HEM IN PLACE: ON DELICATE FABRICS, PIN AND HANDBASTE THE HEM.

- Cut the thread approximately 22 inches (or your arm length)—any longer and it will get tangled. Rethreading shorter lengths of thread is ultimately quicker—pulling long thread through every stitch takes more time.
- Cut the thread diagonally on one end. This makes threading the needle easier.
- Turn the garment to the wrong side. Get comfortable—lay the garment across your lap.
- Begin by securing the thread on the seamline using three or four overhand stitches with a *single strand of thread (not double)* (Figure 15.16).
- Continue stitching the hem in the direction outlined for each hem stitch.
- Take the finest stitches possible, as hem stitches *must* look invisible from the correct side of the fabric.
- Don't pull hand stitches too tight or the hem will look puckered.
- When the hem stitching is completed, finish as you began with three or four overhand stitches and clip the thread.
- When the hem is completed, press in place— this completes the *SEW, CLIP, PRESS* method of hem stitching.

HEM STITCHES

There is no set formula for which hem stitch to choose; this is the designer's choice. The main criterion for choosing the hem stitch is the fabric itself—this is your best guide. Invisible hem stitching is perfected through practice, so sample first before launching into any project.

The five hem stitches described here—blindstitch, slipstitch, hidden slipstitch, catchstitch, and hidden catchstitch—can all be used to sew invisible hand-stitched hems. Choose the appropriate hem stitch for your project from the chart in Figure 15.9.

Blindstitch

A blindstitch is a stitch that is not only invisible from the correct side but almost invisible from the wrong side as well. A blindstitch can only be applied to a folded edge; these two go hand in hand, as seen in Figure 15.16.

A blindstitch can also be used to attach facings, pockets, and trims to the garment surface. Care is needed to make sure the stitches are invisible and strong enough to hold the pockets to the garment when the pockets are used for functional purposes.

Stitch right to left if you are right-handed or left to right if you are left-handed (Figure 15.16).

- Fold and press the ¼-inch seam allowance to the wrong side.
- Pin and handbaste the hem in place.

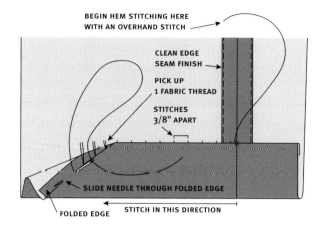

BEGIN HEM STITCHING HERE WITH AN OVERHAND STITCH

CLEAN EDGE SEAM FINISH

PICK UP 1 FABRIC THREAD

STITCHES 3/8" APART

SLIDE NEEDLE THROUGH FOLDED EDGE

STITCH IN THIS DIRECTION

FOLDED EDGE

- Begin by attaching the thread on the seamline of the wrong side of the garment.
- Place the needle back into the previous needle hole, and slide the needle along into the folded hem edge for ⅜ inch and pull the needle out of the fabric.
- Directly opposite where the needle has come out, pick up a small stitch (one fabric thread) on the garment and pull the thread through the fabric.
- Then place the needle back into the previous needle hole and slide the needle ⅜ inch along into the folded edge.
- Continue stitching in this rhythm until the hem is completed.

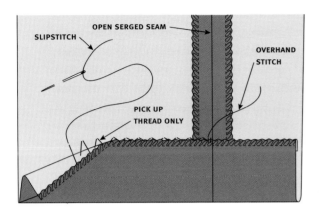

15.17A SLIPSTITCH

SLIPSTITCH
OPEN SERGED SEAM
OVERHAND STITCH
PICK UP THREAD ONLY

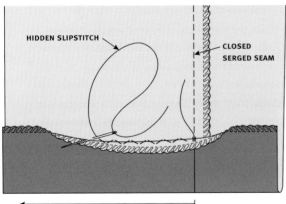

15.17B HIDDEN SLIPSTITCH

HIDDEN SLIPSTITCH
CLOSED SERGED SEAM

STITCH IN THIS DIRECTION

Slipstitch

This stitch is one of the mostly commonly used hand stitches for stitching hems. With practice, a slipstitch can glide along quite fast. However, it is important that the stitches be invisible from the correct side of the fabric. A slipstitch can also be stitched as a hidden slipstitch. The only difference is that the stitches are between the hem and the garment. Refer to Figure 15.17.

- Stitch from right to left if you are right-handed and left to right if you are left-handed (Figure 15.17a).
- Attach the thread to the seam with a few overhand stitches.
- *With a single thread*, take a small stitch in the garment a scant ¼ inch to the left of the seamline and pick up one fabric thread. Move to the left again a scant ¼ inch and slide the needle from the back to the front of the hem.
- Continue to stitch the hem in this rhythm of stitching until the hem is completed.
- The stitches will look like small Vs and should be approximately ⅜ inch apart when finished.

Hidden Slipstitch

For a hidden slipstitch, roll back the hem edge ¼ inch toward you and secure the thread on the side seam, ready to slipstitch (Figure 15.17b).

Catchstitch

A catchstitch forms small x stitches to catch the hem edge to the garment. This is an excellent hem stitch to use on heavier-weight fabrics; however, it is not limited to stitching heavyweight

fabrics only. The hem finish can be left as a raw edge or serged. Notice in Figure 15.18a that the hem edge has been left raw. When a catchstitch is stitched over the raw hem edge, it eliminates bulk and ridges from appearing from the correct side of the fabric. In this case the catchstitch combines the hem finish and the hem stitch all in one stitching process. This is an excellent finish to use when the garment is lined. A catchstitch can also be stitched as a hidden catchstitch, but do apply a hem finish before hand stitching the hem (Figure 15.18b).

- Stitch left to right if you are right-handed or right to left if you are left-handed (see Figure 15.18a).
- After attaching a single thread on the seam with a few overhand stitches, move the needle to the right by 3/16 inch. Then take a small stitch (one thread from right to left) in the garment directly above the hem edge. The garment stitches *must* be small so they don't show on the correct side of the garment.
- Take the next stitch in the hem, ⅛ inch below the hem edge and to the right 3/16 inch. Angle the needle right to left to take a small stitch in the hem. A couple of stitches can be picked up in the hem, as they will not show.

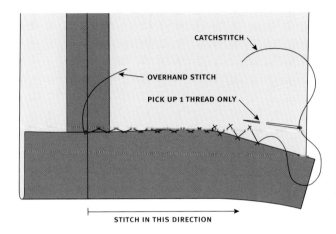

15.18A CATCHSTITCH

CATCHSTITCH

OVERHAND STITCH

PICK UP 1 THREAD ONLY

STITCH IN THIS DIRECTION

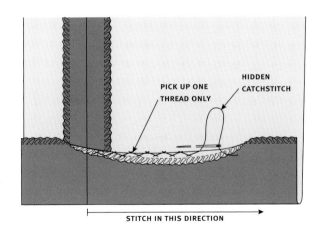

15.18B HIDDEN CATCHSTITCH

PICK UP ONE
THREAD ONLY

HIDDEN
CATCHSTITCH

STITCH IN THIS DIRECTION

- Continue to alternate the stitches from garment to hem until the hem is completed. The distance between each stitch on the garment side should be ⅜ inch.

> **NOTE**
> A catchstitch is an *ideal* stitch to use on the hem of pants, as it prevents high heels from getting caught in the hem. Try it out and you will see how strong this stitch is.

Hidden Catchstitch

For a hidden catchstitch, roll back the hem edge ¼ inch toward you and secure the thread on the side seam, ready to catchstitch (see Figure 15.18b). Using a hidden catchstitch will prevent a ridge from showing on the correct side of the fabric.

Narrow Rolled Hem

A hand-stitched narrow rolled hem adds a couture finish to an expensive garment. Hand stitching a rolled hem is very time-consuming and thus cannot be used in mass production. It is a finish that is ideal for lightweight, sheer fabrics. Use a small-sized hand needle and silk thread for fine fabrics. Just put on your favorite music, get comfortable, and stitch the night away. A narrow rolled hem can be stitched to any hem shape. Follow along with the stitching order in Figure 15.19.

- Allow ⅝ inch hem allowance.
- Stitch a row of staystitching ⅜ inch above the hem edge. This helps to roll the hem edge.
- Trim off the raw edge close to the stitching just a short length at a time as you stitch.
- Roll the hem allowance (below the stitch line) up and over again so the row of stitching is on the folded edge.
- Using a small needle, begin from the seamline and stitch a blindstitch or slipstitch from right to left (left to right if you are left-handed). Figure 15.16 shows how a blindstitch looks as it is stitched.
- Sit comfortably with the garment in your lap, hold the hem taut, and continue stitching.

MACHINE-STITCHED HEMS

Machine-stitched hems are popular in casual clothes. Because they take less time to stitch than hand-stitched hems, they are cost-effective in production.

On machine-stitched hems, the topstitching is visible from the correct side of the garment and can become a design feature. When other parts of the garment, such as the seams, pockets, collars, and bands, have been topstitched, the hems are often topstitched as well. The jeans the designer is wearing in Figure 1.1 illustrate this point.

It is the designer who decides on the placement of the topstitching. There are no rules as to the position; however, the topstitching is guided by the hem allowance, which was addressed

15.19 HAND-STITCHED NARROW ROLLED HEM: THIS IS AN IDEAL HEM TO USE FOR CIRCULAR HEMLINES.

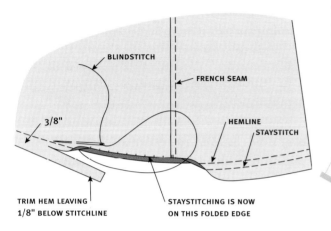

15.19 HAND-STITCHED NARROW ROLLED HEM: THIS IS AN IDEAL HEM TO USE FOR CIRCULAR HEMLINES.

earlier in the text. The finished width of the hem can be as narrow as ½ inch or as wide as 2 or 3 inches. Let the fabric and the shape of the hem guide the hem allowance width. Refer to Table 15.1 for guidance in adding the hem allowance. Also look at Figure 2.9.

Before stitching the hem, preparation is essential. The finish can be a folded edge or serged. The shape of the hem is the guide. After the hem finish is attended to, prepare the hem by following the steps outlined in Figure 15.15. Thread the upper and bobbin threads in the same thread color, check the stitch tension and stitch length, and then topstitch the hem parallel to the hemline.

Machine-stitched hems for three hem shapes will be explained: straight, curved A-line or flared, and angled.

Folded Edge Hem

A folded edge finish is best suited to straight hems and not suitable on curved and flared hemlines. It would only add bulk, as curved edges don't lie flat with a folded edge. If your hem is a curved A-line or flared, a serged finish would be a better choice. Refer to Figure 15.20 for the following stitching order.

- Press the hem edge over ¼ inch to the wrong side.
- Measure and pin the width of the hem allowance, parallel around the entire hemline. Use your tape measure, as accurate measuring is important—wobbly topstitching *does not* look professional.
- Stitch from the wrong side of the garment so you can see what you are doing. Begin stitching from the seamline—start and end with a backstitch.
- The hem can also be topstitched from the correct side. To do this, handbaste the hem in place, measuring the hem width accurately.
- Machine stitch following the handbasting stitches, then remove them after the hem is completed.

Twice-Turned Hem

A twice-turned hem only suits straight hems. If your hem is a curved A-line or flared, don't waste your time trying this hem! A twice-turned hem folds over twice and has a folded edge finish. Both turnings are equal widths. This method is often used on the hems of jeans. Take a look at the jeans in Figure 15.1d of the Style I.D.; a twice-turned hem would be used

there. It is also an excellent hem to use on sheer fabrics to prevent the hem finish from shadowing on the correct side of the garment. The finished hem width can be ½ inch or wider.

To stitch, fold half the hem allowance to the wrong side of the garment and press in place. Fold the hem over again, pin, and handbaste. With the wrong side facing up, topstitch or edgestitch the hem. For pants, begin stitching (with a backstitch) from the inseam and end with a backstitch. Don't forget to add double the hem allowance to the pattern.

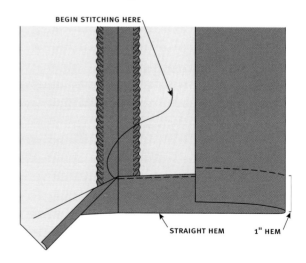

15.20 MACHINE-STITCHED STRAIGHT HEMS: CLEAN EDGE

Twin Needle Hem

Twin needle topstitching is an excellent method for stitching hems in knit fabrics, because the zigzag, back-and-forth motion allows the knit hem to stretch but its use is not restricted to knits only. Twin needle hems can be stitched in woven fabrics, and they also work well on denim. Stitching on angled corners is difficult, so if you are not familiar with this stitch, don't try stitching angled hems with a twin needle.

From the correct side of the fabric, two rows of parallel topstitching are visible. On the wrong side of the fabric, the two rows of topstitching join together as a zigzag stitch. Insert your twin needle into the sewing machine and thread with two threads. In Figure 6.25 and 6.46, twin needle topstitching is also applied to seams. Chapter 2, "Sewing Machine Needle Types," explains twin needles in detail (Figure 2.22b).

15.21 TWIN NEEDLE HEM STITCHING

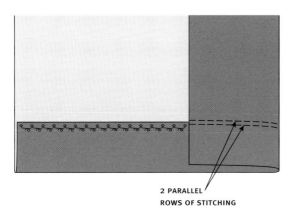

2 PARALLEL ROWS OF STITCHING

On fine knits, tissue stitch the hem if the twin needle stitching does not lie flat. If a knit fabric is used, the hem edge does not need to be finished. For woven fabric, serge the edges or use a folded edge finish. Turn the garment to the correct side and stitch the hem. Twin needle stitching *must* be done from the correct side of the fabric, as the stitches are not the same on both sides. Refer to Figure 15.21 to see both sides of the twin needle hem stitching.

Serged Curved A-Line or Flared Hem

If the silhouette of the garment is A-line or flared (that is, widening gradually at the side seam), then reduce the width of the hem allowance. The hem will sit smooth and flat with a serged finish. There is no real benefit in adding a Hong Kong finish or hem tape when the hem is machine stitched. A folded edge finish is not ideal on curved hemlines. The reason is that an ease stitch needs to be applied along the folded edge to curve the hem allowance, and this only adds bulk.

The hem is machine stitched following the stitching order for the folded edge hem in Figure 15.20. There is one difference—the edge is serged rather than folded over. Figure 15.10 shows how to prepare the hem edge for a curved (A-line) and flared hemline so it sits smooth and flat from the correct side of the garment. After the machine basting has been applied, eased, pressed, and turned back, the hem can be machine stitched in place. Figure 15.22 illustrates how the hem should look, on both side of the fabric, when it is completed.

15.22 MACHINE-STITCHED CURVED/A-LINE AND FLARED HEMLINES WITH A SERGED HEM FINISH

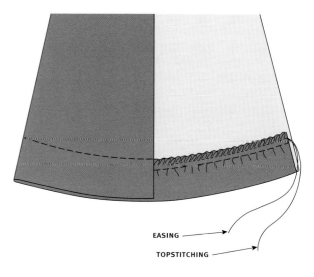

EASING

TOPSTITCHING

Angled Machine-Stitched Hem

An angled machine-stitched hem needs to be correctly prepared before stitching. The hem finish applied can be a folded edge or serged. To reduce bulk, the angled corner of the hem needs to be stitched with a mitered corner.

Mitered Corner

A **mitered corner** is a neat and easy way of eliminating bulk on corners. After the bulk is cut away from the corner, the seam is stitched on the bias grain (Figure 15.23a). Notice in Figure 15.1b that the jacket has an angled hem to form the slits on the front jacket. The corners of the slits would be stitched with mitered corners. The corner is cut off at the patternmaking stage before the garment is cut in fabric (see Figure 15.23a).

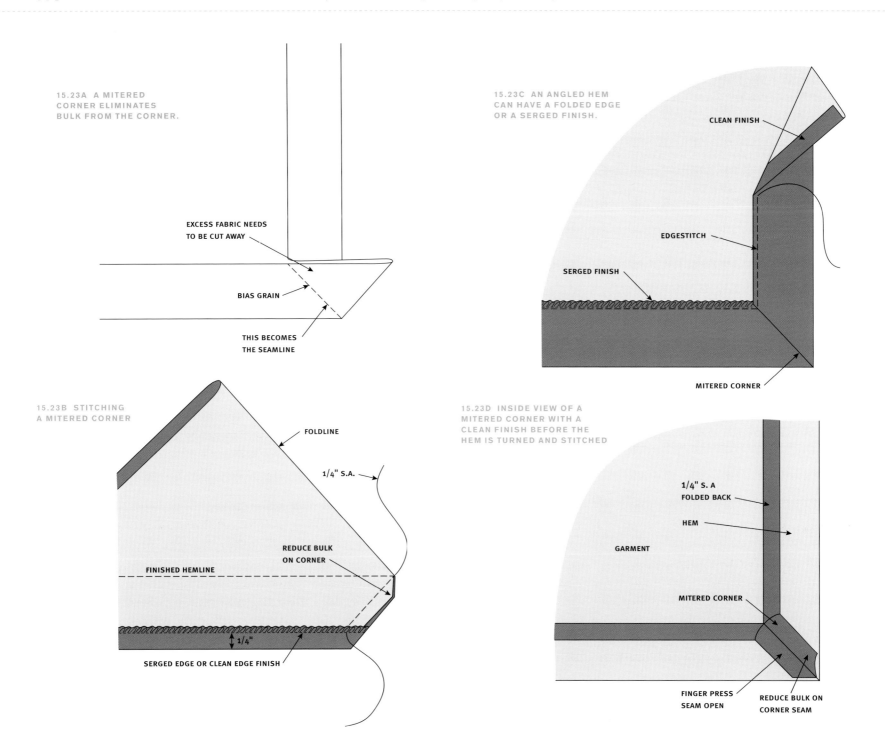

15.23A A MITERED CORNER ELIMINATES BULK FROM THE CORNER.

EXCESS FABRIC NEEDS TO BE CUT AWAY

BIAS GRAIN

THIS BECOMES THE SEAMLINE

15.23B STITCHING A MITERED CORNER

FOLDLINE

1/4" S.A.

REDUCE BULK ON CORNER

FINISHED HEMLINE

1/4"

SERGED EDGE OR CLEAN EDGE FINISH

15.23C AN ANGLED HEM CAN HAVE A FOLDED EDGE OR A SERGED FINISH.

CLEAN FINISH

EDGESTITCH

SERGED FINISH

MITERED CORNER

15.23D INSIDE VIEW OF A MITERED CORNER WITH A CLEAN FINISH BEFORE THE HEM IS TURNED AND STITCHED

1/4" S. A FOLDED BACK

HEM

GARMENT

MITERED CORNER

FINGER PRESS SEAM OPEN

REDUCE BULK ON CORNER SEAM

- Fold the bias edges together with the correct sides facing (see Figure 15.23b).
- Stitch a ¼-inch seam allowance across the diagonal corner.
- If you want a clean edge, finish stitching the mitered corner ¼ inch back from the edge (this is the seam allowance) (Figure 15.23b). Then press the ¼-inch seam allowance to the wrong side before stitching the hem in place (Figure 15.23c).
- If you want a serged hem finish, then serge first. Then stitch the mitered corner seam to the edge of the serging, as illustrated in Figure 15.23b.
- Trim the corner seam to reduce bulk, and finger-press open, as illustrated in Figure 15.23d.
- Turn the garment back to the correct side. Use a point turner to sharpen the corner; press.
- If the garment has hem slits, mirror image both sides to make sure they are equal lengths—this is important to achieving a professional-looking garment.

Narrow, Rolled, Machine-Stitched Hem

A narrow, rolled, machine-stitched hem adds a classy look to any garment. A special foot can be purchased that rolls the hem in one stitching process; however, many design schools don't provide them. This hem technique is ideal to use on circular skirts, collar edges, ruffles and flounces, and curved shirt hems. A narrow rolled hem is also an excellent hem finish for fine, sheer fabrics. It is not a good hem stitch to apply to heavyweight fabrics.

No matter what shape the hem is, straight, curved, circular, or angled, the same three-step stitching technique applies when stitching a narrow rolled hem. The sketches in Figure 15.24 illustrate a narrow, machine-stitched rolled hem stitched to a curved shirt hemline. If you refer back to the striped shirt in Figure 6.28a, you'll notice that its hem is curved in the same way as in these figures.

- Allow ⅝-inch hem allowance.
- From the correct side of the fabric, stitch one row of staystitching ⅜ inch above the hem edge (Figure 15.24a). (It is tempting for students to skip this step, but it really *must not* be skipped! The staystitching adds stability and support in the following steps.)
- With the correct side facing up, fold the hem allowance to the wrong side along the staystitching (the staystitching is now the foldline).
- Edgestitch ⅟₁₆ inch back from the foldline from the correct side of the fabric. The closer you stitch to the foldline, the narrower the final hem will be,

as this defines the finished hem width. Trim the excess seam allowance as close to the edge-stitching as possible. Using appliqué scissors helps to cut closer to the stitching. Take a quick look at these scissors in Figure 15.25a.
- With the wrong side facing up, fold the hem over again and edgestitch directly on top of the last row of stitching; press the hem (Figure 15.24c).

Angled Narrow Rolled Hem

For an angled hemline, each edge must be stitched *separately*, in two easy steps, as illustrated in Figure 15.24d. Use the same stitching order described in the previous section, "Narrow, Rolled, Machine-Stitched Hem." Stitch both sides directionally; this means stitching in the same direction in which the other edge was stitched. Clip the threads, leaving a few inches. Place both strands of thread through the eye of the needle, slide the needle through the folded edge for ½ inch, and clip the threads (Figure 15.24d).

Lettuce-Edge Hem

Lettuce edge is a small, neat hem stitch that can be stitched to woven or knit fabric edges that are shaped or straight. It is such a versatile stitch; it can be stitched to many edges such as hems, collars, ruffles, or flounces. A serger stitches a narrow, fine hem edge. Rayon threads can be used to add sheen to the finish.

The stitch on the lettuce edge has a back-and-forth action, similar to zigzag stitches, except closer together. Any zigzag (back-and-forth)

15.24A FIRST ROW OF STITCHING

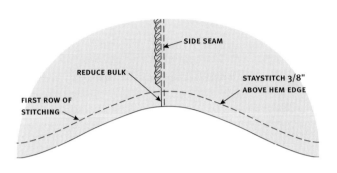

SIDE SEAM

REDUCE BULK

STAYSTITCH 3/8"
ABOVE HEM EDGE

FIRST ROW OF
STITCHING

15.24B SECOND ROW OF STITCHING

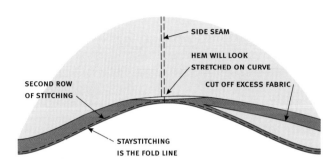

SIDE SEAM

HEM WILL LOOK
STRETCHED ON CURVE

CUT OFF EXCESS FABRIC

SECOND ROW
OF STITCHING

STAYSTITCHING
IS THE FOLD LINE

15.24C THIRD ROW OF STITCHING

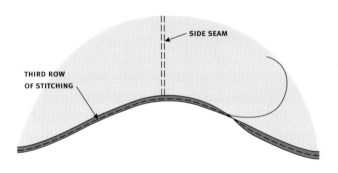

SIDE SEAM

THIRD ROW
OF STITCHING

15.24D AN ANGLED, NARROW, ROLLED MACHINE-STITCHED
HEM IS STITCHED IN TWO STEPS.

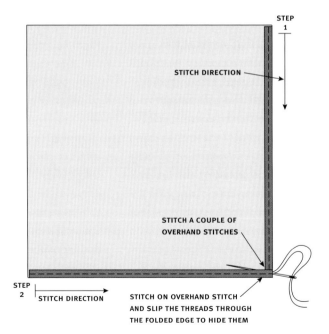

STEP
1

STITCH DIRECTION

STITCH A COUPLE OF
OVERHAND STITCHES

STEP
2   STITCH DIRECTION

STITCH ON OVERHAND STITCH
AND SLIP THE THREADS THROUGH
THE FOLDED EDGE TO HIDE THEM

NOTE

Fishing line can be inserted between the
rolled edges in the last stitching process.
Fishing line weights vary so try 25 lbs—this
is a good, average weight that flutes the
edges in a gorgeous way and adds structure
to the hemline.

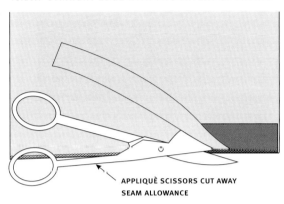

15.25A STRAIGHT EDGE WITH TWO LAYERS OF FABRIC

APPLIQUÈ SCISSORS CUT AWAY
SEAM ALLOWANCE

15.25B LETTUCE EDGE: STRETCH THE HEM AS YOU
STITCH TO FORM CURLS.

PATTERN TIP

Add an extra ¾-inch hem allowance if the
hem edge is folded back, as Figure 15.25a
illustrates (this is eventually cut off).

stitch allows seams and hems in knit fabrics to
stretch. It would not be suitable as a hem finish
on bulky sweater knits.

Figure 15.25a is stitched with two layers of
fabric folded together to stabilize the edge. The
edge is pressed ¾ inch back before stitching.
Figure 15.25b shows a single layer of lightweight
knit fabric stretched as you stitch to form the
curls. The more the fabric is stretched, the more
fluted, like a lettuce leaf, the hem will look.

IMPORTANT

First stitch a sample cut on the same grainline as the hem on the garment to which it
is being stitched. This is important to the
success of a lettuce edge, as the width of
the stitching, density, and tension may need
adjustment to suit each fabric type.

- Match the thread color or combine three different
  tones for an interesting effect.
- With the correct side facing up, place the hem
  edge under the serger foot. Align the knife with
  the hem edge and hold the fabric taut as you
  stitch along the folded edge. The knife will trim
  off any excess fabric.
- When returning to the beginning, overlap as few
  stitches as possible, raise the foot, and release
  the tension disc.
- Carefully pull the garment back out of the machine, leaving 6 to 7 inches of thread.
- Finish the threads by threading them through a
  needle and completing a few overhand stitches.
- Carefully cut off the extra ¾ inch of fabric with
  appliqué scissors (see Figure 15.25a).

FALSE HEMS

Knowledge of how to stitch a false hem is worth-
while, as you never know when it will be useful.
The asymmetrical coatdress pictured in Figure

15.1a illustrates the need for a false hem. The
curved edge of the coatdress would not work as
a turned-back hem.

False hems are cut like a separate facing and
are needed on garments for various reasons:

- Any *shaped* hem edge, such as a scallop hem
  edge, needs a false hem (see Figure 15.1a).
- Fabric shortage may be an issue. When you
  run out of fabric, stitch a false hem. A false
  hem can be stitched to a straight or shaped
  edge.
- If the hemline has been cut on a border, there
  may be no room for a hem allowance (see
  Figure 2.11).
- If a heavyweight fabric hem is too heavy to
  turn back, a bias-cut false hem facing can
  be stitched from a lighter-weight fabric to
  reduce bulk.
- If pants are too short, a false hem can be
  added to lengthen them:
  - Carefully seam rip the hem stitches from the
    hem to let down the hem for the extra length.
    Then press the foldline from the hem.
  - When the hem is let down, the foldline may
    not press out and this can be a problem.
    After the foldline is pressed, stitch a false
    hem to lengthen the pants.
  - Follow the instructions from Figure 15.26.

Bias-Cut Hem Facing

A hem facing is cut following the shape of
the edge it is stitched to. As an alternative to
stitching a shaped facing, a bias-cut facing can
be stitched as a false hem. The A-line curved

hemline illustrated in Figure 15.26 has a bias-cut facing stitched as a false hem. The bias-cut facing is steam-pressed into the required shape.

There are some restrictions when using a bias-cut facing. The scalloped hem edge in the coatdress in Figure 15.1d could *not* be stitched with a bias-cut facing. A shape such as this must be cut to mirror image the shape of the garment edge.

The hem that is going be stitched is an A-line skirt hem. Before proceeding, make sure the skirt is fully stitched together in-the-round. The hem is the last stitching process in the stitching order. Follow along, referring to Figure 15.26.

- Allow plenty of length in the facing; cut the bias width to the hem allowance of your choice—1 to 1½ inches. Add ½-inch seam allowance for a clean-edge hem finish. The edge can also be serged.
- Have the garment turned to the correct side. Carefully wrap the bias-cut facing around the hem edge, with the correct sides facing together; don't stretch the bias, as it will twist the hem out of alignment.

- Overlap the excess facing, and pin the hem edges together.
- Mark the seam join—this must be done on the lengthwise grainline. Refer to Figure 6.17 to see how bias grain seams are stitched together.
- Cut the excess fabric from the facing after allowing ¼-inch seam allowances on both sides of the seam join.
- Carefully remove the facing from around the hem edge and join the facing seam; press the seam open.
- Along the top edge of the bias facing, press a ¼-inch seam allowance to the wrong side. If you

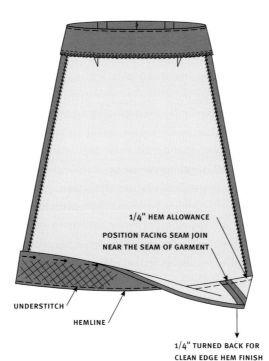

15.26 FALSE HEM: BIAS-CUT HEM FACING APPLIED TO THE HEM OF AN A-LINE SKIRT

1/4" HEM ALLOWANCE

POSITION FACING SEAM JOIN NEAR THE SEAM OF GARMENT

UNDERSTITCH

HEMLINE

1/4" TURNED BACK FOR CLEAN EDGE HEM FINISH

would prefer a serged hem finish, then carefully serge the edge instead. Don't stretch the bias edge as you serge.

- Before applying the false hem, shape the facing to match the garment hem edge. This is done by steam-pressing the hem finish edge to shrink and straighten the edge into a curved shape. Remember, bias grain is flexible and will shape beautifully!
- Again, place the bias facing around the hem edge with the correct side facing together. Position the facing seam close to the side or back seam and pin in place.
- Stitch a ¼-inch seam around the hem edge, understitch, turn, and press the hem. Don't press over the pins, as they may leave a mark; hand-baste the hem in place instead.
- Hand stitch the hem in place.

Scalloped Hem

- Cut a shaped facing that is an exact mirror image of the hem edge shape of the scalloped hemline. The top edge of the facing should be a straight or curved line to mirror the general direction of the hem shape (Figure 15.27a).
- Apply interfacing to the facing, if required.

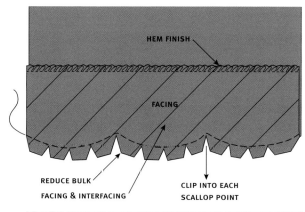

15.27A FALSE HEM: SCALLOPED EDGE

HEM FINISH

FACING

REDUCE BULK
FACING & INTERFACING

CLIP INTO EACH
SCALLOP POINT

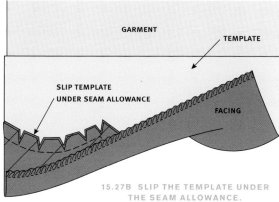

GARMENT

TEMPLATE

SLIP TEMPLATE
UNDER SEAM ALLOWANCE

FACING

15.27B SLIP THE TEMPLATE UNDER
THE SEAM ALLOWANCE.

- Place the correct sides of garment and facing together, and pin in place.
- Stitch a ¼-inch seam around the hem edge; pivot on each scallop point (see Figure 15.27a).
- Clip into each scallop point; the clipping allows the seam allowance to open and spread when the facing is turned to the wrong side and will enable the hem to sit flat on completion (Figure 15.27a).
- To define the scalloped hemline, cut a template with approximately four or five scallops. Cut ¹⁄₁₆

inch off around the scalloped edge so it fits comfortably in between the hem and facing.

- Turn the garment to the correct side, and slip the template between the facing and the garment, under the seam allowance. Push the scalloped hem edge out with the template to define each scallop shape, and press in place (Figure 15.27b).

HORSEHAIR BRAID

Horsehair braid is a very effective sheer polyester mesh used to stabilize and add structure to evening wear such as satin gowns. It is available in heavy and soft weights, in widths from ⅝ inch to 6 inches. Narrow horsehair braid adds a soft structure; wider horsehair is stronger and adds more structure to the hemline. When a hem is stabilized with horsehair braid and stitched in place, hand stitches are less noticeable from the correct side when the garment has been underlined because the stitches are stitched to the underlining rather than to the garment fabric.

Horsehair braid can be stitched to straight hems and shaped. It has qualities of bias grain and will shape easily when pressed to curved and flared hemlines. The circular hem in Figure 15.1c could be stitched with horsehair braid to help stabilize and hold the hem in this shape. The stitching order in Figure 15.28 would be followed to do this. The skirt would need to be underlined so the horsehair could be stitched to the underlining, as Figure 15.28b illustrates. However, if a designer chose to, the hem could be topstitched if an underlining wasn't desired as part of the design.

Horsehair can be steam-pressed to remove any folds. Be sure to remove any bulk from the seams in the hem allowance (see Figure 15.7). To join the seams in horsehair braid, stitch Seams Great to one edge; overlap this edge to hide the other raw edge and to prevent the braid from unraveling (Figure 15.28a). Two stitching methods will show how horsehair braid can be stitched.

HORSEHAIR BRAID STITCHED TO STRAIGHT, CURVED, FLARED, AND CIRCULAR HEMLINES FLAT APPLICATION

- Have the correct side of the garment facing up. Lay the horsehair over the hem allowance, lining up the edges together (Figure 15.28a).
- Stitch them together with a ¼-inch seam allowance. Do not stretch the horsehair as you stitch—if you do, the hemline will look twisted.
- Fold the horsehair braid over to the wrong side of the fabric and press the hem crease.
- Pin, handbaste, and catchstitch the hem to the underlining, as Figure 15.28b illustrates.

HORSEHAIR STITCHED TO STRAIGHT HEM EDGE ONLY

- Serge the hem edge of the garment and with the correct side of the garment facing up, overlap the serged hem finish over the horsehair braid by ¼ inch and edgestitch the two together (Figure 15.28c).
- Fold the horsehair braid to the wrong side, and fold the hem over again so the horsehair is sandwiched between the hem allowance and the garment.

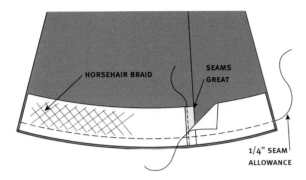

HORSEHAIR BRAID

SEAMS
GREAT

1/4" SEAM
ALLOWANCE

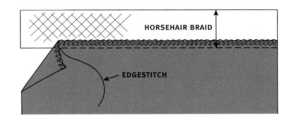

HORSEHAIR BRAID

EDGESTITCH

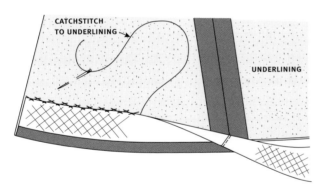

CATCHSTITCH
TO UNDERLINING

UNDERLINING

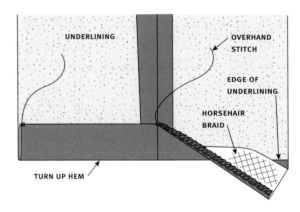

UNDERLINING

OVERHAND
STITCH

EDGE OF
UNDERLINING

HORSEHAIR
BRAID

TURN UP HEM

- Press the hem in place, protecting the fabric with a pressing cloth.
- Catch the hem to the seams and underlining only, using an overhand stitch, and stitching approximately every 5 to 6 inches (Figure 15.28d). The hem must be caught often enough so it does not droop in between the stitches.

CUFFS

Cuffs are an extra length of fabric added to the hemline of the pattern. The extra length is then turned back to form cuffs on the garment hemline. Cuffs can be added to the hem edge of sleeves, skirts, dresses, or pants. Cuffs can be stitched separately as a hem band or cut all-in-one and turned back. Cuffs stitched all-in-one with the garment sit flatter and look less bulky. We suggest not interfacing cuffs, as this may make them too heavy and bulky. Cuffs cut all-in-one will be explained in this chapter. The wide cuffs in the pants in Figure 15.1b look absolutely fabulous made in wool check fabric.

- Stitch the side seams. It is important that they be stitched to the shape of the cuff—if they are not shaped correctly at the pattern drafting stage, then they will not sit well when folded back into cuffs. (Refer to your patternmaking books to get this correct.)
- Stitch the hem finish (Figure 15.29a).
- Turn back the hem on the foldline; place the leg over a sleeve board and move the leg around as you press the foldline. Notice in Figure 15.29a that the fabric width folded back above the fold-

line includes the hem allowance and the width of the cuff.

- From the wrong side, pin and stitch the hem in place—the hem can be hand stitched for a more expensive finish or machine stitched for a budget production finish (see Figure 15.29a).
- Turn the garment to the correct side and fold the cuff back. The cuff can be secured on the *inseam* by stitching-in-the-ditch (Figure 15.29b). The cuff can also be hand stitched using a few overhand stitches to connect the *inside* cuff to the *inseam* (Figure 15.29c). Visible hand stitches would look ugly!

VENT

Vents are used in design on the backs of skirts, jackets, and sleeves. Vents are an important part of functional design. When the garment is worn, the vents open to allow ease of comfort for walking and sitting. Figure 15.30a illustrates three vents in the one ensemble. All the vents are positioned in the seams. The recurring vents also demonstrate two of the design elements: rhythm and repetition. When these elements are used properly, they are pleasing to the eye. To see how important vents are for functional design purposes, refer to Figure 1.4.

- A vent can be added into any seam. First establish the length of the vent. Add a facing to the left side and a facing and extension to the right side (Figure 15.30b).
- Mark matchpoints to mark the stitching placement on the back seam for the vent. This is also the position for clipping into the seam. Also notch

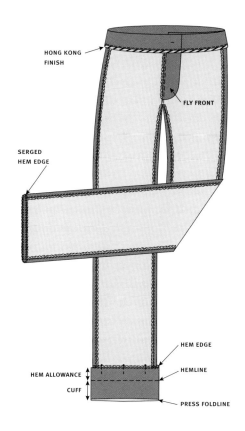

15.29A CUFFED PANTS

HONG KONG FINISH

FLY FRONT

SERGED HEM EDGE

HEM EDGE

HEMLINE

HEM ALLOWANCE

CUFF

PRESS FOLDLINE

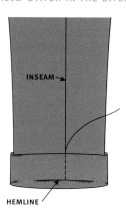

15.29B STITCH-IN-THE-DITCH

INSEAM

HEMLINE

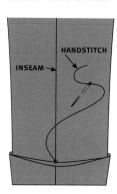

15.29C HAND STITCH

HANDSTITCH

INSEAM

the hem allowance and facing positions (see Figure 15.30b).

The illustration in Figure 15.30b shows the pattern markings, the application of the interfacing, stitching of the darts and zipper, and how the back seam is stitched and clipped. Remember to clip the right side center back seam—otherwise you won't be able to stitch the vent any farther! In the stitching order,

the side seams were stitched next and pressed, and then the waistband applied. This moves us to the next steps needed to complete the vent.

- Once the skirt is stitched in-the-round, the hem edge can be serged.
- Turn both facings at the notches back so the correct sides are facing together. Stitch the width of the hem allowance across the hemline and facing—finish the stitching ½ inch back from

15.30A VENT

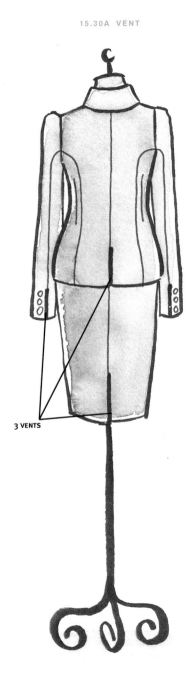

3 VENTS

15.30B IMPORTANT PATTERN MARKINGS
AND INTERFACING APPLIED: DARTS, ZIPPER,
AND CENTER-BACK SEAM ARE ALL STITCHED IN
PREPARATION FOR STITCHING THE VENT.

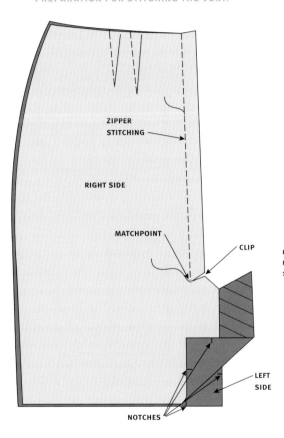

ZIPPER
STITCHING

RIGHT SIDE

MATCHPOINT

CLIP

LEFT
SIDE

NOTCHES

15.30C VENT: STITCHING THE HEM IN PLACE

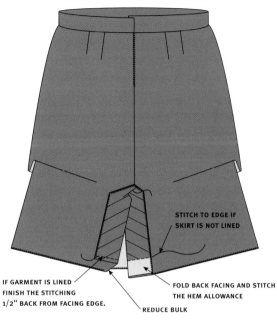

STITCH TO EDGE IF
SKIRT IS NOT LINED

IF GARMENT IS LINED
FINISH THE STITCHING
1/2" BACK FROM FACING EDGE.

FOLD BACK FACING AND STITCH
THE HEM ALLOWANCE

REDUCE BULK

NOTE

When a lining is stitched to the vent, the
lining holds the vent facing in place and no
topstitching is needed. To stitch the lining
to the vent, refer to "Skirt with Vent" in the
section "Open Lining with Waistband" in
Chapter 16.

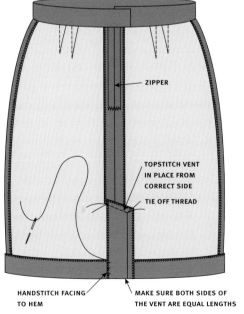

ZIPPER

TOPSTITCH VENT
IN PLACE FROM
CORRECT SIDE

TIE OFF THREAD

HANDSTITCH FACING
TO HEM

MAKE SURE BOTH SIDES OF
THE VENT ARE EQUAL LENGTHS

15.30D INSIDE VIEW OF HOW THE VENT
LOOKS WHEN COMPLETED

the facing edge if a lining is going to be stitched around the vent. If the garment is not lined, then stitch to the edge of the facing (Figure 15.30c).

- The corners of the hem can be trimmed to reduce the bulk (see Figure 15.30c). Once this is done, the hem length cannot be lengthened.
- Turn the facing back to the correct side and sharpen the corners with a point turner; make sure both sides of the vent line up without one side being longer than the other.
- From the correct side, handbaste or pin the topstitching position of the vent; the shape is a mirror image of the facing shape (Figure 15.30d). Refer to Figure 15.30a to see the position of the topstitching from the correct side of the garment.
- Stitch the vent from the correct side; pull the threads back to the wrong side and tie off (see Figure 15.30d).
- If the skirt is not lined, hand stitch the facing to the hem using a slipstitch (see Figure 15.30d).

HEM SLIT WITH FACING

A slit can be added into the garment on any seam, up from the hemline or down from a neckline (Figure 15.31). A hem slit is often used in skirts as an alternative to a vent (Figure 15.31b). Slits are used for functional design purposes in the garment. For example, they are often positioned on the side seam of shorts, capri pants, or long pants to widen the leg opening. Slits are also located on side seams of tops to allow room for the hips. Another popular location for slits is in the center back or side seams of the hem of a skirt, to aid walking and sitting.

Slits also can be used for decorative purposes because the designer thinks they look aesthetically pleasing. In the jacket in Figure 15.1b, the hem slits add a touch of class to the front of the jacket, and they are purely decorative. A facing is added to the slit so it turns back to provide a clean edge rather than joining a seam (which adds bulk). The slit is topstitched at the top edge of the facing to hold it in place. The topstitching is visible, as Figure 15.31b illustrates. For a strapless evening gown, topstitching would look too casual and would detract from the elegance of the garment. Notice that in Figure 15.31a, the topstitching has been omitted; instead, a lining is stitched around the facing edge to hold the hem slit in place. For instruction on how the lining is applied to the facing, refer to "Skirt with Slit" in the section "Open Lining with Waistband" in Chapter 16.

In the stitching order, the interfacing is applied to the facings. The darts and zipper are stitched next, and the seams are stitched together and pressed.

> **PATTERN TIP**
>
> The most important part of the pattern drafting is to mark the matchpoints for the position where the seam divides into the slit. Add the facing and hem allowance to the pattern to allow for the slit. It is best to make the facing and hem equal widths, approximately 1½ inches, so the corner can be stitched into a mitered corner. Notch the hemline and the facing allowance (Figure 15.31c).

> **IMPORTANT**
>
> The hem can also be stitched with a mitered corner to reduce bulk. To do this, turn to Figure 15.23 and follow the stitching order. A serged hem finish is the best option on the skirt, as it reduces bulk.

The waistband is applied, and now you are ready to stitch the hem facing in place.

- Once the skirt is stitched in-the-round, the hem edge can be serged.
- Fold the facings back so the correct sides are together. Stitch across the bottom edge for the width of hem allowance, as illustrated for Figure 15.30c. Reduce bulk on the corner of the hem if the fabric feels thick, as this figure also illustrates.
- Turn the facing back to the wrong side; use a point turner to sharpen the hem corners. Check that the slits are of equal length; if they are uneven, adjust the length.
- Handbaste or pin the top edge of the facing.
- From the correct side of the fabric, stitch the facing to the fabric following the facing shape (see Figure 15.31c).
- Pull the threads to the wrong side and tie them to secure the topstitching.
- Hand stitch the facing to the hem using a slipstitch (Figure 15.31c).

Hem Chart

The chart in Table 15.2 can be used as a guide for choosing the appropriate hem finish and hem stitches for different fabric types. It is impossible

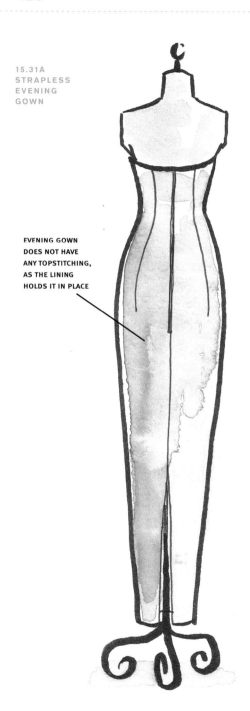

15.31A
STRAPLESS
EVENING
GOWN

EVENING GOWN
DOES NOT HAVE
ANY TOPSTITCHING,
AS THE LINING
HOLDS IT IN PLACE

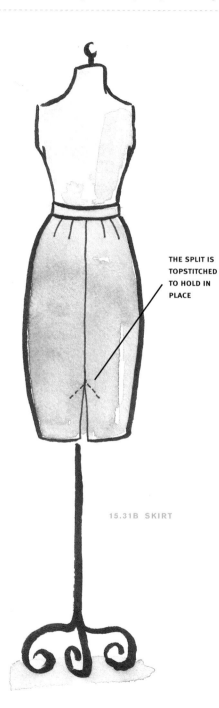

THE SPLIT IS
TOPSTITCHED
TO HOLD IN
PLACE

15.31B SKIRT

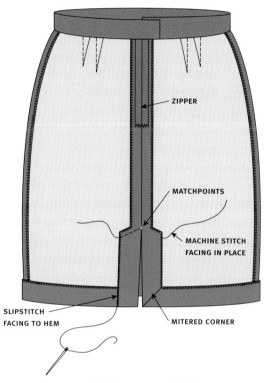

15.31C INSIDE VIEW OF HOW THE HEM SLIT WITH
FACING LOOKS WHEN COMPLETED

ZIPPER

MATCHPOINTS

MACHINE STITCH
FACING IN PLACE

SLIPSTITCH
FACING TO HEM

MITERED CORNER

to cover every fabric type and fabric weight, so this is a general recommendation only. Even when a fabric is listed in this hem chart, we still recommend sampling first to test whether the hem finish and hem stitch are the best choices for the fabric and design.

STITCHING HEMS IN TRICKY FABRICS

Sheer Fabric

Do choose the hem finish and hem stitches carefully, as hems in sheer fabric shadow.

Do sample the hem first to find the *best* option to suit the sheer fabric.

Do use fine lace pins or handbaste the hem to secure in place.

Do try using silk thread for hand stitching hems in fine sheer fabric.

Do also use a fine needle for hand stitching.

Do machine stitch topstitched hems in sheer fabric, with a clean finish.

Do hand or machine stitch a fine, narrow, rolled hem finish, as this works well on sheer fabrics.

Do stitch twice-turned hems on sheer fabric.

Don't stitch most hem tapes to sheer fabrics, as the tape will shadow; however, a lace hem tape shadowing under the hem edge may look fantastic—this is why sampling first is beneficial.

Don't reduce bulk from the hems of sheer fabrics, as this will show from the correct side; hems in sheer fabrics are not bulky.

Lace

Do make use of any scalloped fabric edge as the hemline of the garment (Figure 6.48b).

Do consider appliquéing a scalloped edge from the self-fabric or a lace trim to the hem edge.

Don't machine stitch a once- or twice-turned hem in delicate lace.

Don't stitch a Hong Kong finish, as it will shadow—use sheer Seams Great as a hem finish instead.

Don't topstitch hems in lace.

Satin

Do take special care when stitching hems in satin; always sample the hems in satin first to establish the *perfect* hem finish.

Do use fine lace pins to secure hems in place or handbaste the hem with a fine needle and silk thread.

Do test the fabric first to make sure no hole marks show in the fabric from the pins and needles.

Do consider leaving a raw edge instead of stitching a hem finish in satin when the garment has a lining. Hem finishes can show a ridge from the correct side of the fabric; stitch a catchstitch to enclose the raw edge.

Do stitch a horsehair braid to the hem of an evening gown to add structure to the hem.

Do stitch hems in satin using a catchstitch or slipstitch.

Don't stitch a twice-turned hem in satin, as it would be too bulky and may show a ridge from the correct side of the fabric.

Don't stitch hem tape if it shows a ridge from the correct side of the fabric—test this first!

Beaded Fabric

Do use fine needles and silk thread to hand stitch a hem in beaded fabric.

Do sample the hem first, as the fabric may shadow from the correct side.

Do stitch beaded fabric with care, as it is so delicate to handle.

Do use fine lace pins to secure the hem in place, and handbaste with a fine needle, as hole marks may be left in the fabric.

Do try a Hong Kong finish or Seams Great, then hand stitch the hem using an invisible slipstitch.

Do smash the beads off (gently) with a rubber mallet from any hem edge that is going to be finished with a Hong Kong or Seams Great finish.

Do try a hand-stitched rolled hem on beaded fabric; the beads may need to be gently smashed off first.

Don't machine stitch hems in beaded fabric.

Don't overdesign garments in beaded fabric; let the fabric speak for itself.

Knits

Do think of functional design when it comes to stitching hems in knits; the hem finish and hem stitches must be able to stretch after the hem has been stitched.

Do stitch a hem with twin needle stitching—this is an ideal hem stitch for knits, as the zigzag stitch that forms on the wrong side of the fabric allows the hem to stretch.

Do use a serged hem finish as the hemline of T-shirts.

Do stitch a lettuce-edge finish for hems on fine knits.

Do use a hidden catchstitch to stitch hems in knits. Catchstitching has a back-and-forth (zigzag) movement that allows hems to stretch.

Don't stitch one single row of straight top-stitching around a fitted hem, as the stitches will pop when the garment is worn. Only stitches with a back-and-forth movement allow

TABLE 15.2 HEM FINISHES FOR DIFFERENT FABRICS

Fabric	Hong Kong Finish	Hem Tape Finish	Serged Finish	Clean Edge and Blindstitch	Catchstitch/ Hidden Catchstitch	Slipstitch/ Hidden Slipstitch	Topstitched	Decorative Topstitching
Sheer								
Organza			X (narrow)	X		X	Twice-turned	X
Silk georgette		Seams Great	X	X		X	Twice- turned	
Beaded	X	X		X		X		
Lightweight								
Silk charmeuse	X		X	X		X		
Medium Weight								
Denim			X		X	X	X	X
Satin	X	X			X	X		
Silk dupioni	X	X	X		X	X		
Heavyweight								
Wool		X	X		X	X		
Tweed		X	X		X	X		
Satin		X			X	X		
Knit			X					
Velvet		X			X	X		
Fur					X			
Leather							X	

TABLE 15.2 CONTINUED

Fabric	Narrow Rolled Hem, Hand or Machine Stitched	False Hem	Leather Cement	Lettuce Edge	Twin Needle Stitching	Hem Stabilizer
Sheer						
Organza	X			X	X	
Silk georgette	X			X		
Beaded	X	X				
Lightweight						
Silk charmeuse	X			X		
Medium Weight						
Denim		X			X	
Satin		X				X
Silk dupioni						X
Heavyweight*	*Use raw edge to reduce bulk.					
Wool		X				X
Tweed		X				X
Satin		X				X
Knit				X (lightweight)	X	
Velvet						
Fur		X				
Leather		X	X			

hems to stretch in knits. A straight stitch can be used for circular hems.

Don't stitch hem tape as a hem finish on hems in knit fabrics. The tape will restrict the hem and it won't be able to stretch as the person wearing it walks.

Denim

Do try almost any hem finish and hem stitch outlined in this chapter—denim isn't a tricky fabric to stitch, so be creative with the hem stitches.

Do consider bulk in hems stitched in heavy-weight denim.

Do use topstitching on denim—it *loves* to be topstitched.

Do have fun thinking of creative ideas for stitching hems in denim, as it's a fun fabric to work with.

Velvet

Do treat velvet with care, as it is a delicate and tricky fabric to work with; be patient and take the time needed to perfect hems in velvet.

Do sample the hem finish and hem stitches first in a delicate fabric such as velvet.

Do stitch hem tape as a hem finish, as it eliminates bulk and ridges from showing from the correct side of the fabric.

Do hand stitch hems in velvet. Use a fine needle and silk thread—the stitches should not be visible from the correct side.

Don't place an iron directly on a velvet hem. Hold the iron approximately 1 inch above the hem and steam and stroke the hem to flatten it.

Don't topstitch hems in velvet.

Don't stitch a narrow rolled hem in velvet.

Leather

Do consider placing the hemline on the natural raw edges of a leather skin or hide; leather has no grain, so turn and twist the pattern to get the hem edges in just the right position to create the look you want.

Do topstitch hems in leather.

Do consider leaving a raw cut edge (cut with the rotary cutter), as leather does not fray—be aware, however, that how this looks depends on the quality and weight of the leather.

Do consider using a rotary cutter to cut a decorative hem edge; there are many interesting designs available in rotary cutters.

Do try binder clips (Figure 14.19a) or large paper clips to hold the hem in place; pins leave hole marks in leather. Do test the binder clips to see if they leave a mark on the hem. It may be better to use paper clips on a soft lambskin hem to hold it in place (Figure 15.32).

Do secure hems in place with leather cement. Apply the cement with cotton Q-tips or a small brush to secure the hem in place (see Figure 15.32).

Do edgestitch hems in leather.

Do secure hems in place with leather tape (both sides are sticky; just pull the paper from the tape as you apply the tape to the hem edge).

Do stitch one straight row of stitching ¼ inch away from the hem edge if the garment is going to be lined; then hand stitch the lining to this row of stitching.

Do stitch a false hem in leather using a lightweight fabric, as it will reduce bulk.

Do use a mallet or wallpaper roller to flatten the hem in leather.

Don't hand stitch hems in leather.

Don't press the hem without first protecting the leather with brown paper and turning off the steam.

Don't place cuffs on trouser hems in leather, as they will be too thick and bulky.

Faux Fur

Do stitch a hem in fur, and catchstitch the hem in place.

Do stitch a false hem on heavier furs to reduce bulk, then catchstitch the hem in place.

Don't turn the hem edge under ¼ inch as a clean finish, as fur is too bulky for this type of hem finish.

Don't topstitch hems in faux fur.

Don't trim the fur from the hems (as you do on seams), as it's better left on the hem of faux fur.

Don't stitch a hem finish in faux fur, as the edges will not fray and it is not necessary.

Heavyweight Fabric

Do sample the hem first to see how the finished hem looks from the face of the fabric; check to see if a ridge or bulk is visible along the line of hem stitching.

Do consider stitching a false hem if the hem is too bulky and shows a ridge.

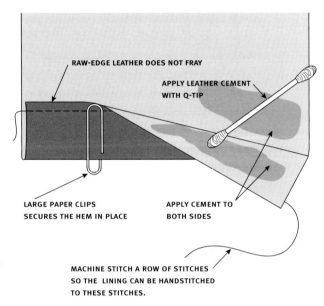

RAW-EDGE LEATHER DOES NOT FRAY

APPLY LEATHER CEMENT WITH Q-TIP

LARGE PAPER CLIPS SECURES THE HEM IN PLACE

APPLY CEMENT TO BOTH SIDES

MACHINE STITCH A ROW OF STITCHES SO THE LINING CAN BE HANDSTITCHED TO THESE STITCHES.

Do consider using hem tape as a hem finish, as the tape reduces bulk on the hem edge.

Don't machine stitch hems in heavyweight fabric; topstitching will draw attention to a bulky hem.

Don't stitch a twice-turned or narrow rolled hem in heavyweight fabrics.

TRANSFER YOUR KNOWLEDGE AND STRETCH YOUR CREATIVITY

Many stitching techniques have been taught in this textbook; this is the time to think back on what you've learned so far. By transferring your knowledge, you will be able to apply some of these stitching techniques to the hem, so the hem becomes the feature. This section will get you started—we encourage you to think of other ideas and stretch your creativity.

Here is a list of some of the stitching skills learned in past chapters. Let's go through them, and apply them to the hem:

- In Chapter 4, we learned to stitch darts. Figure 4.14c illustrates how darts can be stitched up from the hemline to make the hem the feature. Darts are added into the hemline at the pattern drafting stage. How about adding more darts than illustrated, to change the garment silhouette—give it a go to see how it looks.
- Chapter 5 teaches you how to stitch pockets. Have you thought of transferring this knowledge and stitching pockets around the hem edge of a T-shirt so the hem becomes the feature?
- Perhaps you are an expert at applying zippers by now! If so, try the idea illustrated in Figure 15.34a. Stitch several exposed zippers into all the coat seams from the hem up. Notice that the zippers can be unzipped to allow room for walking or zipped up on cold, rainy, and snowy days.
- In Chapter 9, waistbands were discussed, and in Chapter 13 plackets and cuffs were on view. From this stitching knowledge, let's transfer our knowledge and be creative! How about stitching a shirt-sleeve placket to the center front of the denim skirt, up from the hem. Now let's turn a waistband upside

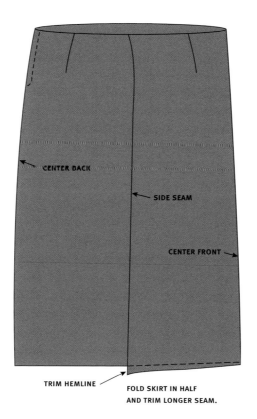

15.33A . . . ONE SIDE OF MY SEAM IS TOO LONG?

CENTER BACK

SIDE SEAM

CENTER FRONT

TRIM HEMLINE

FOLD SKIRT IN HALF
AND TRIM LONGER SEAM.

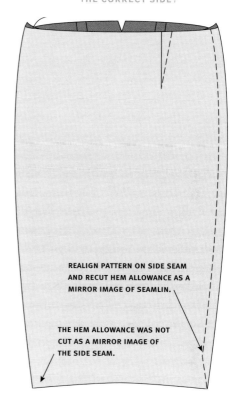

15.33B . . . MY HEM PUCKERS FROM THE CORRECT SIDE?

REALIGN PATTERN ON SIDE SEAM AND RECUT HEM ALLOWANCE AS A MIRROR IMAGE OF SEAMLIN.

THE HEM ALLOWANCE WAS NOT CUT AS A MIRROR IMAGE OF THE SIDE SEAM.

down and stitch it to the tucked hem edge of the skirt. The placket can be opened for ease in walking—how's that for transferring your knowledge?

- Ruffles and flounces can be stitched to any hem edge. They create texture, and the fullness creates a wonderful garment silhouette. You will see this by turning to

Figure 10.1 in the Style I.D. for Chapter 10. The dresses look sexy and romantic in soft, pink hues.

- Chapter 12, on facings, emphasized this very important feature of clothing construction. Look at Figure 12.25 to see how ribbing is stitched to the neckline. Transfer this knowledge and stitch ribbing to the hem edge of a

FUR COLLAR

ZIPPERS IN HEM

UNZIPPED

WAISTBAND

SHIRT
SLEEVE
PLACKET

CUFF JOINED TO
TOP OF STRAPLESS
BODICE

CUFF ON DRESS
CAN BE UNBUTTONED
AND THE DRESS HAS
ADDED LENGTH

15.34A   WOOL COAT

15.34B   DENIM SKIRT

15.34C   KNIT
TOP WITH DENIM
SHORTS

15.34D   STRAPLESS DRESS

garment; it can also be stitched to the sleeve edge. Another idea is to stitch the false hem illustrated in Figure 15.26, to the correct side of the garment as a hem band or as a facing. This too will draw your eyes to the hem, especially if you use line and shape to create a more exciting hem shape.

- And now for Chapter 15—let's take just one stitching technique (cuffs) and transfer this knowledge and stretch our creativity. Figure 15.34d shows an elegant strapless dress. A cuff has been stitched to the hemline and to the top edge of the strapless dress. The wide cuff on the hem is secured in place with buttons and buttonholes. Undo the buttons and let the cuff hang down for a longer length— tall girls will love this design! The cuff on the top edge can also turn up if stabilized correctly.

The popular balloon hemline is a fun hem treatment. This hemline is explained in Chapter 16, "Closed Lining to Control the Garment Silhouette."

STOP! WHAT DO I DO IF . . .

. . . one seam is longer than the other and my hem is not level?

Many students experience this problem, and the following tips may help: If one side is ¼ inch to ⅜ inch longer, the excess can be trimmed off. Figure 15.33a shows how to correct the hem. If one side is ½ inch or more longer, the seam will twist. Carefully rip out the seam and check your pattern seam lengths—if it is not correct, fix it now, as shown in Figure 15.33a. You may want to use the pattern again in the future.

. . . I don't know how much hem allowance to use?

Refer to Table 15.1 as a guide. The fabric weight (the sheerness or heaviness) and the garment silhouette determine the width of the hem allowance, the hem finish, and the stitches used. Sample the hem first in your chosen fabric to establish the best hem allowance for your project.

. . . my garment is too short?

Let the hem allowance down; press. Stitch a false hem with a shaped or bias-cut facing. Figure 15.26 explains how to do this.

. . . I cut my garment too short? How can I lengthen it?

If a false hem does not solve the problem, consider adding a hem band, ruffle, or lace to lengthen the garment. If this solution is not appropriate, you may need to recut your garment.

. . . my hem looks bulky?

Carefully seam rip the hem stitches; press the hem edge so it is lying flat. Stitch a hem tape lace as a hem finish, as this will eliminate bulk. A catchstitch could also be stitched to a raw edge to reduce bulk. Try reducing the width of the hem allowance, as this also reduces bulk.

. . . my hem looks puckered?

If you were stitching a curved or flared hemline, did you add the basting stitches needed to ease the hem edge first? If not, go back and complete this step, outlined in Figure 15.10. The other option is to snip the thread on the hem stitches to loosen the stitching, and then restitch that part of the hem. Carefully take the hem stitches out, and press the hem edge flat. Then reduce the hem allowance and restitch the hem.

A hem can also pucker because the hem edge is too tight when it is folded back and has not been cut in a mirror image of the seamline. So, check the pattern to see if this is causing a puckered hem. If you don't cut the hem allowance as a mirror image, the hem will *never* lie flat—it will always look puckered. This aspect of patternmaking is illustrated in Figure 15.4. To solve this problem, recut and restitch the seamline—a small amount will be lost from the side seam, but it's better to have a slightly narrower skirt than a puckered hem. Follow the instruction in Figure 15.33b.

. . . I'm not sure which hem finish to choose from the many available options?

First sample all your options in the fabric you are using. After years of experience, we still sample all hem choices that suit the fabric and style. Take a look at them, and then choose the best hem. Many creative people are visual, so stitching a sample that can be looked at and touched can be very helpful. Ask your instructor's opinion, and invite other students to critique your work.

Then if you are still not sure, sleep on it—this really does help. Good luck!

. . . I can't find any hem finish that I like?

Sometimes a garment is not going to be "perfect" when the design is finished. Some fabrics are difficult to work with and, in the end, we just have to choose the best hem option from what is physically possible. Remember, life is not always perfect!

SELF-CRITIQUE

This is the time to look at your finished garment and seriously evaluate the hem. Place it on the form or a model, and stand back to view it from a distance. Then answer the following questions:

- Does my hem look level when it is on the form?
- Does the hem lie flat, or does it look puckered?

- Does the completed hem look bulky?
- Is the hem finish appropriate for the fabric type?
- Does the hem shadow or show a ridge from the correct side of the fabric?
- Is my hem hand stitching invisible from the correct side of the garment?
- Is my topstitched hem parallel to the hemline?
- When I stand back and view the garment, does the hem blend with the garment as a whole or does it stand out because of bad stitching?
- Did I stitch enough samples to make an informed decision regarding the best hem finish and hem stitching to use? Did I save them for later reference in my workbook or collection?
- How can I improve on my hem stitching in the future?

REVIEW CHECKLIST

- Do I understand the importance of beginning with correct patterns, with side seams that match together, notches snipped, matchpoints marked, and a smooth, even hemline?
- Do I understand the concept that the fabric weight and silhouette of the garment hemline guide me in choosing the best hem finish and hem stitching for my project?
- Do I understand that using quality thread and the correct size and type of hand stitching needle do make a difference in my hem stitching?
- Do I know how to choose the best hem finish and hem stitching for each fabric weight?

And finally . . .

- We suggest restitching any hem stitching samples that could be improved on or changed for future reference. Then add them to your workbook.

Linings: Covering the Inner Surface

Your garment is beautiful on the outside, and the lining makes it beautiful on the inside. The function of a lining is to cover the interior construction of a garment and also to add warmth, increase comfort, and ensure longer wear. A lining provides a smooth entry and exit from the garment while helping to reduce wrinkles.

The lining should always be compatible with the drape and fabric content of the garment fabric.

It can perfectly match the color of the garment or be a contrasting color or print, adding luxury and excitement. In this chapter we examine, sew, and illustrate the various lining treatments using a variety of methods to apply the linings.

The Style I.D. illustrates several styles of garments from the outside and inside to show how the lining covers the inner surface of the garment.

STYLE I.D.

The styles in Figure 16.1 illustrate how the lining looks. The shape of the linings follow the original garment patterns of the outer garments. For each garment in the Style I.D., the outer garment is on the left and the lining is on the right. Observe how beautiful linings look when they are revealed!

GATHER YOUR TOOLS

Here are the tools needed to stitch linings. By now these essential tools will already be part of your stitching tool kit: lining, thread, tape measure, scissors, hand stitching needles, and point turner.

KEY TERMS

Closed Edge-to-Edge Lining
Closed Lining to Control the Garment Silhouette
Closed Lining with Facing
Closed Partial Lining
Lining
Open Edge-to-Edge Lining
Open Lining with Facing
Open Lining with Waistband
Open Partial Lining
Partial Lining

Style I.D.

PATTERNED
LINING

LINING

16.1A '50S STYLE DRESS

16.1B BALLOON SKIRT

JACKET
LINING

PLEATED
SKIRT

PARTIAL
LINING ON
PLEATED
SKIRT

16.1C PLEATED SKIRT

NOW LET'S GET STARTED
Why Use a Lining?

If the only contribution a lining made was to cover the inner construction, we might not be bothered to stitch a lining at all. We could decide to serge or neaten the seams with a Hong Kong seam finish instead. However, there are many more reasons for adding a lining into a garment than just to cover the inner construction. The following list outlines several reasons why lining a garment is so beneficial. A lining:

- Helps the garment to slip on and off the body with ease.
- Gives the garment a smooth, luxurious feeling of comfort.
- Prolongs the life of the garment.
- Adds a quality finish to the garment.
- Adds warmth.
- Helps the garment retain its shape.
- Prevents the garment from stretching.
- Prevents the garment from clinging to the body.
- Reduces wrinkling in the outer fabric.
- Adds oomph to limp fabrics.
- Helps the garment hang with smooth, flattering lines.
- Protects the skin. Some textiles, such as wool, and the inside of leather have coarse textures that can irritate the skin. Lining garments made with these fabrics will protect the skin.

TYPES OF LINING

Just as there are a variety of fabrics to choose from, there are also a variety of linings. Lining

NOTE

Some silk fabrics such as silk charmeuse, silk georgette, and silk crepe de chine are interchangeable and can double as fabric or lining.

choices are more limited than fabric choices; nevertheless, choosing the correct lining for the garment is important. Linings can be made from many different fabrics, including silk, polyester, cotton, polyester and spandex, flannel, and fleece. The fiber content matters when choosing the lining. Consider a silk lining: one of its attributes is that it breathes, making it comfortable to wear in a hot climate, whereas a polyester lining does not breathe and would feel hot and sweaty in a tropical climate. For this reason, the choice of fiber content and weight of the lining needs to be made with consideration for the wearer. This is how fashion and function meet.

Woven Lining

Just as fabric is categorized into a woven or knit so it is with lining. And just as fabric is categorized into three different weights, lining is similarly classified—as lightweight, medium weight, or heavyweight. A lining should be lighter in weight than the garment fabric; one that is too heavy could distort the look of the garment and feel bulky. The lining should feel comfortable, smooth, and luxurious on the body.

The weight of the lining also needs to suit the purpose and type of garment. For example, a coat needs a heavier-weight lining, whereas a summer jacket may not need lining at all; however, if it was lined, a *breathable, lightweight lining*, such as China silk, would be the appropriate choice. Winter coats need a lining to add warmth and durability, both of which enhance the quality of the garment. Silk satin has a beautiful quality and makes a luxurious coat lining! And there are lots of colors and prints to choose from.

Lightweight Lining

Habotai or *China silk* is a fine, soft, lightweight lining that does not add any bulk under garments. China silk is not a good choice for a coat lining, as it is too limp; however, it is an ideal weight to line skirts and dresses. Don't use China silk to line pants, as it does not withstand the wear and tear—it easily tears away from the crotch seam.

Silk georgette is a sheer lightweight fabric. It is ideal to use as a lining under sheer fabrics, as it helps to retain the soft drape; however, one single layer may not give the opaqueness required. Several layers of silk georgette can be used as the lining. It is available in beautiful tonal colors and prints, which can add a delightful color detail under garments.

Silk crepe de chine is an outer garment fabric available in several weights—two-ply, three-ply, and four-ply—that can double as self-lining. Although it is expensive, it is also long-wearing, making it an ideal choice for linings and other garments. Silk crepe de chine makes a beautiful, luxurious lining. This fabric can be hand washed or dry cleaned.

Bemberg Rayon Lining is a favorite lining fabric because it's good quality, soft to the hand, comfortable, and washable. It also comes in a variety of colors. It can be used to line most garments; however, use a heavier-weight lining for coats and warm jackets. Rayon is an anticling lining, which is another one of its attributes. Ambiance is a lightweight rayon lining that is hand washable and available in an amazing array of colors.

Polyester lining is a lightweight fabric used to line dresses, skirts, pants, or vests. Make sure you purchase a nonstatic lining. Polyester linings do not breathe, but they also don't wrinkle, and are a cost-effective alternative to more expensive silk. Be warned—polyester lining is more difficult to stitch than other linings!

Medium-Weight Lining

Silk charmeuse is a fabulous fabric that can be used for blouses, shirts, and evening gowns, or as a fabulous *medium-weight lining* for jackets, coats, and evening gowns. It drapes beautifully and has a semilustrous face and dull back. We guarantee any customer trying on a garment lined with silk charmeuse will fall in love with the luxurious feel of this fabric next to the skin!

Crepe-backed satin is a medium-weight fabric suitable for lining jackets and coats. It has a smooth, lustrous face and a pebbly, crepe back and is available in silk and polyester.

Twill Lining is a medium-weight fabric suitable for lining jackets and coats, mainly in men's wear.

Microfiber refers to the size of the thread used to make this lining fabric. It can be made from polyester, nylon, rayon, or acetate in many different weights; has a luxurious feel and drape; and is very tightly woven, providing some wind resistance.

Peachskin is a polyester lining that is considered a microfiber. It drapes well and is wrinkle-resistant.

One-hundred-percent cotton is not slippery, so it is best suited to lining skirts and vests that don't need to slip over other garments. A jacket or coat lined in cotton will not slip over other garments easily and may stick to other fabrics and feel uncomfortable.

Heavyweight Lining

Flannel-backed lining is also called Sun Back; it provides a warm lining in coats, as the flannel gives extra warmth and adds weight to the coat. Kasha is another satin-backed flannel lining (52 percent acetate, 48 percent cotton) that is perfect for lining coats and jackets, as the flannel back adds body without bulk.

Fur is an expensive lining, but think of how luxurious a coat would feel with a fur lining! Faux fur can be used for a lining, or a detachable lining. Faux fur comes in different thicknesses: the more fitted the garment, the shorter the pile should be.

Quilted lining is the warmest of all linings and is mostly used in cold-weather coats, jackets, and vests. Quilted lining is padded with polyester batting that traps air. Most quilted linings are available in many fabrications such as acetate, polyester satin, cotton, and faux suede. Any fabric can be turned into a quilted lining by sandwiching batting in between two layers of fabric and topstitch-ing them together (this is called quilting). Batting is also available in silk, which is warm, breathable, and very light in weight.

Stretch Linings

Spandex can be added to either a woven or a knit lining to add a stretch element. It adds stretch in the length, the width, or in both directions. It is important to match the stretch capacity of the lining to the outer fabric stretch capacity. For example, swimsuits are made from fabric that is very stretchy in both directions. Therefore, a swimsuit lining *must* have the same stretch capacity in both directions as the swimwear fabric.

It does not matter if the lining has *more* stretch capacity than the outer knit fabric, but it *must not* have less stretch than the outer knit fabric; if it did, the garment would not function properly because the lining would restrict the stretch capacity. For example, a lining used in a knit dress or skirt only needs to stretch in the width; however, a lining that stretches in both directions can still be used.

Woven/Stretch Lining

Always choose a woven lining with spandex in it if your fabric is woven with spandex. We know it has been said before; *match like with like!* There are fabulous web sites that can help you find a lining with a stretch capacity. Refer to the "Where to Buy" section of this text.

Stretch Knit Lining

Tricot lining is lightweight, fine, and tightly woven. Tricot knits can be sheer or opaque and have a satin, crepe, or brushed surface. This fabric is very strong, comes in a variety of weights, and is ideal for lining knit garments. It is reasonably priced and is available in an array of colors.

Soft lingerie knits make fabulous linings and feel beautiful next to the skin.

Active wear and swimsuit linings can be used as linings for knit garments such as skirts and dresses. Although they stretch in both directions, they can still be used for lining knit garments that stretch only in the width. These linings are available in variety of fibers including polyester/spandex, 100 percent nylon, and nylon/spandex. Colors are limited to white, nude, and black.

Interlock is a knit outer fabric made from 100 percent polyester. It does not have a lot of stretch; there is a little mechanical stretch in the width but this will not give the same stretch capacity as a knit with spandex. Interlock can be used to line knit garments and also woven fabrics, since the stretch is minimal. The little stretch it does have will be comfortable for movement.

Mesh is a stretch fabric that can also be used as a lining. Mesh is sheer, so it would make an excellent lining for garments that only need that touch of sheerness.

Self-fabric as a lining can be an ideal choice, as some fabrics can double as the outer fabric and the lining. This method of lining works best when the fabric is lightweight. Self-fabric is often used to line stretch knit tops and tight knit skirts. Self-fabric as a lining works well on styles made from silk charmeuse, silk georgette,

or crepe de chine. Look to see if any seams or hems can be eliminated and replaced with a foldline instead.

Criteria for Choosing a Lining— Fiber and Function

- Choose a static-free lining; no one wants a lining clinging to their underwear! Rayon and silk make excellent static-free linings.
- Consider the warmth or coolness of the lining. Synthetic linings feel hot and sticky in the heat; on the other hand, silk breathes. Kasha lining is brushed on the wrong side of the fabric and adds warmth.
- Choose the same type of lining as the outer fabric: woven fabric needs a woven lining; a woven fabric with a stretch capacity needs a woven/stretch lining; a knit fabric needs a knit lining—a stretch woven lining may suffice for some knit garments, but test the stretch capacity first.
- Purchase a lining that needs the same care as the outer garment fabric. Don't choose a lining that needs to be dry-cleaned when the outer fabric is machine washable.
- The weight of the lining is important, as the lining needs to cover the construction details. A garment in which the shadows of seams can be seen through the lining does not look professional.
- The lining color is also important for jackets and coats, because when they swing open, the lining is visible. This is an opportunity to apply creativity in design.

THE LINING PATTERN

The first, most important aspect of stitching a lining is to start with the *correct lining patterns.* If you don't have the correct patterns, then the stitching techniques in this chapter will be difficult to follow. The lining pattern affects the fit of the garment. A lining that is too tight will pull the garment out of alignment and will feel uncomfortable; one that is too big will feel bulky and loose, will wrinkle inside, and may even hang below the garment—this is not a good look!

IMPORTANT

Snip all notches and mark all pattern markings. If the fabric and lining are not adequately marked, stitching the lining will be a difficult process.

FULL OR PARTIAL LINING

Garments can be lined with a full lining or a partial lining. When a garment has a *full lining,* the entire inner surface of the garment is covered. Figures 16.1a, b, and c (jacket only) illustrate three garments that have full linings. When the garment has a partial lining, only part of the garment is lined rather than the entire garment. Figure 16.1c shows a partial lining on the pleated skirt. Partial lining can also refer to a garment *part* being lined, for example, a pocket or a collar. This would reduce bulk when stitching fabric that may be too heavy to permit two garment parts to be stitched from the same fabric.

PATTERN TIP

General Pattern Tips

Each stitching method for linings outlined in this text will affect how the pattern is made. Some extra pattern tips will be given for each lining method. Also refer to your patternmaking books for more specific directions. Here are some general pattern tips to get started.

- A lining can be added into any garment (that doesn't mean every garment needs a lining).
- All lining patterns are constructed from the original garment patterns. Figure 16.2 illustrates this point. Even though the pattern plotting illustrated is for a jacket, it is no different for other garments.
- Before making any lining patterns, plot the facings. The lining pattern is the part of the garment pattern is left beyond the facing (see Figure 16.2).
- Notice in Figure 16.2 that a pleat has been added to the back lining. This pleat is added to jacket/coat linings for ease; it opens when the wearer stretches, bends, and reaches. If a pleat is not added, the constant movement of the sleeves will eventually cause them to pull away from the armholes.
- The hem of the finished lining sits approximately halfway on the garment hem

allowance for an open lining, as illustrated in Figure 16.3a, or finishes slightly above halfway for a closed lining, as illustrated on the left side of the garment in Figure 16.3b. Open and closed lining methods are explained later in this chapter.

- With a closed lining, a 1-inch pleat is incorporated in the overall length of the lining for functional design purposes. The pleat prevents the lining from being too tight when stretching, reaching, or bending while wearing a jacket or coat, preventing the lining from pulling away from the hem. The pleat is illustrated in Figure 16.3b.
- Transfer all the same pattern markings and grainlines from the outer garment pattern to the lining pattern. Notice in Figure 16.2 that the armhole and sleeve cap notches from the garment pattern are transferred to the lining pattern. Notches have also been placed on the front facing and lining so these pieces can be matched correctly during the stitching process. The placements for both the back pleat and the center-back facing are notched, as these two points are stitched together when the lining is inserted.
- Differentiate between the lining and the outer garment patterns by marking the lining pattern using a different-colored pen.

This makes the lining pattern easily recognizable and helps prevent the lining pattern from being picked up and cut accidentally as a garment pattern. In this chapter, the lining patterns are indicated by diagonal green lines, as seen in Figure 16.2.

- On skirt and pant linings with a facing or waistband, the back darts can be stitched as tucks instead of a traditional dart. This allows more "ease" across the back hip area.
- When lining a garment that is gathered or pleated around the waistline, eliminate the gathers and pleats as they add bulk to the waistline. Take a look at Figure 16.1a; notice that the '50s-style dress lining is not gathered. To reduce bulk, fold out the fullness from the waistline of the lining pattern; the lining skirt shape will still be flared or circular. The lining hemline will still allow plenty of width so the lining moves with the natural flow of the dress. The measurements for the lining and garment waistlines should be equal lengths after the garment is gathered. Make sure the lining pattern fits the hip measurement and is not too tight—remember the design must be functional!

The stitching methods for full linings include:

- Closed edge-to-edge lining
- Open edge-to-edge lining
- Open lining with facing
- Closed lining with facing
- Open lining with waistband

- Closed lining to control the garment silhouette

The Difference Between Open and Closed Linings

Garments stitched with a full lining can be stitched with either a closed or an open lining.

When the lining is open, all lining and garment seams need to be finished. The lining and garment hems are then finished and stitched separately, as illustrated in Figure 16.3a. The lining hem can be machine stitched with a once-turned hem (see Figure 15.20 and 15.22). The garment hem is hand stitched using one of the stitching

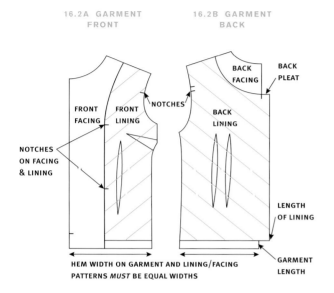

16.2A GARMENT FRONT

16.2B GARMENT BACK

BACK FACING

BACK PLEAT

FRONT FACING

FRONT LINING

NOTCHES

BACK LINING

NOTCHES ON FACING & LINING

LENGTH OF LINING

GARMENT LENGTH

HEM WIDTH ON GARMENT AND LINING/FACING PATTERNS *MUST* BE EQUAL WIDTHS

16.2C SLEEVE

ALL NOTCHES MUST MATCH ARMHOLE NOTCHES

SLEEVE LINING

SLEEVE LINING LENGTH

GARMENT SLEEVE LINING

SLEEVE WIDTH ON GARMENT & LINING PATTERNS *MUST* BE EQUAL WIDTHS

IMPORTANT

The finished length of the lining *must* always be shorter than the garment hemline—it is never a good look to see a lining hem hanging below the garment hem edge!

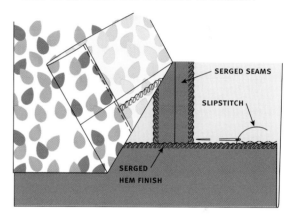

16.3A OPEN LINING: NOT ATTACHED TO GARMENT

SERGED SEAMS

SLIPSTITCH

SERGED HEM FINISH

IMPORTANT

Always use the Sew, Clip, Press method when stitching linings.

methods illustrated in Figure 15.9. An example of an open lining is seen on the sheath dress and skirt in Figure 16.9.

To close a lining, the garment hem is first hand stitched in place. A catchstitch, illustrated in Figure 15.9, is an ideal stitching method to use, as it encloses the raw hem edge. The lining is then hand stitched to the garment hem, as illustrated in Figure 16.3b. The seams do not need to be finished unless the fabric frays. The jacket in Figure 16.1c has a closed lining.

A lining hem can be machine or hand stitched to the garment hem edge. In this chapter, the hand-stitched method is explained because we believe students have more control over the lining using this method. The method of machine stitching the lining to the garment hem is most often used in production.

Table 16.1 helps to define the lining method to choose for each garment type—the lining method chosen is mainly garment driven.

GENERAL STITCHING ORDER FOR A LINING

• Although many different styles can be lined, the general stitching method for most linings is the same. Before the lining is stitched into the garment, the lining and garment are each stitched

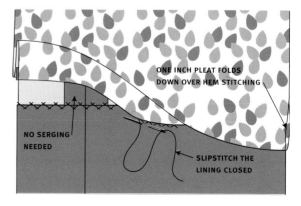

16.3B CLOSED LINING: ATTACHED TO GARMENT

ONE INCH PLEAT FOLDS DOWN OVER HEM STITCHING

NO SERGING NEEDED

SLIPSTITCH THE LINING CLOSED

TABLE 16. HOW THE GARMENT MOVES AFFECTS WHETHER IT IS AN OPEN OR CLOSED LINING

Stitching Methods	Full Lining	Closed Lining (seam and hem finishes not necessary)	Open Lining (seam and hem finishes necessary)
Edge to-edge			
Vest	X	X	
Cape	X	X	
Loose Jacket	X	X	
Strapless Bodice	X	X	
Dress	X		X
Pants	X		X
Skirt	X		X
Lining With Facing			
Pants	X		X
Skirt	X		X
Dress	X		X
Jacket/Coat with straight/A-line hemlines	X	X	
Jacket/Coat with flared/ circular hemlines	X		X
Lining with Waistband			
Pants	X		X
Skirts	X		X
Lining to Control Garment Silhouette			
Any garment		X	
Partial Lining			
Pant			X
Skirt			X
Jacket/Coat			X
Garment Parts			
Collar		X	
Flounce		X	
Peplum		X	
Pocket		X	
Pocket Flap		X	
Waistband		X	

separately. Figure 16.4 illustrates a coat lining fully stitched and ready to be inserted into the coat. Figure 16.5 is the coat fully stitched, ready to be lined. The method for stitching a jacket or coat lining will be outlined later in the text.

- Serge open or closed seams if the lining is an open lining. The seams do not need to be serged when the lining is closed; however, if the lining fabric frays, you may wish to serge the seams.
- When pressing the lining, check the temperature setting of the iron before placing the iron directly on the lining fabric. Many linings are heat sensitive. Set the iron at the correct setting for the lining fabric, and check the temperature before placing it on the garment. You don't want the lining to melt!
- Press all the seams as they are stitched, taking care to clip, trim, or grade the seams as needed. Pressing from the wrong side of the garment, using a tailor's ham to shape the curve of princess seams or darts.

Each stitching method for full linings will be explained. For each stitching method, the garments are illustrated turned inside-out to show the inside view of each lining.

FULL LINING
Closed Edge-to-Edge Lining

When stitching a closed edge-to-edge lining, the outer garment fabric and lining look exactly the same on both sides of the garment except that one side is lining and the other side is the garment fabric. Figure 16.6 illustrates a vest, cape, and jacket stitched with edge-to-edge

16.4 FULLY STITCH THE COAT

16.5 FULLY STITCH THE LINING

HANDSTITCH
FACING
IN PLACE

UNDERLINING

THE POSITION WHERE FACING IS
CLIPPED ON A CLOSED LINING

POSITION WHERE FACING IS
CLIPPED FOR AN OPEN LINING

STAY STITCH DIRECTION

CLIP

PRESS 1/2" BACK
TO WRONG SIDE
OF FABRIC

CREASE LINE

PRESS 1/2" SEAM ALLOWANCE
TO WRONG SIDE OF COAT

PATTERN TIP

The outer garment fabric and the lining are cut as duplicate shapes using the same patterns. The outer garment fabric and lining are stitched separately, then they're both joined together. Figure 16.7a shows the lining and garment as duplicate shapes being stitched together. When the garment is completed, one side of the garment is the outer fabric and the other side is the lining. Notice the absence of a facing in this style of lining. This is a quick and easy lining method that is cost-effective to use in production.

VEST

Figure 16.6a shows an inside view of the vest lining.

- Fully underline the front vest; this is especially important if buttonholes and buttons are stitched as the closure. The back vest can also be underlined, or narrow fusible or sew-in tape can be applied around the neckline, armholes, and back hem edge to prevent the seams from stretching in the stitching process (see Figure 16.7a). Refer to Figure 3.15.

- Stitch darts, pockets, shoulder seams, or any other seams to complete the front and back of the outer garment fabric and the lining—do not stitch the side seams closed at this stage (see Figure 16.7a).

- Press all seams open; slit the darts if there is too much bulk, and press open (see Figure 16.7a).

- Place the correct sides of the lining and fabric necklines together; match the shoulder seams,

linings. This method of lining can also be called "bagged out" lining. Both sides of the garment *must* be perfectly aligned together when they are stitched edge-to-edge. This lining method *does not* have any ease built into the lining. For this reason it is best suited to garments that are loose in fit and worn open with an edge-to-edge closure. This method of lining is also suitable for smaller garments such as a vest or strapless bodice that are easily aligned together. It is dif-

ficult to achieve perfect alignment using this method of lining on complicated styles; lots of seamlines and intricate stitching can pull the lining out of alignment very easily. The garments in Figure 16.6 are illustrative of simple designs without intricate stitching that stitch successfully with an edge-to-edge closed lining.

When stitching the outer garment fabric to the lining, stitch all the seams with the outer fabric on top; this helps to keep the lining aligned.

16.6A VEST   16.6B CAPE   16.6C JACKET

FIGURE 16.6 EDGE-TO-EDGE LININGS

and pin in place. Stitch a ¼-inch seam allowance around the neck and center front; clip curved seams, and trim or grade any bulky seams (see Figure 16.7a).

- Turn the garment to the correct side and understitch the neckline; turn the seam allowance toward the lining to understitch (Figure 16.7b).

- This next step is important! It sets you up to complete the lining successfully—with the garment and lining pieces perfectly aligned together—so don't skip it! From the correct side, smooth the outer garment fabric over the lining. Let the lining hang beyond the fabric edges if it needs to; the lining is often wider due to the understitching. Pin the fabric and lining together around the edges and trim off any overhanging lining (Figure 16.7c).

- Place the wrong sides of the garment and lining together; match the shoulder seams and armhole notches, and pin in place. Stitch the armhole seam using a ¼-inch seam allowance; clip the seam and grade, if bulky (Figure 16.7d).

- Turn the garment to the correct side by pulling the fronts through the shoulders toward the back.

- Understitch the armholes. This is a two-step process: begin stitching from each underarm, finishing at the shoulder seams. If the shoulders are narrow, it may be difficult to understitch right up to the shoulder seams. In that case, just understitch as far as possible. When completed, press the armholes.

- Pin front and back side seams together by placing the correct sides of the outer fabric and lining together. Stitch the side seams using a ½-inch seam allowance; begin stitching from the fabric

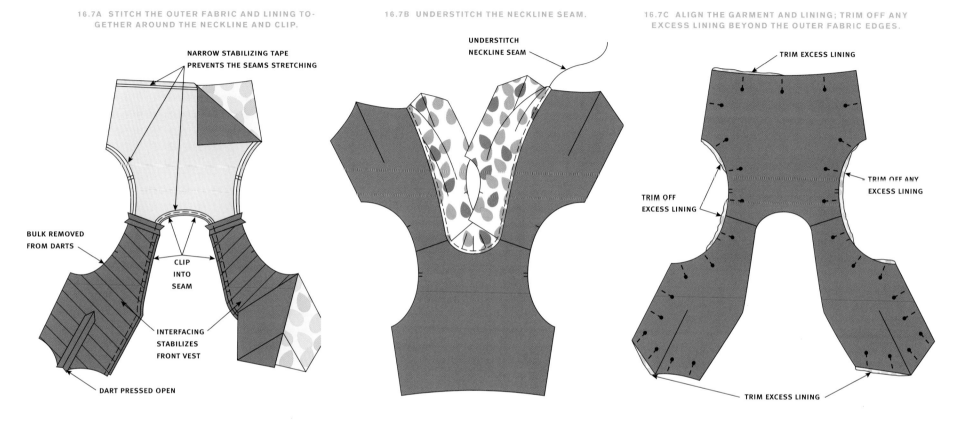

NARROW STABILIZING TAPE
PREVENTS THE SEAMS STRETCHING

BULK REMOVED
FROM DARTS

CLIP
INTO
SEAM

INTERFACING
STABILIZES
FRONT VEST

DART PRESSED OPEN

UNDERSTITCH
NECKLINE SEAM

TRIM EXCESS LINING

TRIM OFF ANY
EXCESS LINING

TRIM OFF
EXCESS LINING

TRIM EXCESS LINING

end and turn the underarm seams toward the lining as you stitch. On one side seam (either side), leave a 6-inch opening in the middle of the lining seam, as illustrated in Figure 16.7e. The garment will eventually be turned through this opening to the correct side.

- Fold the side seams over so the underarm is on the fold and the side seams line up together. Cut diagonally across the corners of the underarm seam to reduce bulk, and press the side seams open. Figure 16.7e indicates where the bulk needs to be removed.

- Place the correct sides of the lining and the outer fabric hem edges together; match darts and seamlines together. Stitch a ¼-inch seam around the hem edge; clip corners and curved seams, and grade any bulky seams (see Figure 16.7a).

- Turn the vest to the correct side by pulling the garment out through the side seam opening (Figure 16.7f). Use a point turner to sharpen any corners. Do not understitch the hemline, as this is an impossible task!

- Press the vest hemline; make sure the seamline

is pressed ¹⁄₁₆ inch back toward the lining so the lining is not visible from the correct side of the garment.

- Close the side seam by stitching an edgestitch to close the opening. This is illustrated on the left side of the vest side seam in Figure 16.6a.

Strapless Bodice

The bodice (garment fabric) is fully underlined and boned on all seams before the lining is inserted (see Figure 6.41). It needs to be noted that the boning can be stitched to either the garment

16.7D STITCH THE ARMHOLE SEAMS.

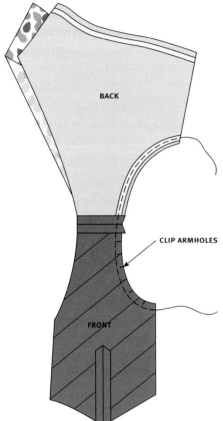

16.7E STITCH THE SIDE SEAMS OF THE GARMENT AND LINING.

16.7F STITCH THE HEM EDGES OF THE OUTER FABRIC AND LINING TOGETHER.

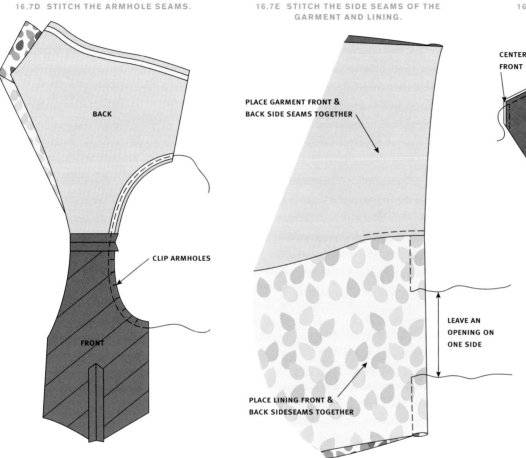

> **PATTERN TIP**
>
> Cut the bottom edge of the lining pattern ⅛ inch shorter than the outer garment pattern. Doing so ensures that the lining will not hang below the outer fabric and that seamlines will be tucked slightly toward the lining so it is not visible from the face of the garment.

fabric or lining. Both methods work well—this decision is fabric driven. (Underlining adds stability and strength, reduces wrinkling and transparency, prevents shadowing and seam allowances from showing through and stabilizes loosely woven fabrics.

The strapless bodice is then fully lined edge-to-edge with a closed lining or left open at the waist if a skirt is added. Strapless dresses need a crisp, tightly woven, firm lining.

Deciding which closure will be used as this affects the stitching order.

ZIPPER

- The zipper would be stitched in the center back seam first.
- The seams are stitched and boned (Figure 6.41).
- While the garment is laying flat, place correct sides of the bodice and lining together. Pin the lining to the bodice top and bottom edges (leave

the center back seams open), matching seamlines together.

- Stitch using a ¼-inch seam allowance.
- Clip, trim, and grade the seam allowances as necessary and press.
- Handstitch the lining to the zipper tape (Figure 16.10b).

OTHER CLOSURES

- A different stitching order is followed for buttons/loops and grommets lacing (see Chapter 17).
- Leave an opening on one side of the lining for several inches for turning (Figure 16.7c).

- Place bodice and lining together and stitch around all edges.
- Clip, trim, and grade the seam allowances as necessary.
- Turn bodice through opening, press and hand-stitch opening closed.

> **NOTE**
> _____
> Refer to the stitching instructions for the fifties-style dress when joining a strapless bodice to a skirt (Figures 16.10).

Cape

The lined cape is constructed in the same manner as the above-described garments: the cape is stitched, and then the lining is stitched (see Figure 16.6b).

- Leave the pocket openings on the outer fabric and lining unstitched.
- If the cape has a collar, stitch the collar to the cape next.
- With the correct sides together, pin and stitch the lining to the cape around the outside edges, leaving an opening near the side seam or center-back hemline.

> **PATTERN TIP**
> _____
> When shoulder pads are used, the lining needs a slight adjustment. Measure the width of the shoulder pad and take this width off the height of the shoulder seam. Make sure the sleeve cap is also adjusted so the sleeve fits the new armhole measurement. Refer to your patternmaking books for more information.

- Clip, grade, and trim the seam allowances; press all seams.
- Catchstitch the collar or hood seam allowances to the lining seam allowances (see Figure 16.15b).
- The two openings on the front of the cape for the hands are machine stitched to the lining from the inside of the cape. Or use a slipstitch or blind-stitch to secure the lining to the garment. Top-stitching around the opening can further secure the lining to the cape.
- Turn the lining seam allowance under on the opening at the side seam or center back hemline and slipstitch closed.

Jacket with Sleeve

The lined edge-to-edge jacket is stitched using the same stitching order as the vest, except of course, there is a sleeve. This jacket could also be considered reversible. Refer to Figure 16.6c to see an inside view of the jacket lined edge-to-edge.

- Stitch the front and back of the jacket together at the shoulder seams and side seams.
- Stitch the sleeves together and insert into the jacket armscye.
- Repeat the previous steps for the lining, leaving an opening in one of the side seams to turn the jacket through as shown in Figure 16.7e.
- Place and stitch the shoulder pads (if they are going to be used) along the shoulder seam (Figure 14.17).
- Sew the lining to the jacket around the center front and the neckline (see Figure 16.7a).
- Understitch the lining to the seam allowances at

the center front, stitching as far as possible up to the neckline area—the presser foot will not fit all the way to the neckline (see Figure 16.7b). Under-stitching prevents the lining from rolling to the correct side of the garment even with excellent pressing skills.

- Stitch the lining to the jacket at the bottom edge of the jacket, understitching the seam allowance to the lining as far as possible. Clip, grade, and trim all seam allowances to reduce bulk.
- Turn the jacket out through the side seam opening, with the lining side facing up and the garment fabric underneath.
- Pin the lining sleeve in place, matching underarm and shoulder seams together; handstitch the lining to the garment at the shoulder seam and underarm seam to secure the lining to the garment.
- Hand stitch or machine edgestitch the opening in the side seam closed.
- Slipstitch the lining to the wrists (Figure 16.8).
- Give the jacket a final press.

Open Edge-to-Edge Lining (Dresses, Skirts, Pants)

This method of using an open edge-to-edge lining is simple to stitch. Garments stitched with this lining have the top of the garment stitched edge-to-edge while the hem of the lining is shorter in length and left to hang freely or open and is not attached to the garment hem. This ensures that the lining will not pull the garment fabric out of alignment. Edge-to-edge linings with the hemline open are illustrated in the two garments in Figure 16.9a and b. When garments are stitched using this lining method,

FIGURE 16.9 USING A PRINT FABRIC FOR A LINING

16.8 EDGE-TO-EDGE LINING—JACKET
WITH SLEEVE: SLIPSTITCH THE SLEEVE LINING TO
THE OUTER FABRIC SLEEVE EDGE.

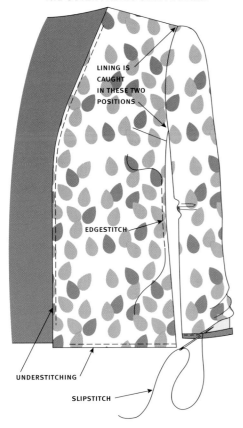

LINING IS
CAUGHT
IN THESE TWO
POSITIONS

EDGESTITCH

UNDERSTITCHING

SLIPSTITCH

The following styles have an edge-to-edge
open lining—do refer to them as you stitch:

- '50s dress with waistline (see Figure 16.1a in
  the Style I.D.)
- Sheath dress (see Figure 16.9a)
- Skirt (see Figure 16.9b)

'50s Dress with Waistline

It must be noted that an edge-to-edge lining is
ideal for dresses, and this is the case for the '50s-
style dress in Figure 16.1a, where the lining is a
spot print. Notice in this lining there is no facing;
stabilizing tape has been used instead (Figure 3.15).
Even though this lining method is an ideal choice
for a dress, the choice of which lining to use is ultimately the designer's, as shown in Figure 16.9.

- Look at the stitching order for the vest in Figure
  16.7a–f. There is no need to leave an opening on
  the side seam, because the dress has a center
  back zipper and this gives access for turning the
  lining to the correct side (Figure 16.10b).

CONTINUE WITH THIS STITCHING ORDER

- Stitch the outer fabric skirt side seams only;
  stitch the lining side seams *and* the center-back
  seam up to the notched position that marks the
  position of the zipper length.
- Place the correct sides of the waistlines together,
  matching the side seams together. Pin in place,
  and stitch a ½-inch seam. Press the seam allowances up toward the neckline (Figure 16.10a).
- Notice that the skirt seams are finished; because
  the lining is open, the seams will be visible. There

a ridge from any seam joins will not be visible
on the correct side of the garment (which is the
case when a facing is stitched to a lining). This
lining method is also ideal for lining pants without a waistband that have a side or center-back
invisible zipper. This method is best suited to
light- to medium-weight fabrics—pants and
skirts made in heavyweight fabrics may cause
the lining to roll to the correct side at the waistline, and this is not a good look!

16.9A SHEATH DRESS
LINING

16.9B SKIRT
LINING

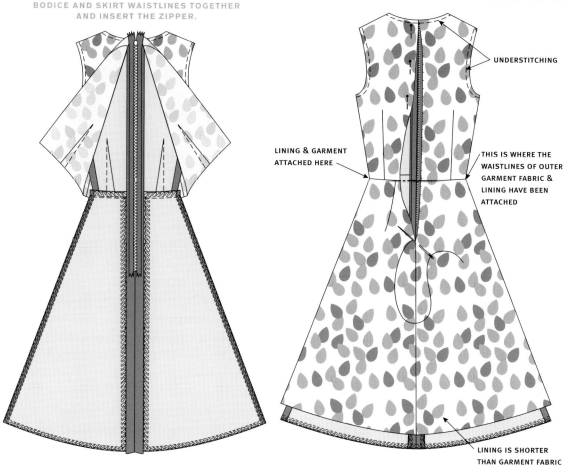

UNDERSTITCHING

LINING & GARMENT ATTACHED HERE

THIS IS WHERE THE WAISTLINES OF OUTER GARMENT FABRIC & LINING HAVE BEEN ATTACHED

LINING IS SHORTER THAN GARMENT FABRIC

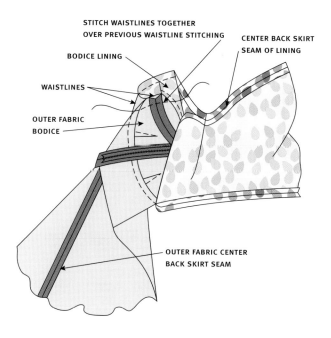

STITCH WAISTLINES TOGETHER OVER PREVIOUS WAISTLINE STITCHING

CENTER BACK SKIRT SEAM OF LINING

BODICE LINING

WAISTLINES

OUTER FABRIC BODICE

OUTER FABRIC CENTER BACK SKIRT SEAM

is no need to finish the bodice seams, as they will not be visible.

- Stitch an invisible zipper into the center back of the garment. Take time to match the waistline seams together horizontally; make sure the waistline seams are still turned up when the zipper is inserted (Figure 16.10b). Use the lightest weight available. (See the "Where to Buy" section of this book.)

- Stitch the bodice and skirt lining together around the waist and press (see Figure 16.10b).
- Fold the center back lining seam allowance to the wrong side; fold the top edge of the zipper tape (at the neckline) back in between the outer garment fabric and lining. If a soft lingerie zipper was not used, this will be difficult! Pin the lining edge to the zipper tape back ⅛ inch from the stitching; slipstitch the lining to the zipper tape (see Figure 16.10b).

- From the inside attach both garment and lining waistline seams together, at the side seams, and anchor them by machine stitching ½ inch or so on the previous seam stitching. Both seams must be facing up toward the neckline when they are stitched together; you will need to twist the seams around to do this (Figure 16.10c).

Sheath Dress

The sheath dress in Figure 16.9a is designed with a low neckline large enough to slip over the head; therefore, a side zipper is applied instead of a back zipper. Although this decision would be mainly fabric driven—cutting a center-back seam could disrupt the flow of the fabric

16.11A SHEATH DRESS WITH DARTS, SHOULDER SEAMS, AND NECKLINE STITCHED AND UNDERSTITCHED.

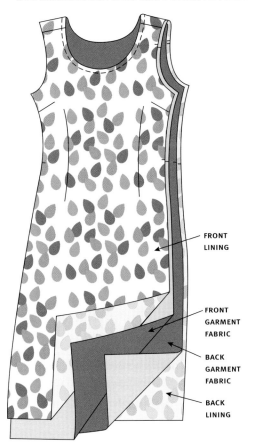

FRONT LINING

FRONT GARMENT FABRIC

BACK GARMENT FABRIC

BACK LINING

16.11B STITCHING THE ARMHOLES OF THE SHEATH DRESS

ARMHOLE SEAM

SHOULDER SEAMS

THESE TWO SIDES OF THE GARMENT ARE SANDWICHED IN BETWEEN THE OTHER SHOULDERS

PULL ON THESE TWO SHOULDERS TO TURN THE GARMENT TO THE CORRECT SIDE OF THE FABRIC

pattern—the choice of where to place the zipper is ultimately the designer's, depending on the fabric used.

- Follow the stitching order for the vest, as outlined in Figure 16.7a, b, and c, earlier. Do not stitch the armhole. Having completed these steps, Figure 16.11a illustrates how the dress should look (from the lining side).

CONTINUE WITH THIS STITCHING ORDER

- Take the left shoulder of the outer fabric and lining and wrap it around the left lining shoulder and armhole; match the shoulder seams and notches together. The correct sides of the fabric will be facing together and the right shoulder will be sandwiched in between the left side of the garment.
- Pin the armholes in place and stitch a ¼-inch armhole seam; take care not to catch the sand-

wiched shoulder seam that is in between as you stitch. Clip the curved seam ready for turning (Figure 16.11b).

- Pull the shoulders sandwiched in between out from between the other shoulder seams to the correct side. Repeat this stitching order to complete stitching of the other armhole.
- Stitch the right-hand side seam only. Refer to Figure 16.7e when stitching the side seam; clip the corner at the top edge to reduce bulk. Don't clip the underarm seam where the zipper will be inserted.
- Insert an invisible zipper in the left side seam, fold the lining seam allowance to the wrong side, and slipstitch the folded edge ⅛ inch back from the zipper stitches (Figure 16.10b).
- From the correct side, machine stitch-in-the-ditch on the side seams to secure the lining in place (see Figure 12.8). The lining could also be catchstitched to the garment side seam by hand in between the lining and outer fabric.

Open Lining with Facing (Skirts, Pants, Coats with Flared or Circular Hemlines)

An open lining with a facing is a lining that is stitched to the facing, but left open to hang freely on its own at the hem. Figures 16.12a and b illustrate a skirt and pant with a facing/lining. A center-back zipper has been inserted in the skirt, and the facing/lining is slipstitched to the zipper tape (see Figure 16.12a). The pant has a side zipper, and the facing/lining is also hand stitched to the zipper tape (see Figure 16.12b).

The goal of the facing is to finish the edge of the garment and to provide some support to the area to which it is stitched. Always check by sampling first to see if the seamline that results from joining the facing and lining together produces a visible ridge on the correct side of the garment. If a ridge does show, then choose another lining method or apply an underlining, which may help diffuse any ridges (sample first to check this out).

Pant and Skirt

The garment has stabilizing tape at the waistline (Figure 12.14b); darts and side seams have been stitched and pressed, and the zipper inserted before applying the facing. The facing is stabilized and sewn together at the side seams (Figure 16.13a). The lining seam allowances are stitched up to the notches for the zipper opening and pressed open (see Figure 16.13b). Notice the lining hem is stitched.

Figures 16.12a and b show a skirt and pant with a facing/lining stitched to the waistline. The facing may be cut from any fabric such as self-fabric, lining fabric, a contrasting color or print; however, do make sure a print or contrasting color does not shadow to the correct side.

- Staystitch the lining and clip (Figure 16.13a).
- The lining is stitched to the facing, matching center-front notches and side seams (Figure 16.13a).
- Seam allowances are pressed up and understitched (Figure 16.13b).
- The lining seam allowances are stitched up to the notches for the zipper opening and pressed open.

16.12A **BACK SKIRT LINING**

16.12B **FRONT PANTS LINING**

- With the correct sides together, pin the facing/lining to the garment at the waistline.
- Stitch; clip, trim, or grade the seam as necessary, and press.
- Understitch the garment seam allowances to the facing; press.
- Turn the facing to the inside of the garment; slipstitch the facing/lining to the zipper tape (see Figure 16.12a).
- From inside the garment handstitch the facing to the darts and seams to hold it in place.

Flared Jacket or Coat

It is always best to have an open lining on any garments that have wide flared or circular hemlines; this is usually the only time a jacket/coat lining is left open at the hem. When this is the case, the garment and lining hems are stitched separately, and the lining hem is left to float free while the garment hem is hand stitched to the garment. If the garment is circular, some of the fullness can be folded out of the lining pattern to reduce the bulk that the lining hem width may cause. When

16.13A STITCHING THE FACING TO THE LINING

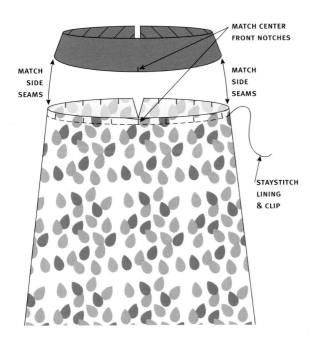

MATCH CENTER
FRONT NOTCHES

MATCH
SIDE
SEAMS

MATCH
SIDE
SEAMS

STAYSTITCH
LINING
& CLIP

Closed Lining with Facing

Jackets and Coats

Jackets and coats usually have a closed lining with a facing. In a closed lining, the lining hem is stitched to the garment hemline, as illustrated in Figure 16.3b. Notice the pleat, which is incorporated in the length of the lining for ease (see Figure 16.4). Refer to "General Pattern Tips," earlier in this chapter, for more information.

Lining a jacket may seem like a challenging

16.13B STITCHING THE FACING TO THE LINING

SEAM
ALLOWANCE
PRESSED
UP

FACING

MACHINE STITCHED HEM

PATTERN TIP

- The jacket or coat lining is always made from the original pattern, as illustrated in Figure 16.2.
- A jacket lining needs a pleat added beyond the center back for ease of movement. The pleat is measured 1 inch out beyond the center back and cut on the fold in a jacket (Figure 16.2b). For a coat, reduce bulk with a center-back seam (see Figure 16.5).
- A pleat is also incorporated into the overall length of the garment and sleeve lining patterns. This is done by adding an inch to the finished length of the lining. The pleat is added to both the garment and sleeve hems for ease of movement (see Figure 16.2).
- The finished lining hemline should sit midway on the hem allowance (with the pleat included). All the sketches of linings in this chapter illustrate this clearly.
- It is important that the hem widths of the lining and garment patterns have the identical measurements, because the two are joined together and must be equal. If the lining is cut wider than the garment, then the lining will be bunched and bulky; if it is tighter, it will pull the garment out of alignment. Either way, it could spoil the final look of the jacket or coat (see Figure 16.2).

the lining is open, make sure the seams and hem have been finished. The lining hem is stitched first before the lining is inserted into the garment. Refer to Chapter 15, Figure 15.10, for details on how to stitch curved hems. Notice in Figure 16.3a that the finished lining hem sits halfway on the garment hem allowance. The exact position where the hem edge of the lining joins to the facing is where the facing is clipped into the seam allowance for ½ inch. The clip is illustrated on the right side of the coat in Figure 16.5. Look ahead to see how to stitch the facing to the jacket or coat edge, as shown in Figure 16.15, and how to stitch the lining to the facing as shown in Figure 16.17.

stitching project—and it is. However, it is not as hard as it looks. To stitch a successful jacket, the lining pattern *must* be correct; otherwise, the lining cannot be inserted correctly nor will it sit correctly within the jacket or coat.

The jacket or coat is completely stitched

16.14A STITCH THE BACK PLEAT IN
THE JACKET LINING.

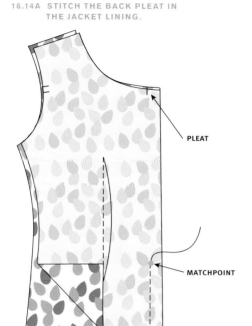

PLEAT

MATCHPOINT

16.14B STAYSTITCH THE BACK NECK.

PRESS
THE
PLEAT

before the lining is inserted. Figures 16.4 and 16.5 clearly illustrate the stitching that must be completed before sewing the lining to the jacket or the coat. It is also possible to stitch the lining to the facing first and then stitch the facing to the garment edges. Both stitching methods are valid.

Have the entire coat stitched, clipped, and pressed, ready to insert the lining (see Figure 16.4).

- Fully stitch the lining; begin by stitching the back pleat on the jacket, as illustrated in Figure 16.14a. The coat pleat is stitched with a center-back seam to reduce bulk, and this is illustrated

in Figure 16.4. Stitch and press all the seams and insert the sleeves.

- Press the pleat in place from the correct side of the lining; the folded edge is turned to the right as you look at the pleat (Figure 16.14b). Staystitch the front and back necklines; the back staystitching will hold the pleat in place. Figure 16.4 illustrates the staystitching around the front and back necklines with the seam allowance clipped; the lining is now ready to insert into the coat.

- Press ½-inch seam allowances to the wrong side of the sleeve and lining hem edges (see Figure 16.4).

- At this juncture, if the jacket has a collar this is

the time in the stitching order to stitch the collar to the neckline.

- Stitch the entire facing to the garment neckline, down the front and across the facing for the width of hem allowance (Figure 16.15a); stop stitching ½ inch back from the facing edge, leaving the ½-inch seam allowance free—*if this is not done, the lining cannot be successfully inserted!* When stitching the facing, make sure the shoulder seams and notches are matching together.

- Reduce bulk on the hem allowance and grade the facing/garment seam, if bulky (Figure 16.15b).

- Turn the garment back to the correct side so the facing is sitting behind the front and back jacket; sharpen the front corners with a point turner.

- Press the facing in place. Sometimes, if a heavy-weight fabric is very bulky, excellent pressing is not enough to keep the facing from rolling to the front of the garment. If this is the case, the facing can be understitched by hand using a catchstitch (Figure 16.15b).

- Clip ½ inch into the facing, which is the full width of the seam allowance. The position of the clip is ½ inch below the finished hem edge, as illustrated on the coat in Figure 16.16.

NOTE

Another alternative is to turn the facing back about an inch from the facing/lining seam and lightly slipstitch or catchstitch the facing to the garment; make sure the stitches aren't visible from the correct side of the garment.

16.15A JACKET OR COAT: STITCH THE FACING AROUND THE EDGE, INCLUDING THE HEM.

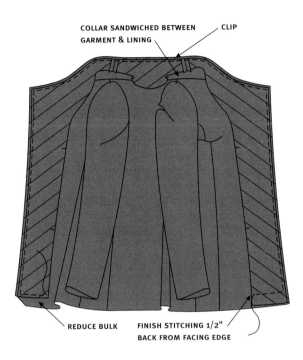

COLLAR SANDWICHED BETWEEN GARMENT & LINING

CLIP

REDUCE BULK

FINISH STITCHING 1/2" BACK FROM FACING EDGE

• Turn the seam allowance on the facing (below the clip) under the facing to the wrong side and invisibly slipstitch it to the hem. Refer to the fully stitched coat on the left side in Figure 16.4 to see how this looks.

• Complete stitching the jacket/coat hem by hand stitching a hidden slipstitch or catchstitch (see Figure 16.16).

• Insert the shoulder pads and the sleeve head, and stitch in place (see Figure 16.16). Refer to Chapter 14, "Sleeve Heads" and "Shoulder Pads" for additional information.

• Place the correct sides of the lining and facing edges together. Pin the center-back pleat to the center-back lining, shoulder seams and notches together, and then pin in between these points. Stitch directional beginning from the center-back seams and continuing around the back and down the front; end with a backstitch at the previously clipped point on the facing (Figure 16.17). Press the seam allowance in toward the garment.

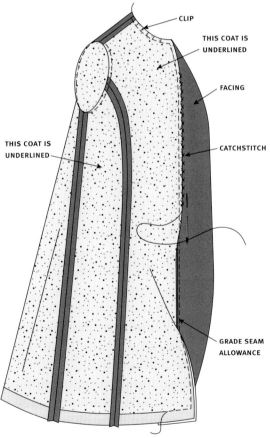

CLIP

THIS COAT IS UNDERLINED

FACING

CATCHSTITCH

THIS COAT IS UNDERLINED

GRADE SEAM ALLOWANCE

16.15B USING THE CATCHSTITCH AS AN UNDERSTITCH

16.16 HAND STITCH THE GARMENT HEM AND CLIP THE FACING.

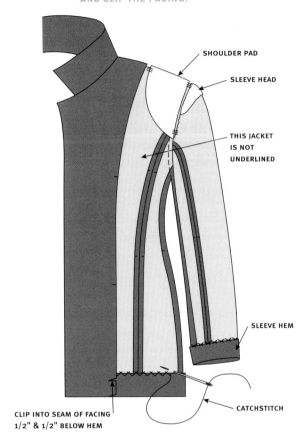

SHOULDER PAD

SLEEVE HEAD

THIS JACKET IS NOT UNDERLINED

SLEEVE HEM

CATCHSTITCH

CLIP INTO SEAM OF FACING 1/2" & 1/2" BELOW HEM

• Hand catch the shoulder seams of the garment and lining together; the shoulder pad will be in between, so stitch through all layers (Figure 16.18).

• Machine stitch the garment and lining underarm seams together (machine stitching is stronger at this point than hand stitching). To do this, follow the illustration in Figure 16.10c. Although the instructions explain how to stitch the waistline

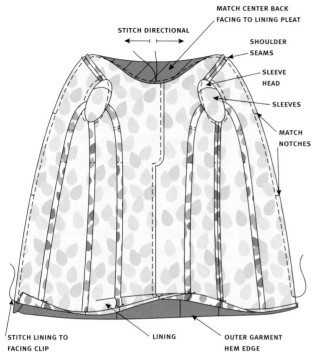

16.17 STITCH THE LINING TO THE FACING.

STITCH DIRECTIONAL

MATCH CENTER BACK
FACING TO LINING PLEAT

SHOULDER
SEAMS

SLEEVE
HEAD

SLEEVES

MATCH
NOTCHES

STITCH LINING TO
FACING CLIP

LINING

OUTER GARMENT
HEM EDGE

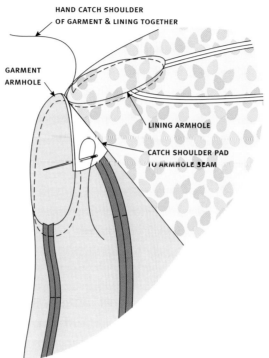

16.18 HAND CATCH THE SHOULDER SEAMS TOGETHER.

HAND CATCH SHOULDER
OF GARMENT & LINING TOGETHER

GARMENT
ARMHOLE

LINING ARMHOLE

CATCH SHOULDER PAD
TO ARMHOLE SEAM

16.19 SLIPSTITCH THE LINING HEM TO
THE GARMENT HEM.

AFTER LINING IS
HANDSTITCHED
TO HEM PRESS
LINING DOWN
TOWARD HEM

LINING
CREASELINE

PLEAT

TURN PLEAT DOWN
& HANDSTITCH TO FACING

seams together, the same method is used to stitch the underarm seams together.

- Also handstitch the garment and lining shoulder seams together (Figure 16.18).
- To close the lining, pin the lining crease line ½ inch over the garment hem edge. When this is done you will be left with an excess length of lining; this excess will become the pleat. Hand stitch the lining to the garment hem using a slipstitch. This is illustrated on the left side of the jacket in Figure 16.19.
- Turn the lining down toward the hem edge to form a pleat, and invisibly slipstitch the pleat to

the facing/lining above the hem as illustrated on the right hand of the jacket in Figure 16.19.

- Press the entire garment and sleeve pleats in the hem of the lining with a crease line.

Open Lining with Waistband

Pants and Skirts

An open lining with a waistband is ideal for skirts and pants with a waistband, as it leaves the lining to hang freely so it will never pull the garment out of alignment. Figures 16.20a, b, and c give an inside view of how the lining is stitched to the waistband of a pant and skirt.

The method of stitching the lining is the same regardless of whether the waistband is contoured or straight.

- Fully stitch the outer fabric for the skirt or pants—stitch darts and side seams, and insert the center-back or fly-front zipper. Press all seams.
- Fully stitch the lining—darts, side seams, center-back seam up to the notch that marks the end of the zipper length—and machine stitch the hem. Press all seams.

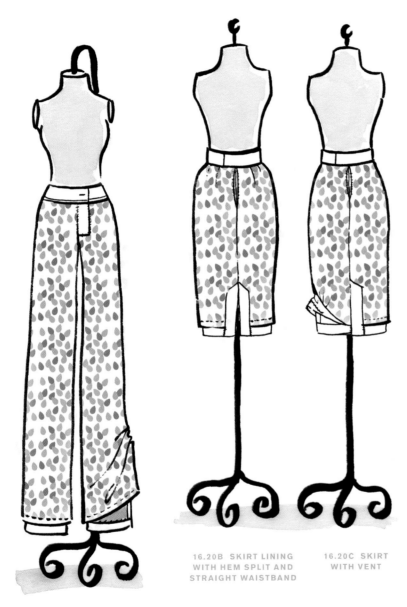

16.20A **PANTS LINING WITH FLY-FRONT AND CONTOURED WAISTBAND**

16.20B **SKIRT LINING WITH HEM SPLIT AND STRAIGHT WAISTBAND**

16.20C **SKIRT WITH VENT**

- The lining is now ready to be inserted into the skirt or pants. This is done before the waistline is completed.
- Machine or handbaste the lining to the garment at the waistline seam allowance with the wrong sides together (Figure 16.21).
- Continue with the construction of the waistband; refer to Chapter 9 for further details.
- Hand stitch the garment hem, and machine stitch the lining hem. Refer to Chapter 15 for further details.

Pants with Fly-Front

In production on the lining pattern for the fly-front pants is adjusted to stitch the lining to the fly front facing; use a ½-inch seam allowance for easy sewing around the curved facing seam and to reduce bulk. Stitch the pants; then:

- Cut both lining fronts the same, eliminating the fly-front facing so the lining will be cut on center front with a ½-inch seam allowance. Notch the zipper opening.
- The section of the front lining that needs to be cut away so the lining can be stitched around the facing is illustrated in Figure 16.21. To avoid cutting away the wrong side, after stitching the lining together (leave the front seam open for the zipper length), place the lining inside the pants. With the wrong sides facing, pin the waistlines, matching center backs, notches, and side seams together.

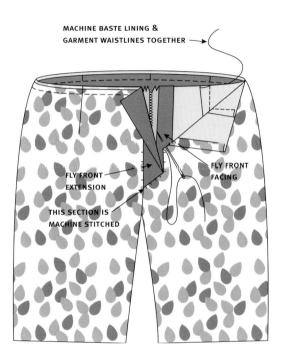

MACHINE BASTE LINING &
GARMENT WAISTLINES TOGETHER

FLY FRONT
EXTENSION

FLY FRONT
FACING

THIS SECTION IS
MACHINE STITCHED

- Cut away the fly facing on the right-hand side of the garment (leave a ½ inch seam allowance, looking at the sketch) in Figure 16.21. If your fly-front is stitched left over right, it will look opposite to this sketch.
- Machine baste the lining to the waistline of the pants.
- From the inside, machine the bottom of the fly front extension to the lining.
- Slipstitch the lining to the center front on the left side, which is the seamline for the fly-front extension.
- On the right-hand side turn the ½-inch seam allowance to the wrong side of the lining

and pin the folded edge to the facing (not the extension). Slipstitch the lining to the front facing as illustrated on the right side of the pants in Figure 16.21.

Skirt with Hem Slit

Figure 16.20b illustrates a skirt with a waistband with a center-back slit in the skirt. Notice the straight silhouette of the skirt. The slit has been stitched up from the hem of the skirt to enable the customer to walk. This is functional design. The skirt in Figure 16.12a has an A-line silhouette; notice there is no slit, as there is adequate width in the skirt to walk with ease.

> **PATTERN TIP**
>
> It is important for a skirt with a hem slit or vent to have an extra ¼ inch of length added to the center-back seam of the lining pattern for ease (Figure 16.22a). This will prevent the lining from being too tight from the end of the zipper to the top of the slit. This extra length ensures the back seam will lie flat when the garment is worn. Add all notches to help achieve a smooth stitching process.

Fully stitch the outer skirt: stitch darts, apply interfacing to the back facing, stitch the zipper, and stitch the back seam to the matchpoints, which are ½ inch back from the seam edge. Stitch the outer skirt side seams, and hand stitch the garment hem as illustrated in Figure 16.22b. Notice the hem has been clipped and stitched at the back in exactly the same way it was done for the jacket facing in Figures 16.5 and 16.16.

> **IMPORTANT**
>
> Marking the matchpoints is important, as the lining will be stitched from this point around the facing.

- Stitch the lining shell as illustrated in Figure 16.22c. Notice the lining hem has also been machine stitched.
- Staystitch the cut-out corner of the lining ¹⁄₁₆ inch inside the seam allowance, and clip into the corners (see Figure 16.22c).
- Turn the garment and lining to the wrong sides. The next section must be stitched in two steps—the right side, then the left side. Otherwise, it will be impossible to stitch this section!
- Turn the lining around so the correct side of the cut-out section and skirt facing are placed together. Place the lining matchpoint directly to the center-back seam matchpoint of the skirt, and pin together. Begin stitching at this point. Stitch across the top of the facing, as illustrated in Figure 16.22d, pivot at the corner, and continue down the side of the facing to the clipped position on the facing.
- Repeat this stitching process for the other side.
- Turn the lining to the correct side and machine baste the waistlines together, ready for stitching the band to the waistline. Figure 16.21 illustrates the waistlines machine basted together.
- Hand stitch the skirt lining around the zipper tape (see Figure 16.20b).
- At the hem, below the clip, turn under the ½-inch seam allowance and stitch.

16.22A ADD EASE INTO THE CENTER-
BACK SKIRT PATTERN.

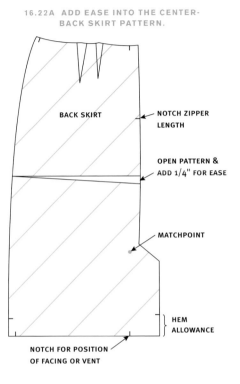

16.22A ADD EASE INTO THE CENTER-
BACK SKIRT PATTERN.

BACK SKIRT

NOTCH ZIPPER
LENGTH

OPEN PATTERN &
ADD 1/4" FOR EASE

MATCHPOINT

HEM
ALLOWANCE

NOTCH FOR POSITION
OF FACING OR VENT

16.22B STITCH THE OUTER GARMENT
PIECES TOGETHER

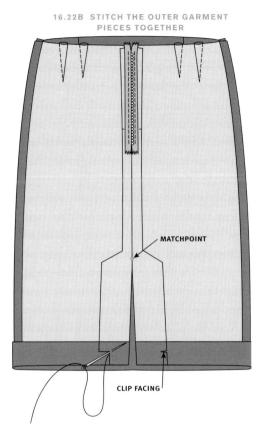

MATCHPOINT

CLIP FACING

16.22C STITCH THE LINING

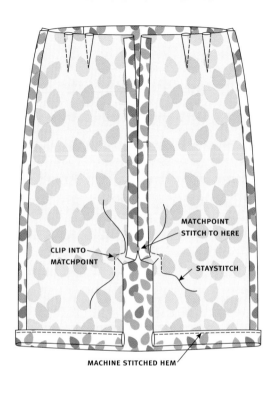

MATCHPOINT
STITCH TO HERE

CLIP INTO
MATCHPOINT

STAYSTITCH

MACHINE STITCHED HEM

Skirt with Vent

Figure 16.20c shows a back view of the lining stitched to a vent. Any style of skirt, pant, or dress can have a vent (or slit) inserted in the seamline up from the hem. Notice the lining is stitched around the vent to the vent facings; the lining pattern needs to be altered to accommodate this, as previously discussed. Also see Figure 16.22a.

Complete the stitching for the skirt and lining in Figures 16.22e and f.

• Stitch the vent facing and extension together

from the matchpoint to the extension folded edge (Figure 16.22f).

• Stitch the right-hand side (looking at the sketch) of the lining to the slit (or vent facing) (see Figure 16.22d). Now the left-hand side of the lining needs to be stitched to the left side of the facing (see Figure 16.22g).

• Place the correct sides of the lining and facing together.

• Pin the matchpoints together; begin stitching from this point down to the hem and press to complete the stitching order.

• At the hem, below the clip, turn under ½ inch seam allowance and handstitch to hem (Figures 16.22f and g).

Closed Lining to Control the Garment Silhouette

Usually a lining is stitched to the garment following the garment shape so it doesn't pull the garment out of alignment. The method of stitching the closed lining to control the garment silhouette is an exception to this "lining rule." When the lining controls the garment silhouette, it is meant

16.22D STITCH THE LINING TO THE SKIRT FACING.

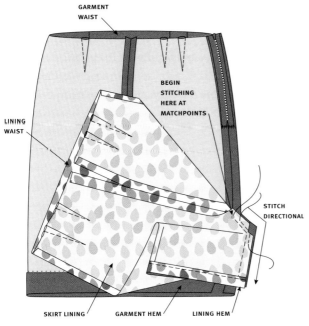

GARMENT WAIST

BEGIN STITCHING HERE AT MATCHPOINTS

LINING WAIST

STITCH DIRECTIONAL

SKIRT LINING   GARMENT HEM   LINING HEM

16.22E STITCH THE LINING AND OUTER GARMENT PIECES TOGETHER: SKIRT WITH VENT–LINING.

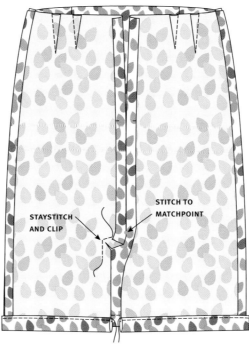

STAYSTITCH AND CLIP

STITCH TO MATCHPOINT

16.22F OUTER FABRIC

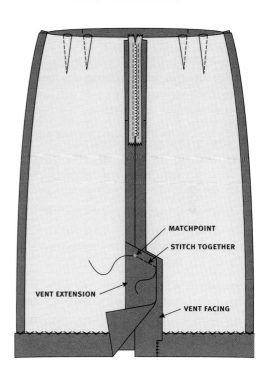

MATCHPOINT

STITCH TOGETHER

VENT EXTENSION

VENT FACING

16.22G STITCH THE LINING TO THE CENTER-BACK SEAM OF THE SKIRT.

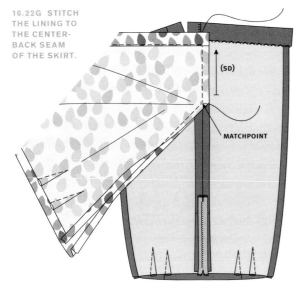

(SD)

MATCHPOINT

to secure the garment shape and hold it in place. This method of lining can be applied to a skirt, dress, jacket, sleeve, collar, or any other garment part—there are no rules here. The skirt in the Style I.D. in Figure 16.1b illustrates a balloon skirt with the lining controlling the silhouette.

Look ahead to Figure 16.28b for another example.

Balloon Hem
The final look is dependent on the fabric weight and drape. For example, if you stitch a balloon hem in lightweight linen, it will create an entirely different look than such a hem in lightweight silk georgette because of the stiffness and the fabric weight. Fit a muslin in a similar fabric as the outer garment first, so the exact ratio of fullness to lining can be established.

This style of skirt looks far more attractive without a back seam. A back seam would only disrupt the flow of the beautiful hemline. Instead, insert a zipper on the side seam.

PATTERN TIP

To achieve this look, the lining is cut smaller, narrower, and shorter to control the outer garment silhouette, as illustrated in Figure 16.23a. Once they are joined together, the lining holds the hem edge underneath to the wrong side and forces the outer fabric to pouf out. A shorter, narrower lining can also be stitched to a longer, fuller sleeve; the pattern for this variation is illustrated in Figure 16.23b.

16.23A CUT THE LINING SMALLER, SHORTER, AND NARROWER THAN THE OUTER SKIRT FABRIC.

OUTER SLEEVE FABRIC

16.23B OUTER SLEEVE FABRIC

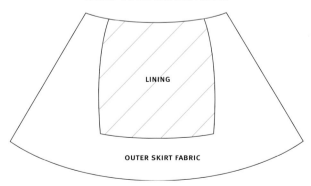

LINING

OUTER SKIRT FABRIC

* Stitch an invisible zipper in the side seam.
* Join the side seams of the garment together, and gather the waist and hem edges (Figure 16.24a).
* Join the lining side seams together; on the zipper side of the lining, leave the zipper length open so it can be hand stitched to the zipper tape at the end. Press all the seams open. Now both the lining and garment fabrics should be in-the-round (Figure 16.24a and b).
* Place the correct sides of the garment and lining hem edges together. Stitch a ½-inch seam in-the-round around the hem edge (Figure 16.24c); trim back to ¼ inch to reduce bulk. Turn the seam allowance up toward the lining and understitch (Figure 16.24c).
* Handbaste both the garment and lining waistlines together, ready to stitch the waistband; match the garment and lining side seams perfectly together, as this is part of aligning any garment.
* Refer to Chapter 9 for instructions on stitching the waistband.
* The lining is then slipstitched to the zipper tape, as illustrated in Figure 16.10b.

Sleeves

* On the sleeves, stitch clear ¼-inch elastic in the seam allowance around the sleeve seam-line so it clings to the arm when the garment is worn.
* Wrap the elastic around the arm so it fits snugly. Don't add any extra length.
* Stretch the elastic as you stitch it into the seam allowance, using a three-stitch zigzag stitch. (Refer to Chapter 6 and Figure 6.32.)

PARTIAL LINING

The decision to partially line a garment depends on the style and weight of the fabric. A partial lining keeps the garment lightweight, still covers the construction details of the lined area of the garment, and helps to keep specific areas of the garment, such as at the knees of pants, from stretching out. Any garment can be partially lined—skirts with pleats, jacket, pants, or a dress.

One example of a garment that is suitable for partial lining is a pleated skirt, illustrated in Figure 16.1c. Figure 16.25a is the same skirt from the inside, showing the partial lining. From the outside of the garment you would never know it was partially lined! Pants can also be stitched with a partial lining down to shorts level as illustrated in Figure 16.25b. The reason for the partial lining in pants will be explained further on in the text.

Stitching a partial lining is not necessarily less work than stitching a full lining, as you can see from the coat in Figures 16.25c and d. Every seam in this coat has been finished with a Hong Kong finish. A coat such as this can be an artistic creation by using contrasting or complemen-

NOTE

Clear elastic can need to be stitched in the same way to a balloon hemline if the garment is made from knit fabric. The clear elastic stabilizes the hemline and prevents it from stretching.

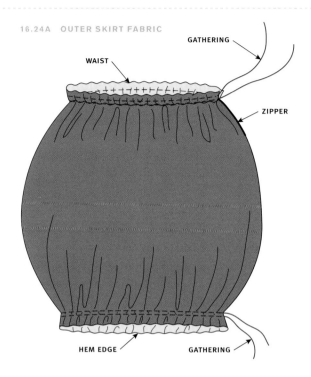

16.24A OUTER SKIRT FABRIC

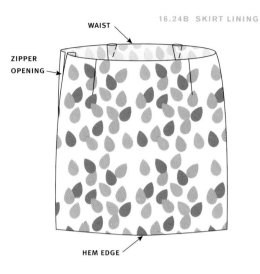

16.24B SKIRT LINING

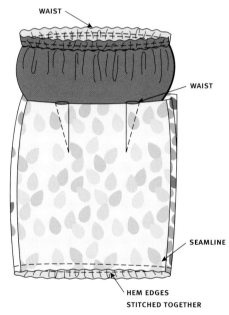

16.24C STITCH THE HEM EDGES TOGETHER.

when the garment is worn. Regardless of this, it is still classified as an open partial lining.

Jacket/Coat

A partial lining is often used in place of a full lining in lightweight jackets that need to "breathe" but still should slip on and off easily. The areas of the jacket that are partially lined are an extended front facing and the back shoulder area (which covers the entire upper back of the garment and is also stitched into the armhole seam). The edges of the facings and the armhole seam are finished with a Hong Kong finish. Occasionally, the sleeves are also lined. Figures 16.25c and d show how a partial lining looks on the inside of a coat on the front and back.

After the partial lining is stitched to the jacket/coat, the back lining is left open. The front facing can be handstitched or machine stitched (in-the-ditch of the Hong Kong finish) to the garment seamline approximately every 5 inches. Notice in Figure 16.25d that these stitches are indicated using a heavier short line. If there is no front seamline, then turn back the facing and lightly catchstitch the facing to the garment; check the face of the garment, as these stitches must not be visible!

Pleated Skirt

A partial lining in a pleated skirt is sometimes called a stay because it helps to stabilize the areas of the pleats that have been trimmed to reduce bulk while also covering the seams. It ends just below the zipper area or approximately at the hips. If darts are hidden in the pleats, they are

tary colors for the lining and the bias binding. The inside of the coat is as beautiful as the outside—the coat looks good enough to be worn inside out!

The garment is constructed and the area of partial lining determined. The lining pieces are plotted from the garment pattern, and assembled. The lower edges of the partial lining pieces are finished. With some fabrics, a Hong Kong finish or serging may show on the front of the garment, causing a ridge when pressed, so be sure to sample the finish first.

Open Partial Lining

An open partial lining is a partial lining that is left open around the lining edges rather than being stitched to the garment to close the lining. If the

partial lining has a facing, as in the coat in Figure 16.25d, the facing needs to be secured every so often to the garment to prevent it from flapping

transferred to the lining and stitched. Secure the partial lining by handstitching it at the side seams. The partial lining allows the skirt pleats to flip open when walking without being restricted by a lining (see Figure 16.25a).

Pant

A partial lining in pants is used to prevent "bagging out" in the knee or seat area of the pants. The pants pattern is used to draft the lining pieces, but their length can range from shorts length to approximately 5 inches below the knee. A partial lining in warm-weather clothing makes the garment more breathable and prevents shadowing through to the front undergarments. A neutral, skin-toned lining can be a good option, as it will not shadow from the face of the fabric.

Dress

A partial lining can also be a good option when a difference in sheerness and opaqueness is wanted in the design. Look ahead at Figure 16.28c.

Closed Partial Lining

Garment Parts

A closed partial lining can be used on one side of a garment section instead of two layers of the outer fabric. Examples of garment parts where this

lining method could be used are pockets, pocket flaps, collars, flounce, peplum, or waistband. When two pieces of fabric are stitched together to form a pocket, pocket flap, waistband, or collar, the garment part can look bulky because of the fabric weight used. Even though the seam may be clipped and graded, the section can look bulky after stitching, and this detracts from the beauty of the garment. To reduce bulk, a lighter-weight fabric such as a lining can be stitched to the underside of the garment piece. There are other reasons for stitching a lining to garment parts, among them: a lining stitched to pockets reinforces the pocket and adds interest with a contrasting color lining under pocket flaps; a lining in collars pro-

vides a design detail; lining flounces provides a clean finish rather than a rolled edge.

The lower edges of the partial lining pieces are stitched, graded, clipped, and understitched; most important, the ridge of the seam *must* not show on the front of the garment.

Pockets

Pockets have been extensively covered in Chapter 5. The goal of any pocket applied to the surface of a garment is to be as flat as possible (as well as durable, if it is a functional pocket). For comprehensive details refer to Chapter 5.

Underside of Pocket Flaps

- Use the lightest-weight, all-bias fusible interfacing (or sew-in) for the flaps, regardless of the

16.25A PLEATED SKIRT WITH PARTIAL YOKE LINING

16.25B PANTS WITH PARTIAL LINING

16.25C COAT BACK WITH PARTIAL LINING

16.25D COAT FRONT WITH PARTIAL LINING

type of interfacing being used on the rest of the garment.

- Cut the lining layer with the lengthwise grain going across the flap.
- When stitching, keep the edges aligned even though the under flap is slightly smaller. Stitch with the lining layer on top; handbaste before stitching, if necessary.
- Clip, trim, and grade the seam before turning; press.
- Topstitch the flap if desired, before continuing with construction of the garment.

Collars

When constructing coats and jackets, the under collar is often cut from a different fabric such as the lining fabric to reduce bulk. The under collar can be cut from a contrasting fabric as a design detail, with the ultimate goal of achieving a bulk-free collar. The under collars for tailored men's jackets and coats are made from wool felt, which can be purchased precut in several basic colors. For extensive stitching information on collars, refer to Chapter 11.

Inside Hoods

Lining the hood of any garment should also reflect the functional aspect of the hood—lining for warmth, such as a hooded wool jacket; for luxury, such as the hood of an evening cape; or to cover the wrong side of the fabric.

When preparing to line a hooded garment, the lining and garment hoods are constructed separately, and both are pressed. The two hoods are then stitched together along the outer edges, and understitched to keep the lining from rolling to the front of the hooded garment. Sample this first; the understitching will show when the hood flips over on the back of the garment, and this may not look very nice. If you delete the understitching, make sure the seamline is well-pressed. If the hood has a center-back seam, lightly slipstitch the lining to the outer hood seamline from inside the hood.

Some design tips for you:

- Garments such as a duffle coat, traditionally made from wool, have hoods lined with plaid flannel for warmth and softness.
- Lining an elegant evening cape made of velvet or wool with a luxurious fabric such as silk charmeuse allows the cape to drape easily over the garments worn underneath.
- A functional hood in a garment such as an active-wear fleece garment has the hem of the hood turned back and topstitched as a casing for the drawstring. Stabilize and stitch the button-

hole openings for the drawstring before turning back the casing (Figure 9.12b). Line the hood with a wind-resistant lining (such as microfiber) designed for active wear, and plot the lining pattern piece without the turned-back hem/casing allowance.

Peplum

A peplum is a separate, shaped section below the waistline that is joined to the bodice with a seam (see Figure 16.26a). In many respects, a peplum is a lot like a collar, only joined at the waist rather than the neckline. The peplum is a style that comes and goes in fashion, and the shape and design of this detail present opportunity for creative pleating, tucking, gathering, and more. The peplum can be lined with self-fabric if the fabric is the appropriate weight, or a contrasting lining fabric can be used—remember, the choice of lining is always a fabric-driven decision.

PATTERN TIP

Cut the outer fabric hood slightly larger than the hood lining; this is the same pattern principle outlined previously. This ensures that the lining fits comfortably inside the outer fabric hood and does not hang over the seam edge. When two pieces of fabric are placed together and rolled over, the under side needs to be cut slightly smaller so it fits comfortably inside the outer shape after they are stitched together.

The jacket and lining are both stitched separately, and the two are joined together before stitching the peplum to the waistline seam.

- Stitch the peplum seams; press. Stitch the lining seams; press (Figure 16.26b).
- Staystitch both lining and outer fabric peplums separately around the waistline to prevent the upper edge from stretching while being stitched to the jacket (Figure 16.26b).
- Place the correct sides of the peplum and lining together; pin and stitch the outer edges. Clip and trim the seam allowance (Figure 16.26b). Under-

16.26A JACKET WITH A PEPLUM AND A FLOUNCE

PEPLUM

FLOUNCE

16.26B STAYSTITCHING

STAYSTITCHING

CLIP

16.26C UNDERSTITCHING

HANDBASTE

UNDERSTITCHING

16.26D SLIPSTITCHING

BACK LINING PLEAT

SLIPSTITCH

▲▼▲▼ **PATTERN TIP**

Make upper and under peplum patterns following the same pattern principle as for the upper and under collar patterns in Chapter 11; refer to Figure 11.4.

stitch the seam allowances to the peplum lining and press (Figure 16.26c).

- Turn the peplum to the correct side and press and handbaste waistlines together (Figure 16.22c). Pin the peplum to the jacket, lining up the notches and the side seams together—keep the jacket lining free, and machine stitch the waistlines together (Figure 16.26d).
- Clip and trim the seam allowance. Press the seam allowances up into the garment (see Figure 16.26d).
- Slipstitch the pressed lining edge over the peplum at the waistline seam (see Figure 16.26d).

Flounce

The jacket in Figure 16.26a has a lined flounce, which adds quality to the garment. Attend to the pattern by preparing upper and under flounce patterns. The *upper flounce pattern* needs to be cut ¹⁄₁₆ inch narrower than the upper flounce pattern; this ensures that when stitched, clipped, turned, and pressed, the seamline will roll slightly to the under flounce and not be visible from the correct side of the fabric.

- Handbaste the inner flounce circles together.
- Stitch to the wrist using ¼-inch seam allowance.

- The sleeve lining is slipstitched to the wrist seamline as shown in Figure 16.26d.

Waistband

A shaped or a two-piece waistband is often lined on the back side of the band to reduce bulk. A lined waistband also adds comfort if the fabric is scratchy, such as wool or beaded fabric, or if fabric is in short supply. The under waistband can be lined with lining fabric and the edge finished with a Hong Kong finish to further reduce bulk, as shown in Figure 9.7c. Refer to the construction of the waistband in Chapter 9.

FINAL PRESSING OF LINED GARMENTS

If you have been following the stitching method of *SEW, CLIP, PRESS* all along, minimal pressing will need to be done at the end of the garment construction. If you have not, the pressing will be much more difficult, and impossible to do in certain areas of the garment without taking it apart.

Even with our many years of experience of sewing and pressing, we take the final coat or jacket to our dry cleaners and have them give it a good press. For a nominal cost, the final garment has a well-set shape that is retained over many times of wear.

LINING TRICKY FABRICS
Sheer Fabric

Do choose a lining for sheers carefully, as the color of the lining will shadow and may be visible from the correct side of the fabric. Choose a lining for its weight and fabric surface; a shiny or mat surface will be evident through the sheerness.

Do consider using two layers of self-fabric as the lining; this ensures the lining will be the perfect color match to the garment.

Do consider cutting the lining a different length to add contrast to the garment. The skirt in Figure 16.28c illustrates how this looks in design. Several different lengths of linings in contrasting tones can be used under a sheer skirt.

Lace

Do preview different linings under lace, as the lining will show through and have an impact on the final look of the lace. For example, silk charmeuse will give the lace a shiny, opaque look, whereas silk georgette will provide a dull, sheer look to the lace.

Do use a quality lining for lace, as it will be visible from the correct side.

Satin

Do match the lining weights together; use a heavier-weight lining for heavyweight satin and a lightweight lining for lightweight satin.

Do consider using silk satin charmeuse as the outer fabric and the lining, as the weights combine well together and the lining will feel luxurious next to the skin.

Beaded Fabric

Do use one of the beautiful silk linings available; silk satin charmeuse gives a fabulous soft, silky feel next to the skin.

Do use a quality silk lining in a quality beaded fabric that will last a lifetime.

Don't use heavy, bulky linings in a beaded garment.

Knits

Do make sure you use a stretch lining in knit garments.

Do look at the variety of knit linings that can be found on the Internet; some lovely, soft knit linings are available in a variety of colors. Refer to the "Where to Buy" section of this book.

Do consider using a lingerie knit fabric as a lining, as it feels soft and luxurious next to the skin.

Don't use a woven lining that lacks a stretch element, as this will restrict the garment fabric from stretching.

Do stitch clear elastic to a balloon hemline to stabilize the hemline and prevent it from stretching. Refer to Chapter 6, "Stretch Seams."

Denim

Do think carefully about stitching a full lining into a denim garment; denim rarely needs to be lined.

Do consider using 100 percent cotton for a partial lining in denim garments.

Do line garment parts such as pockets and

pocket flaps with an edge-to-edge closed lining to reduce bulk, especially in heavyweight denim.

Velvet

Do consider using silk satin charmeuse as a lining in velvet. A luxurious fabric needs a luxurious lining.

Leather

Do realize that leather garments need a lining because:
- People may not like the feel of animal skins against their bodies.
- Lining conceals imperfections in the leather.
- Lining prevents the leather from stretching.
- Lining hides the inside construction.
- Lining prevents "crocking" (color rubbing off onto other surfaces and marking them).

Do choose a *quality lining* made from strong fibers; leather has a long life and often outlasts the lining. China silk, for example, is a rather fragile lining so it's not suitable to line leather.

Do edgestitch the hem of the leather garment and then hand stitch the lining into the edgestitching.

Don't hand stitch the pleat to the facing of a jacket or coat, as suggested in Figure 16.19, because this is difficult to do on leather. An alternative stitching method is to ease stitch the lining 3 or 4 inches up from the hem edge, pull the stitches into easing, and then machine stitch the lining to the facing. The pleat is still there, but stitched using a more appropriate method for leather.

Faux Fur

Do stitch fur lining into jackets and coats, as it is cozy and warm and a great choice for garments worn in cold climates. Fur will be too bulky for buttons and buttonholes, so add a front facing in an alternative fabric (Figure 16.27). Fur could be stitched as the sleeve lining; however, a sleeve lining could also be made from smooth, silky fabric. This will ensure that the jacket or coat slips on and off with ease.

Heavyweight Fabric

Do consider the weight of the lining for the purpose of the garment.

Do consider the weight of the final garment when considering what type of lining to use; fur, fleece, and wool linings all add weight to the garment.

Do use a good-quality lining for long-lasting wear; silk fibers last longer than synthetic fibers.

TRANSFER YOUR KNOWLEDGE

Any garment can be lined using the same pattern and stitching principles outlined in this chapter.

- Transfer your knowledge of how upper and under collar patterns are made. This concept can be transferred into any garment part that is going to be lined.
- Transfer your knowledge of stitching a partial lining to any other garment part.

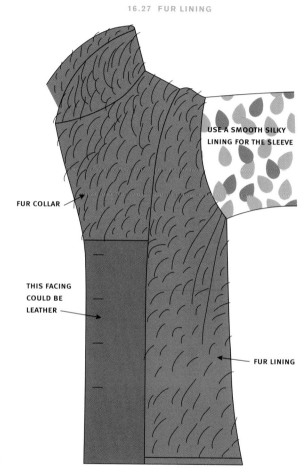

16.27 FUR LINING

USE A SMOOTH SILKY LINING FOR THE SLEEVE

FUR COLLAR

THIS FACING COULD BE LEATHER

FUR LINING

Place two fabric pieces together and stitch, clip, grade, understitch, turn, and press; use a point turner to sharpen any corners.
- Insert a very narrow bias piping (without cording) between the lining and the garment edge it is being joined to—it provides a lovely detail.

STRETCH YOUR CREATIVITY

Here are some ideas to add extra "pizzazz" to the inside of the garment!

- Think creatively when purchasing lining—different colors, fabric patterns, stripes, checks, or plaids can be used as the lining.
- Think creatively and combine several different linings to create one extraordinary lining, as illustrated in the coat lining in Figure 16.28a.
- The body lining in a jacket or coat could have a plain-colored lining and the sleeves could be made from a striped lining.
- The wool knit skirt in Figure 16.28b is nipped, tucked, and draped into an interesting asymmetrical shape. The lining underneath is made in a lightweight patterned jersey knit stitched as a smaller lining to control the outer skirt shape.
- Line a leather jacket with a soft lace—one that is not scratchy or irritating to the skin. An important aspect of functional design is that the lace be comfortable. This idea can look amazing when the lining is cut longer and left hanging below the garment hem edge (the opposite of how traditional linings are cut). In Figure 16.28c, the jacket is made from leather and the hem edge has been cut to take advantage of the natural leather skin edges. The lace lining is only attached to the underarm and shoulder seams of the leather, which would adequately hold it in place. This could be done with a stitch-in-the-ditch.

- Thinking creatively about linings may be the selling point for your garment; a creative lining may attract a customer to choose your garment over another garment.

STOP! WHAT DO I DO IF . . .

. . . my lining is too short?

A band of self-fabric or contrast-colored lining can be added to the hem edge of the lining. Also consider stitching a piece of lace the extra width you need to the lining hem edge. Alternatively, consider stitching a ruffle to the lining hem edge, as long as it doesn't add bulk, or stitch a false hem on the lining.

. . . my lining is too tight, and the outer fabric does not sit well because of this?

We suggest seam ripping the lining and taking it out of the garment. First check the lining pattern to see if the pattern was too tight for the garment. Adjust the lining pattern to the correct size and, if possible, recut and restitch the lining. A panel or a godet can also be added to the lining to add extra width. Don't be hard on yourself—use it as a learning experience!

. . . my garment should have been lined but wasn't—can I add a lining after the garment is finished?

This depends on the style of the garment—it would be easy to add a lining to skirts or pants with a waistband. Simply remove the waistband, insert the lining, and restitch the waistband. Skirts or pants with a facing could easily have

a lining attached to the edge of the facing. It would also be easy to add a lining to the facing of a jacket with a facing; the lining could be constructed from the pattern pieces (but remember to remove the facing area from the pattern).

. . . my lining is hanging below my garment?

Remove the hemline of the lining, press and measure carefully, cut the lining shorter, and re-hem it.

. . . my lining is too wide at the hem and won't fit into my garment!

First check your lining pattern—it could be incorrect. Inaccurate stitching of the lining is often a reflection of incorrect patterns. Go back to the seam allowances and restitch to make the seam allowances bigger, seam rip the old stitches, and press the seams again. Measure the lining to the garment hem edge to make sure it fits this time before attaching it. The opposite can also be done if the lining is too tight around the hem edge: let out the seams, seam rip the stitches, and press the seams before attaching the hem of the lining to the garment.

SELF-CRITIQUE

- Did I begin with the correct lining pattern?
- Did I snip notches and mark matchpoints on the lining?
- Did I choose the best lining method for the type and style of garment?
- Did I choose the right weight and type of lining for my garment?

Stretch Your Creativity

LEATHER
JACKET

LACE LINING
HANGING
BELOW JACKET

KNIT
SKIRT

PARTIAL
SELF LINING

PATTERNED JERSEY
LINING TO CONTROL
THE SILHOUETTE

16.28A COAT

16.28B SKIRT

16.28C LEATHER JACKET

- When my garment is placed on the form, does the lining pull the garment out of shape?
- Does my lining hem hang below my garment hem?

REVIEW CHECKLIST

- Do I understand how correct patterns with notches and matchpoints set me up to accomplish correct stitching and help the garment be perfectly aligned?
- Do I understand how the lining pattern is made from the original garment patterns?
- Do I understand that linings are made in different fibers, weights, and hand?

- Do I understand that a lining adds quality and longevity to a garment?
- Do I understand that not all garments need to be lined?
- Do I understand that a lining needs to suit the function and wear-and-tear of the garment?
- Do I understand that a partial lining reduces bulk in garment parts?
- Do I understand the concept of a partial lining and the reasons for choosing this method of lining?
- Do I realize that a fabulous lining fabric that feels luxurious to the hand may be a good selling point?

- Do I understand how fashion and function *must* go hand in hand when considering whether to line a garment, and if so, which lining to choose?

Stitching a lining is a challenging process for the fashion design student; however, with practice it will get easier. Follow up on what you did not understand. Perhaps ask an instructor to explain what mystifies you. Learning to sew is a process, so keep practicing and never give up! Having an excellent knowledge of clothing construction empowers the designer. Having knowledge of how to stitch linings will take you one step further toward your goal of being an excellent fashion designer.

17

Closures: Closing the Garment

In this chapter we consider the final sewing methods that bring closure to the garment. Depending on the type of closure used, these elements can be a focus of the design or quite insignificant. However, they are an important consideration for the designer, as they facilitate dressing and undressing, as well as warmth and coolness when wearing a garment.

A variety of closures will be discussed that offer many design options for the design student to explore. The faithful "button and buttonhole" will be outlined along with ties, tabs, toggles, loops, tab-loop, snaps, hooks and eyes, lacing, and belts.

Each closure should complement the fabric and design. When considering garment closure, functional design is very important—the closure needs to be user-friendly.

STYLE I.D.
The Style I.D. illustrates various closures that can be used in design:

• Symmetrical double-breasted coat with button and buttonhole closure (Figure 17.1a).
• Symmetrical single-breasted coat with button and buttonholes closure, tie-belt, and tab belt carriers (Figure 17.1b).
• Symmetrical single-breasted jacket with button-and-loop closure (Figure 17.1c).
• Asymmetrical jacket with diagonal bound buttonhole and one large button; the rest of the closure is concealed snaps (Figure 17.1d).

GATHER YOUR TOOLS
Gather the following supplies in a variety of different sizes: snaps, hook and eyes, buttons,

KEY TERMS
Asymmetrical
  Closure
Bias Loops
Buckram
Buttonholes
Buttons
Closure
Concealed Closure
Dome Button
Double Breasted
Edge-to-Edge
  Closure
Extension
Faced Bound
  Buttonhole
Flat Button
Full Ball Button
Garment Center Line
Garment Off-Center
  Line

Grommets
Half Ball Button
Hook and Eye
In-Seam Buttonhole
Lacing
Machine-Stitched
  Buttonhole
Sew-through Button
Shank Button
Single Breasted
Snap Fastener
Structured Belt
Symmetrical
  Closure
Tab-Loop
Tabs
Tie-Belt
Toggle
Traditional Bound
  Buttonhole

and a variety of other closures that interest you. Other essential tools that designers use when stitching closures are tape measure, pins, thread, needles, scissors (and embroidery scissors), buttonhole cutter, and Glover's needle. Be sure to have some interfacing (black as well as white) available at all times, too.

NOW LET'S GET STARTED

Knowing the stitching order of the garment is vital to effective and efficient sewing. Continually having to use a seam ripper to undo the stitches because you have missed an important step weakens the fabric and frustrates the student. Take the time to learn the stitching order so it becomes natural, as it ultimately saves time!

Depending on the style of closure, the stitching order may be organized slightly differently. Embellishments are not added to the stitching order, as they can be stitched first, last, or during the stitching process. Bound buttonholes are stitched early in the stitching order. The final stitching order may need to be individualized for each garment.

Let's go over what has been stitched so far:

- Stabilizer applied
- Darts stitched
- Pockets applied
- Seams stitched
- Tucks and pleats stitched
- Zipper, waistband, ruffles and flounces, collars, facings, and cuffs all stitched
- Sleeves inserted
- Hem stitched
- Lining inserted

17.1B SINGLE-BREASTED COAT WITH TIE-BELT

17.1A DOUBLE-BREASTED COAT

17.1C JACKET WITH BUTTON-AND-LOOP CLOSURE

17.1D ASYMMETRICAL JACKET WITH ONE-BUTTON CLOSURE AND DIAGONAL BUTTONHOLE

Now attend to the closure, which is the last process in the stitching order other than attending to the finishing touches of the garment. You'll need to put time and thought into the closure for your design in the sketching stage; these ideas will be developed further when the pattern is drafted. At this stage, the stitching order to be used and the supplies needed also require consideration.

Types of Closures

There are many different types of **closures**. The key to the success of any closure is choosing one that gives you the look and function you want and suits the fabric surface as well as the fabric weight. Then make the patterns to correlate with the closure design, followed by quality stitching.

Buttons and **buttonholes** are the most common closure used in fashion design. So many fabulous buttons are available today—you just have to look on the Internet to see the variety available. These can become the focus of the garment. Other closures, such as **snap fasteners**, **hooks and eyes**, **tabs**, **tab-loops**, **toggles**, **lacing,** and belts add to the list of favorite closures used in fashion today. All of these closures will be highlighted in this chapter.

Functional design is so important when considering the type of closure to use—the fabric should suit the design, and the closure should suit the fabric. These two aspects *must* be in sync for the garment design to be successful.

How to Choose the Appropriate Closure for the Garment

Let the design and fabric guide your choice. Consider the look you want to achieve—business, evening, or casual wear; the closure influences the design and needs to suit the occasion. Consider the purpose of the closure and the security needed. For example, if snaps are used to close a coat, then the snap size is important; the snap needs to be strong enough to securely hold the coat closed and not pop open. This is how fashion meets function. A complicated closure on coats and jackets may be annoying to take off and put on all day; think functional design—complicated closures could inhibit sales.

The fabric weight needs to hold the particular closure without caving in. For example, a large heavy button stitched to a lightweight fabric will affect how the garment sits on the body. Again, consider functional design—the garment part being closed should dictate the type of closure needed. Any area of a garment where there is stress, such as a waistband or fly-front closure, needs to be secure (four-hole buttons will be stronger than two-hole because of the extra stitches).

The laundering of the garment also dictates the type of closure needed. If buttons are used, then the material from which the button is made is important; if the garment is washable and can be thrown in the dryer, make sure the type of closure used is also washable and dryer safe. Imagine having a *machine-washable, dryer-safe* shirt, with mother-of-pearl, rhinestone, or glass buttons that

are delicate and need gentle hand washing; the extra care needed for laundering could dissuade a customer from purchasing the shirt.

Be aware that synthetic buttons don't tolerate a hot iron, and that leather and wood buttons cannot be hand washed or dry cleaned. Buttons that cannot be dry cleaned need to be removed first or covered by the dry cleaner, which adds to the cost of cleaning the garment.

NOTES

Fashion rules are made to be broken; design students may change this direction to add a different twist.

CLOSING THE GARMENT

A women's garment is closed with the right side lapping over the left side, while men's clothing is closed in the opposite way: left over right. One exception to the "right over left" rule is a fly-front/waist closure on women's pants and jeans when the closure direction is interchangeable (Figure 17.2a). The "right over left" direction continues around the body to the back; the closure in the back then becomes left over right (looking from the back view) (Figure 17.2b).

Key Button Placements

There are key points where buttons need to be placed so fashion and function meet. *Neck, bust, waist,* and *hips* are the key closure positions that relate to the body and its movement; these are

17.2A BACK VIEW

17.2B FRONT VIEW

IMPORTANT

Buttonholes are stitched on the right side of the garment, and buttons on the left side (Figure 17.3).

the parts of the garment under stress. Buttons stitched in these key positions will ensure the garment does not gape when worn (Figure 17.3).

- On blouses, dresses, jackets, and coats, place the last button up a distance from the hem edge to allow room for the customer to sit, bend, and walk (see Figure 17.3).
- On skirts with front buttoning, begin at the waist, then place a button and buttonhole a couple of inches below the waistline to prevent gaping.
- On a belted dress, don't place a button on the waist; instead, place buttons at least 1½ inches above and below the belt. A small snap can be stitched at the waistline to help secure the waist in place.
- Buttons and buttonholes are usually placed an equal distance apart; however, this is *not* a rule, and designers may prefer them grouped in twos or unusually spaced (see Figure 17.3).

STITCHING SUCCESSFUL CLOSURES BEGINS WITH THE CORRECT PATTERN

Having the correct patterns for closures sets the student up for successful stitching and a final garment that functions at its best. Each type of closure, whether buttons, snaps, hook and eye,

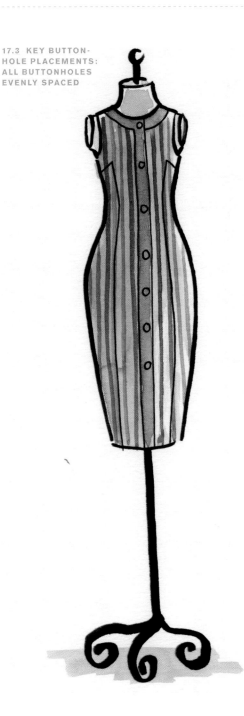

or tabs, has an impact on how the pattern is made. For any closure, whether symmetrical or asymmetrical, the location of the closure must be defined first by drawing a line at this position on the pattern. These lines can be labeled **garment center line** for a symmetrical design and **garment off-center line** for an asymmetrical design (Figure 17.4).

Symmetrical Designs

A **symmetrical closure** is one in which both sides of the garment are the same. For example, the **single-breasted** and **double-breasted** coats in the Style I.D. are both symmetrical closures. Take a look at both these coats in Figures 17.1a and b.

Asymmetrical Designs

An **asymmetrical closure** is one in which the garment fastens to one side. This means that the front pieces of the garment will be cut differently. The jacket in Figure 17.1d of the Style I.D. is asymmetrical and buttons to one side.

After the position of the closure is defined, an extension is added to the pattern to enable the garment to overlap and button (or snap, hook, etc.) together. This is the next step toward stitching a closure that functions well.

EXTENSION FOR CLOSURES

Most closures need an extension in order to close, and this has an impact on how the pattern is made and the stitching techniques used. Figures 17.5a and b indicate the extensions that are needed to enable garments to close. Some

> **IMPORTANT**
>
> For *all* garments to close accurately and correctly, *both* garment center and garment off-center lines must be brought directly together when buttoned. Look at Figure 17.4 to see how each garment closes directly on these lines, indicated in red.

closures don't need an *extension*, as they are an **edge-to-edge closure,** which means the edges are butted together without overlapping (Figure 17.5a).

The extension is added at the patternmaking stage. Garments that close with buttons and loops only need one extension on the left-hand side of the garment while the right side sits on center front (Figure 17.5b). Notice that the loop protrudes out beyond center front and is the extension.

Button and buttonhole closures *must* have an extension added to both sides in order to button closed. Notice that the buttonholes in Figure 17.5c overlap into the extension, and the buttons are stitched on the right side extension. The seam allowance is then added out beyond the extension. In the sketching stage of developing your design, start to think of how your garment will close and define this early on.

Width of Extension

An important part of proper garment functioning is having the correct extension added in the right place at the correct width for each style of closure. In school, an average extension width of

1 inch is usually taught. This width suffices for practice muslins; however, it will be *too narrow* for an extension for larger buttons and *too wide* for smaller buttons. If the correct width of extension is not added, the garment *will not* close properly.

The extension width equals the button diameter, as indicated in Figure 17.6. In this figure, the button is 1 inch in diameter and so the extension is also 1 inch. The extension is added out beyond the garment center or off-center lines, and the seam allowance is added out beyond this. When the garment closes, the two lines *must* be placed directly together.

Single-breasted and double-breasted button closures both have extensions, but a double-breasted extension is wider to accommodate two rows of buttons. The buttons are placed an equal distance from the garment center or off-center lines. Refer to Figures 17.4a and d.

Closure Chart

Take a look at the chart in Figure 17.7, which illustrates some basic closures: buttons, snaps, and hook and eyes. The chart shows what sizes are available for each. The sizes available for purchasing covered button kits (to cover your own) are also indicated in the chart.

If you are not 100 percent sure of the size button you want, then cut a few circles from pattern paper to approximate the possible sizes. Place them on the pattern or your muslin, stand back, and observe whether the size fits the proportion of the overall garment. And don't forget the key placement position for buttons!

17.4A   SYMMETRICAL CLOSURE: DOUBLE BREASTED

17.4B   SYMMETRICAL CLOSURE: SINGLE BREASTED

GARMET CENTER LINE

GARMENT CENTER LINE

SNAPS

GARMENT OFF CENTER LINE

GARMENT OFF CENTER LINE

17.4C   ASYMMETRICAL DESIGN: SINGLE BREASTED

17.4D   ASYMMETRICAL DESIGN: DOUBLE BREASTED

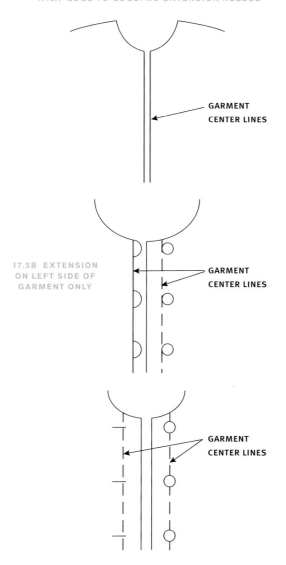

17.5A EDGE-TO-EDGE: NO EXTENSION NEEDED

GARMENT CENTER LINES

17.5B EXTENSION ON LEFT SIDE OF GARMENT ONLY

GARMENT CENTER LINES

GARMENT CENTER LINES

17.5C EXTENSION ON BOTH SIDES OF GARMENT

BUTTONS

A button is a three-dimensional form; it has width, height, and length. Buttons are manufactured from a broad range of materials such as plastic, wood, metal, gold, silver, pewter, brass, copper, horn, mother-of-pearl, ceramic, shell, glass, ivory, porcelain, rhinestone, rubber, bone, and an array of synthetic materials such as polyester or nylon. They may also be covered with fabric.

Buttons can be functional or decorative, or both, depending on their purpose. For example, the buttons in Figure 17.2 on the skirt and pant waistbands are purely functional; whereas all the buttons in the designs in the Style I.D. are both functional (for the closures) and decorative.

Buttons *must* close a garment securely yet slip comfortably through the buttonhole so the customer does not struggle when opening or closing the garment. Buttons that are not stitched securely pop off after several wearings.

Button Sizes

Buttons are measured in lignes (abbreviated *L*), which is the traditional European sizing. Buttons can also be purchased according to the diameter measurement; they are available from ³⁄₁₆ inch to 2½ inches in diameter. Refer back to Figure 17.7, which provides a helpful guide for defining button sizes.

Button Shapes

Many beautiful, creatively shaped buttons are available in the marketplace. The designer can spend hours defining "just the right button"

> **IMPORTANT**
> Always *notch* the extension position, especially if a collar is being stitched to the neckline (see Figure 17.6).

for the garment. Like fashion designers, button designers push their creative limits to come up with new and exciting buttons. The general shapes in which buttons are manufactured are:

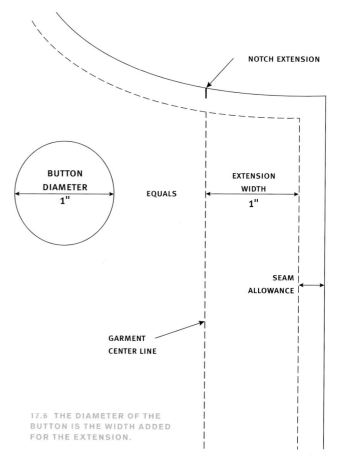

NOTCH EXTENSION

BUTTON DIAMETER 1"

EQUALS

EXTENSION WIDTH 1"

SEAM ALLOWANCE

GARMENT CENTER LINE

17.6 THE DIAMETER OF THE BUTTON IS THE WIDTH ADDED FOR THE EXTENSION.

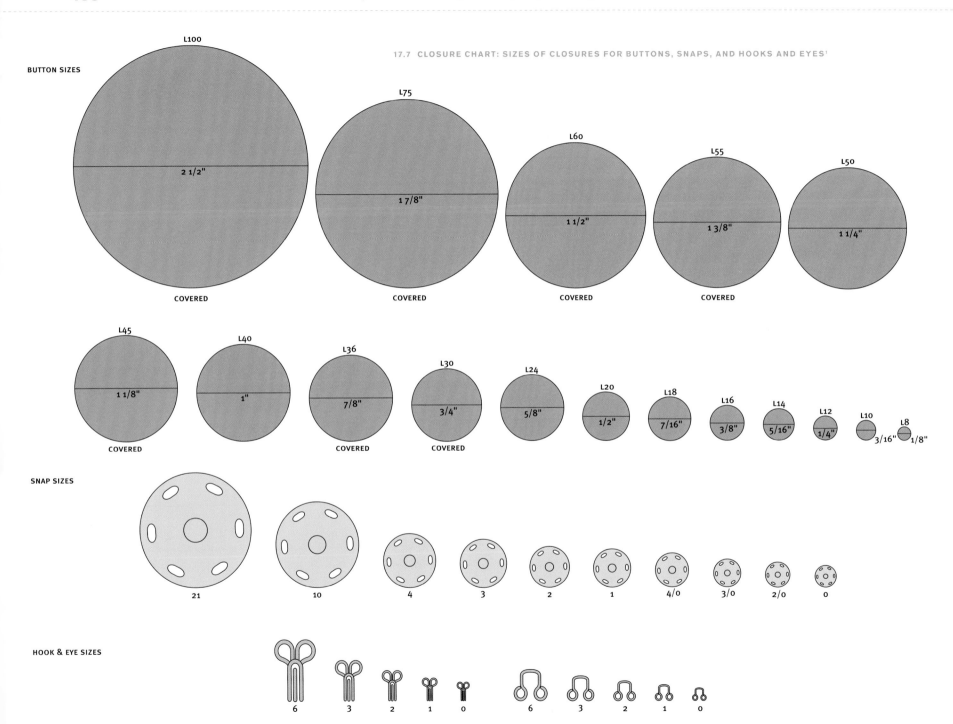

BUTTON SIZES

17.7 CLOSURE CHART: SIZES OF CLOSURES FOR BUTTONS, SNAPS, AND HOOKS AND EYES[1]

L100 — 2 1/2" — COVERED
L75 — 1 7/8" — COVERED
L60 — 1 1/2" — COVERED
L55 — 1 3/8" — COVERED
L50 — 1 1/4"

L45 — 1 1/8" — COVERED
L40 — 1"
L36 — 7/8" — COVERED
L30 — 3/4" — COVERED
L24 — 5/8"
L20 — 1/2"
L18 — 7/16"
L16 — 3/8"
L14 — 5/16"
L12 — 1/4"
L10 — 3/16"
L8 — 1/8"

SNAP SIZES

21   10   4   3   2   1   4/0   3/0   2/0   0

HOOK & EYE SIZES

6   3   2   1   0   6   3   2   1   0

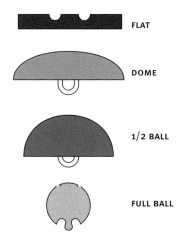

FLAT

DOME

1/2 BALL

FULL BALL

- **Flat Button** (Figure 17.8a)
- **Dome Button** (Figure 17.8b)
- **Half ball Button** (Figure 17.8c)
- **Full ball Button** (Figure 17.8d)

Buttons can be made to look distinctive by using color and texture. Covered buttons made in self- or contrasting fabrics can be made to complement your garment. Figure 17.9 illustrates three different styles of buttons. Before any buttonholes can be stitched, the button *must* be chosen; then the buttonholes can be stitched to fit exactly to the size of the button.

BUTTONHOLES

A buttonhole allows an opening in a garment; it has a slot in the middle large enough to slip over a button to hold the garment closed. In this section, three different types of buttonholes will be explained: the traditional bound (and faced bound) buttonhole, the in-seam buttonhole, and the popular machine-stitched buttonhole. The illustrations in Figure 17.9 show

each of these options.

Buttonholes can be stitched by machine or by hand. Hand-stitched buttonholes look magnificent but require time and expertise to stitch. They are mainly stitched by tailors on high-end men's and women's tailored suits and coats. If you pass by a tailor's shop, take a look at how beautifully the buttonholes on these garments are stitched.

Traditional bound buttonholes are a favorite of ours and look fabulous stitched to woolen and cashmere coats (Figure 17.9a).

An **in-seam buttonhole** is not used as often in design, but nevertheless it is an excellent choice (and easy to stitch), as it's an opening in the seam. An in-seam buttonhole can only be stitched if the seam is placed in the appropriate position for the buttonhole (Figure 17.9b).

Machine-stitched buttonholes are the most common type of buttonholes used in production. They can be stitched to shirts, blouses, dresses, jackets, coats, waistbands, and cuffs (Figure 17.9c).

Stabilizing the Buttonhole Area

Before buttonholes are stitched, always stabilize the buttonhole/button areas on the garment and/or facing. The stabilizer prevents the buttonhole from stretching in the stitching process and creates a firm foundation for the button; this becomes evident when the garment is worn and gives the garment a structured, professional look. Refer to Chapter 3, "Interfacing Garment Parts." Take a look at Figure 3.2, which indicates the key application points for stabilizers. Buttonholes and buttons are one

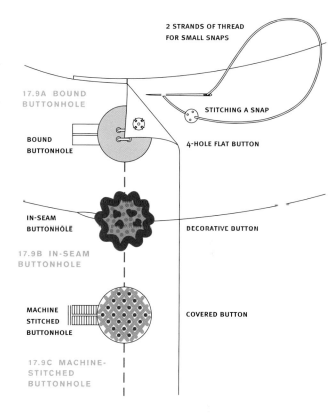

2 STRANDS OF THREAD FOR SMALL SNAPS

17.9A BOUND BUTTONHOLE

BOUND BUTTONHOLE

STITCHING A SNAP

4-HOLE FLAT BUTTON

IN-SEAM BUTTONHOLE

DECORATIVE BUTTON

17.9B IN-SEAM BUTTONHOLE

MACHINE STITCHED BUTTONHOLE

COVERED BUTTON

17.9C MACHINE-STITCHED BUTTONHOLE

of the key areas.

Length of the Buttonhole

The length of the buttonhole is *always* determined by the button size. To calculate, measure the diameter of the button and add ease—the ease allows room for the buttonhole to easily slip over the button without feeling too tight. The amount of ease differs, depending on the shape of the button.

Here are some guidelines to follow when calculating the buttonhole length:

- For a flat button, add ⅛ inch of ease to the button diameter (Figure 17.10a).

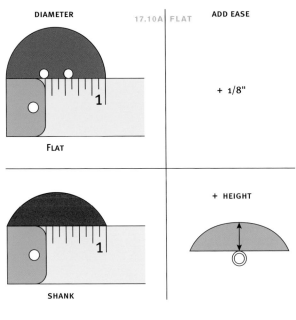

DIAMETER 17.10A FLAT ADD EASE

FLAT

+ 1/8"

+ HEIGHT

SHANK

17.10B SHANK

- For a **shank button**, the height of the button is the *ease*; this is added to the button diameter for the total buttonhole length (Figure 17.10b).
- For a full circle button, slip the tape around the button, hold firmly in your hand, and note the measurement; add ⅛ inch of ease to this measurement.

Position of Buttonholes

The distance between the top edge of the garment and the first button placement needs to be calculated by adding ¼ inch to half the button diameter. Use your tape measure to determine the distance down from the top finished edge of the garment for the first button placement. Refer to Figure 17.11 to see the width. For example, if

the button is 1 inch diameter then the distance down from the top edge would be ¾ inch.

Mark the next button on the waistline (if not belted) and divide the remaining space evenly for the amount of buttons planned. Place a button as close to the bustline as possible; it can be placed *slightly* above or below the bust. Refer to Figure 17.3.

It is advisable to handbaste garment center or off-center lines on both sides of the garment, as Figure 17.11 indicates. Doing this in the beginning will be handy for two reasons: For fittings, this prevents any *guessing* about where the garment closes. By bringing the two lines together the garment can be pinned closed for fittings. The handbasting stitches also direct the position to stitch the closure; again, no guessing! Carefully remove the basting stitches after the closure is completed.

Marking Buttonholes

Buttonholes are applied on the right-hand side of the garment and stitched from the correct side of the fabric. The position and length of the buttonhole needs to be clearly marked using a thread mark, chalk mark, or pin mark (see Figure 17.11).

> **IMPORTANT**
> Always stitch a test buttonhole, especially for unusually shaped or textured buttons, to check the buttonhole size/button ratio before proceeding.

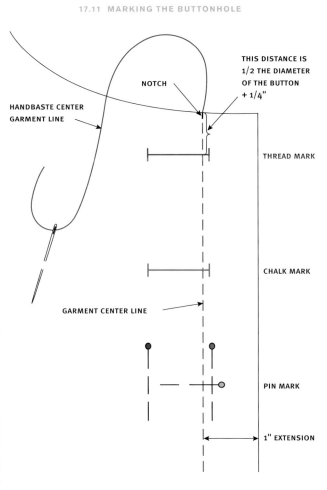

17.11 MARKING THE BUTTONHOLE

THIS DISTANCE IS 1/2 THE DIAMETER OF THE BUTTON + 1/4"

NOTCH

HANDBASTE CENTER GARMENT LINE

THREAD MARK

CHALK MARK

GARMENT CENTER LINE

PIN MARK

1" EXTENSION

Direction of Buttonholes

Buttonholes can be stitched diagonally, horizontally, or vertically; however, the horizontal direction is the most secure (Figure 17.12). This is important for a fly-front with a button opening; the buttonholes need to be stitched in a horizontal direction and four-hole buttons stitched for more security. Look at the direction the buttonholes are stitched in the fly-front in Figure 17.2a.

Diagonal buttonholes draw attention to the garment as a design feature. The diagonal direction is ideal for bias-cut garments; this means they are stitched on the straight grain, which helps to stabilize the buttonhole. Position the buttonhole ⅛ inch over the garment center (or off-center) line and mark in a diagonal direction (see Figure 17.12a).

For *horizontal buttonholes*, begin the buttonhole ⅛ inch beyond the garment center (or off-center) line toward the garment edge (Figure 17.12b). Buttonholes on cuffs, narrow collars (11.8c), and waistbands (Figure 9.3b) are *always* stitched horizontally, in the direction of the cuff and collar or tab length. Refer to Figure 13.16.

Vertical buttonholes are usually stitched to a placket, narrow bands, or lightweight or sheer fabrics with a narrow twice-turned facing. There are no set rules for the direction; however, buttons do pop out of vertical buttonholes more easily than from horizontal buttonholes, so the length of the buttonhole is important. Smaller-sized buttons are generally stitched to bands and plackets. The width of the band is directed by the button size. Double the width of the button diameter to calculate the width of the band needed. For example, a ½-inch button would need to have a 1-inch-wide band. Notice also, in Figure 11.8, that the mandarin collar has a horizontal buttonhole stitched to the collar and vertical buttonholes stitched to the front band.

Vertical buttonholes are stitched directly on the garment center line (or off-center garment line) on the right-hand side of the garment, as indicated in Figure 17.12c. The buttons are stitched on the left side of the garment directly in the same position. As a reference, turn back to Figures 17.4b and c to see how this looks in design.

MACHINE-STITCHED BUTTONHOLES

SEW Smartly, *CLIP* Carefully, *PRESS* Precisely when stitching buttonholes.

Machine-stitched buttonholes are the quickest type of buttonhole to stitch on clothing. If an automatic buttonhole stitch is not available on your sewing machine, you can still sew buttonholes using a zigzag stitch. Some school machines have a dial that guides you through this procedure—follow those instructions. The buttonhole on completion should be ¼-inch wide and a little wider for thicker fabrics. Figure 17.12 illustrates machine-stitched buttonholes.

Cutting the Buttonhole Open

Fray Check can be carefully applied to the buttonhole before cutting; this will prevent the buttonhole from fraying if accidentally snipped. To cut buttonholes open, place the wooden block on a flat surface, and lay your buttonhole on top of this. Take your buttonhole cutter (this was illustrated in Figure 2.1, as it is an essential tool) and position the sharp end directly in the middle of your buttonhole. (When the buttonhole is stitched, there should be a slight gap between both bars.) Hold the buttonhole cutter

NOTE

Cord or gimp can be placed in the buttonhole as a filler to strengthen and raise the stitches; it also prevents larger buttonholes from stretching. The colors available are limited; however, when stitched correctly, the gimp should not show. Snip the gimp from the end of the buttonholes when completed.

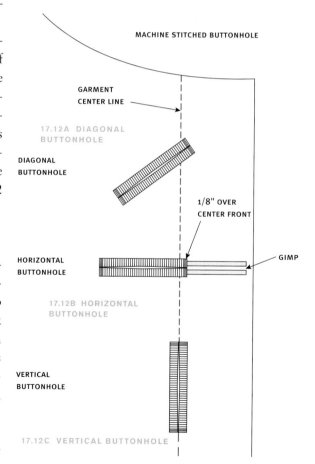

MACHINE STITCHED BUTTONHOLE

GARMENT CENTER LINE

17.12A DIAGONAL BUTTONHOLE

DIAGONAL BUTTONHOLE

1/8" OVER CENTER FRONT

HORIZONTAL BUTTONHOLE

GIMP

17.12B HORIZONTAL BUTTONHOLE

VERTICAL BUTTONHOLE

17.12C VERTICAL BUTTONHOLE

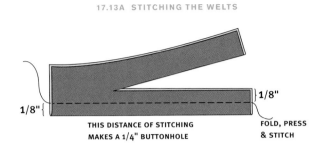

17.13A STITCHING THE WELTS

1/8"

THIS DISTANCE OF STITCHING
MAKES A 1/4" BUTTONHOLE

1/8"

FOLD, PRESS
& STITCH

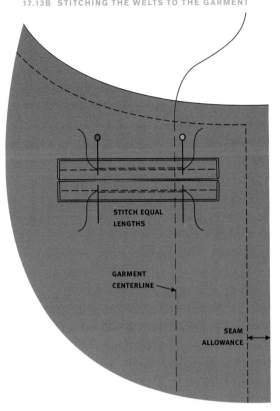

17.13B STITCHING THE WELTS TO THE GARMENT

STITCH EQUAL
LENGTHS

GARMENT
CENTERLINE

SEAM
ALLOWANCE

17.13C SLASH THE BUTTONHOLE OPEN.

SLIT
BUTTONHOLE

UNDERLINING

vertically, not at an angle, and push down on it to cut open the buttonhole. Take your embroidery scissors (illustrated in Figure 2.1) and carefully cut the final length.

BOUND BUTTONHOLES

A traditional bound buttonhole adds a professional couture finish to jackets and coats and looks very classy. Bound buttonholes are formed from two strips of fabric (called welts) cut on straight or bias grains. After the two strips of fabric are stitched, slit, and turned, the facing is attached to the back of the buttonhole. This can be done in two ways: by hand stitching, or by machine-stitching windows into a facing, which is then applied by stitching-in-the-ditch around the buttonhole from the face of the garment. The latter method is called a *faced bound buttonhole*. When completed, both types of buttonholes will look exactly the same from the face of the garment.

Bound buttonholes are stitched in the garment earlier in the stitching order of the garment, before the facing is applied; for this reason, determine your button size early, then add the correct extension to the pattern. Every

bound buttonhole should look identical in size and shape.

If you choose a large button for your jacket or coat, machine-stitched buttonholes may be a poor choice. Large machine-stitched buttonholes (over 1½ inches in length) can look stretched and ugly. For larger buttons, bound buttonholes are recommended; alternately, snaps can be stitched as the closure, under the button, and the button stitched on the garment surface.

For bound buttonholes, use self–fabric (see Figure 17.9a), or as a design feature, choose a contrasting fabric, stripes, checks, or leather for the welts. It is important to use fabric that is not too bulky.

Traditional Bound Buttonhole

- Mark the buttonhole placement (see Figure 17.11).
- Cut two narrow strips, called welts, in one long piece of fabric on straight or bias grain and 1½ inches

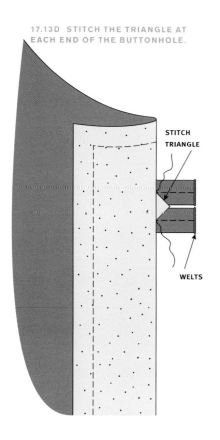

STITCH TRIANGLE

WELTS

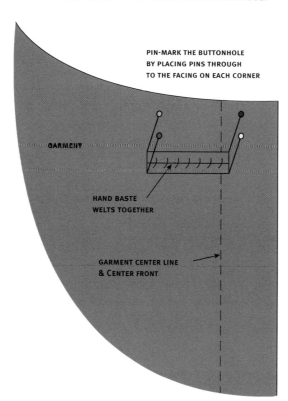

PIN-MARK THE BUTTONHOLE BY PLACING PINS THROUGH TO THE FACING ON EACH CORNER

GARMENT

HAND BASTE WELTS TOGETHER

GARMENT CENTER LINE & CENTER FRONT

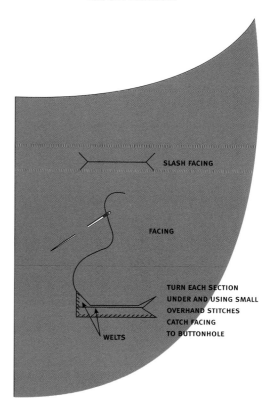

SLASH FACING

FACING

TURN EACH SECTION UNDER AND USING SMALL OVERHAND STITCHES CATCH FACING TO BUTTONHOLE

WELTS

---

wide. Add an extra 1 inch length for each buttonhole. Cut the strips of fabric in one long length.

- With the wrong sides together, press the fabric in half.
- Open the fabric and apply half interfacing, if needed; this is dependent on the fabric weight—definitely stabilize bias grain strips, but straight grain strips may not need stabilizing.
- Refold the fabric again and, using a 2.0 stitch length, stitch back from the folded edge *half the width* of the finished buttonhole width. Stitching ⅛ inch will result in a ¼-inch finished bound

buttonhole. As the length of the buttonhole increases, so too can the width increase; there are no rules, but consider the overall proportion (Figure 17.13a).

- Cut off the excess fabric width of each welt, leaving an equal stitching width (see Figure 17.13a).
- On the correct side of the fabric, position the welts on the placement mark; butt the cut edges together, and pin in place (Figure 17.13b).
- Chalk or pin-mark the finished length of the buttonhole on the welts (see Figure 17.13b).
- Using a small stitch length (1.5), stitch directly on

top of the previous row of stitching for *exactly* the buttonhole length; begin and end with a backstitch; otherwise, pull the threads to the wrong side and tie off. *Both* stitching lengths *must* finish *exactly* at the same squared point. If they don't, the buttonhole will look askew when finished (see Figure 17.13b).

- From the wrong side of the fabric, slit the garment fabric down the center of the stitching, stop ¼ inch from each end, and then slash directly into the corners. Use small embroidery scissors to do this. If the corners are not cut *to the* stitching, the buttonhole will not look squared on completion (Figure 17.13c).

- Push the welts through to the wrong side; align the folded edges together.
- On the correct side, handbaste the welts together with an overhand stitch. Don't remove the basting stitches until the buttons are stitched (Figure 17.13e).
- With the correct side facing up, fold the garment back to expose each triangular corner. Using a shorter stitch length (1.5), stitch across *both* ends. Trim the welts back to ¼ inch to reduce bulk (Figure 17.13d).
- Press the buttonholes; use a pressing cloth to protect the fabric surface.

Finishing the Facing

Use one of the following methods to complete the bound buttonhole facing.

Handstitched/Slashed Facing

- From the correct side, pin the garment and facing together, smoothing the garment fabric over the facing.
- From the correct side of the garment, pin-mark each corner of the buttonhole by pushing the pins vertically through to the wrong side of the fabric; replace with horizontal pins to pin-mark at each corner (see Figure 17.13e).
- On the facing side, carefully slit in the middle of the pins; finish ¼ inch back from each end, and cut diagonally into each corner (Figure 17.13f). This is the same procedure explained in Figure 17.13c and now done on the facing.
- Fold each small section underneath to expose the welts; use a small needle and single strand

of thread to catch the facing to the buttonhole. Use a small overhand stitch and catch into every previous stitch (see Figure 17.13f).

Window Buttonhole Facing

A buttonhole facing has a window stitched to the back of the facing; this is completed before the facing is stitched to the garment.

- Mark the buttonhole placement on the facing.
- Cut a small piece of lightweight fusible interfacing and draw the buttonhole shape ¹⁄₁₆ inch smaller than the final buttonhole shape. (Color match the interfacing as close to the garment fabric as possible.) Draw the center line as well (Figure 17.14a).
- Position the correct side of the interfacing to the correct side of the facing. Line up the marked buttonhole positions together (see Figure 17.14a).
- Use a small stitch length (1.5) and stitch around the window shape; begin stitching on one side, pivot on each corner, and finish by overlapping the stitches by ¼ inch—the over-lapping stitching *must* be directly on top of the previous stitches. This must be a perfectly stitched window with the length and width *exactly* the same size (see Figure 17.14a).
- Carefully cut in the middle of the window and diagonally into each corner up to the stitching; if the corners are not cut *to* the stitching, the buttonhole will not look squared. This is the same cutting procedure illustrated in Figure 17.13c.

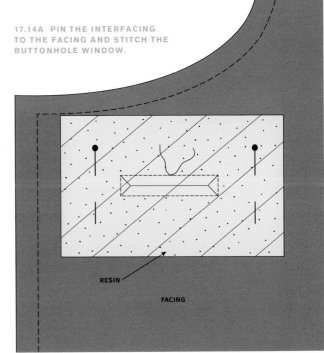

17.14A PIN THE INTERFACING TO THE FACING AND STITCH THE BUTTONHOLE WINDOW.

RESIN

FACING

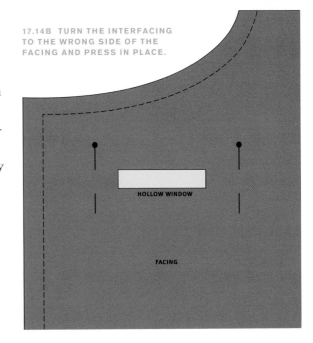

17.14B TURN THE INTERFACING TO THE WRONG SIDE OF THE FACING AND PRESS IN PLACE.

HOLLOW WINDOW

FACING

- Turn the facing to the wrong side of the fabric. If the interfacing is too wide, trim so it fits comfortably behind the facing.
- Carefully press the interfacing to the facing to get a neatly finished window (Figure 17.14b).
- The facing is now stitched to the garment, edgestitched, and pressed.
- Pin and handbaste the window directly behind the bound buttonhole (see Figure 17.14b).
- From the face of the garment, stitch-in-the-ditch around the window of the bound buttonhole to attach the facing in place (see Figure 17.14c).

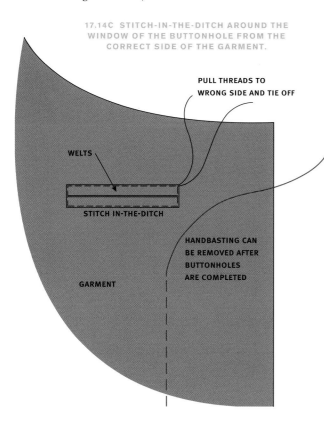

17.14C STITCH-IN-THE-DITCH AROUND THE WINDOW OF THE BUTTONHOLE FROM THE CORRECT SIDE OF THE GARMENT.

PULL THREADS TO WRONG SIDE AND TIE OFF

WELTS

STITCH IN-THE-DITCH

GARMENT

HANDBASTING CAN BE REMOVED AFTER BUTTONHOLES ARE COMPLETED

IN-SEAM BUTTONHOLES

An in-seam buttonhole is such a quick method to use. The buttonhole can be vertical, horizontal, or diagonal as long as the seam is the same direction. An in-seam buttonhole has a slot left open in the seam; notch the opening before you stitch (Figure 17.15).

- Stabilize the buttonhole opening with a narrow fusible stabilizing tape applied to both sides of the opening (see Figure 17.15). Refer to Chapter 3, "Stabilizing Tapes."
- Stitch the seam and backstitch at each end of the opening; the opening must be secure so it does not split open with wear and tear (see Figure 17.15).
- Press the seam open—for this type of buttonhole, the seams *cannot* be closed.
- If the facing has a seam, then leave the same opening in the facing and slipstitch garment and facing together around the opening.
- If the facing does not have a seam, then slit the facing and hand stitch around the buttonhole edge in the same way as you would for the traditional bound buttonholes in Figure 17.13f.

CONCEALED CLOSURE

A **concealed closure** is buttoned together, with one row of topstitching to define the closure (Figure 17.16). A separate band with buttonholes is stitched to the right-hand side of the facing (Figure 17.17a). When the garment is buttoned, the buttons are hidden between the garment and the facing. The buttons need to be flat so they don't add bulk. Use buttons that are approximately ⅞ to 1 inch in diameter—don't use

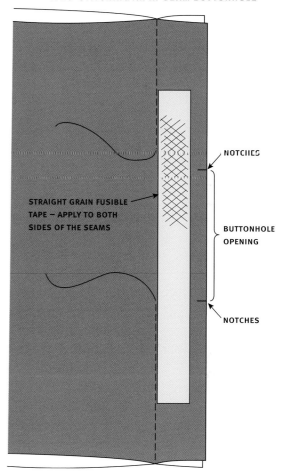

17.15 STITCHING AN IN-SEAM BUTTONHOLE

NOTCHES

STRAIGHT GRAIN FUSIBLE TAPE — APPLY TO BOTH SIDES OF THE SEAMS

BUTTONHOLE OPENING

NOTCHES

extra-large buttons (as the button size increases, so does the band size). Notice in Figure 17.16 that when the garment is unbuttoned, the buttons show on the left-hand side.

- Apply half interfacing to the band, and have the facings interfaced. Fold the wrong sides of the band together and press along the foldline.

17.16 CONCEALED FRONT CLOSURE

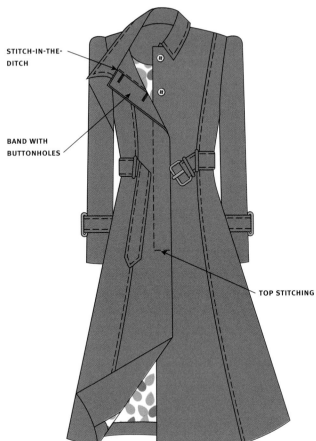

STITCH-IN-THE-DITCH

BAND WITH BUTTONHOLES

TOP STITCHING

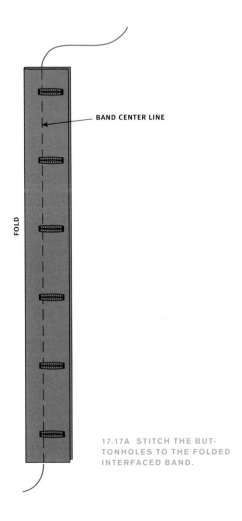

BAND CENTER LINE

FOLD

17.17A STITCH THE BUTTONHOLES TO THE FOLDED INTERFACED BAND.

- Stitch the buttonholes horizontally; handbaste the band center line first, then plan horizontal buttonhole placement in the same way as horizontal buttonholes are placed in Figure 17.12b. The buttonholes should just fit in the space and may finish at the seamline (see Figure 17.17b).
- Slit the buttonholes open before the band is applied.
- Place the correct side of the band on top of the correct side of the smaller facing; match the edges together and staystitch in place around three edges, as indicated in Figure 17.17b.
- Next, to hold the band to the facing, machine stitch in between each buttonhole (stitching all three layers of fabric together). Stitch in a horizontal direction; begin stitching from the seam edge and stitch up to the level of the buttonholes. Leave the needle down in the fabric, pivot, machine stitch back to the edge, and clip your threads. In Figure 17.17b, the stitching is indicated on the band/facing and labeled "stitching."
- Staystitch the corner of the larger facing and clip; an angled seam is stitched at this point. Refer to Figure 6.14 to stitch an angled seam. Make sure matchpoints are marked.
- Place the correct side of the smaller facing/band to the correct side of the larger facing, matching the neck edges together as illustrated in Figure 17.17c. Stitch from the neck edge down, pivot at the corner, and complete the stitching. Press the seam outward; don't serge the seam closed if the garment is lined. Figure 17.17d shows the finished

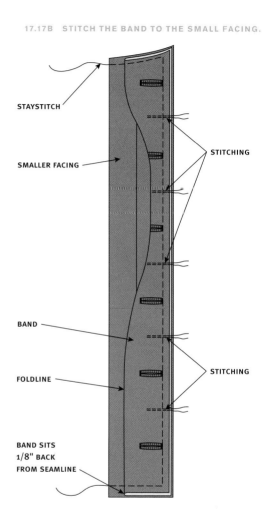

17.17B STITCH THE BAND TO THE SMALL FACING.

STAYSTITCH

SMALLER FACING

STITCHING

BAND

FOLDLINE

STITCHING

BAND SITS
1/8" BACK
FROM SEAMLINE

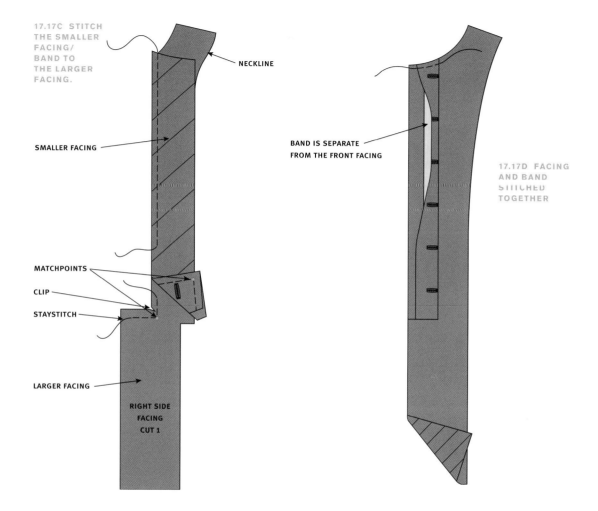

17.17C STITCH
THE SMALLER
FACING/
BAND TO
THE LARGER
FACING.

NECKLINE

SMALLER FACING

BAND IS SEPARATE
FROM THE FRONT FACING

17.17D FACING
AND BAND
STITCHED
TOGETHER

MATCHPOINTS

CLIP

STAYSTITCH

LARGER FACING

RIGHT SIDE
FACING
CUT 1

facing. Notice that the buttonholes just clear the facing/band seam join.

- Stitch the facing to the garment, grade the seams, clip the corners, and understitch (Figure 17.17e). Refer to Chapter 12 for more information on stitching facings.
- On the wrong side, handbaste the band/facing seamline through to the correct side. From the

correct side, topstitch; begin from the top of the band and follow the shape of the band (see Figure 17.16).

- Stitch the buttons to the left side of the garment to correspond with the buttonholes (see Figure 17.16).

BIAS LOOPS

Look at Figure 17.1c in the Style I.D. to see a

jacket with buttons and loops as the closure. The loops slide easily over a shank button (dome, half ball, or full ball). Flat buttons do not work well, as the button needs to be lifted from the fabric surface for the loop to sit under the button.

Bias loops are formed by stitching lengths of narrow bias tubing made in self-fabric or contrasting fabric and forming them into half-

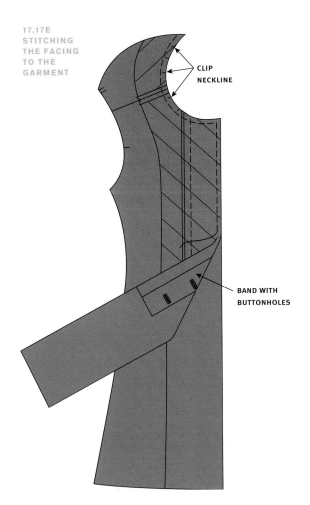

CLIP
NECKLINE

BAND WITH
BUTTONHOLES

Stitching the Loops

The tubing can be turned by using a loop turner. A loop turner is illustrated in Chapter 2, "Gather Your Tools," and is an essential sewing tool to have in your sewing kit. Tubing can also be turned with a needle and thread, and both methods will be outlined and illustrated in Figure 17.18.

- Begin by making a sample loop to get the fabric width/filling ratio just right for each fabric type. Remember, bias stretches; therefore, sampling the loop size first is essential.
- Fold the bias strip in half with the correct sides facing (do not press). Shorten the stitch length and stitch a row of stitches parallel to the fold-line; taper the stitching out ½ inch from the end if you are going to turn the tubing using a needle and thread (Figure 17.18a).

PATTERN TIP

- Cut the bias strip in one long length; to calculate the length, ascertain the length of one loop, add seam allowance, and multiply this loop length by the total number of loops required.
- To cut the width of self-filled tubing (which does look the nicest), add three times the finished loop width and double the measurement. For example, if the finished loop width is ³⁄₁₆ inch, add three time this width and double this measurement; the final cutting width of the loop is 1½ inches.

circle loops. The type of fabric needs to be taken into consideration. Lightweight smooth fabric works best; for example, fine lightweight cotton batiste will make much finer loops than wool crepe. Don't make loops in heavyweight fabric because they will look too thick and bulky. Other creative ways of using tubing and loops will be in "Stretch Your Creativity," later in this chapter.

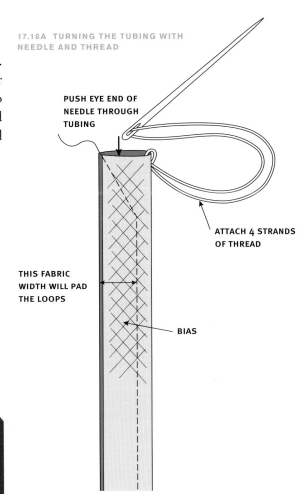

PUSH EYE END OF
NEEDLE THROUGH
TUBING

ATTACH 4 STRANDS
OF THREAD

THIS FABRIC
WIDTH WILL PAD
THE LOOPS

BIAS

- If you plan on using a loop turner, then don't angle the end stitching; instead, stitch straight to the end and clip the corners, as illustrated in Figure 17.18b.

Turning the Loops

- To turn with needle and thread, use a blunt-end tapestry needle and secure two double stands of thread to the slanted end of the

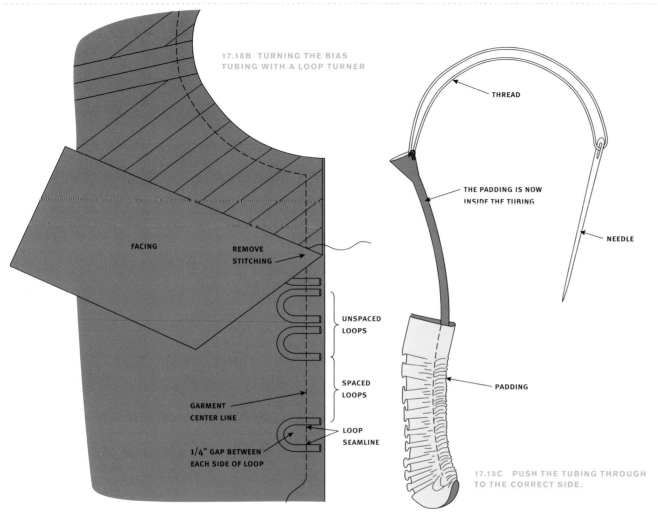

17.18B TURNING THE BIAS TUBING WITH A LOOP TURNER

FACING

REMOVE STITCHING

UNSPACED LOOPS

SPACED LOOPS

GARMENT CENTER LINE

LOOP SEAMLINE

1/4" GAP BETWEEN EACH SIDE OF LOOP

THREAD

THE PADDING IS NOW INSIDE THE TUBING

NEEDLE

PADDING

17.18C PUSH THE TUBING THROUGH TO THE CORRECT SIDE.

Forming the Loops

- Trim off the tapered end of the tubing, and cut the required lengths for each loop. (Sample first to size the loop length to your button.)
- The placement of the loops is the designer's choice—they can butt together or be spaced. It is important that the distance for the placement of each loop be measured evenly (Figure 17.19).
- The loops are stitched on the right-hand side of the garment center line and stitched to the *correct side* of the fabric. To form the loops, shape into half circles (see Figure 17.19).
- Space each loop with ¼ inch between each side of the tubing. Place the raw edges of the loop toward the garment edge and pin in place; staystitch in place just inside the seamline (see Figure 17.19).
- Position the facing on top of the loops with the correct sides of the fabric facing together. Then stitch and understitch the facing in place (see Figure 17.19).

tube. Insert the eye of the needle into the tube (see Figure 17.18a).

- If using the loop turner, slide it up through the bias tubing, as illustrated in Figure 17.18b. Have the lower movable part of the hook facing down as you insert the loop turner. Hook the curved section over the top edge of the tubing. Push the fabric up; as you

do, the hook will clasp around the fabric as you continue to push the fabric up through the loop turner (see Figure 17.18b).

- For both methods, gradually push the fabric through the needle or loop turner. It takes time to get it started; however, once the end is sufficiently turned, the narrow tubing pulls through quite easily (Figure 17.18c).

> ### NOTE
>
> The designer has a choice in choosing the type of closure when using buttons and loops. Since there is no extension, the closure can be edge-to-edge and butt together, as illustrated in Figure 17.20. Figure 17.21 has an extension on the left side for the closure. An edge-to-edge closure will not fully cover the body, and a camisole or some other type of garment may need to be worn underneath—this is not a style for a winter climate, but a great summer style!

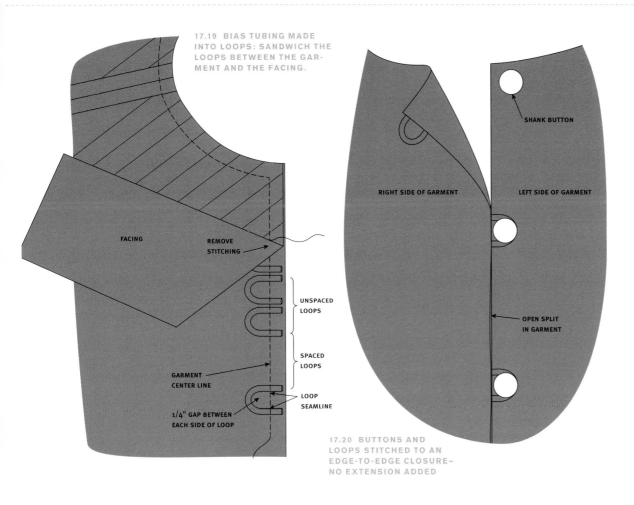

17.19 BIAS TUBING MADE INTO LOOPS: SANDWICH THE LOOPS BETWEEN THE GARMENT AND THE FACING.

17.20 BUTTONS AND LOOPS STITCHED TO AN EDGE-TO-EDGE CLOSURE— NO EXTENSION ADDED

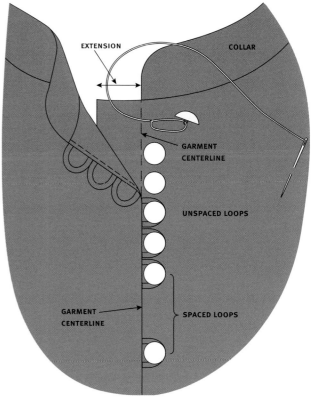

17.21 BUTTONS AND LOOPS STITCHED TO THE FRONT OF THE GARMENT WITH EXTENSION ON THE LEFT SIDE ONLY

TAB-LOOPS AND TABS

Tab-loops and tabs are two other popular closures that look fabulous on more casual garments. Tab-loops and tabs are inserted into the seam following the same stitching method as for the bias loops in Figure 17.19. Just transfer your knowledge and here is another closure you can stitch. To see how a tab-loop and tab closures look in design, refer to Figure 17.22.

Tab-loops are formed from edge-stitched belt loops, which were taught in Chapter 9; refer to the section "Belt Loops," and Figure 9.16 there. Belt loops are used on a waistband to carry the belt and to keep it in place. Tab-loops and tabs can be used as an edge-to-edge closure, or the closure can have an extension, as it does in Figure 17.22. To see how an edge-to-edge closure would look, refer to Figure 17.20. Figure 17.23 illustrates how to form belt loops into tab-loops and stitch in place.

Tabs can be cut to any size, but do size them to fit with the overall proportion of the garment. Cut two pieces per tab and cut one interfacing. To stitch tabs, follow the illustration in Figure 17.24. Apply the interfacing to one side of the tab. Place the correct sides together and stitch a ¼-inch seam around the three sides, leaving the end open for turning. Clip the corners to reduce bulk. Turn the tab to the correct side and use your point corner to sharpen the corners and

17.22 TAB-LOOP AND TAB CLOSURES CAN BE STITCHED AS AN EDGE-TO-EDGE CLOSURE OR STITCHED WITH AN EXTENSION ON ONE OR BOTH SIDES OF THE GARMENT.

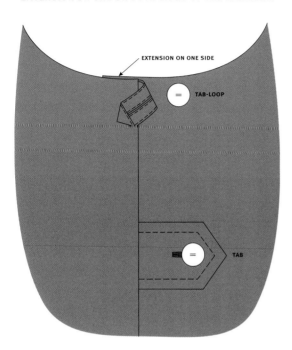

EXTENSION ON ONE SIDE

TAB-LOOP

TAB

17.23A STITCHING TAB-LOOPS

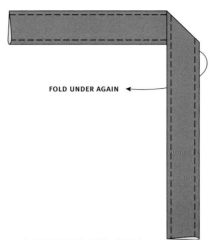

FOLD UNDER AGAIN

17.23B STITCHING TAB-LOOPS

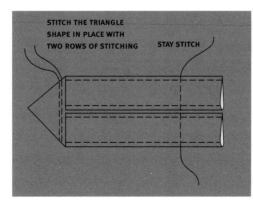

STITCH THE TRIANGLE SHAPE IN PLACE WITH TWO ROWS OF STITCHING

STAY STITCH

17.24 STITCHING A TAB

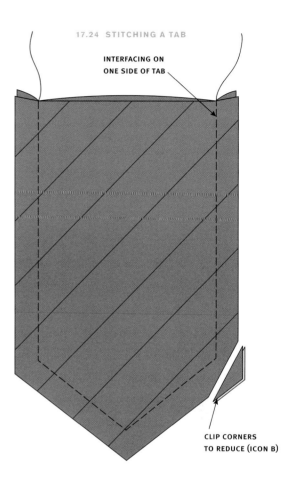

INTERFACING ON ONE SIDE OF TAB

CLIP CORNERS TO REDUCE (ICON B)

press. Tabs can also be topstitched; then stitch the buttonhole before inserting into a seam as illustrated in Figure 17.22.

STITCHING BUTTONS

Any button used for opening and closing the garment needs to be stitched securely so that it doesn't pop off after the first, second, or third wearing.

Marking the Button Placement

- *Always* pin the garment closed first by

bringing the garment center (or off-center) lines together (lapping right over left) (Figure 17.25).

- For horizontal buttonholes, place the pin through to the left side of the garment exactly on the center garment line. This will be ⅛ inch in from the end of the buttonhole (Figure 17.25a).
- On vertical buttonholes, place a pin through the center of the buttonhole to the other side

of the garment; this is the button position (Figure 17.25b).

- Unpin the closure, carefully lift off the over-lapping side, pin-mark the button position, and stitch the button in place.

Single Breasted

The buttonholes are stitched to the right side of the garment. Stitch the buttons on the left-hand side of the garment directly on the garment

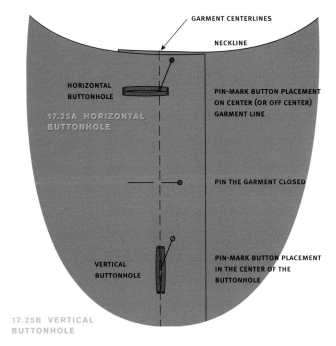

GARMENT CENTERLINES

NECKLINE

HORIZONTAL
BUTTONHOLE

PIN-MARK BUTTON PLACEMENT
ON CENTER (OR OFF CENTER)
GARMENT LINE

17.25A HORIZONTAL
BUTTONHOLE

PIN THE GARMENT CLOSED

VERTICAL
BUTTONHOLE

PIN-MARK BUTTON PLACEMENT
IN THE CENTER OF THE
BUTTONHOLE

17.25B VERTICAL
BUTTONHOLE

center (or off-center) line. Look at the coat in the Style I.D. in Figure 17.1b as a reference.

Double Breasted

Buttons and buttonholes are stitched to both front sides of double-breasted closures. So follow the instructions carefully for stitching button and buttonholes to a double-breasted coat. The coat we are describing for the closure is the coat in the Style I.D. in Figure 17.1a. The instructions move from the right to the left sides; follow this procedure to ensure correct buttoning.

- Stitch the buttonholes on the right-hand front of the garment (Figure 17.1a).
- Pin the garment closed by placing the two garment center (or off-center) lines together.

Pin-mark each button position through to the *left-hand side* of the garment to correspond with each buttonhole (Figure 17.25a). Stitch the buttons in place.

- Unbutton the coat and stitch two buttonholes to the *left-hand side* of the garment, *one at the neckline* or, as an option, *one on the waistline*. These two buttons help to hold the garment securely closed. The neckline buttonhole is indicated on the coat in Figure 17.1a in the Style I.D. The buttons that correspond with these buttonholes are stitched to the facing on the right-hand front. They *must be flat* so they don't add bulk. Buttons stitched to the garment surface can be decorative and any shape—this is the designer's choice.
- Button the coat closed again; pin the garment center lines together, and turn the garment to the wrong side.
- Pin-mark the two left-side button positions through to the facing on the *right-hand side* of the garment and stitch the buttons in place; these buttons will always be hidden underneath the coat.
- Turn the coat to the correct side and button it up. The second row of buttons is stitched to the garment surface and doesn't need buttonholes; it is purely decorative. Double-breasted closures are symmetrical; the buttons are placed at equal distances on each side of the garment center- or off-center line (see Figure 17.4a and d) and lined up horizontally. Securely stitch this row of buttons; if shank buttons are stitched, build another shank to help the buttons sit

upright on the garment. Figure 17.21c shows you how to stitch a shank button with an inbuilt shank.

What Thread to Use

A safe choice is to color match the thread to the button rather than to the fabric, especially for two-hole and four-hole buttons where the thread color is visible. Stitch buttons with two strands of thread. The final length of the threads should be no longer than 16 inches; thread that is any longer than this will get very tangled. Waxed nylon thread (weight C) is excellent for stitching buttons securely to jackets and coats, but the colors are limited.

Stitching Shank Buttons

Dome, half ball, and full ball buttons are all considered shank buttons. They have a small ring or bar called a *shank* that protrudes from underneath the button (Figures 17.8b, c, and d). The thread passes through the shank, then through the garment fabric so they connect together. The shank holds the button slightly away from the fabric to allow room for the other side of the garment to fit comfortably underneath without feeling tight when the buttonhole is slipped over the button.

For stitching shank buttons, follow the illustration in Figure 17.21.

- Secure the thread to the fabric surface.
- Place the button in position with the shank in a vertical direction that allows horizontal stitches.

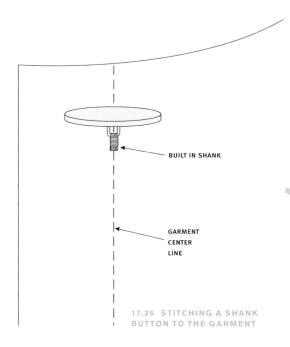

17.26 STITCHING A SHANK BUTTON TO THE GARMENT
- BUILT IN SHANK
- GARMENT CENTER LINE

Stitch the stitches parallel to the garment center line.

- Pass the needle alternately through the shank and the garment fabric, completing about 8 stitches.
- Finish by securing the thread under the button; take a few backstitches and clip the thread.
- To make an additional shank for thicker fabric: when stitching the button, stitch loosely so there is a gap between the shank and the fabric, bring the thread up under the button, and wind around the thread to make a firm shank (see Figure 17.26).

Stitching Sew-through Flat Buttons

Sew-through buttons can be two-hole or four-hole buttons. The needle and thread are pushed through the holes to attach the button to the garment. Flat buttons need a built-in shank to extend the height of the button so there is room for the other side of the garment to fit comfortably under the button after it is buttoned (see Figure 17.27).

Stitch the button with horizontal stitches; make sure all the stitches on every button go in the same direction.

- Attach the thread to the correct side of the garment with a few overhand stitches in the button position (Figure 17.27a).
- Push the needle up through one hole and back through the other hole (repeat again for four-hole buttons).
- Place a tapestry needle through the thread at the top of the button and pull taut; this is necessary for building in the shank (Figure 17.27b).
- Continue to place the needle up into the hole and back down again; as the needle comes back down, push the needle into the fabric under the button and take a small stitch.
- Continue to stitch in this manner to attach the button; the number of stitches depends on the fabric weight and on the size and function of the button. For example, a large button stitched to a coat

will need more stitches to secure it than a small button stitched to a silk georgette blouse.

- Remove the tapestry needle and pull the button outward so it is taut. This leaves a small gap of thread between the button and garment. Wind the needle thread around these threads to build the shank (Figure 17.27c). Or, stitch a chain stitch around the threads, as shown in Figure 17.31c.
- To finish stitching the button, slip the needle under the button, take a few backstitches, and snip the thread. The thread is not finished on the facing side of the garment; the facing stitches need to appear invisible in case the neckline is worn open (Figure 17.27d).

In production, flat sew-through buttons are attached by machine rather than by hand.

Covered Buttons

Custom-made buttons covered with fabric or leather add an elegant finish to a garment. Covered buttons are useful when "just the right" button can't be found. Covered buttons are all *shank buttons* and are available in a wide range of sizes, from ⅜ inch to 2½ inches in diameter, and in flat or half-ball shapes. The closure chart in Figure 17.7 shows the sizes available. The instructions for how to cover the button are written on each packet. Some businesses also offer a covering service. (See the "Where to Buy" section in this text.)

Each button has two separate pieces that form one button; the top section is metal and covered with fabric, while the bottom section

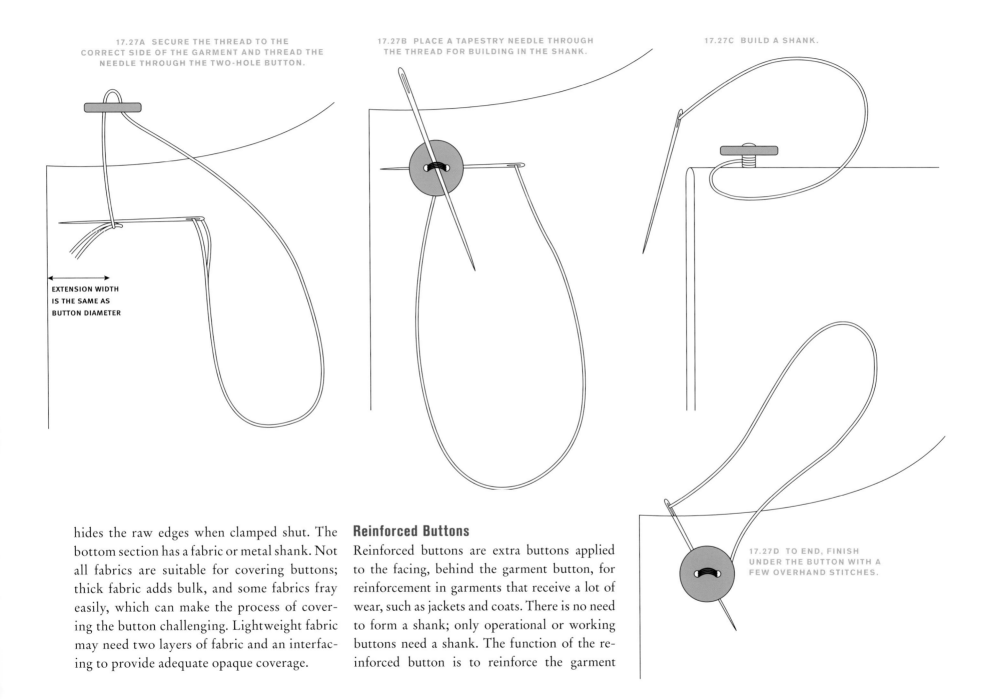

17.27A SECURE THE THREAD TO THE CORRECT SIDE OF THE GARMENT AND THREAD THE NEEDLE THROUGH THE TWO-HOLE BUTTON.

EXTENSION WIDTH IS THE SAME AS BUTTON DIAMETER

17.27B PLACE A TAPESTRY NEEDLE THROUGH THE THREAD FOR BUILDING IN THE SHANK.

17.27C BUILD A SHANK.

17.27D TO END, FINISH UNDER THE BUTTON WITH A FEW OVERHAND STITCHES.

hides the raw edges when clamped shut. The bottom section has a fabric or metal shank. Not all fabrics are suitable for covering buttons; thick fabric adds bulk, and some fabrics fray easily, which can make the process of covering the button challenging. Lightweight fabric may need two layers of fabric and an interfacing to provide adequate opaque coverage.

Reinforced Buttons

Reinforced buttons are extra buttons applied to the facing, behind the garment button, for reinforcement in garments that receive a lot of wear, such as jackets and coats. There is no need to form a shank; only operational or working buttons need a shank. The function of the reinforced button is to reinforce the garment button. Use a *small*, flat, two-hole or four-hole button, approximately L16 or L18. Match like with like—two-hole reinforcement button with two-hole garment button and, likewise, four-hole buttons combined together. Line up the reinforcement button behind the garment button on the facing. Sew directly from one button to the other.

SNAP FASTENERS

Refer to the closure chart in Figure 17.7 to see the snap fasteners available. A snap fastener has two round discs, one *male* and one *female,* that snap together to connect. Snaps are available in sizes 2 to 21, in black, silver, or clear nylon. Snaps can also be covered; this can be a fabulous couture finish to a garment. Snaps are designed to use as closures for a variety of reasons. Match the snap size to the fabric weight and amount of hold the garment needs for the closure to function.

A small, ¼-inch, clear nylon snap (size 2) looks invisible when stitched to the corner of the lapped extension. Look at Figure 17.9 to see the placement for this snap. Small snaps can also be used to hold the garment closed in between buttons (such as the waistline where a belt is worn); use the size and color that are least conspicuous, but be sure the snap will hold the garment securely closed.

On coats, use larger covered snaps such as size 10 (smaller sizes will not be strong enough to hold the garment closed). Snaps can be the closures themselves or be stitched behind a decorative button, as in Figure 17.28. In this case, the button is purely decorative and the snap

holds the garment closed. Snaps make an excellent replacement closure for really large buttons, since buttonholes for very large buttons look unattractive and have the potential to stretch.

- Always stitch the female snap to the right-hand side of the garment and the male to the left side (see Figure 17.28). Use two strands of thread for small snaps and four strands for larger snaps.
- Begin by securing the thread to the fabric with a few overhand stitches; stitch approximately four overhand stitches through each snap hole, then slip the thread under the snap and up into the next hole and stitch several overhand stitches again.
- Pull the threads taut as you stitch and finish with a couple of overhand stitches on the edge of one of the stitches that has secured the snap. After the snaps are stitched, there should be *no* stitches showing on the garment side of the fabric.

Covered Snaps

Choose a fabric in a contrasting color or one that blends with the garment fabric. Silk satin charmeuse is an ideal fabric weight; any designer would feel proud to show off silk-covered snaps in a garment that hangs open. The colors available are vast and most fabrics can be color

> **NOTE**
> Snaps will not hold a waistband or fly front securely closed—these application points need buttons and buttonholes.

RIGHT SIDE OF GARMENT

LARGE SQUARE BUTTON IS A NON-WORKING BUTTON

MALE SNAP

FACING

4 STRANDS OF THREAD ARE USED TO STITCH LARGE SNAPS

LEFT SIDE OF GARMENT

matched. Heavyweight, thick fabrics will preclude the snaps from functioning.

- Cut two circles of fabric to cover the snaps. Cut one circle ¼ inch wider than the snap (to cover the *male* snap). The other circle is cut $\frac{1}{16}$ inch wider than this circle and will cover the *female* snap.

17.29A　PLACE THE FEMALE
SNAP FACEDOWN.

17.29B　PULL THE THREAD
INTO GATHERS.

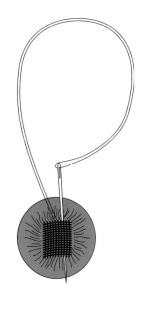

17.29C　PULL THE FABRIC TAUT TO
SECURE IT AROUND THE SNAP.

17.29D　PLACE THE CIRCLE OVER
THE MALE SNAP.

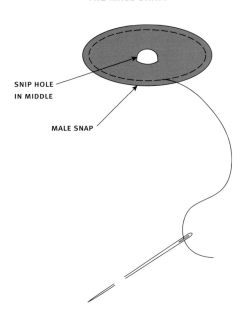

SNIP HOLE
IN MIDDLE

MALE SNAP

- With double thread stitch a running stitch around both circles, ⅛ inch in from the edge; leave the thread and needle attached (Figure 17.29a).
- Place the female snap facedown in the middle of the wrong side of the larger circle; pull the running stitches into gathering to enclose the snap (Figures 17.29a and b).
- Stitch large back-and-forth stitches to catch the fabric until it is firmly secured on both snaps; leave the needle and thread intact (see Figure 17.29c).

- Gently push an awl through the center of the smaller circle; larger snaps will need a little scissor snip in the middle of the circle. Apply Fray Check to prevent fraying. Pull the correct side of the fabric over the male snap; pull up the gathering stitches until taut. Snap both pieces together, then finish off the back of the male snap in the same way the female was finished in Figure 17.29c.

- The snaps are now ready to stitch to the garment—good-quality thread and good-quality stitching is a *must*! Make sure the snap is securely stitched with even stitches and the thread is pulled taut through each of the holes, as illustrated in Figure 17.28. No stitches should be visible from the correct side of the fabric.
- Stitch the male snap to the facing and the female to the garment (Figure 17.28).

Shoulder Strap Keepers

Shoulder strap keepers are very functional, as they hold lingerie straps in place under garments with low necklines and narrow garment straps. Straps popping out from under the garment or falling off the shoulder can spoil the look of an elegant garment. To prevent this from happening, stitch strap keepers—any customer would be delighted to find them in the garment! Cut two short lengths of ¼-inch twill tape to the required length. Finish one end of the keeper

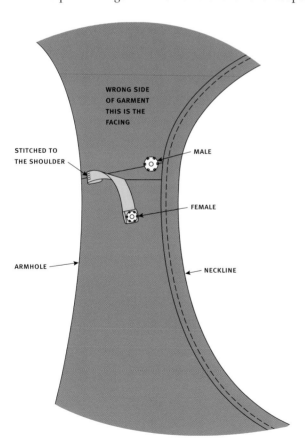

STITCHED TO
THE SHOULDER

WRONG SIDE
OF GARMENT
THIS IS THE
FACING

MALE

FEMALE

ARMHOLE

NECKLINE

17.30 MAKING SHOULDER STRAP KEEPERS

by folding twill tape over twice and catch with small overhand stitches. Place the male disc over the folded edge and stitch in place; use a smaller needle for small snaps so the eye of the needle fits comfortably through the holes (Figure 17.30). Fold the other end of the tape over twice and stitch to the armhole side of the shoulder facing seam using an overhand stitch. Stitch the female snap to the shoulder seam nearest the neckline.

HOOKS AND EYES

Hooks and eyes come in pairs; one side is the hook and the other the eye. They are available in sizes 0, 1, 2, 3, and 6 in black or white enamel and nickel; color match as closely as possible to the fabric color. Hooks and eyes are the last details to be stitched to the garment.

A small hook and eye can be stitched as a closure support. Size 0 will look inconspicuous stitched to the top edge of the waistline where a lapped or centered zipper has been stitched. The hook and eye prevents gaping at the top of a closure (invisible zippers do not need hooks and eyes). Larger silk- or gimp-covered hooks and eyes can be used as the main closure on jackets and coats (Figure 17.7).

Since hooks and eyes are hand stitched, they are not often used in mass–produced garments. They are definitely a couture finish.

- Turn the garment inside out. Stitch the hook on the right hand side of the garment; position the hook ⅛ inch down and 1/16 inch from the garment edges (Figure 17.31a).
- Secure a double length of thread (12-inch final

length) to the facing. Position the hook facing up. Work blanket stitches around circular rings; stitch closely together to completely cover the metal (Figure 17.31a).
- Don't cut the thread—instead, slip the needle in between the garment fabric and facing, surfacing at the end of the hook; then stitch a few overhand stitches to secure the end of the hook to the fabric (Figure 17.31b).

Thread Chain
- An eye is stitched on the opposite side of the facing at the same height, just next to the seamline. Figure 17.31a shows you the position. To stitch a thread chain eye, secure a double thread with a few overhand stitches; take another stitch in the fabric to form a loop (Figure 17.31b).
- Slip your thumb and the first two fingers of your *right hand* through the loop to hold it open; secure the garment firmly with your left wrist and hold the needle thread taut with your left hand (Figure 17.31c).
- Use your *right hand* forefinger to pull the needle thread through the loop to form a new

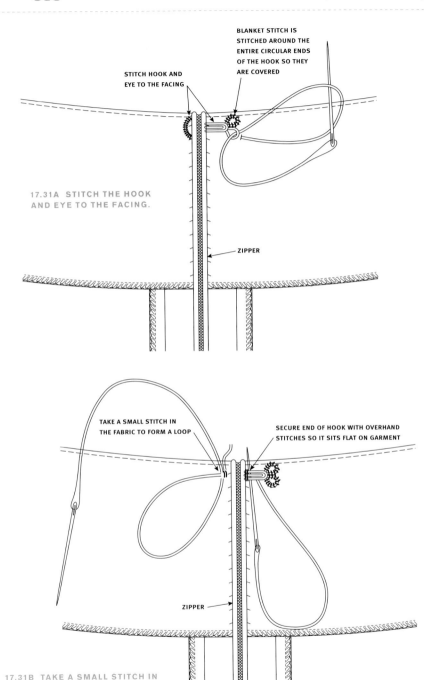

STITCH HOOK AND
EYE TO THE FACING

BLANKET STITCH IS
STITCHED AROUND THE
ENTIRE CIRCULAR ENDS
OF THE HOOK SO THEY
ARE COVERED

ZIPPER

**17.31A STITCH THE HOOK
AND EYE TO THE FACING.**

TAKE A SMALL STITCH IN
THE FABRIC TO FORM A LOOP

SECURE END OF HOOK WITH OVERHAND
STITCHES SO IT SITS FLAT ON GARMENT

ZIPPER

**17.31B TAKE A SMALL STITCH IN
THE FABRIC TO FORM A LOOP.**

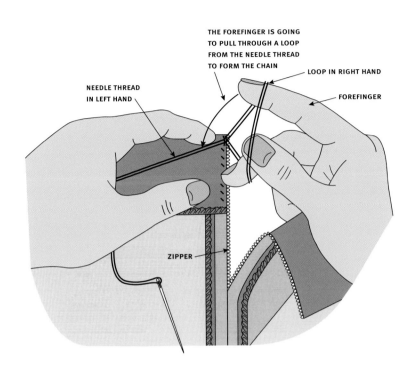

THE FOREFINGER IS GOING
TO PULL THROUGH A LOOP
FROM THE NEEDLE THREAD
TO FORM THE CHAIN

NEEDLE THREAD
IN LEFT HAND

LOOP IN RIGHT HAND

FOREFINGER

ZIPPER

17.31C FORMING THE THREAD EYE WITH A CHAIN STITCH

IMPORTANT

Always match the size of the hook and eye to the function for which
it is being used. Hooks and eyes *can* be stitched as the main closure
but need to be strong enough to secure the garment closed without coming undone. For example, a size 6 hook and eye will hold
a bustier closed, but sizes 0 to 3 will not. Hooks and eyes are *not*
strong enough to keep waistbands closed; use a hook and bar closure
instead (see Figure 8.13).

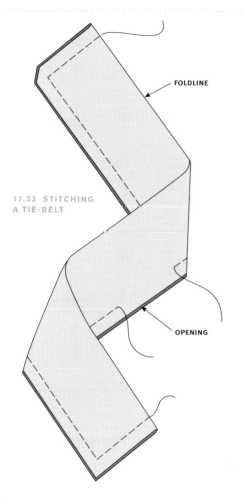

17.32 STITCHING
A TIE-BELT

FOLDLINE

OPENING

loop; tighten the loop to the fabric to form the thread chain. Continue working the chain for the ¼-inch length (see Figure 17.31c).

- To finish, place the needle ¼ inch down into the fabric and end with a few backstitches in the seamline.
- If a metal eye is used, it can be blanket stitched to the garment in the same way as the hook.

Hook-and-Eye Tape

Hook-and-eye tape can be purchased and stitched

to the right and left sides of a closure. Colors are limited to black and white, but the white tape can be dyed. The hooks used are size 2.

BELTS

Belts can be the final finishing touch to the garment; in fact, they would be the last item to stitch in the closure. Belts can be stiff and structured, with a buckle, or softly tied—a style called a tie-belt. Instructions for both types of belts will be outlined.

Tie-Belt

A **tie-belt** can be used on all kinds of garments and tied around the waistline, under the bust, on the front or back of the garment, around the wrist, or slotted through loops in a neckline. The coat in Figure 17.1b in the Style I.D. has a black contrasting tie-belt. Notice, too, that shorter ties encircle the wrists.

Cut the tie-belt so it fits comfortably around the waist with enough length to loop over and tie. A tie-belt can be cut on the fold, on any grainline; however, the grainline will affect how the tails drape. Bias-cut belt ties are wavelike and fall softly; straight grain belt tails fall straight. Interfacing is not needed in softly tied belts.

- Place the correct sides together, and stitch a seam around the edge; leave a 2-inch opening in the middle; backstitch at each point (Figure 17.32).
- Trim the corners to reduce bulk.

- Turn the tie-belt to the correct side with a loop turner, or use a ruler to help turn the tie-belt if you have one on hand. From the correct side, press along the seamline with the point of the iron.
- Lay the tie flat and press again so the seamline is perfectly aligned and does not show on one side more than on the other. Slipstitch the opening closed.

Structured Belt

A tie-belt can be made into a **structured belt** using **buckram** to stiffen it so the belt won't cave in around the waistline. Buckram, available in different widths for belts, is made from a tightly woven, stiffened cotton fabric. The buckle needs to be slightly wider than the finished belt width. **Grommets** need to be applied to the belt when the buckle has a prong. Grommets provide a circle opening for the belt prong to enter. They need to be applied along the lapped side of the belt, giving a variety of closure lengths. Match the grommet size to fit the prong. Grommets and the hardware needed can be purchased online. The appendix "Where to Buy" at the back of this book is a useful resource.

To calculate the length of a structured belt, take the waistline measurement and add several more inches (approximately 8) and 1 more inch for attaching a buckle. Cut the belt wide enough so that when it is stitched, turned, and pressed, the belt is slightly wider (⅛ inch) than the width of the buckram. The end of the belt and the buckram should be identical in shape.

After the belt is stitched, turned, and pressed, slip the buckram into the belt slot—be patient—it will take time to push the buckram in. Cut off 1 inch from the buckram length to reduce the bulk so the belt can wrap around the buckle and be secured with overhand stitches, as illustrated in Figure 17.33. The coat in Figure 17.16 has a structured belt, which gives it a classy tailored look.

The fabric surface needs particular care when stitching closures. Delicate fabrics, such as satin, sheers, beaded, and velvet fabrics, need to be handled with care. Take extra care in choosing the type of closure for these fabrics. It doesn't hurt to be reminded—the design needs to suit the fabric and your closures should suit the fabric—stitching decisions are *always* fabric-driven.

STITCHING CLOSURES IN TRICKY FABRICS
Matching Stripes, Plaids, Patterns, and Repeat Patterns

Do perfectly line up the right and left sides together, matching the plaid, stripe, and check horizontally and vertically. Remember, they will *never* match perfectly unless cut perfectly!

Do stitch bound buttonholes in stripes. Redirect the grainline to the opposite grain for welts to show difference, then they don't need to match exactly to the garment stripe.

Do be careful applying tabs as closures on checks, stripes, and plaid fabrics, as they will need to be perfectly matched. Try cutting them on the bias grain to prevent having to match them; this will also add uniqueness to the design.

Sheer Fabric

Do stitch twice-turned bands (double extension turned over twice) on shirt fronts in sheer fabrics; the extra layer of fabric will equal the interfacing, and color matching of the interfacing will not be an issue.

Do machine stitch buttonholes in sheer fabrics; use a fine sewing machine needle and place tissue paper underneath to stabilize.

Do use bows and ties as closures in soft, lightweight, sheer fabrics.

Do stitch bias loops as closures for sheers, but make sure the seam allowances are carefully and evenly trimmed to a minimum to reduce shadowing.

Don't stitch bound buttonholes, as the seam allowances will be visible in between the garment fabric and facing, and this is unattractive.

Lace

Do sample machine buttonholes in lace first to see how they blend with the surface of the lace. Use organza under the buttonholes as the interfacing. Machine-stitched buttonholes would be applied to a flat-surface lace blouse, but not to an evening gown. Elastic loops are a better option on lace evening dresses; traditionally, they are used as a closure on lace wedding dresses. The loops sit ½ inch apart and stretch over lots of tiny buttons. (See the "Where to Buy" section of this book.)

Do use a fine machine and hand needle when working with lace.

Do use delicate hand stitches when stitching buttons to lace or any other closures.

Don't stitch bound buttonholes or any other closures in lace where seams will shadow from the correct side of the fabric; always remember the integrity of the fabric—the closure must suit the fabric!

Satin

Do use bias loops or elastic loops with half ball buttons as the closures on satin; however, bias loops in heavyweight satin fabrics may look bulky.

Do stitch glamorous decorative buttons—such as pearl, glass, jeweled, or covered buttons—on satin garments.

Do use a *new* correctly sized sewing machine needle when stitching delicate fabrics such as satin; also use a fine hand sewing needle.

Do use tie-belts in soft silk satin fabrics.

Don't stitch buttonholes onto satin fabrics without sampling first, as the surface is delicate and threads pull easily; however, buttonholes can be stitched as openings on blouses and shirts in lightweight silk satin.

Beaded Fabric

Do use a thread eye when hooks and eyes are being applied to fine sheer fabrics.

Do use loops for closures on beaded fabric; however, use a fabric with a smooth surface, such as silk satin, because beaded fabric would not stitch and turn smoothly into bias loops.

Do use soft ties and bows as closures on beaded fabric, but think about using a smooth, lightweight complementary fabric such as silk satin or georgette; don't stitch these closures to the fabric surface but, rather, inset them into a seam or use as a tie around the waist.

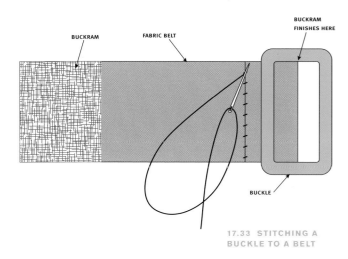

BUCKRAM FABRIC BELT BUCKRAM FINISHES HERE

BUCKLE

17.33 STITCHING A BUCKLE TO A BELT

Don't try to stitch machine buttonholes to the surface of beaded fabric; the beads would get in the way and it would be a rocky road!

Knits

Do use machine-stitched buttonholes in knit fabrics, but make sure the interfacing is cut on the stable grain so the buttonholes don't stretch in the stitching process (see Figure 3.10).

Do use a *stretch stitch* when stitching knit ties or loops; stitches "pop" when a stretch stitch is not used.

Don't stitch loops in heavyweight knit fabric.

Denim

Do try almost any closure in denim. Denim is a wonderful fabric to work with; however, sample the closure first to be sure it suits the fabric weight.

Do stitch any type of buttonhole, tab, tab-loop, snap fastener, tie, and belt in denim.

Don't stitch bias loops in denim, as they may be too heavy and hard to turn.

Velvet

Do carefully choose the closure for velvet, as it is a pile fabric; any closure added, such as a tab, would need to be cut in the same direction as the garment fabric.

Do use bias loops inserted into the seam as a closure in velvet; however, keep in mind that the weight of the velvet may preclude this type of closure from working, so sample first.

Do use a contrast fabric such as silk charmeuse for loops.

Do stitch in-seam buttonholes in velvet, but sample first to get the correct size opening.

Do stitch a sample buttonhole first on velvet fabric to see how it looks because the machine foot can leave marks on the fabric—choose another type of closure if this happens.

Do stitch covered snaps as closures in velvet; they would be an *ideal* closure.

Don't stitch bound buttonholes in velvet; however, if you really want to, use an alternative *nonpile* fabric.

Leather

Do mark the buttonhole position on the wrong side of the leather.

Do sample first to check that the buttonhole size is correct.

Do use tab-loops, tabs, belts, and buckles as closures in leather. They can be inserted into seams or topstitched to the surface.

Do stitch buttons to leather using waxed nylon thread (weight C).

Do stitch traditional bound buttonholes, as they look fabulous in leather! Use a leather machine needle. Mark the buttonhole length on the welts and not on the leather garment. Follow the stitching order for the traditional bound buttonhole with the following difference: slit the facing ⅛ inch longer than the buttonhole length; don't turn the edges under, leave them flat; and use a *fabric glue stick* to secure the facing to the buttonhole area (pins can't be used in leather). Stitch-in-the-ditch around the buttonhole from the face of the leather, as Figure 17.14c illustrates. The leather can be neatly trimmed closer to the stitches on the facing. Pull the threads to the wrong side, tie off, and slip them through the two layers of leather using a Glovers needle.

Don't stitch bias loops, as leather has no bias grain.

Don't use snaps on leather; hand stitching does not look attractive on leather.

Faux Fur

Do use fur hooks and covered snaps for an uncomplicated, clean closure on faux fur.

Don't machine stitch buttonholes in fur, as the hair will get tangled and messy.

Heavyweight Fabric

Do stitch *faced* bound buttonholes in heavyweight fabric, as this method reduces bulk.

Do stitch large covered snaps on heavyweight fabrics; they eliminate bulk. Stitch them as the working part of the closure, and stitch the button as decorative design.

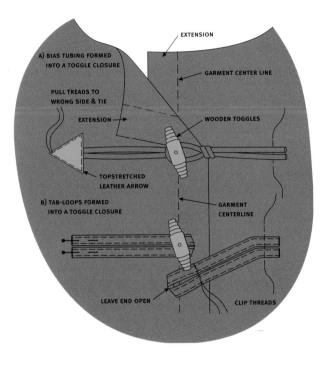

A) BIAS TUBING FORMED
INTO A TOGGLE CLOSURE

EXTENSION

GARMENT CENTER LINE

PULL TREADS TO
WRONG SIDE & TIE

EXTENSION

WOODEN TOGGLES

TOPSTRETCHED
LEATHER ARROW

B) TAB-LOOPS FORMED
INTO A TOGGLE CLOSURE

GARMENT
CENTERLINE

LEAVE END OPEN

CLIP THREADS

17.34B TAB-LOOPS FORMED
INTO A TOGGLE CLOSURE

Do use tabs and tab-loops, but sample first to check whether the fabric is too bulky. **Don't** use bias turned loops in heavyweight fabrics, as they will be too bulky.

TRANSFER YOUR KNOWLEDGE

- Use the same pattern tips and stitching techniques for other placement positions for closures. For example, a garment could

have a closure across the shoulder or down the sleeve. A button and buttonhole closure could also be down the side seam of any garment.

- A tie around the waist can be applied the same way above the wrist of the sleeve. This is part of the design in the coat in Figure 17.1b. The tie can be slipped though belt loops and tied, buttoned, or fastened.
- The same stitching method used for making bias loops can be used for making a tie-belt; simply use larger proportions. The tie-belt will look rounded and padded. Three pieces of bias tubing can also be braided into a tie-belt.
- Do you realize that a bound buttonhole is a smaller version of a welt pocket? Refer to "Welt Pockets" in Chapter 5, and look at Figure 5.11 and compare.
- Stitch a tab to the collar, hem band, or pocket. The coat in Figure 17.1b in the Style I.D. has a tab stitched to the collar as part of the closure. Also use tabs as the belt keeper, as indicated on the design in this coat.
- Use the same *in-seam* buttonhole stitching technique and, transferring your knowledge, stitch a larger slot in princess seams (or any other seams) and insert any style of belt through the slots.

STRETCH YOUR CREATIVITY

- Group small buttons of different compositions (glass, pearl, metal) together as a surface texture on the fabric.

- Stitch different-sized buttons to one garment.
- Be creative with button placements—group them in twos or threes—there are no rules, but do maintain functional design.
- Attach an extra flared section to the bottom of a skirt length and add bias loops. Stitch buttons to the skirt, and button the flared section to the skirt for a longer length; the flare can easily be removed for a shorter look. This is illustrated in Figure 17.1c in the Style I.D.
- The following figures illustrate how some of the closures in this chapter can be stitched in different proportions and used as other creative closure designs.
- In Figure 17.34, a warm all-weather jacket could have either of these toggle closures. Toggles are often used as closures on heavyweight fabrics and casual styles of jackets, coats, and sweaters. A toggle closure needs two bars; the left bar holds the toggle and the right bar forms the loop for the closure. Toggles can be formed using bias tubing (Figure 17.34a) or belt loops formed into a longer tab-loop and stitched to the garment surface (Figure 17.34b). A leather arrow is stitched to cover the raw edges; the bars could also be inserted into a seam and the arrow omitted. Use a double lapped extension for toggle closures.
- Figure 17.35 illustrates a tab-and-buckle closure. This would be fabulous on a leather jacket. Attach a buckle to the left-side tab; then topstitch both tabs to the garment surface. There are many styles of buckles available; choose the buckle first, and then size

the tab to fit the buckle. The buckle could also have a prong for a more secure closure; apply grommets to the opposite tab for the prong to slide through.

- Figure 17.36 has an edge-to-edge bow closure. This is an ideal choice for a loose jacket closure on the neckline. The belt loop is cut longer to tie; the tie would need to be hand stitched to the back of one buttonhole so it would not be lost when untied.
- Lacing is a favorite closure among design students, especially for a bustier. In Figure 17.37, bias tubing is used for the lacing; however, a

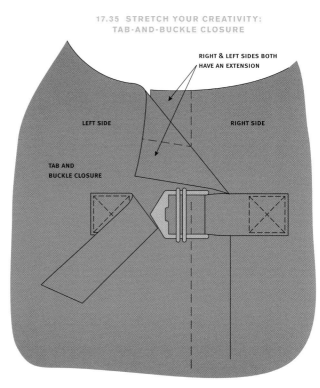

17.35 STRETCH YOUR CREATIVITY: TAB-AND-BUCKLE CLOSURE

RIGHT & LEFT SIDES BOTH HAVE AN EXTENSION

LEFT SIDE

RIGHT SIDE

TAB AND BUCKLE CLOSURE

> **IMPORTANT**
>
> **Functional design should always be the highest priority for the design student when thinking about how a closure works and feels on the body.**

longer belt loop or leather lacing could be used instead. Grommets are applied on both sides of an interfaced edge-to-edge closure. Grommets are sturdier than eyelets, and the back of eyelets can be scratchy next to the skin.

STOP! WHAT DO I DO IF . . .

. . . I don't know what style of closure to choose for my design? Are there any guidelines to help me choose the best closure to suit my design?

Yes, refer to the section "How to Choose the Appropriate Closure for the Garment." Also, sketch different closure options to visualize what looks aesthetically pleasing to the eye. Sample different closures on your fabric to get direction and clarity.

. . . my buttonholes are too big?

From the wrong side of the garment, hand stitch one end of the buttonhole with an overhand stitch to make the buttonhole smaller.

. . . my buttonholes are too small?

It would be best to purchase a smaller button to fit the buttonhole; seam ripping buttonhole stitching from the garment surface would weaken the fabric and cause the fabric to fray. Another option would be to stitch snaps as the

---

closure, hand stitch the buttonhole together with invisible stitches, stitch a large button over the buttonhole, and then stitch covered snaps as the closure. Then, hesitantly, we would say . . . if the buttonhole is machine stitched, you could carefully add on some more stitches to lengthen the buttonhole. You would need exactly the same thread color and begin by overlapping a few stitches, then off you go! Carefully slit the buttonhole extension with embroidery scissors.

. . . I forgot to add an extension to my pattern and the garment is too tight to close?

An extension can be added to the front of the garment as a band, which will have a seam join. Cut the extension/band on the fold with equal width underneath, attach half or full interfacing to stabilize, and then stitch vertical buttonholes.

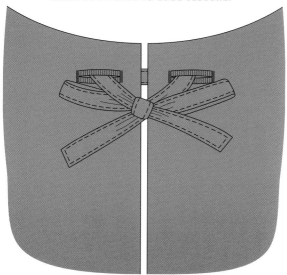

17.36 BELT LOOP MADE INTO A TIE: THE TIE IS SLOTTED THROUGH TWO BUTTONHOLES AND TIED INTO A BOW AS AN EDGE-TO-EDGE CLOSURE.

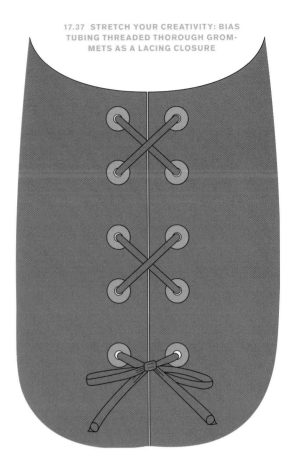

17.37 STRETCH YOUR CREATIVITY: BIAS TUBING THREADED THOROUGH GROMMETS AS A LACING CLOSURE

. . . my hooks and eyes won't stay closed down the front of the garment?

Use a larger size, say size 6. Perhaps the hooks and eyes are too small to hold the closure together. Remember, the closure needs to be strong enough to keep the garment securely closed—this is functional design.

. . . I accidentally snipped the machine buttonhole stitches when cutting the buttonhole open; can I fix it?

Yes you can! Take a needle and double thread in the same thread color as the buttonhole stitches. Attach the thread on the facing side with a few overhand stitches, bring to the correct side, and add a few very close overhand stitches over the stitches that were snipped. Finish the stitching on the facing side on the edge of the buttonhole stitches.

SELF-CRITIQUE

Take a look at your finished garment and, in particular, look at the closure. Assess whether the closure is well-stitched and functional. Here are some other questions to help you critique your closure:

- Does the closure suit the design and fabric weight?
- Did I add the correct extension width for the button or other type of closure?
- Does my closure sit flat, or is it puckered or askew?
- Does the closure keep the garment securely closed, or does it allow the garment to slip open easily when the body moves?
- Did I use a stabilizer under my closure to prevent it from stretching?
- Did I place the closures (buttons, snaps, tabs, etc.) in the key placement points for a woman's body?
- Did I use the recommended amount of thread strands with adequate stitches to secure the buttons and snaps in place?
- Did I follow the stitching method of *SEW, CLIP, PRESS* while stitching my closures?

REVIEW CHECKLIST

- Do I understand how correct patterns (the extension in particular) set me up to accomplish correct stitching and the correct fit of the garment?
- Do I understand that the style of closure directs me in the extension I need to add for my closure?
- Do I understand how helpful it is to hand-baste the *center* or *off-center garment line* before stitching the closure?
- Do I understand the difference between a symmetrical closure and an asymmetrical closure?
- Do I understand that garments can close edge-to-edge, with a single extension, or with an extension added to both sides of the garment?
- Do I understand that the extension width is determined by the diameter of the button?
- Do I understand that women's buttoning is traditionally right over left, and that this direction continues around the body to the back of the garment?
- Do I grasp the important concept that the fabric weight and drape also guide me in choosing the closure along with the design?
- Do I understand that multiple samples may need to be tried before finally deciding on the best closure?
- Do I understand how fashion and function *must* go hand in hand when considering the closure of the garment?

Finishing Touches: All Sewn Up!

What needs to be done to finish the garment? Even though this is the last step, the finishing touches of sew, clip, and press should have been carried out during the stitching order. All the steps leading to this final stage are reviewed and examined in each chapter.

Final tweaking and careful completion of details from the inside out raise the garment from ordinary to extraordinary! In this chapter, to ensure that no step has been overlooked, work

from the completed checklist for review. After completing this chapter, you can take pride in saying, "My garment is finally all sewn up!"

STYLE I.D.
The Style I.D. shows the completion of the garment. Notice the front, side, and back are all on view, as all aspects of the garment are important. It's not only the stitching that's on view but also the fit and the look of the final design (Figure 18.1).

GATHER YOUR TOOLS
Iron, pressing cloth, and your **thread clippers** are the main tools needed to attend to the finishing touches. Attending to the finishing touches *should not* involve stitching, as this should all have been completed. However, it may be useful to have a needle and thread handy just in case one or two stitches have come apart or a hem stitch is missing. At this stage, use a hand stitch for any repairs, as it could be difficult to get back inside the garment to stitch with the sewing machine.

KEY TERMS

Iron
Press
Pressing Cloth
Needle Board
Ironing Board
Tailor's Ham
Sleeve Board
Seam Roll
Crease Line
Thread Clippers

NOW LET'S GET STARTED

During the stitching process, the *SEW, CLIP, PRESS* method of constructing garments has been encouraged. Now when you finish the garment there should not be very much to attend to, beyond clipping and a final press. If you haven't used this method throughout the construction process of your garment, by this stage you will realize how important it was. Trying to get back inside a garment to press and clip threads is an impossible task, especially if the garment has a closed lining. It is also impossible to get inside collars, cuffs, pocket flaps, and facings if they haven't been perfectly turned and pressed before they were stitched to the garment.

Before attending to the finishing touches, we encourage you to understand your fabric before giving it a final press. Burning a hole or scorching the garment at this stage is very upsetting and many students do this, especially when rushing to complete a garment due that very day.

FINISHING TOUCHES THAT NEED ATTENDING TO

In production, quality control takes care of looking over the final finished garments to ensure that they meet standards. In class, the teacher provides quality control. However, we encourage students to assess their own work as well. The finishing touches are important to the final look of the garment.

Clip All Threads

It's amazing how those threads just seem to appear when you think you have snipped them

18.1 STYLE I.D.: BEADED GOWN

all. Of course, few threads should be evident at this stage if the *SEW, CLIP, PRESS* method of stitching has been followed. Don't be tempted to pull any stray threads with your hands to snap them off, as this could pull the stitching apart. Use thread clippers to clip the threads carefully. We know of many students who have rushed this step, grabbed large shears, and accidentally snipped a hole in the fabric just cutting an unwanted thread off! If you have not already used thread clippers, please do purchase a pair and begin to use them. Turn the garment inside out, place on a flat surface or on the form, and carefully clip any threads left hanging after machine or hand stitching or from serging (Figure 18.2).

In production, individuals called finishers attend to the final details of the garment before it undergoes the final pressing. Part of their responsibility is to clip the threads and take care of any hand stitching such as buttons, hooks and eyes, or snaps. If the threads are not clipped, they will still be hanging there when the customer purchases the garment. A customer may be tempted to pull the thread, and the consequences of this could be a seam ripped apart. And what will a customer do then? *Yes*, they will return the garment, and this in turn gives the company a bad name for not having quality stitching. So attending to the finishing touches is important!

Pressing Tips

- Always let the iron heat up to the correct temperature for your fabric.
- Test the iron temperature by pressing a sample first.

- Make sure the base of the iron has been cleaned of any sticky deposits, such as those left by bits of fusible interfacing. Often this type of residue can be removed without the aid of cleaning products, so try this first: Turn off the steam, heat the iron, and rub several layers of scrap muslin over the affected areas to remove the residue. A cleaning product is available to remove stubborn residue from the bottom of an iron.
- *Always use a pressing cloth when placing an iron on the correct side of the fabric!* The quality of work done in construction pressing (remember, *SEW, CLIP, PRESS*) determines how much final pressing is needed.
- The care and respect given to the garment during construction also affects how much final pressing is needed. Good pressing is essential to good sewing!

18.2 CLIPPING THE THREADS INSIDE THE BEADED DRESS

LINING

WRONG SIDE OF BEADED DRESS

The Final Press

Turn your garment to the correct side of the fabric, as the final pressing is done on the outside of the garment. Take the time needed to press carefully. Place a large piece of pattern paper under garments that may drape on the floor when being pressed (Figure 18.3).

To begin, the entire garment is pressed on grain—just as there is directional sewing, there is directional pressing. Curves should be pressed over a **tailor's ham**, zippers should be closed, and basting stitches removed. No creases are needed in the sleeves—use a **sleeve board** or a **seam roll.** (Refer to Chapter 2, "Pressing Equipment," to view these pressing items, and to the section on "How to Press a Garment" there for further pressing instructions.)

- Dresses should be pressed from the neck down: collar, sleeves, shoulders, facings, bodice front, bodice back, and skirt. Often, applying steam directly above the area that needs pressing is sufficient to remove wrinkles.
- To press trouser **crease lines,** first check on the body where you want them placed. If the waistline has tucks, then the creaseline follows on from the tuck down the length of the pants. Press crease lines with care, for once pressed it is hard to unpress the creases.
- While the garment is pressed and still warm, place it on a hanger to cool down rather than in a pile with other clothes, as this will only put creases back into the garment.
- Place your garment in a garment bag to

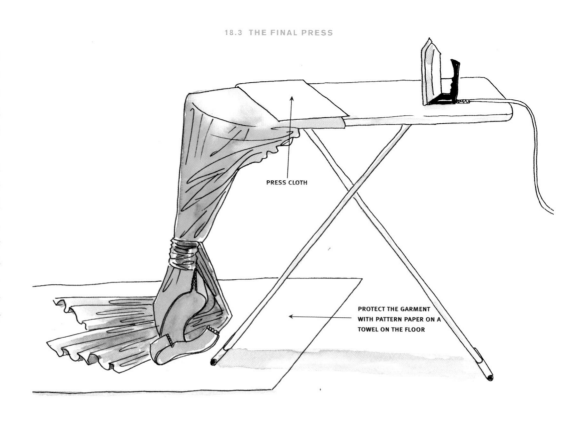

PRESS CLOTH

PROTECT THE GARMENT WITH PATTERN PAPER ON A TOWEL ON THE FLOOR

carry home (Figure 18.4). Don't squish it in your bag because if you do, you will need to repeat the final pressing process again and that is a waste of time!

In production, some garments are lightly steamed while they are still on the form or on a hanger.

PRESSING TRICKY FABRICS

It cannot be stated often enough: the fabric is the basis on which all decisions are made for pressing. Knowing the fabric content and care requirements of your fabric is *essential* when giving tricky fabrics a final press. Different fabrics require different temperature settings, and some fabric surfaces need special attention when pressing. Fabrics such as denim press easily, and don't require the use of a pressing cloth, while other fabrics may need a pressing cloth to protect the fabric surface from the iron and heat. Fabrics such as velvet cannot have a hot iron placed directly on the fabric surface. If pressed directly, the pile surface would be left with a definite iron mark. Always set the iron heat to the temperature setting for each fabric type, and then proceed by sample pressing first. Refer to Chapter 2 for more pressing tips.

STOP! WHAT DO I DO IF . . .

. . . my iron was too hot and I burned a hole or scorched the fabric in my garment in the final pressing stage? Can I do anything about this?

Not really! This often happens to students when they don't do a pressing sample first. One thing you can do is to carefully seam rip the burnt garment section out, then recut and restitch the piece back into the garment. This is a big job but worth doing if you have extra fabric and your garment is going to be in a fashion show. The other option is to add a decorative trim to the garment to cover the hole; this could be lace, a bow, a braid, or other appliqué.

. . . my garment already looks pressed; do I still need to give it a final press?

This means you have obviously pressed every dart and seam, collar, and cuff throughout the entire stitching process and carried your garment to and from school in a garment bag. Congratulations—this does need applauding! No, don't press the garment any more; it's been pressed adequately.

. . . I can't get into my garment to press the seams, collar, cuffs, and darts, and they don't lie flat—and, oh yes, my garment is lined—what can I do?

Unfortunately, this is almost an impossible task with a closed lining. It is too hard at this stage to get back into the garment to press the darts, seams, and collar after it is completed. However, you can seam rip the lining from the hem to get back inside the garment. Slip the garment over the **ironing board** and carefully get back inside the garment and press the seams and darts. Pull the collar corners out carefully with a pin point to sharpen the corners, roll the collar in your hand to get the seam perfectly aligned, and press again.

SELF-CRITIQUE

Place the garment on the form, stand back, and take a good long look at it. Check that every detail has been attended to. Congratulations, you have now finished your project!

- How would you rate your final product? (Circle one)
  Excellent /Very good /Good /Fair/ Unacceptable
- If you answered anything less than "Excellent," in what ways could you improve when you sew your next garment?

Make a list of the areas for improvement.

_____

_____

_____

_____

- If your answer was "Excellent," then list some sewing techniques you've never stitched before that would stretch your creativity and transfer your knowledge:

_____

_____

_____

_____

_____

_____

_____

- Look at your final project; can you see what a difference it has made by using the *SEW, CLIP, PRESS* method of stitching that was suggested in Chapter 2? If you don't recall reading this, we suggest going back to read page 51 in the chapter again before stitching another garment.
- Can you see that precise patternmaking and quality stitching result in an excellent garment—one that, when it appears on the catwalk, will make people gasp because it looks so fabulous!
- If you gave up halfway on pressing as you stitch, then next time try the *SEW, CLIP, PRESS* method. It does make a huge difference to the quality of a garment.

18.4 THE FINAL WRAP

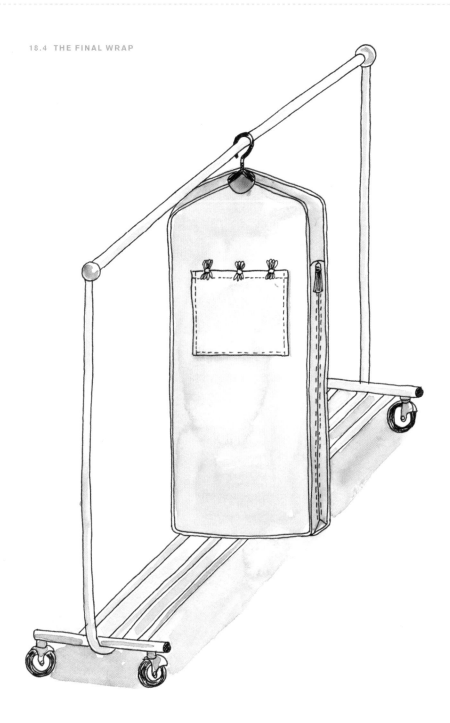

REVIEW CHECKLIST

- Did I choose the right fabric for the design?
- Did I stabilize the areas needing structure with the correct weight and type of stabilizer?
- Is my stitching straight, and was the proper stitch tension used?
- Did I use the *SEW, CLIP, PRESS* method of stitching?
- Do the darts and seams lie flat and are they well pressed?
- Do collar, cuffs, and pocket corners look squared; do seamlines sit directly in the middle of the seam or do they roll forward to the correct side of the garment?
- Did I attend to reducing bulk during the stitching process?
- Do the pockets look symmetrical on both sides of the garment; are they stitched securely?
- Is pocket stitching even and are welts of equal width?
- Is the centered zipper actually centered?
- Is the lapped zipper welt an adequate width or is it too wide?
- Does the invisible zipper open and close easily or is it stitched too close to the coils, putting additional stress on the garment?
- Is the invisible zipper invisible, or does the zipper tape show on the correct side of the garment?
- Is the bottom of the invisible zipper inserted into the seam without puckering or pleating?

- Are the tucks evenly spaced and stitched straight?
- Are the tucks an equal width and depth?
- If topstitched, are the pleats stitched evenly?
- Are the pleats correctly hemmed and bulk free?
- Is the waistband properly stabilized?
- Does the waistband extension face the correct direction?
- Does the waistband have the correct closure and does it lie flat?
- Are the ruffles stitched with even, well-distributed gathering, or does the gathering look bunched?
- Does my collar sit well on the garment and did I use the correct weight of interfacing to add the required structure or did I leave this aspect out?

- Do the facings lay flat and adequately finish the garment edge?
- Do the cuffs fit to the wrist properly or are they too tight or too loose? Are the cuffs structured with an interfacing and the buttonholes or loops stitched in the correct position?
- Do my sleeves round the arms beautifully, with the easing evenly distributed and no little puckers evident on the sleeve cap?
- Do my hem stitches on the hem show on the correct side of the garment? Is my topstitched hem stitched straight?
- Does the lining sit well? Is the lining too tight or too loose? Does any lining hang below the hem from the correct side of the garment?

- Have I used the best type of closure for the design? Does the closure function well, so that buttonholes easily slip over buttons, and snaps, hooks, and eyes securely hold the garment closed?
- When I stand back and view the overall garment, does it look well pressed?
- When I stand back and view the overall garment, are any threads left hanging?
- Did I experiment by sampling to make an informed decision on the type of stabilizer, seam stitching, hem stitching, and pressing?

Congratulations, your garment is finally all sewn up! Place it in the garment bag for the final wrap.

GLOSSARY

Accordion Pleat: A very narrow pleat, wider at the bottom than at the top.

All-in-One Facing: A facing used to finish the neckline and armhole edges at the same time. It is commonly used in areas where separate facings would overlap, creating a bulky appearance.

All-in-One Sleeve: A sleeve with no armhole.

All-Purpose Zipper: A zipper that is closed at the bottom; most often used in a skirt or neckline openings, and trousers, slacks, or pants. Also known as a *conventional zipper.*

Armhole Facing: A fabric piece cut the same shape and on the same grainline as the armhole edge it is finishing.

Asymmetrical Closure: A closure on one side of the garment and not centered.

Asymmetrical Darts: Darts that originate from different positions on either side of the garment.

Awl: A pointed, metal instrument used to make small holes within areas of the pattern or garment.

Backstitch: (1) A permanent hand stitch used to stitch a seam. (2) A technique of machine stitching forward and backward to secure a seam so it does not unravel during the construction process.

Band: A feature used as a finish for the edge of garment sections, as an extension of a garment edge, or applied as a decoration.

Belt Loop: Fabric or other material, such as leather strips, constructed to hold a belt in the desired position on a garment.

Bemberg Rayon Lining: An excellent all-purpose quality lining that is anti-cling and breathable, with a soft silky touch.

Bias: The grainline that runs at a 45-degree-angle to the lengthwise and crosswise grainlines.

Bias Binding: Strips of fabric cut on the bias grain.

Bias Binding Finish: An edge finish that stitches a narrow bias-cut fabric strip to enclose a raw edge.

Bias Facing: Bias fabric strips cut and pressed to match the shape of the area to which it is being applied.

Bias Loops: A closure made of bias tubing formed into half circles.

Bias/Roll Collar: A straight, rectangular, bias-cut collar that rolls over and drapes around the neckline.

Blanket Stitch: An embroidery stitch, usually sewn by hand, that is evenly spaced, with one stitch exactly like the stitch next to it. The needle is inserted at right angles to the edge of the fabric and brought out at the edge so that each time the stitch is repeated, the needle passes over the previously stitched thread.

Blend: A combination of natural and manufactured fibers.

Blind Tuck: A type of tuck in which the foldline of one tuck touches the stitching line of the adjacent tuck.

Blindstitch: A hand stitch used through a folded edge. It is nearly invisible from the correct and wrong sides of the fabric.

Block Fusing: Lengths of fabric and interfacing fused together, and then treated as one piece of fabric.

Bobbin: A small spool used on the sewing machine inside the bobbin case; approximately 50 or more yards of thread that creates the bottom stitch of a well-balanced stitch.

Bodkin: A tool used to thread elastic or draw a string through casings wider than ⅜ inch.

Boning: Plastic or metal strips stitched on the inside of a strapless garment to support and add structure.

Bottom Stop: A metal tab at the bottom of the zipper that prevents the slider from running off the zipper.

Box Pleat: Formed by two side pleats, placed side by side, and turned away from each other.

Breakpoint: The beginning of the roll line on the front of the garment where a notched or shawl collar rolls over.

Broadcloth: A tightly woven fabric with a faint rib, available in different weights and fibers.

Buckram: A very stiff, coarse, open-weave fabric used to stiffen parts of a garment, such as a belt.

Bulk: Thickness in seams that needs to be reduced.

Bulky Seam: A thick seam.

Bust Point: The apex, or center point, of the bust.

Button: A three-dimensional form that has width, height, and length, and is usually paired with a buttonhole or loop and used as a closure; it can also be a decorative element on the garment.

Buttonhole: A finished opening paired with a button (or other type of closure) to secure a garment closed.

Canvas: A stabilizer used for tailoring men's and women's garments.

Casing: A foldover edge or a separately applied piece of fabric used to create a "tunnel" within which to enclose drawstring ties or elastic.

Catchstitch: A hand hem stitch that forms small x stitches.

Centered Zipper: A zipper in which the teeth are centered beneath the basted seamline, and top stitched ¼ to ½ inch parallel to the seam.

Chiffon: A lightweight, sheer fabric made with tightly twisted yarns of silk, polyester, or other fibers and used for evening wear.

Clean-Edge Finish: Fabric edges topstitched to finish the raw edges of a seam or hem.

Clear Elastic: Stretchy elastic made from 100 percent polyurethane.

Closed Cuff: A cuff stitched in-the-round that does not open and does not need a placket.

Closed Edge-to-Edge Lining: A lining in which the outer garment fabric and lining are exactly the same shape.

Closed Lining to Control the Garment Silhouette: A lining that is cut smaller than the garment piece and used to control the shape of the garment silhouette.

Closed Lining with Facing: A lining that is stitched to the facing and to the hem.

Closed Partial Lining: A lining used on a section of the garment (yoke, pocket, or flap) to reduce bulk.

Closed Ruffle or Flounce: A ruffle or flounce that is stitched in-the-round.

Closed Serged Seam: A seam in which both seam edges are serged together and pressed to one side.

Closure: Whatever is used to fasten the garment so it will close.

Collar: The part of a shirt, blouse, dress, jacket, or coat that encircles the neckline.

Collar Stand: The height to which the collar stands up.

Collars Stitched with Front or Front/Back Neck Facings: A necessary finish to the garment when the collar is worn open.

Collars Stitched with No Neck Facing: A collar designed to remain closed rather than being worn open.

Collection: A group of garments designed and presented for a particular season.

Concealed Closure: A hidden closure.

Concealed Placket: A lapped placket with concealed closures.

Continuous Placket: A separate binding stitched to enclose the raw edges of a slit; traditionally in a sleeve wrist.

Contour Dart: A vertical dart that adds shape to the bust, waistline, and hips of a garment without a waistline seam. Also known as a *fish-eye* or *double-pointed dart.*

Contoured Cuff: A wider shaped cuff.

Contoured Waistband: A band of fabric shaped to coincide with the contour of the rib cage or upper hip, and cut in two pieces.

Convertible Collar: A collar designed to be worn open or closed.

Cord 1: In a zipper, the slightly rolled portion of the zipper tape, exposed above the top stop, to which the teeth or coils are attached.

Cord 2: A filling made with yarns twisted together and used in piping or tucks.

Corded Tuck: A tuck in which the cord is placed inside the foldline of the tuck before the tuck is stitched.

Cotton Batiste: A lightweight, sheer, delicate fabric with a plain weave.

Courses: In knit fabric, the crosswise grain composed of loops. This terminology is used only with knits.

Cowl: A neckline finish cut on the bias.

Crease Line: A crease made by folding the fabric and pressing.

Crepe-Backed Satin: A fabric in which one side is a lustrous satin and the other side is textured crepe.

Cross Tuck: A decorative arrangement of rows of tucks stitched crosswise and lengthwise on the fabric.

Cuff: (1) A separate straight or shaped piece of fabric stitched to the hem of sleeves or pants.

(2) An extra length added to the garment hem and turned back.

Curved, A-Line, Flared Hem: A shaped hemline (as opposed to straight).

Cut-in-One Waistband: An extension of the garment shape at the top of the waistband.

Cutting: The action of slicing fabric using scissors, a rotary cutter, or a cutting machine.

Dart: An amount of fabric taken from the flat garment to create shape.

Dart Base: The beginning of the dart.

Dart Leg: The sides of the dart, which are equal in length and are indicated on the pattern or garment by the stitch lines.

Dart Point: The end of the dart, which releases the maximum fullness to contour the garment over the body.

Dart Transformations: The process of transferring darts into other construction details through pattern alteration.

Dart Tuck: A tuck that is not stitched to the dart point.

Darted Placket: A topstitched placket with a dart at the top of the slit and used on sleeves.

Decorative Design: An element that is included in a design for its aesthetic value.

Decorative Facing: A facing that is turned to the correct side of the garment, functioning as trim as well as a facing.

Decorative Two-Piece Waistband: A waistband cut in fabric and lining to accommodate the decorative shape.

Designing: The process of visually arranging and rearranging the design elements into an aesthetically pleasing design.

Dome: A quarter-circle button.

Double Breasted: Overlapping closure usually with two rows of buttons.

Double Topstitched Seam: A seam that combines two rows of topstitching, an edgestitch, and a welt.

Draping: A method of designing a garment by manipulating fabric on a dress form.

Dress Form: A physical replica of a women's body shape with no head or arms, but sometimes with legs.

Dropped Shoulder Sleeve: A sleeve that extends from the bodice over the upper arm.

Ease: The process of joining a slightly larger garment piece to a smaller garment piece by evenly distributing the fullness along the seam where the pieces are joined.

Edge Application: A method used to stitch ruffles and flounces to the garment edge.

Edgestitch: A topstitch applied 1/16 inch away from the seamline.

Edge-to-Edge Closure: A method of closing the garment in which the center fronts are butted together and do not overlap.

Edge-to-Edge Cuff: A cuff that is stitched to the entire length of the wrist, including the placket.

Elbow Dart: A dart that allows the arm to bend in a straight, fitted sleeve; it may be designed as one or several smaller darts.

Embroidery Scissors: Scissors that are approximately 4 to 6 inches in length and are used for detailed cutting.

Encased Elastic Waistband: A length of elastic that is zigzag stitched to the upper edge of a garment waistline, and then turned to the inside.

Enclosed Seam: A narrow ¼ inch stitched seam inside a collar, cuff, or waistline that is not visible.

Exposed Teeth Zipper: A zipper with enlarged teeth and wide tape that shows on the correct side of the garment, usually at center front or center back.

Extended/Self-Facing: A facing cut in one piece with the garment.

Extension: An extra width of fabric typically used for closures.

Fabric: Material constructed from fibers that can be woven, knitted, felted, crocheted, braided, or plaited.

Face of the Fabric/Garment: Another way of saying "the correct side of the fabric or garment."

Faced (Folded Edge): Two layers of fabric folded together, as in a ruffle.

False Hem: The hem allowance cut as a separate facing.

Fashion Designer: A person who designs clothing.

Flannel-Backed Lining: A warm lining consisting of satin on one side with a napped, flannel-like finish on the other side.

Flap: A shaped garment piece stitched to the garment section by one edge. It can be functional, hanging downward, covering a pocket, or decorative, as a design detail.

Flat Application: Stitching while the garment lies flat.

Flat Button: A button approximately ⅛ inch in height.

Flat Insertion: A technique in which the sleeve is stitched to the armhole before the side seams are stitched.

Flat-Felled Seam: A seam with a clean finish on both sides of the fabric.

Flounce: A circular shape of fabric with inner and outer circles. When the inner circle is straightened, the outer circle flutes.

Fluted Ruffle: A narrow strip of bias-cut fabric ease stitched down the center to give a wavelike effect.

Fly-Front Zipper: A zipper application in which fabric is used as a lap to cover the front opening in a tailored garment such as a man's or woman's trousers.

Fold-Back/Gauntlet Cuff: A wide, flared, fold-back cuff that is stitched to a contoured cuff.

Fold-Over Waistband: A waistband formed by turning over the raw edge of the waistline and stitching it to the garment, forming a casing.

French Cuff: A straight, wide cuff folded back and fastened with cuff links.

French Dart: A dart that forms a curve extending from the lower side seam in a diagonal line toward the bustline. Also called a *curved dart*.

French Seam: A small, narrow enclosed seam stitched to sheer, lightweight fabrics.

Full Ball: A circular button.

Full Interfacing: Interfacing that is applied to an entire section of a garment to provide support, reinforcement, and shaping.

Full Lining: Fabric that covers the entire inner surface of the garment.

Functional Design: An element that is included in the design to enable a garment to work physically on the body.

Functional Facing: Fabric that is attached to the raw edge of a garment section in order to finish that edge. It will not be visible on the correct side of the garment.

Fusible Interfacing: An interfacing with resin-like tiny dots on one side that become fused to the garment fabric when heat is applied.

Fusing: Using an iron to adhere a stabilizer to the fabric using heat, steam, and pressure.

Garment Center Line: The center front or back of the garment.

Garment Off-Center Line: The closure position on an asymmetrical design.

Garment Silhouette: The outline shape of the garment.

Gathered Sleeve: A type of sleeve in which the top of the sleeve is gathered to the desired fullness between the notches.

Gathered Wrist: A type of wrist finish in which gathering is used to add fullness.

Gathering: A technique used to create fullness by drawing up two rows of basting stitches into small folds.

Glovers Needle: A leather hand stitching needle.

Godet: A triangular piece of fabric inset into a seam to add fullness.

Grading: (1) To reduce bulk by trimming the seam allowance to different widths.

(2) Using specific measurements to increase or decrease patterns into different sizes.

Grainline: A pattern marking that indicates how to place the pattern on the fabric.

Grommets: Brass, nickel–plated, or oxidized black metal rings with holes in the middle to accommodate lacing or used for decorative design.

Gusset (One-Piece): A diamond-shaped piece of fabric designed to be inserted into the slash of an underarm seam to allow freedom of arm movement.

Gusset (Two-Piece): Two triangle-shaped pieces of fabric designed to be inserted into the slash of an underarm seam to ease restrictiveness of a fitted bodice and sleeve for freedom of arm movement.

Habotai or China Silk: A soft, lightweight lining, tightly woven with very fine yarns.

Hairline Seam: A narrow seam overcast with zigzag stitches; an alternative to a French seam for sheer fabrics.

Half Ball: A half-circle button.

Half Interfacing: Interfacing that is applied to only half of a garment section.

Handbasting: Temporary stitches used in the construction of a garment and later removed.

Hand/Finger-Press: To press with the hands or fingers rather than using an iron; steam can also be applied.

Hand-Stitched Hem: The least visible stitching of the hem to the garment, using a single thread and hand-sewing needle.

Hem: All these components: the hem allowance, hem finish, and hem stitches make up the hem.

Hem Allowance: The width added below the hemline that is turned back to form the hem.

Hem Edge: The raw edge of the hem.

Hem Finish: The hem edge neatened.

Hem Slit: An opening in a seam up from the hem edge.

Hem Stabilizer: Interfacing, canvas, or horsehair braid applied to the hem to add shape and structure.

Hem Tape: Lace or rayon tape used as a hem finish.

Hemline: The finished bottom edge of the garment.

Hidden Catchstitch: The finished hem edge rolled back ¼ inch and sewn using a catchstitch so the stitching remains hidden.

Hidden Slipstitch: The finished hem edge rolled back ¼ inch and sewn using a slipstitch so the stitching remains hidden.

Hong Kong Finish (or Bound Finish): A method of finishing a seam or hem in which the raw edges are encased with a binding.

Hook and Eye: A small metal fastener; one side is a hook that catches over a bar (or handmade eye) to close the garment.

Horsehair Braid: Sheer, bias, synthetic mesh used to stabilize and structure hems and other edges.

In-Seam Buttonhole: An opening in the seam for a buttonhole.

In-Seam Pocket: A pocket stitched in the seam.

Interfacing: Fabric that is used to support, reinforce, and give shape to garments.

Intersecting Seam: Two seams that cross each other.

Inverted Pleat: The reverse side of a box pleat, with two side pleats folded to meet each other on the correct side of the fabric.

Invisible Casing: A length of elastic that is zigzag stitched to the raw edge of a waistline, turned to the inside of the garment. No stitching is visible on the correct side of the garment.

Invisible Zipper: A zipper that, when closed, gives a seamlike finish; only the very small pull shows.

Invisible Zipper Foot: A special sewing machine foot used for installing invisible zippers; it is designed with grooves that hold the coil out of the way so that the needle can stitch alongside the chain or coil.

Ironing Board: A board with a padded, heat-resistant work surface used for pressing.

Keyhole Opening: A circular shape usually on the neckline.

Kick Pleat: A pleat that gives fullness to a skirt at the knee to the hem.

Kimono Sleeve: A wide, loose sleeve cut all-in-one with the front and back of the garment.

Knife or Side Pleat: A crisply pressed pleat in which the fold of the fabric is turned to one side.

Knit Fabric: Fabric constructed of interlocking loops that has stretch. Lycra is often added to retain the shape of the knit.

Knit Interfacing: Interfacing made with interlooping yarns that give it a stretch capacity.

Lacing: A long strip of fabric or leather threaded through pairs of holes (grommets) to secure the garment closed.

Lapped Seam: A seam in which one seam allowance is trimmed off, lapped over the other, and topstitched; it is best suited to nonfraying material such as leather.

Lapped Zipper: A zipper that is stitched between two sides of the garment. One side is stitched on the folded seam edge; the folded edge of the other side forms a tuck concealing the entire zipper.

Lettuce-Edge Hem: A method of finishing a hem that serges a small balanced stitch; when the edges are stretched, they look fluted.

Lining: A lighter-weight fabric constructed similar to the garment. It covers the inner construction and adds warmth and body.

Machine-Stitched Buttonhole: Two parallel rows of close zigzag stitches that form two narrow bars; each end of the bars is finished with a wider bar.

Machine-Stitched Hem: A method of finishing a hem on a sewing machine, with stitching that is visible on the correct side of the garment.

Mandarin Collar: A narrow collar band that stands up around the neckline.

Manufacturing: The production of garments.

Matchpoints: A pattern marking that indicates the points that must come together when stitching a seam.

Melding: A pressing process that sets the stitches into the fabric after stitching.

Microfiber: A soft, lightweight fabric with a silky feel composed mostly of ultrasoft polyester fibers.

Mirror Image: An exact reflection of a shape.

Mitered Corners: A diagonal seam stitched on a corner to reduce bulk.

Mock Seam: A seam that is formed by stitching a tuck.

Narrow Bias Facing: Bias strips of fabric used in curved areas in place of a shaped facing.

Narrow Rolled Hem: A narrow, twice-turned hem that may be machine or hand stitched.

Natural Fibers: Any fiber derived from animal or vegetable sources.

Neckline Facing: A fabric piece facing cut in the same shape and on the same grainline as the neckline edge it is finishing.

Needle Board: A flat board consisting of a rigid top nap formed by short, blunt wires embedded upright in the base; it supports the nap of fabrics, preventing them from being crushed during pressing.

Netting: A stiff open-mesh fabric used under garments to add structure.

Nonfusible Interfacing: A type of sew-in interfacing.

Nonwoven Interfacing: Interfacing produced from a bonded fabric created with synthetic fibers that have been chemically or thermally compressed together with the use of heat.

Notched-Extension Cuff: A cuff stitched to the wrist from one placket edge to the notched extension.

Notched Lapel Collar: A tailored L shape two-piece collar that rolls back onto the garment.

Notches: Small marks or clips placed on the outside edge of a sloper, pattern, or seamline to identify pattern and fabric pieces that need to be matched together.

Notions/Trims: All the supplies, other than the fabric, needed for constructing garments.

On Grain: A process whereby pattern grainlines are placed parallel to the selvage of the fabric regardless of whether the grainline is lengthwise, horizontal, or bias.

One-Piece Cuff: A cuff cut in one piece, then folded in half to become one cuff.

One-Piece Waistband: A waistband cut in one piece with a foldline in the middle.

Open Cuff: A cuff that opens with a closure.

Open Edge-to-Edge Lining: A lining in which the garment and lining are exactly the same shape, but the hem lining is shorter in length and left to hang freely.

Open Lining with Facing: A lining that is stitched to a facing; the hems are not stitched together but left to hang freely.

Open Lining with Waistband: A lining inserted into the waistband seam. The garment and lining hems are left to hang freely and are not attached.

Open Partial Lining: Fabric that covers only part of the garment. The edge of the lining is left to hang free of the garment and is not attached.

Open Ruffle or Flounce: A ruffle or flounce

constructed in one length and not stitched together.

Open Serged Seam: A plain seam with both edges serged separately and pressed open.

Overhand Stitch: A small diagonal stitch used to attach fabric parts together.

Overhand Tuck: A narrow, decorative tuck produced on curved lines using accurate hand stitching and measuring.

Overlap: The end of the waistband that is flush with the placket of the zipper. It is extended with straight or shaped end.

Partial Lining: Fabric that covers only a section of the garment.

Patch Pocket: A shaped piece of fabric applied to a surface of a garment. It can be self-faced, unlined, interfaced, lined, or self-fabric lined, and can be functional or purely decorative.

Patternmaking: The process of drafting garment patterns mathematically.

Peplum: A shaped garment section attached to the waistline of a blouse or jacket.

Peter Pan Collar: A circular flat collar that sits around the neck, with two rounded collar ends that meet at center front.

Pickstitch: A topstitch sewn by hand using embroidery thread. A smaller stitch is visible on the face of the fabric, with a longer stitch underneath the fabric.

Pin-Mark: Placement of pins in the fabric to mark a certain position.

Pin Tucks: Tucks that are stitched parallel and close to the edge of a fold in the fabric.

Piped Seam: A bias-cut piece of fabric, with or without cording, that is inserted into a seam as a decorative trim.

Pivot: Stitching to a point and swinging the fabric around 180 degrees.

Placket: A finished opening in a garment section.

Pleat: A folded amount of fabric (in one or two directions) around the garment, stitched or unstitched and held securely along the joining seamline, such as a waistline.

Point Turner: A tool used to accomplish angled corners on collars, cuffs, etc.

Pressing Cloth: A square of cotton, muslin, or organza that is placed on the fabric surface before ironing to protect it and prevent the iron from leaving shine marks.

Princess Seam: A seam sewn in the front and the back of a garment from the shoulder or armhole to give a formfitting shape; it is used instead of darts.

Production: The process of producing garments.

Pull Tab: The pull that moves up and down the zipper, opening and closing it. Also known as a *slider.*

Quality Control: The process of ensuring that garments are manufactured with consistently high-quality stitching.

Quilted Lining: A warm lining produced by topstitching layers of lining and polyester batting together, trapping air within the layers.

Raglan Shoulder Pad: An oval-shaped shoulder pad, rounded at the shoulder edge, and molded to fit over the shoulder point.

Raglan Sleeve: A type of sleeve (cut in one or two pieces) with slanting seams from front and back necklines to the armhole.

Raw Edge: The cut fabric edge with no finish.

Reinforced Button: An extra button applied to the facing behind the garment button for reinforcement.

Release Tucks: Tucks that release fullness in the garment.

Research Trends: Forecasting, tracking, and analyzing the general direction of fashion.

Roll Line: The point on a roll-over collar at which the collar rolls over.

Roll-Over Collar: A collar that stands up around the neckline and then rolls over onto the garment.

Rotary Cutter/Mats: A cutting tool with a round blade, resembling a pizza cutter. It can only be used on special cutting mats, which protect the work surface.

Ruffle: A straight strip of fabric, lace, or ribbon gathered into fullness on one edge and applied to a garment.

Saddle Stitch: An evenly spaced topstitch sewn by hand using embroidery thread.

Safety Stitch: A seam that is stitched simultaneously with a chainstitch and an overcast stitch on a serger.

Sample: An example of the finished garment or seam technique.

Sample Hand: A highly skilled person who makes the first sample garment during the design process.

Scallops: A series of half circles used as a decorative edge.

Scissors: A cutting tool, available in various sizes. Bent-handled dressmaker's shears have offset blades that allow the blade to rest flat on the cutting surface, preventing the fabric from lifting away from the cutting surface.

Seam: A line of permanent stitching that joins two pieces of fabric together.

Seam Allowance: The space between the seamline and the edge of the pattern or the space between the seamline and the cut fabric edge.

Seam Application: An element that is inserted into a seam.

Seam Roll: A firm cylinderlike cushion covered with cotton on one half and wool on the other half, and used to press long narrow seams.

Seam Slippage: A garment construction problem in which yarns separate, pulling away from the seams.

Seamline: On the face of the garment it is a line; on the wrong side of the garment it is a seam.

Seams Great: A lightweight, sheer stabilizing tape made from 100 percent nylon.

Self-Fabric as Lining: Fabric that doubles as both outer fabric and lining.

Selvage: The firmly woven edges on both sides of a woven fabric.

Separate Casing: A band of fabric constructed separately from the garment; the elastic is inserted into the band, and the band is stitched to the garment.

Separating Zipper: A zipper constructed with individual, vertical pin or bar stops that lock together, enabling the slide to join and separate the teeth or coils together; most often seen on sweaters, jackets, and jeans.

Serging: The technique of using a serger, which simultaneously cuts and overcasts the raw edges of a fabric with several threads. This can be used as a seam finish.

Set-in Shoulder Pad: A layer of padding made from materials such as cotton batting, felt, or foam that supports the shoulder of a garment with set-in sleeves.

Set-in Sleeve: A sleeve joined to the garment by means of a seam that encircles the arm over the shoulder.

SEW, CLIP, PRESS: The rhythm of stitching used in garment construction; sew the seam, clip the threads as you sew, and press the seams as you stitch.

Sew-in Interfacing: A woven stabilizer that is not fusible.

Sewing/Construction: The making of garments.

Sew-through Button: A button with two or four holes in the center; a needle and thread is passed through the holes to attach it to the garment.

Shank Button: A button with a small ring or bar, called a *shank*, which protrudes from underneath the button.

Shaped Dart: A dart that can be angular and squared or shaped in a curve, creating an interesting line detail to a garment.

Shaped Facing: A facing that matches the area to which it is being sewn. It is often used on necklines and sleeveless armholes.

Shaped Hem: A curved, circular, or angled hemline.

Sharp Hand Stitching Needle: A needle with a sharp point, a round eye, and medium length.

Shawl Collar: A design in which the front jacket/coat collar is cut all-in-one with the back collar.

Shell Tuck: A decorative tuck, formed by hand or machine stitching, that produces a scallop by overstitching the fold at determined intervals.

Shirring Elastic: Elastic sewing thread.

Shirt Collar: A type of collar traditionally used on men's and women's shirts.

Shirt-Sleeve Placket: A type of placket traditionally used on men's shirts.

Shoulder Dart: A dart used to shape the curved area on the back of the garment between the armhole and the neckline.

Silhouette: The overall outline, contour, or shape of the garment.

Silk Charmeuse: A soft, satin-weave fabric, shimmery on the face with a dull finish on the back.

Silk Dupioni: A crisp, lustrous silk fabric with an irregular, knobby texture.

Silk Georgette: A sheer fabric with a dull creped fabric surface; it is an excellent choice for evening wear.

Silk Organza: A stiff, sheer, lightweight fabric.

Single Breasted: Having one row of closures.

Single-Layer Pocket: A pocket that is top-stitched to the surface of the garment; on casual garments, it is usually made of lightweight fabric.

Sit-Flat Collar: A collar that sits flat on the shoulders; the collar shape is almost identical to the garment shape.

Sketching: The technique of using paper and pencil to communicate garment designs.

Skirt Marker: A tool used to level a hem.

Slashed Opening: (Can also be called a slit). A slitlike opening in the garment, usually at the neckline or wrist, finished with a facing or placket.

Sleeve Board: A small-scale wooden ironing board with rounded, padded ends used for pressing sleeves, short seams, and hard-to-get-to areas of a garment.

Sleeve Cap: The curved top section of the sleeve from the front to the back.

Sleeve Ease: The additional allowance of fabric at the sleeve cap, biceps, elbow, and wrist, which allows body movement.

Sleeve Finish: The various ways a sleeve can be completed.

Sleeve Head: Strips of fabric or batting that lift and support the sleeve cap and enhance the sleeve's shape.

Slipstitch: A quick and easy hand stitch used to stitch hems.

Slot Seam: A seam that features two open tucks folded to the center of the seam.

Smooth Hemline: Drawing a level hemline in the patternmaking stage.

Snap Fastener: A pair of interlocking discs used to fasten clothing together.

Spaced Tucks: Tucks separated by a determined amount of space between the foldline of one tuck and the stitching line of the next.

Specialty Fabric: Any fabric that is difficult to work with and requires extra care and attention when it is cut or stitched.

Stabilizer: Anything that could be used to add structure to the fabric, such as interfacing, boning, wire, fishing line, netting, or tulle.

Stabilizing Tapes: Narrow ¼-inch to ½-inch-wide fusible or sew-in tape applied to the seamline to prevent the seams from stretching.

Stand-up Collar: A collar that stands up around the neckline and does not roll over.

Staystitching: A single row of permanent stitches applied just inside the seamline to add reinforcement before the garment pieces are stitched together.

Steam Iron: An iron that holds a limited amount of water, which produces steam when heated; it is used for pressing seams, hems, and completed garments. Industrial irons are gravity fed from large tanks of water and produce a continuous stream of steam.

Stitch Directional: A method of sewing the garment in which seams on both sides of the garment are stitched in the same direction.

Stitch-in-the-Ditch: The technique of sewing a row of stitches inconspicuously from the correct side of the garment in the seamline.

Stitched-Down Casing: Casing that is turned to the inside of the garment and edgestitched or topstitched to secure it to the garment.

Stitched In-the-Round: A method of sewing the garment together that involves stitching all seams together so the fabric piece is circular.

Stitching Guideline: A line woven into the zipper tape that directs the stitching.

Straight Hem: A hem that folds back and sits flat.

Stretch Seam: A seam sewn with stretch stitches on knit fabrics, providing stretch that matches the stretch capacity of the knit.

Structural Design: All the seams that are stitched to hold the garment together.

Surface Application: An element that is stitched to the correct side of the garment, which is the fabric surface.

Symmetrical Closure: A design in which the closure is centered on the garment.

Symmetrical Darts: Darts that are the same on both sides of the garment.

Synthetic Fiber: Any fiber created by pushing a chemical or combination of chemicals through the holes of a special device, and then into another chemical solution or air, which hardens it into strands.

Tab: Two pieces of fabric shaped with a point at one end.

Tab-Loop: A belt loop shaped into a loop and used as a closure.

Tailor's Ham: A firm, rounded, or oval cushion with a wool or cotton covering that provides a pressing surface to shape darts, sleeve heads, lapels, collars, and curved areas.

Tape: In a zipper, the fabric portion to which the teeth or coils are attached; it is usually made of cotton, cotton blends, stabilized nylon, or polyester knit.

Tape End: The very top and bottom edges of the zipper tape.

Tension: The balance of the upper and lower threads when stitching.

Thread: Flexible strands made from fibers or filaments in many combinations and used in hand or machine stitching.

Thread Carrier: An alternative to a belt loop, made of several strands of thread covered by a blanket stitch for reinforcement.

Thread Clipper: A device with short blades used to clip threads when stitching.

Toggle: A type of button used as a closure. It looks like a barrel and is often made of wood.

Top Stop: The plastic or metal tab at the top of the zipper, which keeps the zipper slide from being pulled off.

Topstitched Pocket: A pocket attached to the garment by stitching through all layers.

Topstitching: One or more rows of stitches stitched on the correct side of the garment. It can also be used to hold the facing to the garment in place of understitching.

Traditional Bound Buttonhole: A buttonhole in which narrow strips of fabric (called welts) cover the opening and meet in the middle (like lips) to form the buttonhole. It is mainly used on tailored garments such as jackets and coats.

Tricot: A stable knitted fabric that can be sheer or opaque and is often used for lingerie.

Trim: (1) A decorative embellishment added to the garment. (2) To cut away excess material with scissors.

Tuck: A fold of fabric (usually placed on the lengthwise grain so it lies flat) that is stitched down all or part of the way.

Tucked Wrist: A type of wrist closure in which tucks are stitched in the wrist to add fullness.

Tulle: A fine lightweight mesh used for bridal veils.

Tweed: A heavyweight textured woolen fabric with colored, stubby yarns.

Twice-Turned Hem: A hem that is folded over twice.

Twill Lining: A strong, sturdy lining, with a diagonal parallel weave.

Twill Tape: A narrow, sturdy, straight-grain stabilizing tape woven with herringbone twill.

Twin Needle Stitching: A technique in which two machine needles stitch two rows of parallel topstitching simultaneously on the face of the fabric and zigzag stitches underneath. Also known as *double needle stitching*.

Two-Piece Cuff: A cuff formed from two fabric pieces that are stitched together.

Under Collar: The collar piece that sits underneath the upper collar and is slightly smaller.

Underlap: The extension of the waistband that allows for an opening.

Underlining: An extra layer of fabric or interfacing fully applied to the wrong side of the fabric to stiffen, reinforce, or add warmth. The two layers are then stitched as one.

Understitching: A row of stitches sewn close to the seamline of a facing or under collar edge to keep the seamline from rolling to the outside.

Unpressed Pleat: A pleat that is formed in soft folds, and is not pressed.

Upper Collar: The collar piece that is visible on the garment and is cut slightly wider than the under collar.

Velvaboard: A flexible base with polyester bristles embedded upright in it, used to "press" napped fabrics and prevent crushing of the nap.

Vent: A lapped opening directed up from the hem edge of skirts, sleeves, and jackets to allow for comfortable movement.

Waist Dart: A dart that reduces the waistline and refers to the fullness to the hip area.

Waistband: A band of fabric, usually fully interfaced, that is seamed to the waistline of skirts or pants and fastened to hold the garment firmly around the waist.

Waistband (Two-Piece): A waistband cut in two pieces that can accommodate a decorative shape. A lighter-weight fabric is generally used for the under waistband to reduce bulk.

Waistline Facing: A facing with a finished edge that rests on the natural waistline, and must correspond with the shape of the waistline.

Waistline Stay: A firmly woven tape or grosgrain ribbon stitched to the inside of a waistline to prevent stretching and to stabilize the waist; it also relieves stress and strain on the closure of strapless garments.

Wale: A lengthwise grain composed of loops. This term is used in place of *grainline* when speaking of knit fabrics.

Waxed Nylon Thread: A strong-quality thread used for stitching buttons.

Welt: A double fold of fabric stitched to the lower and upper cut edge of the pocket.

Welt Seam: A seam that is topstitched on the fabric surface ¼ inch away from the stitched seamline.

Woven Fabric: A fabric produced on a loom by weaving lengthwise and crosswise yarns in three basic weaves—plain, twill, and satin. It does not stretch, unless a stretch property, such as Lycra, is added to the fabric.

Woven Interfacing: Interfacing constructed with two sets of yarns (warp and weft) formed by weaving.

Wrist Finish: The stitching technique used to finish the raw edge of the wrist.

Zipper: A fastening device that makes a complete closure by means of interlocking teeth or coils.

Zipper Coil: A continuous strand of flexible nylon or polyester twisted in a spiral and attached to a woven or knitted tape.

Zipper Foot: A sewing machine foot used in sewing all-purpose zippers or separating zippers.

Zipper Teeth: Interlocking metal or plastic pieces, more rigid than coils, that fasten together and are attached to a cotton or cotton-blend tape.

APPENDIX: WHERE TO BUY

As Cute as a Button
www.ascuteasabutton.com
What to buy: Buttons

Atlanta Thread and Supply
www.store.atlantathread.com
What to buy: Thread, cording for piping, shoulder pads, and many other sewing supplies, as listed in Chapter 2, "Gather Your Tools."

Baer Fabrics
www.baerfabrics.com
What to buy: Underlining, interfacings, custom covered buttons, and all notions

Clotilde
www.clotilde.com
What to buy: FrayBlock, pleaters, and Velvaboard

Clover, Fabric Depot
www.clover-usa.com, www.fabricdepot.com

What to buy: All notions

Candlelight Valley Fabrics
www.candlelightvalleyfabrics.com
What to buy: Stretch Bemburg rayon knits and woven fabrics

The Crowning Touch Inc.
www.crowning-touch.com
What to buy: For turning bias tubing

Denver Fabrics
www.denverfabrics.com
What to buy: Lining, knits, woven fabrics, silk charmeuse, faux fur, and microfiber

Fashion Fabrics Club
www.fashionfabricsclub.com
What to buy: Silk charmeuse, silk dupioni, organza, and more . . .

Fashion Leather International
www.fashionleather.com
What to buy: Leather and fur

Greenberg & Hammer Inc.
www.greenberg-hammer.com
What to buy: This company has a huge selection of online supplies mentioned in this textbook as tools for the designer. Here is a list of all the supplies, and much more that can be purchased: Home sewing machines, pressing equipment, dress forms, bobbins, scissors, rotary cutters, awl, pins, Chaco-liner, seam ripper, thread (Gutermann), DMC embroidery floss, thread clippers, loop turner, pins, hand sewing needles, Glovers needle, tapestry needle, interfacing, organza, muslin, linings, horsehair, ribbon and lace hem tapes, elastic, hooks and bars, hooks and eyes, hook-and-eye tape, fur hooks, cement, grommets (gold, brass, and nickel) and grommet tools, shoulder pads, buttons, custom-made covered buttons, covered button kits, boning

(riglene boning and other types), cording, piping, buckram, batting, elastic and zippers, skirt makers, snaps, and more . . .

Haberman Fabrics
www.habermanfabrics.com
What to buy: SeamsGreat (in black, white, and ivory), other notions, and great fabrics

Leonard Adler & Co Inc.
www.leonardadlerco.net
What to buy: Skeins of waxed nylon thread (C weight), interfacing, underlining, and notions

Londa's Creative Threads
www.londas-sewing.com
What to buy: SofKnit Interfacing

Louise Cutting (Cutting Corners)
www.cuttinglinedesigns.com
What to buy: Underlining, interfacings, stabilizing tape, and specialty interfacings (check availability, as stock changes)

Lucy's Fabrics
www.lucysfabrics.com
What to buy: ¼-inch clear elastic, fashion knits, and knit lining

Mendel's Far Out Fabrics
www.mendels.com/fasteners
What to buy: Elastic loops

Outdoor Wilderness Fabrics Inc.
www.owfinc.com
What to buy: Grommets (brass, nickel-plated, and oxidized black), brass grommet heavy setter tools, and metal hardware

Prym-Dritz
www.dritz.com
What to buy: Craft fabric glue and nylon snaps

The Sewing Emporium
www.sewingemporium.com
What to buy: Teflon zipper feet and adhesive-backed Teflon sheets

Stan's Sewing Supplies
www.stanssewingsupplies.com
What to buy: Two-sided leather hemming tape (for stabilizing seams and hems in leather) and zippers of every kind, including invisible separating zippers

Tandy Leather Factory
www.tandyleatherfactory.com
What to buy: Eco-Flo (Eco-wise, water-based leather cement), leather, and other leather products

Thai Silks
www.thaisilks.com
What to buy: Fabulous silks, including silk knits, silk charmeuse, silk dupioni, and silk lining

Twins Pleating Service
www.TwinsPleating.com
What to buy: Custom pleating of fashion fabric by special order

Leather, Suede, Skins, Inc.
www.leathersuedeskins.com
What to buy: Leather and suede

Zipperstop
www.zipperstop.com
What to buy: Custom-order zippers

NOTES

Chapter 1

1. Richard Sorger and Jenny Udale, *The Fundamentals of Fashion Design* (Lausanne, Switzerland: AVA Publishing, 2006), 28.

2. Alix Sharkey, "Boy Wonderful: Once Hailed as Fashion's Wunderkind, Zac Posen Has Come Into His Own as a Mature, Confident Couturier," *WYNN* no. 2 (Spring 2006): 86–90.

3. Mizuho Inoue, "World Changers: Coco Chanel," www.wc.pdx.edu/chanel/chanel.html (accessed December 1, 2007).

4. Sanjay S. Chaudhari, Rupali S. Chitinis, and Dr. Rekha Ramkrishnan, "Waterproof Breathable Active Sports Wear Fabric," Synthetic & Art Silk Mills Research Association, Mumbai, India, www.sasmira.org/sportwear.pdf (accessed January 16, 2008).

5. Connie Long, *Sewing with Knits* (Newtown CT: Taunton Press, 2002), 13, 110.

Chapter 2

1. Claire B. Shaeffer, *High-Fashion Sewing Secrets* (Emmaus, PA: Rodale Press, 1997), 165.

Chapter 3

1. Hilary Alexander, "The 'Little Black Dress' Comes Home." www.telegraph.co.uk/fashion/main.jhtml?xml=fashion/2006/12/08/efhepburn08.xml (accessed December 3, 2007).

2. Marcy Tilton, "Armani Jackets: The Inside Story." www.taunton.com/threads/pages/600248.asp (accessed January 12, 2007).

3. Debbie Ann Gioello and Beverley Berke, *Fashion Production Terms* (New York: Fairchild Publications, 2003), 199, 314.

Chapter 6

1. "The Look of Giambattista Valli," *In Style* (February 2000), 112.

Chapter 17

1. Debbie Ann Gioello and Beverley Berke, *Fashion Production Terms* (New York: Fairchild Publications, 2003), 199.

INDEX